AF505270

Artifact and Assemblage

EDITED BY

Curtis Runnels, Daniel J. Pullen,
and Susan Langdon

Artifact and Assemblage

The Finds from a Regional Survey
of the Southern Argolid, Greece

VOLUME I

*The Prehistoric and Early Iron Age Pottery
and the Lithic Artifacts*

Stanford University Press   Stanford, California

Stanford University Press, Stanford, California
© 1995 by the Board of Trustees of the
Leland Stanford Junior University
Printed in the United States of America

CIP data appear at the end of the book

Stanford University Press publications are
distributed exclusively by Stanford University Press
within the United States, Canada, Mexico, and
Central America; they are distributed exclusively by
Cambridge University Press throughout the
rest of the world.

Preface

The present volume presents the results of analyses of the prehistoric artifacts collected from surface sites in the Southern Argolid, a remote peninsula in the northwest Peloponnese of Greece (Fig. 0.1). These artifacts were collected from archaeological survey sites investigated, beginning in 1972, by teams from Indiana University and the University of Pennsylvania, and, between 1979 and 1983, by teams from Stanford University. This project, known in the literature as the Argolid Exploration Project, was conceived originally by Michael H. Jameson and Thomas W. Jacobsen and their colleagues. Jacobsen directed the survey in 1972, and Jameson, with Tjeerd H. van Andel and Curtis Runnels, directed the Stanford survey from 1979 to the present. The project was conducted under the auspices of the American School of Classical Studies at Athens and the Greek Ministry of Culture.

The purpose of the Argolid Exploration Project was to carry out a study of the cultural ecology of the entire region. The many studies that have been undertaken by the project include excavations at the prehistoric site of Franchthi Cave, the Classical and Hellenistic town of Halieis, and geological, geomorphological, anthropological, historical, and archaeological surveys of various kinds. A general volume that lays out the results of this large project for a broad readership (*Beyond the Acropolis: A Rural Greek Past*, by Tjeerd H. van Andel and Curtis Runnels, 1987) and the final report on the survey project as a whole (*A Greek Countryside: The Southern Argolid from Prehistory to the Present Day*, by Michael H. Jameson, Curtis Runnels, and Tjeerd H. van Andel, 1994) have been published by Stanford University Press. The reader is directed to the latter volume for an extended discussion of the goals and history of this large and ambitious project.

From the beginning of the project it was the intention of the directors that the artifacts collected from the survey sites should be treated in the same manner as artifacts recovered in the excavation of stratified deposits. To that end, all of the artifacts that were collected were saved and analyzed by specialists. The artifacts remain in Greece, where they are curated by the Archaeological Museum of Nafplion in storerooms in the town of Kranidhi, in the Southern Argolid.

Our objectives have been to analyze regional artifact production and to document shifting patterns of trade and cultural contact from period to period. Along with the results of the environmental survey and the study of settlement patterns, the results of our studies of the artifacts are the principal source of data for the conclusions that are presented in our published reports and monographs. For this reason we have been determined to present full reports on all of the artifacts collected in the course of the survey. The full publication of all of the artifacts from the archaeological survey also serves the purpose of permitting scholars to utilize our findings in their own research without the onerous obligation of visiting the storerooms in Greece. The present volume, *Artifact and Assemblage: The Finds from a Regional Survey of the Southern Argolid, Greece, Volume 1: The Prehistoric and Early Iron Age Pottery and the Lithic Artifacts*, is the first of two projected volumes intended to present the conclusions derived from the specialist study of the artifacts, and it includes all of the stone artifacts, the Neolithic and Bronze Age ceramics, and the Early Iron Age pottery. The second volume, *Artifact and Assemblage: The Finds from a Regional Survey of the Southern Argolid, Greece, Volume 2: The Historical Pottery, Coins, Architectural Members, and Other Artifacts*, being edited by Mark Munn, includes studies of the Classical, Hellenistic, Roman, Medieval, and Turkish pottery, the terracotta figurines, coins, metal objects, and architectural pieces, and the other historical *disiecta membra* recovered from the survey during the many years of survey work.

In a project of this size, complexity, and duration there are many people who have helped the editors and authors along the way. Although it is never possible to acknowledge the valuable assistance of every individual, we would like to thank the many persons who since 1979 have contributed to the study of the Southern Argolid and to the production of this volume. Special thanks are offered to the artists who prepared the numerous technical drawings of often very plain and uninteresting artifacts, the kind hardest to capture in a drawing, over a period of years. For the drawings not prepared by the present authors, we gratefully acknowledge and warmly thank Eric Brunnemann, Janet Douglas, Penelope Mountjoy, and Priscilla Murray. No less daunting a task was the photography, and we also wish to thank Craig Mauzy, who made and printed the photographs. Michael H. Jameson and Tjeerd H. van Andel, the co-directors of the survey, have supported and encouraged the study and publication of the artifacts from the beginning of the project. Many specialists made visits to our laboratory—the remains of an abandoned schoolhouse, a drafty and inconvenient hulk appreciated mainly for its magnificent view—to identify the numerous classes of artifacts collected by the survey teams, and we would like to thank especially Angelika Dousougli, Ann Foley, Elizabeth Wace French, Catherine Perlès, Jeremy Rutter, Karen D. Vitelli, and Kostas Zachos. Mark Munn, who is editing the second volume of survey artifacts, was responsible, with Mary Lou Zimmerman Munn, for the operation of the laboratory. Last, but not least, we wish to thank the many Stanford undergraduate students and other volunteers who worked to collect the artifacts in the field and who assisted the specialists in every stage of the sorting, classification, and study of the artifacts.

C. R.
D. J. P.
S. L.

Contents

A Note on Tables, Figures, and Appendixes   ix

Introduction   1

Curtis Runnels, Daniel J. Pullen, and Susan Langdon

1 The Pottery of the Neolithic, Early Helladic I, and Early Helladic II Periods   6

Daniel J. Pullen

The Early Neolithic Period, 6. The Middle Neolithic Period, 6. The Late Neolithic Period, 7. The Final Neolithic Period, 7. The Early Helladic I Period, 10. The Early Helladic II Period, 19. Conclusions, 39.

2 The Pottery of the Early Helladic III and Middle Helladic Periods   43

Gullög C. Nordquist

The Early Helladic III Period, 43. The Middle Helladic Period, 45.

3 The Pottery of the Late Helladic Period   52

P. A. Mountjoy

The Late Helladic II Period, 52. The Late Matt-Painted Pottery, 53. The Late Helladic IIIA1 Period, 53. The Late Helladic IIIA2 Period, 53. The Late Helladic IIIB Period, 54. The Late Helladic IIIC Early Period, 55. Coarsewares/Cooking Pots, 55. Unpainted Pottery, 56. Figurines, 56.

4 The Pottery of the Early Iron Age and Geometric Periods   57

Susan Langdon

The Protogeometric Period, 58. The Early Geometric Period, 60.
The Middle Geometric Period, 61. Middle to Late Geometric Pottery, 62.
The Late Geometric Period: Late Geometric I, 63. The Late Geometric
Period: Late Geometric II, 64. The Subgeometric Period, 69. Three Figurines
from the Geometric Period, 71. Conclusions, 72.

5 The Lithic Artifacts: Flaked Stone and Other Nonflaked Lithics   74

P. Nick Kardulias and Curtis Runnels

Survey Methods and the Lithic Assemblage, 75. Flaked-Stone Laboratory
Procedures and Computer Coding, 75. Flaked-Stone Chronology, 85.
Bronze Age Flaked Stone, 93. Flaked Stone of the Historic Periods, 97.
Discussion: Flaked-Stone Artifacts, 103. Conclusions: Flaked-Stone
Artifacts, 108. Ground Stone, Polished Stone, and Other Nonflaked
Artifacts, 109. Conclusions: Nonflaked Lithic Artifacts, 136.

Conclusions   140

Curtis Runnels, Daniel J. Pullen, and Susan Langdon

Appendixes

1. Pottery Catalogue   147
2. Assemblage Tables for Chapters 1–4   223
3. Concordance of Catalogue Numbers, Inventory Numbers, and
   Figure Numbers   320

Figures   335

References Cited   465

Index   473

A Note on Tables, Figures, and Appendixes

As a guide to the various kinds of documentation contained in this volume, we offer this note. The tables referred to in Chapters 1 and 5 (the only tables in the volume, apart from Appendix 2) are to be found within the text of those chapters. All figures, both the line drawings and the photographs, will be found at the end of the volume, immediately prior to the Index. *Line drawings* of the ceramics treated in Chapters 1–4 (Figs. 1–64) and of the lithics treated in Chapter 5 (Figs. 65–117) precede the *photographs* of the ceramics treated in Chapters 1–4 (Figs. 118–36). There are no photographs of the lithics.

Descriptions of the individual ceramic objects in Chapters 1–4 are presented as catalogue entries in Appendix 1, the Pottery Catalogue, and are referred to (in text) by **boldfaced** catalogue numbers. These same catalogue numbers are used to identify the objects in Figs. 1–64 and 118–36, which are arranged virtually in catalogue-number order at the back of the book. Lithic artifacts are generally not individually catalogued, a tradition followed here; references to the lithic objects in Figs. 65–117 are thus made directly from the text of Chapter 5.

The Assemblage Tables given in Appendix 2 present all ceramic materials for the periods represented by Chapters 1–4, that is, the Neolithic Age, the Bronze Age, and the Early Iron Age, in summary fashion, by date, for each site. When an object of a particular date from a site has been studied in detail and catalogued in Appendix 1, its **boldfaced** catalogue number appears in the appropriate table in Appendix 2, in the righthand column. The site numbers used in the Assemblage Tables of Appendix 2 utilize the standard AEP numbering system of a single letter, from A to G, which designates a region of the Southern Argolid, followed immediately by a sequence number for that region, which indicates the particular site. The site number (for example, F32) forms the initial part of the individual object's AEP inventory number, which appears in the individual catalogue entries of Appendix 1. In order to facilitate cross-references between the original AEP inventory numbers and the catalogue numbers used in this volume, a concordance of catalogue numbers and figure numbers to the AEP inventory numbers has been provided, as Appendix 3.

With these various types of documentation we hope that the reader will be able to read about the Southern Argolid ceramics on a regional level, in the appropriate chronological chapters, and then identify specific objects of interest from a particular site through the use of the appendixes and the figures.

Artifact and Assemblage

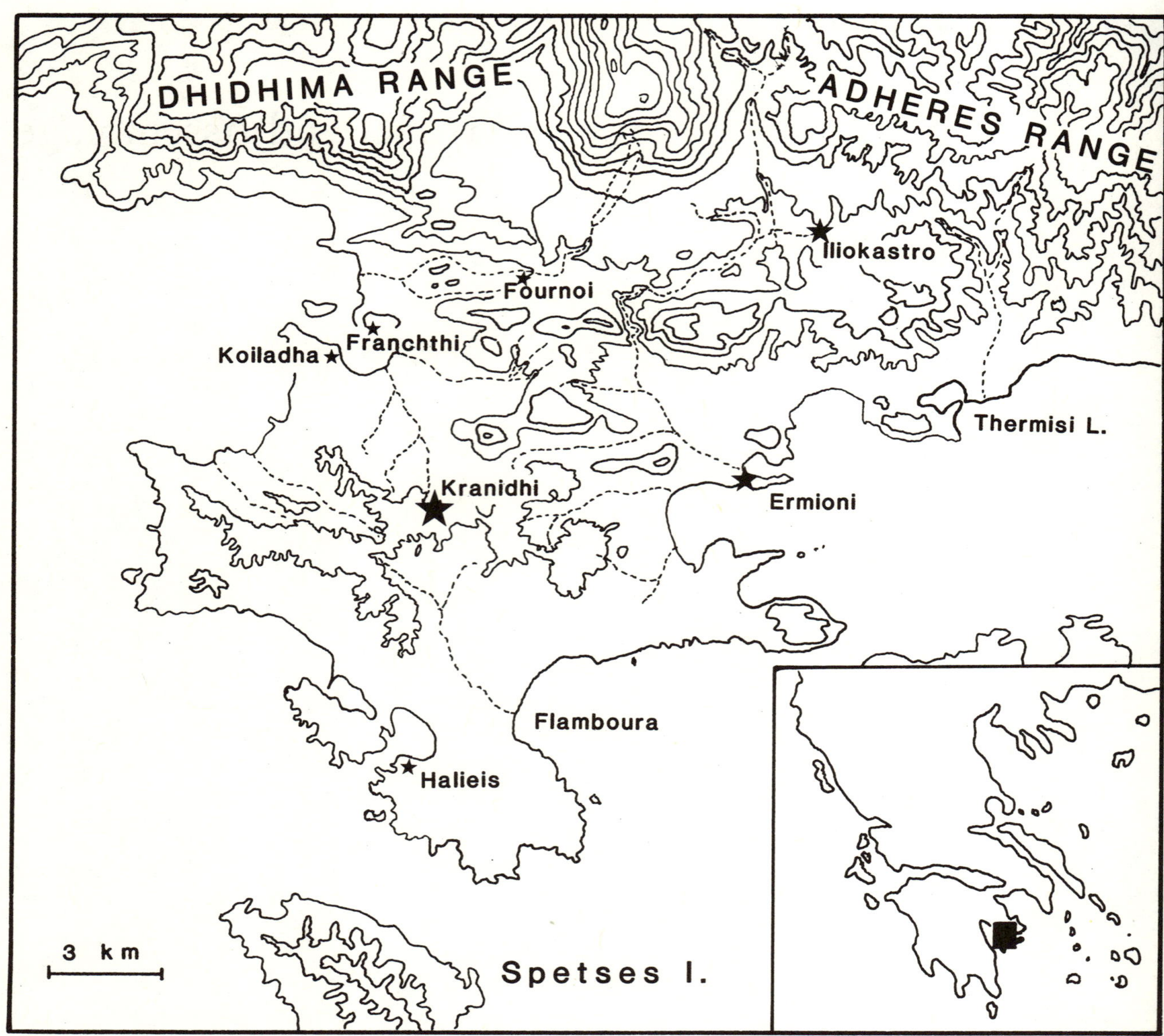

Fig. 0.1. The Southern Argolid. Halieis and Franchthi are archaeological sites; Kranidhi, Ermioni, Koiladha, Fournoi, and Iliokastro are modern towns; Flamboura is a regional place name.

Introduction

Curtis Runnels, Daniel J. Pullen, and
Susan Langdon

This volume presents the finds from a regional archaeological survey of the Southern Argolid from 1972 to 1983. The full publication of survey finds is a significant departure from traditional archaeological practice. Topographical and regional surveys in the modern sense have been conducted in Greece since the 1950's, but the artifacts recovered from these surveys have usually not been accorded full documentation and publication. The reason for this is simple: artifacts collected from the surface are usually very fragmentary and greatly worn by natural forces, making them difficult to compare with artifacts in good condition recovered from tombs or well-preserved buried deposits. It is particularly difficult to judge the shape of pottery vessels from sherds, and such surface decoration as may have embellished them has often been completely removed by natural processes. Moreover, surface finds are unstratified, and the dating of such materials may be very difficult or impossible, making comparison with materials in published *corpora* of objects from stratified deposits a risky business at best. For these reasons, surface artifacts have been regarded as useful only for broadly dating sites and assigning functions to them, and the artifacts were usually discarded after inspection, and thought not worthy of separate study and publication.

The purpose of the present volume is to change the approach that is taken to surface materials. Nearly 50,000 artifacts were collected from approximately 328 archaeological sites in the Southern Argolid from a region no more than 225 square kilometers in area (Fig. 0.1). Even so, this number represents but a fraction of the total number of artifacts to be found on the surface. Only 20% of the region was intensively searched, yet recent efforts to count the number of artifacts seen in the course of searching quite small areas of relatively remote countryside indicate that the number of artifacts to be found on the surface can be numbered in the hundreds of thousands (e.g. Cherry et al. 1988; Wells, Runnels, and Zangger 1990). Although there are areas where surface artifacts are rare (Runnels 1988a), it is clear that the surface of many parts of Greece is rich in artifacts, and the interpretive potential of the surface scatters of artifacts in the study of larger patterns of settlement history and economy must now be recognized by archaeologists.

Part of the reason for the extraordinary preservation of artifacts in the Southern Argolid can be explained by the local conditions. The Southern Argolid is an arid land with little vegetation, and surface conditions, although subject to erosion and other disturbances, are relatively stable. Once artifacts are brought to the surface by plowing, animal burrowing, or erosion they may remain in their positions for long periods of time. It is also clear that some low-density scatters of artifacts were deposited on parts of the landscape as the direct result of past human activities, for instance those connected with agriculture and pastoralism, where they remain to the present day (Cherry et al. 1988: 170–76; Wells, Runnels, and Zangger 1990: 237–38).

There are many problems that make the analysis and interpretation of surface assemblages very difficult, particularly the poor preservation of artifacts exposed at the surface for thousands of years, but these problems do not diminish our commitment to the full study and publication of the artifacts from surface sites. This is so for three principal reasons. First, most of the sites we discovered will be destroyed by natural processes and human activity in the near future, and it is unlikely that they will ever be tested by excavation. Our sample of artifacts may be the only record of the cultural materials from these sites, and it is imperative, therefore, that we publish these finds so that our attributions of date and function for many sites are substantiated by the evidence.

Second, many sites in our study area are quite small, and consist of a single cultural component (e.g. Late Roman) representing a period of occupation often of short temporal duration. Thus some chronological control is possible, and assemblages recovered from the surface of such small sites in many cases belong to a single occupation period, although some uncertainties about chronology will always remain. Our careful study of the assemblages revealed that numerous single-period sites were recorded in the survey. Although some may be assigned only broadly to periods, such as Early Helladic I-II (a broad period, perhaps as much as 500 years in length), others could be assigned to much shorter periods, such as the Late Classical to Early Hellenistic period (ca. 50–70 years). This finding gave us reason to believe that the many sites found in our survey could be ordered chronologically, and the assemblages from them could be studied as samples from sites of specific periods.

Third, the large number of artifacts and sites in the Southern Argolid gives us a substantial sample of artifacts from a small, isolated region. The coarse and fine ceramic wares and the stone tools we recovered there can be compared with those from better-known regions such as the Argive Plain and Attica, particularly as the results of many other regional surveys become available. In the Southern Argolid, our assemblages can be compared with those from Franchthi Cave (excavated by T. W. Jacobsen and his colleagues) and Halieis (excavated by Michael H. Jameson and Wolf W. Rudolph). Such comparisons will permit the analysis in the future of regional products, and provide evidence of evolving patterns of cultural contact and trade. An attempt to provide such evidence is found in the following pages.

A systematic approach to sampling was followed during the collection of artifact assemblages from the Southern Argolid. It is our contention that the samples obtained by the survey are representative and can be used for detailed study of the sites in question. The details of the survey procedure are given elsewhere (Jameson, Runnels, and van Andel, 1994, Chapter 4), but a brief recapitulation here is useful. The surveys in 1972 and 1979–82 used different methods to collect surface materials. In 1972, artifacts were for the most part collected from the surface in an unsystematic manner. The team members simply walked about the site and picked up diagnostic artifacts (i.e. recognizable feature sherds or lithic artifacts) that came to their attention. Although the specific definition of diagnostic material naturally varies by chronological period, a broadly inclusive definition (e.g. rims, handles, bases, decorated fragments) compensated for the relative inexperience of newly trained students. On some sites a more systematic approach was employed. A grid, for instance, was laid out over several of the larger sites, and all of the artifacts were collected from selected squares. Beginning in 1979, the earlier survey sites were revisited and new samples were taken. All sites discovered between 1979 and 1983 were systematically sampled by means of randomly selected transects that crossed the site, and the artifacts within these transects were collected. The teams also carefully searched for and collected diagnostic artifacts on the site as a whole after the random sample was taken. This procedure was made more systematic by dividing the site into quadrants and collecting diagnostics separately from each quadrant. An average of 4.7% of the area of each site was sampled by the random transects, and this accounted for an average area of ca. 92.8 m² for each site. The results of the collections made in 1972 were compared with those made in the course of the reexamination of the sites. Sufficient materials had been collected in 1972 to adequately date the sites. The systematic, random samples, however, added significantly to our understanding of sites. Undecorated sherds and very fragmentary artifacts were used to identify the function of the site. Pieces of cooking ware, or storage vessels, or small fragments of millstones and pressing beds were often retrieved in the course of the systematic sample collection, but were overlooked during the collection of diagnostic artifacts. The latter are almost always decorated sherds from fine-ware vessels, and these give an incomplete picture of the full inventory of material culture at a site.

All of the 1972 sites were visited and sampled more than once. Many of the sites discovered in 1979–82 were revisited when possible, and new samples were taken. The revisiting of sites, when the combination of sampling techniques is taken into account, is sufficient in our estimation to ensure that we obtained an adequate sample of artifacts for interpretation.

The detailed studies of the artifacts, covering the ceramic artifacts of the Neolithic, Bronze, and Early Iron Ages, are presented in the first four chapters of this volume. A diachronic study of the lithic artifacts, in Chapter 5, includes the historical as well as prehistoric artifacts, because the sample of lithics, particularly the ground stone, is too small to warrant a site-by-site treatment, or to permit the historic material to be placed in a separate chapter. The primary division in Chapter 5 falls between the flaked-stone artifacts of obsidian and flint, which are largely although not completely prehistoric in date, and the ground-stone artifacts, chiefly querns, which are about equally divided between prehistoric and historic periods.

The artifacts in each chapter are treated typologically (whether by shape, ware, raw material, or technique of manufacture) rather than by site of discovery. In so doing, we hope to emphasize the regional nature of our samples. In order to facilitate the reader's reconstruction of the ceramic finds from each site, assemblage tables (Appendix 2) record all prehistoric and Early Iron Age pottery found at each site, including materials not described in the general pottery catalogue (Appendix 1). Cross-references in the catalogue (Appendix 1) to individual objects allow users to shift directly between the typological narratives in the chapters, the catalogue (Appendix 1), and the assemblage tables (Appendix 2). Appendix 3 contains a concordance of original inventory numbers to the catalogue numbers, which is useful for specialists who wish to examine the original artifacts stored in Greece. The lithic artifacts do not require detailed catalogue entries, and the relevant data are presented instead in summary tables in the text.

A final word about the work in the field laboratory may be useful. Analysis of the ceramics began after the ceramic material collected on sites in the survey area was brought into the laboratory. The primary goal of the analysis was to date the artifactual material as closely as possible. At this time every artifact was recorded on one of three recording sheets: an artifact summary sheet giving counts and weights for the collection units; a nonpottery ceramic form recording rooftiles, loom weights, and other objects; and a pottery recording sheet for identified vessels represented by potsherds. The following information was recorded for all sherds: method of manufacture (hand, wheel, or mold), fabric (fine, medium, or coarse), extant portion represented by the sherd, surface treatment (e.g. paint, slip, black glaze, plastic or incised decoration, burnishing), vessel shape (open vs. closed, and type if identified), and probable date. We hoped that by comparing the characteristics of unknown pieces with dated ones, more sherds could be identified, and to a certain extent this hope was realized. Appendix 2 summarizes, in the form of tables, the collected totals of sherds for the prehistoric and Early Iron Age material that were collected from each site. More detailed analyses were undertaken during two full study seasons in 1982 and 1983, when all of the specialists collaborating in the analysis of the artifacts were able to go over the artifacts together.

The study of the ceramics reported in this volume is the work of four individuals: Daniel J. Pullen for the Neolithic, Early Helladic I, and Early Helladic II pottery; Gullög C. Nordquist for the Early Helladic III, Middle Helladic, and Late Helladic I pottery; Penelope A. Mountjoy for the Late Helladic II through Late Helladic IIIC; and Susan Langdon for the Early Iron Age and Geometric pottery. Although we have attempted to be consistent, it is inevitable that we would approach our materials in different ways. We decided that because the Mycenaean (Late Helladic) materials are similar to Mycenaean material from elsewhere, the publication of the Late Helladic material must conform as closely as possible to the publication format of Mycenaean material from other regions, for comparative purposes. For this reason, Chapter 3 differs slightly in style from the other chapters. For Chapters 1, 2, and 4 the ceramics are less readily comparable to other areas, or material from these other areas is not well published, and we have supplied rather more detailed presentations of the ceramics therein.

General discussions of the pottery are to be found in Chapters 1–4. Detailed catalogue entries are found in Appendix 1, where a continuous numbering sequence has been used for ceramic artifacts of all periods. Specific objects are referred to by the catalogue numbers of Appendix 1. Likewise, catalogue numbers are used in the assemblage tables of Appendix 2 to identify objects from a particular site that are discussed in detail elsewhere in this volume.

We characterize the Neolithic and Early Helladic I and II ceramics primarily by shape and decoration, and we follow this approach in order to facilitate the attempt to determine the functions of the sites from which the material comes. The characteristics of shape and decoration are for the most part the principal means of initially identifying the material as Neolithic or Early Helladic. Fabric is taken into consideration, of course, and some periods, especially Early Helladic I, offer very distinctive fabrics not seen in other periods. Other approaches to classification could have been taken, for instance classification by wares (fabric and decoration), which is the method used in Chapter 2.

The Early Helladic III and Middle Helladic ceramics present a wide variety of fabrics that seem to be rather significant. Unlike the Middle Helladic period, the Early Helladic II period does not offer many distinctive fabrics, and thus shape is used as the organizing factor. The Mycenaean material is arranged by shape within each chronological subdivision of the Late Helladic period. The pottery of the Early Iron Age is organized according to shape, from open to closed, larger to smaller vessels; and the coarse wares are described after the fine wares. Specific descriptions of shape appear in catalogue entries only when a sherd seems to be an unusual variation of a standard type, or is not easily identified from its illustration.

Catalogue entries are organized in a standard manner. Catalogue number, object title, and illustration references appear on the top line. The inventory number is given in parentheses, followed by the extant portion represented by the sherd and its relevant dimensions (all dimensions in this volume are in metric measure unless otherwise specified). Fabric is described next, and, for non-Mycenaean material, color descriptions are given based on the Munsell Soil Color Charts (1975 edition). Detailed descriptions of shape and decoration conclude each entry.

Paint is not indicated on the illustrations of the Neolithic, Early Helladic I, or Early Helladic II material because it was generally poorly preserved, and the great quantity of plastic and incised decoration made it difficult to depict. Paint is indicated on the illustrations of the Early Helladic III, Middle Helladic, Late Helladic, and Early Iron Age material. Special problems are encountered in the illustration of survey material, in particular deciding the most effective means of rendering an important, but badly worn sherd. In cases where line drawings are intended to document the actual shape and state of a sherd, a photograph is provided to offer a clearer sense of its appearance. A related issue is the fact that many illustrations are necessarily interpretive (e.g. setting the orientation of a rim or handle), and dates for sites that are based on such interpretations must accordingly be very broad.

The methods of our analyses have been patterned after those used in the study of large bodies of materials retrieved in the course of systematic excavations. Nevertheless, ours is a pioneering study in its own right, an attempt to chart new ground by treating on their own terms artifacts and assemblages that have been often overlooked by earlier generations of archaeologists. Whether our efforts have been successful is for the reader to judge, and we must now finally deliver the results of our studies, as did Gibbon, to the "curiosity and candour of the Public."

CHAPTER I

The Pottery of the Neolithic, Early Helladic I, and Early Helladic II Periods

Daniel J. Pullen

This chapter covers the pottery of six distinct periods in Greek prehistory: the Early, Middle, Late, and Final Neolithic periods and the Early Helladic I and II periods. The pottery of each of the six periods is considered in a separate section below. The catalogue for all the periods covered in this chapter appears in Appendix 1.

The Early Neolithic Period

Although the Early Neolithic period is not represented in the collections of the survey, excavations at Franchthi Cave (site C13) have produced extensive evidence for this period, both inside the cave and along the (present-day) shoreline in front of and below the mouth of the cave (Jacobsen 1969, 1973a, 1973b, 1976).

The Middle Neolithic Period (1–5, Figs. 1, 118)

The Middle Neolithic period is represented by ceramics from D3 and E14, in addition to the excavations at Franchthi Cave. D3 is the Dhidhima Cave, a rock-shelter-like formation, and E14 is the Mouzaki cave to the south of Ermioni. Only sherds of the group of wares known as Urfirnis, and in only three shapes, have been identified from the survey.

The Urfirnis fabrics are fine to medium, with small inclusions, and are mostly hard-fired to an even color (see Vitelli [1974] and Cullen [1985] for further details of Urfirnis pottery characteristics). Surfaces are covered with the Urfirnis slip, ranging from orange to black-brown, and then burnished, in one instance in a vertical "scribble" fashion (3). No pattern-painted Urfirnis examples were detected.

The major parts of the pedestaled bowl shape (Weinberg 1937: 501 and 501 fig. 10) are represented by examples from three separate vessels: a rim 1, a sherd preserving the junction of the bowl and pedestal 2, and a pedestal base 3. The carinated bowl 4 could also have stood on a pedestal, but need not (Weinberg 1937: 501). The plate or shallow bowl 5 with its straight sides is not a common shape in the MN repertoire.

The Late Neolithic Period (6–11, Figs. 1, 118)

Late Neolithic pottery has been identified at four survey sites, D3, E5, E14, and G9, as well as from the excavations at Franchthi Cave. D3 and E14 continue from the Middle Neolithic. E5 is an open-air site near Ermioni, and G9 is the Kotena Cave on the slopes of Mt. Dhidhima's foothills. At none of the sites was material identified as Late Neolithic very plentiful (D3 had 11 definite and two possible Late Neolithic sherds, the others only one or two definite), and, as is usually the case with small numbers of sherds from a surface survey, the identification of the presence of a phase such as Late Neolithic remains tenuous.

A greater variety of wares has been identified for the Late Neolithic, compared with the Middle Neolithic, including black burnished **6**, matt painted **10**, and polychrome **8**. Lavezzi (1978: 418) notes the "remarkably wide range of fabrics plainly in contemporaneous use" at Late Neolithic Corinth.

Shapes identified in the Late Neolithic material are primarily bowls: carinated **6** and **7**; a vertical walled, probably deep bowl **8**; and one with a flaring rim **9**. A small burnished loop handle **11** would have come from a closed vessel, but its dating to LN is not certain.

The Final Neolithic Period (12–68, Figs. 1–4, 118)

The presence of a phase at the end of the Neolithic in the fourth millennium B.C. had been suspected for several years, e.g. at Eutresis (Caskey and Caskey 1960), but it was not until Renfrew's (1972) work on the Early Bronze Age that the period was formally defined and named as the Final Neolithic. The Final Neolithic is marked by regional variation in ceramics; for our purposes the Final Neolithic of southern Greece is represented by material from excavations at Athens (Immerwahr 1971), Aigina (Walter and Felten 1981), Phlius (Biers 1969; material in Corinth Museum), and those sites included in Phelps' (1975) study of the Neolithic sequence of the Peloponnese, such as Alepotrypa. The Final Neolithic assemblage is characterized by a lack of matt, pattern, and polychrome painted pottery, the presence of pattern burnished, slipped and burnished, and numerous plain coarse wares, some with applied plastic or incised decoration.

The Final Neolithic is represented at a number of sites in the survey, but at most sites the number of sherds is quite small. Only three sites had more than five definite FN sherds: C15 (8), C29 (15), and G9 (127). Final Neolithic is also present at Franchthi Cave. The other sites had fewer than five definite or possible FN sherds, or sherds which may belong to the earliest part of the EH I period: A6, A33, A51, B5, B8, B9, B20, B39, B41, B46, B53, C2, C8, C11, C24, C25, C37, D3, E4, E5, E6, E9, E13, E14, E74, F5, F6, F9, F14, F20, F32, F49, and G11. But taken together, the sherds from these latter sites constitute a sizable amount of material, which, considered in conjunction with the sherds from the three principal FN sites, demonstrates the widespread nature of FN activity in the Southern Argolid. A number of the sites are located in the Koiladha Valley and lower Fournoi Valley near Franchthi Cave, a situation very different from earlier Neolithic occupation of the region. The other major FN site is Kotena Cave (G9), close to the Iliokastro basin. The remaining sites are generally to be found toward the eastern and southern coasts of the Argolid, but not in any detectable clustering like that around Franchthi Cave.

The small amounts of Final Neolithic material at any one site contributed to the difficulty of isolating it from material of other periods, especially from Early Helladic I. Indeed, at only two sites, C25 and C29, was no material of the EH I period found. The large body of material from

Kotena Cave, G9, and comparisons with Final Neolithic material excavated at Franchthi Cave and the Acropolis at Halieis, though, have allowed for the effective identification of the Final Neolithic ceramics here.

Fabrics of the Final Neolithic were generally semicoarse to coarse, with many inclusions, some of which could be quite large, e.g. **38** with inclusions $>$ 0.005 m. Fine or semifine fabrics with few, small inclusions were very uncommon: **50**, a tubular lug, and **68**, a pattern burnished sherd whose fabric is similar to the Early Helladic I quartz and volcanic tempered fabrics. The tempers used include limestone or other related calcium carbonate material in small amounts in roughly two-fifths of the catalogued material, but the number of sherds that did not react to the dilute hydrochloric acid is probably more significant, given the extensive limestone bedrock of the Southern Argolid (Vitaliano 1987). Some quartz was readily identifiable, and the volcanic minerals characteristic of the succeeding Early Helladic I period were remarkably absent, but without petrographic thin section analysis the identification of the other tempering agents was not attempted.

The biscuit was unevenly fired in all but six of the catalogued pieces. The colors of the breaks were usually red, reddish brown, reddish yellow, or yellowish brown (10R 4/8, 5/6-8; 2.5YR 4/4-8, 5/6-8, 6/8; 5YR 2.5/1, 3/2, 4/1, 4/4-6, 5/6-8, 6/4-8; 7.5YR 5/6, 6/4-6), with the majority 2.5YR 4-6/6, 4-5/8 (red, light red, reddish brown). The cores tended to be darker, with indeterminate gray and black in the majority and low value and chroma readings for hues 2.5YR, 5YR, and 7.5YR (e.g. dusky red, dark reddish brown, and dark reddish gray).

The Final Neolithic assemblage encompasses a wide variety of open and closed shapes, plastic and impressed decoration, and surface treatments.

Most bowls either are of the spreading variety with straight walls **12–14** or have incurving walls **16–19**, though carinated **15**, and deep, almost vertical-sided varieties **20** and **21** also occur. The pierced-rim vessel **22** is probably an open vessel, though it and similar uncatalogued pieces are so irregular that it is difficult to determine whether one is a bowl or a jar. The bowl with pierced rim, known as a "cheese pot," is widespread in the Aegean in Final Neolithic (Renfrew 1972: 155). The spreading bowls range in diameter at the rim from ca. 0.20 to 0.35 m, and the incurving bowls all cluster around 0.26 to 0.29 m. The large deep bowl **21** gives a diameter of ca. 0.44 m below the rim, but because the orientation is not secure, the rim diameter is only approximate.

The distinction between incurving bowls such as **18–20** and simple "hole mouth" jars such as **23** and **24** is, perhaps, not very great, depending primarily on whether the rim is thickened, as in the jars, suggesting a link with jars such as **26** and **27** with distinct necks. The jars, then, range from the simple thickened rims **23** and **24** to tall flaring necks such as **31**. Usually there is a smooth transition from rim to neck to shoulder, as in **28**, but offset necks, e.g. **27**, or necks distinguished by a groove at their base, such as the rolled rim of **26**, also occur. The rim diameters of jars vary from 0.15 to 0.36 m, with several in the 0.28–0.32 m range, similar to the incurving bowls.

Bases are flat **35–39** or hollow **40** and **41**. While all the bases in the catalogue have tentatively been identified as coming from open vessels, this is surely the case only for **35** and **41**, which have burnished and slipped interiors, respectively. The three measurable flat bases have diameters of 0.12 and 0.17 m; the nonmeasurable bases seem to fall within the same range. The two hollow bases have diameters of 0.07 and 0.10 m.

One sherd **61** has been worn to an almost circular shape, perhaps from use as a burnisher or as a stopper. Though the sherd is of Final Neolithic date, its reuse cannot, of course, be dated.

A variety of handles and lugs have been identified as belonging to Final Neolithic vessels. Vertical handles range from narrow, e.g. **42**, perhaps from a jug neck, to wide and thin, such as **44**, from the maximum diameter of some large closed vessel. Handle **64**, an incised wide vertical strap handle of U-shaped section, may come from an askos or from another asymmetrical shape. Horizontal handles, too, vary from **45**, a small loop handle from an open vessel, to larger, thicker handles **46** and **47** from closed vessels and **48** from an open vessel. The tab handle **49** is from some large vessel, and though the orientation is not certain, it probably extended above the rim, with the center cut out. Some of the lugs and the knobs are most likely functional, e.g. **50**, a horizontally pierced lug, or the large knobs **54** and **56**. Other lugs, e.g. double-horned lugs **17** and **51**, are perhaps more decorative, but could well function as lifting supports.

Plastic decoration consists of plain horizontal ridges with sharp arrises **18, 58**, and **59** and plain rounded ridges such as **57**, which bends at a 90° angle. More common are plastic ridges, both pointed and rounded, with impressions and incisions. Single rounded ridges with slashes **61**, pairs of pointed ridges at angles with incisions **60**, and pairs of rounded ridges at angles with finger impressions **62** are found, as are more complicated patterns. **14** has a horizontal plastic band with impressions, with an angled impressed band below it (probably the band continued around the vessel in a zigzag pattern), and **16** and **30** have multiple horizontal bands with impressions. Large raised bands occur: **21** has a very wide band at the rim, with three horizontal rows of finger impressions unevenly spaced, and **63** has the edge of a band on which are incised at least two diagonal grooves. Other plastic decoration includes the row of three pellets on jar **29**.

Incision occurs by itself, as in handle **64** with rows of oblique and perpendicular slashes and longitudinal grooves, and in the two body sherds **65**, with herringbone, and **66**, with uneven chevrons formed by grooves with irregular oval impressions.

Surface treatments are generally plain, or at least smoothed, but burnishing regularly occurs. Burnishing is the most common surface treatment, usually on an unslipped surface. In some instances, e.g. on the interior of deep bowl **21**, the surface has been smoothed with readily visible marks of the tool, and a slight luster imparted to the grooves. This compaction of the surface does not always result in a lustrous surface, e.g. base **38**, where the surfaces are cracked and crazed due to the burnishing of an extremely coarse fabric, with the temper coming through to the surface. In other instances the burnishing is well done to a high, almost glossy luster, e.g. handle **42**. Burnishing occurs on both interiors and exteriors of bowls and several jars have a narrow band of burnishing on the interior lip or rim, in addition to the exterior, such as **27**.

Burnishing usually appears by itself, but in several instances it was used as a contrast to or in conjunction with other treatments. The wide raised bands of **21** and **63** are plain, i.e. unburnished, in contrast to the heavily burnished surfaces below. In a few instances a red slip has been applied to either exterior or interior, and the surface was then heavily burnished, e.g. **18** and **29**; more common was a light burnish on a red slip, such as **41, 44, 48, 58, 61**, and **65**. One example of a black burnished surface, the handle **42**, may be due to overfiring, since the biscuit is a dark gray color (5YR 4/1).

Pattern burnishing is a very characteristic feature of the Final Neolithic, as defined by Renfrew (1972: 77–79); two examples, both rather worn, are catalogued here. **67**, a body sherd from an open vessel, seems to have an underlying cream slip on top of which are heavily burnished red stripes, though neither the order of application nor the pattern is distinct. It is unclear whether the red stripes are added paint or whether the burnishing has caused the color change. On the closed vessel body sherd **68** the vessel was clearly slipped red and burnished in stripes, and then a second, pale (white?)

color was added to the nonburnished area; this process agrees with Immerwahr's description (1971: 7, 11), where a "fugitive matt white . . . has mostly flaked off" the surfaces of red slipped pattern burnished vessels from the Athenian Agora. This is similar to the ware from the Final Neolithic deposits at Franchthi Cave that Jacobsen (1973b: 273–74) has labeled "crusted ware." A third sherd, a rim from a jar or flaring bowl **34**, has a cream slip on top of which is a solid red paint that is highly burnished to a luster. This could be from a pattern burnished vessel like **67** and **68**, but need not be, since the pattern burnish variety of the red slipped and burnished ware is much less common than the solid burnished variety. This red-on-white pottery has been found at Franchthi Cave in conjunction with the crusted ware (Jacobsen 1973b: 273).

In the catalogue several pieces, **18**, **29**, **32**, **41**, **48**, **64**, and **68**, are dated Final Neolithic to Early Helladic I, generally by the presence of red slipped and burnished surfaces, a characteristic treatment of the Early Helladic I period. The handle **64** is perhaps from an askos, a shape common in EH I as well, but the fabric seems to fit with the other Final Neolithic pieces. The body sherd **68** is pattern burnished, but the fabric, as noted before, seems closer to Early Helladic I examples.

The affinities of the Southern Argolid Final Neolithic material with material from elsewhere in the Aegean can be detailed only in general terms. Absent from the Southern Argolid assemblage are such distinctive Final Neolithic features as the rolled rim bowl (the "Kum Tepe Ib" type) or the shouldered bowls. The few open bowls found are of a spreading wall variety, with little curve evident; these are widespread in their distribution and occur in many wares throughout the Final Neolithic. The carinated or "collared" bowl **15** finds general parallels in early FN bowls from Alepotrypa and elsewhere, though in our example the shoulder is not markedly set off (Phelps 1975: 322–24). The pierced-rim vessel **22** has already been identified as an example of the FN "cheese pot"; Coleman (1977: 17–18 Type C3) identifies them as "baking pans" or "hearths."

Hole-mouth jars, i.e. without a distinct neck, like our **23–25**, are found generally in the later part of the Final Neolithic, according to Phelps (1975: 339). Simple bands, usually single, are found on the upper part. Jars or pithoi with thickened rims and plastic bands at the rim are also common in the later phases of the period. Jars with collars or other distinct necks as **26–28** and **31** are found throughout the Final Neolithic at many sites, though jars with more gently sloping necks are generally later in FN.

The plastic decoration of plain and impressed applied bands, in single or multiple varieties, is found throughout the Aegean, from the Ionian islands to the eastern Aegean islands, in the Late Neolithic through Early Bronze Age phases. The grouping of bands into patterns, as opposed to single horizontal bands, is to be found more often in the Final Neolithic, but this feature is by no means restricted to this period. The pattern-burnished, crusted, and red-on-white painted surface treatments tend to be earlier than later in Final Neolithic.

The Early Helladic I Period (69–212, Figs. 4–12, 118, 119)

Unlike what was found in the preceding Neolithic periods, the Early Helladic I is well represented in large quantities at a number of sites. There are 15 sites with ten or more definite Early Helladic I sherds: A6 (83), A33 (48), C11 (48), A9 (29), F32 (24), B24 (18), B81 (18), B39 (14), C15 (13), F9 (13), F45 (13), E6 (12), B41 (11), C17 (10), and E13 (10); eight sites with five to nine EH I sherds: B9 (7), E4 (5), E5 (5), E9 (9), E16 (5), E74 (7), F6 (6), and G9 (7); and 19 sites with fewer than five EH I sherds. Altogether, then, evidence for the EH I period is extensive and plentiful. In

Table 1.1. Presence of Quartz, Volcanic Minerals, and Lime

in Early Helladic I Pottery from the Southern Argolid (N = 123)

Quartz	Volcanic Minerals	Lime	Number	%
yes	yes	yes	4	3.2
yes	yes	no	45	36.6
yes	no	yes	27	22.0
yes	no	no	23	18.7
no	yes	yes	0	0.0
no	yes	no	3	2.4
no	no	yes	17	13.8
no	no	no	4	3.2

addition to the Early Helladic I material, there is a large body of ceramics we have labeled either Early Helladic I-II or Early Helladic I: Blegen Class A. This material does not fit into Early Helladic I ceramic categories typical for the Southern Argolid; rather, it is similar to Blegen's Class A (Wace and Blegen 1916–18; Blegen 1921), i.e. EH I slipped, typical of the Northern Argolid and Corinthia, and seems to develop into Early Helladic II ceramics (including those of the Southern Argolid). The Early Helladic I ceramics common in the survey area are more related to Saronic Gulf and Cycladic pottery, and do not seem to have a great deal of influence on later ceramics in the Southern Argolid and Northern Argolid. For this reason, then, I have distinguished Early Helladic I from Early Helladic I: Blegen Class A and Early Helladic I-II, the former referring to the local and the latter two to the ceramics similar to those of the Northern Argolid and Corinthia.

The Fabrics

The typical Southern Argolid Early Helladic I ware is a red-orange quartz or quartz and volcanic mineral tempered gritty clay, covered with a thick red slip, and then burnished to a high luster. Both open and closed shapes occur in this ware.

Macroscopic examination of the pottery indicates that several of the minerals in the fabric are of volcanic origin, and probably derive from andesite, a common volcanic stone used for millstones in the Southern Argolid. A major source of andesite is the island of Aigina (Runnels 1981).

The Early Helladic I fabrics can be divided into three principal groups, based, respectively, on the presence of quartz, the volcanic minerals, and lime. Table 1.1 presents the frequencies of quartz, volcanic minerals, and lime for 123 catalogued samples for which the information is available (no claim for a statistically valid sample is made, but the relative frequencies do, I believe, hold for the entire Early Helladic I collection).

The presence of quartz appears to be the defining factor for the local Southern Argolid EH I fabric, for of the 21 sherds without quartz temper, 18 fall into the Early Helladic I: Blegen Class A or Early Helladic I-II categories; only five of the 99 quartz-tempered sherds (and none with volcanic minerals) have been placed into the Early Helladic I: Blegen Class A or Early Helladic I-II categories.

Volcanic minerals and lime seem, to a large degree, to be mutually exclusive; only four sherds have both, out of 96 that have either, compared to 48 volcanic-tempered with no lime and 44 lime-tempered but with no volcanic minerals. Quartz temper does not seem to be affected by the choice of lime temper, for roughly the same number of quartz-tempered sherds have lime (27, or 22%) as do not have lime (23, or 18.7%).

The three fabric groups, then, are:

Fabric I: Quartz and volcanic minerals, and rarely also lime
Fabric II: Quartz without volcanic minerals, and with or without lime
Fabric III: No quartz or volcanic minerals, but usually with lime; this includes most of the Early Helladic I: Blegen Class A and Early Helladic I-II material

There does not seem to be any correlation between the two quartz-tempered fabrics (I and II) and shape, surface treatment, or added decoration. The only significant difference between Fabrics I and II is that a higher percentage of the Fabric I sherds are evenly fired (32 out of 49, or 64%), whereas sherds of Fabric II are more often unevenly fired (34 out of 50, or 68%). The presence of lime may have something to do with this, for 34 out of 48 (71%) of lime-tempered sherds are unevenly fired, compared to 34 out of 75 (45%) sherds without lime.

The two quartz-tempered fabrics have the same range of colors, with most sherds reading approximately 2.5-5YR 4-5/4-6-8, i.e. red, yellowish red, and reddish brown, on the break. The core color readings for Fabric II, because they are more numerous, tend to be more widespread, but generally they fall in the 5YR 4/2-4 range. The Fabric I sherds have core color readings that are lower in value and chrome (i.e. darker) and cluster more tightly at 5YR 3-4/2-3, but the differences are slight. In both fabrics the cores are rarely black or just gray, unlike the cores of the Neolithic fabrics. For the most part Fabrics I and II will be considered together, as there are very few differences between them.

Fabrics I and II are relatively rare in the northern Argolid, but have been found, for example, at Lerna, where Early Helladic I is poorly represented (Wiencke 1989: 495 n.1), and at the Nemea Valley, where an occasional piece has been found at Tsoungiza Hill and in the regional survey of the Nemea Valley Archaeological Project (personal observations). Rather, the fabrics seem to have a wide distribution along the Saronic coast of the Argolid, where they are relatively plentiful. On Methana (my thanks to Dr. Christopher Mee for this information) and farther north, the fabrics have been recognized on surface survey and other known sites.

Fabric III, without quartz or volcanic temper, often has lime (17 out of 21, or 81%) and is unevenly fired (17 out of 21, or 81%). Several of the Fabric III sherds (six) have a silver inclusion that is platy, like mica. Only one of the Fabric I sherds and four of Fabric II had the silver inclusions. The colors of the fabric and core tend to be lighter and less red, with the colors on the breaks clustering around 2.5-5YR 5-6/8 and on the cores around 5-7.5YR 4/1-2.

The Shapes

Although the Early Helladic I Fabrics I and II are distinctive enough to be used as indicators of the time period, certain shapes and surface treatments, too, can be readily associated with the Early Helladic I assemblage.

The study of Early Helladic I shapes is hampered by a lack of comparative material. Early Helladic I material has been found in limited quantities at Asine, Korakou, Mycenae, Perachora, and Zygouries in the Argolid-Corinthia, Asea in Arcadia, Kolonna on Aigina, Eutresis and Lithares in

Boeotia, and Asketario, Palaia Kokkinia, and other Attic sites. Only the material from Perachora has been published in any detail, albeit in preliminary reports (Fossey 1969). Recently Dousougli (1987) has published EH I material from three Argive sites: two surface collections (Makrovouni to the north of Argos and Talioti to the north of Asine) and one test excavation (Kephalari Magoula north of Lerna). But the Southern Argolid assemblage does not correspond closely to the assemblages from sites such as Perachora or Kephalari Magoula.

Bowls are classified by their shape into shallow (radius greater than interior height), spreading (straight, angled walls), hemispherical (radius equals interior height), incurving (maximum diameter below rim), and deep (vertical walls) and by size arbitrarily into small, with rim diameters usually up to 0.25 m; medium, with rim diameters 0.25–0.35 m; and large, with rim diameters greater than 0.35 m. In some shapes, though, a different scale is used when there are clusters of rim diameters that do not fit the arbitrary divisions at 0.25 and 0.35 m.

Shallow Bowls (69–79, Figs. 4, 118)

The shallowest bowls are from a special Early Helladic I shape: the fruitstand. Two examples, **69** and **70**, have the characteristic shallow bowl, flaring rim that turns down, and incision on top of the rim. Both examples are in Fabric III and are plain. The true fruitstand is generally on a large, tall pedestal (Dousougli 1987: 184 Abb. 12, 202 Abb. 27 nos. 163–68, 204 Abb. 29 nos. 176–83), but the bowl can also be on just a flat or raised base (e.g. Dousougli 1987: 202 Abb. 27 no. 166). The incision on the rim takes many forms, including herringbone, feathered lines, hatched triangles, and irregular lines (Dousougli 1987: 185 Abb. 13, 202 Abb. 27 nos. 164, 165), but the rims can be plain. Whether or not the incision, when present, goes completely around the rim is not clear. Several fruitstands appear to have handles on top of the rim (e.g. Dousougli 1987: 184 Abb. 12 nos. 42, 43), but no examples of such handles have been identified in the Southern Argolid collections. Only one fragment of the distinctive junctions of bowl and pedestal with decoration (e.g. Dousougli 1987: 185 Abb. 14 no. 48) has been found in the Southern Argolid at site C15 (uncatalogued). Dousougli (1987) suggests a late EH I date for the fruitstand, and this is confirmed in the excavations at Tsoungiza Hill in the Nemea Valley (Pullen 1987).

The more common shallow (i.e. radius greater than interior height) bowls **71–79** generally have a simpler shape: the wall curves gently to a simple rounded or flattened lip. Two examples have thickened rims: the rim of **76** appears to be incurving, though it is just thickened like **79**. Rim diameters of shallow bowls range from 0.17 to 0.43 m, with most around 0.30–0.33 m. Shallow bowls appear in all three fabrics:

Fabric I: **74–76, 78, 79**
Fabric II: **71, 72, 77**
Fabric III: **73**

71 appears to be related to the Early Helladic I: Blegen Class A by its red slipped and burnished surface.

Two shallow bowls have added plastic decoration. **73** has a long vertical lug (unpierced) below the rim. **74** has a horizontal impressed taenia band below the rim.

The shallow bowls are usually slipped and burnished: only **74** and possibly **79** are plain, though this could be a function of preservation of surface materials. All but one of the slipped examples appear to be slipped on both exterior and interior: **73** has a red-brown slip on the exterior and on the lip, but a plain interior. The slips range in color from a bright red to red-brown. Burnishing is usual on top of the slip, but despite poor preservation only **72** can be said to be not burnished to the extent that the results of the process are visible.

Spreading Bowls (**80–87**, Fig. 5)

Spreading bowls **80–87** have straight, angled walls. The rims are generally plain, with flat, **84** and **86**, or beveled, **85**, lips. **81** has a groove on a flat lip, while **80** has a groove on the exterior below the lip. **82** has a straight exterior wall, but the rim is greatly thickened on the interior; the lip is rounded and has a groove like **80**. A number of spreading bowls have a slightly thickened rim and rounded lip like **83**. **86** had a horizontal handle, oval in section, perhaps similar to that on **89**. Only four rim diameters were measurable, ranging from 0.21 to 0.37 m. Spreading bowls occur in all three fabrics:

> Fabric I: **83**
> Fabric II: **80–82, 85, 86**
> Fabric III: **84**

Plastic decoration was limited to a trumpet lug on **84**, of which the right-hand flaring vertical element and a horizontal ridge running to the left are preserved. Other "trumpet lugs" (cf. below **109–17**) from the Southern Argolid often have only one flaring end, or a very long horizontal bar, unlike those of Perachora (Fossey 1969: 58 fig. 3 no. 20, 63 fig. 5 no. 17).

Incised decoration occurs on the flat lip of **87** in the form of impressed triangles alternating directions in order to form a kerbschnitt pattern. Incised lips appear to be another feature characteristic of EH I.

Spreading bowls appear plain, **80**, **81**, and **86**, or slipped and burnished, **82** and **83**. **84** is slipped only on the interior, but both exterior and interior are burnished. **85** is slipped red on the exterior only, and burnishing was not apparent. Slips range in color from red to red-brown.

Hemispherical Bowls (**88–96**, Figs. 5, 6)

Hemispherical bowls **88–96** have a radius equal to interior height. Of course with only sherds preserved it is difficult to judge whether a vessel would have fit into this category, but the category can be thought of as distinct from incurving, shallow, or spreading bowls. As in the spreading bowls, the rims are generally simple (only **88**, **91**, and **94** have thickened rims), and the lips are either rounded, **88**, **90**, **92**, **93**, and **95**, or flattened, **89**, **91**, **94**, and **96**. One bowl, **89**, has a horizontal handle, oval in section with a small horizontal ridge running lengthwise. Most of the rim diameters range from 0.27 to 0.35 m, but diameters up to 0.54 m occur. Hemispherical bowls occur only in Fabrics I and II:

> Fabric I: **90, 91, 94–96**
> Fabric II: **88, 89, 92, 93**

No plastic decoration, other than the ridge on the handle of **89**, or impressed decoration was found on hemispherical bowls. All the catalogued examples are slipped red to red-brown, and most are burnished. **93** and **95** are too worn for us to determine whether they are slipped on both exterior and interior. **94** is burnished to a very high luster, almost glossy in sheen.

Incurving Bowls (**97–125**, Figs. 6–8, 118)

The incurving bowl, **97–125**, is certainly the most common open shape of the Early Helladic I period in the Southern Argolid. The degree of incurve of the wall, the sharpness of the curve, and the shape of the rim and lip all vary a great deal. A number of bowls have gentle, slight incurves, e.g. **99**, **102**, and **120**; others curve in more, e.g. **100**, **104**, **106**, and **122**; and still others are sharply incurved, as in **110** and **111**. Rims can be simple, such as those on **99** and **102**, but more often they are thickened to the exterior, as in **107**, **115**, and **124**, to the interior, as in **101** and **111**, or to both the exterior and interior, e.g. **105** and **121**. Lips can be rounded, **98** and **106**, though flattened lips are more common, whether horizontal, **124**, or beveled, e.g. **115** and **123**. **119** has an incurving wall, but the rim is turned out to form a band for impressions and slashes. Rim diameters cluster into three sizes: 0.20–0.24 m (four examples), 0.26–0.33 m, especially around 0.29 m (seven examples), and 0.36–0.46 m, especially 0.38–0.41 m (nine examples). No handles were observed for incurving bowls. Incurving bowls occur in all three fabrics:

Fabric I: **97**, **100–104**, **118**, **120–122**
Fabric II: **98**, **99**, **106**, **108**
Fabric III: **105**, **107**, **109–117**, **123**, **124**

The incurving bowl continues into the Early Helladic II period as the most common bowl form, in both small and large varieties. The large number of the EH I examples that have been classed into the Early Helladic I: Blegen Class A and Early Helladic I-II categories (**98**, **105**, **109–117**, **123**, and **124**) is not surprising, as they probably represent late EH I or pieces transitional to EH II, anticipating developments in the Southern Argolid Early Helladic II.

Plastic decoration is usually found on those pieces assigned to the Early Helladic I: Blegen Class A and Early Helladic I-II category; only **105** of this category did not have plastic decoration, and only **118** and **120–122** of those sherds which are not in this category have plastic decoration. Plastic decoration includes trumpet lugs **109–117**, decorative lugs **118**, impressed taenia bands **119–122**, and plain horizontal ridges **123** and **124**. The trumpet lugs in all but one instance (**117**) have preserved only one flaring end. The horizontal bar can be a plain ridge as in **109**, **112–114**, and **117**, or can be an impressed taenia band **110**, **111**, and **116**. Since the horizontal bars of the trumpet lugs seem to be rather long, those sherds with just a plain horizontal ridge, **123** and **124**, or impressed taenia band **119–122** could conceivably also be part of trumpet lugs. While the flaring ends of the trumpet lugs are generally well formed, in **114** the end seems to be formed by bending and curling the horizontal ridge. All the taenia bands, whether with or without the flaring trumpet end, are of the impressed variety, without slashes or separate overlapping discs. The only exception is **119**, where slashes are used in conjunction with finger impressions on an outturned rim.

Incised decoration occurs only on the flat beveled lip of **125**: diagonal slashes form an irregular set of chevrons.

Again, the surfaces are left plain, as in **97**, **101**, **103**, **111**, **115**, **118**, **120–122**, or one or both surfaces are slipped and usually burnished. **107** is just burnished with no slip, and **104** is slipped red on the interior only, but both interior and exterior are burnished. The interior and lip only are slipped and burnished on **116** and **124**. On **123** both exterior and interior are slipped, on **113** only the exterior is slipped, and no burnishing was detected. The exterior and interior of **114** are slipped, but only the interior burnished. Both exterior and interior are slipped and burnished on **99**, **100**, **102**, **105**, **108**, **112**, and **117**. The slips used are red, red-brown, brown, and, on **99**, red mottled to black.

Deep Bowls (**126–128**, Fig. 8)

Only three examples of deep bowls, **126–128**, are catalogued here. The walls are virtually vertical, but each of the rims is different. **126** has a rim greatly thickened to the exterior, the rim of **127** is slightly thickened and barely curves out, while **128** is also slightly thickened, but curves in slightly. Only two rim diameters are measurable: 0.24 and 0.255 m. Only Fabrics II and III were used:

> Fabric II: **127, 128**
> Fabric III: **126**

No plastic or incised decoration was noted on any deep bowl. One deep bowl, **127**, is plain, one, **128**, is burnished only on the interior, and the third, **126**, does not have its surfaces preserved.

Jars (**129–164, 166–173**, Figs. 8–11, 118)

There are remarkably few closed shapes among the Early Helladic I material from the Southern Argolid. Three varieties of jars were recognized: jars with very flaring rims, jars with flaring rims, and jars with insloping necks and thickened rims. No jugs were identified, and only one askos is suggested by an incised handle. The presence of other shapes is more tenuous.

Jars were categorized on the basis of their neck and rim shape into: very flaring, with rims greater than 45° from vertical, **129–132**; flaring, with rims less than 45° from vertical, **133–148**; and insloping necks, **149–154**. Below the neck the reconstruction of the various shapes is difficult. **133**, one of the more completely preserved examples, has a rather wide shoulder, short insloping neck, and a flaring rim, all in a continuous curve. **134–136** have virtually no shoulder, and no distinct neck other than the point of constriction and inflection below the rim. In **137–138** and **148** the neck area appears to be rather tall, but there again may be virtually no shoulder. That there are a number of jars with necks offset from shoulders is indicated by shoulders such as **156** and especially by decorated shoulders such as **157–162**. Here the junction of the neck and shoulder is emphasized by an incised groove. It is not possible to determine which of the jar rim/neck types, very flaring, flaring, or insloping, belongs with the grooved shoulders.

The diameters of the jar rims vary quite a bit. The jars with very flaring rims have rim diameters of 0.23, 0.24, and 0.34 m. The flaring-rim jars have rim diameters that cluster into three groups: 0.15–0.17 m (three examples), 0.22–0.25 m (six examples), and 0.28–0.35 m (three examples). The jars with insloping necks have rim diameters ranging from 0.19 to 0.38 m. The rim diameters both of the flaring-rim jars and the insloping-neck jars fit well with the diameters at the junction of neck and shoulder of the decorated shoulders **160–161** (diameters at shoulder 0.25 and 0.40 m); the shoulders **157–159** do seem to be a bit small for the rims catalogued here, but we really have no idea how short or tall the necks would have been.

Jars with very flaring rims, jars with flaring rims, and jars with insloping necks occur only in Fabrics I and II. All the incised jar shoulders **157–162** and incised body sherds which are probably from jars (cf. below), **163, 164, 166–173**, are also only in Fabrics I and II (the fabrics of **167–173** were only quickly examined for presence of quartz and/or volcanic temper, hence they are placed generally into Fabrics I-II). Indeed only jar **156**, with a flaring neck unlike any others, is in Fabric III. No jar rim, shoulder, or probable incised body sherd has been placed into the Early Helladic I: Blegen Class A or Early Helladic I-II category.

> Fabric I: **131, 136, 139–141, 143–147, 149–151, 154, 155, 160, 162–166**
> Fabric II: **129, 130, 132–135, 137, 138, 142, 148, 152, 153, 158, 159**
> Fabric III: **156**

Dousougli (1987) publishes few jars from Early Helladic I, none of which provides any close parallel for the Southern Argolid jars. The material from Perachora provides some comparanda to our material. Two Perachora jars, one from Phase Y (Fossey 1969: 61 fig. 4 no. 22) and one from Phase Z (Fossey 1969: 66 fig. 6 no. 1), have rims which could be considered very flaring, as are our **131** and **132**. There are several flaring rims from Perachora (Fossey 1969: 56 fig. 2 nos. 1, 16–19 from Phase X; 58 fig. 3 no. 17, called a bowl or "large jar," also from Phase X; 61 fig. 4 nos. 1–3, 21, 23, 25–30 from Phase Y). Only one example of the insloping, thickened rim jar is illustrated from Perachora, though it is called a "heavy, apparently deep bowl" and is unlike anything else published from there (Fossey 1969: 63 fig. 5 no. 1). Missing from the Southern Argolid are the collared jars (e.g. Fossey 1969: 56 fig. 2 nos. 9–14; 61 fig. 4 nos. 16–20) and jars with flaring necks (such as Fossey 1969: 56 fig. 2 nos. 2–7; 61 fig. 4 nos. 4–15). Fossey does remark (1969: 61) on three examples from Perachora Phase Y on which the neck and shoulder are separated by a "single or grooved line scored around the shoulder" (e.g. Fossey 1969: 61 fig. 4 nos. 10, 18, and 23).

Several of the rims and offset shoulders of the Southern Argolid jars have Cycladic parallels in the Early Cycladic I Grotta-Pelos culture, such as "necked jars" from Phylakopi and Grotta, Naxos (Renfrew 1972: 156 fig. 10.2 nos. 2 and 8), and Early Cycladic II Keros-Syros culture footed jars (Benaki Museum 1978: 141 no. 163 = Goulandris Collection no. 231 and Benaki Museum 1978: 142 no. 164 = Goulandris Collection no. 232), as well as from the eastern Aegean, e.g. Kum Tepe Ib (Renfrew 1972: 74 fig. 5.3 no. 10). None of the parallels is exact, and as the reconstruction of the entire profile of the Southern Argolid jars is problematic, as discussed above, such parallels are to be thought of in general terms.

No added plastic decoration was used for the jars. Rather, incised decoration seems to be quite common. Jars from the Southern Argolid that have a shoulder distinct from the insloping neck generally mark the junction with a groove, as in **157–162**. Usually additional incision decorates the shoulder, but never the neck (unlike the Cycladic examples cited above, which can have incised decoration on neck and/or shoulder). Small oblique impressions form a "feathered" line, **159** and **160**; pairs of diagonal lines form chevrons, **157** and perhaps **162**; and irregularly spaced vertical slashes also form a feathered line, **161**.

Incision is rare in the Perachora material in the earlier Phases X and Y (Fossey 1969: 56, 61), but much more common in Phase Z "despite the small amount of material" (Fossey 1969: 66). Of particular note in the Perachora Phase Z material is a jar (Fossey 1969: 66 fig. 6 Jar no. 10) with shoulder marked off from the neck by a "feathered" groove and stamped triangles following angled incised lines down the shoulder, and a jug (Fossey 1969: 66 fig. 6, Jar no. 11), which appears to have a groove at the base of the neck and sets of three incised lines forming chevrons. In addition, incision at Perachora occurs on frying pans (as in Phase Y examples, Fossey 1969: 66 fig. 6 Frying pans nos. 1 and 2) and on handles, one of which is surely an askos (Fossey 1969: 66 fig. 6 Handle no. 3).

A number of incised body sherds, **163–164**, **166–173**, are likely to come from jars. All are from closed vessels and illustrate the schemes of incised decoration. **163** and **164** have stamped spirals in addition to incised lines (see also below, **206**, for possible frying pan with stamped spirals or circles). Feathered lines are common, whether on both sides of an incised line, **166**, or on a curved line, **171**. Groups of incised lines either parallel, **169**, **170**, and **172**, or converging, **168** and **173**, seem to be placed on the diagonal. **169** may have a pattern of hatched triangles with the different orientations of parallel lines. **171** appears to have a feathered curving line tangential to a straight line, though these could well be two converging lines, one of which is feathered.

Stamped spirals occur in the Cyclades (especially on pottery from Syros) and on varieties of pyxides, jars, and frying pans from the mainland with affinities to the Cyclades. Stamped spirals begin toward the end of the Early Helladic I period (Bossert 1960; Coleman 1985: 218–19).

The majority of the very flaring and flaring jar rims, **129–148**, neck/shoulders, and body sherds are slipped red and burnished. **134** is plain, and **133** is slipped and burnished on the exterior only. Several have slips that are not the usual bright red: **135** is black, **137** is red-brown, **141** is orange, and **140** is mottled red to black. On many of these rims the burnishing is done to a very high glossy luster, e.g. **129, 130, 132, 136, 139, 140, 142, 145–147**.

The jars with insloping necks seem to be slipped red and burnished on the exterior and lip, and not always on the interior. **150** is slipped red and burnished on the exterior and lip, but the interior is burnished only; **151** is slipped all over, but only the exterior and lip are burnished; **153** is plain; and **152** and **155** are slipped red and burnished on the exterior and lip, but the interior is plain. On **149** the slip is preserved only on the exterior. Only **154** had slip all over, and may have been burnished all over.

On the jars with incised shoulders the exterior is slipped red, and often burnished. **159** preserves red slip and burnish on the interior of the neck portion. Of the incised body sherds, all are slipped red and burnished on the exterior only; **169**, though, is the only plain piece, and it may be from a handle.

Miscellaneous Body Sherds, Handles, Lugs, and Knobs
(**165, 174–188**, Figs. 11–12, 119)

Body sherd **165** has a raised band on which is incised an irregular herringbone pattern. The raised band is plain, but the area below is slipped red. Closed body sherd **188** has two applied ridges, which are perhaps vertical. The red slip is almost like red Urfirnis of Early Helladic II, and though the fabric is Fabric II, it has been placed into the Early Helladic I: Blegen Class A category.

Handles come from both open, **86, 89**, and **180**, and closed, **175–179**, vessels. The most common shape seems to be a wide handle, either horizontal, **86, 89, 176–179**, or vertical, **175** and **180**, and oval or wide and thin in section. As mentioned above, **175** probably comes from an askos or other asymmetrical shape. **174** is a large open vessel with the scar of a handle attached with a dowel, part of which remains in the hole. Handles occur in all three fabrics:

Fabric I: **174, 177, 179, 180**
Fabric II: **176, 178**
Fabric III: **175**

Incision occurs on several of the handles, in the form of lines running parallel or converging along the length of the handle. At the base of **176** and **177** are incised lines that seem to set off the handle. All the handles are slipped red on the exterior; only **177** is also burnished. The slips of **175** and **178** are similar to Early Helladic II Urfirnis, and these have been placed into the Early Helladic I-II and Early Helladic I: Blegen Class A category.

Three lugs **181–183**, all in Fabric II, are all pierced. Two lugs **181** and **183** are half round, and the third rectangular. **181** comes from a closed vessel that was incised and slipped red and burnished on the exterior. **182** is plain, and the vessel form is indeterminate, like **183**.

Knobs, **184–187**, also occur in Early Helladic I. Only **184** can be said to be definitely from a closed (pithos?) vessel. **186** is more like a pellet; **187** may be worn down and not originally truncated at an angle. **184** and **185** are in Fabric II; **186** and **187** are in Fabric I. **184** and **187** are burnished; **185** is plain.

Bases (**189–205**, Fig. 12)

Bases are generally of two types: hollow, **189–191**, or flat, **192–205**. It was often not possible to determine with confidence whether a base is from an open or closed vessel. **189** and **192–194** all had finished interiors, suggesting open vessels, and **195–199** all had interiors left plain, while exteriors (and bottoms!) are slipped and burnished, suggesting closed shapes. Diameters of the three hollow bases measure 0.07, 0.09, and 0.12 m; diameters of the flat bases cluster at 0.05–0.06 and 0.08–0.15 m.

> Fabric I: **189, 198, 199, 203–205**
> Fabric II: **190–193, 195–197, 200–202**
> Fabric III: **194**

Only **201** was placed into the Early Helladic I: Blegen Class A category. **194** may not be Early Helladic I, and the heavy burnishing suggests an earlier date.

Several of the bases are plain: **191, 201, 203–205**. Both interior and exterior are slipped and burnished on **189**. **192** and **194** are burnished on both interior and exterior. The exterior and bottom are slipped and burnished with a plain interior on **195, 197**, and **199**, the exterior only on **196** and **198**. **193** has slip on the exterior and bottom, but the entire vessel is burnished.

Flat base **205** has the deep impression of a mat on its bottom.

Miscellaneous Shapes (**206–212**, Figs. 12, 119)

A small flat sherd **206** of Fabric I, with portions of two stamped spirals or circles and an incised tangential line, may come from a frying pan. The surface is slipped red and burnished.

Several knobs to stands were either in Fabrics I and II (e.g. **208**) or were slipped red as in Early Helladic I: Blegen Class A (e.g. **207**). See below the section on stands in the Early Helladic II period (**633–646**).

An Early Helladic I red slipped and burnished sherd of Fabric I, **209**, probably from a closed vessel, had a hole drilled through it after firing. Though this could represent a mend hole, the sherd seems to be worn down in a manner suggesting that it was suspended, perhaps as a weight.

Three spindle whorls **210–212**, all conical in shape, were recovered, two from the same site (**211** and **212** from C25), where they were the only EH I artifacts found. **210** is in Fabric I, and **211** and **212** are in Fabric II. All were plain.

The Early Helladic II Period (**213–617**, Figs. 13–37, 119–124)

Sites of the Early Helladic II period in the Southern Argolid are very widespread and have produced much material. More ceramics identified as Early Helladic II have come from more sites than any other prehistoric period, and only the Late Classical and Late Roman phases of the historic period seem to be more plentifully represented in the Southern Argolid than is EH II. The quantity of material collected by the survey is large, with seven sites having more than 50 EH II sherds, including site F32 with more than 600.

The Early Helladic II assemblage from the Southern Argolid resembles that of the northern Argolid and Corinthia in shapes, decorative features, and surface treatments. What distinguishes the Southern Argolid are the relative proportions of various shape elements and decorative features. For instance, pedestaled feet for bowls and sauceboats are relatively rare at sites such as Lerna, Tiryns,

Zygouries, and Asine, but much more common in the Southern Argolid. The small incurving bowl known as a "saucer" is found at virtually all Early Helladic II sites in the survey area, but in fewer numbers than in the northern Argolid and Corinthia. Other differences include a greater use of yellow-blue slip and burnish ware, incision and impression for decoration, and the krater with out-turned lip in the Southern Argolid, compared to the northern Argolid and Corinthia. Taken together, the features in the Southern Argolid EH II assemblage suggest closer affinities with the Saronic Gulf and Attica than with the Argive Plain and Corinthia. This is not surprising, given the location of the Southern Argolid midway between the Saronic Gulf and the Argive plain. This problem of the affinities of the Southern Argolid EH II assemblage will be further discussed below.

The Fabrics

The fabrics of the Early Helladic II material were difficult to categorize, unlike the Early Helladic I material. Only a few distinctive fabrics stood out: that associated with the yellow-blue slipped and burnished ware; the "Corinthian green" fabric; and a few examples of Early Helladic I Fabrics I and II that were used for shapes usually dated to Early Helladic II.

The fabric of the yellow-blue slipped and burnished pieces is generally a semifine hard, but unevenly fired, biscuit. Colors range from 5YR 5-6/6 (yellowish red to reddish yellow) on the breaks to 5YR 5/1-4 (gray, reddish gray, and reddish brown) at the cores, though a number of examples fall into the grays. The pieces are covered with a thick slip that tends to be yellow or reddish yellow (7.5-10YR 7-8/6-8), though when the slip is worn, it leaves a distinctive blue-gray color to the surface (does not appear on Munsell Soil Color charts). Occasionally it appears as if the blue-gray color was deliberately sought. The slip is then burnished or polished to a luster, though nothing like the glossy reds of the Early Helladic I period. The yellow-blue slipped and burnished ware seems to be rather brittle, and vessels tend to break into very small pieces. A number of yellow-blue slipped and burnished pieces were recovered in the survey, though few are catalogued here, owing to their fragmentary condition. A glance at the assemblage tables under Early Helladic II will illustrate the quantity of yellow-blue slipped and burnished pieces. At site A6 nearly 10% of the Early Helladic II pieces are yellow-blue slipped and burnished. The percentages are lower for other sites. There does seem to be a pattern wherein the Southern Argolid sites of the eastern and coastal areas have a higher percentage of the ware than do the western and inland sites, as Table 1.2 illustrates.

The "Corinthian green" fabric is found at sites in the Corinthia such as Corinth, Korakou, and Zygouries, but seems to be rare farther south. The fabric tends to be semifine to semicoarse, and in color tends to fall around 10YR–5Y 7/2-3 (light gray, very pale brown, pale yellow), with a "greenish" cast. Three pieces catalogued here are from a small incurving bowl **226**, and small bowls or sauceboats **526** and **531**.

Other fabrics will be discussed under the shape categories below. Plastic and incised decorations take many forms, and they, too, will be discussed under the shape categories below.

The most common surface treatment is the application of the black paint known as Urfirnis. Rarely in our collections is the paint metallic or lustrous on its own. The paint also appears mottled black to red, red-brown, brown, and, rarely, in red, but black is by far the most common. Only one small pattern painted piece that might be assigned to Early Helladic II was picked up on the survey.

Table 1.2. Distribution of Yellow-Blue Slipped and Burnished

Wares at Early Helladic II Sites in the Southern Argolid (N = 54)

Site	Number Yellow-Blue Slipped and Burnished	Total EH II	% Yellow-Blue Slipped and Burnished
A6	20	215	9.3
A6/9	1	39	2.6
A9	1	20	5.0
A33	1	31	3.2
B24	1	98	1.0
B39	0	22	0.0
B41	4	63	6.3
C11	3	88	3.4
E4	2	37	5.4
E5	2	37	5.4
F5	2	33	6.1
F6	1	74	1.4
F20	3	109	2.8
F32	13	650	2.0

The Shapes

The discussion and catalogue of the Early Helladic II pottery have been arranged by shape, beginning with open shapes, then closed, followed by vessel portions not limited to either open or closed categories or to a single characteristic shape (e.g. feet, bases, and handles), and, finally, non-vessel ceramics such as stands, hearthrims, and rooftiles. Within shape categories, the catalogue is arranged either by size or by major decorative feature.

Sauceboats (**213–224**, Figs. 13, 119)

The sauceboat is one of the most distinctive ceramic shapes of the Aegean, and is one of the defining characteristics of the Early Helladic II period. Even relatively small sherds can be easily identified by the complex curves unique to this shape. Unfortunately, most of our examples are fragmentary, and no meaningful profiles could be reconstructed.

The Lerna Type II sauceboat (Caskey 1960: 290; Fahy 1964: 25), with its rounded bowl, horizontal handle, downturned lip, and ears of the spout forming a 45° angle, appears to be the most common shape of the Southern Argolid sauceboats. Fahy notes in her study of the sauceboat (1964: 25) that this is "by far the most common" type. Spout **213** is from a Type II sauceboat, as are probably handles **223** and **224**. The reserved patch under the handle of **224** is very typical of Peloponnesian sauceboats when painted with Urfirnis, whereas at Ag. Irini, Kea, for instance, this area of the sauceboat is usually painted (D. Wilson, personal communication). When the sauceboats are covered with the yellow-blue slip and burnished, the entire vessel is covered. The sauceboat rims presented here as **214–222** give the range of rim forms of the bowl found in the Southern Argolid. The most common rim form is **214**, with its slight thickening as it begins to curve in to a pointed lip. The slight thickening below the rim helps distinguish sauceboats from bowls that seem to lack this feature. Some sauceboats appear to be rather shallow, as **217** (perhaps a Type I?), whereas others, **220–222**, are probably from the deep Type III sauceboat. **219** is rather peculiar with its carinated rim.

The fragmentary state of the sauceboat material makes the restoration of shapes difficult. Generally, the bowl of the sauceboat is more rounded than are the similar-sized small incurving bowls (e.g. **225–242**). The foot is particularly difficult to identify, for both the ring foot and the pedestal foot can be used for either the sauceboat or the small bowl. Ring feet and pedestal feet are both common in the Southern Argolid. Fahy (1964: 25–26, 104–5), places the sauceboats with a "high foot" into her Type IIA and notes that the pedestal foot is preferred for sauceboats in Attica, Boeotia, and the islands of Naxos and Syros. The ring foot is more commonly used in the northern Argolid and Corinthia (except for northeast coast sites such as Isthmia and Kalamaki); indeed the pedestal is very rare there. The Southern Argolid sauceboats would seem to fit into Type IIA, with a preference for pedestal feet, though ring feet do outnumber pedestal feet.

Sauceboats tend to be in a fine to semifine fabric, about half of them evenly fired. Colors on the break are in the reddish-yellow area of the Munsell charts, 5YR 6/6-8 and 7.5YR 6-7/6, though browns, 7.5YR 4/2, 5/4, and 10YR 7/4 also occur, and at the core gray or pink, 7.5YR 7/4. The two yellow-blue slipped and burnished sauceboats **214** and **215** have evenly fired gray semifine fabrics. One unique fabric, **222**, is probably not local with its red color (2.5YR 5/8) and silver inclusions.

Most of the handles found are of the horizontal, slightly upswung variety with subrectangular sections, **214**, **223**, and **224**. The vertical handle usually associated with Type III sauceboats or with yellow-blue slipped and burnished sauceboats is rare in the Southern Argolid and none is catalogued here.

Sauceboats for the most part are painted black with Urfirnis that can be quite lustrous, e.g. **217** and **221**. As noted above, the black covers the entire vessel except for the reserved area under the handle, as on **224**. **216** is painted red on the exterior and interior and then scribble burnished on the exterior; in appearance this is an Early Helladic I surface treatment, and this piece may therefore be a rather early example of a sauceboat. The unusual fabric of sauceboat **222** is painted with red Urfirnis on the exterior, but left plain on the interior. Two yellow-blue slipped and burnished sauceboats are catalogued here, **214** and **215**; **214** is slipped yellow on the exterior, including the area below the horizontal handle, and blue on the interior, and both surfaces are burnished; and **215** is just slipped yellow (wearing to blue) and burnished.

Small bowls: shallow, incurving, and inturned (225–243, Fig. 13)

The small bowl is more plentiful than in previous periods, and comes in three principal varieties: shallow, as in **227** and **228**, where the radius is much greater than the interior height of the vessel; incurving, as in **225**, **226**, and **229–233**; and inturned, where the actual point of inflection between body and rim can be determined, as in **234–242**. This shape is also known as a "saucer."

The only complete profile of a small bowl, inturned bowl **238**, has a ring foot. **228**, a shallow bowl, probably rested on a flat or hollow bottom, though a very small ring foot is possible. As noted above under the discussion of the sauceboat, the large number of pedestals suggests that sauceboats, and probably small bowls, too, rested on them, in addition to ring feet. Small bowls on pedestals are found in Attica, Boeotia, the Saronic Gulf and the islands, and only very rarely in the northern Argolid and Corinthia away from the northeast coast (cf. Hatzipouliou-Kalliri 1983: 370–71, P297 and Pl. 39; Theocharis 1953–54: figs. 8–10 for sauceboats and fig. 12 for bowls on pedestals).

The walls of the small bowls curve inward to the area of the rim. At the rim, the wall can thicken

Table 1.3. Frequency of Painted Decoration on Small Bowls of the Early Helladic II Period from the Southern Argolid (N = 70)

Bowl shape	Plain	Solid painted	Painted bands
incurving	9	34	0
shallow	11	6	0
inturned	1	9	0

and continue its inward curve, e.g. **227**, **229**, **233**; the curve can change so that the rim curves in more sharply, as in **230** and **232**; or the rim can actually be turned in, as in **234–237** or **239** and **240**. The maximum diameter of the bowl is usually below the rim for incurving and inturned bowls. Lips are pointed, **225**, **227**, **228**, **239**, **240**, **242**, rounded, **230**, **232**, **234**, **238**, **241**, flattened, **229**, **233**, **243**, or beveled **226**, **231**.

Four bowls are unusual for having their rim inturned to horizontal, **234–237**. All have rim diameters of 0.20 m. **235–237** have semifine fabric, **234** medium. The fabrics of **235** and **236** appear unusual in their colors. **235** and **237** are covered with mottled slips of a distinctively greenish cast, 2.5Y 5/4 (light olive-brown) and 10YR 4-5/3 (brown), respectively, and burnished to a very high, glossy luster. **234** and **236** are painted red, and **236** seems to also be burnished. These bowls are related to ones from Thebes (Demakopoulou and Konsola 1975: 59 fig. 6, nos. 9 and 14).

Rim diameters of the small bowls range from 0.07 to 0.23 m. The shallow and inturned bowls have diameters of 0.13–0.15 m, and the incurving bowls of 0.07 and 0.13–0.23 m.

The fabrics of the small bowls vary from semifine to semicoarse, with and without lime, and are more often unevenly fired than evenly. As is the case with many Early Helladic II fabrics, the colors of the biscuit on the break tend to be in yellowish red or reddish yellow (5-7.5YR 5-6/6-8) and if unevenly fired, the cores are often gray (5YR 4-6/1) or generally darker. One example of "Corinthian green" fabric, **226**, is catalogued here, with a semifine biscuit evenly fired to 10YR 7/3 (very pale brown). The fabrics of the two yellow-blue slipped and burnished examples **241** and **242** do not differ from the others.

The most common surface treatment for the small bowls is to be painted black (Urfirnis): **225**, **226**, **228**, **230**, **231**, **240**. Brown Urfirnis occurs in solid, **239**, and in one instance, **243**, on the interior, on the lip, and on an exterior band. Traces of slip, not of the Urfirnis variety, were found on **229**, and its fabric and shape suggest it may be early if not EH I. **238** is painted red-brown on the exterior, but the interior is left plain; **232** is painted red and apparently burnished; and **241** and **242** are slipped yellow and burnished. Plain small bowls also occur: **227** and **233**.

243 may be painted with just a band on the exterior rim because of its added plastic decoration of a taenia (impressed applied band) below the maximum diameter. Painted bands on the rims of small bowls were otherwise not detected in the Southern Argolid, whether due to preservation or to preference. In a sample of 70 noncatalogued small bowl rims preserved to a height on which all but the widest bands would be apparent (i.e. greater than half the vessel height, in which case they would hardly be painted bands), none had painted bands (Table 1.3). The lack of painted bands contrasts with the situation at Tiryns, where, in order to classify the large number of banded small bowls, a rather elaborate typology has been devised, a typology based on combinations of plain, narrow, and wide painted bands, and solid painted interiors and exteriors (Weisshaar 1981, 1982, 1983).

Flaring rim bowl (**244**, Fig. 13)

One unusual rim, **244**, comes from a small flaring bowl. The wall curves in slightly, but the rim thickens and flares out to a pointed lip. The fabric fits with other small bowls, but the surface is painted red (Urfirnis), suggesting a date earlier in Early Helladic II.

Spreading bowls and basins (**245–254**, **263**, Figs. 14, 15)

Spreading bowls and basins are characterized by straight, splayed walls. The rims of spreading bowls are generally simple as in **245**, **246**, and **251**, slightly thickened to the exterior as in **247–250**, **253**, and **254**, or slightly thickened to the interior as in **252**. The diameters of the rims cluster in three size groups: 0.15 m (one example), 0.29–0.33 m (six examples), and 0.38–0.46 m (three examples). The form of the base is not known. The fabrics are medium to semicoarse (the small spreading bowl **245** is in a semifine fabric), and usually unevenly fired. Colors of the biscuit on the break are around yellowish red and reddish yellow (2.5-7.5YR 5-6/6-8), and the cores are often gray or reddish gray.

263 appears to be a spreading bowl, but it is unlike any of the others. Below the rim on the exterior is a row of impressed triangles. The decoration, and to an extent the shape, relate it to the outturned bowls **428–444**.

253 and **254** have taenias, in both cases composed of overlapping discs in a horizontal row, just below the rim. On **254** each disc overlaps the disc to the right, as do the majority of such taenia; on **253** the discs overlap to the left.

A variety of surface treatments occurs on spreading bowls and basins: plain, **248** and **254**; exterior plain and interior painted in a thick black wash of Urfirnis, **245**; exterior slipped or painted a thin black wash and interior painted black Urfirnis, **246** and **251**; interior plain and exterior painted solid with Urfirnis, **247**, or with a band at the rim on the exterior, **252**; and one case of red slip, **249**.

Large bowls or basins (**255–262**, Figs. 15, 119)

Related to the large spreading bowls or basins of the previous section and large incurving bowls such as **369–374** are bowls or basins with incurving sides but without the incurve resulting in the maximum diameter occurring below the rim. The rims of these bowls are all thickened, from slightly as in **256**, thickened to a triangle as in **257** and **258**, or very thickened to a "T" as in **255**. The rim diameters range from 0.46 to 0.72 m. The fabrics are redder than on the spreading bowls, with most having biscuit colors on the break of 5YR 3/3-4 (dark reddish brown), or 2.5YR 4-5/6-8 (red). The uneven firing of most is probably due in part to the thick walls.

All examples of these large bowls or basins have taenias of various kinds below the rim. **255**, **256**, and **261** have impressions on an applied ridge. **258** and **260** have a taenia of overlapping discs to the right, **262** overlapping discs to the left. **257** appears to have a very wide taenia of overlapping discs to the left, though the discs are so indistinct that the taenia may just be impressed to resemble overlapping discs. **259** has a ridge that has been impressed from below to form a scalloped pattern.

Plain, **256–258** and **260**, and painted surfaces occur. **255** is painted red on the interior and lip, but the exterior is just slipped. **259** is painted black on the lip and in bands on the interior and exterior; the exterior band of paint extends to below the taenia. **261** seems to be plain on the interior, but the exterior is too worn for us to tell what treatment it had.

Deep bowls (264–267, Figs. 15, 119)

A few bowls appear to have virtually vertical walls, but this may be a factor of orientation, in which case **264** and **265** would be grouped with the spreading bowls and **266** and **267** would be grouped with the large bowl or basins of the previous category. **266** has a taenia of two sets of impressions on an applied ridge, **267** a taenia of diagonal slashes on an applied ridge. **264** and **267** are plain; **265** and **266** are slipped.

Shallow bowls (268–281, Fig. 16)

Shallow bowls have a radius greater than their interior height and curving walls, but not curving in so much that the maximum diameter is below the rim. Usually the wall thickens toward the rim, but there are exceptions, e.g. **272** and **273**, and probably **276** and **278**. **272** and **273** have grooves on the exterior just below the lip. Thickening of rims can be to the exterior, as in **269**, **270**, **275**, **280**, and **281**, or to both exterior and interior, as in **268**, **271**, and **279**. Most of the lips are flattened and either horizontal or beveled: **268–270**, **272**, **275–278**, **280**, and **281**. The rim diameters of the shallow bowls can be divided into a group of medium diameters, 0.25–0.29 m (five examples), and a group of large diameters, 0.34–0.41 m (five examples). The fabrics are medium or semicoarse and usually contain some lime. **270** and **275** have silver inclusions: **272** has some gold inclusions, perhaps some volcanic mineral, and has thus been dated Early Helladic I to II. The colors of the biscuit on the break range from red (2.5YR 4-5/8, 5/6), yellowish red (5YR 4-5/6), reddish brown (5YR 4-6/4), reddish yellow (5YR 6/6, 7.5YR 6-7/6), to brown (7.5YR 6/4); most are unevenly fired and the cores appear gray (5YR 3-4-5-6/1, 10YR 5/1), reddish brown (5YR 4/4), brown (7.5YR 5/4), or reddish yellow (7.5YR 6/6) in color.

Three sherds have projecting lugs formed by extending the rim to the exterior and thus a wide lip. **276** and **277** have projections which, seen from above, form a triangle, and the curve of the ends suggests that both lugs were originally doubled. The triangle is pierced vertically at its widest point on both. The second triangle would have been pierced also. Such double-pierced lugs are found in Early Helladic I and Early Helladic II strata (e.g. Caskey and Caskey 1960: 140 and plate 47 no. III.9, 156 and plate 48 no. VIII.42; Dousougli 1987: 197 Abb. 24 no. 128 and 200 Abb. 26 no. 159).

279 has the left part of a trumpet lug formed by the thickening of an applied horizontal ridge. **280** and **281** have little diagonal impressions (more like little nicks removed) right on the exterior of the thickened rim.

Several of the shallow bowls are plain, **272**, **273**, **277**, **278**, and **280**, and two appear to have just a slip, **270** and **276**. **268** is slipped on interior and exterior, but the lip is painted red; **275** and **279** have the lip and interior painted red-brown, and **279** is also burnished. **271** is painted black on the exterior. Only **274** and **275** are solidly painted, in black and brown, respectively.

Miscellaneous bowls (282 and 283, Fig. 16)

282 appears to be deeper than are the shallow bowls, and because it is not incurving it has been called a hemispherical bowl. It has a flat horizontal lip and an applied horizontal lug ending to the right. **283** does not fit well in either the shallow bowl or the incurving bowl category; it, too, appears to be hemispherical. The rim is very slightly thickened, the lip flat. It is slipped.

Incurving bowls (284–425, Figs. 16–23, 119, 120)

As is apparent from the profile drawings, there is a continuum in the shape of bowls in the Southern Argolid from shallow to incurving. The division is, to a certain degree, artificial, and there are several pieces categorized as "shallow" that fit well with the incurving bowls, and vice versa. Bowls like **283** represent overlaps among the categories.

The incurving bowl is by far the most common shape in the Early Helladic II period in the Southern Argolid. In order to make the discussion more manageable, I have broken down incurving bowls by major added plastic or incised decoration into:

> without plastic or impressed decoration, **284–308**
> with ridges or appliqué, **309–327**
> with ledge lugs, **328–329**
> with tubular handles, **330–340**
> with taenia, **341–388**
> with impressions, **389–425**

Incurving bowls without plastic or impressed decoration (**284–308**, Figs. 16, 17)

The rims of incurving bowls without plastic or impressed decoration are all thickened to some degree, except for **295** and **302**. Rims can be slightly thickened as in **286–292**, thickened to the interior like **307** (very uncommon), thickened to the exterior, as in **284**, **285**, **293**, **294**, and **308**, or thickened to both exterior and interior as in **296** and **297**, even to a "T" as in **306**. Most of the curves of the wall are gentle, but sharp incurves as **288** or **291** are possible. **291** is really a shallow bowl, but the sharply incurving rim places it in this category. Likewise **296** has straight walls, as do basins, but the rim curves in sharply. The rim diameters cluster into two groups: medium diameters ranging from 0.20–0.31 m, averaging 0.265, and large diameters ranging from 0.36–0.46 m, averaging 0.405. Fabrics of the incurving bowls without plastic or impressed decoration are mostly medium or semicoarse, though semifine and coarse also occur, have some lime, and are unevenly fired. **286**, **287**, **290**, and **301** have silver inclusions. Colors of the biscuit on the break are mostly yellowish red (5YR 5/6), reddish yellow (5-7.5YR 6/6-8), red (2.5YR 4-6/6, 5/8), or brown (7.5YR 4/6, 5-6/4), and colors of the core are gray (5YR 4-5-6/1, 7.5YR-N5/0, 5/1) or brown (5YR 5/4, 5-7.5YR 3/2, 5-6/4, 10YR 5/3).

By definition there is no added plastic or impressed decoration. A number of the incurving bowls without plastic or impressed decoration are plain, **285**, **292**, **293**, **297**, and **302**. A couple of examples are self-slipped, **288** and **290**; **288** is also burnished. **295** and **304** are red slipped and burnished. Solid paint is found in black Urfirnis, **284** and **291**?, red, **286** and **308**, black interior and red exterior, **287**, red-brown, **305**, and brown, **294**. **296** is painted red only on the interior, **300** and **307**? red-brown only on the lip, and **301** red-brown only on the exterior. **306** is painted with brown Urfirnis on the exterior and lip, with a self-slipped interior. Yellow-blue slip and burnish occurs on **289**.

Incurving bowls with ridges or appliqué (**309–327**, Figs. 18, 119)

Like the incurving bowls without plastic or impressed decoration, the incurving bowls with ridges or appliqué have a range of degree of curvature, from negligible, as in **311** and **319**, to sharply incurving, as in **309** and **315**. Rims are unthickened, as in **310**, slightly thickened, as in **316**, and thickened to interior and exterior, as in **321** and **322**. Again, two groups of rim diameters can be distinguished: medium diameters ranging from 0.23–0.33 m, averaging 0.273, and large diameters, 0.41 m (three examples). The fabrics are mostly semicoarse or fine and have some lime, and only about half are unevenly fired. The colors of the biscuit on the break are mostly reddish yellow (5YR

6/6-8, 7.5YR 6-7/6), yellowish red (5YR 4-5/6), and brown (7.5YR 5/2, 6/4); the cores are generally gray (5YR 5-6/1) or red-gray (5YR 4-5/2). Two bowls, **323** and **326**, have silver inclusions.

All the bowls have a ridge (except **326** and **327**; see below), but the ridges vary. All ridges but one are applied plastic elements. The ridge on **312** is formed by a wide groove on the exterior of the thickened rim. Most ridges are horizontal, but that on **314** definitely curves, and perhaps that on **311** does, too. Most ridges are small and shallow, but some are almost tall enough to be considered ledge lugs, as **311**, **314**, **316**, **319**, and **321**. Most of the sherds on which are found the ridges are small (max. pres. W. is 0.07 m on **319**), and the ridges occupy the full width of the extant sherd. On several, however, the ridge ends abruptly and without any ornamentation, both to the left, **315**, **316**, and **320**, and to the right, **318**, **322**, and **326**. Two bowls catalogued here provide evidence that ridges are used in combination with other decoration. On **324** the ridge ends to the right, and the horizontal line of the ridge is continued by a row of diagonal slashes. This is similar to the incurving bowls with tubular handles, **330–340**, and with ledge lugs, **328** and **329**. The ridge on **325** appears to end to the left in a vertical impression, widening and flattening the ridge to give the semblance of a "trumpet lug." **317** and **319** also appear to end with an impression of some sort, perhaps like **325** (cf. Dousougli 1987: 200 Abb. 26 no. 160 from EH I stratum at Kephalari). The presence of so many ridges ending abruptly and plainly suggests that trumpet lugs and other applied horizontal elements can have decoration only on one end and end abruptly on the other.

326 and **327** are included in this group of incurving bowls. **326** has the end of a ridge, perhaps a plain one or a taenia as **341** to **388**. **327** has at least two applied buttons at the maximum diameter.

As in the incurving bowls without plastic or impressed decoration, there is a variety of surface treatments on these bowls, including plain, **310**, **318**, **324**, and **326**. Urfirnis paint in black occurs on **311**?, **312** (exterior only), **314** (exterior only), **317**, **319** (interior and lip), and **325**, in red-brown or brown on **316** (lip only) and **323**. A number of examples are self-slipped but not burnished, **313**, **314** (interior only), **315**, **320**, and **322**. Yellow-blue slip and burnish occurs on the interior and lip of **309** and possibly on **311** (could also be black Urfirnis). Burnishing is apparent only on the exterior of **316** in an irregular manner, with a plain interior and a brown painted lip.

Incurving bowls with ledge handles (328–329, Figs. 19, 119)

Two large incurving bowls have high, horizontal ridges that form ledge handles. These are related to both the incurving bowls with horizontal ridges, **311**, **314**, **316**, **317**, **321**, and especially **324**, and to incurving bowls with tubular handles, **330–340** below. On **328** the lip is folded over to the interior to form a thickened rim; on **329** the rim is thickened to the exterior. On **328** the entire width of the lug, 0.07 m, is preserved. The line of the ledge handle is continued by a taenia of impressions on an applied ridge. On **329** only part of the ledge handle is preserved on the right, and to the left at a higher level than the handle is a row of oblique slashes. **328** is self-slipped on the exterior. **329** is painted black Urfirnis on the interior and lip, and self-slipped on the exterior.

Incurving bowls with tubular handles (330–340, Fig. 19)

A number of large incurving bowls have a wide vertical strap handle, almost like a tube, attached either at the rim, e.g. **337**, or just below the rim, e.g. **331**. The rims of these bowls are of the usual forms, from slightly thickened, as in **332** and **333**, to thickened to a "T", as on **338**. The rim diameters range from 0.36–0.42 m; the unmeasurable rims would seem to fall close to that range, as do the two ledge-handle examples from the previous section (0.38 and 0.43 m). The fabrics are semicoarse to coarse, and unevenly fired. The colors of the biscuit on the break are mostly reddish yellow (5-7.5YR 6/6-8), though red (2.5YR 5/8), pink (7.5YR 7/4), and light brown (7.5YR 6/4) also occur. The cores are brown (7.5YR 5/2-4, 4/2) or gray (5YR 6/1, 5/2, 7.5YR-N5/0).

The handles are all wide, at least 0.05 m in width at the attachments, but they narrow at their farthest projection. The handles tend to sag or droop downward slightly. **330**, **333**, **339**, and **340** have taenias of impressions on an applied ridge that continue the line of the upper handle attachment, just like the ledge handles **328** and **329**. **330** also has a horizontal row of diagonal slashes to the right of the handle opening. Most of the other examples are not preserved well enough to determine whether they, too, had taenias; **331** and **332** suggest that not all do.

The same range of surface treatments as on the other varieties of incurving bowls occurs on these bowls: plain, **337**; burnished, **330** (exterior only) and **339** (interior and lip only); slipped, **333** (exterior); and painted red, **334** and **340**, or black, **336** and **338** (interior only). **335** is slipped and burnished.

Dousougli publishes three examples of incurving bowls with tubular handles from the surface at Makrovouni (1987: 180 Abb. 10 no. 30, 181 Abb. 11 nos. 40, 41).

Incurving bowls with taenia (**341–388**, Figs. 19–21, 119, 120)

The most common decoration of incurving bowls is the taenia. Taenias occur on the full range of rim forms of incurving bowls, from simple rims as **350**, to slightly thickened as **366**, and thickened to a "T", as **351**. Only a few small incurving bowls like **341** have taenias. Large bowls are the size most commonly decorated with taenias. The medium bowls have rim diameters that range from 0.24–0.33 m, averaging 0.287, and the large bowls have rim diameters that range from 0.35–0.67 m, averaging 0.43. The division between medium and large bowls is a bit arbitrary; there is really a continuum of sizes, but with a definite cluster around 0.38 to 0.40 m (ten examples). The fabrics are about half semicoarse and half evenly divided between medium and coarse. Most examples are unevenly fired. **359**, **374**, and **384** have silver inclusions. Colors of the biscuits on the breaks are mainly yellowish red (5YR 4-5/6-8), red (2.5YR 4-5/6-8, 3/6), reddish yellow (5YR 6-7/6-8), and reddish brown (5YR 2.5/2, 4/3-4, 5-7.5YR 5/4); colors on the core are mostly grays (5YR 3-4-5-6/1), reddish brown (5YR 3/2-3, 4-5/3-4), reddish or pinkish gray (5YR 4-5-6/2, 7.5YR 6/2), or brown (7.5YR 5/2).

The taenias are for the most part located below the rim and above the maximum diameter. There are some taenias right at the rim, e.g. **341**, **349**, **357**, and **363**, and some located at or below the maximum diameter, often as a second taenia, e.g. **342**, **352**, **359**, and **365**. There is usually one taenia on a vessel, but taenias can be doubled, e.g. **357** and **358**, or two taenias can be separated by space as in **352**, **365**, and **380**. On only two bowls, **347** and **359**, does the taenia end, like many of the horizontal ridges of **309–326**, but **347** may be early if not Early Helladic I.

There are three basic types of taenias in the Southern Argolid (see also **255–267** above): finger impressions and moulding on an applied band, slashes on an applied band, and individual discs on clay laid in an overlapping pattern. Sometimes it is difficult to distinguish among the three types, as the finger impression or slash can be used to imitate the overlapping discs. Finger impressions and moulding on an applied ridge constitute the most common type of taenia (roughly two-thirds); taenias of discs overlapping to the right are also common, but taenias of slashes on an applied ridge or discs overlapping to the left are much less common.

The taenias of finger impressions on an applied band are sometimes formed to imitate a twisted-rope pattern, either to the left as in **351**, **355**, and **361**, or to the right as in **369**; a scalloped pattern where the waves are formed by pressing the finger up from the lower edge of the applied band as in **341**, **380**, **383**, and **384** (the best example is **259**, already considered above); or overlapping discs as in **362**, **364**, **377**, and **383**. Otherwise the finger impressions are usually fairly deep on the band, and sometimes placed at a slant. The taenia formed by slashes on an applied ridge is not very common; **368** and **381** are the only two examples catalogued here. **381** imitates discs overlapping to the left.

Individual discs, not always round or retaining their original shape, are usually laid in a horizontal row, from right to left, overlapping the previously laid disc to the right, as in **342**, **344**, **348**, **349**, **356**, **357**, **365**, **366**, **372–375**, **387**, and **388**. Rarely are the discs laid in the opposite direction, as in **346**.

Weisshaar has devised a typology of taenias (1981: 229 Abb. 74 and 230; revised in Weisshaar 1983: 336 and 338 Abb. 7) wherein he has five major types, with one main type divided into three. His taenia types are: (a) plain applied ridge; (b) overlapping discs divided into (b1) narrow, closely spaced discs, (b2) widely spaced discs, and (b3) wide, closely spaced discs; (c) finger impressions on an applied ridge; (d) slashes on an applied ridge; and (e) oblique slashes forming a rope pattern. He does not distinguish impressed ridges imitating either overlapping discs or a rope pattern, nor does he distinguish between discs overlapping to the left and discs overlapping to the right.

On **373** a row of diagonal slashes occurs on the thickest part of the rim, just above the taenia of overlapping discs.

For the most part, the incurving bowls with taenia are plain, **341**, **345**, **349**, **350**, **352**, **357**, **361**, **363**, **367**, **373**, **377**, and **383**. Several are self-slipped, **351**, **353**, **360**, **366**, **369**, **382**, and **368** (exterior only?), **388** (exterior only?), and **371** (interior and lip). Paint is not very common, and appears in black on exterior and interior on **343**, on the interior only on **381** and perhaps **346**, possibly on the exterior only on **354**, in red or red-brown on exterior and interior on **362**, on interior and lip on **359**, **365**, **384**, and perhaps **370** and **380**, and on the exterior and lip on **372** (interior not preserved). **355** and **378** are burnished just on their lips, and burnishing appears on **374** (interior not preserved). Many examples were too worn to determine the presence of any surface treatment. No yellow-blue slipped and burnished examples were noted.

Incurving bowls with impressions (**389–425**, Figs. 21–23, 120)

The incurving bowl with a horizontal row of usually diagonal impressions just above the maximum diameter seems to be a distinctly Southern Argolid shape; Dousougli (1987) does not publish any examples from Kephalari, Makrovouni, or Talioti, and Weisshaar published from Tiryns (1982: 453 Abb. 69 no. 1) only one large incurving bowl with nicks at the rim, not at all like our examples.

The forms of these bowls are slightly different from the incurving bowls of the previous categories. The walls tend to curve in more sharply, such as **390**, **400**, **407**, and **415**. Several appear as if the lower part of the wall were straight, like a spreading bowl or basin, e.g. **397**, **399**, **404**, **409**, **416**, and **423**. Of course more gently, continuously curving walls occur, too, as **394**, **410**, and **422**. The rim forms tend to be thickened, though the great thickening of the "T"-rims does not occur here. Some bowls have a sinuous, almost S-shaped profile that relies in part on the thickening to exterior of many rims, such as **407**, **409**, and **411**. A few examples have nearly vertical walls with incurving rims, **412** and **421**; these also are impressed only with triangles, not slashes. Only medium and large incurving bowls have the impressions, but very large bowls (greater than 0.45 m) do not seem to have them. The rim diameters fall into two groups: 0.24–0.32 m, averaging 0.279, and 0.35–0.43

m, averaging 0.38. Unfortunately, fabric descriptions were not recorded for this category, other than **404** and **418**, but no sherd had been set aside as being unusual in its fabric.

The impressions generally occur in a single horizontal row just below the slightly thickened to exterior rim and above or just down to the maximum diameter; on **411** the impressions are over the maximum diameter. Two rows of impressions on a sherd, as **402**, are uncommon. The impressions are formed either by slashing and gouging or by a stamp, generally triangular. The slashes are oval or oblong, sometimes deeper at one side or one end, and usually set at a diagonal with the upper end to the right. Vertical slashes, **396** and **404**, and slashes diagonal to left, **389** and **422**, do occur. The triangular stamps are of three kinds, or at least are employed in three different ways. Small, evenly formed triangles, **391** and **401**, are not common. Large triangles are impressed so that only the top apex is apparent, either widely spaced as **412**, or so closely spaced that they overlap and form a zigzag, as **405**, **420**, and **421**. The third type of triangular impressions is irregularly formed, with the bottom and one side much longer than the third side, as if the stamp were dragged or impressed obliquely, **400**, **403**, **407**, **415**, and **416**.

Surface treatments, when surfaces are preserved, include plain, **407**; yellow-blue slip and burnish, **391**, **409**, and **421**; burnish, **416**; and slipped, **397**, **410**, **399** (exterior only), **403** (exterior not preserved), and **420** (interior only, and burnished). Painted examples also occur in black, **404**, **394** (lip only), and **412** (exterior worn); brown, **418**, **398** (interior only); red-brown, **414**, **424**, and **417** (interior not preserved); red, **406** (lip only); and indistinguishable paint.

Spouted bowls (426–427, Fig. 23)

Two bowls have fragments of spouts. **426** is an incurving bowl with an oval hole at the maximum diameter. Around the hole is an applied ridge forming the spout; the ridge extends to the right horizontally. Below the horizontal ridge is a taenia of impressions on an applied band. The surfaces are not preserved. **427** is included here because of the spout, though the rim is flaring. The hole is oval, and the spout is a U-shaped applied piece. To the right of the top of the spout is a horizontal slash, perhaps the beginning of a row of slashes. The exterior and a band on the interior are slipped yellow-orange, probably a variation of yellow-blue slip and burnish finish.

Outturned bowls with impressions (428–444, Figs. 23, 24, 121)

The outturned bowl or krater is a distinctly Southern Argolid shape. The wall usually slopes in toward the rim, with little curvature evident. The rim is turned out so that on the interior there is a sharp line marking the rim off from the wall, but on the exterior the transition is less pronounced. A row of impressions, most often stamped triangles, appears on the exterior, below the outturned rim. Dousougli publishes only one example (1987: 215 Abb. 32d) that actually comes from the survey area, probably our site F32; she suggests an EH I date, but this cannot be supported. From Tiryns come a few EH II examples, with stamped triangles and paint (Weisshaar 1981: 241 Abb. 84 no. 7), impressions (Weisshaar 1981: 241 Abb. 84 no. 12), solid painted (Weisshaar 1981: 241 Abb. 84 no. 15), and EH II pattern painted with vertical lugs (Weisshaar 1981: 243 Abb. 86 no. 2). An example from a supposed EH III level at Tiryns (called Schicht III in 1981) has, according to the published drawing (Weisshaar 1981: 247 Abb. 89 no. 13), a completely different orientation, with a wall that slopes out, not in, though the outturn of the rim, the stamped triangles, and black paint are similar to ours. Another example from Tiryns, from the "Bereich der Apsidenhäuser," has diagonal slashes (Weisshaar 1981: 250 Abb. 91 no. 6), but this material is probably mixed EH II and EH III.

The lower portion of the outturned bowls is problematic. At some point the wall must turn or curve back to a base or foot. The profile may be similar to that of a large footed bowl from an EH II level at Tiryns with a large ring foot, almost straight-spreading lower wall, insloping upper wall, and outturned rim (Weisshaar 1981: 231 Abb. 77 no. 1).

When the walls of the Southern Argolid outturned bowls curve, it is a convex curve, as in the incurving bowls, e.g. **435** and **442**, but the straight insloping wall is much more common. The outturn of the rim results in the backside of the rim becoming the lip beveled to the interior; in one instance, **432**, this surface was impressed. The actual lip (the topmost area between the exterior and interior surfaces of the vessel) is rounded, e.g. **432**, **435**, **437**, and **440**, or flattened and beveled to the exterior as in **433**, **436**, **438**, and **441**. The range of rim diameters for the medium-sized bowls is 0.22–0.32 m, with average diameter around 0.26, and for the large bowls is 0.35–0.64 m. Unfortunately, fabric descriptions were recorded for only three examples, **437**, **440**, and **442**, and they fall into the usual Early Helladic II fabrics of medium to semicoarse, unevenly fired, reddish-yellow biscuit to brown or gray core.

Stamped triangular impressions are the most common decoration, and in all but one (**432**) occur on the exterior just below the outturned rim. The triangles are usually small and somewhat regularly impressed, **431**, **434–436**, **439**, and **444**, though small triangles impressed more deeply to one side are found on **430** and **437**. Large triangles are impressed usually with the top apex deeper and the bottom edge not apparent, **438** and **440**. Two rows of small, evenly impressed triangles with their apices to the interior are on the interior rim/lip of **432**. Slashes also occur, usually at a diagonal to the right, as in **428**, **429**, **441**, and **443**, but also to the left, as in **433**. The slashes on **442** appear to be impressed, or at least have one corner and are deeper at the top. **442** also has a curving applied band located well below the row of slashes.

The most common surface treatment is black Urfirnis paint, **429** (interior and lip), **431**, **435** (lip only preserved), **438**, **440**, and **444** (interior worn). Paint also occurs in brown, **430**, **441** (interior worn), red-brown, **443** (exterior only), and indeterminate color, **434**, **442** (interior only?). No definite plain examples were noted. A brown slipped and burnished example, **437**, is probably a variation on the yellow-blue slip and burnish.

Miscellaneous bowls with impressions (**445–448**, Figs. 24, 121)

Four miscellaneous bowls are catalogued here, mainly because their type of decoration relates them to the incurving bowls with impressions and outturned bowls with impressions. **445** is the rim of a large shallow? bowl with greatly thickened rim. On the lip is an incised herringbone pattern of three sets of bars. It is painted red. **446** is from a flaring, probably shallow bowl with rim turned out and down, similar to the Early Helladic I fruitstands. The fabric is quite different, with many small vacuoles, as if some of the temper had been burned out. The lip, or top of the rim, is incised with three rows of alternating diagonal slashes, giving the appearance of herringbone but without connecting lines. I have dated this piece to Early Helladic II Early or possibly EH I. **447** is the closest in shape to the outturned bowls, with a tall, convex wall, but the rim is more thickened to a "T." On the exterior below the rim are two rows of large triangles impressed so that only the top is visible. On the lip or top of the rim are two rows of large impressed triangles with apices facing each other and forming a kerbschnitt pattern. It is painted black. **448** has an incurving wall with outturned horizontal rim, and looks like both the outturned bowls above and the pithoi **450–482**, below. On top of the flat lip are two rows of small impressed triangles with apices facing each other, forming a kerbschnitt pattern. On the exterior below the rim is a small applied ridge with small impressed triangles (not shown in the illustration).

Pithoi (**449–484**, Figs. 25–29, 121)

A large number of large storage vessels, or pithoi, were recovered from the Southern Argolid survey. Most of the pithoi are characterized by an insloping or incurving wall with a very thick, triangular-section rim whose flat top is beveled to the interior and whose interior side is a straight continuation of the inside of the wall, e.g. **451**, **463**, **464**, and **476**. Several pithoi have an outturned rim, the top of which is also flattened and beveled to the interior, e.g. **450**, **458**, **462**, and **477**. In neither type is there a distinct neck.

A few vessels do not fit into either of the two types outlined above. **449** is very similar to the outturned bowls, but the thick wall seems to be concave, not convex, and slopes in more steeply. Its small size (rim diameter 0.17 m), too, marks it as unusual. **454** is more jarlike, with a distinct neck that is greatly thickened above the wall of the body. This vessel may be later, though. **455**, too, appears to be a jar with flaring neck, but it is much bigger than similarly shaped jars (e.g. **502–507** with rim diameters of 0.11 to 0.18 m, compared to 0.35 m for **455**). **471** has a rim thickened to the exterior and interior, forming a very rounded shape. **473** is thickened to a "T." **479** has a slightly thickened rim, but with no outturn. **484** and **485** have flaring walls (the wall of **485** is almost vertical), **484** with only a slight thickening to the exterior, **485** much more so. The diameters of the rims of the pithoi range from 0.26 m to more than 0.70 m, with no clear grouping.

The majority of pithoi have a coarse fabric, some have semicoarse, and only two have medium. Three-fifths are unevenly fired. The fabric colors are redder than those of smaller shapes such as incurving bowls. Colors of the biscuits on the break are red (2.5YR 4/6-8, 5-6/8), reddish brown (5YR 4-5/3, 5-6/4), brown (7.5YR 5/2-4, 6/4, 10YR 6/3), or gray (5YR 4-5/1, 10YR 5/1); only three are reddish yellow (5YR 6/6) or yellowish red (5YR 4/8), as is typical of the bowls. Core colors are reddish brown (2.5-5YR 5/4, 5YR 3/3), brown (7.5YR 4/6, 5/2), and red or pink (2.5YR 4-5/6, 7.5YR 7/4).

Applied plastic decoration occurs on some pithoi. Taenias of slashes on an applied ridge are found on **450** and **453**. Taenias of overlapping discs to the right are found on **458** and **477**. **462** has a taenia of finger impressions on an applied ridge in combination with a row of triangular impressions below the taenia and three rows of small impressed triangles on the wide top of the rim. **466** has a scar where some long (>0.09 m) horizontal attachment, perhaps a handle, has broken off. Another possibility is just a ledge handle like that on **474**, which ends to the right.

Incised and impressed decoration occurs on a few pithoi. **462** has already been described, in the preceding paragraph. Four other rims have impressed decoration on top of them. **479** has on top of its rim, beveled to the interior, a pattern of incised hatched triangles; this pattern is quite common on hearth rims (see below, **657–661**). **480** has a stamped herringbone pattern on top of the horizontal lip. The herringbone pattern has four sets of bars, and appears to be impressed by a cylinder stamp. The stamped herringbone pattern has parallels on some hearth rims (**652**). **481** also has a stamped herringbone pattern; there are at least five sets of bars to this example. **482** is an elaborate kerbschnitt pattern on a wide horizontal lip. There are at least six rows of triangles, each triangle oriented 180° from its neighbors on all sides. Thus the triangles alternate apices pointing to the exterior with apices pointing to the interior. The triangles are stamped at an angle, so that the one apex that points either to the interior or to the exterior is deeper. This pattern is not found on any other Southern Argolid piece.

There seems to be a distinct style of painting pithoi using a thin black (Urfirnis?) wash. Irregular horizontal bands are painted around the lip and/or rim to just below the rim, e.g. **458–460**, **465**, and **468**; on the body of the pithos are painted large irregular loops, as **483** and **470**. The interior is not painted on these examples. One red-wash example, **450**, is catalogued here. On solid painted examples, too, generally only the exterior and/or the lip is painted, and not the interior. This occurs in red-brown, **452** and **473**, black, **454** and **462**, and red, **477**. Only one black example, **472**, is painted on the interior. **478** is painted red and burnished; **455** is burnished only on the exterior, and **467** is burnished on the interior, but the exterior surface is not preserved. **484** has a horizontal band of thin wash just below the rim and an irregular thin wash that streaks in a diagonal direction below that. Four plain pithoi are catalogued here: **451**, **457**, **464**, and **469**.

Jars (**486–515**, Figs. 30, 32, 121)

Jars in the Southern Argolid are quite similar in shape to jars found in the northern Argolid and Corinthia. I have divided the Southern Argolid jars into four types: insloping neck, **486**, splayed neck, **487–501**, flaring neck, **502–508**, and collared, **509–513**. The jar with an insloping neck, **486**, is similar to the Early Helladic I jars with flaring rims, and indeed this example is burnished, but the fabric fits in with the other Early Helladic II jars.

Jars with splayed necks have an offset neck whose wall is fairly straight. The rims are usually simple and unthickened, and the lips are rounded, e.g. **487** and **498**, pointed as in **491**, everted as in **492**, or flattened to one side as on the interior of **489**. The diameters of the rims range from 0.11 to 0.22 m, with five examples at 0.14 m. The fabrics are more often semicoarse, and about half are unevenly fired. The colors of the biscuit on the break are (light) brown and pink (7.5YR 4-5-6-7/4), red-brown (5YR 3/2, 5/4), reddish yellow (5YR 6/6-8, 7.5YR 6/6), yellowish red (5YR 5/8), or red (2.5YR 5/8); colors of the cores are gray (5YR 5/1, 7.5YR-N4-5/0, 10YR 5/1), red-brown (5YR 5/3-4), or gray-brown (10YR 5/2). None of the jars with splayed necks has plastic or incised decoration. Most of these jars are plain, **492–497**; three are self-slipped, **488**, **498**?, and **499** (exterior and lip interior); two are burnished on the exterior and only the interior of the lip, **489** and **490**; and three are painted, one brown on the exterior, **501**, and two black, **487** (exterior only) and **491**.

Jars with flaring rims have an offset neck whose wall curves out in a flare, **503** and **505**, or whose rim turns or flares out, **502**, **504**, and **506**. The rims are rounded. **507** has a thickened rim on the exterior that gives an exterior profile of a flaring rim jar. **508** is perhaps a flaring rim jar, with a splayed neck and slightly flaring rim. The rim diameters of the jars with flaring rims range from 0.11 to 0.18 m, as do the jars with splayed necks. The fabrics are again mostly semicoarse; all but one are unevenly fired, with colors of the biscuit on the break in brown (7.5YR 5/4-6, 6/4), red-brown (5YR 4/3), reddish yellow (5YR 6/6), and red (2.5YR 4/8), and colors of the cores in gray (7.5YR-N3/0, N5/0, 10YR 6/1) or brown (7.5YR 4-5/2, 10YR 7/4). No plastic or incised decoration was noted on these jars. Four jars were plain, **503–506**; one was painted red-brown on the exterior, **502**; one was painted in a thin black wash on the exterior and a band on the interior, **508**; and **507** was burnished at least on the exterior.

Collared jars all had very short necks, either vertical, **509**, or slightly splayed, **510–513**. **509–511** and **513** have rounded lips, **512** has a flat lip. The rim diameters for **509–511** are 0.12–0.14 m;

for **512** and **513**, 0.20 and 0.21 m, respectively. The fabrics are like those of the above two jar categories. The plastic decoration of **512** will be discussed with **514** and **515**, below. The exteriors of all five collared jars are painted with Urfirnis, and all but **509** have a band on the interior of the neck. **512** is painted with a band on the exterior and interior, and on the exterior below the ridge.

Three jars exhibit added plastic decoration. **512** has a tall applied ridge on the shoulder. The neck above and the shoulder below the ridge are painted, but the ridge is plain. **514** is a jar shoulder that has a taenia of an applied ridge impressed at an angle; it is plain. **515** has an applied ridge on the exterior of the junction of the neck and shoulder and a second, vertical ridge that runs from the first one down the shoulder. Both ridges are square in section. There are traces of a red-brown slip on the exterior.

Jug (**516**, Fig. 31)

Jugs were very difficult to identify from the survey. A number of jug handles were recovered, but it was not possible to assign them definitely to a specific time period. One jug neck and spout of Early Helladic II date was identified, **516**. The neck seems to be cut away at the rear to form the spout. The fabric fits with the jars, above. The exterior and a small band at the interior of the rim are painted black (Urfirnis).

Ring feet (**517–578**, Figs. 32, 33)

The ring foot is the most common type of base for the Early Helladic II period in the Southern Argolid. Although most ring feet seem to be for open vessels of some kind, a few closed vessels, too, utilize them. For our purposes a ring foot for a closed vessel was determined by a plain interior in contrast to a decorated exterior; eight examples fit this definition, **548**, **549**, **557**, **560**, **561**, and **572–574**. A number of those ring feet called "open," especially "open?," may also be from closed vessels, but in the absence of explicit proof they are left as "possibly open." It is difficult to associate ring feet directly with a specific shape, but **517–541** are most likely from small to medium incurving bowls or sauceboats. Occasionally, enough of the wall curve is preserved to suggest that the shape is more likely a sauceboat, to judge from the more rounded lower portion of Type II sauceboats compared to bowls. The ring feet can be divided into vertical and splayed types. Splayed ring feet have a definite constriction where the foot is attached to the underside of the vessel, e.g. **520**, **532**, **557**, and **571**. Vertical ring feet have no or very little constriction at the junction of base and vessel, e.g. **530**, **553**, **555**, and **565**. Splayed feet are much more common than vertical ring feet. **519** has an offset ring foot that appears to be partially molded into shape while being turned; the pontil emphasizes this impression. **532** and **558** preserve evidence for the method of attaching ring feet to the vessels. The vessel and/or the ring base are incised with diagonal slashes, and added clay is used to smooth over the join. The diameters at the base of the 62 catalogued ring feet range from 0.025–0.19 m, averaging 0.095, but two clusters, one at 0.04–0.065 m (19 examples) and one at 0.10–0.12 m (25 examples), are noticeable. The fabrics are semicoarse (26 examples), medium (19), coarse (ten), and semifine (seven), and are mostly unevenly fired (50 examples). The colors of the biscuit on the break are reddish yellow (5YR 6/6-8, 7.5YR 6/6; 22 examples), red (2.5YR 3-4/6, 6/6, 4-5-6/8; 16 examples), yellowish red (5YR 5/6-8; nine examples), reddish brown (2.5YR 3/4, 5YR 4/3-4, 5/3; five examples), brown (7.5YR 4/6, 5-6/4; four examples), and pink (5-7.5YR 7/4; four examples). The colors of the core are grays (2.5YR-N5-N6/0, 5YR 3-4-5-6/1, 7.5YR-N5/0; 13 examples), red-brown (5YR 3/2, 3-4-5-6/3, 4-5/4; 13 examples), reddish gray (5YR 4-5/2; ten examples), brown (7.5YR 4-5/2, 5/4; seven examples), pinkish gray (5-7.5YR 6/2; two examples) and red (2.5YR 4/6, 5/2; two examples). **526** and **531** are "Corinthian green" fabrics, with colors 2.5Y 7/2 (light gray) to 5YR 7/4 (pink) and 5Y 7/3 (pale yellow), respectively.

No plastic or incised decoration was noted on the ring feet. More ring feet are plain (23 examples) than painted (14) or slipped (14). Red paint, **517** (exterior plain), **519**, **521** (exterior plain), **537** (interior plain?), and **541** (exterior plain), and black paint, **522**, **523**, **525**, **526**, **533**, **540** (exterior only), **544**, **558** (interior only), and **569** (interior only), are used. Several ring feet are slipped in red and burnished, **542**, **543**, and **545**, or slipped yellow-blue and burnished, **529**, **535** (exterior), **536**, and **573**. Self-slip occurs on **547**, **548** (exterior), **549** (exterior), **552** (interior), **557** (exterior), and **566**.

Pedestals (**579–607**, Figs. 33, 34)

The pedestal is a popular base for small vessels, though larger vessels were supported by pedestals also, as in **606** and **607**. Pedestals are tall, and often have a flaring base, as in **584**, **586**, and **587**. The demarcation between ring feet and pedestals is sometimes arbitrary; pedestals such as those on **591–593** could be considered as ring feet. Generally, the lowest point of the vessel wall is at least a centimeter above the base of the foot in order for the foot to be considered a pedestal. There seem to be three sizes of pedestals, based on the relative size of the diameter at the junction of pedestal and bowl, suggesting three sizes of vessels: small, as in **579–594** and **600–604**, medium, as in **595** and **596**, and large as in **598**, **599**, and **605–607**. The base diameters of the pedestals range from 0.04–0.25 m, but they can be divided into groups similar to those just discussed (**594** has a small junction diameter, but flares greatly to 0.11 m). The fabrics are about evenly divided among medium (11 examples), semicoarse (nine), and semifine (eight). The colors of the biscuit on the break fit with those of incurving bowls and sauceboats: reddish yellow (5YR 6/6-8, 7/8, 7.5YR 7/6; 12 examples), brown (7.5YR 4/2, 5-6/4; five examples), yellowish red (5YR 5/6-8; four examples), red (2.5YR 4/6-8, 5/6; four examples), pink (7.5YR 7/4; three examples), and reddish brown (5YR 4/3; one example). The colors of the core are gray (2.5YR-N5/0, 5YR 4-5-6/1, 7.5YR-N4-N5-N6/0; 15 examples), pinkish gray (5-7.5YR 6/2; two examples), reddish brown (5YR 4/3; two examples), brown (7.5YR 5/4, 10YR 6/3; three examples), reddish gray (5YR 5/2; one example), and black (one example).

There are no pedestals with plastic or impressed decoration. No one surface treatment seems to dominate. Five pedestals are plain, **579**, **589**, **593**, **596**, and **600** (interior not preserved); two are self-slipped, **604** and **607** (interior); two are slipped red, **591** and **599** (exterior); and two are slipped and burnished, **583** (exterior) and **594**. Red paint is found only once, **588**, but black paint is found on **582**, **585**, **590** (bottom only preserved), **598** (worn), **603** (plain interior), **605**, and **606**. Yellow-blue slip and burnish occurs on four pedestals, **580** (exterior only?), **584**, **601**, and **602**.

Hollow bases (**608–610**, Fig. 34)

Three hollow bases are catalogued here. It is difficult to determine whether they are from open or closed vessels, let alone to assign them to a vessel shape, but their size indicates that they were probably medium to large, most likely jars. The fabrics are medium, reddish yellow or reddish brown near the surfaces to gray or reddish brown cores. **610** may have been painted on the exterior; the other two are plain.

Flat bases (**611–616**, Figs. 34, 121, 122)

Flat bases appear to have some added clay to form the resting surface. The relatively straight, splayed walls suggest that they were used for open vessels, and **612–614** are painted or slipped on the interior, confirming that suggestion. **615** and **616** are included here because of the mat impressions on their bottom (**616** is very fragmentary, and only its flatness and the presence of the mat impression indicate that it might be a base). **613** and **614** are unusual for their added decoration. **613** has a taenia of discs overlapping to the left just above the flat base. The interior is slipped and burnished. **614** had a very complicated history of manufacture. The original flat base was impressed by a mat, then covered up by a thin layer of clay to form a new flat base, which extended over the edge to form the ridge at the base of the wall. The mat impression was recovered only after the piece was accidentally dropped and some of the masking clay came off. Subsequent dropping of other pieces did not reveal any other hidden mat impressions. This ridge was then impressed. There were at least two taenias on the lower wall, both of them finger impressions on applied bands. After firing, a hole was drilled through the body of the wall from both sides, perhaps for mending.

Plate (**617**, Fig. 34)

One example of a flat vessel with slightly thickened rim, **617**, was found on the survey. Dousougli (1987: 186 Abb. 15 no. 54) publishes a similar plate from the surface collection at Makrovouni.

Pan (**618**)

Early Helladic II "baking pans" were found at many sites, but the poor quality of the fabric and the thin bottoms do not preserve very well. The pans are round or oval and have large, slightly rounded, thin bottoms and straight walls that are thicker and better finished (Blegen 1921: 13 and 13 Fig. 15). Catalogued here is an example of a pan rim that rises up to a tab handle, **618**, a typical feature of the baking pans.

Handles: askos and jug (**619–622**, Fig. 34)

619 is probably from a jug. It is an irregular subrectangle in section and has an added pellet and two diagonal slashes on the upper surface. **620–622** are wide vertical handles with incision that probably come from askoi, though some jugs with such handles are known from elsewhere. **620** and **621** may be of EH I date, to judge from the surface treatments. Incision is in the form of grooves, in either parallel, **622**, converging, **621**, or diagonal, **620**, patterns.

Handles: tubular (**623**, **624**, Fig. 34)

Two wide vertical strap handles, like those on incurving bowls **330–340**, seem to come from closed vessels, each probably a large jar. Both of these examples are plain. Tubular handles also occur on the saddle-type stands **635** and **637**.

Handles: miscellaneous (**625**, Fig. 34)

Several horizontal handles that swing up slightly were recovered. This example, **625**, has a rectangular section, with raised margins, and is painted red. Dousougli publishes a similar handle from a closed vessel from the surface at Makrovouni (1987: 192 Abb. 19 no. 98).

Lug (**626**, Fig. 34)

A trumpet lug from an open vessel, **626**, pierced longitudinally, is covered with yellow slip and burnished. The vessel shape from which it came is not known.

Knob (**627**, Fig. 35)

Several large knobs on constricted necks and with a slightly rounded top could be dated to Early Helladic II by fabric or by surface treatment. Like **627**, these knobs probably came from large jars or pithoi.

Spoons (**628**, **629**, Figs. 35, 122)

Little terracotta spoons were occasionally recovered. Our two best preserved examples are catalogued here as **628** and **629**. The handles are wide and flat, and on the end is a slight groove. The bowls are not completely preserved, but they would have been rather shallow. **629** is painted black.

Scoop (**630**, Fig. 35)

A number of scoop fragments were found. The handles are long, wide, and flat, e.g. **630**, and the bowls are relatively shallow. The handles sometimes narrow toward the end, and a segment from this section would be indistinguishable from the lower, rectangular section of the dipper handle (e.g. **631**). **630**, like most scoops, is painted, here in black Urfirnis.

Ladle (**631**, Fig. 35)

Ladles were found on several EH II sites. The handles are rectangular in section at their lower end, then, after a slight bend, change to round in section. The end of the handle is turned back to join the underside of the handle, forming a loop. The bowls of ladles are rarely preserved on the survey, but are much deeper than those of the scoops. The ladle published here, **631**, is plain, but many are painted red or black.

Seal or plug (**632**, Figs. 35, 122)

A small terracotta cone with three vertical grooves, **632**, was recovered. In shape it seems to be similar to seals, and the grooves may aid in handling. The bottom is rounded, probably owing to wear, and any design that had been on it has disappeared. The cone could conceivably be a plug or stopper.

Stands (**633–648**, Figs. 35, 36, 122, 123)

At least four different kinds of stands have been identified from the Southern Argolid, but it is not possible to reconstruct completely all four types. One type is represented by two different kinds of knobs or legs, **638–640** and **641–644**, one type by corners formed by bending slabs of clay, **645** and **646**, and one type is a table of some sort, **647** and **648**.

One type of stand, the "saddle-type," is represented by a number of large fragments, **633–637**, and can thus be related to the stand found in the Keramidaki (Gymnasium) area of Ancient Corinth (Wiseman 1967: 26 and 27, fig. 10), though our examples do not flare up in so pronounced a manner as does the Corinth example. The most complete example, **633**, preserves about one-quarter of the stand and, along with **634** and **635**, provides evidence for their manufacture. A large rectangular slab of clay was laid out. Two cuts on each short end would mark the gap between the legs on each side, but this part was not removed; rather, it is folded up underneath, as is clearly seen in the photograph of the rear of **633**. The entire slab is then folded over into an arch, the center section kept thick and low, and the edges are thinned and stretched to form the higher parts. The outer edges of **633** and **634**, as in many other examples, are nicked or impressed. Over the low midsection of the saddle can be a vertical taenia, usually impressions on an applied band, **633**, or a wide vertical strap or tubular handle, as in **635** and **637**. The legs are pear-shaped, **633**, or oval, **634** and **636**. **634** also has a mat impression on the bottom. All of the examples are plain.

Three knobs, **638–640**, are on constricted stems. **638** has a hollow triangular-section stem, **639** an oval-section stem, and **640** a round-section stem. **639** appears to be attached to a thick, curving wall; **640** may be obliquely attached. The curving ends of the knobs do not make good resting surfaces. The knobs are probably from stands similar to those from Tiryns, which have two rounded legs supporting a wide, curving clay slab that forms the third support (Müller 1938/1976: 65 and pl. XXV no. 10–12). Above the two legs are two knobs on constricted stems that project up at an angle, similar to our **638–640**. Legs **641–644**, all of which rise at an angle, may be supports for stands like these. All the knobs and legs are plain except for **640**, which is slipped or painted red, perhaps Ur-firnis.

645 and **646** appear to be corners of stands of some sort. **645** has a resting surface for two sides, but an open bottom, and a corner of a rectangular cutout on each side. **646** is a folded slab of clay, with the exterior corner pinched to form a ridge. It is not possible to reconstruct the original form of these stands.

647 is a corner of a small table. A triangular leg rose to support one corner of a rectangular surface that seems to be slightly concave. Along the edge of the upper surface and the top of the sides are rows of oval slashes. **648** is a triangular leg similar to **647**, but it is not clear if it comes from a similar object.

Hearth rims (**649–665**, Figs. 36, 37, 123, 124)

Fixed terracotta hearths were apparently a feature of EH II houses. We have recovered many examples of three different shapes (round, keyhole, and Figure-8), and with stamped or incised decoration on the rim. The rims are generally wide and low, with a shallow basin. The underside is round and unfinished, reflecting the ground surface on which it rested.

The most common shape is the round hearth, **649–662**. **663** is a corner of a hearth that probably was square at one end and round on the other, i.e. keyhole shaped. **664** has a reverse curve, which suggests the rim was in the shape of a Figure-8. **665** is included here on the basis of its similarity to **654**, but it may not be a hearth rim. No hearth could be measured for rim diameter. Fabrics were coarse, except for two semicoarse examples, and most were unevenly fired. Colors of the biscuit on the break are reddish yellow (5YR 6/8, 7.5YR 6-7/6; four examples), brown (7.5YR 5/4-6; three examples), reddish gray (5YR 4-5/2; three examples), red (2.5YR 5-6/8; two examples), yellowish red (5YR 5/6-8; two examples), and reddish brown (5YR 3/2; one example). Colors of the cores are brown (7.5YR 4-5/2, 5/4; six examples), reddish brown (5YR 5/3-4; two examples), gray (2.5YR-N4/0, 5YR 6/1; two examples), reddish gray (5YR 4/2; one example), and grayish brown (10YR 5/2; one example).

All the hearths are decorated with either stamped or incised patterns on top of the rim. The patterns on **649–653** seem to be produced by a roller or cylinder with the pattern cut into it. **649** and

652 have stamped herringbone patterns. **653** has a herringbone pattern that alternates with a row of diamonds. **651** has nested diamonds, perhaps flanked by herringbone as **653**. **650** has a curvilinear pattern where the curves become tighter in parts, and straighter in others, perhaps indicating concentric circles or spirals. **654** and **656** have single rows of large, stamped triangles. **662** has a two-level rim: the upper is not preserved, but on the lower part is a row of alternating small, stamped triangles. **655** has a herringbone pattern, but it seems to be incised, not stamped. The most common decoration is incised hatched triangles, as in **657–661**, and perhaps **663**. **664** has hatched triangles that may be stamped. On the interior basin of **664** and **665** are traces of slip; **655** is actually slipped red and burnished on the interior basin.

Rooftiles (**666–677**, Figs. 37, 124)

Early Helladic II rooftiles of the type found at Lerna were picked up at seven sites: A6, A33, B24, F5, F6, F20, and F32. The tiles have a distinctive form: they are made of clay spread out on a bed of chaff that is apparent on one side, the other side being smoothed (see uncatalogued example on Fig. 124), then cut into the rectangular shape. The cuts do not always penetrate the thickness of the tiles, and a small projection along the bottom with an unfinished edge is left, contrasting with the smooth edge above the projection (see details of tile edge on Figs. 37 and 124). No complete tile was recovered; the largest piece measured 0.145 m along the rim and 0.155 m wide. Table 1.4 presents the dimensions of the uncatalogued rooftiles.

The rooftiles range in thickness from 0.007–0.020 m (with one up to 0.026 m). There appears to be a break in the thickness range at 0.013 m; 12 tiles have their maximum thickness below that, and ten have their minimum thickness above. There are two thicknesses of tiles at other Early Helladic II sites, and we may have a similar situation here.

The fabrics are mostly coarse and evenly fired. The colors of the biscuit range from red (2.5YR 5/6) to very pale brown (10YR 8/3). All the tiles are plain.

The manufacture of the tiles on a bed of chaff has left many plant impressions on one side of the tiles. Prof. Julie Hansen, of Boston University, has examined 68 latex molds made from the tiles, some of which have more than one impression on them. A total of 29 latex molds had identifiable grains that include:

> wheat: three grains of either emmer or bread, three rachis fragments
> barley: four definite (one of which is twisted in the manner of the lateral grains of six-row barley,
>   *Hordeum hexastichum*), 16 possible, one rachis fragment
> barley or oats: two small grains
> oats: three possible grains

Prof. Hansen cautions that it is impossible to tell from this evidence whether the three cereals were actually grown as crops; oats, for instance, are a common contaminant in cereal crops.

Conclusions

Although it is dangerous to equate ceramics with peoples, as has been all too easily done in the past, nevertheless the history of ceramics in the Southern Argolid does to a certain extent reflect the history of the human societies that manufactured, utilized, and discarded them. Within the Southern Argolid, the ceramic assemblages from contemporary sites seem to be remarkably homogeneous, with the greatest differences due to size: the larger sites have more materials and a greater variety of

Table 1.4. Dimensions of Early Helladic II Rooftiles

from the Southern Argolid (dimensions in meters)

AEP inventory number	Corner or rim	Maximum preserved length	Maximum preserved width	Thickness
A6-83-x	Corner	0.165	0.135	0.013–0.018
A6-5-10	Rim	0.110	0.080	0.009–0.015
A6-8-18	-	0.110	0.080	0.011–0.013
A6-83-x	Rim	0.105	0.110	0.011–0.018
A6-83-x	Rim	0.155	0.135	0.013–0.017
A6-83-x	Rim	0.080	0.065	0.007–0.013
A6-83-x	Rim	0.070	0.040	0.008–0.015
A6-83-x	Rim	0.080	0.080	0.009–0.016
A6-83-x	Rim	0.085	0.060	0.010–0.017
F20-5	Rim	0.065	0.075	0.013–0.016
A6-72-218	Rim	0.125	0.090	0.010–0.020
F32-A3-22	Rim	0.050	0.060	0.012–0.014
A33-1-x	-	0.060	0.040	0.010–0.011
F5-351	-	0.045	0.040	0.009–0.013
A33-81-1-28	Rim	0.055	0.040	0.011–0.012
A6-72-x	Rim	0.025	0.045	0.009–0.011
A6-83-x	-	0.065	0.060	0.017–0.019
A6-72-216	-	0.070	0.075	0.011–0.013
A6-8-19	Rim	0.040	0.050	0.013–0.020
B24-123	Rim	0.125	0.085	0.015–0.026
F6-74	Rim	0.040	0.065	0.012–0.013
A6-83-x	Corner	0.095	0.110	0.010–0.016
A33-81-1-x	Rim	0.060	0.085	0.013–0.015

materials. The homogeneity of the ceramic assemblages validates our claim that the Southern Argolid is a region, and can be studied on such a scale. The degree of similarity of the ceramic assemblage in the Southern Argolid to ceramic assemblages elsewhere in the Aegean varies through time and space; both types of variation, that is, the degree of similarity through time and across different geographical regions, suggest changes in the extra-regional contacts of the Southern Argolid. The pottery of the Neolithic through Early Helladic II periods presented in this chapter demonstrates better than the pottery from other periods these variations in similarity through time and space.

The Neolithic material from the survey is rather sparse, but when ceramic material from the excavations at Franchthi Cave is also considered, the similarities of the Middle Neolithic and the Late Neolithic assemblages to those from other Peloponnesian sites are striking, as both Vitelli (1974) and Cullen (1985) have demonstrated. Interaction between the inhabitants of the Southern Argolid and those of other regions of the Peloponnese in the Middle and Late Neolithic periods was evidently quite strong. The picture in the Final Neolithic is less clear, owing primarily to the comparative lack of published material from other sites and regions. Certainly the pottery of the Southern Argolid shares a number of features, such as crusted ware, pattern-burnished ware, and cheese pots, with pottery from sites throughout the Aegean, but these similarities are not so many. Indeed, the Final Neolithic and the following Early Helladic I periods both portray rather independent ceramic assemblages. Certainly there was contact, for the lack of specific ceramic parallels does not indicate a lack of contact among peoples (Rutter 1982). The Final Neolithic ceramic assemblage from the Southern Argolid can quite clearly be placed within the overall context of the Final Neolithic in the Aegean, on the basis of general parallels of fabric treatments, shapes, and decorative treatments, but the lack of numerous specific parallels, which is not characteristic of other periods, does suggest that there was a certain independence to the Southern Argolid ceramic assemblage. The Final Neolithic settlement pattern, which appears to be one of several small settlements perhaps of short duration, along with cave occupation (e.g. Franchthi Cave and Kotena Cave), has been interpreted as indicating a "pioneer" expansion period when people were moving into previously unexploited territories (van Andel and Runnels 1987; Runnels and van Andel 1987), or one that had a major transhumant component (Jacobsen 1984). Final Neolithic society may not have been organized in such a way as to promote extensive contacts among regions, at least among the producers of ceramics.

The rather unique appearance of the Southern Argolid Early Helladic I ceramic assemblage is most likely not due to the same causes as is the uniqueness of the ceramic assemblage of the Final Neolithic. The Early Helladic I period is truly a time of expansion of settlement, in terms of both quantity and size of sites. It has been suggested a number of times that there was an influx of population at this time (e.g. Caskey 1971), most likely from the east, and the great similarity of the Southern Argolid pottery to that of the Cycladic islands would support such a view. As stated at the beginning of these conclusions, however, changes in pots are not the same as changes in people. The similarities of the Early Helladic I material to material from the Cyclades, as in the case of the Final Neolithic period, are of a general nature. Similarities in shapes and especially surface and decorative treatments have been indicated above, but exact correspondences between the Southern Argolid assemblage and assemblages from specific sites within the Cyclades are very few. But as in the Final Neolithic, of course, ceramics of the Early Bronze I period in the Cyclades (and on the mainland, for that matter) have not been extensively published, and for the Cyclades we have the added problem that the majority of assemblages are from tombs, not domestic contexts. There are a number of similarities between ceramics from the Southern Argolid and ceramics from several sites in the Saronic Gulf (mostly unpublished surface sites, including several on Methana; I would like to thank C. Mee for showing me some of this material; see also Pullen 1984), and it may be that the Southern Argolid is part of a larger region exhibiting a ceramic assemblage distinct from other regions such as the Argive plain/Corinthia or the Cyclades. The Southern Argolid pottery suggests to me an initial stimulus from the Cyclades in terms of shapes, decoration, etc., but then a rather independent development subsequent to this stimulus. By the end of the Early Helladic I period in the Southern Argolid, the ceramics seem to be moving closer to those from the northern Argolid and Corinthia, though many of the features of the final, "Talioti" phase of Early Helladic I ceramics from the Argive plain and Nemea Valley are not present in the Southern Argolid, at least not in appreciable quantities (Dousougli 1987; Pullen 1987). Until contemporaneous ceramic assemblages from the Saronic Gulf and from other regions are published, this proposed shift in orientation of the Southern Argolid ceramics from the Cyclades to the mainland of the Peloponnese during the Early Helladic I period must remain a suggestion.

In the Early Helladic II period the ceramics of the Southern Argolid seem to be quite close to the ceramics of the northern Argolid and Corinthia in terms of fabrics, individual shapes, and decorative treatments. What is striking about the pottery from the Southern Argolid is that while for the individual artifact a comparable piece can be identified from any one of a number of sites outside the

Southern Argolid, the situation on the level of the entire ceramic assemblage is quite different. Certain shapes and decorative techniques have different popularities in the Southern Argolid than at contemporary sites in the northern Argolid and Corinthia. The picture may be skewed slightly by the great amount of material from the central Fournoi Valley focus group of sites, which alone constitutes nearly one-fourth of the prehistoric pottery. This group of sites seems to be involved in some kind of large-scale, specialized production, as evidenced by the proportionately great quantities of medium to large incurving bowls, often decorated with incision as with applied plastic bands. In stone tools, too, the Fournoi Valley focus of sites presents an unusual picture (cf. below, Chapter 5). But even when the predominance of the Fournoi Valley cluster is taken into account, the Southern Argolid ceramic assemblage is still distinct from that of the northern Argolid and Corinthia. There is little in the way of comparison with material from the Cyclades, but again, as is the case with pottery of the Early Helladic I period, there seem to be a number of similarities to the assemblages of pottery from the Saronic Gulf. The location of the Southern Argolid on the sea route between the Argive Gulf and the Saronic Gulf would of course allow contact with sites located in both regions. Despite the great amount of interregional contact and "internationalism" that characterize the Early Bronze 2 period (especially when compared to previous periods; cf. Renfrew 1972), a number of distinct regions have been identified on the mainland during the Early Helladic II period, at least in ceramic terms: Boeotia and central Greece (Konsola 1984); Kea and eastern Attica (Wilson 1986); and the Argive plain and Corinthia. I would add the Southern Argolid and Saronic Gulf as an additional ceramic region for the Early Helladic II, though further work in the Saronic Gulf may indicate that this area should not be included with the Southern Argolid.

The detailed discussions of the ceramic assemblages from the Southern Argolid, as presented in this and the following chapters, provide the documentation for one aspect of the history of the Southern Argolid, that of the changing degrees of similarities of ceramic production in the Southern Argolid with other regions through time. As shown in this chapter, the Southern Argolid ceramic assemblage in the Middle and Late Neolithic periods is close to those of other Peloponnesian sites, is rather independent in the Final Neolithic period, receives a major influence from the Cyclades in the Early Helladic I, and by the Early Helladic II period returns to close connections with the Peloponnesian sites, though maintaining its own distinctive regional interpretation of ceramic features. These variations in the ceramic assemblages, when related to variations in other categories of materials, help to explain change in the history of the Southern Argolid.

CHAPTER 2

The Pottery of the Early Helladic III and Middle Helladic Periods

Gullög C. Nordquist

This chapter includes pottery dated to the Early Helladic III and Middle Helladic periods, the two treated separately below. Since the major cultural and ceramic break of the Early Bronze Age falls not at the end of Early Helladic III but at the transition from Early Helladic II to Early Helladic III, we decided to group the Early Helladic III pottery with that from the Middle Helladic. Late Helladic I pottery is discussed within the section on Middle Helladic ceramics, since the ceramics of the Late Helladic I period belong to the Middle Helladic tradition, technologically and stylistically.

The Early Helladic III Period (678–711, Figs. 38, 39, 125)

Early Helladic III pottery was found at eight sites. A larger amount of EH III pottery was recovered at sites A6 (12 sherds) and E13 (29 sherds), both of which also yielded a respectable number of MH sherds. Early Helladic III activity is probably also attested at site E9 (seven sherds) and possibly at F5 (four sherds), while the other sites yielded only occasional and sometimes dubious EH III sherds: F6 (two sherds), and F32, G6, and G9 (one sherd each). The similarity with the EH III material from the central Argive plain, as known from, for example, Lerna and Asine, should be noted. Among the material from the survey there were no clear examples of either local fabrics or vessel types peculiar to this part of the Southern Argolid, although this may be due to the difficulty in recognizing such as yet poorly understood pottery. Future excavations will probably uncover more of the local ceramic.

The Fabrics and the Shapes

Early Helladic III vase typology is based on the pioneering work of the early excavators, such as Wace and Blegen (1916–18), Blegen (1921, 1928), and Frödin and Persson (1938). Lately, Rutter (1979, 1982, 1983, 1986) has added studies on the material from Lerna. Shape and ware references are to Rutter 1986.

To make it possible to tie in the EH III material from the Southern Argolid with that from the central Argive plain, the sherds have been categorized primarily to the classes of pottery determined by fabric and surface treatment of Rutter, on the basis of the EH III pottery from Lerna, and secondarily to shape.

It is to be noticed that this material from the Southern Argolid has strong similarities to that from the central plain. It has not been possible to establish any local EH III pottery traditions, owing to the limited amount of sherds—only in two cases were more than ten EH III sherds found at one site (sites A6 and E13). Evidence for pottery imported from outside the Argive region is to be found in the gold mica fabric. This was recognized within three classes: Solidly Painted and Unburnished (**690**), Solidly Painted and Burnished (**697**, **699**, and **702**), and Dark-on-Light Painted (**705**). Gold mica fabric has been recognized as Aiginetan in its Middle Helladic context (Zerner 1978: 148–58; 1986: 64–66). There is no reason to suppose another origin for the EH III gold mica pottery.

The following classes of EH III pottery were recognized:

Solidly Painted and Unburnished ("Smear ware") (**678–694**, Figs. 38, 125)

A fine to coarse clay with round gray, black, and angular white, sometimes also brown, inclusions and very little mica (Rutter 1986: 30, 34). The color of the biscuits was generally 7.5YR 6-7/4, 5YR 5-6/4-6, or 2.5YR 6/6 (pink to reddish yellow or red), and of the cores, 5YR 6/4, 7.5YR 2-5/4, or 10YR 3-6/1 (brown to gray). The vases were coated with an uneven dull paint, varying in color between 7.5YR N3/ or 10YR 4-3/1 (gray/dark gray) to 2.5YR 5/6 (red) or 7.5YR 6/4-6 or 5YR 4/3 (light to reddish brown to reddish yellow). One sherd, **689**, had three distinctly colored layers, pinkish gray in core and near the surface, and light red in between. The pithos(?) sherd, **686**, had large white and gray and black inclusions in addition to straw temper, and was painted with a dull red paint.

Among the closed shapes should be noticed the narrow-necked jars **678–681**, **685**, and **689** of Rutter's type XVII.1, with trianguloid handles, and a pithos, **686**. Among the open shapes were various bowls, such as bowls with horizontal handles of Rutter's type XIII.3, **687**, **688**, **690**, **692**, and **693** (**690** possibly of a gold mica fabric) and of type XIII.4, **682** and **694**. **683** and **684** were sherds with applied bands with impressed rope pattern.

Solidly Painted and Burnished (**695–703**, Figs. 38, 125)

Clay similar to that of the preceding class, semifine to semicoarse, often gritty, with gray, red, and white inclusions and very little mica; biscuits 5YR 5/6 to 7.5YR 6/4 (yellowish red to light brown) and cores 2.5Y N5/, 10YR 4-5/1 (gray), 7.5YR 6/2 (pinkish gray) to 7.5YR 7/4-6 (pink to reddish yellow). The surfaces were solidly covered with an unevenly applied paint, burnished in patches. The paint varied in color from 5YR 5/3-6/6 and 2.5YR 4/8 to 5YR 3/1 (red to very dark gray) to 2.5YR 4/4, 5YR 5/4 (reddish brown) or 2.5YR N2.5/ (black) (Rutter 1986: 34). Three sherds, **697**, **699**, and **702**, were of a semifine gold mica clay, with white, black, and gray inclusions, biscuit 5YR 6-4/6 (light reddish brown to reddish yellow) and cores 2.5Y N5/ (gray) or 2.5YR 5/6 (red). The paint used on the surfaces was rather dull, 2.5YR 4/6-5YR 4/6-5YR 3/1 (red to very dark gray), 5YR 4/6 (yellowish red) to 7.5YR 5/4-2 (brown) in color, with traces of burnishing.

The shapes were narrow-necked jars of Rutter's types XVII.1 (**695–697**) or general form XVII, **698**. Among the open vessels should be noted a bowl with horizontal lugs, **699**, a shoulder-handled bowl of Rutter's type XII.2, **700**, a tankard, **701**, a cup or kantharos, **703**, and a pedestaled vessel, **702**, of gold mica fabric.

Dark-on-Light Painted (**704–707**, Figs. 39, 125)

The Dark-on-Light Painted sherds were semifine to semicoarse with gray, white, and sometimes brown inclusions, and very little mica; biscuits 5YR 6/8, 5YR 5/4-6/6 (yellowish red or reddish yellow) to 7.5YR 6/2 (pinkish gray) and cores 10YR 4/1 (gray) to 5YR 5/4-6/6 (reddish brown or yellow). The paint used for painted surfaces and for patterns was of the same type as for the classes above, 5YR 4/2-3, 7.5YR 5/2-4 (dark reddish gray to reddish brown), used in filled semicircles on interior rims (Rutter 1986: 31). The shapes were open, mainly bowls, **704–707**. Also here a sherd of gold mica fabric was found, **705**, with white inclusions and painted with a dull red paint (Rutter 1986: 34).

Fine Burnished (**708–709**, Figs. 39, 125)

No certain sherd of Fine Gray Burnished (Rutter 1983, 1986: 34) was recognized, owing perhaps partly to the worn state of much of the material. Fine Burnished Non-Gray was represented by **708** and **709**. The former was a rim of an open vessel, and the latter a body sherd with handle from a shoulder-handled bowl of Rutter's type XII.1 (?).

Medium Coarse Burnished and Medium Coarse Unburnished (**710–711**, Figs. 39, 125)

Medium Coarse Burnished and Medium Coarse Unburnished were represented by one sherd each, the burnished rim with handle from a deep rounded bowl, **711**, and the unburnished fragment of a small jar, **710**, with a pared exterior.

The Middle Helladic Period (**712–824**, Figs. 39–43, 125–127)

The pottery of the Middle Helladic period in this study includes the Late Helladic I pottery as well, the reason being that the materials found in the Southern Argolid survey from these periods belong almost totally to the Middle Helladic tradition. The character of the material, as surface finds, also naturally meant that it is impossible to establish any chronological classifications of divisions based on stratigraphy. The pottery differs little from stratified finds in the main Argive plain, but in the absence of excavated stratified sequences of pottery from the Southern Argolid it seems better not to try to divide the pottery of the late MH tradition securely on either side of the arbitrary border between the Middle Helladic and Late Helladic periods.

Altogether, 242 Middle Helladic sherds were identified at 19 sites:

F5	103 sherds	E74	4 sherds
E13	60 sherds	E5	3 sherds
E9	31 sherds	B5	2 sherds
A6	17 sherds	F4	2 sherds
E76	7 sherds	B43	2 sherds
F26	6 sherds		

A9, B25, B39, B83, B98, F15, F23, F32   1 sherd each

The sherds were naturally often worn and sometimes less easy to diagnose. As seen from the above distribution of the quantity of Middle Helladic pottery, the sites can be grouped into four classes. F5 (Fournoi) was the largest, with 103 sherds and one spindle whorl (**824**). The second group, with a good representation of MH pottery, consists of two sites in the Ermioni area, E13 and E9, with 60 and 31 sherds, respectively; a second spindle whorl (**823**) was found at E13. A third group consists of three sites, A6, E76, and F26, with between 6 and 17 sherds. The last group includes 13 sites with fewer than five sherds each.

The Fabrics

The Middle Helladic pottery was first recognized as such by Wide (1896) in his excavations of the graves at Aphidna. Its classification is based on the early work by Wace and Blegen (1916–18), Blegen (1921, 1928), Frödin and Persson (1938), and others, and was further advanced by D. French and E. French (1971), D. French (1972), Buck (1964), and Howell (1968), all working in the same tradition. This classification system was based mainly on the various surface treatments and surface colors of the vessels. As has been pointed out by Zerner (1986: 58), however, this method is less suitable for the very varied character of the Middle Helladic pottery. A property like color may vary within the same group of pottery, even the same vessel, because it is dependent on the varying kiln conditions; shape is also of less help, since the same shape occurs in several fabrics. Instead, Zerner (1986) has recently suggested a classification based on fabrics, and enforced this with petrographical analyses of some of these fabrics. This work is still in progress, and the suggested classification suffers from some inconveniences in both terminology and grouping (Maran 1987). But potentially it offers a scope for further studies toward a better understanding of the Middle Helladic pottery workshops and their output. The fieldwork for this study of the MH sherds from the Southern Argolid was done before the work of Zerner was available. It will in some respects make use of the results reached by her, while adhering in the main to the more traditional method of classification.

The sherds have been divided according to the more or less traditional Middle Helladic categories of Gray Minyan, Dark Burnished, Yellow Minyan, plainwares, Monochrome Matt-Painted, Matt-Painted Bichrome, and coarse wares. The well-defined classes of Lustrous Decorated (Zerner 1986: 66–67; cf. below) and Gold Mica fabrics (Zerner 1986: 64–66; cf. below) have been treated separately. Within the text of each ware the prevalent fabrics are discussed.

I have preferred to refrain from introducing a more exact shape terminology, awaiting the important publication of the Middle Helladic pottery from Lerna by Carol Zerner, and to a lesser extent Asine and other central Argive sites. It seems reasonable that the much needed redefinition of terminology for the MH pottery should be based on these large, partly well-stratified find groups rather than surface finds.

In the following, a large percentage of the Middle Helladic sherds found in the survey area are catalogued. Sherds too small or too worn, or otherwise undiagnostic body sherds, have been used only in the tables.

Gray Minyan (**712–720**, Figs. 39, 126)

This group was fairly homogeneous, of a type belonging to that group of Gray Minyan that falls into Zerner's Dark Tempered fabric (Zerner 1986). The clay, in color 2.5Y 4/0-1 (dark gray) over 10YR 4-5/1 or 7.5YR N6/ (gray) to 7.5YR 6/1 (pinkish gray), was tempered fine to semifine with mostly small to occasional medium-sized angular black, white, and occasional gray inclusions and little mica, and well-fired, with platy or pasty breaks. Surfaces were burnished, and 24 sherds were identified as gray Minyan.

Open shapes were most common (17 of 24), usually cups or small bowls, e.g. **716**, with a rim diameter up to 0.15 m, and medium-sized bowls with a rim diameter of 0.15–0.20 m, **713**, **717**, **719**, and **720**, usually angular in profile. Cups with high handles from the later MH period were also present, **714**, **715**, and **718**. Of special interest was the small handmade jar from site F26, **712**. The Gray Minyan vessels were mainly handmade (17 out of 24), but the precise manufacturing method was often uncertain, since surface treatments, such as smoothing and burnishing, have usually destroyed all traces of the method of building the individual pot. A technical detail worth noting is the method of fastening a strap-handle to the surface of a body of a cup with high handles, **718**: a couple of incisions were cut in order to facilitate the fastening of the handle. In this case the method was less successful since the handle has in fact broken loose from the body. Decoration occurred only as horizontal incised lines or grooves on the shoulder of bowls and cups with high handles, **713**, **714**.

The date of the Gray Minyan pottery from the Argolid survey is late middle to late MH, into the Shaft Grave period in the case of the jar **712**, or in Zerner's chronology, based on the Gray Minyan and Dark Burnished pottery from Lerna, phases 4, 5 and 6 (Zerner, no date).

Dark Burnished wares (721–727, Figs. 39, 126)

Of the various types of dark burnished wares found, three are particularly noteworthy. One of these, Argive (Black) Minyan or Micaceous Dark Burnished fabric (Zerner 1986: 63), was found in four cases. The clay was hard and grainy, tempered semifine to semicoarse, with mainly white and black inclusions and silver mica. Cores were 5YR 5-6/3-6 (reddish brown/yellowish red/light brown) with biscuits and surfaces 10YR 4-3/1 to 5/1-3 (very dark gray to grayish brown). Surfaces were highly burnished with traces of the tool visible. The only decorations were the typical grooves on the shoulders of open vessels: handmade basins, cups, small or medium-sized bowls, such as **722** and **726**, or large bowls, **723**, with angular profiles.

Another Dark Burnished ware, also found in four cases, two of them catalogued (**724** and **725**), was a fairly soft, somewhat sandy clay, tempered fine to semifine, with small to medium black, gray, and white, and very little mica. Cores were 10YR 6-5/1-3 to 5YR 6/4 (grayish brown to reddish yellow) with biscuits and surface 10YR 6/1-2 to 7.5YR 4/6 (grayish brown to reddish yellow). It was burnished to a softer shine than the preceding, and was similar to the finer version of Zerner's Dark Burnished fabric (1986: 62–63). The sherds were from handmade, medium-sized, open vessels.

A coarser variant of the preceding was found in the base of a closed vessel **721** and the bowl rim **727**, with many small to medium-sized mainly gray, black, and white inclusions and very little mica. Cores were 10YR 3/1-2 (dark gray to very dark grayish brown) to 2.5Y 4/8-5YR 5/6 (red), with biscuits and surfaces 7.5YR 5/4 to 5YR 5/4 (brown to reddish brown).

Yellow Minyan (728–745, Figs. 40, 126)

Yellow Minyan pottery was fairly frequent, with 41 sherds. The term covers a number of various late Middle Helladic wares, continuing in the Late Helladic fine ware, often difficult to distinguish from the late Middle Helladic variants (French and French 1971: 26; D. French 1972: 28; Rutter and Rutter 1976: 9, n. 10; Dickinson 1974: 113). Here the term Yellow Minyan is limited to the yellow, usually burnished, fine ware. The same type occurred also as matt-painted as well as in coarser versions, listed below under plainwares.

The clay was tempered fine, occasionally semifine, with either no inclusions visible to the eye or very few small black and white inclusions and very little mica. Core color was from 5YR 6-7/4-6 to 7.5YR 7/4 (reddish yellow to pink) over 7.5YR 7/4, 2.5YR 7/2 and 5YR 7/2-3 (pink to pinkish gray) to 7.5YR 6/4 (light brown) or 10YR 6-7/3-4 (pale or very pale brown). Biscuits were often in the same color as the cores, or more in the 5YR 5/4 to 6/6-7/6 range (reddish brown to reddish yellow). The Yellow Minyan belong mainly to Zerner's group of Dark Tempered fabrics (1986: 60–61). Surfaces were usually covered with an even, thin, technical slip, produced through smoothing and burnishing, 7.5YR 7/4-6 (pink to reddish yellow) to 10YR 8-7/3 (very pale brown), whereas applied slips often were difficult to distinguish. In one case, **742**, the surface was vitrified, indicating either a production site or secondary firing. The surfaces were smooth, usually burnished, sometimes to the typical soapy surface (e.g. **732**, **733**); the open vessels are burnished on both exterior and interior. Variants occurred. Two sherds, **741** and **742**, had a break consisting of layers like a sandwich, from the core 5Y 8/2 (reddish pink), the biscuit 2.5Y 8/2 (white), finally another layer of 5Y 8/2 (reddish pink), and the surface was slipped(?) 2.5Y 8/2. Three other sherds were of a reddish yellow or red (5YR 7/4-6 or 5YR 5/4) to strong brown (7.5YR 4/6) in surface color, i.e. of the type sometimes called Red Minyan, **729**, **739**, and **740**.

The open shapes predominate: 35 sherds were from open vessels, cups, and small to medium-sized bowls such as **730–738**, **743**, and **744**, bowls on a high foot, e.g. **741** and **742**, and cups with high handles, **739** and **745**. Closed shapes were represented by five sherds only, e.g. **728** and **729**. One is of uncertain shape. The vessels were more often wheelmade than were the Gray Minyan: 28 cases, against 12 cases of probably handmade. The sherds belonged to the late MH III and LH I period (cf. Davis 1979: fig. 9; Dietz 1982: fig. 121).

Plainwares, burnished and unburnished (746–755, Figs. 40, 126)

The material is too small to make a closer identification of all wares possible, but two categories could be distinguished. The first is a coarser fabric of Yellow Minyan character: a usually burnished yellow fabric ("Coarse Yellow Minyan"), cf. **746**, **748–751**, **753**, and **754**, semifine to semicoarse, with white, black, gray, and brown inclusions and very little mica, the cores 7.5YR N5/ (gray) over 10YR 5/1-2 (gray to grayish brown) to 7.5YR 7/4 (pink), the biscuits in the same or more in the 5YR 6/4-6 range (light reddish brown to reddish yellow), the surfaces usually paler, 10YR 6/3-4 (pale brown to light reddish yellow). Vessels are often well burnished, often with tool traces, but may be left unburnished. The type was similar to French and French's "Oatmeal" fabrics (French and French 1971; D. French 1972). The bowl on high foot, **754**, had a thick dull white slip, which had been slightly burnished. **746** from site E13 had a vitrified surface, perhaps secondary-fired or indicating a ceramic workshop. The mostly open vessels could be grooved around the shoulder or foot, e.g. **748**, **751**, and **754**. Open vessels were usually burnished on both exterior and interior. The same type of clay was matt-painted, cf. below.

The second category of plainwares is a semifine to semicoarse clay with gray core between red biscuit; with gray, brown, red, and white inclusions and very little mica. Cores were 2.5Y N6/ or 10YR 5-6/1 (gray) to 7.5YR 6/0-2 (gray to pinkish gray), biscuits and surfaces 2.5YR or 5YR 5-6/6 (red) in the bowl (?) **752**, the closed vessel **747**, and the bowl on high foot **755**, the last two red-slipped and burnished, slip 5YR 5/6 (yellowish red).

The vessels were handmade, mostly open, such as a cup, **749**, and medium-sized bowls, **748** and **752**. **750**, **751**, and **753–755** were two-handled bowls of the typical late Middle Helladic type (Dietz 1982: 80–81; Nordquist 1987: figs. 49–51), **751**, **754**, and **755** at least, on high foot. **746** was probably a jug.

Monochrome Matt-Painted (756–783, Figs. 41, 126)

It is of course impossible to say whether a sherd is from a non-matt-painted vessel, or is a part of a matt-painted vessel that happened to be without decoration. Fabrics used were various fine wares of the fine Dark-Tempered fabric (Zerner 1986), either burnished, **756**, **768**, **774**, **778**, or un-burnished, **764**, **773**, **775**. Also coarser fabrics, described above, were Matt-Painted, either burnished, **758**, **762**, **765**, **769**, **771**, **776**, and **777**, or unburnished, **759**, **763**, **767**, **770**, and **772**. Of these, **758**, from site E13, was vitrified.

Among other types of fabrics may be mentioned: **761**, a semifine clay with gray, white, and small straw-like white inclusions, traces of vegetable temper, and some mica; core 7.5YR N5/ (gray), biscuit 5YR 6/6 (reddish yellow), and surface 7.5YR 7/4 (pink); **766**, a semicoarse, very hard and gritty clay with white, brown, red and gray inclusions and occasional mica; core 7.5YR 7/2 (pinkish gray), biscuit 7.5YR 7/5 (pink), and surface 7.5YR 7/6-5YR 7/5 (reddish yellow). The paneled cup **780** was of a semifine, fairly soft clay with gray, black, and white inclusions and very little mica; 5YR 6/6 (reddish yellow), surface 10YR 6/3-4 (pale brown to light reddish brown). It was slightly vitrified. The paneled cups **781–783** were of a semifine hard clay with brown or red, black, gray, and white inclusions and very little mica; core 2.5YR 5/2, 10YR 5/1 (grayish brown to gray), biscuit 7.5YR 6/4, 5YR 6/6 (light brown to reddish yellow), and surface 7.5YR 8/4, 10YR 8/2 (pink or white). The three cups are of the type established by Davis as the mainland paneled style (Davis 1978).

Other open shapes that appeared were various types of smaller shapes, probably cups (**774** and **775**), cups with high handles (**768**, **769**, and **776**), a wide-mouthed bowl (**772**) and other bowls (**773** and **777**).

Among the closed shapes can be noted small to medium-sized jugs/jars, e.g. wide-mouthed jars Buck C2 (**757**) or jars Buck C5 or C9 (**760**) (Buck 1964). Open shapes were represented by, for example, cups or small bowls (**774**, **775**, **779**), cups with high handles (**768**, **769**, **776**), egg or paneled cups (**780–783**), and wide bowls (**772** and **777**).

The paint was the typical matt, manganese-based, Middle Helladic type (Farnsworth and Simmons 1963: 395–96). Paint color varied from black (2.5YR N2.5/) or very dark gray or grayish brown (5YR 3/1, 10YR 3/1-4/4), dark brown or brown (7.5YR 3-4/2-4 or 5/2, 10YR 5/3, 2.5YR 3-4/2, 5YR 4-3/2-3) to lighter shades, such as light brownish gray or pale brown (10YR 6/2-3) or pinkish gray (5-7.5YR 6/2).

The following motifs occurred (references are to Buck 1964):

1. horizontal band: neck (**765** and **772**), body (**774**), base (**778**).
2. horizontal parallel lines: below rim (**773**), neck (**757**, **760**, and **769**), top of shoulder (**758**), and body (**756**, **759**, **761**, **771**, **775**, and **779**).
3. horizontal ladder band, Buck no. 67: foot (**763**).
4. group of vertical lines: interior neck (**757** and **765**).
5. horizontal simple or double zigzag, e.g. Buck no. 4A, 5: shoulder? (**756**, **761**, and **772**), body (**771**), horizontal triple zigzag, Buck no. 6A: shoulder (**765**).
6. pendant triple triangle, Buck no. 38: shoulder (**757**), body (**766**).
7. curvilinear: shoulder (**760**).
8. filled pendant semicircles: body (**756**).
9. multiple semicircle (?), Buck no. 90: body (**775**).
10. alternating circle sections: base (**778**).
11. plant motif, cf. Buck no. 129: shoulder (**762**).
12. small pendant semicircles, Buck no. 57: body (**781**).
13. pendant dots: body (**774**).

Applied pellets were used on handle attachments, **769**.

Matt-Painted Bichrome (**784–785**, Figs. 42, 127)

The few sherds of Matt-Painted Bichrome that were recognized seem all to belong to the mainland type, dated to the LH I period (French 1972: 33–34; Davis 1979: 256–57, 1986: 6–7).

Lustrous Decorated: mainland variety (**786–788**, Figs. 42, 127)

The Minoan connections of this group have been shown by Zerner (1978: 166–70, 1986: 66–67, Rutter and Zerner 1984: 77–79). Clay analyses have shown that it was produced in the Peloponnese (Zerner 1986: 67; Jones 1986: 420–24), probably as the product of a specialized manufacturing center, producing handmade vessels for the trading network, and the type has been recognized at several sites mainly in the Peloponnese, e.g. Lerna (Zerner 1978: 166–70), Ag. Stephanos (Rutter and Rutter 1976), and Asine (Nordquist 1987: 49–50). The fabric was well-fired, usually tempered semifine to semicoarse, with small angular white, occasional red or brown inclusions and little mica. Colors: cores 7.5YR 5/2 to 5YR 6/4-6 (brownish gray, light reddish brown, to reddish yellow), biscuits and surfaces 5YR 5/6 (yellowish red), or 7.5YR 7/4 (pink). The interior surfaces of closed vessels showed the typical deep parallel incisions after being scraped with a hard-edged tool.

The fabric may be decorated in Dark-on-Light or Light-on-Dark style as well as in polychrome. The lustrous paint was 5YR 2.5-3/1, 5YR 4/6-8, 2.5YR 3/2, 10YR 3/2-4 (black to dark reddish brown or red). Additional chalky white was used on the handle, **787**. Two of the Lustrous Decorated sherds belonged to the typical small jars, the handle, **787**, and the neck and shoulder, **786**. The third sherd was a body of a small open vase, **788**.

Lustrous Decorated: imports (?) (**789–790**, Fig. 42)

Two Lustrous Decorated sherds, both from closed shapes, do not fit the pattern of the mainland version, but may be imports, perhaps from Crete.

Gold Mica fabrics (**791–817**, Figs. 42, 43, 127)

Fine to coarse fabrics, with shiny gold-colored plates of mica (biotite) sparsely scattered on the outside have been recognized as coming from Aigina (Zerner 1978: 148–58; 1986: 64–66). Three main types of Gold Mica fabrics occurred in the material from the Southern Argolid: 1. matt-painted; 2. red or black slipped and burnished; and 3. coarse. In its finer versions, the clay was usually light buff, almost green, in color, sometimes fired to a reddish-yellow color. Cores: 7.5YR N7/, 2.5Y 8-7/2, 5YR 6/1, 10YR 5-7/1 (white or gray) to various shades 5YR 5-6/4-6, 7.5YR 6/4, 10YR 6/2-4 (light or pale brown) or 7.5YR 7/6, 5YR 7/4 (pink to reddish yellow or brown); biscuits and surfaces often 10YR 7/3-4 or 2.5Y 8-7/2 (pale brown to gray) or 5YR 2-6/4-6 (pink to reddish brown). Inclusions were small and angular, giving the clay a rather sandy touch: white, red-brown and black, together with a little silver mica, and notably gold and black mica.

Gold Mica Fabrics: Matt-Painted (**791–801**, Figs. 42, 127)

The paint was matt, varying from 2.5YR 3/0-2, 5YR 4/1 (very dark gray), 7.5YR 3/2, 5YR 3/2-3, 2.5YR 3/4-6 (dark or reddish brown), 5YR 5/2 (reddish gray), to 2.5YR 4/6 (red) (Zerner 1986: 64). Of the closed vessels **791–796**, **792**, **795** and probably **796** were wide-mouthed jars. **801** was a two-handled bowl of the typical late Middle Helladic type; **797–799** were broad-rimmed bowls, **797** with unusual decoration.

The following motifs occur:

1. Horizontal band: below rim (**798** and **800**), neck (**795**).
2. Horizontal parallel lines: neck (**792** and **796**), body (**793**).
3. Vertical parallel lines: across rim (**797**).
4. Zigzag, Buck no. 6A: shoulder (**795** and **801**).
5. Pendant triple triangles, Buck no. 37: shoulder (**792**).
6. Double wavy lines: shoulder (**791**, **798**, and **799**).
7. Filled pendant semicircles: below rim (**797**).

Gold Mica fabrics: red-slipped ware (**802–811**, Figs. 42, 127)

The red-slipped and burnished vessels were covered with a dull, slightly burnished striated slip, which varied in color even on the same sherd from 10YR 4/1 (black), 5YR 3/1-2 to 5/6, 2.5YR 4-3/4 (very dark gray or dark reddish brown), to 7.5YR 7/6, 2.5YR 5-4/6-8, 10YR 8/3 (reddish yellow or red). The black color is according to Zerner (1986: 64) more common in LH I, but occasionally the slip on the same vessel may range from red to black in color, cf. **807**. All sherds of this type belonged to vases from the latest Middle Helladic into the LH I period: bowls with everted rims **802**, **803**, and **805**, broad-rimmed bowls **804–808**, and the bowl on high foot **810**.

Coarse Gold Mica fabric (**812–817**, Figs. 43, 127)

The Coarse Gold Mica fabric was tempered with small to medium, occasionally large, gray, white, and brown inclusions, with some silver mica and large plates of gold mica visible in the surface. Color: cores 2.5YR N5/, 7.5YR N6/, 10YR 6/1-2 (gray) or 5YR 6/4 (light reddish brown), biscuits 2.5YR 5-6/4-6, 5YR 5/6-8 (reddish brown to red). Surfaces were smoothed but not burnished. The vessels, usually medium to large jars, were handmade (Zerner 1978: 158–68, 1986: 64–65). Potter's marks are found on three bases, **814–816**, dating the vessels into the LH period (Zerner 1986: 65; Bikaki 1984).

Other coarse wares (**818–822**, Figs. 43, 127)

Coarse wares are underrepresented in this study, because they are difficult to date, especially as worn sherds. Here are only included those that are most likely to date to the Middle Helladic period. Potter's marks were found on the base **819** and on the handle **820** (Bikaki 1984). Several types were found, all closed vessels:

1. A coarse light and fairly hard clay with gray, black, white, and red (burned clay) inclusions and various amounts of mica; 7.5YR 7/4-8/2 (pink to pinkish white) in color, **818**.
2. A coarse clay with shiny black and transparent, light red, gray, and white inclusions and little mica; core 2.5YR 4/2-4, 5YR 3/1-2 (very dark gray, weak red to reddish brown), surface 5YR 4/1-2 (dark gray to dark reddish gray) or 5YR 4/3-4 to 2.5YR 4/6 (reddish brown to red), **819**, **822**. Possibly Cycladic imports.
3. **820** and **821** contained white and small to medium black, large red (clay), gray inclusions and little mica; the core 7.5YR 5/4 (brown), 10YR 6/2 (light brownish gray), the biscuit 2.5YR 5/6 (red) to 2.5YR 5/8 (red).

Terracotta whorls (**823–824**, Figs. 43, 127)

Two terracotta whorls were found. One, **823**, was of the biconical type known from the whole Bronze Age, and the other, **824**, was concave-conical, a type common in Lerna IV but found also in Lerna V (Banks 1967: 486–551). The whorls were burnished, but otherwise undecorated.

CHAPTER 3

The Pottery of the Late Helladic Period

P. A. Mountjoy

A total of 1241 Mycenaean sherds were recognized at 59 sites, of which 45 sites produced under 20 sherds each. The largest amount of Mycenaean pottery was found at F5 (Profites Ilias: Fournoi) followed by E74 (Asprokhoma).

F5	257 sherds	E9	52 sherds
E74	151 sherds	C11	38 sherds
F4	93 sherds	B38	35 sherds
B21	79 sherds	B25	34 sherds
B41	76 sherds	E5	27 sherds
E13	72 sherds	F21	22 sherds
A6	60 sherds	C3	20 sherds

Most of the material could be assigned to LH III, LH IIIB being the most frequent and LH IIIC the rarest. The Mycenaean pottery classified as LH I, that is, pottery decorated with lustrous black or orange paint on a buff or greenish clay and slip, was not found on the survey. This need cause no surprise, since it is only one of several wares in use during this phase and forms a very small proportion of the whole range of LH I pottery. The other LH I wares, which included Matt-Painted, Polychrome Matt-Painted, and Gray and Yellow Minyan, continue to be manufactured in the Middle Helladic tradition and are presented in Chapter 2.

The framework for the classification of Mycenaean pottery was initiated by Wace and Blegen (1916–1918) and by Blegen (1921, 1928), but expanded into its present form by A. Furumark in his monumental work (1941a, 1941b). Although subsequently revised as a result of information provided by new material (Mountjoy 1986), Furumark's work still forms the international basis for the classification of Mycenaean pottery and, as such, is employed here. Since Mycenaean pottery has been well published in numerous excavation reports (particularly from the Argolid), a less detailed presentation of the pottery from the survey is necessitated here than for the Early and Middle Helladic material. Unlike the coarser pottery of the earlier phases, the well-levigated clay of Mycenaean pottery lends itself less successfully to the use of the Munsell Soil Color Charts for color description; recourse has not been had to them in this section.

The Late Helladic II Period (825–841, Figs. 44, 128)

Late Helladic II has been identified at only ten sites; pieces from all these sites have been illustrated here, except for two late Matt-Painted jar necks from B89 and B96.

The Late Helladic IIA sherds include single pieces from a piriform jar or bridge-spouted jug decorated with ogival canopy **825**, a squat jug with hatched loop **826**, a rounded cup with stone pattern **828**, and a Vapheio cup with foliate band **829**. The Vapheio cup belongs to Type III (see Coldstream 1978: 393, 395 for a definition of the types). The trough-shaped section of the handle **827** suggests that it belongs to a bridge-spouted jug (see Mountjoy 1986: 27, fig. 24.1 for an illustration of the shape). Two monochrome goblet bases **830–831** are shown; they are not domed underneath, in the manner of the later goblet and kylix, but are raised concave; they are also painted monochrome on the underside, a feature of this period (for an example from Korakou see Mountjoy 1986: 35, fig. 35.13).

Characteristic sherds belonging to Late Helladic IIB include **832**, a Vapheio cup decorated with foliate band, and four goblet sherds **833–836**; **833**, with a chevron under the handle, belongs to the Ephyraean type (Frizell 1980: fig. 6.95–6); **834**, decorated with lily, could belong to this period or to Late Helladic IIIA1, since the same motif is used in both periods.

The Late Matt-Painted Pottery (837–841, Figs. 44, 128)

The deposits from the Athens wells (Mountjoy 1981: *passim*) and Ayia Irini, Kea (Cummer and Schofield 1984: 46) show that Late Matt-Painted pottery with sparse decoration continued into Late Helladic II and Late Helladic IIIA1. The Late Matt-Painted from the survey includes jar necks with angular rim **837–838** (Mountjoy 1981: fig. 12.125–27) and one (from B96) with lipless rim (Mountjoy 1981: fig. 12.121–24), which is too worn to illustrate. Two decorated body sherds **839–840** are shown, to which there are parallels from the Athens material (Mountjoy 1981: pl.11.113, 11.114), and a krater base **841**, whose shape and monochrome decoration also find parallels in the Athens wells (Mountjoy 1981: fig. 23.283).

The Late Helladic IIIA1 Period (842–855, Figs. 45, 128)

Pottery of this period has been identified at ten sites; pieces from all of them are included here, except for E74 and B25/42, which produced cup and goblet rims too worn to illustrate. Apart from the piriform jar **842**, kraters **843** and **855**, and cups **844–846**, all the pieces illustrated belong to the goblet, which is one of the most popular shapes in this period. The small diameter of **844** suggests that it belongs to a cup rather than a goblet, while the profile suggests the deep semi-globular type of FS 213 (see Mountjoy 1985: 154, fig. 5-2.18 for the shape). The groove around the interior base of **846** is a common feature of Late Helladic IIIA1 shallow cups. Of the four common Late Helladic IIIA1 motifs (stipple, spiral, scale, and net), stipple is represented here on one of the cups **845** and a possible spiral on the goblet **849**. The narrow and taller stem of **854** suggests the transition from the goblet to the kylix, which first appears during this period (for a transitional example from Prosymna and for the Late Helladic IIIA1 kylix, see Mountjoy 1986: 65, fig. 75.2, and 66, fig. 76). **855** is an early version of the ring-based krater FS 279; the beginning of the horizontal handle can be discerned.

The Late Helladic IIIA2 Period (856–877, Figs. 45, 128)

Predictably, most of the sherds identified from this period belong to the kylix and the stemmed bowl, particularly the monochrome varieties. Sherds from 12 sites are illustrated here; a further seven sites have produced Late Helladic IIIA2 monochrome kylix or stemmed bowl sherds, easily recognizable as belonging to this phase from their bright-orange lustrous paint (French 1965: 183). These sites are B43, B97, B98, C11, E3, F1, and F29. The material published here includes a piriform jar sherd **856** decorated with foliate band and a sherd from a large coarse stirrup jar **857** decorated with wavy line or octopus. A mug sherd **858** has the typical Late Helladic IIIA2 ridged rim (Mountjoy 1986: 85–86). The kylix sherds include three decorated ones **859–860, 862**, and a monochrome rim **864**. The pronounced lip to the rim of **859–861** is typical of the Late Helladic IIIA2 kylix. A further group of monochrome rims **865–868** could belong to the kylix or the stemmed bowl; two decorated stemmed bowl rims **870–871** are published, the wavy band on **871** being a typical Late Helladic IIIA2 stemmed bowl decoration (Mountjoy 1986: 91–92). Other decorated stemmed bowl sherds include an example with a narrow decorative zone filled by ogival canopy **874**; there is a parallel to the decoration from Scimatari in Boeotia (Mountjoy 1983: 62 fig. 23.30). **875** and **876** have several narrow belly bands flanked by a wider one, a system of banding that normally appears on closed shapes, but that is used in Boeotia on open shapes, such as stemmed and deep bowls, in Late Helladic IIIA2/B, and has been called the Boeotian stripe (Mountjoy 1983: 17). **875** and **876** do not appear to be Boeotian imports, but the possibility should not be ruled out, since this system of banding is not used in the Argolid.

The Late Helladic IIIB Period (**878–923**, Figs. 46, 47, 128)

The sherds illustrated here come from 15 sites; another four sites (B25/42, B98, F26, F58) have also produced Late Helladic IIIB sherds, while 13 other sites (B2, B38, B49, B84, C1, C37, E4, E5, F15, F16, F20, G22, G23) have yielded kylix stems or bases, mostly unpainted, that date to Late Helladic IIIA2 or Late Helladic IIIB, and just possibly to Late Helladic IIIC.

The piriform jar is represented by a single sherd decorated with tricurved arch **878**, while the stirrup jar, neck-handled jug, and spouted conical bowl are represented by single linear pieces **879**, **881**, and **923**; **879** belongs to the large coarse ware stirrup jar FS 164. The linear rim **880** could belong to an amphora or hydria FS 69, 128, or to a large jug FS 105. The krater sherds include a rim decorated with paneled pattern **883** and several bases from both FS 9 **887–889** and FS 281 **890. 887** is unusual in being pierced round the base underneath; the holes do not go right through but terminate in bumps on the outside in a manner suggestive of decoration. **883–886** illustrate the variety in the shape of the krater rim. Three mug sherds **891–893** could be identified, of which **893** is decorated with tricurved arch with fill and **892** with paneled pattern and lozenge fill; **891** could belong to a deep bowl, but the rim band is rather broad and the angle of the rim not quite right for this shape, hence the assignation to mug.

Ten sherds belonging to the kylix, **894–903**, are illustrated. Motifs represented are the whorl-shell **894, 896, 898**, the panel **900** and **901**, flower with panel **899**, and a possible version of multiple stem **897. 900**, decorated on one side only, belongs to the Zygouries type; **901** may also belong to this type, but too little is extant to be sure. A stem and a base **902–903** are published. **904** belongs to a monochrome carinated kylix; its upright lipless rim suggests a Late Helladic IIIB date.

The deep bowl is the commonest shape among the Late Helladic IIIB sherds, apart from the unpainted kylix. Patterns represented include antithetic spiral **905**, whorl-shell **906–907**, and tricurved arch **909**. Enough sherds from **905** are present to allow a reconstruction on paper, but the height is only an estimation; moreover, the sherds are all very worn and it is impossible to tell whether the vase had a monochrome interior, which would date it to Late Helladic IIIC; the flare of the lip is slight, which suggests that, although the vase could be Late Helladic IIIC (see Podzuweit 1979: 416, fig. 37 for Late Helladic IIIC Early flaring rims), it is more likely to be Late Helladic IIIB. Four bases **912–915** are published, of which **912** and **915** are ring and **913** and **914** are raised concave. **916** belongs to a Group B deep bowl with deep band below the rim and monochrome interior (see Wardle 1973: 315–16 for a description of the Group B bowl); it is Late Helladic IIIB2.

Several stemmed bowl sherds could be identified, including a rim with panel pattern **917**. The single deep rim band of **918** is uncanonical, since the stemmed bowl normally has a narrow band on the rim and a deeper one below it as **917** and **919**. **917–919** have the typical lipped rim of this shape. The handles **920** and **921** belong to the stemmed bowl, not the deep bowl, on the criteria of their thick walls and the interior banding, since deep bowls rarely have interior body banding apart from that on the lip and in the base (Mountjoy 1976: 88, fig. 66). One base is included, **922**. A spouted conical bowl base **923** is shown; since the handles are not present, it is not possible to say whether it comes from FS 300 or FS 301.

The Late Helladic IIIC Early Period (924–945, Figs. 48, 128)

Pottery of this period could be identified at six sites (B21, C19, E3, E13, F5, G9). It is all illustrated here. The two amphora/hydria sherds are tentatively assigned to this period: the rim **925** has only a slight hollow and could belong to Late Helladic IIIB (see French 1969: 135), while the decoration of **926** could be a Late Helladic IIIC streamer or antithetic loop, but too little of the decoration is extant to be certain; however, the appearance of the sherd with thin whitish slip and red-brown paint does suggest a Late Helladic IIIC date. A collar-necked jar body sherd with bivalve **924** is shown and some krater sherds **927–929**. The bivalve **924** is probably a filling resting in a larger ornament, since, if it is used alone, it is generally set sideways, not vertically. The monochrome interior of **928–929**, as that of the deep bowl sherds, is a criterion of Late Helladic IIIC in the Argolid, although it is possible that monochrome interiors began elsewhere in late Late Helladic IIIB (French 1969: 135); this may also be the case in the Southern Argolid. One kylix base **930** is classed as Late Helladic IIIC because of its reserved edge (see parallels from Phylakopi, Mountjoy 1985: 180, fig. 5.15.179–82).

Deep bowl sherds **931–944** are illustrated. There are three monochrome examples **942–944** to which there are parallels from Lefkandi Phase 1b (Popham and Milburn 1971: 335 fig. 1.1). **942** illustrates the typical Late Helladic IIIC flaring rim, while **943** has a reserved area between the handle stubs, another Late Helladic IIIC feature. The remaining deep bowl sherds all have a monochrome interior; decoration includes antithetic spiral **931** and **936**, running spiral **934** and stemmed spiral **937**, as well as paneled pattern **940**, zigzag **938**, and wavy line **939**. The rim **932** with straight heavy lip could belong to a stemmed bowl, but the stemmed bowl normally has a knobbed lip, hence this sherd is classed here. The stem of a stemmed bowl **945** is shown; it has a reserved center base, another Late Helladic IIIC feature (see Popham and Milburn 1971: 336 for this feature on a kylix of Lefkandi Phase 1b).

Coarsewares/Cooking Pots (946–972, Figs. 49, 50)

A pithos rim **946** is illustrated. The cooking pot includes the tripod type **947–952** and the button base type **953–958**. The rims of the tripod type **947–949** are all very everted, while the legs vary from medium round **951** to large oval **949**; **952** has an incision at the handle base. The button base cooking pot, a one-handled type, is illustrated by the rim **953** and a selection of bases **954–958** (for complete examples see Mountjoy 1981: 58 and fig. 6.27–29). Bases can be flat **954** or raised **955** and **957**.

A selection of miscellaneous coarse rims and bases **959–972** is illustrated. The rims include a closing shape with everted rim **959**, the everted rims **960** and **961**, and two heavy thickened rims **962** and **963**. **964–967** are raised concave bases, **968** flat concave, **969** and **970** ring, and **971** and **972** flat.

Unpainted Pottery (973–1011, Figs. 50, 51)

973–975 belong to medium-sized jugs; they are too thin-walled to come from the larger amphora or hydria. The splaying rounded rim of **973** suggests a Late Helladic IIIB date (Wardle 1969: 283, fig. 8.86). An alabastron rim **976** is illustrated; it is worn and could once have been painted; its sharply everted rim presupposes a Late Helladic IIIA2/IIIB date (Mountjoy 1986: 73, fig. 83; 99, fig. 118). **977–979** come from kraters; the tall everted rim of **977** belongs to the stemmed type and probably dates to Late Helladic IIIA1 (Mountjoy 1986: 61); the shorter rims **978** and **979** come from FS 281 and may be Late Helladic IIIB. A lipless conical bowl **980** is illustrated (for Late Helladic IIIA1 parallels, see Mountjoy 1981: fig. 10.94, 97). **981–985** belong to the shallow cup; the sharply everted rims **981** and **982** suggest a Late Helladic IIIA1 date (compare decorated examples Mountjoy 1986: 62, fig. 72.1, 3), whereas the less everted rims **983** and **984** could belong to Late Helladic IIIA2 (compare Mountjoy 1986: fig. 100); the base **985** has Late Helladic IIIB parallels (Mountjoy 1976: 99, fig. 12.136–42). **986** belongs to a dipper, and **987–990** to Late Helladic IIIA1 goblets; the stems **989** and **990** are too short for the kylix (Mountjoy 1986: 65, fig. 75). **991** and **992** come from the carinated kylix FS 267, the sharp everted rims suggesting a Late Helladic IIIA1 date rather than Late Helladic IIIA2. **993–998** belong to the rounded kylix. A selection of kylix stems and bases **999–1005** is illustrated. **1003** has the flat base that occurs on kylikes of rough ware (Wardle 1969: 288; for a definition of polished, standard, and rough wares, see ibid. 281); **1002**, **1004**, and **1005** have a hollowed base (Wardle 1969: 288, 289); **1005** is unusual in having a beveled edge. A deep bowl base **1006** is illustrated; the well-articulated ring foot dates it to Late Helladic IIIC Early (see Mountjoy 1986: 150, fig. 189 for decorated examples). **1007** belongs to a large basin, and **1008** and **1009** to shallow angular bowls; the everted rim of **1008** suggests a Late Helladic IIIA2 date, whereas the flaring lip of **1009** is more likely to belong to Late Helladic IIIB (Wardle 1969: 287, fig. 11.111–14). The stemmed bowl rim sherd **1010** with an angular knobbed rim is Late Helladic IIIA1-2, while **1011** has the canonical Late Helladic IIIB stemmed bowl rim; its surface is very worn, and it may once have been painted.

Figurines (1012–1015, Fig. 129)

Four fragments belonging to figurines were recovered from E13, B21, F4, and B9. **1012** is a Proto-phi figurine but belongs to a transitional group between Naturalistic and Standard Proto-phi (French 1971: 112). The arms are heavy bulges, with the division between body and arm clearly shown; the arm is an applied strip edging the body. The stem is hollow, the top of the hollow coming just above the break. **1013** belongs to the Hollow Psi type. The hollow of the stem reaches nearly to the waist. The lower part of the raised arms can be made out (French 1971: 126). **1014** is classified as Phi B, since it has a circular body, high waist, and thin stem (French 1971: 116). **1015** is a polos head.

CHAPTER 4

The Pottery of the Early Iron Age and Geometric Periods

Susan Langdon

Previous excavation and survey in the Argolid have shaped a general picture of a vibrant and prosperous area in the Late Bronze Age and early Iron Age. This view derives largely from study of the major settlements of the northwestern Argive plain region. The results of the Southern Argolid survey project augment this picture with a more richly detailed investigation of the southeastern part of the peninsula. Of the 328 sites of all periods identified by the survey, 33 include material of Geometric or Subgeometric date, with a total of 1283 Geometric sherds collected. A meaningful articulation of changing settlement patterns can be drawn from nine sites that each produce over 65 identified Geometric sherds: 331 at C12, 127 at B2, 125 at B17, 106 at A9, 100 at C17, 92 each at B16 and E9, 82 at G1, and 66 at F32. Another five assemblages are attested by the presence of from 14 to 36 Geometric sherds (36 at F5, 16 at C27, 15 at C11, and 14 each at E3 and E40). Nineteen sites produced seven or fewer early Iron Age sherds. That these small concentrations represent more than a mere hum of background activity is confirmed by their verification as Geometric sites from one survey season to the next. Such sites may represent farmsteads or minuscule communities of brief duration that later opted for synoikismos with one of the larger villages such as Halieis, Hermion, or Vista (C12).

In the following discussion of pottery wares and styles, the term "Argive" is used in the conventional manner, to refer to the pottery tradition and culture defined in the production of the Argive plain and the centers that surround it. "Local" and "Southern Argolid" refer to the region of the survey. The period designations Protogeometric, Geometric, and Subgeometric will be abbreviated as PG, G (Early, Middle, and Late as E, M, L), and SG.

The local fabric resembles that of pottery found across the Argive plain. It is usually fired medium hard, although it can be powdery at the surface, and is well-levigated with tiny, evenly distributed vacuoles, occasional micaceous particles, and usually white inclusions varying from small to large; often red, brown, and black inclusions are present as well. In color the fabric is generally of a warm buff or orange-beige tone (7.5YR 7/4-6/4), occasionally going more pink (near 5YR 6/6) or greenish (10YR 6/4-7/4). There is a slight tendency for this color to vary through time from a predominance of warm pinkish tones in the Protogeometric and Early Geometric periods (5YR 6/6; the possibility of Attic imports among these is discussed below), to a paler and more gray tone in Middle Geometric (10YR 4/3-6/4 being prevalent), to an average of 7.5YR 7/4-7/6 as the norm in the Late Geometric and early seventh centuries. This observed trend may reflect a general raising of firing temperatures or slight changes in kiln construction through the Geometric period. Tests done on Argive sherds by the Louvre for Courbin revealed that the more greenish color (10YR 6/4) results from firing at about 950°C, while the more usual buff tone (7.5YR 7/4) is obtained at 1000° (Courbin 1966: 456). Foley has distinguished the local fabric of the eastern Argolid as "generally orange . . . much darker than anything from the central plain with the exception of Asine. . . ." (1988: 68), an observation with which this survey study concurs only for the late Geometric period. For most of the period, variations often produce tones that can be more cool or yellow rather than orange.

The term "paint" is used throughout in an incorrect but conventional way, just as, alternatively, "glaze" is used by some authors, to designate the slip or engobe applied decoratively to Geometric pottery. The paint varies considerably from sherd to sherd, with Protogeometric and Early Geometric often showing a metallic sheen that is rarely found in later periods. In Middle Geometric and Late to Subgeometric the paint is sometimes thickly applied, yielding a crackled effect. More often it is faded or worn off to a greater or lesser extent, sometimes leaving behind a "ghost" of the original pattern. The color of the paint varies as widely as its quality, being fired to shades of red and brown as commonly as black, and often varying on the same vessel.

Because sherds found on the surface tend to be small, and tend to preserve isolated body parts (rim, handle) without the more important relationships of parts to the whole, the information they can offer on vessel shapes is random and incomplete. What they can contribute concerning their dates and the general chronological ranges of sites is more readily accessible, particularly from preserved motifs and decorative schemes, and more useful for one of the ultimate goals of the project: an outline of the demographic history of the Southern Argolid. The following catalogue is therefore organized first by date, from Protogeometric to Subgeometric, and second by shape, from open to closed and from larger to smaller vessels. Specific shapes and motifs are discussed under the chronological sections in which they most naturally fit. References to parallels mentioned in the text can be found under the catalogue entries in Appendix 1. A site-specific analysis of the survey area in Geometric times will be presented in a separate study.

The Protogeometric Period (1016–1035, Figs. 52, 130)

The Protogeometric period is represented at only one site, E9 Sambariza, a maghoula (an artificial mound) with an important Late Helladic settlement. In the early Iron Age the site is primarily Protogeometric, with light but apparently continuous representation through the Late Geometric period. The Protogeometric (PG) pottery fabric looks distinctly different from that which typifies the Southern Argolid in later Geometric. This PG fabric tends to be hard-fired, well-levigated, and very fine with sparse white inclusions, minute vacuoles, and micaceous particles; its color falls within a range of pinkish buff to pinkish orange. The paint frequently appears quite lustrous and metallic. In general, the pottery in both fabric and form is reminiscent of Attic PG, and this isolated coastal site on the southeastern shore of the Argolid might have originated as a settlement from Attica.

As at all sites and phases of Geometric, open shapes are the most fully represented, and in specifics of design these PG sherds show great affinity with Attic wares. The particular decorative system of **1016**, a skyphoid krater with a panel of cross-hatching flanked by sets of concentric circles corresponding to Desborough's Type IIA skyphos, is a favorite of Attic PG production (Desborough 1952: 80, 82–83). Parallels from Tiryns and Asine are rather late, and Wells has pointed out the rarity of this system in Phase 1 Asine, where it does not become usual until Phase 4 (1976: 48, 108). The unusual "wheel spoke" motif within concentric circles of krater body **1017** is paralleled on an

LPG krater at Lefkandi. Fragment **1019** from the lower body of a krater or skyphos may preserve part of a reserved area of foot and lower body; if just a band, it may indicate a type common at Asine, which is primarily black with a central zigzag between horizontal reserve bands (Wells 1976: 182–83, 187, 200 no. 278). The mostly solid black body with a low, and apparently single, reserve band is rare.

Skyphoi **1018** and **1020** have a broader space between rim bands and concentric circles than is usual at Asine, but the scheme is paralleled at Argos. The lack of lower body and foot makes these vessels undatable precisely. Skyphos body fragment **1021** preserves a dilute zigzag with vertical downward strokes set between a pair of horizontal bands, a decorative system corresponding to Desborough's skyphos Type IVa (1952: 80, 86–88). This scheme is known in Athens, Corinth, and the Argolid, where it is very popular at Asine, and continues into EG in all three regions. Without lip or foot the small fragment cannot be dated more precisely, but its very high quality of execution should be noted. Lower skyphos body **1022**, of a deep bowl shape, preserves three horizontals.

Two non-joining fragments of deep, thin-walled, open shape **1023**, probably a skyphos, preserve a cross-hatched panel between rather widely spaced multiple vertical bands. This unusual scheme, with a solid lower body not separated from the panel by horizontals, is found in Laconian PG skyphoi. The presence of Laconian imports in the Argolid in PG times has been established at Asine (Wells 1976: 42, 64, 83), where a fragmentary Laconian trefoil oinochoe preserves the same decorative scheme as **1023** (Wells 1976: 83 no. 526). The fabric of the latter appears grittier and more calciferous than does local southern Argive ware, an observation that corresponds with a comparative technological study of a Laconian sherd from Amyklai and an imported Laconian fragment at Asine (Wells 1976: 229 no. 526; 138, 145, 146, 148). Comparison was also made with several Geometric sherds from the Amyklaion in the University of Missouri's Museum of Art and Archaeology, and although the fabric color of **1023** is not as red as those, it is more likely an import than a local imitation. Connections between Laconia and the Argolid have been noted previously (Desborough 1972: 241, 243), and in fact Coulson has suggested that a similar fragment from Sparta might be an Argive imitation (1985: 50 fig. 7). The survey can thus add evidence from the Southern Argolid to this picture of activity across the Argolic Gulf.

Five rims from Sambariza, of which four are catalogued as **1024–1027**, present an intriguing puzzle. Their solid painted bodies with banded rims (except for **1024**, without banding), and low, sharply outturned lips, appear to be kantharoi of the traditional Attic PG type (Desborough 1952: 102–6). As such, they provide a strong representation of a shape otherwise not common in the Argolid, with rare occurrences documented at Tiryns and Mycenae. Wells reports no examples of the Attic type at Asine (1976: 66), but finds instead solid black skyphoi with banded rims, best represented in Phase 3 (her nos. 674–78) and Phase 4 (nos. 850–57). Because the Sambariza fragments do not preserve handles, it is difficult to judge whether they are to be seen as Attic kantharos types, even Attic imports, or as skyphoi of the Asine Type II banded form. None of the Asine solid skyphoi with exterior-banded rims preserves a handle; solid skyphoi with handles in Phase 1 (nos. 287–91) but without exterior banding are posited as the ancestors of the Phase 3 and 4 vessels. The Sambariza rims are likely not all contemporary. The high shoulder and short lip of **1024** are reminiscent of the kantharos from an LPG grave at Argos (Protonotariou-Deilaki 1971: pl. 66g), while the plump lower bodies of **1026** and possibly **1027** recall the kantharos from an EG grave at Tiryns (Gercke and Naumann 1974: 22, fig. 19) and several from Corinth (Weinberg 1943: 13 nos. 39–42). Although noting the possibility that the handleless banded rim sherds of Sambariza and Asine may be skyphoi and not kantharoi, we will continue to use the more traditional designation, noting the uncertainty of identification.

Cup rim **1028** with dilute zigzag and solid body finds close parallels with high-footed Attic cups, and with examples believed to be Attic imports at Asine (Wells 1976: fig. 152 no. 363) and Argos (Courbin 1954: 176, fig. 34, 177). This type does not continue into the Early Geometric period.

Rim **1030** of a closed vessel has been identified as a neck-handled amphora on the basis of the Attic form, which customarily has a painted rim and reserved neck. The hollowed form of **1030** is unusual, although it can be paralleled in two early amphorae at Asine, from Phases 1 and 2 (Wells 1976: 35, 82). It must also be noted that our fragment may date rather to LHIIIC, as paralleled in a hydria from the Klepsydra well (Smithson 1982: pl. 22b).

Two body fragments from closed vessels have sets of concentric circles made by multiple compass-brush. Body fragment **1032** from the shoulder of a small oinochoe preserves an area of solid brown paint that probably extends over the entire neck. Below and just touching this is a set of thin concentric circles with a broader outermost circle. This scheme is unusual in small oinochoai, but it can be paralleled in a larger version from Nea Ionia. The space between lower solid black body and concentric circles is not usual. The fragment of a solid black neck from a closed vessel, **1033**, may be from a PG belly-handled amphora, although the angle of the shoulder, the presence of a tiny ridge at the base of the neck, and the extension of the black matt paint onto the shoulder suggest also an oinochoe or small amphora of the Early Geometric period. **1034**, a small vertical strap handle with horizontal banding, does not curve inward at the top sufficiently to attach to a lekythos neck, and is more likely from a small trefoil oinochoe. Coarse jug rim **1035** is datable to Protogeometric by its combined features of a rectangular handle attached to a flaring rim above a straight neck. The closest parallels for the shape are two smaller PG vessels from Nea Ionia and several jugs from Asine.

The Early Geometric Period (1036–1039, Figs. 52, 130)

In view of the general scarcity of Early Geometric sites in the northwestern Argolid, it is unsurprising to find only one certain EG site in the southern region. Only four sherds, all from E9 Sambariza, can with any certainty be assigned to this period, although many of the undiagnostic body sherds from the site might well be EG. Although survey results are not sufficiently sensitive to distinguish chronological phases of PG and EG at a site as small as Sambariza, particularly in the latter period, a smooth continuity can probably be assumed here as at other sites such as Argos, which show no great change from PG to EG.

Skyphos **1036** is likely of local manufacture. Although in color it resembles some of the putative Attic imports here, the fabric is quite soft and easily scratched, and the paint adheres poorly to the surface. Both Argos and Attica provide good parallels for this EGI shape with its broadly oriented handle.

Cup rims **1037–1039** and a fourth uncatalogued cup body fragment (E9-225) are thin-walled vessels with metallic-looking brown paint with an olive tinge, much like that of some of the PG pieces. In contrast to the more vertical PG forms, the short outturned rims suggest an EG date. These few representative examples provide an apparent continuity at the site from PG to MG, although it seems clear from the decline in diagnostic sherds that there was a rather dramatic reduction in its size from the ninth century on.

The Middle Geometric Period (1040–1067, Figs. 53, 54, 130, 131)

Aside from Sambariza, where Middle Geometric material is also present, there are up to five newly inhabited sites in the MG period. The small site of B17 is believed to be a group of early graves on the basis of the nature, the quality, and the uniform dating of the vessels found here. Of the 130 sherds identified from the site, only five are non-Geometric. The cemetery appears to have been in use only from the beginning of Middle Geometric through Late Geometric I. There are several fragments of kraters like that from the Berbati grave, including **1040** and **1041**, which feature short everted rims with reserved bands. Flaring ribbed pedestals **1042** and **1043**, and body fragments **1045–1047** belong to the same shape. Of these sherds **1042**, **1046**, **1047**, and uncatalogued handle B17-A-35 share similar fabric, thick paint fired to a chocolate-brown, and wall thickness, and perhaps come from the same krater. A similar but earlier version of this krater type exists in an Attic example from the Kerameikos (Kübler 1954: pl. 84, inv. 930). The single reserve band under the panel on **1045** dates the vessel to Early to Middle Geometric. The dogtooth motif of body fragment **1048**, never as popular in Argive painting as in Attic, becomes even less so in Late Geometric; this fragment with careful and even execution is likely of MGII date.

The only settlement of size is A9, a maghoula in the Flamboura valley. The pottery here revealed a concentration in the Middle through Late Geometric I phases, with very little representing LG II. Pedestal rim **1044** corresponds with the MG krater type well documented at B17 (**1042–1043**) and best known in the krater from Berbati. A second such pedestal from this site (**1069**) has been catalogued as MG to LG because of its straighter profile; it may in fact be closely contemporary with **1044**.

Especially abundant at this site are skyphoi and cups. The MG drinking vessels in the Southern Argolid follow closely the varied models of the Argive plain in their dependence on Attic forms. Lips become more vertical, the decoration simple but carefully executed. The hard-fired, fine, deep-pinkish fabric and lustrous black paint of rims **1049**, **1050**, and **1051** are of especially high quality, and may in fact indicate either imports or close imitations of Attic cups. The continuation of horizontals below the lip of **1050** is more characteristic of Attic than of Argive skyphoi. Attic import skyphos **1049**, painted neatly without benefit of multiple brush and with a rather outturned lip, must be LGI rather than LGII. Small skyphos or cup rim **1052** has a very similar scheme, also zigzagged by hand. Fragment **1053**, a ring foot with a sharply delineated profile below a broad deep bowl, is paralleled in a MGII skyphos from Argos, but might also represent a globular pyxis.

Pyxis fragment **1054**, with its inset rim, is best paralleled in a MGII vessel from the settlement at Lefkandi believed to be a northeastern Peloponnesian import (Popham and Sackett 1979: 48; Coldstream 1968: 169, n. 13). Body fragment **1055**, the shoulder of a globular pyxis similar to **1054**, has an unusual decoration of alternating black and hatched horizontal bands paralleled in rare MG examples from both Argos and the Kerameikos. Pyxis lid rim **1056** documents the occurrence of the characteristic Argive globular pyxis at yet a third site in the Southern Argolid.

As discussed below in reference to later periods, the coarsewares tend to display more independent, local forms than does the fine painted pottery, and in survey study their identification and dating inevitably entail a certain amount of guesswork. Coarse krater or storage vessel rim **1057** illustrates such a problem, and is here dated to MG chiefly because of its provenience in the uniform assemblage of site B-17. Its well-modeled rim with indented edge perhaps anticipates the interest in adding fillets below rims as found later in **1183–1185**.

Unlike **1057**, the fine closed vessel fragments datable to MG follow the standard Argive MG repertoire and offer little sense of local production. An amphora strap handle (**1060**) with an X design, and probably a second X originally above it, attests the presence in this area of the most popular MG strap-handle treatment. A more unusual decoration is found in slightly smaller handle **1061**, in which the vertically bisected handle is banded horizontally, a variation on the more common angle-banded form. **1063** and **1064** are shoulder fragments of oinochoai, whose dark-ground scheme and horizontal orientations indicate MG dates. Oinochoe neck **1065**, with its panel of three horizontal zigzags painted freehand, similarly betrays an early date and Atticizing affinities.

Amphora body sherd **1062** contains a vertical dotted lozenge chain flanked by sets of concentric circles enclosing a reserved St. George's cross, a scheme imitating contemporary Cycladic work. Although at least one imported Cycladic example has turned up in the Argolid at Argos (Courbin 1966: pl. 151 left), the fabric of **1062** appears to be local. The mastos oinochoe (**1066**), a well-documented form in both Attic and Argive EG-MG, may be datable to later MG by its precise articulation of the mastos with painted circles, a change from the earlier practice of absorbing the relief form into the decoration or covering it with solid paint (Courbin 1966: 311). Attica may not have conformed to this trend, however, as an EGII cup from the Kerameikos shows a distinct emphasis of the mastoi by concentric circles within a design panel.

Middle to Late Geometric Pottery (1068–1097, Figs. 54, 55, 131, 132)

A number of the catalogued sherds are not sufficiently preserved to be dated more closely than to a general MGII-LGI category. Skyphos ring feet **1078**, **1079**, and **1082** preserve little of the informative vessel wall. Cup or kotyle rim **1083** with a panel of chevrons on the shoulder belongs to a type with a "nick" in the rim, which develops from MGII onward. The dating depends on the curve of the lower bowl, missing here, and the number of horizontals below the panel, which increase into the LG period. In the present example, the width and spacing of these horizontal bands suggest a small number and hence an earlier date. **1083** is not a local product, and the pinkness of the fabric suggests an Attic origin.

Various body fragments preserve motifs that are introduced in Middle Geometric II and continue to be popular into the Late Geometric. Hatched quatrefoils with stars (**1074**, **1075**) and the double axe alternating with vertical bars (**1076**) begin a distinguished career in this region. Open vessel shoulder **1081**, a skyphos or kantharos with a red-glazed interior, has a panel of wavy sigmas corresponding to the design scheme of the pottery found outside Grave G II/I at Mycenae. Coldstream has dated these vessels to MGII, Courbin to LGI. A skyphos (**1077**) with eight-pointed star above the handle attachment continues a MG Attic type and may be an Attic import. **1084**, a highhandled kantharos, is an exceptional form in the Argolid, although a couple of examples have been found at Tiryns. A plate with round handle and dotted rim, **1085**, represents a rare type for the Argolid, but corresponds to an example from a MG deposit at Berbati.

Certain sherds have been catalogued as MG to LG simply for reasons of caution. A ribbed krater pedestal, **1070**, and a rope krater handle, **1072**, both from Iliokastro (G1), represent forms that have their greatest popularity in MG; they have been included in this larger category primarily because there is little other evidence for material earlier than LGII from this site. A second twisted handle with a thick chocolate-brown to black paint, **1091**, seems to have been vertically oriented, recalling the popularity of rope handles on amphorae and oinochoai in MGII.

The survey yielded a remarkable number of fragments from cylindrical stands, a vessel form uncommon elsewhere in the Argolid or the rest of Greece. Probably intended to support kraters, their form as documented at Argos changes little from Early through Late Geometric (Courbin 1966: 232–34). The cylindrical body becomes gradually more concave, and both upper and lower rims become more differentiated, with the bottom achieving a slightly larger diameter and the upper an often sharper angle than earlier. Their differentiation from amphora necks depends on a few consistent details: the stands rest on the angle of the mouth, with the rim flaring up from the bottom and down from the top. Most decisive is the regular presence of a raised ridge or fillet below the rim, which is extremely rare on an Argive amphora and usually includes a corresponding dent on the inside. Like amphora mouths, the stands from Argos have decorated rims, bearing either vertical strokes with X's or a continuous zigzag. The stands of the Southern Argolid have solid-painted rims and occasionally bands on the body near the rim.

With few dated examples to compare, and little preserved evidence of body decoration on the survey finds, stand fragments **1086–1090** can be dated only generally to MG to LG. One example, **1067**, is more securely dated to MG because of its very flat rim. Body fragment **1089**, decorated with a double axe between verticals, closely resembles a MG example from Argos. Of the 14 stand fragments found by the survey, nine come from a single site, Vista (C12), and another two from Mases (C17), just across the bay. It is tempting to speculate that they were manufactured locally for a specific use at these sites.

A few coarsewares among the survey finds have been grouped with this transitional period, although as presumably local products the difficulty of finding satisfactory parallels in excavation material leaves these dates open to question. On amphora or hydria **1092** a round handle was attached to the lower part of the neck. Particular to the Southern Argolid is the cylindrical neck with flaring rim, found in the larger vessel **1094** as well. Typical of the Argive plain amphorae are a more flaring neck and a higher attachment of the strap handle. If these two local examples are from hydriae rather than amphorae, they attest a form unusual in the Argolid in either handmade or painted examples. An incised zigzag on the lip of **1093** documents locally a coarseware decoration known elsewhere in the Argolid since EGI. An unpainted example from a coarseware amphora or jug (**1095**) preserves one of two strips of clay that were once twisted together to form a rope handle.

Pithos rim **1096** with its horizontal rim above flaring shoulder may belong to the baggy form represented by Argos pithos C.3966 of LGI date. (Sherd **1096** illustrates the hazards of cataloguing survey pottery with poorly preserved surfaces; cf. **461** above.) Rim **1097** with sloping rounded rim is reminiscent of a LG pithos type of simpler profile known from Tiryns, which Foley considers an Argos, and not local Tirynthian, type. It is perhaps to be expected that vessels of this size were not traded around the Argolid but made close to the site of use, and may not therefore reflect standardized types but local variants. The two pithoi of the Flamboura maghoula suggest a cemetery area near the settlement. Pithos burials varied in use pattern around the Argolid, being rare at Geometric-period Argos but the preferred method of burial at Tiryns and Nauplia (Foley 1988: 35–43). Documenting such burial customs is beyond the scope of surface collection, and it is not possible with this material to define the mortuary habits of the Southern Argolid. The dates of these two pithoi may be set into the MG-LGI range that the other pottery of Flamboura suggests.

The Late Geometric Period: Late Geometric I
(1098–1112, Figs. 56, 132, 133)

The Late Geometric I phase in the Southern Argolid is represented almost entirely by krater fragments, with several splendid examples showing the high quality of work available in the area. The percentage of imports from the Argive plain that number among these is difficult to establish on the basis of surface finds, but most have such close parallels to the northwest that there are surely imports of pottery as well as artistic influences represented here. Krater fragments **1098–1101** are possibly from the same vessel, and are certainly from the same type, with their symmetrical panel decoration down to the middle of the krater and solid black or banded below. Other examples of this style are known from Mycenae, Argos, and Dendra. The thin meander of **1104**, the one-legged birds in triples (**1106** and **1107**), and the vertical squiggles on the shoulder of **1103** date these vessels to Late Geometric I. Krater rim **1102** is comfortable as a LGI large skyphos shape, but its decoration with vertical hatched columns is found only in Attic LG and on a unique amphora neck from Corinth (Pfaff 1988: 41); the fabric seems local. **1103** is so far without parallel for shape. Its short vertical collar on a broad shoulder recalls an unusual EG pyxis from Mycenae (Desborough 1955: 241, pl. 47a), although its decoration suggests an LGI date. In both Attic and Argive LGI, stacked chevrons with the points at the top are the norm; **1105** shares its more rare "upside down" chevrons with a krater from Mycenae, Gr. 53-338. The vertical dotted lozenge chain of krater **1108** likely dates to LGI, owing to the relatively narrower shoulder than on the LGII kraters.

The simple thin meander of body sherd **1112** dates it to LGI, although the placement of this motif on the body rather than on the neck or shoulder of the vessel is unusual. The sherd does not preserve a painted interior surface, but since the Argive decorative scheme generally does not employ metopes on closed shapes or meanders in the belly zone, it is reasonable to assume that this is rather a krater or pyxis fragment. The well-executed hatched meander on amphora neck **1110** is a standard decorative scheme in both Attic and Argive amphorae from EG-LGI, becoming gradually replaced by more varied and inventive motifs. A rather remarkable find is a large double handle (**1109**), apparently of a quite sizable funerary vessel. Although its fabric is consonant with local material, its form is Attic and might reveal a connection with the Atticizing workshop of Asine. Its presence, together with the small but fine collection of MG and LGI material from B17, strongly supports a cemetery group.

Body sherd **1111**, of the size and shape of a large amphora neck, has an unparalleled combination of motifs. A pair of angle-hatched ribbed leaves stands vertically beneath a section of what appears to be a broad angle-hatched battlement meander; below are two horizontals and a solid area. Single vertical leaves in a continuous row are common on the bodies of Attic closed vessels, as is the particular leaf form, yet no parallel has so far been located for such a motif within a meander. An angle-hatched key meander with checkerboard rectangles as filler ornaments is found on an amphora neck in Athens. The solid painted area below suggests a date in LGI rather than in LGII. Together, the fabric, both paler and browner in color than that typical of the Southern Argolid, and this unusual motif suggest an imported vessel.

The Late Geometric Period: Late Geometric II
(1113–1197, Figs. 57–62, 133–136)

By the eighth century the Argolid enjoyed a general prosperity that manifested itself in part through a new individuality of pottery styles distinct from Attic. This cultural self-definition extended to a deeper level in the Argolid plain, where the general uniformity of earlier pottery styles gave way to distinctive ceramic production at several centers. The ramifications of this trend for the Southern Argolid are discussed below. One of the questions that this survey project sought to clarify in its study of the Geometric-period pottery is the traditional interpretation of a cultural and commercial dichotomy between the northwest Argolid and the southern peninsula. Defined as geographically separated from the plain region by the Dhidhima range, this area has been perceived both as a backwater cut off from the prosperity and cultural ingenuity of the west, and as an autonomy affiliated north and east with its neighbors in Aigina, Attica, and the islands. A consideration of the evidence for life in the eighth and seventh centuries in the Southern Argolid must approach the material in light of these two issues.

Kraters (1113–1138, Figs. 57, 58, 133)

For the LGII and Subgeometric periods, the survey produced a remarkably large number of kraters, which in some cases comprise as much as a third to a half of all identified Geometric sherds (see assemblage tables). To some extent this phenomenon is an archaeological mirage created by overzealous collection of the eye-catchingly large and patterned fragments. However, even sites sampled by total-collection procedures revealed significant differences in component shapes among rims, handles, and bases of all identified shapes. The following table compares the percentage of krater parts among the six major LGII sites:

Site	Percent of identified sherds	Percent of diagnostic sherds
B16	53	64
G1	42	50
C17	38.7	45
F32	37	37.5
B2	34	22.7
C12	29	27

The very great variety of krater shapes characteristic of Argive LGII production makes it difficult to distinguish local products from those imported from the northwestern Argolid. Nevertheless, a certain group emerges as particular to the survey area, and indeed close parallels for the shape are lacking. Three LGII krater rims (1113–1115) share details of shape and a rather severe approach to decoration for this time. These are broad of shoulder, with a very short vertical collar rim that is flattened on top without a noticeable thickening of the rim, much as in slightly earlier rim 1103, of local manufacture. Rim 1113 has a solid black shoulder with streaky horizontal bands on the neck and evenly spaced verticals on the shoulder; 1114 has nearly the same scheme, but a gap to the left of the vertical banding may indicate a panel decoration. Rim 1115 has a continuous series of short vertical strokes on the shoulder that seems to continue around the vessel. Although its vertical shoulder squiggles belong to a LGI decorative scheme well documented at Mycenae and Argos, rim 1103 has the same short vertical collar neck as these three and likely stands at the beginning of the local series. Although its short neck and rim flare out rather more than those of the rest of this group, the solid black shoulder of 1119 is of the same austere decorative approach as these local kraters, and it may be considered as part of this line.

Other details seem to characterize the kraters of this region as well. Stirrup handles are little in evidence, only one fragment (1137) having been securely identified in the collected material. Although the use of pedestals generally died out by LGII in the Argive plain, pedestaled kraters are still being produced in the south. Flaring pedestal rim fragment 1138 is covered in a streaky black paint that looks quite late, but its well-modeled profile with sharp ridge below the rim, reminiscent of stands, argues for a date still within the eighth century. A narrow cylindrical pedestal with banding (**1136**) is also rather carefully executed, with a paint and fabric that closely resemble the LG pottery. Krater pedestal **1071**, classified as MG to LG for lack of close comparisons, is most likely of LG date because of its sharply articulated profile and small size. Despite this new line of local kraters, there was still a market for wares from the Argive plain. LGII kraters **1116**, **1117**, and **1120–1124** can be securely traced to the production of Argos and vicinity. The rich decorative treatments and motifs of **1116**, **1121**, **1123**, and **1128**, for example, stand fully within the mainstream of Argive tradition.

Other Shapes

Skyphoi vary greatly in shape and proportion for the whole of the LG period, and when a piece is fragmentary it is often best to date it on the basis of decoration. Indeed, when a sherd preserves only a small section of rim and shoulder, it may not be possible to distinguish a skyphos rim from a kantharos. Such is the case with **1139** and **1140**, which have apparently high rounded shoulders and relatively short outturned lips. **1139** is best paralleled for decoration and perhaps form in an Argive LGI kantharos (C.2466), yet here has been assigned to LGII in case it is a later deep skyphos. **1140**, with a profile nearly identical to **1139**, has a shoulder panel of vertical zigzags found more often on kantharoi than on skyphoi. Rims **1141–1145** are the tall flaring skyphos forms that came into vogue in LGI. **1141** and **1142** may represent the earlier end of the scale when the lips are mostly vertical; in **1143–1145** they begin to splay out to the width of the shoulder or beyond. This type generally has a simple decoration of horizontals and dots on the rims, although there are exceptions, like the birds of **1143** and the blind lozenges of **1144**. The vertical strokes above the latter are unusual. The solid black skyphos **1146** represents still another popular version of the shape, with a short vertical lip and relatively deep bowl, a form that extends into the Subgeometric period in Argos (Courbin's LGIIc). **1194** has a more strongly everted rim than **1146**, and is therefore catalogued as LGII-SG.

Bases **1149** and **1151** illustrate two late trends of the skyphos foot. Both flat bottoms and distinct foot profiles occur in LGII, while the kantharos tends to retain a ring foot. Unlike the standard Argive LG flat cup base, foot **1152** is nearly discoid in form and has a reserve band at the bottom akin to the developments in Attic cups at the end of LG and into the seventh century. Its fine pinkish fabric supports its identification as Attic.

The pyxis, always a popular shape in the Argolid, never became thoroughly standardized, as the variety of shapes found on survey reflects. Of the five fragments so identified for the LGII period, none belongs to the flat form that was most typical of LGII. Flat-bottomed pyxis **1155** is an Attic import. Two pyxis feet attest the continuation of the footed form into LG and SG: **1156**, a high conical foot with center of underside reserved, and **1195**, the stem of a plainware pyxis. Knob **1158** does not preserve enough of its conical lid profile to suggest its pyxis form. The globular pyxis established in the Early and Middle Geometric periods becomes increasingly rare in the Argolid, but is known in an example from the survey (**1157**), which preserves the blank handle area with two horizontals below. An example of the same shape from Asine is decorated with panels of horizontal hatched zigzags and may suggest what the main decorative panel of **1157** looked like.

Motifs

In general, the motifs of LGII pottery in the Southern Argolid compare closely with the repertoire of the Argive plain: dotted and blind lozenges (**1126**, **1133**, **1139**, and **1144**), bands of alternating X's and verticals (**1132**), hatched multiple zigzags (**1134**), Atticizing triple outline leaves (**1131**), concentric circles (**1171**), hatched meanders (**1172**), and gear patterns (**1171** and **1172**). More unusual and perhaps local ideas are panels of aligned dots (**1147** and **1148**), although similar treatments have been found at Asine and Tiryns, and a so-far unparalleled "fence" motif on amphora neck sherd **1165**. Uncatalogued fragments preserve further motifs: tangential blobs, double axes between verticals, eight-pointed stars, and a badly preserved example of what might be a diagonal cross in triple outline.

Figural sherds are not common among the decorated fragments, but examples of birds and horses are catalogued. Although the seven catalogued LGII sherds with bird decorations recall the popularity of birds attested in the pottery of the Argive plain in this period, it is notable that few seem locally produced. Krater rim **1118**, though a typical Argive shape, bears rows of disconnected blobs that are characteristic of Attic, Euboean, Cycladic, and Boeotian pottery, and in fact occur in nearly every region except the Argolid. Panels in which a triangle projects from the side frame above a bird's tail are equally at home in these regions. Similarly, body fragment of small krater or skyphos **1127** uses a scheme characteristic of a skyphos type with birds in square metopes popular throughout Attica, Euboea, Boeotia, and the Cyclades. The sherd preserves a two-toed bird facing left, certainly the right of a pair of antithetical birds in one or two metopes, with a solid lower vessel body just below the figural panel. Asine is known to have imitated this skyphos type (Frödin and Persson 1938: fig. 224 no. 6). Although not enough is preserved of **1127** to trace its origin, its light to medium tan fabric, like that of **1118**, is consistent with a non-local source.

Small closed vessel fragment **1177** sets a bird high on the shoulder above a banded body, perhaps of a footed pyxis such as that in a grave at Tiryns. Alternatively, an amphoriskos from Amoriani bears a similar decoration although in an extremely rare shape (Foley 1988: 65). The light-brown fabric is not necessarily out of the local range, but may indicate an origin in the western Argolid.

The survey has produced only two examples of the favorite Argive figural motif, the horse. A body fragment from Mases C17 (**1129**) is of remarkable thickness, and is apparently not painted on the inside; it more likely comes from a large pyxis like Argos C209 than from a krater, because the horse panel is located on the belly rather than on the shoulder of the vessel. The angle-hatched verticals in the panel behind the horse are paralleled in examples from Tiryns and Argos, and the hatched vertical zigzags in the upper zone may be a variation of the motif seen in krater C.4656 from Argos (Courbin 1966: pl. 115). The horse, part of a horseleading composition, resembles examples from Tiryns and Argos (Courbin 1966: pl. 136 C.4524) with its long thin neck, notched muzzle, and stiff brushlike mane. The vessel is an import from the Argive plain region. From A9 Flamboura comes a poorly preserved krater body sherd, **1130**, with the legs of a horse facing left. Behind it are the tail and three verticals of the triglyph panel frame; in front and in back of the rear legs are sloppily executed vertical chevron stacks, and behind the front legs is a fish in double outline angled upward to the horse's belly. This is certainly the right half of a symmetrical scheme either of horses facing a central horseleader or of isolated horses in panels flanking a central non-figural panel. The somewhat peculiar form of the fish in double outline with fins has parallels in kraters and skyphoi from Argos, and the general carelessness of execution of horse and chevrons suggests a date late in LGII.

Imported Vessels

For most of the Geometric period the Argolid had only slight trade with neighboring regions that can be documented through either exported Argive pottery or wares imported into the Argolid. The situation changed little in Late Geometric. The imports increased somewhat but were almost exclusively Protocorinthian. The situation in the Southern Argolid offers a rather different picture. Imports of Attic and island products continue to trickle in, perhaps even more steadily than earlier, and are all the more remarkable for being surface finds. Moreover, eighth-century imports from Corinth are represented in only one or two sherds, while connections with other sites in the Argolid were more active than ever.

Foley (1988) has suggested that pottery from Tiryns and Asine is sufficiently distinct from the pottery of Argos to indicate local production centers. Mycenae and Dendra also appear to show differences from Argos, but in such small samples these inferences are riskier. The survey finds reveal strong links with these sites. The large LGI krater from C12 (**1098**) finds a close parallel at Dendra, and the horse fragment **1129** resembles specific horses of Tiryns. Links with Asine are especially strong, and recall traditions of the close relationship between the Dryopians of Asine and those living in communities of the eastern Argolid. The "ladder column" popular in Asine is found in examples (**1169** and **1170**) from two southern sites, and a number of amphorae from C12 can only be matched at Asine in their application of strong, spare motifs to a blank neck: a cross-hatched triangle (**1164**), a large meander (**1166**), and circles with inscribed crosses (**1167**). A small krater from Asine, a pedestaled form unusual for LGII, is paralleled at B2 (**1136**). Similarly, a small globular pyxis type known from Asine is found also at Southern Argolid site B16 (**1157**), representing rare examples of this pyxis form in LGII. In other words, at a time when certain small towns and villages in the plain are finding an artistic "voice" distinct from Argos, the Southern Argolid is maintaining active links with these sites. The ease with which Tiryns and Asine could move their pottery by boat down the coast to the bays of Koiladha and Halieis no doubt had much to do with these contacts. Such commercial and cultural ties joining the smaller towns, while Argos was attempting to establish its hegemony in the Argolid, may reflect the symptoms of independence that Argos apparently needed to crush out of Asine in the destruction of ca. 710 B.C.

Several other vessels come from farther afield. Vertical kantharos rim **1154** is an Attic import with parallels in the Athenian Agora and the Kerameikos. The "open" decorative scheme of the vessel that leaves the rim blank dates it somewhat later than the Kerameikos kantharos. Also from Attica come flat-bottomed pyxis **1155** and two SOS amphora rims, **1163**, and an uncatalogued rim from the same site. Two plates with triple outline leaves (**1159**) and hatched leaves with triangles (**1160**) have schemes found in both Attic and Parian production. Their warm pinkish fabric and red-fired paint, as well as the use of a cream slip on **1159**, certify them as imports. Possibly of island origin is the large body fragment **1168**, which has no interior paint and could be from either a krater or a belly-handled amphora. Preserved decoration includes a bird with a hatched body separated by multiple vertical bands from the handle zone, in which the handle decoration extends down on the body as a hatched "leaf." Below the bird is a panel with a triple X. An affinity for continuing handle decoration down on the body is found in Cycladic amphorae from Delos, including one that Courbin thought Argive (1966: pl. 151 right). The separation of bird from handle zone by one broad and several thin verticals occurs on "Parian" amphorae (Coldstream 1968: pl. 37–38) but also on Euboean (1968: pl. 41e). Rim **1125** may be a foreign import as well. The tall straight rim offset from a broad shoulder resembles the Argive krater type with tall vertical neck and high-swung strap handles (e.g. Courbin 1966: pl. 28, 29), although the notable thinness of **1125** exceeds that of most kraters.

The motif of a ringed oval vaguely recalls the Argive "water symbol" (e.g. Courbin 1966: pl. 65 C.1146, C.756, pl. 37 C.2362) but only exceptionally occurs on a rim. A Cycladic kantharos from Delos with ringed dots between groups of verticals, but without the bulging shoulder of the present example, suggests an island origin for **1125** if it is a kantharos.

Among the smaller shapes are several vessels readily identified as originating outside the Southern Argolid. Skyphos **1143** has a nearly exact parallel at the Argive Heraion, and related pieces come from Aigina and Tiryns. The body fragment of a votive plaque (**1162**) is by the same hand as pieces from Aigina, the Argive Heraion, and an unpublished fragment from Halieis. A delicate kotyle rim fragment (**1153**), apparently preserving part of a bird in the handle zone, represents a rare Early Protocorinthian import.

Coarsewares (1178–1188, Figs. 60, 61, 135)

Geometric coarsewares from a surface context pose a real challenge for recognition and identification. On a multi-period site they are difficult to distinguish from Archaic and other coarsewares. Relatively few examples from excavated Geometric contexts have been published, and the chances of meeting an unparalleled local variation among the usually handmade forms are great. Nevertheless, among the survey material are several coarseware sherds that share convincingly Late Geometric features. In general, fabric is evenly tempered with large to small white, red, orange, gray, and black inclusions, and varies in color from a warm pinkish-brown surface not unlike that of the finewares (7.5YR 6/4-7/4) to a gray or blue-gray core (7.5YR 5/2-7.5YR N7/). Some examples (**1179** and **1184**) have been given an extremely smooth washed or self-slipped surface.

Courbin has distinguished two classes of Argive pithoi: an earlier form often with high relief bands (MGI) to which type **1096** might belong, and a second type with a smooth unbanded body. This latter form evolves from baggy or ovoid shapes, seen here in **1178** with flaring rim and short neck and possibly in **1179**, whose rounded shoulder is beginning to drop, to a lighter, more cylindrical version often with flat horizontal rims like **1182**. Pithos handles, rare in the Argive plain and slightly more common in Corinth and Athens, are represented in at least one example from the Southern Argolid, **1180**, a broad, flat strap handle with a central inset. Five similar coarseware handles with insets containing incised braid patterns are likely from smaller vessels such as hydriae and amphorae, although the larger might possibly come from pithoi: **1181**, **1186**, and three uncatalogued handles B28-28, B16-All-2-7, and B16-63. This "rope" effect, created by diagonal incisions, has been traditionally cited as Corinthian, although examples are known from Perachora, the Argive Heraion, and Athens. Whereas these handles usually feature a twisted or rolled piece in the inset, the examples found on survey are imitated by incisions on flat clay, and may be a local rendition of a popular form.

Clearly a local favorite is the jar or storage container with flaring lip and molded fillet below (**1183–1185**). A similar form in an earlier and finer jar from Mycenae may indicate the origin of the form. The handmade jug or jar bases **1187** and **1188** with flat disc forms are unparalleled among typical Argive jugs, which have simply flattened bottoms (cf. Courbin 1966: pls. 91–95 various).

The Subgeometric Period (1189–1212, Figs. 62–64, 136)

As in many other regions of Greece, the Argolid in the early seventh century poses numerous problems. Sites seem to be in recession, pottery production is on the decline, and painting styles have lost interest and vitality. The difficulty of detecting a seemingly vanishing population is exacerbated by the fact that seventh-century pottery is simply not well enough known to be identifiable, and much of what is assumed to date from the late eighth century may in fact be a little later. Coldstream (1968: 146) found a Subgeometric phase of Argive pottery detectable only in kraters, particularly those of the so-called "Fusco type," while Courbin did not systematically distinguish a true Subgeometric phase but identified a LGIIc that was characterized by a decadence of the Geometric tradition. The problem of identifying and understanding a SG period in the Argolid is beginning to take new shape, aided by the recent publication by Foley (1988). New evidence produced by the Argolid survey enhances the developing picture.

A number of krater fragments from survey sites parallel vessels from the northwestern Argolid that have been designated LGII, but which could easily be seventh century. Rim fragments **1189, 1190, 1191,** and **1200** are of the heavy, tall, vertical form flattened on top that Bommelaer has ascribed to Argos workshops at the end of the eighth century. Representatives of the so-called Fusco type are also present in **1201, 1202,** and **1203.** Aside from these kraters, which seem to demonstrate a continuity of contact and importation from the Argive plain, are several that are new and certainly local. Stamnoid krater or stamnos rims **1198** and **1199** indicate a new kind of storage container, perhaps not quite continuing the same function as the traditional kraters. The deep open bowl **1204,** which may have had a decorated lower body, provides a profile unrelated to earlier forms. Krater rim **1205,** with its heavy black appearance and newly rigid lines, stands clearly on the threshold of the Archaic kraters, as does the remarkable flaring pedestal with rounded rim, **1192.**

Preceded by only a single earlier example (**1085**), plates and bowls, shapes that never enjoy much popularity in the Argolid, begin to appear in greater numbers in this region, with an example datable to LGII or SG (**1161**) and three others more likely of SG date. The shallow rim of **1161** is broad and flat with fugitive dogteeth around the perimeter and looks SG in decoration but corresponds with a LGII dish profile from Argos. Vessel rims **1207–1209** share no consistency of form. Shallow plate **1207** has features paralleled in a votive deposit in the Athenian Agora but can be tied to the Argolid by its fabric and a closely similar unpublished example in Argos. Bowl rim **1208** seems also to be a local product, best paralleled in a smaller version from a LG pithos burial at Nichoria, which the excavators suggest is Argive on the basis of fabric (McDonald et al. 1983: 109). The incurving wall and thin streaky paint of bowl rim **1209** indicate a SG date, but no precise parallels have so far come to light.

Decorative motifs characteristic of the early seventh-century pottery of other centers were used in the Southern Argolid as well. The sloppy use of multiple brush to render parallel zigzags has been noted on the rims of kraters and is well under way in LGII. The further disintegration of zigzags into squiggles appears on a large body sherd (**1197**), more likely SG than LG. Clearly new in the seventh century are the large, loose net pattern of **1211** and the movement of alternating blocks of "mattress" zigzags to the body of a closed vessel, as in **1212.**

Body fragment **1210** from a large vessel, either krater or amphora, is a tantalizing mystery. The matt-painted figure of a serpentine creature rises out of what may be a handle break; the alignment of the break with the star above suggests that the figure had a long, compactly curving body and perhaps a second head extending symmetrically to the right. With its orientalizing sinuous curves and outline body with dotted eye, it recalls a SG bird head on a sherd from Mantinea, or the head of a horse on a seventh-century amphora from the Argive Heraion (Courbin 1966: pl. 87 left). Yet the fragment must be from an imported vessel. The star rosette is replaced in the seventh-century Argolid by the dot rosette, and the rather gritty greenish fabric is not local. A survey of snake heads from a number of Protocorinthian and related seventh-century vases (Gabrici 1913: 334 fig. 135) reveals a prevalence of dotted outlines and triangular heads showing two eyes—in short, nothing like the serpent of **1210**. The head of a quadruped on a Cypriot Geometric Bichrome krater from Ayios Iakovos (Dikaios and du Plat Taylor 1936: 111, figs. 3–4; Karageorghis and Gagniers 1974: 146, XV.2), with its leaf-shaped ears, dotted eye, and long toothy jaws with protruding tongue, bears a striking resemblance to **1210**, although the star rosette is not a Cypriot filling ornament and **1210** is certainly not Bichrome. The comparison does, however, suggest eastern Mediterranean regions as the source of our sherd's motif.

In fact, the best parallel for a snake with an "ear," toothy jaws, and protruding tongue is a Rhodian amphora from Exochi. On each side of the shoulder winds a serpent with head curving down and lined with dots, but otherwise rendering a horned viper similar to **1210**. For other horned serpents with teeth-lined jaws, one must go to seventh-century Cretan bronzework, such as a Gorgoneion from Dreros (Marinatos 1936: pl. 29) and a helmet in the Norbert Schimmel collection in New York (Mitten and Doeringer 1967: no. 29), where the concepts if not the styles parallel the **1210** serpent. The precise origin of **1210** remains uncertain, but it is probably an import from a Cycladic, Rhodian, or even Cretan site. It reminds us that even in a well-trodden area like the Argolid, surprises still wait to be found.

Three Figurines from the Geometric Period (1213–1215, Figs. 64, 136)

Two figurine fragments from F32 have been included here among the Geometric material, although their incomplete condition precludes precise identification. Head **1213** retains flakes of thick reddish paint in insufficient quantities for us to determine whether the surface was completely covered. Broken just at the top of the neck, the head had perky ears and a narrow muzzle, the lower jaw of which recedes slightly. It most resembles a dog, but may be a deer or even a bull; it lacks the mane or forelock that distinguishes Geometric horse figurines. A thin horizontal scratch marks the mouth, and two vertical lines are the nostrils, features that occur occasionally among Mycenaean terracotta animals. The eye holes created by impressing a triangular stick or reed deeply into the clay are unusual for both Mycenaean and Geometric terracottas, where eyes are generally shown in paint or applied as pellets. Although rare, drilled or impressed eye holes are known in Geometric bronze figurines, such as the charioteer from Delphi that Rolley believes to be Argive (Sarian 1969: 660 fig. 14). Fragment **1214** comprises the front half and neck of a quadruped torso with splayed legs. Differences in color of fabric and paint and a coarser texture indicate that this is from a different figurine from **1213**. Dark-red paint remains in small patches on **1214** and may once have covered the body with stripes. The elongated torso with wide break patterns for the legs and neck suggests a Geometric date for the animal.

Our bronze bull, **1215**, bears the distinction of being the only known bronze bull of the Geometric period from the Argolid. It was picked up from the surface in the early 1970's by a local farmer, who showed survey members where it was found on the Flamboura maghoula (A9), and allowed us to make a plaster cast; it remains in his possession.

Although lacking any Argive Geometric bronze bovine companions, the bull's elongated torso and high-swung rump with long tail hanging against the rear legs are paralleled in the Geometric horse type characteristic of the Argolid. The flattened rear feet and pointed front feet correspond with a horse from Kalaureia; most of the horses known from the Argolid are attached to stands or tripod handles, and so lack comparable features. The proportions of **1215** resemble those of several Argive Geometric figurines, notably horses from Olympia and the Argive Heraion. An Archaic bull figurine from Kalaureia with much greater detail and more natural proportions illustrates the later development of the bull in the Argolid. The presence of this Geometric bronze figurine at A9 supports the site's identification as a sanctuary.

Conclusions

One of the major issues addressed by our survey project is that of the relationship of the Southern Argolid to the Argive plain region in the northwest. To what extent is the traditional view of the Southern Argolid —as a backwater overshadowed by the leading centers in the Argive plain—borne out in the archaeological record? A useful approach to this question is offered by the combined evidence of the LG kraters and their SG counterparts. Examining the extent to which the Southern Argolid relied on its own craftsmen for its primary conspicuous vessel of ritual and daily use may suggest the answer to the larger question of autonomy and the relative health of the region in the seventh century.

It can probably be assumed that merchants from Argos and such nearby pottery centers as Asine would have brought their wares by sea, stopping in at the two good harbors on the southern coast, Koiladha and Halieis. A third bay, that of Hermion, has not yet yielded such clear information for the Geometric period. Sites located farther inland obtained their vessels overland from these two or three centers. In the archaeological record this distributive pattern would be expected to show up in a greater concentration of non-local vessels at bay or coastal sites, with a larger representation of local variations appearing in the inland sites. Although the Southern Argolid is such a small area that there hardly exists an "inland" on the map, in actuality the stretches of unaccommodating shoreline on the south and the Dhidhima and Adheres ranges create sufficiently isolated pockets to make this a viable model.

Three sites support this model: Mases (C17), the large LG domestic and probably sanctuary site situated on the Koiladha bay; Vista (C12) just across the bay, which may have been the settlement that supported the sanctuary; and Halieis, apparently settled first in Late Geometric, although the amount of excavated Geometric material is small and most of the site has not been explored to that depth. The general dearth of LG material found in this half of the survey area, however, suggests that Halieis had absorbed the population of the area. The same situation may be true of Hermion, which likely had a Late Geometric settlement of some size, although the lack of excavation and the present town obscure such information. The region along and to the east of Koiladha bay contains the fullest concentration of Late Geometric activity. Major inland sites for testing krater distribution are B2, B16, F32, and G1. A comparison of the sherds from these sites reveals that the majority of kraters imported from elsewhere in the Argolid occur at the three large sites around Koiladha bay (C12, C17, and B2). Kraters believed to have been of local Southern Argolid production, with no parallels outside this area, turn up in a ratio of 2 to 1 at the sites east of the Koiladha region, in particular at Iliokastro G1. This picture is generally supported by comparison with other shapes, which shows that pottery imported from Attica and other non-Argive sources is found only at the three sites near Koiladha bay and at the A9 Flamboura sanctuary. Confirmation of this trend comes from Halieis, where much of the seventh-century pottery is imported, especially from Attica, Laconia, and Corinth (Foley 1988: 74).

Against this background emerges a clearer picture of the Southern Argolid in the early Iron Age.

During Late Geometric the two large sites on Koiladha bay were receiving pottery from Argos, Asine, Attica, and elsewhere. Sites to the east and south include a greater proportion of local types during the later eighth century. The basic problem of the apparent eclipse of pottery in Subgeometric has long bedeviled seventh-century studies, not least in the Argolid. The Southern Argolid survey data seemingly confirm the phenomenon: most of the eighth-century sites also have Archaic and Classical material, yet few show a distinct Subgeometric phase. To judge by the identified pottery, no part of the survey area served as a refuge for the early seventh-century inhabitants of the Southern Argolid. Rather, it seems that the locally observed gap between Geometric and recognizable Archaic should be closed by factors other than depopulation. Possible explanations could involve a lower date for the end of the Geometric style, or more likely a breaking off of relations with western Argive pottery workshops in favor of local products and the occasional Corinthian imports. Predominating among recovered Subgeometric sherds are types for which parallels are still lacking. Thrown back on its own resources with the decline of pottery production in the Argive plain, the Southern Argolid was beginning to rely more heavily on its own workshops. In this light the perceived status of the Southern Argolid as a Geometric-era backwater is dissipated by the emerging evidence of longstanding and active connections with its illustrious neighbors on the plain.

CHAPTER 5

The Lithic Artifacts: Flaked Stone and Other Nonflaked Lithics

P. Nick Kardulias and Curtis Runnels

This chapter is concerned with the 6857 lithic artifacts recovered in the course of the Southern Argolid survey in 1972 and 1979–82. Flaked-stone artifacts of obsidian, flint, and other materials account for 6553 of this number, and the remaining 304 artifacts are of ground or polished stone from material other than obsidian or flint.

The analysis of the lithics has two goals. Primarily, the description of tools and debitage provides the backdrop for a further discussion of the implications of the study of the lithic assemblage for various aspects of past society in the Southern Argolid. Secondarily, the analysis attempts to extract from the lithic assemblage inferences about economic aspects of lithic technology, for example procurement of raw resources, exchange networks, transport of material, and hierarchical arrangement of sites in a trading network. The ability to discriminate between centralized and decentralized exchange systems for the procurement and distribution of raw material (especially obsidian) and completed artifacts is an important economic consideration. In a centralized system a single site or restricted number of sites may regulate the importation of a resource, the production of finished or semi-finished artifacts from that material, and the distribution of finished items. In a decentralized system, by contrast, procurement, production, and distribution may be handled independently by many sites in a region.

At a general level there are a number of observations about stone-artifact usage through time that are of considerable interest. Both flaked- and ground-stone artifact technologies have a long history in the Southern Argolid and elsewhere in Greece, beginning in the Middle Palaeolithic (Runnels 1988a; Pope, Runnels, and Ku 1984) and continuing through the entire prehistoric sequence into the historic period. The majority belong to the Neolithic and Bronze Age, but a significant presence may be discerned in the historical periods, despite the introduction of metal tools (Runnels 1982). Querns, mortars, and similar tools first enter the archaeological record in substantial quantities in the Mesolithic and Neolithic, and are an enduring feature of food processing well into the twentieth century (Runnels 1981).

The nature of survey data permits examination of a region in an extensive manner, both spatially and chronologically. The information from our investigations clearly suggests the presence of both flaked and ground stone in most periods in the region, and indeed allows us to trace the evolution of lithic technology through time. Although the numbers of artifacts from any one site are limited, the individual components can be compared with those from sites elsewhere in the Aegean that have substantial lithic assemblages, and the latter can serve as reference points indicating how representative our lithic industries are, i.e., does our surface collection reflect the range of artifact types, if not the relative abundance, of stone tools for particular periods? From such comparisons, inferences about resource procurement and exploitation of the environment can be drawn.

Survey Methods and the Lithic Assemblage

Two phases of the Argolid survey affected the collection of samples. Systematic field work was undertaken in 1972 under the auspices of the University of Pennsylvania and Indiana University, and again between 1979 and 1982 as the Stanford AEP (Jameson, Runnels, and van Andel 1994). In the initial season, 1972, the collection procedure at sites being recorded did not follow a consistent pattern. Some effort was made to be discriminating in the gathering of lithic artifacts, but discrepancies arose. At small sites, virtually all flaked stone was collected, while at some of the large lithic scatters a grid was laid out and alternate units were completely collected. During the 1979–82 seasons the AEP survey adopted a systematic format for the sampling of sites. This system involved both random samples and a separate search for diagnostic artifacts at each site (Runnels 1983a; Jameson, Runnels, van Andel 1994). The two methods followed during the major phases of the survey thus collected disparate samples from the various sites. In order to obviate this problem and to search for further diagnostics, most of the 1972 sites were revisited and more systematically sampled in the later phases of the project. Great care was taken to find flaked-stone artifacts while making these collections. In an orientation session prior to fieldwork in each season, staff members trained fieldwalkers in the recognition of different categories of artifacts. Under the guidance of specialists, the students inspected cleaned specimens to become familiar with characteristic artifact landmarks. This inspection was carried out first in the laboratory, then in the field at sites known to possess ceramics and lithics. As a result, field teams became adept at the recognition of even small flakes. We feel confident that fieldwalkers overlooked few lithics during the systematic intensive collection of 1-m-wide random transects during the 1979–82 survey. Nonetheless, the problem of sampling remains, and it is not possible to state unequivocally that the lithics available for analysis from each site are directly comparable between sites in terms of quantity. Because of verification visits, however, we assume such discrepancies to be few, so that our samples provide a fairly accurate comparative data base concerning the amount of flaked stone on the survey sites.

Although archaeological materials were processed as they were brought in from the field, two study seasons (1982 and 1983) were required to undertake thorough examination of all the finds. Furthermore, because we could not remove any materials from Greece for specialized analysis, we were somewhat limited in the scope of examination one could employ, and in fact only macroscopic examination could be undertaken.

Flaked-Stone Laboratory Procedures and Computer Coding

Our laboratory procedures for flaked-stone artifacts began with an initial classification by category (type of blank) for each sample within a site. All complete flakes, cores, blades, and designated tools were then measured. Where present, we recorded platforms and utilization, for both complete and fragmentary items. Any artifact exhibiting a modified edge was examined with a 15-power hand lens. Each such piece was perused at least twice before we made a final determination of its status. Many of the modified edges proved to have been unintentionally altered. The purposefully re-

Table 5.1. Summary of Flaked-Stone Artifacts, by Type and Material

Material	Nodule	Core	Crested Blade	Debris	Flake Cortical	Flake	Blade	Other	Total
Obsidian	0	96	58	144	1299	2140	521	1	4259
Chert	87	171	0	745	459	810	16	0	2288
Glass	0	0	0	0	0	0	0	2	2
Other	3	0	0	0	1	0	0	0	4
Total	90	267	58	889	1759	2950	537	3	6553

touched pieces were then described in a precise manner, listing a series of traits (see Fig. 65 and below) that describe the form of the worked edge(s). The terminology we use is consistent with that used in European Palaeolithic archaeology (Movius et al. 1968; Brézillon 1971; Crabtree 1972). The diagnostic specimens were assigned commonly used functional labels (e.g. scraper), while the others were referred to by morphological rubrics. Along with these retouched artifacts, the cores and blades were treated in a detailed manner. For the entire collection, all pertinent data were recorded on analysis sheets that became our sole links with the artifacts once we returned to the United States. A total of 6553 pieces (986 retouched) from 139 sites and seven isolated findspots was processed in this fashion (see Tables 5.1 and 5.3). To assist in the analysis of the flaked stone collected during the survey, the recorded data were transposed by means of a numeric code into a format amenable to manipulation by SPSS. A total of eleven variables is included in the program:

1. Case number (running count)
2. Site number
3. Sample number
4. Material
5. Category (type of blank)
6. Tool type (retouched items)
7. Condition (amount of blank extant)
8. Measurements (length, width, thickness)
9. Platform
10. Cross section
11. Utilization

Some of the variables, particularly the first three and the eighth, are self-explanatory. The others, though, require fuller definitions and discussion of the respective values in order to trace the evolution of our thinking with regard to the specific analytical techniques and assumptions we have adopted.

Material

In terms of raw material, 4259 specimens (65%) are of obsidian, 2288 (34.9%) are of flint or other siliceous rock, two are of glass, and four are of metamorphic rock. Although no detailed compositional analysis has been conducted, the obsidian is presumed to be from Melos, the Cycladic island approximately 150 km southeast of the Argolid that is the nearest source for obsidian. The excavations at Franchthi Cave showed that Melian obsidian was imported into the Southern Argolid as early as the late Upper Palaeolithic (Perlès 1979; Renfrew and Aspinall 1990); it appears in abundance in the Mesolithic and is found in substantial quantities through the Neolithic. Obsidian continues to be the dominant raw material during the Bronze Age (Table 5.13). Analysis of the flaked-stone artifacts from Lerna near Argos revealed a return to the use of chert late in the third millennium, which continued to the end of the Middle Bronze Age (Runnels 1985a), but such a pattern is not as pronounced in our sample. This is probably because sites of the Middle Bronze Age in the Southern Argolid are very rare.

There are several local sources of flint and chert in the Southern Argolid that yield tabular forms thinly bedded in limestone. In addition, nodules and cobbles are widely found as float in local streams (van Andel and Vitaliano 1987). Most of this material is highly fractured, with numerous veins and inclusions, making knapping a difficult task. The predominant colors are red, brown, and gray or grayish blue (see Table 5.2).

The two glass artifacts are made on small fragments of clear bottle or jar glass. Runnels (1975, 1976) has recorded the use of such tools in the Argolid; they represent essentially ad hoc implements that fulfill an immediate need.

Category

This variable serves as a basic divider within each material type. During the recording phase of the analysis, the process involved sorting out the individual pieces according to the blanks represented in the site or sample bag. A key reason for this procedure, beyond imposing typological boundaries, is to see if specific blank types tend to be selected for particular retouched items. Conversely, if certain kinds of blanks are regularly avoided in the retouching process, we can learn something about the available flaking technology and local or regional traditions in stone-tool manufacture, or about the access to and abundance of various materials, especially imported stone. Each of the blank types is listed below, accompanied by a description of specific characteristics.

Nodule/unworked stone. Field workers were instructed to collect any stone that might have indications of human manipulation. Once an item was returned to the lab and processed (washed and labeled), the lithic analyst had to record the material, since no labeled items were discarded. As a result, some unmodified specimens have been included in the sample.

Core or core fragment (e.g. Fig. 67, 1; Fig. 75, 1). Included in this category are complete flake and blade cores, various segments of broken cores, and smaller pieces removed in an attempt to rejuvenate the core. The segments can be proximal (flanks, often with all or part of the platform), medial, or distal portions. Overhang removal flakes preserve one or more negative blade bulbs on the dorsal surface, usually at an angle perpendicular to the flake's own axis of force; these represent efforts to trim the edges of blade-core platforms so as to allow for further blade production. Spent or broken cores were rarely modified to accommodate some other function. In an analysis of blade cores from the Argolid, Van Horn (1980) asserts that the conical type is Neolithic in age and the tabular form is characteristic of the Bronze Age. Our work indicates that the two types represent slightly different ways of producing blades, or they may reflect two distinct stages in the reduction sequence during which tabular cores acquire conical shape as blades are removed. Nevertheless, the two types of core appear to be contemporary in the Southern Argolid and to belong to the Final Neolithic and the Early Bronze Age.

Lame à crête. Since crested blades (lames à crête) are direct products of the reduction se-

Table 5.2. Flint colors; colors are given as they are found in *The Rock-Color Chart* (New York: Geological Society of America, 1963)

Red	Black
5 R 4/2 grayish red	5 YR 2/1 brownish black
5 R 3/4 dusky red	5 G 2/1 greenish black
10 R 8/2 grayish orange pink	N2 grayish black
10 R 4/2 grayish red	
10 R 3/4 dark reddish brown	
10 R 5/4 pale reddish brown	
10 R 6/6–4/6 moderate reddish orange to moderate reddish brown	
5 RP 6/2 pale red purple	

Brown	Gray
5 YR 3/2 grayish brown	N5 medium gray
5 YR 5/2 pale brown	N6 medium light gray
5 YR 3/4 moderate brown	
5 YR 4/4 light moderate brown	
5 YR 6/4 moderate light brown	
5 YR 8/4 moderate orange pink	
10 YR 6/2 pale yellowish brown	
10 YR 2/2 dusky yellowish brown	
10 YR 6/6 dark yellowish orange	

Green	Blue
5 G 4/1 dark greenish gray	5 PB 5/2 grayish blue
5 Y 6/1 light olive gray	
10 GY 5/2 grayish green	
10 Y 6/2 pale olive	

quence leading to the creation of blade cores (Bordaz 1970: 51; Crabtree 1972: 72), they are technically core-preparation fragments. They have been singled out here, however, for individual description because of their unique landmarks and the fact that they can be utilized or retouched to serve other purposes. Typically, crested blades exhibit triangular cross section and a series of flake scars with an axis perpendicular to the central arris on the dorsal surface. These blades are the first that are detached from a core, and their removal leaves behind smooth facets for subsequent prismatic blades.

Spall/debris. These terms refer to the byproducts of debitage. They are usually quite angular pieces on which the typical flake landmarks (bulbs, platforms, etc.) are absent. The continual reduction and reworking of cores tend to produce such irregular, shattered pieces. This is especially true for grainy cherts that have many impurities and fracture lines. Debris fragments were largely ignored as blanks for tools. Occasionally, however, the dividing line for the analyst between debris and small-core fragments is hard to draw.

Cortical flake. Subsumed under this heading are all flakes with any evidence of cortex. Primary decortication flakes have cortex covering at least 50% of the dorsal surface; secondary decortication flakes have less than half of the dorsal surface encased in cortex and include pieces that might otherwise be considered tertiary flakes except for a small cortical patch. The size range varies a great deal. The presence of numerous cortical flakes, along with finished items, implies the full spectrum of flaking activity. As with crested blades, this situation may suggest centralized or decentralized exchange systems, depending on the number of sites that have a high proportion of such material. At certain sites, large cortical flakes tend to be passed over in the selection of blanks for retouching in favor of small tertiary flakes. The fact that such a significant amount of material evidently was viewed as waste indicates that access to sufficient quantities of obsidian imported from an exotic source, probably Melos, was assured.

Plain flake. The term designates any flake lacking cortex, and includes secondary, tertiary, and trimming flakes produced by both percussion and pressure. Tertiary flakes are often favored for the manufacture of finished tools. Secondary flakes have a maximum dimension greater than 1.75 cm. Tertiary flakes fall in the range 1.75–0.50 cm, and trimming flakes are smaller than 0.50 cm.

Blade/bladelet (e.g. Fig. 66, 1). Two key traits distinguish blades from other blanks: (1) high length to width ratio, and (2) detachment from a specially prepared core (Bordaz 1970: 51). The long, thin flakes that are produced characteristically exhibit a uniform appearance, with a varying number of long, smooth dorsal facets. The manufacture of blades represents a stylistic tradition beginning in the late Upper Palaeolithic and is refined through time, culminating in the symmetrical Bronze Age cores and consistently fine blades struck from these nuclei (Van Horn 1980). If any lithic technology can be said to have operated on a mass-production basis, the blade industry is the most likely candidate. Mesoamerican examples of such a level of manufacture exist both in the archaeological (Holmes 1919: 214–27, 323–24; Millon 1967; Spence 1981; Zeitlin 1982; Shafer and Hester 1983) and ethnohistoric (Tylor 1861; Sahagun 1961; Clark 1982) records. The primary reason for the widespread popularity of blades (especially of obsidian) in both the Old World and the New World is the degree to which they can serve as blanks for a variety of tools. In our sample, retouch has formed the following tool types on blades: notches, end scrapers, projectile points, backed items with the opposing margin retaining its original sharp edge, geometrics, truncated pieces, and denticulates (probable sickle elements). Most blades in our sample, however, are not retouched. Obsidian's perfect conchoidal fracture and homogeneous texture made it the ideal material for blade production. The implications of obtaining obsidian through importation are discussed below.

Tool Type

In designating retouch, a conservative approach was deemed appropriate, since the pieces had lain on the surface for extensive periods of time before being collected during the survey. On the ground, these artifacts were subject to the vagaries of animal hooves, human trampling, crushing and fortuitous flaking by machinery, and transportation and consequent damage by weathering and erosion. These natural factors produce flaking patterns which, though mostly erratic and thus fairly easily discerned, can on occasion provide a more regular appearance. Tringham et al. (1974) suggest that such unintentional damage is easily distinguished from purposeful working. Other studies (Runnels 1976; Schiffer 1979; Miller 1982; Mallouf 1982; Moss 1983), however, indicate that drawing

Table 5.3. List of Flaked-Stone Tool Types

Retouched flakes and blades (N = 359)

direct, one edge	143
direct, two edges	39
inverse, one edge	27
inverse, two edges	7
alternating	51
opposed	23
bifacial	6
distal only	24
distal and one edge	32
proximal only	7

Retouched pieces (N = 37)

proximal and one edge	11
proximal and two edges	1
unifacial, covering one face	2
entire perimeter retouched	6
distal and proximal retouch	2
inverse and one edge	1
inverse and proximal end	1
distal, proximal, and one edge	2
backed piece	11

Scrapers (N = 34)

end scraper on plain piece	13
end scrpaer on retouched piece	10
side scraper on plain piece	9
other	2

Notch (N = 53)

denticulate	16
plain notch	30
shouldered piece	7

Piercing tools (N = 119)

perçoir/bec	119

Pieces with silica gloss (N = 16)

on plain piece	3
on retouched piece	13

Truncated pieces (N = 139)

single, with retouch	67
single, without retouch	63
double, with retouch	2
double, without retouch	6
retouch on break	1

Geometrics (N = 11)

rectangle	5
triangle	1
trapezoid	3
other	2

Engraving/incising tools (N = 3)

burin	3

Points (N = 15)

bifacial foliate	2
hollow-based bifacial	1
tanged bifacial	9
Mousterian point	2
unidentified	1

Scaled pieces (N = 62)

pièce esquillée	62

Multiple tools (N = 136)

notch/perçoir	14
truncation/notch/perçoir	2
notch with retouch	14
multiple perçoir	21
perçoir with retouch	44
truncation/perçoir with retouch	10
truncation/notch	8
double truncation/notch	1
multiple notch	3
rectangle/perçoir	1
truncation/perçoir	12
multiple percoir/truncation	1
end scraper/notch	2
side scraper/truncation	1
piece esquillée/perçoir	1
backed piece/perçoir	1

Miscellaneous (N = 2)

batonnet	1
gunflint	1

this line is not an easy matter. None of these reports fully addresses time as a factor. Even if the experimentally trampled artifacts are recognizable as such after one episode, or after an extended period (up to one year), this presumption does not take into account the unknown length of time that the survey lithics were exposed to these forces. Because they may have been exposed for years, the repeated trampling to which they would thus have been subject may well have had the effect of regularizing the appearance as more flakes were removed, eliminating the random distribution of the accidental damage. As a result, a decision was made from the outset of the analysis to discount as retouch anything that did not fall within fairly restricted parameters and, thus, provide clear-cut evidence of purposeful working. By our definition, retouch minimally consists of at least three medium (0.10–0.15 cm) or large (> 0.15 cm) adjacent flake scars oriented in the same direction that modify the outline of a blank toward one or more characteristic forms. Using such criteria, we ran the risk of possibly overlooking a retouched piece, classifying it instead as debris, but avoided the more egregious error of artificially inflating the various tool categories. The extraneous alteration to which surface materials are subject made this decision necessary.

In establishing the various categories under the tool type variables, we followed two approaches. The first simply involved a description of the location and extent of retouch. If the retouch was significantly diagnostic, so as to fall under or be identified with widely used typological terms, then the specimen was labeled accordingly. These terms include the following: scraper, notch, denticulate, perçoir, truncated piece, geometric, piece with silica gloss, burin, projectile point, and pièce esquillée. We call retouched pieces all those specimens that have labels describing only location of retouch. In addition to this basic list, terms have been combined to designate various multiple-use tools. Table 5.3 lists all the tool types. In an overall sense, the discussion of tool types will concentrate on morphological as opposed to functional elements. The latter aspect is not precisely ascertainable without examination for micro-wear use marks under a powerful microscope (see Keeley 1980), and so, even though functional terms are often used (e.g. scraper), they are employed as generic references rather than to imply particular usage.

The 64 tool types reflect the combined morphological/functional perspective employed in describing retouch. Many of the labels refer to the position of the retouch on the blank (e.g. right distal edge) and pinpoint the extent of working. As mentioned above, some of the terms are the same as those defined for other cultural areas (e.g. prehistoric France, Brézillon 1971), a tactic adopted as a matter of convenience; no relationship to artifacts found in another place is thereby implied. These latter groups require some clarification of the criteria used to define them:

Perçoirs (e.g. Fig. 90, 2). Brézillon (1971: 280) says that this form is characterized by a pronounced tip, commonly formed at the distal end of a piece by the retouch of two concave, converging edges. In our sample, this retouch often is direct on one edge and inverse on the other. Most of these perçoirs are made on small obsidian flakes that can be held only between thumb and forefinger. Several artifacts that might otherwise be labeled becs were placed in this category, since the types did not appear to be sufficiently distinct to warrant separate designations. The factors of small size and brittle material pose the serious question of the utility of such implements. Perhaps microwear studies, with their demonstrated ability to determine use (Semenov 1964; Hayden 1979; Keeley 1980; Odell and Odell-Vereecken 1980), could help overcome this difficulty, but they were not possible for the present study. Examination of use wear on lithics has proved valuable in other studies. At the Labras Lake site in western Illinois, Yerkes (1987: 135–36 and figs. 30, B-5 and B-8) examined a number of stone tools similar in appearance to the perçoirs in our sample. He determined that some of these pieces were used to pierce holes in dry hides. Other functions included scraping wood and dry hide. At Cahokia, pointed tools similar to perçoirs were hafted and used to drill holes in shell (Yerkes 1983). Winters (1969: 54) identified microperforators with a concave edge and small spurs like perçoirs as tools used by prehistoric Indians to shape arrow and spear shafts. We suggest that perçoirs in the Southern Argolid served as general-purpose piercing, scraping, and carving tools to work wood, hide, shell, bone, and ivory, and perhaps to incise pottery.

Sickle elements (e.g. Fig. 66, 2). This general category was divided into two types based on the presence or absence of gloss, which forms on chert as the result of a polishing process accompanying abrasion. Meeks et al. (1982) indicate that this polish results from abrasion between the tool margin and soil particles and/or opal phytoliths from plant stems. Other work by Unger-Hamilton (1985) indicates that microscopic striations appear on sickle elements used to harvest plants from tilled soil, and may aid in distinguishing between gathering wild crops and early domestication. On obsidian pieces, the abrasion produces a dull, matted surface. Those pieces retouched so as to produce a serrated, or denticulated, edge, with the other edges roughly truncated for fitting into a haft, but without gloss, are termed denticulates (Fig. 78, 2). Although most traits indicate that they were used in sickles, these artifacts lack the definitive gloss. The specimens possessing the requisite surface may be retouched or not, but are clearly sickle elements in either case. The majority of both denticulates and pieces with gloss come from sites with Bronze Age components, indicating an important role for lithic technology alongside metal tools. Van Horn (1977) suggests the presence of denticulated tranchets during the Early Helladic in the Argolid. Although these are similar to sickle elements in most aspects, including the presence of gloss, he argues that the squared teeth indicate an adze-like rather than a sawing action, and thus a function other than harvesting of plants. Careful examination revealed no such implement in our sample.

Pièces esquillées (e.g. Fig. 71, 4). These distinctive pieces are generally square to rectangular in outline, with rather large converging scalar flake scars, originating from opposite ends, evident on both surfaces. They give the appearance of having been battered from both ends. The precise function of these artifacts is enigmatic. Semenov (1964: 150) provides a possible clue with his illustration of an experimental flint chisel having the same general landmarks as a pièce esquillée. Since most of the survey specimens are of obsidian, a relatively soft worked material is implied, if in fact they were used in this manner. Runnels (1985: 374, footnote 27) suggests that these artifacts may be tinder flints; experimentation with the use of flint and obsidian struck against metal created flaking patterns similar to these scaled items. Morphologically, the scaled, typically bifacial flaking tightly defines pièces esquillées and clearly distinguishes them from other lithic artifacts. Within the class, however, there is considerable variation in size and in the direction and number of flake scars.

Projectile points (e.g. Figs. 77, 1; 89, 3). Where they are found, these artifacts can act as horizon markers. The Mousterian point from site B27 (Fig. 67, 2) is clearly Middle Palaeolithic in date (Bordes 1962; Plate 10, No. 5 for a comparable piece). A foliate point from B85 (Fig. 71, 1) seems to belong to the same period. Points similar in size and shape from Kokkinopilos in Epiros and Thessaly have been assigned a late Middle Palaeolithic age (Dakaris and Higgs 1964; Runnels 1988a). Along with those from several other survey sites, the material from Franchthi Cave, and an isolated Levalloisian flake (Bialor and Jameson 1962), these points and their associated assemblages are the evidence for the Palaeolithic from the Argolid. Whether this reflects a highly nucleated settlement pattern or the burying of sites by alluvial and colluvial sediments, thus obscuring them from sight, is discussed in detail elsewhere (Jameson, Runnels, van Andel 1994).

The one hollow-base obsidian point from F32 is a diagnostic Bronze Age type and correlates with the other EH material from the site. The nine tanged points (eight obsidian, one chert; e.g. Figs. 76, 4; 77, 1, 3–4; 78, 1; 80, 4; 83, 8) come from six sites that have EH or FN-EH components. The resemblance of several of the specimens to the Saliagos type (Evans and Renfrew 1968) and what Diamant (1977) calls a "B/C"-type places them in a general late Neolithic to early Bronze Age framework; the tanged points from Lerna also belong to the same period (Runnels 1985). Although the ceramic representation of the Neolithic component is rather weak, these points are quite diagnostic for the transition from Final Neolithic to the Early Bronze Age.

Backed pieces (e.g. Figs. 74, 1–2, and 78, 4). Small backed blades and flakes are commonly associated with an Upper Palaeolithic industry (Bordes 1968: 225; Perlès 1987a). Of the eight sites for which such material was collected, five may be Upper Palaeolithic, while the other three have a Neolithic-EH component. Other than this artifact category, there are few specific types in the Argolid that can be systematically used to characterize an Upper Palaeolithic industry. In general, one must fall back on more generalized criteria, such as overwhelming predominance of flint over obsidian, small size of the artifacts, and small well-formed cores, especially pyramidal/conical blade cores. Additionally, site location also seems to be important, since four of the locations are caves, while one (F25) is also a large Middle Palaeolithic lithic scatter.

Gunflint (Fig. 72, 6). This thick, trapezoidal specimen is finely made on a large blade segment of non-local chert. The gunflint was retrieved from B102, a large quarry site that may have been used from Middle Palaeolithic times to the early historical era and possibly later (although local residents have no knowledge of any recent quarrying activities at the site). The gunflint is of a high-quality black flint, decidedly unlike the poor-quality reddish-brown chert outcropping at B102. This piece may represent hunting activity along the maquis-covered summit of a chert quarry area in the last century.

Condition

This variable refers to the extant portion of the blank, whether it has undergone further modification or not. The four categories are (1) complete, (2) nearly complete, (3) fragment, and (4) not applicable. Thus, a specimen identified as a trapezoidal geometric would be listed as complete if the artifact is visible in its entirety as the piece appeared when it was first produced. The fact that the original blade blank is no longer fully extant does not preclude the completeness of the one artifact fashioned on it. The fourth category is employed when it is difficult to determine the degree of completeness, as is often the case with debris or spalls.

Platform

The degree and nature of platform preparation provides some indication of the sophistication of the technique employed in the manufacture of flakes, blades, etc., and can be used as one hallmark for particular traditions. The platform can also provide a rough estimate of the stage in the reduction sequence when the blank was removed from the core. Platform types are plain ($N = 788$), point ($N = 30$), dihedral ($N = 42$), faceted with three flake scars ($N = 308$), and faceted with more than three flake scars (also called multiple; $N = 39$). Table 5.4 lists platform types found on dated lithic sites.

Cross section

This feature was recorded primarily for only two categories of artifacts, blades and cores, but it is more applicable to the former. The cross section of a blade indicates to some degree the technical

Table 5.4. Types of Platforms by Period

	Flakes				Blades			
Period	Plain	Point	Dihedral	Faceted	Plain	Point	Dihedral	Faceted
Middle Palaeolithic	99	3	8	13				
Upper Palaeolithic	7		1		1			1
Neolithic	100	1	8	17	2			5
Bronze Age	216	13	7	125	25	1	2	61
Historical	61	4	2	22	1	1	2	12
Total	483	21	26	177	29	2	4	79

Table 5.5. Types of Cross Section for Blades by Period

Period	Triangular	Trapezoidal	Multiple	Other
Middle Palaeolithic	1	1		
Upper Palaeolithic	3	6		
Neolithic	14	19	1	1
Bronze Age	68	206	17	21
Historical	20	54	6	2
Total	106	286	24	24

expertise and the regularity of the technique employed by the artisan. The values under this variable include the following: (1) triangular (N = 193), (2) trapezoidal (N = 365), and (3) multiple (more than two dorsal ridges; N = 35). Single rather than binomial terms (e.g. plano-triangular) are employed for simplicity. Table 5.5 shows the cross sections of blades from dated sites.

Utilization

The minute flake scars and/or crushing along a margin resulting from usage present what might be called a nibbled appearance that exhibits some continuity on the edge. By the greater degree of regularity exhibited by the flake scars, this wear pattern is distinguished from the erratic crushing and shattering that occur as the result of fortuitous elements in the environment. A knottier issue is clearly demarcating the limit between utilization and small, limited retouch. For the purposes of this study, which established rather strict criteria for identifying retouch, utilization is identified primarily on the basis of its dissimilarity to systematic working, i.e. very tiny, irregular flake scars of limited extent. For coding purposes, this trait was simply marked present or absent (see Table 5.6).

Flaked-Stone Chronology

Since all of the examined lithic artifacts were gathered from the surface and were found in association with other materials, it is difficult to assign most of them to precise cultural periods. Virtually all survey sites exhibit more than one cultural component. Except in a few cases, lithic material cannot be treated as a chronologically sensitive indicator, and the dating of lithics is therefore conservative. Lithic artifacts are not used as index fossils unless they can be dated by comparison with items from excavated, stratified, and dated contexts. Barring this good fortune, the material from each site, flaked stone included, is assigned to temporal components on the basis of association with datable items, such as pottery, coins, and architecture. In the case of site B27 the lithics were independently dated by uranium/thorium series assay, utilizing pedogenic calcium carbonate scraped from the artifacts themselves. In general, however, flaked stone found on a site with Classical ceramics, for example, was assigned to that component rather than to an otherwise unrecognized prehistoric component. This approach avoids the sort of a priori reasoning that presumes that flaked stone in any quantity must represent a prehistoric, especially pre-Bronze Age, component. Flintknapping, along with other stone-working methods, persisted into the twentieth century, and certainly provided a significant portion of the artifact inventory in the first and second millennia B.C., a fact that has been largely neglected in the heartland of Classical antiquity (Runnels 1982).

The process of assigning dates to sites in the sample operates at three levels. First, there are two sites dated on the basis of radiometric assay (U/Th series). B27 and F25 yielded dates of circa 55,000 B.P., firmly in the Middle Palaeolithic (Pope, Runnels, and Ku 1984). Site B85 is dated by association with a Pleistocene paleosol that may be older than 55,000 B.P. Second, there are distinct groups of sites linked in time by similar artifacts. For example, barbed and tanged projectile points appear in Final Neolithic and Early Bronze Age contexts, and backed bladelets belong to a late Palaeolithic/Mesolithic tradition. The third technique involves determining the date of the site and its nondiagnostic lithics on the basis of ceramic chronology. There are a total of 105 ceramically dated sites with flaked stone (3651 obsidian, 943 flint). This method gives us seven Neolithic sites (Table 5.10), 33 Bronze Age sites (Table 5.13), and 65 historic sites (see Table 5.16) with lithics.

The archaeological sequence in the Southern Argolid begins with the Middle Palaeolithic and

Table 5.6. Utilization of Flakes and Blades, by Period

Period	Flakes		Blades	
	Utilized	Unutilized	Utilized	Unutilized
Middle Palaeolithic	8	403	1	1
Upper Palaeolithic	3	46		9
Neolithic	35	418	7	28
Bronze Age	42	2601	49	263
Historical	45	376	19	63
Total	133	3844	76	364

Table 5.7. Middle Palaeolithic Flaked Stone, by Site and Material

Site	Obsidian	%	Chert	%	Total
B27	0	0	253	100	253
B85	3	7.0	40	93.0	43
F25	8	1.7	474	98.3	482
Total	11	1.4	767	98.6	778

continues to the present. The different cultural periods are represented by different quantities of find-spots and sites. Lithics are found on sites of every cultural period, but they are less common in some periods (Table 5.20). In the Mesolithic there are only two sites, one at Franchthi Cave and one at F35, the latter an undated site. In all, 139 of the 298 survey sites, or a little less than half the sites, yielded flaked-stone lithics, a total of 6449 artifacts. An additional seven locations (findspots not designated as sites) with 104 pieces of chipped stone make the total 6553. Most of the latter findspots represent areas that were discovered prior to 1979 and could not be relocated.

The flaked-stone data are summarized below by period. Within each temporal category, we considered several factors as critical for characterizing the assemblage. These factors include the raw material, technology, and type. Raw-material categories have been explained above. Technology refers to the group of techniques used to work stone and "implies a systematic control of minute and distinguishable detail" (Crabtree 1972: 94). A key aspect of any lithic analysis is the attempt to discern patterns that reflect the manufacturing process (i.e. reduction sequence). Variations in technology suggest changes in production methods, and these alterations can be of chronological, cultural, and economic significance. By type we mean defined by a cluster of morphological attributes (i.e. dimensions, outline, cross section). Some common terms (e.g. scraper) for various types of stone tools imply particular uses, but since our research could not entail the microscopic examination necessary to determine specific applications, we employ these labels only as conventions. We do not wish to engage here in a protracted discussion of the type concept (for a good recent summary, see Adams 1988). Suffice it to say we subscribe to the view that the classification process is essentially an arbitrary one in which individual specimens are grouped together on the basis of criteria defined by the analyst. These categories gain greater credibility when supplemented by experimental data.

Middle Palaeolithic Flaked Stone

This period marks the earliest known occupation of the region. The four sites that belong to this period (see Tables 5.7 and 5.8) are found in four different geographical zones (for site locations, see Runnels and van Andel 1987). Franchthi Cave (C13) yielded flakes and tools that may be MP, but they were found in small numbers (ca. 15) in the lowest levels of excavation and in mixed surface units (Perlès 1987a); nonetheless, there is probably a MP component at Franchthi Cave. F25, which lies in a Pleistocene terrace at the mouth of the Katafiki Gorge, is the location of a major outcrop of the grayish-blue chert of moderate quality; people visited the site to extract chert and fashion tools, and in MP times it could have served a double purpose, as a spot from which to observe migrating herds of animals that passed through the narrow gorge from the uplands to the broad, fertile Ermioni Valley. B85 lies on an eroded red-bed deposit on the coastal plain at Petrothalassa and may be a hunting camp. B27 is a buried site exposed by recent erosion in a streambed some two kilometers SE of Franchthi Cave; the lithics are unrolled, and the site is probably best regarded as an in situ tool-making location. Two sites, F25 and B27, were radiometrically dated to ca. 55,000 B.P. (Pope, Runnels, and Ku 1984; Jameson, Runnels, and van Andel 1994: Appendix 1).

This small sample of sites exhibits numerous similarities, despite the lack of geographic proximity. The obsidian at two sites appears to be later than MP. At B85 the obsidian was found at the edge of a red bed and hence may be intrusive. F25 obsidian artifacts include a tanged projectile point that is LN-EH in date. At the only sealed site, B27, there is no obsidian. The flint is local in origin, either grayish blue or dark reddish brown in color (Table 5.2); flint of both colors is found in the region in the form of small nodules. The size of this raw material and its less than ideal tractability probably account in part for the small dimensions of artifacts, especially when compared with other parts of Greece and Western Europe (see Bordes 1961 and Theocharis 1967). The lithics from B27 are typical of the Greek Middle Palaeolithic industry and have characteristic sidescrapers, Levallois flakes, Mousterian points, and a variety of small retouched pieces (Figs. 67–70). The retouched tools at B85 (Fig. 71), F25 (Figs. 81–84), B27, and C13 are similar. Among the few diagnostic tools are two bifacial foliates from B85 (Fig. 71, 1 and 5) that are similar to specimens found widely in Greece (Runnels 1988a: 282).

Upper Palaeolithic Flaked Stone

Only one survey site, C6, appears to be predominantly UP in date. It is located on a rocky promontory south of Koiladha and Franchthi Cave. Although currently a littoral site, at the time of prehistoric occupation it would have overlooked a broad coastal plain to the west and may have been a hunting camp. Of the 92 artifacts retrieved from the site, 37 (40.2%) are obsidian and 55 (59.8%)

Table 5.8. Dimensions of Middle Palaeolithic Flaked-Stone Lithics by Site (Dimensions in Millimeters)

Site	Length			Width			Thickness		
	N	X	SD	N	X	SD	N	X	SD
					FLAKES				
B27	59	2.2	1.0	59	1.9	0.8	59	0.5	0.3
B85	18	2.8	1.5	18	2.1	0.8	18	0.9	0.3
F25	64	2.8	1.1	64	2.1	0.8	64	0.7	0.3
					TOOLS				
B27	17	2.3	0.9	17	2.0	0.7	17	0.6	0.3
B85	12	2.9	1.6	12	2.1	0.8	12	0.9	0.3
F25	30	2.9	1.0	30	2.2	0.7	30	0.8	0.4

Table 5.9. Upper Palaeolithic and Mesolithic Flaked Stone, by Site and Material

Site	Obsidian	%	Chert	%	Total
C6	37	40.2	55	59.8	92
F35	19	21.3	70	78.7	89
Total	56	31.0	125	69.0	181

are flint (Table 5.9). The obsidian resembles Melian obsidian, and the flint is local, chiefly a fine-grained, dark-brown material. The percentage of retouched tools (16.3%) is high.

The range of tool types from C6 includes five retouched pieces, one sidescraper, three truncated flakes, one perçoir, three pièces esquillées, and two backed blades (Fig. 74). Only the backed blades are diagnostic UP tools (Bordes 1968; Perlès 1987a). The higher percentage of truncated flakes in this period over the MP (3.3% to 0.7%, respectively) may indicate an initial trend toward the manufacture of geometric microliths that are important elements of post-Pleistocene lithic assemblages. By way of comparison, the main tool types in the UP levels at Klithi Cave in Epiros are backed bladelets, end scrapers, burins, and notches, in decreasing order of abundance (Bailey et al. 1984: 20). The discrepancy between the assemblages at C6 and those at Klithi Cave may be the result of differences in regional environmental setting and between a closed and an open site.

The artifacts from C6 bear a strong resemblance to those of the late Palaeolithic industry in nearby Franchthi Cave, which contains many small-scale retouched implements, most notably the backed bladelets. The small number of tools from the highly eroded site C6 cannot be used to draw wide-ranging conclusions, but the rather narrow range of tool types, and the presence of backed bladelets, may point to the presence of a hunting stand at this site. Hunters on this promontory, a spur of the Koiladha range of hills in the late Pleistocene, would have had an unobstructed view over the coastal plain. The site, if it is Palaeolithic, would have been a special-purpose site tied to the main camp at Franchthi Cave.

A single backed bladelet (Fig. 78, 4) was found at E80, a small cave or rock shelter in the Katafiki Gorge. This is the only other findspot that yielded artifacts of probable UP date. Backed bladelets, however, continue to be used in the Mesolithic period at Franchthi Cave, and an early Holocene date for C6 and E80 cannot be ruled out. Whatever date may be the true one, it is readily apparent that UP materials are strikingly rare in the Southern Argolid. Franchthi Cave remains the only large and well-dated site for this period. The lithics from C6 and E80 add nothing to our picture of this period.

Mesolithic Flaked Stone

The Mesolithic is represented in Greece at very few sites (e.g. Franchthi Cave and Sidari, the latter on Corfu). This paucity of evidence makes an understanding of post-Pleistocene adaptations in Greece quite problematic, and compounds our difficulties in comprehending the advent of domestication in the Aegean. For the Argolid survey, the immediate problem is the small body of material that is available for comparison with surface lithics. The dearth of comparanda makes the identification of Mesolithic surface sites highly tentative. Lacking stratigraphic associations, it is difficult to recognize this period in the survey lithics. Ammerman (personal communication 1981) suggests that the characteristic setting for Mesolithic sites in southern Italy is rockshelters or caves just below the summits of ridges, but investigation of numerous similar overhangs in the Argolid yielded no Mesolithic sites.

Only one site, Koukou Cave (F35), produced lithics that may be aceramic early Holocene (Table 5.9 and Fig. 91). A collection of artifacts, almost all of them flakes, from this site resemble materials from the lower Mesolithic deposits in Franchthi Cave (Perlès 1987b). The most diagnostic tool types at this site are the notched or denticulated flakes and the backed pieces. Though the aceramic character of the collection from F35 reinforces the impression that this is an early Holocene site, the simple nature of these notches and backed pieces is not diagnostic. In the absence of faunal remains or independent evidence of date, it is not possible to be certain that F35, or any other surface material in the Argolid, is in fact a Mesolithic site.

At F35 obsidian makes up 21.3% (N = 19) of the total, approximately double that in Mesolithic levels at Franchthi Cave. The tool types at F35 range from retouched pieces (N = 7, 7.9% of all lithics and 41.2% of the retouched tools) to backed blades (N = 4, 4.5% and 23.5%), notches (N = 2, 2.4% and 11.8%), truncated flakes (N = 2, 2.4% and 11.8%), an end scraper (N = 1, 1.1% and 5.9%) and a perçoir (N = 1, 1.1% and 5.9%). The retouched tools comprise 19.1% of the total.

Neolithic Flaked Stone

Seven sites constitute this subsample (Tables 5.10 and 5.11). Components defined by ceramics include Middle, Late, and Final Neolithic. The bulk of the material, however, belongs to the Late and Final Neolithic. None of the lithics is certainly MN in date. The sites are widespread: one near Ermioni (E14), two outside Koiladha (C15 and C29), one in the Dhidhima sinkhole (D3), one in the Fournoi Focus (F14), and two in the Iliokastro uplands (G7 and G9).

At Franchthi Cave and in other major Neolithic sites in Greece, lithics comprise an important segment of the artifact assemblage. Flaked-stone tools enjoyed an enhanced status in some ways, because agricultural activity required new implements or more intensive use of old types. Mesolithic

Table 5.10. Neolithic Flaked Stone, by Site and Material

Site	Obsidian	%	Chert	%	Total
C15	120	87.6	17	12.4	137
C29	71	86.6	11	13.4	82
D3	176	63.1	103	36.9	279
E14	2	100.0	0	0	2
F14	5	3.0	162	97.0	167
G7	0	0	24	100.0	24
G9	2	66.7	1	33.3	3
Total	376	51.2	318	45.8	694

Table 5.11. Dimensions of Unretouched Neolithic Blanks, by Material
(Dimensions in Millimeters)

Material	Length			Width			Thickness		
	N	X	SD	N	X	SD	N	X	SD
Obsidian flakes	107	1.7	0.7	107	1.4	0.7	107	0.4	0.2
Chert flakes	60	2.1	0.8	60	1.6	0.6	60	0.6	0.3
Obsidian blades	35	1.6	0.6	35	1.0	0.3	35	0.3	0.1

people, for example, used sickle elements to cut a variety of grasses and other plants, but these tools were much more abundant in the Neolithic period as the harvesting of crops became a central feature of the subsistence cycle.

The material of choice for flaked stone in the Neolithic was obsidian (N = 376, 54.3%, compared to N = 317, 45.7%, for flint), but not by a great margin. The situation of the survey sites differs significantly from that of Franchthi Cave, where obsidian makes up 40% of the lithics in the Early Neolithic and reaches 95% by the Final Neolithic (Jacobsen 1976: 80). The discrepancy may be due in part to the presence of non-Neolithic components at most of the surface sites. The only site where flint artifacts outnumber obsidian is F14 (five obsidian, 162 flint) in the Fournoi Valley; none of the 21 retouched tools from this site is particularly diagnostic.

The percentage of tools among the flaked-stone artifacts from these seven sites (16.3%, N = 113) is low (Table 5.12; Figs. 76, 77, 92). There is considerable variation between the Neolithic sites in this regard, however, with 24.0% at D3, 15.9% at C29, and 3.7% at C15. The differences may reflect variable site functions and chronology. D3 in the Dhidhima sinkhole is used today by shepherds and may have served a similar function in antiquity. The tools from D3 include an array of retouched pieces, six perçoirs, three tanged projectile points, and three pièces esquillées (Fig. 77). These artifacts may have been part of the range of weapons and tools employed by shepherds at this site. In addition to the working of hide or bone, ethnographic evidence indicates that herders spend considerable time working wood during idle hours, and many of the retouched pieces may have served as scrapers, much as glass fragments do today (Runnels 1975, 1976). At the other extreme, C15 is an open site south of Koiladha and may have been a flintknapping site. The three retouched pieces and two notches (3.6% of the total of 137 artifacts) from this site are not diagnostic. The impression is of expedient use of *ad hoc* tools in tasks not requiring specially adapted implements. Another possibility is that craftsmen prepared but did not use blanks at this site.

Perçoirs form a significant part of the assemblage in the Neolithic. These pointed tools tend to be made on small obsidian flakes and blades; their function is difficult to ascertain. Tools similar in appearance were used to carve soft semiprecious stones at the Bronze Age site of Tepe Hissar in Iran (Bulgarelli 1977), to carve seals (Gorelick and Gwinnett 1981), and to work shell, bone, wood, and hides at Archaic and Mississippian sites in the American Midwest (Yerkes 1983, 1987). The lack of contextual association for the survey lithics makes it difficult to resolve this issue of use. Circumstantial evidence, however, may provide a clue. The appearance of perçoirs in some number in the Late and Final Neolithic may signal the introduction of a new technology to which these small boring/incising tools were well adapted. Working of wood, bone, shell, antler, and hides, and perhaps the incision of decoration on pottery are possible candidates.

A diagnostic tool type that belongs to the Neolithic is the barbed and tanged point. There are four obsidian specimens in our sample (Figs. 76, 4; 77, 1, 3–4). This type of point is broadly diagnostic for the Late Neolithic in the Cyclades, where it is common on sites of the Saliagos culture (Evans and Renfrew 1968). It is found on mainland sites in contexts ranging in date from Late Neolithic to EH II (Diamant 1977; Runnels 1985a: 372). These small points are probably arrowheads; we assume them to have been used in hunting and warfare. Wild game would certainly have supplemented the Neolithic diet, and such well-made obsidian points would enhance the hunters' chances of bringing down the prey; tests indicate that well-made projectile points penetrate animal hide and flesh more deeply and with less chance of bouncing off the surface (Odell and Cowan 1986). As Runnels (1985a: 381, footnote 29) suggests, however, there is evidence indicating the use of arrowheads as implements of war. The points probably served both functions.

Compared to the foraging phases, the Neolithic lithics assemblage exhibits a greater degree of specialization and suggests modification of the pattern for exploiting the environment. There is a much greater reliance on obsidian than before, and this indicates both the relative ease in obtaining this material and a preference for its properties (i.e. ease of flaking, and extremely sharp, though brittle, edges). It seems that the distributional pattern found in the Bronze Age begins in the Neolithic, with most of the obsidian found in the western part of the Southern Argolid, centered around Franchthi Cave and the Fournoi area.

Table 5.12. Neolithic Tool Types, by Material

Tool type	Obsidian	Chert	Total
Not retouched	306	275	581
Retouched pieces	36	26	62
Notches	3		3
Perçoirs	7	10	17
Sickle elements		1	1
Single truncations	11	2	13
Double truncations	2	1	3
Arrowheads	4		4
Bifacial pieces	2		2
Pièces esquillées	4	1	5
Backed pieces	1	1	2
Multiple tools		1	1
Totals	376	318	694
	(54%)	(46%)	

Table 5.13. Bronze Age Flaked Stone, by Site and Material

Site	Obsidian	%	Chert	%	Total
A6	23	88.5	3	11.5	26
A9	50	96.2	2	3.8	52
A33	9	100.0	0	0	9
B7	15	93.8	1	6.2	16
B24	52	63.4	30	36.6	82
B28	131	92.9	10	7.1	141
B39	3	100.0	0	0	3
B41	4	80.0	1	20.0	5
B81	23	71.9	9	28.1	32
C8	122	86.5	19	13.5	141
C11	11	84.6	2	15.4	13
E4	3	33.3	6	66.7	9
E5	2	50.0	2	50.0	4
E13	6	46.2	7	53.8	13
E16	2	100.0	0	0	2
E74	4	28.6	10	71.4	14
F4	22	68.8	10	31.2	32
F5	14	73.7	5	26.3	19
F6	45	93.8	3	6.2	48
F9	11	20.0	44	80.0	55
F13	38	77.6	11	22.4	49
F15	2	50.0	2	50.0	4
F16	8	66.7	4	33.3	12
F17	4	80.0	1	20.0	5
F18	0	0	3	100	3
F19	95	86.4	15	13.6	110
F20	98	96.1	4	3.9	102
F21	2	100.0	0	0	2
F22	31	93.9	2	6.1	33
F30	11	64.7	6	35.3	17
F32	2106	98.7	28	1.3	2134
F45	8	50.0	8	50.0	16
F51	30	90.9	3	9.1	33
Total	2985	92.2	251	7.8	3236

Bronze Age Flaked Stone

The largest single category of sites in the survey belongs to the Early Bronze Age. There are 33 lithic sites at which Early Helladic ceramics are found (Table 5.13). In accord with our conservative approach, other sites with Bronze Age components represented by less than 50% of the diagnostic ceramics are excluded from consideration. Bronze Age lithic sites are located at Kheli Nisiou, Flamboura, Petrothalassa, Pikrodhafni, the Ermioni Valley, the area around Koiladha, and the Fournoi Complex, where there are 17 sites (see Runnels and van Andel 1987 for site locations). The increase in number of sites in the EH I-II period indicates more intensive exploitation of the environment, including lithic resources. This process of ecological intensification involved the use of exotic as well as local materials. Obsidian from Melos dominates the Bronze Age lithic assemblage (2985 artifacts, 92.3%) and from this fact we infer the significance of procurement expeditions and exchange. The emergence of complex polities by MH times, if not earlier, certainly stimulated long-distance trade. Although the quarrying of obsidian on Melos was not regulated in the Bronze Age (Torrence 1986: 214–16), once the material reached the Greek mainland the evidence suggests regulated dispersal within small regions from a central place.

Lithics continued to be used for important tools in the Bronze Age, even though implements made of other materials either increased in quantity (pottery) or appeared for the first time (e.g. metals; Van Horn 1976). The introduction of metallurgy did not displace flintknapping as the key process for the production of many tools because bronze remained a relatively expensive commodity throughout the Bronze Age (Runnels 1982). Sickle elements, projectile points, knives, and other tools for everyday use continued to be made of stone to the end of the Mycenaean period. It is likely that the large centers, such as Mycenae, Tiryns, and Asine, had access to more metal. In areas of secondary importance, such as the Southern Argolid, however, stone would have served many of the functions that metals coopted in the more affluent areas. From a practical standpoint, the residents of the Southern Argolid had ready access to abundant obsidian through the long-established contact with Melos, and may have seen little advantage in adopting bronze tools in large quantities. Alternatively, bronze or its constituent elements may have served as a medium of exchange, and the residents of the Southern Argolid may not have been able to afford to immobilize these fluid assets by using metal tools to any great extent. If elites controlled access to metal, they may have been reluctant to relinquish the valuable commodity for use in prosaic tools for which stone was quite suitable.

Obsidian (N = 2985, 92.2%) far exceeds flint (N = 248, 7.7%) in the Bronze Age lithic assemblage. F9 is the only site with a substantial number of lithics at which flint exceeds obsidian; the reason for this anomaly in the pattern is not clear. These proportions differ from the Neolithic sites in the survey, but resemble the proportions found at Franchthi Cave in the Final Neolithic (95% obsidian, 5% chert). The dominance of obsidian parallels the conditions at Lerna in the northern Argolid and Agios Stefanos in Lakonia. As at those sites, extensive use of obsidian in the Southern Argolid indicates the interplay of two key factors. First was the realization of and preference for the superior tractability and sharp edges of obsidian. The knappers had a choice of materials and opted for obsidian, despite its brittle nature, because it suited the tasks at hand, i.e. cutting, scraping, penetrating, and incising. Second, from the quantities of obsidian found, we infer relatively easy access to Melos and an unimpeded flow of the material throughout most of the Bronze Age. This situation indicates that external contacts for the region may have been much easier by sea than over land; it was simply easier and faster to sail to Melos for obsidian than to obtain chert directly or by intermediate exchange from quarries in the northern Argolid or elsewhere in the northeastern Peloponnesos.

As van Andel and Runnels (1987: 22) argue, the Southern Argolid is somewhat isolated, and has the characteristics of an island in its contacts with other regions, because the best routes in and out of the area are by sea. We suspect that an economic motive played a key role in the extensive use of obsidian in southern Greece during this period. Chert blades were imported to Lerna as finished products from some distant source (Runnels 1985a). Perhaps obsidian was worked at Lerna and other sites for the return trade. This argument would not exclude the probability that functional qualities were of equal importance (e.g., flint was always preferred for sickle elements). Fine pressure-struck flint blades were imported to Franchthi Cave from an unknown source already in the Early Neolithic. Imported flint blades, although made from flint different from that found in the Neolithic, continued to be imported to Peloponnesian sites in the Early Bronze Age (Runnels 1983b, 1985a). Some evidence for return traffic in prepared obsidian blades can be adduced from the distribution of obsidian cores and blades found in the Argolid survey. Cores are concentrated at the Fournoi sites, but the rather rare blades were found in significantly greater numbers at small outlying sites (Jameson, Runnels, and van Andel 1994: Chapter 6). Blades struck from the many cores found at sites such as Lerna (Runnels 1985a) may have traveled even farther from their place of manufacture. The centralized manufacture of pressure blades from obsidian may have been a distinctive southern Greek craft activity, and the blades may have been widely traded, perhaps to northern Greece along the trade routes for the flint blades.

Retouched artifacts made up 14.3% (N = 462) of the Bronze Age survey (Table 5.14). This percentage marks a slight drop from the Neolithic and may be due to the much larger size of the sample; with more pieces, there is a greater likelihood of encountering more flaking detritus. The tools range over a wide variety of types. The five end scrapers and three sidescrapers mark the first appearance of these types since the Palaeolithic in the sample. A number of types are characteristic of this Bronze Age assemblage. Perçoirs, either as single or multiple tools, constitute the largest category by far (N = 165, 35.7% of all retouched tools, 5.1% of all lithics; see Figs. 89, 2 and 90, 1–4). We have already discussed possible functions for these tools. By way of additional circumstantial evidence, pins of ivory and bone, some with elaborate carved decoration, are known on Greek Bronze Age sites, particularly in the EH and MH periods (Banks 1967). The perçoirs, if utilized for carving and incising, would have been useful tools for this craft. Denticulates (N = 12, 2.6% and 0.4%) and pieces with silica gloss (N = 8, 1.7% and 0.2%) provide evidence for cereal or grass cutting and are much more numerous than in the Neolithic sample. The difference between the two periods may reflect several factors. First, in the Neolithic, Franchthi Cave is perhaps alone in being a permanent habitation. Inhabitants at other sites may have engaged in specialized activities, e.g. resource procurement or pastoralism. Second, with a wider distribution of agricultural implements in the Bronze Age we may have distinct communities, whereas in the Neolithic the residents of a central settlement simply visited the various sites and did not farm in those peripheral areas. The greater number of clearly recognizable sickle elements in the Bronze Age supports the argument that there was a shift at the beginning of the Bronze Age to intensive cultivation of cereals. Such a shift has been recognized throughout the eastern Mediterranean area at the end of the Neolithic, which can be coupled to widespread social and economic change (van Andel and Runnels 1988). In the Southern Argolid there is a marked concentration of settlement in the early Bronze Age on the best arable land (Runnels and van Andel 1987), and this can be plausibly interpreted as a shift from Final Neolithic pastoralism to plow cultivation of arable land for cereal production (Jameson, Runnels, and van Andel 1994: Chapter 6).

Table 5.14. Bronze Age Flaked-Stone Tool Types, by Material

Tool type	Obsidian	Chert	Total
Not retouched	2584	192	2776
Retouched pieces	108	24	132
End scrapers	5		5
Side scrapers	2	2	4
Denticulates	10	2	12
Notches	21	4	25
Shouldered pieces	5		5
Perçoirs	137	16	153
Batonnet	1		1
Sickle elements	2	4	6
Single truncations	67	2	69
Double truncations	1		1
Geometrics	7	1	8
Burins	1		1
Tanged arrowheads	2		2
Hollow-based	1		1
Pièces esquillées	17	2	19
Backed pieces	1		1
Bifacial pieces		1	1
Multiple tools	13	1	14
Total	2985	251	3236
	92%	8%	

Of the three projectile points in the collection, two are tanged and barbed and one is a concave or hollow-base type. The former type belongs with the Late Neolithic tanged points, while the latter is a Bronze Age type (Runnels 1985a). Hollow-base projectile points have been found in good Helladic contexts at Mycenae (Mylonas 1965; Van Horn 1976), Lerna (Runnels 1985a) and Agios Stefanos (Kardulias 1992). Although the Bronze Age lithic assemblage is much larger than that of the Neolithic, Bronze Age sites yielded few projectile points. This small number in a period with considerable evidence for warfare and hunting is perplexing, and is unlike the situation from excavated sites. Among the 393 lithics from the later excavations at Agios Stefanos are 15 projectile points, 3.8% of the total compared to only 0.002% (N = 5) for Lerna III and 0.09% for our survey material.

Small-scale geometric tools (Figs. 78, 3; 80, 2; 89, 9) are found in the Bronze Age sample. There is a total of eight (five rectangular, one triangular, and two trapezoidal) such tools fashioned on snapped or truncated portions of obsidian blades. Careful, minute retouch, both inverse and direct, created the symmetrical shapes. These geometric tools may have been used in composite implements such as sickles or reaping knives, but they are probably arrowheads (Runnels 1985a). Small notches form another common type in this period, and may have been used in woodshaving.

Finally, there are more multiple tools (pieces with more than one retouched facet, e.g. notch-perçoir) among the Bronze Age lithics, a fact that suggests Helladic peoples engaged in a wider range of tool-using behavior than did their predecessors; perhaps even in this small area of stone-tool usage we have indirect evidence of a more complex scheme for exploiting the environment. Tools are somewhat more specialized than before. Of the 64 total tool types, there are specimens in 19 categories for the MP, 26 for the Neolithic, and 45 for the Bronze Age. The greater number of Bronze Age types is probably due in part to the large size of that assemblage, but an enhanced degree of specialization cannot be discounted.

The production of blades was also an important aspect of Bronze Age stoneworking. Certain techniques had developed in the Palaeolithic, but the refinement of the technology occurred in the Neolithic and Bronze Age, especially in the latter. Through experimentation and the use of ethno-historic accounts, scholars have reconstructed the techniques used by Mesoamerican craftsmen to produce large quantities of standardized obsidian blades (Clark 1982). Tests by Runnels indicate Bronze Age Aegean knappers may have secured prismatic cores in a clamp or hand-held support and pressed off blades with a copper-tipped pressure flaker. Core preparation involved the removal of crested blades to prepare the underlying surface. Cores were tabular to conical in outline, and blades were removed from one face only, in a very regular manner. Platform preparation involved roughing the proximal end of the core by abrasion or faceting (removal of some flakes to create a good striking/pressing surface). The method produced highly regular, parallel-sided blades, with a typical trapezoidal or triangular cross section. Experiments by Runnels have shown that hand-held cores can also be successfully flaked to produce fine pressure blades.

The Bronze Age sites in our sample yielded 308 obsidian and four flint blades. We will concentrate on the obsidian blades; of the 308 pieces, only two are complete and four nearly complete. Obsidian blades comprise 9.5% of all Bronze Age lithics and 10.3% of all Bronze Age obsidian. As Runnels (1985a) has suggested for Lerna, it is misleading, on the basis of such numbers, to label Bronze Age collections as blade industries. The production of blades was clearly important, but it was not the sole focus of stoneknappers. The fact that 74.7% (N = 230) of the blades are unretouched underscores this point. Of the blades that are retouched, the modal category (N = 19) is single truncation (Fig. 89, 7). In the smaller Neolithic sample (N = 35), 65.7% of the blades exhibit no retouch. Thus the knappers went to considerable trouble to produce blades, most of which were evidently to be used without further modification. Since most of the blades appear at sites without cores, perhaps many of these unretouched blades were intended for export to other settlements in the region. It was, perhaps, as an exchange commodity that obsidian acquired its greatest economic significance.

The technical expertise apparent in Bronze Age obsidian blades has led scholars to consider the role of craft specialists in the production of these blanks. There is abundant evidence to indicate that knappers in some large, prehistoric Mesoamerican sites were full-time artisans. In the Aegean some have argued for the existence of full-time obsidian workshops in the Bronze Age at Agios Kosmas (Mylonas 1959: 144), Phylakopi (Mackenzie 1898: 24; Bosanquet 1904: 218), Mallia (Van Effenterre and Van Effenterre 1969), and Knossos (Warren 1972: 393). Recently Runnels (1985) and Torrence (1979, 1986: 162) have countered this argument, suggesting that part-time specialists, or even domestic production, can account for much of the material found at Aegean sites. The relatively small number of blades from Bronze Age sites covering nearly 2,000 years of occupation in the Southern Argolid seems to support the part-time specialist thesis, but excavation of sites in the Fournoi Complex would be necessary to resolve the issue. Runnels has inferred the presence of part-time specialists, or what Clark calls "attached" specialists, both at Lerna, from the degree of standardization exhibited (Runnels 1985a), and in the Southern Argolid, from the centralized concentration of cores (Runnels and van Andel 1987; Jameson, Runnels, and van Andel 1994: Chapter 6). Clearly it was the product, hence the centralization of material, rather than the specialist, that was controlled, at least on the Greek mainland.

Even if the working of obsidian was a sporadic enterprise, we can discern certain patterns. Most of the material, including blades and cores (see Figs. 85–87 and 93) is in the Fournoi area. Inhabitants of sites in this valley may have been the key importers, processors, and distributors of obsidian in the Southern Argolid during the Bronze Age. Obsidian knapping may have been only a small part of the economic system that required skilled craftsmen—but required them for only a limited time each year. Nonetheless, the evidence indicates consistency in the production of obsidian blades in the Southern Argolid and elsewhere in the Aegean. Table 5.15 compares the width and thickness of blades from various sites. The Neolithic blades from the Southern Argolid are somewhat smaller and finer, and their dimensions exhibit tighter clustering around the mean than is seen in those from Kephala on Kea. The Bronze Age blades in our sample are narrower than both the Neolithic pieces and the blades from other Bronze Age sites in Greece. The coefficients of variation for both dimensions suggest a uniformity in production technique that is shared with other Bronze Age sites. There are several possible explanations for such widespread uniformity. To some extent, artisans in the Aegean shared common production techniques (encompassing morphology and style) in a variety of media such as pottery and lithics. Alternatively, the regularity we see may be dictated by parallel but independent solutions to the same problems of how to obtain the maximum number of sharp implements from a given quantity of raw material. Because of the numerous contacts between regions during the Bronze Age, including frequent meeting at the Melos quarries, and the long history of blade production by the third millennium, we place more stress on the common-culture model, although technical elements remain highly important.

In summary, the Bronze Age lithics form the largest part of our sample. A high percentage of perçoirs and multiple tools characterizes the assemblage. In addition, diagnostic types include small geometric tools, denticulates, sickle elements, and hollow-based and barbed and tanged projectile points. Although not predominantly a blade industry, blades (obsidian and chert) make up 9.7% of all lithics, as compared with just over 5% for the Neolithic assemblage.

Flaked Stone of the Historic Periods

Flaked-stone tools did not disappear from site assemblages after the end of the Bronze Age. Runnels (1982) has documented the continued use in the Mediterranean of lithics throughout antiquity, the medieval period, and into the twentieth century. Flaked stone appears in historic contexts at many sites in Greece, such as the Byzantine phases at Agios Stefanos (Kardulias 1992). Until recently, many excavators viewed stone tools as intrusive from earlier levels, but this perspective is no longer tenable.

In the survey samples, 65 of the sites have predominantly historical components (Table 5.16), and 36 lithic sites have historical ceramics only (Table 5.17). We assigned sites to this last category only if diagnostic prehistoric ceramics were completely absent. To eliminate questionable associations we have omitted sites where typologically prehistoric lithics are found with historic ceramics. The historic-period sites span the periods from Late Geometric to Early Modern.

Table 5.15. Comparison of Obsidian Blades (Dimensions in Millimeters)
from Various Aegean Prehistoric Sites

Provenience	N	Mean	Standard Deviation	Coefficient of Variation
			WIDTH	
Southern Argolid (Neolithic)	35	104	29	27.9
Southern Argolid (Bronze Age)	308	86	24	27.9
Agios Stefanos	120	93	29	31.2
Lerna III	318	96	24	25.0
Lerna IV	462	98	29	29.6
Lerna V	189	99	28	28.3
Kephala	128	144	37	25.7
Phylakopi (Total)	1542	104	31	29.8
Phylakopi (obsidian deposit)	409	93	31	33.3
Ayia Irini	960	96	25	26.0
			THICKNESS	
Southern Argolid (Neolithic)	35	28	8	28.6
Southern Argolid (Bronze Age)	308	26	8	30.8
Agios Stefanos	120	26	9	34.6
Lerna III	318	26	7	26.9
Lerna IV	462	27	8	29.6
Lerna V	189	29	9	31.0
Kephala	127	39	16	41.0
Phylakopi (Total)	1543	31	13	41.9
Phylakopi (obsidian deposit)	409	30	17	56.7
Ayia Irini	953	29	9	31.0

Table 5.16. Historical Flaked-Stone Artifacts, by Site and Material

Site	Obsidian	%	Chert	%	Total
A11	1	100.0	0	0	1
A12	6	75.0	2	25.0	8
A14	1	50.0	1	50.0	2
A17	6	100.0	0	0	6
A23	5	100.0	0	0	5
A25	2	100.0	0	0	2
A36	1	100.0	0	0	1
A38	6	100.0	0	0	6
A40	4	100.0	0	0	4
A47	2	66.7	1	33.3	3
A51	3	100.0	0	0	3
A52	2	100.0	0	0	2
A54	1	100.0	0	0	1
B3	0	0	1	100.0	1
B5	29	80.6	7	19.4	36
B6	0	0	1	100.	1
B9	31	67.4	15	32.6	46
B10	21	72.4	8	27.6	29
B14	0	0	1	100.0	1
B16	0	0	1	100.0	1
B20	6	54.5	5	45.5	11
B23	3	75.0	1	25.0	4
B35	7	58.3	5	41.7	12
B38	0	0	1	100.0	1
B50	1	100.0	0	0	1
B55	1	100.0	0	0	1
B67	10	100.0	0	0	10
B68	4	80.0	1	20.0	5
B94	1	25.0	3	75.0	4
B100	9	64.3	5	35.7	14
B102	1	0.6	170	99.4	171
B106	0	0	5	100.0	5
C17	23	82.1	5	17.9	28
C37	9	90.0	1	10.0	10
C39	3	75.0	1	25.0	4
D7	1	6.7	14	93.3	15
E3	2	33.3	4	66.7	6
E6			1	100.0	1
E7	2	40.0	3	60.0	5
E35	0	0	4	100.0	4
E36	12	75.0	4	25.0	16

Table 5.16, *continued*

Site	Obsidian	%	Chert	%	Total
E37			1	100.0	1
E40	0	0	1	100.0	1
E42	0	0	1	100.0	1
E46	2	66.7	1	33.3	3
E51	3	21.4	11	78.6	14
E53			3	100.0	3
E57	0	0	17	100.0	17
E60	0	0	2	100.0	2
E61	7	33.3	14	66.7	21
F1	3	50.0	3	50.0	6
F2	3	50.0	3	50.0	6
F3	8	47.1	9	52.9	17
F24	21	95.5	1	4.5	22
F41	7	70.0	3	30.0	10
F48	10	100.0	0	0	10
F57	0	0	1	100.0	1
G1	5	55.6	4	44.4	9
G11	1	100.0	0	0	1
G20	2	50.0	2	50.0	4
G21	0	0	1	100.0	1
G22	0	0	1	100.0	1
G30	0	0	8	100.0	8
G31	2	12.5	14	87.5	16
G33	0	0	7	100.0	7
Total	290	43.3	379	56.7	669

Perhaps the most striking feature of the historic assemblage is its widespread distribution. Historic sites with flaked stone are found in all areas of the Southern Argolid. Most of the sites (N = 45) have fewer than ten pieces. B102, a quarry or flintknapping site in the Pikrodhafni Valley, has the most material (N = 171), and B9 is next (N = 46). This distribution suggests low-intensity usage over a long time. There seems to have been a drop-off in stone-tool use after the Bronze Age, but there are certain functions for which lithics continued to be most appropriate. The number of distinct tool types, however, shows a considerable reduction from the Bronze Age, a pattern observed elsewhere in historical Europe (Ford et al. 1984). Certain cutting and scraping activities are accomplished efficiently with stone tools; and the cost of metal implements would have made lithic implements viable alternatives into the Early Modern period (Runnels 1982: 370–73). In addition, lithics could be used in threshing sledges; flintknappers produced stones for these implements (called *tri-*

bula in Latin sources) until the present day in various parts of the Mediterranean (Bordaz 1969; Rupp et al. 1984: 140). Up to the 1940's, residents of the Southern Argolid commonly used chert tinderflints (*tsakmaki*) with metal strike-a-lights to produce sparks. This technique for making fire certainly has a long history, and some of the pieces in our sample may be discarded tinderflints (e.g. Fig. 66, 3); such pieces typically have slight traces of metal streaks, but surface exposure may have weathered away this residue. There is one gunflint (Fig. 72, 6) made of high-quality black exotic flint in our sample from B102, a quarry site where bands of chert outcrop, and this site may have been used in the Early Modern and Modern periods for the production of gunflints and tinderflints.

The breakdown by material is 290 (43.3%) obsidian and 378 (56.5%) flint; there is also one glass scraper (0.1%; Fig. 92, 3). This represents a change from the Bronze Age (92.2% obsidian). The situation changes somewhat if we remove B102 (one obsidian, 170 flint) from consideration. The counts then become 289 obsidian (58.2%) and 208 flint (41.8%), but both types of material remain important. Flint is more appropriate for threshing sledges, tinderflints, and scrapers that require durability, whereas obsidian provides superior tractability (i.e. better conchoidal fracture that makes it easier to knap) and sharper cutting edges. One inference to be drawn from these data is that lithics were well integrated into the total tool inventory. People made and used stone tools of different materials depending on the particular task at hand. The procurement of flint and obsidian probably followed several paths. Obsidian could still be obtained directly from Melos, which was also the source for the lightweight Rema stone used for rotary querns in medieval times (see below). Low-grade chert sources abound in the Southern Argolid, and better material could be obtained from elsewhere in the northeastern Peloponnese; although large quarries have not been found, good-quality flint appears at sites such as Nemea and Isthmia in small amounts. Alternatively, knappers could reuse pieces of flint and obsidian they found at the various sites in the region, a practice for which there is evidence in the Aegean region (Runnels 1982). This latter method of procurement eliminated the time-consuming core reduction, because the craftsman could pick up prepared blanks.

A total of 173 specimens (25.9%) of this assemblage exhibits some retouch (Table 5.18). This is a much higher proportion than is seen in any other period, and may reflect a more specialized approach taken by historic residents to their tool needs. Various retouched pieces form the bulk of the tools (N = 85, 49.1% of all retouched specimens). Scrapers (N = 14, 8.1%) are more common

Table 5.17. Historical Flaked-Stone Artifacts,
by Period and Material

Period	Obsidian	Chert	N	Sites
Early Historical				
(Classical-Late Roman)	31	40	71	17
Late Historical				
(Medieval-Modern)	33	147	180	4
General historical				
(ancient to modern)	134	27	161	15
Total	198	214	412	36

Table 5.18. Historic Tool Types, by Material

Tool type	Obsidian	Chert	Total
Not retouched	200	299	499
Retouched pieces	38	47	85
End scrapers	3	8	11
Side scrapers		3	3
Denticulates		2	2
Notches	5	5	10
Shouldered pieces	2		2
Perçoirs	9	9	18
Sickle elements	2	2	4
Single truncations	19	1	20
Double truncations	2	1	3
Tanged arrowheads		1	1
Pièces esquillées	9		9
Multiple tools	1		1
Gunflint		1	1
Total	290	379	669
	43%	57%	

than in the Bronze Age, but there are no geometric tools. Truncated flakes (N = 23, 13.3%), perçoirs (N = 10, 5.8%), notches (N = 5, 2.9%), and multiple tools (N = 15, 8.7%) appear in about the same proportions as in the preceding period. There are two denticulates and four sickle elements with gloss that indicate the possible continued use of stone tools in harvesting. The only projectile point, a tanged specimen from site E3 (Fig. 78, 1), may be recycled from a LN-EH site. There are specimens in 36 of the 64 categories, a reduction from the Bronze Age (45 types), and this also suggests a concerted effort to suit tools to particular functions, or conversely, that a variety of retouched forms could all execute certain activities well. Another significant difference is that blades comprise 26.6% (N = 77) of all obsidian in the historic period and only 10.3% in the Bronze Age; in both periods there are very few flint blades. However, there are many more cores and crested blades in the prehistoric phases. These facts together suggest that obsidian blades were being preferentially recycled in the historic periods from prehistoric sites because they were both useful and easy to recognize. In the Bronze Age, the core-to-blade ratio is 1:4.97 (i.e. ca. five blades for every core), and in the historic period it reaches 1:12.83. This index suggests a greater relative abundance of cores in the Bronze Age and perhaps a larger production and exchange system. In the historic period, no site has more than one core, suggesting that residents in various settlements produced blades for local consumption. This argument hinges on the assumption that the cores and blades at historic sites are not recycled from earlier periods. But even if people reused older blades in the historic periods rather than producing new ones, the notion of localized "manufacture" and consumption still holds, because they would have acquired the material at or near their place of residence.

Historic residents of the Southern Argolid made extensive use of flaked-stone tools. The pattern of use varies from that of the preceding Bronze Age by a drop in quantity while maintaining diversity in types (despite the drop in the number of categories present, from 45 to 36). Expedient reuse of old blanks and tools may have been a common feature of historic lithic utilization, and this practice could explain much of the pattern in the foregoing evidence. The abundance of retouched artifacts may reflect extensive reworking of old lithics found on the surface by post-Bronze Age inhabitants of the region.

Discussion: Flaked-Stone Artifacts

A number of issues, having chiefly to do with the origins of raw materials, the production of tools, and the trade in both, remain to be discussed.

Tool Production and Raw Material

Most of the obsidian implements exhibit a fine degree of workmanship, whereas many of the flint tools demonstrate less morphological consistency. The less-refined appearance of these flint artifacts should not necessarily be construed as indicating a lower level of technological expertise. Rather, the nature of the raw material probably was the determining factor in this variation, as Crabtree (1975: 109) has pointed out in a general statement on the subject. The nature of the local cherts is such that it is quite difficult to locate any sizable piece of homogeneous texture. The rather crude appearance of the chert artifacts is thus a function of a lower degree of tractabiliy than that exhibited by available obsidian. This factor also plays into the smaller dimensions of the putative Middle Palaeolithic to Early Upper Palaeolithic artifacts. For example, a Levallois flake and Mousterian point from site B27 (Figs. 68, 1 and 67, 2) possess all the characteristics of their respective types, except that they are smaller than their Western European counterparts. The radiometric dates associated with these artifacts (ca. 55,000 B.P.), however, place them in the Middle Palaeolithic. The problem is the same one of finding a sufficiently large nodule from which to manufacture implements of adequate size for the rather generalized requirements of Middle Palaeolithic tools. Consequently, the widespread Levallois-Mousterian technique was evidently employed on the available local stone resources, resulting in smaller versions of typical Mousterian artifacts.

In general, later artifacts may provide a more consistent appearance, owing to the increasing use of obsidian, which was obtained in larger sizes. Although the idea of enhanced technical excellence cannot be ignored, craftsmanship seems to have been subordinate to the nature of material in determining the quality of the final product.

Flint and Chert Procurement

Because of the easy access to abundant, albeit low-grade, local chert, a discussion of the acquisition of this resource does not necessarily entail a consideration of exchange. Valley bottoms in the region are strewn with chert cobbles of varying size and quality. In addition, two large procurement sites (B102 and F25) were situated within easy walking distance of various sites, including Franchthi Cave (5 km from B102 and 11 km from F25). All of the identified Palaeolithic implements (Figs. 67–71 and 81–84) were manufactured out of these local cherts. The early residents of the region may simply have procured their own raw materials, rather than exchanging for them between locales.

One Palaeolithic site, F25, is located in an area where the chert both outcrops and appears as stream-transported nodules. This site is also in a strategic position near the Katafiki Gorge, which provides a natural corridor for migrating herd animals between the highland Iliokastro basin to the north and the wide Ermioni Valley to the south. Evidently, the acquisition of both food and tools could be simultaneously accomplished at this site. Such circumstances would be consistent with Binford's embedded-procurement hypothesis, by which "logistically organized collectors supply themselves with specific resources through specially organized task groups" (Binford 1980: 10). In this case, the primary task would have been food acquisition; chert collection would have been a secondary activity that the hunters engaged in once the food quest brought them to the gorge.

Even at the Bronze Age and historic-period sites there is little exotic flint present. The most characteristic type of exotic flint at Neolithic Franchthi Cave is a very-high-quality material called "honey flint" because of its rich amber color. The source of this flint is not known, but may be as far away as Bulgaria or Romania (Perlès 1987b). Bronze Age levels at Tsoungiza in the Nemea Valley have yielded substantial amounts of high-quality flint of various colors, and its source is presumed to be nearby. Flint has proved resistant to various sourcing methods that stress trace-element analysis (Luedtke 1978, 1979; Vickery 1983; Ives 1984). A new technique based on normative mineral composition promises better results and is currently being tested on artifacts and quarries at Flint Ridge in Ohio (Foradas 1989).

The better flint blades in the Neolithic Southern Argolid, and the fine, parallel-sided flint blades in the Early Bronze Age, were imported. This is clear from the absence altogether there of cores, debitage, or debris of the same materials as constitute the large blades (Runnels 1983b, 1985a). The honey-flint blades at Neolithic Franchthi Cave were retouched until exhausted, presumably because supplies were limited (Perlès 1987b). Perhaps a trade in finished flint blades existed along the same lines as the obsidian trade from Melos. Until the geological sources of the exotic flints have been identified, it is not possible to comprehend fully the workings of this trade, or to relate the flint trade to the obsidian-exchange system.

From the Bronze Age on, the use of flint and chert dropped off drastically as obsidian became increasingly available. The rather poor quality of the local cherts would have kept them in the realm of parochial items, uninvolved in the increasingly complex exchange patterns involving obsidian and the igneous and metamorphic rocks from different areas used as millstones (Runnels and Murray 1983; Runnels 1985b). The last widespread use of local cherts was for tinderflints. Various informants in the region have indicated that these rudimentary devices were fairly common up to the 1940's. Once a stone was no longer usable for this purpose, it was simply thrown away, and another one was selected from the numerous fragments in the fields.

Obsidian Acquisition and Trade

The presence of obsidian in the Southern Argolid inevitably leads to a consideration of trade. As mentioned above, the closest source for this material is Melos, and so the discussion must devolve to an examination of plausible procurement systems involving that island. Several studies (Cann and Renfrew 1964; Renfrew et al. 1966) have verified that Melos was in fact a key source for much of the central and western Aegean basin. As Renfrew (1982: 222) states, "Indeed there can be little doubt that Melos was visited directly by voyagers from Crete, the various Cycladic Islands . . . , the Peloponnese and the coasts of Attica." Such was the case with Franchthi Cave in the Argolid from as early as the late Palaeolithic (Renfrew and Aspinall 1990); this activity gained momentum during the Mesolithic (Aspinall et al. 1972). Van Andel and Shackleton (1982) suggest a possible route from the mainland to Melos during the late Upper Palaeolithic that would have required only several short water passages, none longer than 15 km; and the significant increase in obsidian on the mainland in the Mesolithic and later may in fact be related to greater exploitation of marine resources (Renfrew 1972: 290; Jacobsen 1976: 81). In addition, as navigational abilities were enhanced in the succeeding millennia, the journey would have become less onerous, and thus one might expect an increase in the percentage of obsidian at Bronze Age sites, since it is far superior to local stone sources in the Argolid for the production of large blades. This trend is clearly in evidence at Franchthi Cave by the Late Neolithic (Jacobsen 1976), and is dramatically reflected in survey-site F32, one of the major Early Bronze Age settlements in the Southern Argolid. Obsidian comprises 98.7% (2106 pieces) and flint 1.3% (28 pieces) of the lithic industry at F32, demonstrating a clear shift in emphasis from the situation during the Palaeolithic.

Having at least tentatively established the Argolid as falling within a Melian procurement sphere, we find that the next problem requiring our attention is the nature of obsidian dispersal within the study area. Specifically, the concern here is whether the occupants of individual sites undertook separate procurement journeys or whether, instead, certain larger sites regulated the flow of obsidian. Much has been made of this issue in studies of the Mesoamerican obsidian trade. Drennan (1984) suggests that during the Formative Period, obsidian acquisition in the region was of such a small scale (5 kg/person/year) that no elaborate exchange network was necessary or even feasible. Only during the Classic Period, with its complex socioeconomic structure, did obsidian become one focus of a large-scale commercial system. At Teotihuacan, in the Valley of Mexico, there is evidence of obsidian workshops whose products were traded far afield (Millon 1967), although this view has been challenged recently (Clark 1986). Although the situation in the Aegean is quite different in terms of the number of sources and the means of transport, perhaps some general analogy is applicable. If the proposed connection between tunny fishing and obsidian acquisition during the Mesolithic is correct, then individual acquisition of lithic resources by separate expeditions was possible. Although there are eight known Neolithic sites on Melos (Cherry and Torrence 1982: 24), there is no indication of exclusive control of the quarries by native islanders during this period. Ships from the mainland would have had ready access to the material, but the activity was probably on a small scale, with subsequent exchange taking place from a variety of mainland coastal sites to the interior (Runnels 1983b: 419). Torrence (1986: 215) suggests that the exploitation of the Melos quarries was expedient and unorganized, required only a simple technology, and occurred in brief episodes. Furthermore, she argues, different people employed two distinct procurement strategies: (1) "special-purpose" visits by knappers and consumers to obtain raw material, involving careful selection of nodules and the preparation of "macro"-cores (i.e. cores); and (2) haphazard collection of unworked nodules by traders, fishermen, and others who stopped at the quarries only because their travels brought them close to Melos. The first strategy requires logistical organization, whereas the second is simply embedded in an activity of higher priority (Binford 1980), but both are forms of direct access (Torrence 1986: 216). The distribution of obsidian on the Greek mainland may have followed several patterns. Torrence (1986: 218–26) argues for "distribution without exchange," i.e. simple, reciprocal, noncommercial exchange, in the Neolithic and Bronze Age because of easy access to Melos from the mainland and other islands. She views obsidian in the Aegean as commercially insignificant. We are not convinced that that assessment is entirely accurate for the Neolithic period, and our data suggest that the Bronze Age distribution pattern certainly had a different cause. Obsidian remained a relatively cheap commodity in the Bronze Age, but central places seem to have regulated its dispersal inland in the Southern Argolid.

With the advent of complex polities, the potential for more regular, structured exchange ensued. The key question is whether certain large sites in the Southern Argolid came to dominate the scene in terms of obsidian acquisition, becoming central clearinghouses through which the stone was distributed to other settlements in the peninsula. One avenue that may prove fruitful is the presence/absence of crested blades (lames à crête) as indicators of on-site modification of nodules or large blanks into blade cores, as opposed to the importing of prepared cores from elsewhere, as Renfrew (1972: 449) suggests. If crested blades are restricted to a relatively few sites, a model proposing the regulation of obsidian importation by large centers gains some credibility. If, on the other hand, such pieces are widely distributed throughout the region, this may reflect rather unrestricted access through a decentralized economic system (i.e. a continuation of the earlier system). There are 21 sites with a total of 58 crested blades present, but only four sites yielded more than one crested blade. These sites, all of which have EH components, are C8 (three pieces), F6 (two pieces), F19 (two pieces), and F32 (34 pieces). Although this distribution seems to support the centralized-system hypothesis because of the number of crested blades from F32, it must be noted that this site was sampled in 1972 and its direct comparability with other locations may be open to question. Subsequent revisits and re-collection, however, confirm the initial findings. Perhaps it is appropriate to identify F32 tentatively as a major obsidian processing center which, if it did not control, certainly had a major input into, the exchange network involving obsidian, and probably other commodities as well. The distribution of cores and blades also exhibits a marked dominance for F32. Eleven sites have obsidian cores (A6, A33, B7, C11, F4, F5, F6, F19, F20, F30, and F32; total of cores is 62 for these sites), but only five locations have more than one such core. F32 has 43 (69% of all Bronze Age obsidian cores), F6 has five (8%), F19 and F20 each have three (5% for each), and B7 has two (3%); F32, F6, and F19 are in close proximity to one another and may represent different activity areas in one site. Of the 28 Bronze Age sites with obsidian blades (N = 304), only nine have ten or more pieces (F32, N = 84 or 28%; C8 and F20, N = 34 or 11% for each; F19, N = 33 or 10.8%; F13, N = 15 or 5%; F51, N = 14 or 4.6%; F22, N = 11 or 4%; A9 and F6, N = 10 or 3% for each). The discrepancy in the percentages of Bronze Age cores and blades found at F32 may indicate that it was an important production site; cores are generally not moved far from the center of production, and the blades, as finished products, could have been distributed widely from F32, thus creating a more even distribution for this category.

Determining the amount of obsidian imported at any time would aid in assessing the extent and intensity of exchange networks. Luedtke (1979) suggests this can be done by considering factors such as number of tools needed, and weight of the tools and associated debris. This approach offers an avenue for further research with Greek lithics, including those of the survey material.

F32 and Other Bronze Age Sites in the Peloponnese

The nature of survey data often precludes the possibility of detailed comparison with excavated sites. The amount of survey material from particular industries available for analysis is often quite small, and comparative statements thus become specious. For example, in our sample there are a number of sites with only a handful of lithics each, and it is difficult to draw any general conclusions based on such sparse evidence. Several sites, however, have substantial lithics associated with a few major components, and thus make it possible to extend the analysis through comparanda.

Table 5.19. Flaked-Stone Artifacts at Site F32, by Type
and Material

Types	Obsidian	Chert	Total
Not retouched	1884	20	1904
Retouched pieces	53	5	58
End scrapers	4	0	4
Denticulates	7	0	7
Notches	8	0	8
Shouldered pieces	1	0	1
Perçoirs	104	1	105
Sickle elements	1	0	1
Single truncations	29	1	30
Double truncations	1	0	1
Geometrics	2	1	3
Burins	1	0	1
Hollow-based arrowheads	1	0	1
Multiple tools	9	0	9
Miscellaneous	1	0	1
Total	2106 (98.7%)	28 (1.3%)	2134

Site F32 is crucial in this regard because: (1) ceramics indicate the dominance there of EH II
material (> 90% of dated sherds), followed by Late Geometric (8%) and LH and LR (1% each); and
(2) there is a large body of lithic material (2134 pieces of flaked stone, 34% of the total, and 55
ground stone, 20% of that total). Table 5.19 breaks down the F32 lithics into various categories. The
size of this assemblage may be somewhat deceptive, because the 1972 sampling procedure involved
intensive, systematic collection of nonrandom grid squares, whereas in 1979 and later the procedure
entailed intensive, systematic collection from random transect samples. Nonetheless, it is clear that
F32 and associated sites of the Fournoi Focus contain much larger amounts of flaked stone (especially obsidian) than did any other site in the region. From a technological standpoint, the number of
blades (84) and blade cores (43; Fig. 93) suggests an emphasis on the production of such uniform
blanks, as was the case at Lerna (Runnels 1985a), Phylakopi (Torrence 1979), and Agios Stefanos
(Kardulias 1992) in the Bronze Age. Just as at these other sites, though, at F32 the blades do not
form the most abundant category. To define such assemblages as purely blade industries is misleading. Of the blades that are produced, many are not utilized or retouched into specific tool types. The
majority of the tools are fashioned on flakes. Blade production was certainly an important component of lithic technology in the Aegean Bronze Age, but it was not the exclusive focus of flaked-
stone production. In our Bronze Age sample there are 460 retouched artifacts, of which 194 (42.2%)
are made on cortical flakes, 170 (40%) are on plain flakes, and only 93 (20.2%) are on blades (81,
17.6%, on prismatic blades, and 12, 2.6%, on crested blades). At F32, 128 (55.7%) of the 230 retouched lithics are fashioned on cortical flakes, 78 (33.9%) are on plain flakes, and 24 (10.5%) are

on blades (16, 7%, on prismatic blades, and eight, 3.5%, on crested blades). There is a tendency at F32, Lerna, and Agios Stefanos to select smaller flakes for retouch. At all three sites, most of the large decortication flakes seem to have been discarded, suggesting an abundant supply of raw material, obsidian in particular. Generally, greater distance from a source augments the value of lithic materials as labor output for procurement increases (Feder 1980–81), but this axiom does not hold strongly in the Southern Argolid, for the ease of sea travel would have minimized the procurement cost for obsidian.

The amount of obsidian at F32 far exceeds the quantity at any other site in the Southern Argolid. Van Andel and Runnels (1987) argue that the inhabitants of the Fournoi Focus imported obsidian from Melos, and F32 served as both port of entry and major production center of cores and perhaps blades for the entire region. The nature of this exchange network is discussed above. The focus here is on specialization and how it is revealed in on-site lithic manufacture. Our working hypothesis is that a specialized production site will exhibit less variability in tool types than do sites that may be smaller but more generalized in activity (e.g. farmsteads). F32 has specimens in 36 of the 64 total retouched categories. There are no pièces esquillées, only one projectile point, and one piece with silica gloss. In Lerna III there are 79 pièces esquillées, five projectile points, and 58 sickle elements with gloss; the respective figures for Agios Stefanos are four, 15, and nine. The seven denticulates from F32 may be sickle elements, and would make up some of the deficit in agricultural processing tools. These numbers for F32 are all exceptionally low, considering the quantity of lithics, and may imply a stress on lithic production at the expense of other activities. Perhaps we can speak of F32 as an obsidian emporium in the Bronze Age. In this capacity, the site could have serviced the needs of the surrounding region for obsidian artifacts.

In contrast to the quantities of obsidian at F32, the paucity of flint and chert there indicates a different setting and perhaps an alternate form of production for this stone material. The rather uniform natural distribution of low-quality cherts throughout the region may have impeded the development of a single major chert-artifact production center because of universal access to the resource in question. Sites B102, a major outcrop in the Pikrodhafni Valley, and F25, at Katafiki, served as chert quarries, but there is no evidence that access was regulated. F32 and the Fournoi Focus thus seem to offer the only major specialized lithic production centers. Chert and exotic flint were rare (5.5%) in EH II Lerna, but increased steadily afterwards (7.7% in EH III and 12.2% in MH; Runnels 1985a), and we suspect a similar phenomenon occurred in the Southern Argolid, but the survey lithics lack the stratigraphic context necessary to draw such fine chronological distinctions.

Conclusions: Flaked-Stone Artifacts

The flaked stone from the AEP survey forms a large corpus of data that can provide substantial information about human occupation in the Southern Argolid. This report has outlined the analytical procedures employed in an effort to order the diverse material, so that some such inferences can be drawn. As an initial step, this process involved the delineation of 64 tool types, comprising 986 (15%) of the total of 6553 artifacts in the sample. Another consideration is the relative proportion of flint and obsidian. The increase in obsidian artifacts through time indicates an expanding trade system. The persistence of flaked stone into the historic era (Table 5.20) is also an area of concern; for the advent of metallurgy did not lead to the abandonment of lithic technologies, as commonly believed. These are several of the observations that have been made as the result of this study. De-

Table 5.20. Flaked-Stone Artifact Summary,
by Period

Period	Total
Middle Palaeolithic	778
Upper Palaeolithic/Mesolithic	181
Neolithic	694
Bronze Age	3236
Historical	669
Unattributed	995
Total	6553

tailed analysis carefully outlines the relationship among the artifact categories, how these differences are reflected at various sites, and what the variation implies for human exploitation of the environment in the Southern Argolid through time.

Ground Stone, Polished Stone, and Other Nonflaked Artifacts

In this section we present the results of our analysis of the ground, polished, and other nonflaked lithics. To our knowledge, our study is the first attempt to present in detail all flaked and nonflaked lithic artifacts from surface sites in one region of Greece, because nonflaked lithic artifacts are rarely collected in the course of excavations, and even more rarely published in full. Although the importance of collecting and analyzing flaked-stone artifacts is widely recognized in Mediterranean survey work, rarely are attempts made to collect ground-stone and polished-stone artifacts systematically (Runnels 1983c).

The decision was made at the beginning of the survey in 1979 to collect all but the largest stone tools (which were recorded in the field) found on every site. Fieldwalkers were shown the different kinds of raw materials known to have been used for celts, querns, ornaments, and other artifacts, and the significance of the specimens that were found was explained. Fieldwalkers spent part of each day in the laboratory cleaning and sorting the artifacts that were collected in the course of the day, and this activity afforded an opportunity to examine stone tools first hand. We believe that the field crews were sufficiently well-trained to have detected and identified most categories of stone tools. In addition, the implementation of a random-sampling technique on almost every site obviated the problem of unfamiliarity with stone artifacts in the field. The utility of collecting and studying the wide variety of stone tools is enhanced by the use of diagnostic forms and distinctive raw materials. Small, shapeless fragments of andesite and Rema stone were recognized as parts of querns and collected, once the material was shown to fieldwalkers.

As a result of this activity, 304 nonflaked lithic artifacts were collected or recorded in the field between 1972 and 1982. This large sample affords a convenient opportunity to analyze changes in nonflaked-stone technology and use in the prehistoric and historic periods.

Types of Stone Objects

The majority of the nonflaked lithic artifacts are saddle querns, handstones, hopper mills, rotary querns, press beds, and olive crushers. These artifacts will be treated first by discussing the different categories of implement and the materials from which they are made. This will be followed by a discussion of the material by chronological period, to bring out more clearly the significant changes in lithic technology that have occurred.

To summarize the character of the sample, the several types of querns and handstones make up around 55% of the sample, and olive-crushing and -pressing implements comprise about 13%. The remaining 32% of the objects are celts (i.e. stone axes or adzes), vessels, mortars, and miscellaneous or fragmentary objects.

The nonflaked lithics may be grouped into the following broad categories:

Saddle querns (synonyms: metates; grinding slabs; lower stones; millstones). Figure 94 illustrates the principal shapes of querns and the terms used to describe them in this report. The earliest saddle querns from the survey belong to the Late Neolithic period, and they continue to be used, with many modifications, to the end of Classical antiquity.

Handstones (synonyms: manos; upper stones; grinders; rubbers; mullers; Fig. 95). Handstones have roughly the same time range as saddle querns, continuing in use to the end of Classical antiquity. These tools are often no more than expedient implements, unmodified cobbles or stones that were discarded after short periods of use.

Hopper querns (Olynthus mills; Fig. 95). The hopper mill is a specialized form of the saddle quern, and it makes its first appearance in the Archaic period. The greatest period of use is the early Hellenistic period, and it continued to be used early in the Roman era.

Rotary querns (handmills; Fig. 96). Rotary querns were introduced to Greece from the western Mediterranean in the first century B.C. to the first century A.D. and continued in use to the present day.

Press beds and weight blocks (Fig. 113). Stone press beds and weight blocks used for pressing olives and grapes belong to the late Classical period and after. They are found in smaller numbers in the Roman and Medieval periods.

Rotary olive mills or crushers (*trapetum* [sg.], *trapeta* [pl.]; Fig. 97). The Roman trapetum was introduced to Greece in the second century B.C., earlier than the rotary quern. This machine went out of use after the seventh century.

Celts (stone axes and adzes; Fig. 116). The small number of celts (N = 4) belong to the Final Neolithic period. No examples were found in Bronze Age or later contexts.

Vessels (vases and mortars; Fig. 115). Four classes of mortars and vessels were identified. One stone mortar belongs to the Early Helladic I-II period. A second class of mortar with three legs belongs to the Mycenaean period. A small number of simple mortars are Classical in date, and one Classical perrirhanterion (a specialized sacral vessel) was recovered.

Miscellaneous. This category consists primarily of unidentified fragments of stone. In almost every case they were collected because the stone was recognized by the fieldwalkers as being foreign to the area. The majority of these pieces are of andesite, Rema stone, or hard igneous greenstone (see below for discussion of raw materials). The group includes fragments of saddle querns, rotary querns, and handstones of various periods that have been broken up by plowing and erosion.

Table 5. 21. Colors of Artifact Materials. Colors Are Given as They Are Found in *The Rock-Color Chart* (New York: Geological Society of America, 1963)

Andesite	Greenstone
5 B 7/1 light bluish gray	5 G 2/1 greenish black
5 YR 6/4 light brown	5 GY 7/2 grayish yellow green
10 R 6/2 pale red	10 GY 5/2 grayish green
Nisyrean and Oros-type andesite	Sandstone
N4 medium dark gray	5 YR 6/4 light brown
Rema stone	
5 YR 8/4 moderate orange pink	
10 YR 8/2 very pale orange	

Raw Materials

The stone artifacts are made from a wide variety of rocks, some of which are local and some of which appear to have been imported from the islands in the Saronic Gulf and the Cyclades. The different raw materials are dicussed here in their order of importance. The total number of specimens that was classified is 289.

Andesite. Altogether, 168 artifacts, or 58.8% of the sample, are made of various forms of extrusive volcanic lava (andesite, basaltic andesite, or rhyolite), here collectively called "andesite" for convenience. The sources for the wide variety of andesites recorded in the survey are evidently in the islands of Aigina, Melos, Santorini, Nisyros, and probably many other places (Runnels and Cohen 1981; Runnels 1981; Williams-Thorpe 1988). The andesites from the Saronic Gulf and from the more distant Aegean islands of Santorini and Nisyros may be distinguished in a rough-and-ready way by color, texture, and visible mineralogy. The Saronic Gulf andesites are porphyritic, with prominent crystals of plagioclase and Fe-Mag minerals. In color they may be brown, pale red, or bluish gray (Table 5.21). The andesites from Nisyros and other islands in the South Aegean Volcanic Arc may be fine-grained with many prominent vugs, or cavities. They often have a texture that resembles a sponge or metallic slag. In color they appear dark gray or even black (Table 5.21).

Considerable advances have been made recently in our ability to identify the sources of these lavas in the Mediterranean (Williams-Thorpe 1988). Andesites were traded to the mainland to be used for saddle querns and other kinds of mills in the Mesolithic period, about 9,500 B.P., and this trade continued through the Roman period (Runnels 1981). After the seventh century A.D., andesite was used primarily for olive mills, but rarely for querns.

Serpentine and basalt. There are 38 specimens made of this rock, or 13% of the sample. Second in importance to the andesites, these rocks derive from the ophiolite nappe (van Andel and Vitaliano 1987). The ophiolite complex consists of altered mafic rocks that include serpentine, diabase, and basalt, all very weathered and highly fractured. These rocks were used for celts, ornaments, and small handstones. They are hard, dense, and readily available, especially as cobbles in the beds of seasonal streams. In color many are greenish black to grayish green (Table 5.21), and for this reason these are often referred to as altered volcanic greenstones. Greenstones occur along with the sandstones in very small pieces, but they are not particularly suited for making larger vessels or implements.

Sandstone. There are 28 specimens of this rock, or 10% of the sample. Many varieties of sandstone occur as outcrops in the Southern Argolid (van Andel and Vitaliano 1987) and were recorded as part of the survey. The Argolid sandstones, light brown in color (Table 5.21), are often highly fractured and weathered, and they are suitable for manufacturing very small saddle querns and handstones. They were rarely used for other kinds of artifacts, and there is no evidence that any of the sandstone used for artifacts was imported into the Argolid.

Rema stone. A small group of artifacts, 13, or 4.5% of the sample, is made of a distinctive vesicular (i.e. having a sponge-like texture), hydrothermally altered, volcanic rock. This rock, very pale orange in color, sometimes appearing almost white in some lights (Table 5.21), has its only known source in the island of Melos (at the site of Rema at Dhemenegaki: Runnels 1981; Cherry 1982: 300). This material was exploited in the fourteenth century or earlier for rotary querns and for millstones for windmills and watermills. This stone was widely traded in the Aegean until the introduction of the steel roller mill in the twentieth century. The quarries in Melos closed in 1957.

Miscellaneous. A small number of artifacts (42 specimens, or 12% of the sample) are made from metamorphic rocks such as marble, or from rocks found in the ophiolite nappe (van Andel and Vitaliano 1987), such as talc and metallic ores. Some rock types have not been identified. Very-poor-quality marble is found in the Southern Argolid and is quarried today, but some of the marble used for artifacts in the historic periods, if not earlier, may have been imported.

Saddle Querns

Saddle querns are slabs of stone with at least one grinding surface (Fig. 94). They are usually concave in their longitudinal profile and plano-convex in cross section. When wear traces are present they are the result of extensive abrasive wear. Saddle querns are round, ovate, rectangular, or square in outline. The classification and dating of the Argolid saddle querns is based on the comparative study of approximately 200 saddle querns from stratified contexts in the Argolid, Corinthia, and Attica (Runnels 1981; 1985b).

We collected 36 prehistoric (Neolithic and Bronze Age) saddle querns from 16 sites and 35 historical saddle querns from 27 sites (Figs. 98–102; Tables 5.22 and 5.25). The greater number of sites producing saddle querns in the historical period is a reflection of the larger sample of sites from the last 3000 years of the archaeological record. The number of saddle querns per site decreases at more recent sites.

The prehistoric saddle querns belong primarily to the earlier Bronze Age (Table 5.22), undoubtedly because Neolithic and later Bronze Age sites are rare in the Southern Argolid. Only five saddle querns, from C15, C29 (Fig. 98), E14 (Fig. 98), and G9, are Neolithic in date. The quern from E14 may be Middle or Late Neolithic, but the rest belong to the Final Neolithic. These querns cannot be readily distinguished in material or shape from Early Bronze Age querns, but they are smaller in size (Runnels 1985b). The dimensions of the prehistoric saddle querns are given in Table 5.23. The Neolithic saddle querns are significantly smaller than the Bronze Age average. Comparison with the large sample of Neolithic saddle querns from the excavations at Franchthi Cave (C13; Runnels 1981: 101–5) shows that the saddle querns from surface sites are identical. The Neolithic querns are made of andesite, conglomerate, and sandstone, the andesite imported from the Saronic Gulf. Samples of Neolithic millstones from the Southern Argolid have not been tested petrographically, but thin-

Table 5.22. Prehistoric Querns and Handstones, by Site and Period

Site	Quern	Handstone	Date range
A6		3	Bronze Age
A9	2	6	Bronze Age to Archaic
A33	3	8	Early Helladic I-II
B9	1	1	Bronze Age to Hellenistic
B24		3	Bronze Age
B25	1	1	Late Helladic?
B39		1	Early Helladic?
B97	1		Late Helladic?
B98	2		Late Helladic or later
B100	1		Early Helladic or later
C15	1		Final Neolithic-Early Helladic I
C29	1	2	Final Neolithic
E4	3		Early Helladic I-II
E5	3	1	Bronze Age
E9		1	Bronze Age or later
E13	1	1	Bronze Age; numerous specimens noted at site
E14	1		Middle to Late Neolithic
E74		2	Late Helladic
F23	1	1	Early Helladic?
F32	12	32	Early and Late Helladic
F45		1	Early Helladic I
G9	2	1	Late Neolithic-Early Helladic I
Total	36	65	

section analysis of two querns from the Late and Final Neolithic site of Kitsos Cave in Attica points to a source in Aigina (Runnels and Cohen 1981; Runnels 1985b). The andesite used for the Kitsos and Argolid querns appears to be identical, and a common source in Aigina is a strong possibility.

The Bronze Age saddle querns are larger than the Neolithic querns, and are similar to the querns found in the excavations at Lerna, Asine, and Tiryns on the Argive plain (Figs. 98–102; Runnels 1981: 105–17). An exact comparison of sizes cannot be attempted, because the querns from the survey are for the most part fragmentary. The full width of the quern is more often preserved, however, than the length. The mean width of the Bronze Age querns from the survey is 0.16 m (s.d. 0.05 m; Table 5.23) and the mean width for querns from excavated sites in the Argolid varies from 0.18 m (s.d. 0.05 m) to 0.20 m (s.d. 0.07 m) (Runnels 1981: fig. 28). A small group of complete saddle querns from Ermioni Magoula (E13; Table 5.24) dates to the later Middle Helladic and the beginning of the Late Helladic period. Their mean dimensions are extremely close to the means from excavated Argolid Bronze Age sites (Runnels 1981: fig. 28) and perhaps give a better basis for com-

Table 5.23. Prehistoric Querns, by Site and Material
(Dimensions in Meters)

Site	Material	Length	Width	Thickness
A9	andesite	0.30	0.21	0.09
	conglomerate	0.13	0.12	0.05
A33	andesite	0.11	0.11	0.05
	andesite	0.10	0.15	0.06
	greenstone	0.13	0.13	0.06
B9	andesite	0.10	0.12	0.04
B25	andesite	0.14	0.09	0.05
B97	andesite	0.11	0.09	0.05
B98	andesite	0.18	0.15	0.08
	andesite	0.16	0.13	0.05
B100	andesite	0.45	0.24	0.18
C15	andesite	0.14	0.15	0.06
C29	conglomerate	0.18	0.18	0.06
E4	andesite	0.11	0.15	0.08
	andesite	0.12	0.16	0.05
	andesite	0.13	0.13	0.06
E5	conglomerate	0.12	0.17	0.07
	andesite	0.11	0.10	0.05
	andesite	0.22	0.13	0.06
E13	granite?	0.12	0.18	0.05
E14	sandstone	0.07	0.13	0.04
F23	andesite	0.11	0.08	0.05

parison than the more fragmentary specimens. There is no evident difference between the saddle querns from the survey and the querns from excavated sites in other parts of Greece.

The prehistoric querns were manufactured from small boulders collected from stream beds. The cortex, often preserved on the bottom of the quern, reveals the rolled and water-worn original surface. The querns were manufactured in a simple way: a handstone was used to peck a flat grinding surface on one face of the boulder, but the final shape of the quern was obtained only after long use had worn down this surface, making the quern too thin to be used. Some querns show evidence of percussion and impact scars on their edges, and some shaping was evidently accomplished by flaking the blank with a hammerstone in a manner similar to flintknapping (Runnels 1981: 137–42), but this was only a preliminary stage.

The Bronze Age querns are almost all made of andesite similar in appearance to Saronic Gulf andesites. This material, foreign to the Southern Argolid, was probably more easily recognized and collected in the field. The preference for andesite for saddle querns, however, is confirmed by the sample from excavated sites (e.g. Runnels 1981: fig. 39). Neolithic querns in Attica were imported

Table 5.23, *continued*

Site	Material	Length	Width	Thickness
F32	andesite	0.26	0.17	0.09
	andesite	0.33	0.21	0.09
	andesite	0.21	0.26	0.07
	andesite	0.20	0.26	0.09
	andesite	0.19	0.27	0.15
	andesite	0.25	0.21	0.05
	andesite	0.14	0.17	0.07
	andesite	0.22	0.17	0.06
	andesite	0.12	0.20	0.06
	andesite	0.13	0.13	0.06
	sandstone	0.32	0.21	0.11
	sandstone	0.13	0.17	0.06
G9	andesite	0.14	0.08	0.09
	sandstone	0.10	0.18	0.06
X		0.17	0.16	0.07
s.d.		0.08	0.05	0.03
Neolithic only				
X		0.12	0.13	0.06
s.d.		0.05	0.04	0.02

from Aigina, and many of the Bronze Age querns were probably derived from the same source. The original determination of Aigina as a source was made on the basis of thin-section analysis, and the attributions have been confirmed recently by chemical analysis (Williams-Thorpe, personal communication, 1987).

The prehistoric saddle querns were used with simple handstones, often no more than a cubical or spheroidal stream cobble of hard igneous greenstone. The Neolithic querns are too small to have been used effectively to grind flour for bread. Probably, they were used for a variety of purposes, such as grinding mineral pigments, clay, or salt, or for sharpening and smoothing celts, shells, and bone implements (Runnels 1981: 146–58). As an experiment, in 1983, we ground down a *Spondylus* shell on an andesite quern. It took approximately 40 minutes of grinding, using wet sand as an abrasive, to get the shell thin enough to make a hole through the center without shattering the piece.

The Bronze Age querns show much variation in size, and probably served a multitude of uses. The larger querns, however, were used with large handstones to grind cereals to produce flour for

Table 5.24. Bronze Age Saddle Querns at E13, Ermioni Magoula (Dimensions in Meters)*

X and s.d.	Material	Length	Width	Thickness
	andesite	0.16	0.21	0.07
	andesite	0.35	0.25	0.12
	andesite	0.28	0.19	0.07
	conglomerate	0.24	0.22	0.06
	conglomerate	0.22	0.20	0.06
X		0.25	0.21	0.08
s.d.		0.07	0.02	0.03

* Only one specimen was collected; the others were measured on the site.

bread (Figs. 100–101). The grinding surfaces are often polished over their entire area by extensive, abrasive use-wear. The use of the same kind of saddle quern in the Classical period for grinding bread flour is well-attested (Moritz 1958).

The small sample from the survey is enough to show that saddle querns continued in use to the end of the Bronze Age. No change in the size, form, or raw material is noticeable during this long period.

In the historical periods, saddle querns continued to be used, and they are found in small numbers at sites of the Roman and Medieval periods (Table 5.25). They were rendered obsolete, however, in the Classical and Hellenistic periods by hopper mills, and by rotary querns in the Roman period.

The historical saddle querns, though they are in principle operated in the same way as their prehistoric prototypes, show many changes (Fig. 103). The most notable difference can be seen in their method of manufacture. Saddle querns that were shaped by flaking and pecking continued to be made into the Roman period, but the majority of historic saddle querns after the Archaic period were carefully shaped by hammer-dressing with a pointed iron tool (Runnels 1981: 75–77, 137–41). Greco-Roman grinding slabs, or lower stones, in the period were thin rectangular slabs (Table 5.26, mean thickness 0.06 m) carefully squared by hammer-dressing. The upper surface, the one used for grinding, was often dressed with parallel grooves or furrows to improve the efficiency of the mill. The handstone was typically shaped like a boat, with a narrow elliptical outline, two pointed ends, and a triangular cross section. The historic saddle quern, cut to specified sizes by skilled stone masons, is common at the site of Halieis in the Southern Argolid, which dates to the end of the late Classical period and the beginning of the Hellenistic period (Runnels 1981: 117–27, figs. 22–26).

The saddle querns from the surface survey are very fragmentary. The small size of the average fragment (Table 5.26, mean length 0.16 m) is the result of post-depositional damage and obviates comparison with complete specimens, which are as much as 0.49 m in length, from the excavations at Halieis (Runnels 1981: table 25). The majority of the survey saddle querns are of andesite (88%, Table 5.26). The andesite used for historic saddle querns, however, comes from a different source or sources than does the andesite used in the Bronze Age. Although andesite from Saronic Gulf sources is still seen, the majority of historic saddle querns are made of a dark-gray, fine-grained bas-altic andesite (Table 5.26: Nisyros and Oros-type andesite). The limited number of thin-section and chemical analyses that have been carried out on Greek millstones point to Nisyros, and to a lesser extent Santorini, as possible sources for this andesite (Williams-Thorpe, personal communication, 1987 and 1988). Nisyros is attested in Classical sources as a source of millstones that were exported to mainland Greece (Runnels 1981: 58–99; Williams-Thorpe 1988). A trapetum from Corinth,

Table 5.25. Historical Querns and Handstones, by Site and Period

Site	Quern	Handstone	Date range
A11		1	Late Roman
A16		1	Classical
A31	1		Hellenistic?
A32	2	1	Late Roman?
A35	2		Medieval to Modern
A40	1		Classical
A42	2		Late Roman
A62		1	Late Classical-Early Hellenistic
A63		1	Late Roman
B1	1		Late Roman or later
B5	3	3	one Classical to Hellenistic, others possibly Late Helladic to Modern
B20	1		Classical to Roman
B23	1	1	Late Classical-Early Hellenistic
B33	2		Late Classical-Early Hellenistic
B38		1	Late Helladic to Modern
B57	1		Late Classical-Early Hellenistic
B62	1		Classical
B78		1	Late Classical-Early Hellenistic
B83	1		Late Classical-Early Hellenistic
B89	2		Late Classical and Hellenistic
B95		1	Late Classical-Early Hellenistic
B96	2		Late Classical-Early Hellenistic
C11	1	1	Late Classical-Early Hellenistic
C12	1	2	Late Geometric to Archaic
C16	1		Late Classical-Early Hellenistic
C17	1	4	Late Geometric to Late Roman
C35		1	Late Roman
C42	1		Late Classical-Early Hellenistic
D3		2	one Late-Final Neolithic, one possibly Archaic-Late Roman
D8	1		Late Classical-Early Hellenistic?

Table 5.25, *continued*

Site	Quern	Handstone	Date range
E6	1		Late Classical-Early Hellenistic, Late Roman
E45		2	Late Roman or later
E57	1	1	Classical to Middle Roman
E62	1		Hellenistic to Late Roman
E70		1	Classical to Late Roman
F4		2	Early Helladic to Late Classical-Early Hellenistic
G2	1		Late Classical-Early Hellenistic
G20	1		Late Classical-Early Hellenistic
G30	1		Late Roman
Total	35	28	

which is made of the porphyritic bluish-gray andesite associated with the Saronic Gulf, has been traced to a source at Marathona in Aigina (Williams-Thorpe, personal communication, 1988).

The trade in Nisyrean andesite began in the late Classical period. About one-third of the saddle querns from the survey are made of Nisyrean-type andesite, and include those from B23 and B33 (Table 5.25), which are dated to the late Classical-early Hellenistic period. Williams-Thorpe (1988: 282–83) and Runnels (1981: 117–27) identified Nisyros as the source of Hellenistic hopper mills, and we may safely assume that saddle querns and handstones were manufactured at the Nisyrean quarries for export with the hopper mills. The rectangular grinding slabs were used with both the hopper mill and the boat-shaped handstone as upper stones. The Nisyros source continued to be exploited in the Roman period (Runnels 1981: 127–30).

Handstones

These stones are roughly of a size that will fit the hand, and they have at least one surface (but often more) that exhibits use-wear (Figs. 99, 104–5). They have the same overall characteristics as querns, but they are smaller in size. Handstones have shapes that may be classified roughly as spherical, conical, discoidal, cubical, rectangular, ovate, or irregular. About half of the handstones resemble very small saddle querns, and there are undoubtedly errors in their classification. A few small saddle querns that were intended by their makers to be used as lower stones, or stationary supports, may have been classified by us as handstones. There are no certain criteria for distinguishing between small saddle querns and handstones (Runnels 1981: 146–55). Nor is it certain that they were distinguished on a consistent basis by their makers or users, and almost every handstone shows clear evidence of being used for multiple purposes. Some (e.g. Fig. 105) have predominantly abrasive use-wear from fine grinding (striations and polish), and others (Fig. 106) have impact damage (fractures, pecking, and crushing) from percussive uses (Runnels 1981: 75–77, 130–58). The usual pattern is a mix of both types of use-wear.

Table 5.26. Historical Saddle Querns, by Site and Material
(Dimensions in Meters)

Site	Material	Length	Width	Thickness
A31	sandstone	0.23	0.14	0.05
A32	andesite	0.11	0.13	0.04
	andesite	0.14	0.10	0.09
A35	andesite	0.17	0.06	0.06
	andesite	0.08	0.06	0.03
A40	andesite	0.13	0.14	0.05
A42	andesite	0.15	0.08	0.03
	andesite	0.09	0.05	0.05
B1	andesite	0.12	0.08	0.05
B5	andesite	0.13	0.08	0.06
	andesite	0.19	0.12	0.05
	andesite	0.17	0.11	0.05
B20	andesite	0.10	0.14	0.07
B23	andesite	0.17	0.13	0.05
B33	andesite	0.17	0.13	0.09
	andesite	0.19	0.22	0.05
B57	andesite	0.16	0.09	0.06
B62	andesite	0.10	0.14	0.06
B83	conglomerate	0.32	0.26	0.14
B89	andesite	0.17	0.16	0.06
	andesite	0.13	0.11	0.04
B96	andesite	0.21	0.17	0.07
	andesite	0.19	0.17	0.08
C11	andesite	0.11	0.09	0.09
C12	conglomerate	0.20	0.13	0.07
C16	andesite	0.14	0.13	0.06
C17	andesite	0.16	0.13	0.07
C42	andesite	0.12	0.13	0.06
D8	andesite	0.22	0.13	0.03
E6	andesite	0.17	0.14	0.05
E57	sandstone	0.13	0.10	0.08
E62	andesite	0.14	0.11	0.11
G2	sandstone	0.14	0.10	0.09
G20	andesite	0.20	0.13	0.06
G30	andesite	0.10	0.12	0.07
X		0.16	0.12	0.06
s.d.		0.05	0.04	0.02

Table 5.27. Prehistoric Handstones, by Site and Material (Dimensions in Meters)

Site	Material	Length	Width	Thickness	Site	Material	Length	Width	Thickness
A6	greenstone	0.13	0.09	0.04		andesite	0.12	0.13	0.05
	andesite	0.13	0.08	0.07		andesite	0.13	0.11	0.05
	greenstone	0.14	0.13	0.06		andesite	0.07	0.16	0.04
A9	sandstone	0.12	0.07	0.05		andesite	0.09	0.09	0.05
	andesite	0.10	0.10	0.05		andesite	0.12	0.10	0.06
	greenstone	0.15	0.08	0.06		andesite	0.13	0.16	0.03
	greenstone	0.08	0.09	0.07		andesite	0.16	0.16	0.04
	andesite	0.10	0.13	0.04		andesite	0.11	0.09	0.05
	greenstone	0.08	0.05	0.03		andesite	0.08	0.12	0.05
A33	andesite	0.18	0.13	0.05		andesite	0.11	0.08	0.04
	greenstone	0.09	0.07	0.04		andesite	0.12	0.07	0.05
	andesite	0.09	0.11	0.04		andesite	0.08	0.10	0.03
	greenstone	0.09	0.05	0.03		andesite	0.09	0.05	0.03
	greenstone	0.09	0.05	0.03		andesite	0.14	0.10	0.05
	greenstone	0.08	0.06	0.03		andesite	0.13	0.15	0.05
	greenstone	0.13	0.06	0.04		andesite	0.09	0.05	0.04
	greenstone	0.10	0.08	0.03		andesite	0.10	0.07	0.04
B9	sandstone	0.07	0.07	0.05		andesite	0.14	0.10	0.03
B24	andesite	0.07	0.07	0.04		andesite	0.10	0.11	0.04
	andesite	0.11	0.07	0.07		greenstone	0.11	0.10	0.08
	andesite	0.06	0.11	0.05		sandstone	0.13	0.14	0.04
B25	andesite	0.09	0.06	0.04		sandstone	0.10	0.09	0.04
B39	sandstone	0.06	0.07	0.02		greenstone	0.12	0.07	0.02
C29	greenstone	0.07	0.05	0.03		basalt	0.06	0.05	0.04
	greenstone	0.06	0.04	0.02		greenstone	0.09	0.06	0.06
E5	andesite	0.15	0.11	0.07		sandstone	0.07	0.05	0.03
E9	sandstone	0.11	0.09	0.05		hematite	0.04	0.04	0.04
E13	greenstone	0.10	0.06	0.03		greenstone	0.06	0.06	0.03
E74	greenstone	0.06	0.05	0.05		andesite	0.05	0.04	0.04
	andesite	0.15	0.18	0.06	F45	chert	0.06	0.05	0.04
F23	greenstone	0.06	0.05	0.05	G9	andesite	0.10	0.09	0.05
F32	andesite	0.09	0.07	0.04					
	andesite	0.10	0.13	0.05					
	andesite	0.11	0.15	0.04	X		0.10	0.09	0.04
					s.d.		0.03	0.04	0.01

Handstones are found on sites of every period. Sixty-five specimens from 16 sites are prehistoric (Table 5.22), and 28 specimens from 19 sites span the historical period (Table 5.25).

The prehistoric handstones are quite small, averaging only 0.10 m in their greatest dimension (Table 5.27). A little over half of them (54%) are of an andesite that resembles Saronic Gulf andesite from Aigina. The remainder are made of hard igneous greenstone (N = 20, 31%), sandstone (N = 7, 10.8%), hematite (N = 1, 1.5%), basalt (N = 1, 1.5%), and chert (N = 1, 1.5%). Greenstones were favored for handstones that were used for percussive tasks because the rock is tough and dense. Suitable cobbles of greenstone, and of other rocks such as sandstone, were picked up in stream beds and used with little or no modification. Most handstones retain portions of their original cortex, which reveals their origin as stream cobbles. Use-wear traces are the only certain way of recognizing handstones from natural stones that were brought to the site but never used.

There is no clear evidence that a particular type of handstone was confined to any particular period. Handstones are common at sites from the Neolithic to the Roman period. Older celts or handstones must have been picked up frequently and recycled, thus finding their way onto later sites (e.g. Fig. 107). Handstones can thus be defined as expedient tools and, as such, are distinct from saddle querns and other types. No change through time was detected. A comparison of the mean values for the dimensions of prehistoric and historic handstones, for example, shows that there is almost no difference in size (Tables 5.27 and 5.28). There is a slight drop in the number of andesite handstones in the historical periods (Table 28: to 43%), with a corresponding increase in the number of greenstone examples (to 39%). The samples are too small, however, to warrant our assigning any significance to this small change.

Hopper Mills

Seven hopper mills belonging to the late Classical-early Hellenistic period were found in the survey (Fig. 95; Table 5.29). The hopper mill, or Olynthus mill, is a large rectangular upper stone with a hopper let into the upper surface (Moritz 1958: 42–52; Runnels 1981: 119–22). A feed slot has been cut through the bottom of the hopper to permit the passage of grain through to the lower stone (a quern, or grinding slab). These large mills have many distinctive features, particularly the cuttings for handles and for pins to secure the mill to a pivot. The grinding surfaces of both the hopper quern and the lower stone are often dressed with furrows or grooves cut in a variety of patterns. The most common patterns are parallel lines and herringbone. They were probably operated, while placed upon a table, by means of a lever, as is illustrated on decorated Megarian-type bowls (Fig. 97).

All seven hopper mills are of andesite (Table 5.30). The examples from B36 and E43 (Fig. 108), both of which are farmsteads of the late Classical-early Hellenistic period, are made of andesites from the Saronic Gulf and Nisyros. It is perhaps significant, although the sample is too small to allow us to draw wide-ranging conclusions, that the three hopper mills from B89 are all of Nisyros-type andesite. B89 is a Hellenistic farmstead that is somewhat later in date than B36 or E43. The three hopper mills and other querns found at Halieis, which was abandoned by 280 B.C., are all made of Saronic Gulf-type andesite (Runnels 1981: table 17). These facts may suggest a preference for andesite from Nisyros beginning in the Hellenistic period (Runnels 1981: 117–27).

It is regrettable that there has been very little organized study of Classical saddle querns and hopper mills. These millstones were produced by craftsmen at specialized quarry sites on the Aegean islands, and they must once have been part of extensive trade networks. The distribution of

Table 5.28. Historical Handstones, by Site and Material
(Dimensions in Meters)

Site	Material	Length	Width	Thickness
A11	greenstone	0.10	0.06	0.03
A16	limestone	0.13	0.07	0.04
A32	greenstone	0.08	0.06	0.04
A62	andesite	0.13	0.13	0.05
A63	andesite	0.07	0.12	0.06
B5	greenstone	0.06	0.06	0.06
	greenstone	0.08	0.07	0.05
	andesite	0.15	0.10	0.06
B23	unknown	0.06	0.06	0.05
B38	greenstone	0.09	0.07	0.05
B78	andesite	0.09	0.06	0.04
B95	andesite	0.13	0.16	0.05
C11	greenstone	0.08	0.06	0.04
C12	greenstone	0.05	0.06	0.03
	greenstone	0.06	0.06	0.03
C17	hematite	0.06	0.05	0.04
	andesite	0.10	0.11	0.03
	andesite	0.09	0.04	0.04
	greenstone	0.08	0.06	0.06
C35	sandstone	0.08	0.06	0.04
D3	andesite	0.10	0.14	0.06
	andesite	0.15	0.11	0.06
E45	andesite	0.11	0.10	0.06
	andesite	0.06	0.13	0.05
E57	sandstone	0.09	0.06	0.06
E70	andesite	0.12	0.12	0.05
F4	greenstone	0.13	0.07	0.06
	greenstone	0.11	0.07	0.05
X		0.09	0.08	0.05
s.d.		0.03	0.03	0.01

Table 5.29. Archaic to Hellenistic Hopper Mills,
by Site and Period

Site	Number	Date range
A9	1	Late Geometric-Archaic or later
B36	1	Late Classical-Early Hellenistic
B89	3	Late Classical to Hellenistic
E43	1	Late Classical-Early Hellenistic
E57	1	Late Classical to Middle Roman
Total	7	

millstones of island andesite to the mainland and finds of querns on shipwrecks are together proof of the existence of the trade in these stones, and the many graffiti found on hoppers and saddle querns are almost certainly masons' marks added at the quarry. This last conlcusion is supported by the cargo of unfinished Nisyrean millstones with matching graffiti on upper and lower stones on the fourth century B.C. Kyrenia shipwreck (Runnels 1981: 119–22, table 23). Recent research has revealed evidence of extensive trade in millstones in the western and eastern Mediterranean in the Roman period (Peacock 1980, 1986). It is likely that Nisyros, and quite possibly Aigina, were involved in long-distance trade in the Roman period, but this possibility remains to be fully documented (Williams-Thorpe 1988).

Both saddle querns and hopper mills were found in houses at Halieis that had been abandoned between 300 and 280 B.C. (Runnels 1981: 117–27). Both types of mill were in use, therefore, in domestic contexts in the late Classical-early Hellenistic period. Three hopper-mill upper stones were found at Halieis, along with 24 saddle querns or grinding slabs. A similar ratio holds for the surface survey (Tables 5.25 and 5.29: seven hopper mills to 35 saddle querns), indicating that hopper mills were probably more expensive for everyday use than were the saddle querns. It is interesting that some of the more complex and more expensive hopper mills were found on isolated farmsteads in the survey, far from the urban centers of Hermion and Halieis. This fact suggests that some farmsteads must have been occupied on a permanent basis, or from time to time had several residents for extended periods. It is otherwise inexplicable why a sophisticated milling device would be maintained on the premises.

The hopper mills on the Kyrenia wreck (Runnels 1981: 117–27, table 23) came in three distinct sizes, one of them quite large (a length of 0.60 m and a weight of 120 kg). Perhaps the hopper mills had a variety of uses that have not been determined, such as the grinding or crushing of metallic ores, or of olives before pressing. The superiority of the hopper mill over the saddle quern is presumably in its greater capacity (because of the hopper), but this advantage is offset by the greater amount and weight of stone that is required. Hopper mills would have been relatively expensive, one presumes, compared to saddle querns. The greater capacity for the milling of grain, however, does not explain the necessity of having at least three separate sizes of mill. Until more research is done, it will not be possible to understand fully the position of the hopper mill in the ancient Greek milling technology and economy.

Table 5. 30. Archaic to Hellenistic Hopper Mills, by Site and Material (Dimensions in Meters)

Site	Material	Length	Width	Thickness
A9	andesite	0.12	0.09	0.09
B36	andesite	0.11	0.10	0.11
B89	andesite	0.11	0.08	0.08
	andesite	0.13	0.07	0.08
	andesite	0.14	0.10	0.10
E43	andesite	0.35	0.20	0.10
E57	andesite	0.21	0.19	0.10
X		0.17	0.12	0.09
s.d.		0.09	0.05	0.01

The Rotary Querns

The rotary quern incorporates two discoidal stones separated by a spindle (Fig. 96). Each stone of the pair has one grinding surface, and the upper stone has a central perforation to permit the spindle to pass through it. The lower stone sometimes has a socket in the center to hold the bottom of the spindle. The upper stone may also have a hopper let into its upper surface to hold the grain, and a cutting for a handle in the hopper or the outer rim of the stone. The grinding surfaces are sometimes dressed with furrows, often in a spiral pattern. The rotary quern is the only type of handmill in Greece to have employed rotary motion in its operation. Small fragments of rotary querns can be distinguished from fragments of other types of querns when they preserve part of the discoidal shape.

There are 29 querns or parts of querns from the survey. They have been separated into two periods, Roman and Medieval-Modern. Fourteen querns are securely dated to the fifth through seventh centuries A.D., although some of the querns may be older. The rotary hopper quern from E6 (Fig. 109; Table 5.31), for instance, was found on a site with some evidence of an Early Roman component. Fifteen querns are assigned to the Medieval to Modern period on somewhat less secure grounds (Table 5.32). Some of the andesite quern fragments were found on sites (e.g. B31, B91, and E70) that had many Late Roman sherds in addition to sherds of Medieval or Modern date. Two facts, however, seem secure: there are no examples of querns having hoppers in their upper stones on post-Roman sites; and a fragment, possibly a quern, from the fourteenth-century site E42 constitutes the earliest evidence for the use of Rema stone from Melos. It is possible that the Rema stone quarries in Melos began to be exploited already in the eleventh century (Runnels 1988c, 1990), but there is no evidence for a Rema stone quern on a Roman site. The hopper querns and Rema querns seem to be secure diagnostic types.

The sample of 29 quern fragments from 22 sites is the largest collection of querns in Greece where the provenience is known (Runnels 1981: 127–30; 1990). This large sample, although not recovered from precisely dated and controlled stratigraphic excavations, is nevertheless of fundamental importance for establishing the chronology of the introduction of the quern to Greece and its subsequent development there.

Interest in rotary querns does not have a long history in archaeology. As recently as 1958 the date and the place of the origin of the rotary quern were uncertain, owing to the lack of archaeological specimens (Moritz 1958), and the picture is only somewhat clearer today. An international conference on querns at the University of Southampton in 1988, organized by David Peacock, brought workers on this subject together, and in light of the discussion at that conference, the broad outlines of the history of the querns are now visible.

Rotary querns in Greece belong to the Roman period, none earlier than the first century A.D. The earliest querns are probably the hopper type, but flat querns appear to be contemporary with hopper querns on the Argolid sites. Some of the hopper querns have handle slots on the upper surface or let into the outer rim of the upper stone (e.g. Fig. 110, B19 and B88). In others the handle slot is let into the interior of the hopper near the rim (e.g. Fig. 111, G30). A diagnostic feature of all the known Roman querns in Greece is the placement of the rynd, a small bar that attaches the upper stone to the spindle on the lower stone. The rynd is essential for the operation and adjustment of a rotary quern, and it is let into the eye from the top of the upper stone on the Roman querns (Fig. 110, B19).

Only fragments of Roman querns were found in the survey, and no specimen preserves the entire

Table 5.31. Roman Rotary Querns, by Site and Material (Minimum Dimensions in Meters)

Site	Type	Diameter	Thickness	Material	Description
A31	flat		0.04	andesite	fragment
A63	flat		0.04	andesite	fragment
B19	flat	0.12	0.05	andesite	upper stone with handle slot
	flat	0.18	0.06	andesite	upper stone with handle slot
B88	flat	0.13	0.05	andesite	upper stone with rynd cutting
	flat	0.12	0.07	andesite	fragment
	hopper	0.13	0.07	andesite	upper stone with rim, handle slot, and rynd cutting
	flat	0.18	0.04	andesite	lower stone with eye; goes with quern above
C11	hopper	0.17	0.08	andesite	upper stone with handle slot and rynd cutting
E5	flat?	0.17	0.06	andesite	lower stone with eye
E6	hopper	0.16	0.09	andesite	upper stone
F57	hopper?	0.09	0.09	andesite	upper stone with rim, handle cutting
	flat		0.07	andesite	upper stone with cutting
G30	hopper	0.14	0.06	andesite	upper stone with rim, handle cutting
X		0.14	0.06		
s.d.		0.03	0.02		

Table 5.32. Medieval-Modern Rotary Querns, by Site and Material (Minimum Dimensions in Meters)

Site	Type	Diameter	Thickness	Material	Description
B9	flat	0.17	0.06	andesite	upper stone with handle slot
B20	flat		0.07	Rema stone	fragment
B31	flat		0.06	andesite	fragment
B91	flat	0.16	0.06	Rema stone	lower stone
B97	flat?		0.05	andesite	fragment
B98	flat		0.06	Rema stone	upper stone
B100	flat	0.21	0.07	Rema stone	upper stone with collar, rynd cutting
E42			0.04	Rema stone	fragment
E45			0.06	Rema stone	fragment
E62	flat		0.08	Rema stone	upper stone with collar, handle slot
E70	flat?		0.05	andesite	fragment
	flat?		0.06	Rema stone	upper stone with collar
E73			0.03	Rema stone	fragment
			0.05	Rema stone	fragment
G31			0.04	Rema stone	two fragments
X			0.06		
s.d.			0.01		

diameter. An estimate of their size, however, is possible. The mean preserved distance from the eye to the rim, the radius, is 0.14 m, and this figure should be doubled for an estimated minimum diameter of 0.28 or 0.30 m (Table 5.31). The Medieval-Modern querns are more fragmentary than are the Roman specimens, but one example (from B100, Fig. 112) preserves nearly one-half of an upper stone with a diameter of 0.21 m (Table 5.32). The complete diameter was greater, and the Medieval-Modern querns are thus approximately the same size as were the Roman querns. The mean thickness of the querns, ca. 0.06 m, is the same in both periods. These numbers are consistent with measurements taken from more complete specimens in Corinth, Isthmia, and Athens (Runnels 1981: 127–30).

In terms of the raw materials, the Roman querns are made exclusively from andesite. Nothing is known of the Roman quern trade in the Aegean from literary sources, and we will not be able to base firm conclusions upon the survey sample. Seven of the Roman querns are made of Saronic Gulf-type andesite, and all four querns from site B88 (Late Roman; Table 5.31) are made of an andesite very similar to the material from Marathona in Aigina (Runnels 1981: 63–98). Three querns from secure Late Roman contexts (Table 5.31: C11, F57, G30) are made of dark-gray, fine-grained andesite that may be from Nisyros (Williams-Thorpe, personal communication, 1988). Production centers in Nisyros, Aigina, and possibly another place in the Saronic Gulf are likely.

Medieval querns are always flat, in sharp contrast with Roman querns, and they have a keyhole-shaped handle slot in the form of a raised collar around the eye on the top surface of the upper stone.

The cutting to hold the rynd is also different from Roman practice. It is let into the inner part of the eye halfway between the top and the bottom surfaces of the stone, having moved down into the eye from its position on Roman querns. The Medieval querns are made from Saronic Gulf-type andesite or Rema stone, with Rema stone being more common. The rotary querns of the Southern Argolid are very similar in form to the securely dated eleventh-century querns found in the Serçe Limani shipwreck, which may have been quarried in Melos (Runnels 1988c, 1990). The Serçe querns were possibly part of the ship's cargo, and if so, they represent the earliest evidence for the transshipment of querns from Melos to lands around the Aegean.

Modern querns, dating from the seventeenth to the twentieth century A.D., are very flat and have a simple collar around the eye (Runnels 1988c, 1990). Handle cuttings consist of simple holes let into the top surface of the upper stone near the outer edge. The cutting for the rynd is always on the bottom of the upper stone. Rema stone is the only raw material used for the manufacture of modern querns, proving that at some point the quarries at Rema in Melos became the sole source for rotary querns in southern Greece.

Further research may cause us to alter some of these conclusions, but for the present it seems possible to distinguish Roman, Medieval, and Modern querns on the basis of raw material, placement of the rynd cutting, and the presence or absence of a distinctive collar and handle slot on the top of the upper stone.

Despite periodic claims to the contrary, there is no archaeological evidence from the Southern Argolid to suggest that the rotary querns were invented in Greek lands. Current evidence points instead to a probable origin in Central or Western Europe, whence it seems to have quickly diffused, perhaps carried with the legions of Rome (Childe 1943; Peacock 1980; Williams-Thorpe 1988). This picture is consistent with the picture in Greece, and we may assume that the quern was introduced during the Civil Wars, which were waged largely on Greek soil, or was brought by Italian colonists beginning in the first century B.C. (Jameson, Runnels, and van Andel 1994: Chap. 2).

The Roman rotary quern was little changed until the Modern period, when it was superseded in the home by the availability of commercially milled flour. The changes that can be inferred from our sample, however, are enough to allow Roman, Medieval, and Modern querns to be identified with confidence. This fact has great usefulness for archaeologists working in Mediterranean lands. The differences between ancient and later querns can allow the dating of even small fragments of querns, which should especially aid the study of surface sites where querns are frequently found. Not only can they be used as an aid to dating sites, but they offer clues to the function of sites, for their domestic function is beyond doubt.

This abrupt changeover from andesite to Rema stone for querns occurred after the seventh century A.D., and is no doubt to be explained by the disruption of seagoing trade at that time. Saracen raids on Crete and Slavic raids on the Greek mainland in the seventh century may have been responsible for the interruption of the trade in andesite for querns (Jameson, Runnels, and van Andel 1994: Chap. 2).

We do not know when the Rema stone source was first discovered (it may have been at any time), but the monopoly of its use for querns must surely be attributed to the Franks. Once established on the Cycladic islands, the Franks searched diligently for raw materials and other resources that could be exploited (Wagstaff 1982), and Rema stone has many qualities to recommend its use. The stone is comparatively light in weight compared with andesite (because of the many voids caused by hydrothermal alteration of the original rock), but its glassy matrix is hard, and thus excel-

Table 5.33. Olive Crushing and Pressing Equipment: Press Beds, by Site and Period

Site	Number	Date Range
A8	1	Late Roman
A60	1	Late Classical-Early Hellenistic
A61	1	Late Classical-Early Hellenistic
B6	1	probably Classical or Hellenistic
B78	1	Late Classical-Early Hellenistic
C11	1	Late Geometric to Hellenistic?
		Bronze Age and Roman materials also present
E26	1	Late Roman
E38	2	Hellenistic
E54	1	Late Classical-Early Hellenistic
G14	1	Hellenistic
Total	11	

lent for grinding flour. The relative scarcity of the rock must also have had its appeal for the exporters, for it allowed a virtual monopoly of supply for good-quality querns. The quarries at Rema were still quite active and profitable in the nineteenth century, and the last querns were produced there as recently as 1957 (Runnels 1981: 87–90, 235–38).

Press Beds and Weight Blocks

In the course of fieldwalking, many stone implements associated with pressing were noted. Fragments of 11 press beds and 13 weight blocks were recorded. Apart from a few fragments that were collected, these objects were left in the field, because of the size of the surviving fragments. They were measured and photographed in situ (Table 5.33).

Press beds are stones with a shallow basin let into the upper surface, and with some sort of channel or spout leading from this basin to the edge of the stone (Fig. 113). Weight blocks are rectangular stones with two rectangular and parallel cuttings let into the upper surface of the stone. Stones with a single cutting were also encountered in the field, but these may have had other uses, for instance as stelae bases (one specimen at A9 preserved traces of lead sheets that were intended to secure the base of a stela), and they are not included with the weight blocks. Fragments of press beds were identified when a part of a rim or a spout was preserved. The counts of press beds, therefore, must be taken as a minimum, because many fragments may have been overlooked. Weight blocks were more easily recognized, because of the careful hammer-dressing of the blocks and the probability that traces of the cuttings would be preserved.

The press beds are made from various grades of conglomerate or limestone. All of the weight blocks are limestone. Because the press beds are fragmentary it is difficult to determine the average diameter of the bed. Two specimens are about 1.0 m in preserved diameter (Table 5.34). Four complete press beds are preserved in situ as part of extensive pressing installations in private houses in the excavated section of the lower town of Halieis (Boyd and Rudolph 1978). These conglomerate press beds, which were built into the house walls, have a diameter of between 0.90 and 1.00 m. Figure 113 illustrates one of these installations; the carefully made cement floor, catch basin, collecting jar, and weight block are typical features.

Many of the press beds from the survey are contemporary with Halieis, belonging to the late Classical-early Hellenistic period around 300 B.C. (Table 5.33). At least three are later Hellenistic (E38 and G14), and two are Late Roman (A8 and E26). None of the press beds is earlier than from the Classical period. The presence of press beds on the survey sites, most of which can be reliably described as farmsteads, is an indication of the expansion and intensification of agricultural production that began in the late Classical period and continued, after an interruption in the middle and late Hellenistic period, into the Roman period.

The weight blocks tell the same story. All but one, from G1, span the same periods as the press beds (Table 5.35). The average length and width of these blocks is 0.81 m by 0.49 m (Table 5.36). They are quite substantial, and functioned to anchor the end of a beam that had one end fixed in a wall. This beam was levered down to press upon the materials stacked on the press bed below. The operation of the beam press has been described often (e.g., Forbes and Foxhall 1978). Although the beam press was supplanted in the Roman world by presses using the principle of the screw sometime after the Hellenistic period, there is no evidence for this innovation on our Late Roman farmsteads. The important point is that these pressing installations were substantial, requiring large blocks of stone and special architectural arrangements to house the machine and to anchor the press bed and the beam.

If we take the number of press beds and the number of weight blocks found on different sites (Tables 5.33 and 5.35), we can estimate that 18 different Greco-Roman farmsteads had such pressing establishments. If we add the trapeta, or olive crushers, from the next section, this number in-

Table 5.34. Historical-Period Press Beds, by Site and Material (Dimensions in Meters)

Site	Material	Length	Width	Thickness
A8	conglomerate	0.53	0.33	0.03
A61	conglomerate	0.13	0.11	0.06
B6	limestone	0.42		0.07
B78	conglomerate	0.15	0.08	0.06
C11	sandstone			
E26	conglomerate			
E38				0.08
G14		1.10		0.20
G34		1.03	0.85	
			X	0.08
Total	9			

Table 5.35. Historical-Period Olive Crushing and Pressing Equipment:
Weight Blocks, by Site and Period

Site	Number	Date range
B78	1	Late Classical-Early Hellenistic
B103	1	Classical or Hellenistic
E7	1	Late Classical-Early Hellenistic
E26	1	Late Roman
E30	1	Late Classical-Early Hellenistic
E38	1	Late Classical and Hellenistic
E50	1	Medieval to Modern, Late Roman present
E52	1	Hellenistic
E70	2	Late Classical, Hellenistic, Late Roman
E81	1	reused in 13th c. chapel
G1	1	Late Geometic to Classical
G14	1	Hellenistic
Total	13	

Table 5.36. Historical-Period Weight Blocks, by Site
(Dimensions in Meters)

Site	Length	Width	Thickness
B78	0.70	0.50	0.36
B103	1.06	0.64	0.26
E7	0.90	0.57	0.36
E26	0.91	0.48	0.34
E30	0.96	0.54	0.29
E38	0.83	0.45	0.20
E50	0.61	0.39	0.28
E52	0.54	0.44	0.33
E70	0.82	0.50	0.25
E81	0.94	0.38	
G1	0.59	0.50	0.47
G14	0.84	0.49	0.30
X	0.81	0.49	0.31
s.d.	0.16	0.07	0.07

creases to 27. This is a substantial number, especially because it is strictly a minimum number of pressing installations that must have existed on these farmsteads, though it must be remembered that these sites are not contemporary. The ratio of sites with presses, however, is similar to that found at Halieis, which is four or five presses in 12 or 13 private houses.

The weight block from G1 is interesting, however, since it may be Archaic in date. It consists of a large boulder with two broken projections that may once have been part of cuttings designed to hold ropes. It is tempting to see here a suspension weight for a beam similar to the one depicted on the famous sixth-century black figure vase painting of an olive press (Forbes and Foxhall 1978: fig. 8). The smaller ashlar weight blocks are a later Classical or early Hellenistic innovation.

The substantial nature of the pressing installations, along with evidence for olive pollen and the local production of transport containers in the Classical, Hellenistic, and Roman periods, points to the use of the press beds for the production of olive oil (Jameson, Runnels, and van Andel 1994: Chap. 6; Runnels and Hansen 1986; van Andel and Runnels 1987: 101–17).

Rotary Olive Mills or Crushers: the Trapetum

The *trapetum* is a rotary olive mill consisting of two principal parts: the *orbis* is a wheel turned on an axle about a central pivot or column (*miliarium*) within a *mortarium*, or basin, to crush olives before pressing out the oil (Fig. 97). The trapetum belongs primarily to the Roman period. Possible trapetum fragments from B78 (Fig. 115) and E7 may be Hellenistic (Table 5.37), but the fragment from B78 is not certainly a mortarium (it may be part of a mortar), and there are Roman sherds in small quantities at E7 in addition to the Hellenistic materials. Trapetum parts were reused in later times (e.g. B5, B107, and D14) and were moved from their original sites, destroying their contex-

Table 5.37. Historical-Period Olive Crushing and Pressing Equipment: Trapeta, by Site and Period

Site	Number	Date Range
B5	1	orbis, Frankish chapel, re-used?
B78	1	mortarium? Late Classical-Early Hellenistic
B91	2	mortaria, Early to Late Roman
B107	1	mortarium, re-used
C11	2	mortarium and orbis, Late Roman?
D14	1	mortarium, re-used
E7	1	mortarium, Late Classical-Early Hellenistic?
E12	1	mortarium, Late Roman
E19	1	mortarium, re-used
E26	1	orbis, Late Roman
E45	1	mortarium, probably Late Roman
F2	1	mortarium, Late Roman
G12	1	mortarium, Frankish, perhaps re-used?
Total	15	

Table 5.38. Historical-Period Trapeta, by Site and Material (Dimensions in Meters)

Site	Material	Diameter	Height	Rim Thickness
MORTARIA				
B91	conglomerate	1.36	0.70	0.24
B107	limestone	1.37	0.97	
D14	andesite	0.87	0.36	0.06
E7	conglomerate	0.92		0.09
E12	limestone	1.50	0.85	0.15
E19	andesite	1.38	0.40	0.14
E45	NA	0.90	0.30	
F2	andesite	1.50	0.85	
G12	andesite	0.98	0.31	
X (large)		1.42	0.75	
X (small)		0.92	0.32	
ORBES				
B5	conglomerate	0.57		0.11
C11	NA	0.40		0.14
E26	andesite	0.52		0.14

tual associations. One-third of the trapeta, however, are associated clearly with Roman sites. The existence of late Hellenistic-early Roman/Greek trapeta, of for example the second or first century B.C., and trapetum and trapetum orbes dating to the first century A.D. at Knossos (Runnels 1981: 132–34; Warren 1988; see also Forbes and Foxhall 1978) suggests that the trapetum was in use by the Hellenistic period. The trapetum is not found at Halieis, however, and the introduction of the trapetum to the Southern Argolid must have occurred after the abandonment of that city in ca. 280 B.C. It is perhaps significant that the earliest Argolid trapeta are found on sites (B78, B91, and E7) in the territory of Hermion that continued to be occupied in the later Hellenistic period after the abandonment of Halieis.

The trapetum has only one known use, to crush olives for pressing, and the presence of this machine, which represents a considerable capital investment, is an indication of a high level of olive-oil production. The large number of specimens proves that the trapetum was common on the large estates and small farmsteads of the Roman period. Something of the scale of the investment involved may be judged from the size. The mortarium came in two sizes, respectively around 0.92 m and 1.42 m in diameter (Table 5.38), and could weigh several tons. The orbes were 0.40–

0.57 m in diameter. More than one center of production is suggested by the variety of materials used in their manufacture, which includes limestone, conglomerate, and Saronic Gulf–type andesite (Table 5.38).

Celts

Ground and polished celts, i.e. stone axes and adzes, are very rare in the Southern Argolid. Only four specimens were collected (Tables 5.39 and 5.40). Two celts, one a miniature, were found on a Final Neolithic site (C29; Fig. 116). A battered handstone from the same site may be a recycled celt, but no trace of a bit was preserved (Fig. 106). Another miniature celt comes from an Early Helladic site (F4; Fig. 116). A fourth possible celt was picked up on C33, a Hellenistic site (Fig. 107). The celt from C33 may have been brought from C29, which is less than 300 m away, and there is evidence that prehistoric celts were often recycled in Classical antiquity (e.g. Theocharis 1973: fig. 240).

Large and small celts of the same type as those found in the survey are numerous in the later Neolithic deposits at Franchthi Cave (S. Diamant, personal communication, 1988). There can be little doubt that the survey celts are all Late or Final Neolithic, and it is highly unlikely that celts were made in the historic period. The miniature celt on F4 may have been picked up at Franchthi Cave, which is a 10-minute walk from the site, but it is possible that celts were still manufactured into the beginning of the Early Bronze Age.

Nothing certain can be said about the four celts in the survey collection. The two miniature celts probably served as bits for small tools, perhaps chisels, rather than as axes. The two larger celts are

Table 5.39. Prehistoric Celts, by Site and Period

Site	Number	Description	Date Range
C29	2	one miniature	Final Neolithic
C33	1	bit preserved	"Hellenistic"
F4	1	miniature	Early Helladic II
Total	4		

Table 5.40. Prehistoric Celts, by Site and Material
(Dimensions in Meters)

Site	Material	Length	Width	Thickness
C29	greenstone	0.06	0.04	0.03
	greenstone	0.02	0.02	0.01
C33	igneous porphyry	0.10	0.05	0.03
F4	greenstone	0.04	0.02	0.01

Table 5.41. Ayios Kosmas-type Mortars, by Site and Period

Site	Number	Description	Date range
A6	3	Ayios Kosmas-type	EH I-II
A33	1	Ayios Kosmas-type	EH I-II
C11	1	Ayios Kosmas-type	EH I-II?
F2	1	Ayios Kosmas-type	EH I-II?
F32	6	Ayios Kosmas-type	EH I-II?
Total	12		

Table 5.42. Mortars and Other Vessels, by Site and Period

Site	Number	Description	Date
A56	1	perirrhanterion	Classical, LR, reused?
B4	1	mortar	LR
B21	1	tripod mortar	LH III B-C
C17	1	mortar?	EH I-LR
E74	1	tripod mortar	LH I-III B
F5	1	relief vase	EH II-LH III
G10	1	mortar	Classical
Total	7		

both heavily damaged by percussive impact. The celts may have been damaged from long use as axes or as the bits of digging sticks; alternatively, this damage may be the result of post-depositional forces.

Mortars and Other Vessels

There are several distinct types of artifacts from the survey that may be broadly described, for want of a better term, as stone mortars or vessels. The largest group of vessels, with 12 specimens, has been described as the Ayios Kosmas-type mortar, and it belongs to the EH I-II period (Table 5.41). The Ayios Kosmas-type mortar has been discussed in detail elsewhere, and we have nothing new to add here, except to say that there is no evidence for the source of these mortars (Runnels 1988b). They are of a dark-gray, fine-grained basaltic andesite that may be from Santorini or Melos (Williams-Thorpe, personal communication, 1987), but this is an as yet untested hypothesis.

Another type of vessel is the Mycenaean tripod mortar (Tables 5.42 and 5.43). Two specimens were found, on sites B21 (Fig. 114) and E74. This kind of mortar is common in Cyprus, Crete, and the Cycladic islands, and on the mainland of Greece, in the Middle and Late Bronze Age (Runnels

1981: 107–8, 1988b: 269–70). The two specimens from the survey are from the earlier and later parts of the Late Helladic period, but they are too fragmentary to be used for drawing any conclusions. It should be noted, however, that they are both made of Saronic Gulf-type andesite, and there may have been a production site for these mortars on one of the islands there.

Three mortars of Saronic Gulf-type andesite were found on sites that range in date from the Early Bronze Age to the Late Roman period (Fig. 115; B4, C17, and G10). These mortars are simple stone bowls. The large mortar from G10 (Fig. 115), a Classical lookout or fortification in the mountains north of Iliokastro, must have served for the pounding of barley or wheat to supply the garrison at this place, a function that is attested in Classical sources (Runnels 1988b, note 17).

The marble fragment from A56 appears to be from a perrirhanterion, a ritual ablution table of the Classical period that may have been reused at this site. Nothing can be ascertained from this single specimen.

One fragment of talc with relief decoration may be from a Mycenaean vase (Fig. 116). It was found on the acropolis at Fournoi (F5) with rich deposits of late Middle Helladic and all phases of the Late Helladic. The original shape of the artifact that produced this fragmentary object has not been reconstructed, and we have found no parallels in published material. The design is consistent with a Late Helladic III date. The finding of a fragment of a valuable prestige artifact at F5 reinforces the conclusion that this site was the center of an important MH and LH settlement in the Fournoi Valley (Jameson, Runnels, and van Andel 1994: Chap. 6).

Miscellaneous Artifacts

Nine pieces of talc are classified as ornaments (Table 5.44). Small, perforated objects of talc, usually in the form of truncated cones, have often been called spindle whorls or beads (Fig. 117). They may also have been weights of some kind, perhaps for garments (Iakovides 1977). As Iakovides makes clear, the majority of these beads have been found in Late Bronze Age contexts. Talc is a mineral found in the ophiolite nappe of the Southern Argolid (van Andel and Vitaliano 1987), and the beads from the survey could have been made locally. The contexts of the survey beads range from the Mesolithic to the Archaic period, but these contexts are not secure. The two truncated con-

Table 5.43. Mortars and Other Vessels, by Site and Material
(Dimensions in Meters)

Site	N	Material	Description	Length	Width	Thickness
A56	1	marble	perirrhanterion	0.24	0.05	0.06
B4	1	andesite	mortar	0.15	0.07	
B21	1	andesite	tripod mortar	0.12	0.11	0.08
C17	1	andesite	mortar?	0.08	0.06	0.07
E74	1	andesite	tripod mortar	0.11	0.11	0.07
F5	1	talc	relief vase?	0.03	0.02	0.01
G10	1	andesite	mortar	0.35	0.29	
Total	7					

Table 5.44. Ornaments, by Site, Material, and Period (Dimensions in Meters)

Site	Length	Width	Type	Date range
		TALC BEADS AND OTHER ARTIFACTS		
A9	0.015	0.014	truncated cone	EH I-II, G-A
B21	0.014	0.019	truncated cone	LH IIIB-C
B21	0.021	0.029	truncated cone	LH IIIB-C
C25	0.010	0.020	truncated cone	FN
E9	0.024	0.015	biconical cone	EH I-LG
F4	0.015	0.023	truncated cone	EH II, LH, A-H
F4	0.070	0.020	perforated disk	EH II, LH, A-H
F35	0.012	0.008	worked fragment	Mesolithic?
F48	0.024	0.020	perforated fragment	MB-F
		PERFORATED GREENSTONE PEBBLE		
C29	0.030	0.020	pendant	Final Neolithic

ical beads from B21 (Fig. 117) appear to be Late Helladic IIIB-C, and are typical examples of Mycenaean beads. The Argolid specimens contribute nothing to an understanding of the function of these beads.

A greenstone pebble with an incomplete perforation was perhaps intended to be a pendant. The ornament was found on the Final Neolithic site of C29 (Fig. 116), and it closely resembles perforated pebbles of the Upper Mesolithic from Franchthi Cave across Koiladha Bay (Jacobsen 1976: 83; Theocharis 1973: fig. 244). The piece from C29 is unique in the collection from the survey, and may be a Mesolithic ornament that was picked up in antiquity and recycled.

Turning to the other miscellaneous stone artifacts, there are some 32 small stone fragments that do not preserve any definite form (e.g. Fig. 116, F32; Table 5.45). They were for the most part recognized in the field by the distinctive character of their raw material, often andesite or igneous greenstone. These raw materials were readily detected as stones foreign to a site, but for the most part these fragments preserve no more than a small trace of a worked or utilized surface. Many of the fragments of andesite, Rema stone, and greenstone are probably parts of saddle querns or handstones that have been broken up by post-depositional forces. The existence of a piece of andesite or other foreign stone on an isolated site may be an indication that a quern or other millstone was once employed at that place, but apart from this simple observation, these fragmentary objects tell us little.

Conclusions: Nonflaked Lithic Artifacts

The lithic artifacts found in the course of the survey may be used to deepen our understanding of the ancient economy of this region. They are also useful for tracing the many changes in lithic technology that occurred before the modern period.

The prehistoric lithic artifacts of the Final Neolithic and the Bronze Age include saddle querns, handstones, and two different types of household mortar. These tools are associated, as far as we know, with the grinding of grain, other plants, and inorganic materials such as salt. No implements could be attributed to the pressing of olive oil, and this finding supports the conclusion that olive cultivation must have played little part in the economy of the Southern Argolid before Classical antiquity (Jameson, Runnels, and van Andel 1994: Chap. 6; Runnels and Hansen 1986). Saddle querns continue in use down to the Hellenistic period, providing, we assume, an inexpensive and traditional means of grinding grain for daily use in small households. The principal difference between prehistoric and historic saddle querns is in their method of manufacture. Historic saddle querns were carefully hammer-dressed at distant quarries before they were exported.

Several distinct changes in milling technology were noted in the late Classical Southern Argolid. Pressing equipment for the production of olive oil, in the form of press beds and weight blocks, makes its appearance by the end of the Archaic period. Hopper mills, a specialized form of the saddle quern for milling bread flour, were also introduced by the beginning of the Classical period. The hopper mills went out of use before the Roman period, but the press beds were used throughout the historical era. The discovery of pressing installations at the site of Halieis and on numerous late Classical and early Hellenistic farmsteads found by the survey is the main evidence for proposing the expansion of olive arboriculture in the Southern Argolid. Once started, this production would be part of the Argolid economy down to the end of the Roman period in the seventh century A.D.

Another major innovation was the introduction of rotary querns and the rotary olive mill (trapetum), in the late Hellenistic and the early Roman periods. Rotary motion in milling was an important innovation in the Mediterranean world, and later in Europe, because it would ultimately permit the application of inanimate sources of power, namely water and wind, to milling. The late appearance of rotary querns and trapeta in the Southern Argolid is an indication that these new forms of

Table 5.45. Unidentified Fragments of Other Stones, by Material and Site

Material	Number	Site	Material	Number	Site
Hematite	2	A33	Andesite	1	C33
	1	B38		1	E6
	1	C8		1	F4
	1	A23		1	F32
	1	A17		1	F57
	3	E3		1	G31
	1	E5	Greenstone	1	B24
	1	E52		1	B38
	1	E63		1	C29
	1	F49	Rema Stone	1	A9
	2	G2	Limestone	1	C17
	1	G4	Slate	1	B73
	2	G5	Sandstone	1	F32
			Marble	1	A15

mills were brought to Greece from the west, most probably by the Roman legions that campaigned in the eastern Mediterranean during the first century B.C., under Sulla, Pompey, Caesar, and Antony (Peacock 1986; Runnels 1990).

Rotary querns are the only form of mill recorded from late Medieval sites (ninth through fifteenth centuries). Olive-oil presses are notably absent, and it is tempting to use these very limited data as additional evidence that the Middle Byzantine return to the Southern Argolid was based upon arable agriculture rather than on olive arboriculture (Runnels and van Andel 1987).

The pattern of exploitation of raw materials from the Neolithic to the Medieval period is also of interest. Andesite for millstones was imported from the Saronic Gulf in the Neolithic period, and in the Bronze Age, the period for which we have the greatest evidence in the Argolid, andesite was the principal raw material for saddle querns and mortars. At least two different kinds of andesite were being imported from as yet unknown sources. The Ayios Kosmas-type mortars in the Early Bronze Age were manufactured by skilled craftsmen and imported to the Argolid as finished implements. This is the first evidence for the specialized production of a stone tool other than flaked-stone artifacts. By the Archaic period, saddle querns were being manufactured by specialized craftsmen at distant quarries, and hopper mills, rotary querns, and trapeta would follow in the Hellenistic and early Roman periods. Different sources of andesite, possibly including Santorini and Nisyros, came into play in the Hellenistic period, and were the dominant sources in the Roman period. Although it is clear that the settlements in the Southern Argolid participated in large trade networks in the Greco-Roman period, the scale and organization of these networks remain to be studied in the same detail as are those in the western Mediterranean (Peacock 1980; Williams-Thorpe 1988).

The last major change in lithic technology occurred in the Middle Byzantine-Frankish period (ninth through fourteenth centuries). The quarries for Rema stone in Melos were opened sometime in this period. The Roman millstone quarries and factories were either lost or forgotten, and Rema stone became the only raw material for the manufacture of rotary querns and other millstones by the eighteenth century.

Watermills are known in Greece in the Late Roman period, and the windmill was introduced to Greece via the Cyclades in the Frankish period (Runnels 1981: 135–36; Vaos and Nomikos 1975). The development of the latter must have prompted the search for a suitable source of stone for millstones, and the hard but lightweight stone from Rema in Melos was the best material, because it was not too heavy to be driven by the mills' sails. Once the quarries were opened, the manufacture of rotary querns developed as a spin-off of the production of large millstones (Runnels 1981: 235–38). Owing to the importance of the introduction of windmills and watermills into the technological repertoire, a careful search was made on every site for pieces of stone that could be identified as being parts of millstones for these kinds of mills. No evidence for watermills before the eighteenth and nineteenth centuries was found, and only a single site, B14 near Kranidhi, is a candidate for an early windmill (Jameson, Runnels, and van Andel 1994: Appendix 1). This site consists of a ruined foundation for a windmill that dates to the thirteenth or fourteenth century. Many small pieces of Rema stone, presumably from a destroyed millstone, were found in the debris of this structure. There are many dilapidated windmills of the nineteenth and twentieth centuries in this same area, and the rarity of earlier ruins may be explained by the continuous rebuilding of windmills on favorable spots.

Many questions about lithic technology remain to be answered, but the utility of collecting stone tools of all kinds from surface sites has been demonstrated. Regrettably, stone tools are often not systematically collected even in controlled excavations of stratified deposits.

The great number of tools that were found, and the numerous types that are documented, together illustrate the usefulness of this class of artifact. The querns and pressing implements provide important clues for interpreting the functions of individual sites, and for reconstructing the economic structure of whole periods. The study of the raw materials opens up new perspectives on trade patterns in the prehistoric and historic eras; and the study of craft specialization, as it is revealed in the forms and methods of manufacture of the artifacts, is only just beginning. The collection of all stone artifacts in the course of fieldwalking when conducting regional surveys, whether or not these artifacts are associated with sites or other findspots, is imperative for the detailed reconstruction and interpretation of the history of a region.

Conclusions

Curtis Runnels, Daniel J. Pullen, and Susan Langdon

The abundance and diversity of the artifacts found in the Southern Argolid survey amply justify the attention given them in these pages. Approximately 21,000 artifacts from over 100 separate sites are described in this volume. In our view, the wealth of data offered in these pages demonstrates conclusively that surface sites, when properly investigated, can be as informative as excavated sites for archaeological interpretations on a regional scale. It is important to make note of the last part of this statement. Though it must be admitted that excavation is required to give a detailed picture of an individual archaeological site, the results of excavation at a single site are inadequate to address questions intended to encompass an entire region, even one as small as the Southern Argolid. Moreover, it is clear that many of the locations that are conventionally called "sites" are something other than habitations (i.e. towns, villages, etc.). Many of the Argolid sites are "special-purpose" sites that served as farmers' huts, storehouses, country shrines, dumps, animal folds, and the like. The investigation of these humble and often ephemeral vestiges of human activity in the landscape gives a clear picture of the extent and variety of human activity that took place in the countryside away from the main settlements.

Isolated artifacts and full assemblages (collections of artifacts from individual sites) were collected from sites in all parts of the Southern Argolid, and it is not an exaggeration to say that *scores* of sites would have required *full* excavation in order to provide samples on a scale comparable to those considered here. This advantage is often overlooked by the critics of regional surveys. They draw attention to the lack of stratigraphic control for materials collected from the surface, and make the unwarranted inference that surface materials are less closely dated, or somehow less useful for interpretation, than materials from excavations. We have endeavored to show that many of the single-period surface sites can be dated with confidence, especially where careful, systematic surface collection permitted us to acquire varied artifact assemblages from many sites of the same period. The quantities and the preservation of the materials presented in this volume compare favorably with materials obtained from many published excavations, and we are prepared to challenge the critics of regional surveys. We claim that, from the point of view of cost, the most economical way to adequately explore an entire region is by systematic, intensive surface survey. Equally important to a survey project, when possible, is the subsequent problem-oriented excavation of sites to clarify points of stratigraphy, date, and function. Owing to a lack of available permits, the Argolid survey was not able to conclude with a campaign of testing to confirm some of our findings through small test excavations. We suggest that long-term survey projects in the future should include a program of test excavation, and we hope that the present policies of administration of archaeological work in Greece can be modified to accommodate this scientific objective.

An important goal in archaeology is the establishment of archaeological cultures. The identification of such cultures, which were defined by V. Gordon Childe as recurrent assemblages of archaeological types, presupposes the investigation of numerous sites and large numbers of cultural materials, but the increasing investments of time and money that are necessary for the study of individual sites through excavation are an obstacle to the identification of archaeological cultures. Regional surveys are a more effective method of studying the large numbers of artifacts and sites that are essential to the process of classifying archaeological cultures, which are fundamental building blocks for archaeological interpretations.

To this end, it is our hope that the publication of these artifacts will serve to stimulate the collection and publication of surface artifacts. Much information was gathered about this isolated and historically little-known area with no great investment of time in the field and little commitment to long-term storage and conservation of the artifacts. An additional benefit of working with surface artifacts is that, although they are usually badly eroded or decayed, they are stable after years of exposure, and the storage of such artifacts presents few problems.

The artifacts collected during the survey were recovered from sites with very different functions spanning a period of more than 50,000 years. Some conclusions based on these finds are now possible. One example that will serve to illustrate this point is the study of the Early Helladic (EH) period in the Southern Argolid (ca. 3100–2100 B.C.). The first phase of this period, Early Helladic I (EH I), is perhaps more important for our understanding of the development of the Early Bronze Age than was previously recognized. There are many sites, some of them relatively large, with Early Helladic I material. Early Helladic I sites are very poorly known from excavations, and the EH I surface sites enrich the archaeological record for this period. It is clear that the expansion of settlement, and the differentiation of sites into different categories based upon function, is a process that began in EH I, although this process continued until the end of Early Helladic II. In addition, the lack of close parallels in other regions for the EH I pottery found in the Southern Argolid emphasizes the relative isolation of the Southern Argolid in this period, and encourages renewed interest in the ceramic similarities among widely separated regions that do exist in the ensuing Early Helladic II. Pullen has shown that the EH II period in the Southern Argolid, which is otherwise unknown from excavation, witnessed a substantial period of settlement growth, with some sites attaining the size and characteristics of small towns. More pottery was produced in this period, and from a larger number of sites, than from any other period before Classical times, perhaps indicating the existence of a sizable population and a successful economy. The EH II pottery in the Southern Argolid resembles that of the Argive plain and Corinthia, but shows even greater affinities with that of the Saronic Gulf and Attica, suggesting close ties with these regions. It was also possible to distinguish the local pottery production of the Southern Argolid. Although the shapes or decoration of the local pottery differed only in small ways from those of the pottery of neighboring regions, this finding suggests that the Southern Argolid was politically independent from other regions at a time when regional interdependence is increasingly noticeable to some scholars (e.g. Renfrew 1972). These conclusions are reinforced by the Early Helladic lithic artifacts. Kardulias and Runnels show that tool types and raw materials, although they are similar to those found on sites in adjacent regions (e.g. Lerna in the Argive plain), reflect easily recognized regional traditions. Melian obsidian is used for the flaked-stone artifacts, and similar techniques are used by local flintknappers, but an entirely different industry was forming, on the basis of tool types that are only infrequently seen outside of the region. A large assemblage of obsidian at one of the Early Helladic II sites is important evidence for the specialized production of lithic artifacts under the control of local elites. Although excavations in Early Helladic sites in other regions have produced evidence of specialized production, the survey has demonstrated the existence of specialized production in the Southern Argolid from evidence available on the surface. This evidence is crucial for the reconstruction of Early Bronze Age trade networks on a regional scale. The nonflaked lithics, particularly the Ayios Kosmas-type mortar, serve to link the Southern Argolid with the islands of the Saronic Gulf and Attica (Runnels 1988a), which neatly confirms the inferences drawn from the study of the pottery.

Among the other important finds from the Early Helladic II sites are many fragments of decorated terra-cotta hearth rims. The hearths represented by these rims were fixed features in EH II houses, and these rims are strong proof for the existence of domestic structures on several of the Southern Argolid sites. Terra-cotta rooftiles in considerable number were also identified on several of the surface sites. These artifacts are poorly known from excavations, and the sample from the survey takes on added significance as a consequence. These rooftiles are perhaps indicators of substantial roofed structures in the EH II period. The presence of such structures on sites otherwise having indications of large size, sites that in addition have restricted access to imported materials and artifacts, provides a basis for the classification of the surface sites into a hierarchy of settlement types (Jameson, Runnels, and van Andel 1994: Chap. 6).

The contribution of surface artifacts and assemblages to regional studies is also illustrated by the analysis of the Middle Helladic (MH) pottery by Nordquist. She demonstrates that MH sites in the Southern Argolid are to be assigned to the end of the period, and this finding suggests that the suspected hiatus of occupation that followed the end of the EH II period in the Argolid was of long duration, perhaps several centuries, and that recovery in the Southern Argolid was a protracted process. This observation serves to support the widely accepted picture of an underpopulated and economically depressed Greece in the Middle Helladic period. Recent research by members of the Nemea Valley Archaeological Project has shown that the latest phases of the Middle Helladic period and the earliest phases of the Mycenaean period (Late Helladic I-II) were marked there also by the establishment of new settlements in remote rural areas that had been previously underpopulated (J. Wright and J. Rutter, personal communication, 1989). The evidence from the Southern Argolid for a hiatus in the Middle Helladic period, followed by the foundation of new settlements immediately before the era of the Shaft Graves at Mycenae, is a valuable addition to the growing body of data necessary for our understanding of the origins of Mycenaean civilization.

Other useful results were obtained for the historic periods. In her study of the pottery, Langdon showed that the Southern Argolid maintained close cultural ties with Argos at the head of the Argolic Gulf during the Early Iron Age and the Geometric period. Imports from Attica and the Cyclades were present from Protogeometric through Middle Geometric times, and in fact seem to have continued steadily and perhaps increased during the Late Geometric period, a finding directly contrary to that in the Argive plain. Although imports into the plain were almost exclusively Corinthian products, this category is represented in the Southern Argolid by only one or two sherds. Moreover, connections with sites in the Argolid other than Argos were more active than ever. As discussed above, independent pottery workshops have been distinguished in Tiryns, Asine, Mycenae, and even Dendra, examples from all of which can be documented in the survey pottery. There is also secure evidence for the local production of pottery during the Geometric period, particularly in the second half of the Late Geometric through Subgeometric periods. Recent studies have suggested that in the Late Geometric, Argos began to dominate the central plain. The most overt expression of this new aggressive spirit may have been the crushing of the town of Asine by Argos ca. 710 B.C., which Pausanias relates (II.36.4–5) was in retaliation for Asine's assistance to Spartan invaders into the Argolid. The historical reality of this eighth-century invasion has been questioned, and the survey has not produced further evidence of the very small amount of Laconian pottery known from the Argolid. It must be recalled yet again that the most important ingredient in the reconstruction of the Southern Argolid is lacking: the record of Geometric settlement at Halieis, which in the Late Geometric must have been one of the major sites in the region. If the evidence of the survey pottery does indeed support a picture of strengthened ties among the smaller Argive towns, it may add to our understanding of what motivated such acts of aggression from Argos.

By the opening of the seventh century, there is a marked decrease in pottery production in the Argive plain, accompanied by a greater reliance on imported, particularly Corinthian, wares. Corresponding to this sign of cultural decline is evidence not only for decreased settlement activity, but for the movement of population out of the central plain. In the eastern Argolid the atmosphere of self-sufficiency suggested by the presence of local pottery production, and perhaps a consolidation of sites in the seventh century, reminds us of traditional stories of immigrants from the Argive plain arriving in the Southern Argolid (Jameson, Runnels, and van Andel 1994: Chap. 2) in the eighth and seventh centuries B.C.

The study of the historic periods has also benefited from the analysis of the lithic artifacts. It was long thought that the use of flaked-stone tools of obsidian and flint died out with the introduction of metal tools and weapons at the beginning of the Bronze Age. But finds of lithic artifacts have been made occasionally on historic-period sites, suggesting that their use continued long after the Bronze Age. Kardulias and Runnels note that the numerous small sites investigated in the course of the survey, many of which are interpreted as individual farmsteads, have produced flaked-stone tools that demonstrate clearly the extensive use of such artifacts in the Greek and Roman periods.

The origin of rotary mills in the historical period has also been a vexing question in Mediterranean archaeology. Evidence for rotary mills has been lacking from excavations of stratified sites in Greece, and the sample of rotary mills in Greece has scarcely changed since the first synthesis on the subject was prepared by Moritz (1958). The recovery of Roman period rotary querns in the Southern Argolid, therefore, is significant. The 29 specimens that were collected constitute the largest sample of rotary querns (handmills) in Greece. This large sample is sufficient to establish a typology and chronology for rotary querns, and it can be shown that querns were introduced into this area in the first century B.C. or later, thus establishing an important *terminus ante quem* for the introduction of rotary milling to Greece. The equally vexing question of the introduction of the trapetum, the Roman olive-crushing mill, is also addressed. The Roman olive mill was introduced into the Southern Argolid in the second century B.C., and not invented, as has sometimes been claimed, by the Greeks in the fifth century B.C.

A further benefit of the analysis of the lithic artifacts is the better understanding of the use of raw materials in different periods. Obsidian was procured directly from the quarries in Melos in the Bronze Age, and the concentration of working debris at Fournoi (F32) points to the centralized control of the production and distribution of obsidian tools once the raw material reached the mainland. Regional trade networks were controlled by higher-order centers in the settlement system, and it was in part from this control that the elites residing at these centers derived their influence and power.

The trade in raw materials included Aigina, as a source of andesite for querns in the Bronze Age, and Aigina and Nisyros together were evidently sites of specialized quern manufacturing in the Greek and Roman periods. Melos was also the dominant supplier of querns and millstones of the distinctive white Rema stone in the late Medieval and early Modern periods. The full implications of the shifting pattern of trade and demand for raw materials have yet to be explored, but the survey data demonstrate that the signatures of such past activities are to be read on the surface today.

In this volume we have attempted to elucidate the patterns of production and exchange, of trade and cultural communication, and of intraregional interaction that are revealed by comparisons within the complete corpus of our artifactual assemblages, from all of the sites that we investigated. Traditional approaches to archaeological interpretation have focused on the finds from individual sites that have been excavated, while in other cases artifacts and assemblages from widely separated excavations are compared. By contrast, we have been able to compare the assemblages from scores of sites closely associated in space and in time, and have been able to extend our conclusions from the level of the isolated, individual site to an entire region. We believe that this volume amply demonstrates both the value of archaeological surveys for regional problems and the value of studying and publishing survey artifacts and assemblages.

Appendixes

Pottery Catalogue

Descriptions of individual ceramic objects from all periods covered by Chapters 1–4 are presented here in Appendix 1 as catalogue entries. General discussions of fabrics, shapes, and decoration are found in the pertinent chronological chapters, where specific references to items listed here in the catalogue are denoted by **boldfaced** catalogue numbers; conversely, items not discussed in the text do not carry catalogue numbers here.

The catalogue entries for all periods are presented in a standard manner, though the entries for the Mycenaean pottery of Chapter 3 are more schematic in order to conform more closely to the standard reporting style used by other Mycenaean specialists. All entries have on their first line a **boldfaced** catalogue number, an object title (generally the specific shape), and references to such illustrations as are given at the end of the volume. The original AEP inventory number is found in parentheses, followed by the portion of the object preserved and its dimensions, expressed in meters. The description of the fabric for the pottery treated in Chapters 1, 2, and 4 includes the relative coarseness of the inclusions (e.g. fine, medium, medium-coarse, and coarse); information about the size, shape, color, and/or type of inclusions, based on macroscopic inspection; and color name, as determined by the Munsell Soil Color Charts (1975 edition). The fabric of the Mycenaean pottery of Chapter 3 is briefly described by color and by degree of coarseness only when not of the fineness characteristic of Mycenaean fabrics. Although all but a few of the objects in the catalogue are illustrated by line drawings of the profile, each catalogue entry describes features of the shape of that object as represented by the sherd, features that are distinctive or unusual for that shape. The Mycenaean pottery of Chapter 3 is described in terms of its standard Furumark (1941a, 1941b) shape number (e.g. FS 279 for the krater shape). Descriptions of the surface treatments are given next, since many surface treatments are difficult to illustrate; this problem is exacerbated by the usually poor condition of the surfaces of the objects. References to comparanda and other parallels have been kept to a minimum and are usually presented only to substantiate the identification of unusual pieces, or pieces difficult to identify. The precise dating of an object concludes its entry.

MIDDLE NEOLITHIC

1   PEDESTALED? BOWL   Fig. 1
(E14-A-1) Rim. D. 0.32, Max. pres. W. 0.045, Th. 0.005. Fine fabric; few lime inclusions; evenly fired, 2.5YR 6/6 (light red). Pedestaled bowl or fruitstand, straight wall sloping out, slightly flattened lip. Orange urfirnis paint, burnished. Weinberg 1937: 501 for shape.
Middle Neolithic.

2   PEDESTALED BOWL   Fig. 1
(E14-11) Sherd preserving junction of bowl and pedestal. D. at junction est. 0.16, Max. pres. W. 0.040. Medium fabric; many tiny inclusions, mostly lime; evenly fired, 5YR 6/6 (reddish yellow). Large pedestaled bowl or fruitstand. Exterior black urfirnis, burnished; interior mottled orange/brown-black urfirnis, burnished. Weinberg 1937: 501; Lavezzi 1978: 436 nos. 17-18.
Middle Neolithic.

3   PEDESTALED BOWL   Figs. 1, 118
(E14-1) Pedestal base. D. 0.22, Max. pres. W. 0.065, Th. 0.0068. Medium fabric; small inclusions, some lime; hard, evenly fired, 5YR 6/8 (reddish yellow). Tapering pedestal base with straight sides. Exterior painted orange [2.5YR 6/8 (light red)] urfirnis, vertical scribble burnishing. Weinberg 1937: 501; Lavezzi 1978: 436 nos. 17-18.
Middle Neolithic.

4   CARINATED BOWL   Fig. 1
(E14-9) Rim. D. est. 0.30, Max. pres. W. 0.040. Medium fabric; small inclusions, some lime; evenly fired, 5YR 4/3 (reddish brown). Carinated bowl with outturned rim, forming overlapping ridge on interior, rounded lip. Exterior streaky brown-black urfirnis, highly burnished; interior plain. Weinberg 1937: 501; Holmberg 1944: 51 fig. 52.
Middle Neolithic.

5   PLATE or SHALLOW BOWL   Fig. 1
(E14-7) Rim. D. 0.27, Max. pres. W. 0.07, Th. 0.008-0.009. Medium fabric; small inclusions, mostly lime; unevenly fired, 5YR 6/6 (reddish yellow) to gray core. Plate or shallow bowl with straight sides, bevelled rim. Black-brown urfirnis.
Middle Neolithic.

LATE NEOLITHIC

6   BLACK-BURNISHED CARINATED BOWL   Fig. 1
(G9-10) Rim. D. 0.26, Max. pres. W. 0.075. Semi-coarse fabric; medium to large inclusions, no lime; dark fired, black to 2.5YR 3/2 (dusky red) [core]. Carinated bowl, flaring rim with slight groove on exterior, rounded lip. Heavily burnished to luster. Lavezzi 1978: 436 nos. 20-21.
Late Neolithic.

7   CARINATED BOWL   Fig. 1
(D3-4-2) Rim. D. indet., Max. pres. W. 0.032. Coarse fabric; some medium sized lime inclusions, other irregular angular inclusions; unevenly fired, 5YR 4/2 (dark reddish gray) to 7.5YR 4/2 (dark brown) [core]. Carinated bowl, slightly flaring rim, rounded lip. Heavy horizontal burnishing.
Late Neolithic.

8   PATTERN PAINTED DEEP BOWL?   Figs. 1, 118
(D3-2-6) Rim. D. est. 0.30, Max. pres. W. 0.03. Semifine fabric; few tiny lime inclusions, occasional medium sized inclusions; evenly fired, 7.5YR 7/4 (pink). Deep? bowl, slightly tapering in sides, rim thickened to exterior. Exterior slipped buff, bichrome blotches of paint (black surrounding red ovals); interior slipped red-brown. Lavezzi 1978: 443 no. 44.
Late Neolithic?

9   BOWL   Fig. 1
(E14-A-7) Rim. D. est. 0.23, Max. pres. W. 0.040. Coarse fabric; medium sized inclusions, mostly lime; unevenly fired, 7.5YR 6/4 (light brown) to gray core. Flaring bowl with bevelled lip. Exterior and lip burnished; interior plain?
Late Neolithic?

10   MATT PAINTED LARGE VESSEL   Fig. 118
(D3-2-10) Body. Max. pres. W. 0.071, Max. pres. H. 0.078, Th. 0.013. Coarse fabric; much small lime and quartz inclusions; unevenly fired, 5YR 6/6 (reddish yellow) to 7.5YR-N6/0 (gray) [core]. Large open? vessel. Exterior uneven vertical matt brown stripes with uneven horizontal burnishing over; interior plain.
Late Neolithic.

11   HANDLE   Fig. 1
(E14-A-6) Handle frag. Max. pres. W. 0.28, Max. pres. L. 0.031, Th. 0.009. Coarse fabric; small and medium sized inclusions, mostly lime; unevenly fired, 2.5YR 5/6 (red) to 5YR 6/4 (light reddish brown) [core]. Small loop handle, probably vertical. Burnished.
Late Neolithic?

FINAL NEOLITHIC

12   SPREADING BOWL   Fig. 1
(G9-5-19) Rim. D. est. 0.20, Th. 0.0045. Semicoarse fabric; small to medium inclusions, no lime; unevenly fired, 5YR 6/8 (reddish yellow) to gray core. Spreading straight wall, bevelled lip. Burnished.
Final Neolithic.

13   SPREADING BOWL   Fig. 1
(G9-1-17) Rim. D. est. 0.35, Max. pres. W. 0.04, Th. 0.011. Semicoarse fabric; many small to medium inclusions, little lime; unevenly fired, 5YR 6/6 (reddish yellow) to gray core. Spreading straight wall, rounded lip. Slipped? burnished?
Final Neolithic.

14   SPREADING BOWL   Figs. 1, 118
(A33-3-7) Rim. D. est. 0.30, Max. pres. W. 0.043, Th. 0.008. Semicoarse fabric; small to large inclusions, little lime; unevenly fired, 5YR 6/4 (light reddish brown) to 10R 5/8 (red). Spreading straight wall, flat lip; below lip narrow horizontal taenia; angled narrow taenia tangential to bottom of horizontal taenia. Interior finished smooth.
Final Neolithic.

15   CARINATED BOWL   Fig. 1
(C15-A-23) Rim. D. indet., Max. pres. W. 0.05, Th. 0.005. Medium fabric; little lime; unevenly fired, 2.5YR 5/8 (red) to 5YR 4/2 (dark reddish gray) [core]. Curving wall with slight carination, slightly flaring rim, pointed lip. Plain.
Final Neolithic.

16   INCURVING BOWL   Figs. 1, 118
(B43-ALL-2-3) Rim. D. 0.27, Max. pres. W. 0.054, Th. 0.007. Semifine to medium fabric; small to few medium inclusions, no lime; unevenly fired, 10R 5/6 (red) to black. Incurving wall, slightly flattened lip; four narrow bands of taenia. Plain.
Final Neolithic.

17   INCURVING BOWL WITH DOUBLE HORNED LUG
                                           Figs. 2, 118
(G9-3) Rim with lug. D. est. 0.28, Max. pres. W. 0.10, Th. 0.011. Coarse fabric; many large inclusions, including lime; evenly fired 2.5YR 4-5/6 (red). Large bowl, incurving sides, rounded lip; approx. 0.015 below lip, large lug 0.09 wide with two upturned protuberances 0.03 high. Rough surfaces. Cf. **51**.
Final Neolithic.

18   DEEP BOWL   Fig. 2
(B53-3-1) Rim. D. 0.26, Max. pres. W. 0.002, Th. 0.011. Medium fabric; small to medium inclusions, no lime; unevenly fired, 2.5YR 6/8 (light red) to 7.5YR 4/2 (brown-dark brown) [core]. Straight wall tapering in slightly, lip bevelled to interior; two horizontal ridges, one just below lip, second 0.017 below lip. Interior red slipped, burnished.
Final Neolithic to Early Helladic I.

19   DEEP BOWL   Fig. 2
(G9-2) Rim. D. est. 0.29, Max. pres. W. 0.045, Th. 0.010. Semicoarse fabric; small to medium inclusions, some lime; unevenly fired, 2.5-5YR 5/6 (red-yellowish red) to gray core. Straight wall tapering in, flattened lip. Burnished.
Final Neolithic.

20   DEEP BOWL OR HOLE-MOUTH JAR   Fig. 2
(G9-5-28) Rim. D. est. 0.25, Max. pres. W. 0.055, Th. 0.011. Semicoarse fabric; medium to large inclusions, no lime; unevenly fired, 10R 5/8 (red) to gray core. Slightly tapering straight wall, flat lip. Burnished.
Final Neolithic.

21   DEEP BOWL   Fig. 2
(D3-1-1) Rim. D. est. 0.44, Max. pres. W. 0.040. Semicoarse fabric; small to medium sized lime inclusions; unevenly fired, 7.5YR 6/4 (light brown) to 7.5YR 5/0 (gray) [core]. Deep bowl? (orientation not certain). Exterior: above heavily burnished surface, raised band approx. 0.057 wide below lip with three rows of unevenly placed wet finger impressions; Interior: smoothed with some burnishing strokes evident.
Final Neolithic?

22   PIERCED OPEN? VESSEL   Fig. 2
(G9-15) Rim, exterior (?) surface not preserved. D. indet., Max. pres. W. 0.06, Th. est. 0.014. Coarse fabric; medium to large inclusions, some lime; unevenly fired, 2.5YR 4/8 (red) to black core. Slightly incurving rim, preserves three holes made before firing just below rounded lip. Surfaces rough (due to preservation?).
Final Neolithic

23   JAR   Fig. 2
(E7-48) Rim. D. 0.31, Max. pres. W. 0.04, Th. 0.006. Medium fabric; small to medium inclusions, little lime; unevenly fired, 5YR 4/1 (dark gray) to 5YR 3/2 (dark reddish brown) [core]. Sloping shoulder, lip thickened to exterior. Exterior burnished.
Final Neolithic.

24   JAR   Fig. 2
(G9-5-16) Neck, shoulder, and rim just below lip. D. 0.23, Max. pres. W. 0.05, Th. 0.012. Semicoarse fabric; medium to large inclusions, no lime; unevenly fired, 2.5YR 5/8 (red) to gray core. Sloping shoulder, slight groove below lip, forming lip thickened to exterior. Exterior smoothed.
Final Neolithic.

25   COLLARED JAR?   Fig. 2
(G9-1-4) Rim. D. 0.18, Max. pres. W. 0.04, Th. 0.008. Semicoarse fabric; few large, many small to medium inclusions, no lime; unevenly fired, 2.5YR 4/6 (red) to dark core. Incurving wall, outturned lip; two grooves preserved, one just below lip. Slightly burnished?
Final Neolithic.

26   JAR   Fig. 2
(G9-1-1 + 12) Rim and non-joining body. D. est. 0.28, body: Max. pres. W. 0.069, Th. 0.015. Semicoarse fabric; no lime; unevenly fired, 2.5YR 4/8 (red) to 2.5YR 6/8 (light red) to gray core. Incurving body, rim rolled or thickened to exterior; large lug 0.01 high. Burnished. Surface pitted as if organic temper burned out.
Final Neolithic.

27   COLLARED JAR   Fig. 2
(G9-1-2) Rim. D. 0.28, Th. 0.009. Medium fabric; small to medium inclusions, no lime; evenly fired, 2.5YR 5/8 (red). Offset shoulder, vertical collar 0.029 tall with two shallow ridges, thickening to lip. Exterior and lip interior burnished.
Final Neolithic.

28   JAR   Fig. 3
(E4-B-7) Rim. D. 0.32, Max. pres. W. 0.07, Th. 0.008-0.010. Semicoarse fabric; small to medium inclusions, no lime; unevenly fired, 5YR 4/6 (yellowish red) to 5YR 4/2 (dark reddish gray) [core]. Wall continuously curving from shoulder to slightly flaring rim; rounded lip. Exterior smoothed; interior of rim burnished.
Final Neolithic.

29   JAR   Figs. 3, 118
(C13-18) Rim. D. est. 0.36, Max. pres. W. 0.085, Th. 0.009. Semicoarse fabric; small to medium inclusions, no lime; evenly fired, 5YR 3/2 (dark reddish brown). Wall continuously curving into vertical rim thickened below rounded lip; horizontal row of pellets on exterior est. 0.015 below lip. Exterior slipped red, burnished to irregular luster. Franchthi Cave.
Final Neolithic (to Early Helladic I?).

30   JAR (or DEEP BOWL)   Figs. 3, 118
(B39-2) Rim. D. indet., Max. pres. W. 0.055. Semicoarse fabric; medium to large inclusions, no lime; evenly fired, 5YR 3/2 (dark reddish brown). Sloping shoulder to vertical? rim; three plastic ridges: two have finger impressions pressed alternately from top and bottom, third has one finger impression with rest of ridge left plain. Plain.
Final Neolithic.

31   JAR   Fig. 3
(E5-A-19) Rim. D. 0.15, Max. pres. W. 0.052, Th. 0.008. Semicoarse to medium fabric; no lime; unevenly fired, 2.5YR 5/8 (red) to 5YR 3/2 (dark reddish brown) [core]. Slightly flaring rim, flattened lip. Exterior plain; interior very rough.
Final Neolithic.

32   JAR   Fig. 3
(C15-A-43) Rim. D. indet., Max. pres. W. 0.03, Th. 0.009. Medium fabric; some lime; unevenly fired, 5YR 5/8 (yellowish red) to 5YR 4/2 (dark reddish gray) [core]. Thick concave wall, rim curving out, rounded lip. Interior burnished.
Final Neolithic (to Early Helladic I?).

33   JAR?   Fig. 3
(B5-8) Rim. D. indet., Max. pres. W. 0.042, Th. 0.011. Coarse fabric; small to very large inclusions, no lime; unevenly fired, 5YR 4/4 (reddish brown) to 5YR 3/3 (dark reddish brown) [core]. Flaring rim to jar. Plain.
Final Neolithic?

34   JAR (or FLARING BOWL)   Fig. 3
(G9-1-7) Rim. D. indet., Max. pres. W. 0.025, Th. 0.008. Medium fabric; small to medium inclusions, no lime; unevenly fired, 10R 4/8 (red) to gray core. Flaring lip. Exterior cream slip, solid red paint heavily burnished to gloss; interior heavily burnished horizontally to luster.
Final Neolithic.

35   FLAT BASE (to OPEN? VESSEL)   Fig. 3
(C15-A-4) Base. D. 0.12, Th. 0.011. Semicoarse fabric; small to very large inclusions, no lime; unevenly fired, 2.5YR 4/8 (red) to 5YR 3/2 (dark reddish brown) [core]. Large open vessel: flat base rounding up to very splayed wall. Interior burnished.
Final Neolithic.

36   FLAT BASE (to OPEN? VESSEL)   Fig. 3
(C25-3) Base. D. indet., Th. 0.007. Medium fabric; no lime; unevenly fired, 2.5YR 5/8 (red) to 5YR 3/1 (very dark gray) [core]. Flat base, concave sides. Exterior burnished, interior worn.
Final Neolithic.

37   FLAT BASE (to OPEN? VESSEL)   Fig. 3
(C25-2) Base. D. 0.12, Th. 0.007; very worn. Semicoarse fabric; little lime; unevenly fired, 5YR 5-6/8 (yellowish red or reddish yellow) to 5YR 3/2 (dark reddish brown) [core]. Vessel shape indeterminate: flat base, splayed slightly concave wall. Poorly finished.
Final Neolithic.

38   FLAT BASE (to OPEN? VESSEL)   Fig. 3
(G9-4) Base. D. at base 0.17, Max. pres. W. 0.08, Th. 0.016. Coarse fabric; medium to very large (>0.005) lime inclusions; unevenly fired, 5YR 5/6 (yellowish red) to gray to black core. Flat base, flaring wall. Surfaces cracked, crazed, and pitted from attempts to smooth and burnish coarse fabric.
Final Neolithic.

39   FLAT BASE (to OPEN? VESSEL)   Fig. 3
(G9-37) Base. D. at base indet., Th. 0.011. Coarse fabric; many medium to large inclusions, no lime; unevenly fired, 2.5YR 2.5-3/2 ([very] dusky red) to black core. Unevenly formed flat base, ridge at bottom of wall part way around base. Exterior and bottom burnished.
Final Neolithic.

40   HOLLOW BASE to OPEN VESSEL   Fig. 3
(G9-26) Base. D. at base 0.10, Max. pres. W. 0.04, Th. 0.0095. Coarse fabric; medium to large inclusions, including lime; evenly fired 2.5YR 5/8 (red). Slightly hollowed base,

flaring wall. Exterior (including bottom) lightly burnished.
Final Neolithic.

41   HOLLOW BASE to OPEN VESSEL   Fig. 3
(C25-1) Complete base preserved. D. of base 0.07, Th. 0.006; secondary burning. Medium fabric; small to medium inclusions, no lime; evenly fired, 5YR 2.5/1 (black). Irregular circular base with concave bottom, splayed straight wall. Exterior burnished; interior slipped red?
Final Neolithic (to Early Helladic I).

42   VERTICAL HANDLE   Fig. 3
(G9-5-15) Handle. Max. pres. L. 0.051, Max. pres. W. 0.027, Th. 0.010. Semicoarse fabric; small to medium inclusions, little lime; even, dark fired, 5YR 4/1 (dark gray). Subrectangular handle, spreading into rim or attachment? Self slip? black, heavily burnished to gloss.
Final Neolithic?

43   VERTICAL HANDLE   Fig. 3
(G9-5-14) Handle frag. Max. pres. W. 0.046, Max. pres. L. 0.059, Th. 0.020. Medium fabric; small inclusions, no lime; unevenly fired, 2.5YR 5/8 (red) to 7.5YR 6/2 (pinkish gray) [core]. Large handle, semicircular in section.
Final Neolithic?

44   VERTICAL? TUBULAR HANDLE   Fig. 3
(C29-ALL-19) Body with handle attachment. Max. pres. W. 0.055, Th. 0.007, handle W. 0.044, Th. 0.008. Medium fabric; unevenly fired, 2.5YR 4-5/8 (red) to 5YR 3/1 (very dark gray) [core]. Closed? vessel with vertical? tubular? handle, thin rectangular section. Traces of slip on exterior?
Final Neolithic?

45   OPEN VESSEL WITH HORIZONTAL HANDLE   Fig. 3
(G9-11) Body with horizontal handle. Max. pres. W. 0.041, handle: Max. pres. W. 0.014, Th. 0.006. Semicoarse fabric; small inclusions, few large lime inclusions; unevenly fired, 7.5YR 6/4 (light brown) to gray core. Small horizontal handle, subrectangular in section. Self slipped surface, compacted and cracked.
Final Neolithic?

46   HORIZONTAL HANDLE   Fig. 3
(C29-ALL-23) Handle. Max. pres. L. 0.057, W. 0.035, Th. 0.009-0.011; surfaces worn. Coarse fabric; medium to very large inclusions; no lime; unevenly fired, 2.5YR 4/4 (reddish brown) to 2.5YR-N5/0 (gray) [core]. Horizontal slightly upswung strap handle, curved in section, thicker at edges.
Final Neolithic?

47   CLOSED VESSEL WITH HORIZONTAL HANDLE
                                                         Fig. 3
(A6-74-36) Body with handle frag. Th. 0.009, handle Max. pres. L. 0.044, W. 0.033, Th. 0.013. Semicoarse fabric; small to medium inclusions, no lime; unevenly fired, 2.5YR 4/8 (red) to 2.5YR-N2.5/0 (black) [core]. Closed vessel with horizontal strap handle, rectangular in section. Burnished.
Final Neolithic.

48   OPEN VESSEL WITH HORIZONTAL HANDLE   Fig. 3
(F6-ALL-3) Body with handle attachment. Max. pres. W. 0.050, Th. 0.007, handle W. 0.041 Th. 0.013. Coarse fabric; many medium to large inclusions, much lime; unevenly fired, 2.5YR 4/8 (red) to 5YR 4/4 (reddish brown) [core]. Horizontal

slightly upswung strap handle, oval in section; four deep unevenly spaced grooves on handle. Exterior slipped red; interior slipped brown?
Final Neolithic to Early Helladic I.

49   TAB HANDLE   Fig. 3
(G9-1-44) Handle, Max. pres. W. 0.053, Th. 0.017. Semicoarse fabric; medium to large inclusions, very little lime; unevenly fired, 5YR 6/6 (reddish yellow) to gray core. Vertical? tab handle, thicker towards center where it is cut out. Plain.
Final Neolithic.

50   TUBULAR LUG   Fig. 3
(B8?-ALL-5) Body with most of horizontal? tubular lug. Max. pres. W. 0.047, Th. 0.006, lug 0.016 high, hole 0.006-0.010; surfaces very worn. Semifine fabric; unevenly fired, 5YR 6/6 (reddish yellow) to 5YR 4/1 (gray) [core]. Small triangular section lug, pierced horizontally.
Final Neolithic?

51   OPEN? VESSEL WITH HORNED LUG   Fig. 3
(E13-2-42) Body with lug. Max. pres. W. 0.068, Th. 0.008-0.009. Coarse fabric; medium to very large lime temper; evenly fired, 5YR 4/4 (reddish brown). Upcurving lug with two (?) horns. cf. **17**.
Final Neolithic.

52   LARGE VESSEL WITH LUG   Fig. 4
(G9-B-2) Body with partially preserved lug. Th. 0.010 - 0.012. Coarse fabric; medium to large inclusions, some small lime; unevenly fired (in lug), 7.5YR 5/6 (strong brown) to gray core. Upturned lug 0.055 x 0.031, pres. 0.014 high. Exterior burnished.
Final Neolithic.

53   LARGE VESSEL WITH LUG   Fig. 4
(G9-5-13) Body with partially preserved lug. Max. pres. W. 0.071, Th. 0.010. Semicoarse fabric; small to medium inclusions, no lime; unevenly fired, 2.5YR 4-5/8 (red) to black core. Circular lug (or handle attachment?) 0.038 x 0.043, preserved to 0.011 high; top surface of lug angled. Exterior slipped? or burnished?
Final Neolithic.

54   KNOB   Fig. 4
(G9-1-26) Body with knob. Th. 0.008, knob: 0.057 x 0.053, Th. 0.010. Semicoarse fabric; medium to large (some very large) inclusions, no lime; unevenly fired, 2.5YR 4/8 (red) to 2.5YR 3/2-4 (dusky red to dark reddish brown) [core]. Irregular circular knob applied to exterior of wall. Smoothed, uneven surfaces.
Final Neolithic.

55   LARGE CLOSED VESSEL WITH KNOB   Fig. 4
(F20-20) Body with raised knob. Max. pres. W. 0.077, Th. 0.018, knob: D. est. 0.04, H. 0.009. Medium fabric; many small inclusions, no lime; unevenly fired, 2.5YR 6/8 (light red) to 5YR 3/1 (very dark gray) [core]. Closed? vessel with raised circular knob. Plain. cf. **53**, **54**.
Final Neolithic?

56   CLOSED VESSEL WITH KNOB   Fig. 4
(C29-ALL-8) Body with raised knob. Max. pres. W. 0.059, Th. 0.008, knob 0.045 x 0.039, H. 0.008. Medium fabric; small to medium inclusions, little lime; unevenly fired, 2.5YR 6/8

(light red) to 5YR 4/1 (dark gray) [core]. Closed? vessel with oval, concave knob. Plain.
Final Neolithic.

57   PITHOS?   Figs. 4, 118
(G9-B-3) Body preserving two applied ridges. Max. pres. W. 0.076, Th. 0.016. Semicoarse fabric; small to large inclusions, little lime; unevenly fired, 7.5YR 6/6 (reddish yellow) to gray core. Large vessel with two applied ridges, 0.022 and 0.016 wide, 0.003 high, angled at 90° to each other. Exterior burnished.
Final Neolithic.

58   LARGE OPEN? VESSEL   Fig. 4
(A33-1-55) Body. Max. pres. W. 0.057, Th. 0.010 - 0.013. Coarse fabric; medium to large inclusions, little to no lime; unevenly fired, 2.5YR 4/4 (reddish brown) to 5YR 3/3 (dark reddish brown) [core]. Exterior: horizontal ridges est. 0.013 apart, 0.004 high; interior: slipped?
Final Neolithic.

59   VESSEL WITH RIDGE   Fig. 4
(G9-5-29) Body. Max. pres. W. 0.04, Th. 0.0055. Shallow ridge 0.014 wide, 0.003 high.
Final Neolithic.

60   VESSEL WITH INCISED RIDGES   Figs. 4, 118
(G9-5-18) Body. Max. pres. W. 0.05, Th. 0.013. Shallow ridges 0.015 wide, 0.003 high, at 60° angle, perpendicular slashes through ridge.
Final Neolithic.

61   STOPPER OR BURNISHER?   Fig. 4
(C29-ALL-13) Body worn to almost circular. 0.032 x 0.034, Th. 0.007 - 0.008. Semicoarse fabric; unevenly fired, 5YR 5/8 (yellowish red) to 5YR 5/1 (gray) [core]. Originally open vessel. Exterior: taenia band of perpendicular slashes on raised band 0.013 wide; interior: red slip.
Final Neolithic (reuse not datable).

62   LARGE CLOSED VESSEL   Fig. 4
(C11-C28-12) Body. Max. pres. W. 0.043, Th. 0.011. Semicoarse fabric; many medium inclusions, mostly quartz, no lime; unevenly fired, 2.5YR 4/6 (red) to 2.5YR 3/0 (very dark gray) [core]. Closed vessel. Exterior: taenia bands 0.013-0.018 wide and 0.006 high meeting at 60° angle; interior worn.
Final Neolithic.

63   OPEN VESSEL   Fig. 4
(D3-2-18) Body. Max. pres. W. 0.03, Th. 0.006. Medium fabric; unevenly fired, 5YR 4/6 (yellowish red) to 2.5YR 5/8 (red) to black core (no Munsell). Open vessel. Exterior: raised band with incised diagonal grooves, lower portion burnished; interior smoothed.
Final Neolithic.

64   INCISED HANDLE   Figs. 4, 118
(F9-1) Handle. Max. pres. L. 0.042, Max. pres. W. 0.039, Th. 0.010. Semicoarse fabric; small to large inclusions, no lime; unevenly fired, 2.5YR 4/6 (red) to 2.5YR 3/4 (dark reddish brown) [core]. Vertical? strap handle, upturned at edges; on top, from exterior: row of very oblique slashes, row of less oblique slashes, longitudinal groove, row of perpendicular slashes. Plain.
Final Neolithic to Early Helladic I.

65   INCISED BODY SHERD   Fig. 4
(B8?-ALL-4) Body. Max. pres. W. 0.032, Th. 0.007-0.008. Semicoarse fabric; medium to few very large inclusions, no lime; unevenly fired, 5YR 6/6 (reddish yellow) to 5YR 4/2 (dark reddish gray) [core]. Vessel shape indeterminate. Exterior: interlocking herringbone design, perhaps stamped?; traces of red slip in grooves.
Final Neolithic.

66   INCISED BODY SHERD   Figs. 4, 118
(F14-1) Body. Max. pres. W. 0.05, Th. 0.008-0.009. Medium fabric; small to medium inclusions, little lime; unevenly fired, 2.5YR 6/8 (light red) to 5YR 5/1 (gray) [core]. Vessel shape indeterminate. Exterior: incised irregular chevrons; between each pair of lines one or two rows of impressed ovals.
Final Neolithic.

67   PATTERN-BURNISHED OPEN VESSEL   Figs. 4, 118
(G9-20) Body. Max. pres. W. 0.035, Th. 0.0065-0.0085. Semicoarse fabric; small to medium (one very large) inclusions, no lime; unevenly fired, 7.5YR 6/4 (light brown) to gray core. Exterior cream slip (7.5YR 7/4 [pink]) with red paint burnished to luster in pattern of stripes?; interior smoothed.
Final Neolithic.

68   PATTERN-BURNISHED CLOSED VESSEL   Fig. 118
(E13-2-50) Body. Max. pres. W. 0.045, Th. 0.003. Semifine fabric; few silver inclusions, no lime; unevenly fired, 2.5YR 6/8 (light red) to 5YR 6/2 (pinkish gray) [core]. Curving wall. Exterior slipped red and burnished in patterns of stripes; traces of second color in non burnished areas.
Final Neolithic (to Early Helladic I? [by fabric]).

EARLY HELLADIC I

69   FRUITSTAND (FLARING RIM BOWL)   Fig. 4
(B39-62) Rim. D. indet., Max. pres. W. 0.025, Th. 0.009. Semicoarse fabric; little lime; unevenly fired, 5YR 6/6 (reddish yellow) to 5YR 4/2 (dark reddish gray) [core]. Flaring rim turning down; three grooves on top, not aligned with circumference of vessel. Plain. Dousougli 1987:184 Abb.12 nos.42-45; 202 Abb.27 nos.163-165; 204 Abb.29 nos.176-179.
Early Helladic I.

70   FRUITSTAND (FLARING RIM BOWL)   Fig. 4
(F32-N-152) Body. D. indet., Max. pres. W. 0.035, Th. 0.008. Medium fabric; no lime; unevenly fired, 5YR 5/8 (yellowish red) to 5YR 5/1 (gray) [core]. Shallow bowl, flaring to horizontal rim (lip not preserved); on top of rim, diagonal grooves. Plain? See **69** for references.
Early Helladic I.

71   SMALL SHALLOW BOWL   Fig. 4
(C11-C19-12) Rim. D. 0.17, Max. pres. W. 0.045, Th. 0.005. Semifine fabric; quartz inclusions, no volcanic; unevenly fired, 5YR 5/8 (yellowish red) to 5YR 5/6 (yellowish red) [core]. Curving wall, rounded lip. Slipped red and burnished (almost urfirnis?). cf. Blegen's AI.
Early Helladic I.

72   SMALL SHALLOW BOWL   Fig. 4
(A9-6-6) Rim. D. 0.19, Max. pres. W. 0.03, Th. 0.006. Medium fabric; quartz? inclusions, some lime, no volcanic; unevenly fired, 2.5YR 5/8 (red) to 7.5YR 5/4 (brown) [core].

Curving wall, rounded lip. Slipped red-brown.
Early Helladic I.

73   MEDIUM SHALLOW BOWL WITH LUG   Fig. 4
(E9-265) Rim. D. 0.26, Max. pres. W. 0.04, Th. 0.007. Medium fabric; no lime; unevenly fired, 5YR 5/6 (yellowish red) to 5YR 4/4 (reddish brown) [core]. Shallow bowl, bevelled flat lip; on exterior, long vertical lug. Exterior and lip slipped red-brown and burnished; interior plain.
Early Helladic I [Blegen].

74   MEDIUM? SHALLOW BOWL   Fig. 4
(F6-5) Rim. D. indet., Max. pres. W. 0.035, Wall Th. 0.011. Coarse fabric; volcanic and quartz inclusions; evenly fired, 2.5YR 4/6 (red). Round lip; horizontal taenia band, impressed. Plain.
Early Helladic I.

75   MEDIUM SHALLOW BOWL   Fig. 4
(A33-81-1-12) Rim. D. 0.30, Max. pres. W. 0.06, Th. 0.009. Medium fabric; volcanic? and quartz inclusions, much lime; unevenly fired, 5YR 3/2 (dark reddish brown) to 5YR 5/4 (reddish brown) [core]. Curving wall, flattened lip. Traces of red slip and burnishing.
Early Helladic I.

76   MEDIUM SHALLOW BOWL   Fig. 4
(G1-A-59) Rim. D. 0.32, Max. pres. W. 0.045, Th. 0.007. Medium fabric; volcanic? and quartz inclusions; unevenly fired, 5YR 5/8 (yellowish red) to 5YR 3/2 (dark reddish brown) [core]. Rim thickened to interior [giving impression of incurving], rounded lip. Traces of red slip.
Early Helladic I.

77   MEDIUM SHALLOW BOWL   Fig. 4
(B43-B45-3) Rim. D. 0.33, Max. pres. W. 0.055, Th. 0.008. Semicoarse fabric; quartz inclusions, some lime; unevenly fired, 5YR 5/8 (yellowish red) to 5YR 5/1 (gray) [core]. Hemispherical wall, rounded lip. Exterior slipped red; interior worn.
Early Helladic I.

78   LARGE SHALLOW BOWL   Fig. 4
(B43-B-1) Rim. D. 0.43, Max. pres. W. 0.055, Th. 0.008. Medium fabric; volcanic and quartz inclusions; evenly fired, 5YR 4/4 (reddish brown). Spreading wall, slightly thickened rim, pointed lip. Slipped red and burnished.
Early Helladic I.

79   LARGE SHALLOW BOWL   Fig. 4
(A6-75-40) Rim. D. indet., Max. pres. W. 0.35, Th. 0.009. Medium fabric; volcanic and quartz inclusions; evenly fired, 5YR 4/6 (yellowish red). Rim thickened to interior, lip slightly rounded. Plain?
Early Helladic I.

80   MEDIUM SPREADING BOWL   Fig. 5
(A33-1-17) Rim. D. 0.21, Max. pres. W. 0.04, Th. 0.005. Semicoarse fabric; quartz inclusions, some lime; unevenly fired, 5YR 4/6 (yellowish red) to 5YR 4/4 (reddish brown) [core]. Spreading wall, groove on exterior below flattened lip. Plain.
Early Helladic I.

8 1 MEDIUM SPREADING BOWL   Fig. 5
(A33-1-19) Rim. D. indet., Max. pres. W. 0.25, Th. 0.008. Semicoarse fabric; quartz inclusions, much lime; unevenly fired, 5YR 4/6 (yellowish red) to 7.5YR 4/6 (strong brown) [core]. Spreading wall, flattened lip with groove on lip. Plain.
Early Helladic I.

8 2 MEDIUM SPREADING BOWL?   Fig. 5
(C17-26) Rim. D. 0.30, Max. pres. W. 0.04, Th. 0.005. Semicoarse; quartz inclusions, much lime, no volcanic; unevenly fired, 5YR 5/6 (yellowish red) to 7.5YR 5/4 (brown) [core]. Straight wall, rim thickened to interior; groove at lip. Slipped red-brown and burnished.
Early Helladic I.

8 3 MEDIUM SPREADING BOWL   Fig. 5
(B9-63) Rim. D. 0.32, Max. pres. W. 0.05, Th. 0.009. Medium fabric; volcanic and quartz inclusions; evenly fired, 5YR 4/6 (yellowish red). Spreading wall, rim thickened, rounded lip. Slipped red and burnished.
Early Helladic I.

8 4 LARGE SPREADING BOWL WITH TRUMPET LUG
Fig. 5
(A6-65-4) Rim. D. 0.37, Max. pres. W. 0.05, Th. 0.010. Medium fabric; few silver inclusions, no lime; unevenly fired, 2.5YR 4/6 (red) to 7.5YR 4/2 (dark brown-brown) [core]. Shallow bowl, flat lip; below rim, trumpet lug (vertical element, ridge to left). Exterior burnished; interior slipped red? and burnished.
Early Helladic I [Blegen].

8 5 LARGE SPREADING BOWL   Fig. 5
(A6-74-19) Rim. D. indet., Th. 0.013. Medium fabric; quartz inclusions, some lime, no volcanic; evenly fired, 5YR 4/4 (reddish brown). Spreading wall, lip bevelled to exterior. Exterior slipped red.
Early Helladic I.

8 6 LARGE SPREADING BOWL WITH HANDLE   Fig. 5
(C11-NW-1) Rim. Max. pres. W. 0.04, Th. 0.012. Semicoarse fabric; quartz inclusions, little lime; unevenly fired, 5YR 5/6 (yellowish red) to 5YR 4/2 (dark reddish gray) [core]. Spreading wall, flat lip; on exterior below lip, stub of horizontal handle, oval in section. Plain?
Early Helladic I.

8 7 SPREADING BOWL WITH IMPRESSIONS   Fig. 5
(B24-ALL-2) Rim. D. indet., Max. pres. W. 0.035, Th. 0.008. Spreading wall, slightly thickened rim, flattened lip. On lip, impressed alternating triangles forming kerbschnitt.
Early Helladic I.

8 8 MEDIUM HEMISPHERICAL BOWL   Fig. 5
(A6-1-14) Rim. D. 0.27, Max. pres. W. 0.04, Th. 0.009. Medium fabric; quartz inclusions, much lime; unevenly fired, 2.5YR 5/8 (red) to 5YR 5/3 (reddish brown) [core]. Slightly thickened rim, rounded lip. Traces of red slip.
Early Helladic I.

8 9 MEDIUM HEMISPHERICAL BOWL WITH HANDLE
Fig. 5
(A33-81-2-2) Rim with handle. D. 0.30, Max. pres. W. 0.075, Th. 0.009. Semicoarse fabric; quartz inclusions; unevenly fired, 5YR 4/6 (yellowish red) to 5YR 3/4 (dark reddish brown)

[core]. Curving wall, flat lip; horizontal handle, oval in section with longitudinal horizontal ridge. Slipped red and burnished.
Early Helladic I.

9 0 MEDIUM HEMISPHERICAL BOWL   Fig. 5
(A6-2-10) Rim. D. 0.31, Th. 0.009. Semicoarse fabric; volcanic and quartz inclusions; evenly fired, 5YR 5/6 (yellowish red). Curving wall, rounded lip. Slipped red.
Early Helladic I.

9 1 MEDIUM HEMISPHERICAL BOWL   Fig. 5
(A6-74-26) Rim. D. 0.32, Max. pres. W. 0.055, Th. 0.008. Medium fabric; volcanic and quartz inclusions; unevenly fired, 5YR 4/6 (yellowish red) to 5YR 3/2 (dark reddish brown) [core]. Hemispherical wall, rim thickened to interior [giving impression of incurving profile], flattened lip. Slipped red-brown and burnished.
Early Helladic I.

9 2 MEDIUM HEMISPHERICAL BOWL   Fig. 5
(E5-B-18) Rim. D. 0.34, Max. pres. W. 0.055, Th. 0.007. Medium fabric; quartz inclusions, no lime; unevenly fired, 2.5YR 5/4 (reddish brown) to 7.5YR 5/4 (brown) [core]. Hemispherical wall, rounded lip. Slipped red (mottled).
Early Helladic I.

9 3 LARGE HEMISPHERICAL BOWL   Fig. 5
(C15-A-25) Rim. D. 0.35, Max. pres. W. 0.045, Th. 0.008. Medium fabric; quartz inclusions, no lime; evenly fired, 5YR 5/6 (yellowish red). Curving wall, rounded lip. Exterior worn?; interior and lip slipped red.
Early Helladic I.

9 4 LARGE HEMISPHERICAL BOWL   Fig. 6
(A6-74-3) Rim. D. 0.39, Max. pres. W. 0.065, Th. 0.012. Medium fabric; volcanic and quartz inclusions; unevenly fired, 5YR 4/6 (yellowish red) to 5YR 3/3 (dark reddish brown) [core]. Rim thickening towards flat lip. Slipped red and burnished (to gloss).
Early Helladic I.

9 5 LARGE HEMISPHERICAL BOWL   Fig. 6
(E5-A-2) Rim. D. 0.045, Max. pres. W. 0.065, Th. 0.010. Semicoarse fabric; volcanic and quartz inclusions; unevenly fired, 5YR 3/4 (dark reddish brown) to 5YR 2.5/1 (black) [core]. Hemispherical wall, rounded lip. Traces of red slip on exterior.
Early Helladic I.

9 6 LARGE HEMISPHERICAL BOWL   Fig. 6
(A33-81-1-31) Rim. D. 0.54, Max. pres. W. 0.09, Th. 0.011. Semicoarse fabric; volcanic and quartz inclusions; evenly fired, 5YR 3/3 (dark reddish brown). Hemispherical wall, flat lip. Slipped red.
Early Helladic I.

9 7 SMALL INCURVING BOWL   Fig. 6
(A33-1-20) Rim. D. 0.20, Max. pres. W. 0.02, Th. 0.007. Semicoarse fabric; volcanic and quartz inclusions; evenly fired, 5YR 3/4 (dark reddish brown). Incurving rim, flattened lip. Plain.
Early Helladic I.

9 8 SMALL INCURVING BOWL   Fig. 6
(B81-2-36/37) Rim, two joining. D. 0.22, Max. pres. W. 0.65, Th. 0.004; very worn. Semicoarse fabric; quartz inclusions,

some lime; unevenly fired, 5YR 5/6 (yellowish red) to 5YR 4/2 (dark reddish gray) [core]. Incurving wall, rim slightly thickened, lip rounded. Surfaces not preserved.
Early Helladic I to Early Helladic II.

99   SMALL INCURVING BOWL   Fig. 6
(A6-74-8) Rim. D. indet., Max. pres. W. 0.03, Th. 0.006. Semicoarse fabric; quartz inclusions, some lime; unevenly fired, 5YR 3/4 (dark reddish brown) to 5YR 5/2 (reddish gray) [core]. Incurving wall, rounded lip. Slipped red to black mottled and burnished.
Early Helladic I.

100   SMALL INCURVING BOWL   Fig. 6
(A6-74-28) Rim. D. 0.24, Max. pres. W. 0.03, Th. 0.004. Semifine fabric; quartz and volcanic? inclusions, some lime; unevenly fired, 5YR 4/2 (dark reddish gray) to 5YR 4/6 (yellowish red) [core]. Incurving rim, rounded lip. Slipped brown and burnished.
Early Helladic I.

101   MEDIUM INCURVING BOWL   Fig. 6
(E4-B-2) Rim. D. 0.29, Max. pres. W. 0.07, Th. 0.005. Medium fabric; volcanic and quartz inclusions; unevenly fired, 5YR 4/6 (yellowish red) to 5YR 3/3 (dark reddish brown) [core]. Incurving wall, rim thickened to interior, lip slightly flattened and bevelled to exterior. Plain.
Early Helladic I.

102   MEDIUM INCURVING BOWL   Fig. 6
(A33-1-3) Rim, two joining. D. 0.29, Max. pres. W. 0.085, Th. 0.005. Medium fabric; volcanic and quartz inclusions; unevenly fired, 5YR 4/6 (yellowish red) to 5YR 3/1 (very dark gray) [core]. Slightly incurving wall, rounded lip. Slipped red and burnished.
Early Helladic I.

103   LARGE INCURVING BOWL   Fig. 6
(E16-15A) Rim. D. indet., Max. pres. W. 0.06, Th. 0.006. Medium fabric; volcanic and quartz inclusions; evenly fired, 5YR 3/2 (dark reddish brown). Incurving wall, rim slightly thickened, lip slightly flattened. Plain.
Early Helladic I.

104   LARGE INCURVING BOWL   Fig. 6
(A6/9-B-20) Rim. D. 0.38, Max. pres. W. 0.09, Th. 0.008. Semifine fabric; volcanic? and quartz inclusions; evenly fired, 5YR 5/2 (reddish gray). Incurving rim, flattened lip bevelled to interior. Exterior burnished; interior slipped red and burnished.
Early Helladic I.

105   LARGE INCURVING BOWL   Fig. 6
(F32-A3-3) Rim. D. 0.38, Max. pres. W. 0.055, Th. 0.008. Semicoarse fabric; silver inclusions, little lime; evenly fired, 2.5YR-N3/0 (very dark gray). Slightly incurving wall, thickened rim. Slipped red and burnished.
Early Helladic I (to Early Helladic II).

106   LARGE INCURVING BOWL   Fig. 6
(A6-65-5) Rim. D. 0.38, Max. pres. W. 0.065, Th. 0.012. Semicoarse fabric; quartz inclusions, much lime, no volcanic; unevenly fired, 5YR 5/6 (yellowish red) to 5YR 4/2 (dark reddish gray) [core]. Incurving rim, rounded lip. Traces of red slip on interior.
Early Helladic I.

107   LARGE INCURVING BOWL   Fig. 7
(F32-A3-2) Rim. D. 0.41, Max. pres. W. 0.045, Th. 0.008. Medium fabric; silver inclusions, little lime; unevenly fired, 5YR 5/8 (yellowish red) to 5YR 5/1 (gray) [core]. Incurving wall, rim thickened in and out. Burnished.
Early Helladic I (?).

108   LARGE INCURVING BOWL   Fig. 7
(A6/9-B-13) Rim. D. 0.41, Max. pres. W. 0.06, Th. 0.008. Medium fabric; quartz and silver inclusions, some lime; unevenly fired, 2.5YR 4/8 (red) to 5YR 4/6 (yellowish red) [core]. Incurving wall, thickened rim, flat lip. Slipped red and burnished.
Early Helladic I.

109   MEDIUM INCURVING BOWL WITH TRUMPET LUG
Fig. 7
(F32-N-136) Rim. D. 0.26, Max. pres. W. 0.055, Th. 0.006. Medium fabric; some lime; evenly fired, 2.5YR 5/8 (red). Incurving wall, slightly thickened rim, flattened lip; below rim, trumpet lug (vertical element, horizontal ridge to right). No surface finish preserved.
Early Helladic I (to Early Helladic II).

110   MEDIUM INCURVING BOWL WITH TRUMPET LUG
Fig. 7
(F32-A7-2) Rim. D. 0.26, Max. pres. W. 0.045, Th. 0.004. Medium fabric; some lime; evenly fired, 2.5YR 6/8 (light red). Incurving wall, rim thickened to exterior; below rim, trumpet lug (vertical element, impressed horizontal band to right, i.e., taenia). No surface preserved.
Early Helladic I to Early Helladic II.

111   MEDIUM INCURVING BOWL WITH TRUMPET LUG
Figs. 7, 118
(F32-64) Rim. D. indet., Max. pres. W. 0.055, Th. 0.006. Semicoarse fabric; silver inclusions, no lime; unevenly fired, 5YR 5/4 (reddish brown) to 5YR 5/1 (gray) [core]. Incurving wall, rim thickened to exterior, lip flattened; below rim, trumpet lug (vertical element, impressed horizontal ridge to right, i.e., taenia). Plain?
Early Helladic I to Early Helladic II.

112   MEDIUM INCURVING BOWL WITH TRUMPET LUG
Fig. 7
(C11-C19-1) Rim. D. 0.31, Max. pres. W. 0.065, Th. 0.007. Medium fabric; some silver inclusions, some lime; unevenly fired, 2.5YR 5/8 (red) to 5YR 3/1 (very dark gray) [core]. Incurving wall, rim thickened in and out to "T"; below rim, trumpet lug (vertical element and horizontal ridge to right). Slipped brown and burnished.
Early Helladic I [Blegen].

113   LARGE INCURVING BOWL WITH TRUMPET LUG
Fig. 7
(F32-S-108) Rim. D. indet., Max. pres. W. 0.05, Th. 0.007. Medium fabric; some lime; unevenly fired, 2.5YR 6/8 (light red) to 7.5YR 5/2 (brown) [core]. Incurving wall, thickened rim; below rim, trumpet lug (vertical element, horizontal ridge to right). Exterior slipped.
Early Helladic I [Blegen].

114   LARGE INCURVING BOWL WITH TRUMPET LUG
Figs. 7, 118
(C11-NE-7) Rim. D. 0.36, Max. pres. W. 0.07, Th. 0.008. Medium fabric; some lime; unevenly fired, 5YR 6/8 (reddish

yellow) to 7.5YR 4/2 (dark brown-brown) [core]. Incurving wall, slightly thickened rim, lip bevelled to interior; below rim, trumpet lug (vertical element, curving from top into horizontal ridge to left). Exterior slipped red; interior slipped red and burnished.
Early Helladic I [Blegen].

115 LARGE INCURVING BOWL WITH TRUMPET LUG
                                                        Fig. 7
(F32-S-99) Rim. D. indet., Max. pres. W. 0.06, Th. 0.007. Medium fabric; much lime; unevenly fired, 5YR 5/6 (yellowish red) to 7.5YR 5/2 (brown) [core]. Incurving wall, rim thickened to exterior; below rim, trumpet lug (upper part of vertical element, ridge running to right). Plain.
Early Helladic I to Early Helladic II.

116 LARGE INCURVING BOWL WITH TRUMPET LUG
                                                        Fig. 7
(F32-N-65) Rim. D. 0.45, Max. pres. W. 0.07, Th. 0.007. Semicoarse fabric; medium to large inclusions, some lime; unevenly fired, 5YR 4/6 (yellowish red) to 5YR 3/2 (dark reddish brown) [core]. Incurving wall, thickened rim (especially to exterior); below rim, trumpet lug (vertical element, impressed horizontal ridge [i.e., taenia] to left). Interior and lip slipped red and burnished.
Early Helladic I [Blegen].

117 LARGE INCURVING BOWL WITH TRUMPET LUG
                                                   Figs. 7, 118
(F32-S-96) Rim. D. 0.46, Max. pres. W. 0.08, Th. 0.07. Semicoarse fabric; small to large inclusions, some silver, little lime; unevenly fired, 5YR 4/4 (reddish brown) to 5YR 4/1 (dark gray) [core]. Incurving wall, slighting thickened rim; below rim, double trumpet lug (two vertical elements connected by horizontal ridge). Slipped red-brown and burnished.
Early Helladic I [Blegen].

118 SMALL INCURVING BOWL WITH LUG   Figs. 7, 118
(B39-1) Rim. D. 0.22, Max. pres. W. 0.085, Wall Th. 0.008. Semicoarse fabric; volcanic and quartz inclusions; evenly fired, 5YR 3/4 (dark reddish brown). Incurving wall, flat lip; on exterior below lip, horizontal lug with four protuberances. Plain.
Early Helladic I.

119 MEDIUM INCURVING BOWL WITH TAENIA   Fig. 7
(A6-75-32) Rim. D. 0.32, Max. pres. W. 0.05, Th. 0.008. Incurving wall, rim rolled to exterior to form taenia with slashes and impressions.
Early Helladic I.

120 MEDIUM INCURVING BOWL WITH TAENIA   Fig. 7
(F32-S-82) Rim. D. indet., Max. pres. W. 0.055, Th. 0.010. Semicoarse fabric; volcanic and quartz inclusions; evenly fired, 5YR 2.5/1 (black). Flat lip; horizontal taenia band, impressed. Plain.
Early Helladic I.

121 MEDIUM INCURVING BOWLS WITH TAENIA Fig. 7
(F32-S-73) Rim. D. indet., Max. pres. W. 0.045, Th. 0.009. Coarse fabric; volcanic and quartz inclusions; unevenly fired, 5YR 4/6 (yellowish red) to 5YR 3/4 (dark reddish brown) [core]. Incurving wall; horizontal taenia band, impressed. Plain.
Early Helladic I.

122 LARGE INCURVING BOWL WITH TAENIA   Fig. 7
(B97-1-2) Rim. D. 0.40, Max. pres. W. 0.05, Th. 0.008. Semicoarse fabric; volcanic and quartz inclusions; unevenly fired, 5YR 4/6 (yellowish red) to 5YR 3/2 (dark reddish brown) [core]. Thickened rim; horizontal taenia band, impressed. Plain?
Early Helladic I.

123 MEDIUM INCURVING BOWL WITH HORIZONTAL RIDGE   Fig. 7
(B9-B11-10) Rim. D. 0.33, Max. pres. W. 0.075, Th. 0.009. Semicoarse fabric; some lime; unevenly fired, 2.5YR 4/8 (red) to 7.5YR 4/2 (dark brown-brown) [core]. Slightly curving wall, rim thickened to exterior, lip flattened; below rim, horizontal ridge. Slipped? (or painted?) red.
Early Helladic I [Blegen].

124 LARGE INCURVING BOWL WITH HORIZONTAL RIDGE   Fig. 7
(C11-SW-23) Rim. D. indet., Max. pres. W. 0.05, Th. 0.009. Semicoarse fabric; much lime; unevenly fired, 5YR 6/6 (reddish yellow) to 7.5YR 6/2 (pinkish gray) [core]. Curving wall, rim thickened to exterior, horizontal flat lip; below rim, horizontal ridge. Interior and lip slipped red-brown and burnished.
Early Helladic I (to Early Helladic II).

125 MEDIUM INCURVING BOWL WITH IMPRESSIONS
                                                        Fig. 8
(B24-96) Rim. D. 0.31, Th. 0.013. Incurving wall, rim thickened to interior and exterior, flattened lip bevelled to interior. On lip, incised irregular chevrons.
Early Helladic I (to Early Helladic II).

126 DEEP BOWL?   Fig. 8
(C11-NW-2) Rim. D. 0.24, Max. pres. W. 0.05, Th. 0.008. Semicoarse fabric; little lime; unevenly fired, 5YR 6/8 (reddish yellow) to 5YR 4/1 (dark gray) [core]. Vertical wall, rim thickened to exterior. Surfaces not preserved.
Early Helladic I? (to Early Helladic II).

127 DEEP BOWL   Fig. 8
(A33-1-18) Rim. D. 0.255, Max. pres. W. 0.025, Th. 0.006. Semicoarse fabric; quartz inclusions, little lime; evenly fired, 5YR 3/2 (dark reddish brown). Vertical wall, slightly thickened rim curving out slightly, flattened lip. Plain.
Early Helladic I.

128 DEEP BOWL   Fig. 8
(F6-27) Rim. D. indet., Max. pres. W. 0.02, Th. 0.007. Semicoarse fabric; quartz inclusions, much lime; unevenly fired, 5YR 3/2 (dark reddish brown) to 5YR 2.5/1 (black) [core]. Vertical? wall, slightly thickened and slightly incurving rim, flattened lip [orientation not secure]. Interior burnished.
Early Helladic I?

129 JAR WITH VERY FLARING RIM   Fig. 8
(E13-81-1-4) Rim. D. 0.23, Max. pres. W. 0.045, Th. 0.009. Medium fabric; quartz inclusions; unevenly fired, 5YR 5/6 (yellowish red) to 5YR 5/3 (reddish brown) [core]. Very flaring rim. Slipped red and burnished (to gloss).
Early Helladic I.

130 JAR WITH VERY FLARING RIM   Fig. 8
(C11-SE-8) Rim. D. 0.24, Max. pres. W. 0.06, Th. 0.007. Semicoarse fabric; quartz inclusions; evenly fired, 2.5YR 5/8 (red). Very flaring rim. Slipped red and burnished (to gloss).
Early Helladic I.

131 JAR WITH VERY FLARING RIM   Fig. 8
(A33-1-4) Rim. D. indet., Max. pres. W. 0.045, Th. 0.007. Semicoarse fabric; volcanic? and quartz inclusions; evenly fired, 2.5YR 3/4 (dark reddish brown). Very flaring rim. Slipped red and burnished.
Early Helladic I.

132 JAR WITH VERY FLARING RIM   Fig. 8
(A33-81-1-38) Rim. D. 0.34, Max. pres. W. 0.075, Th. 0.010. Semicoarse fabric; quartz inclusions; evenly fired, 5YR 5/6 (yellowish red). Very flaring rim. Slipped red and burnished (to gloss).
Early Helladic I.

133 JAR WITH FLARING RIM   Fig. 8
(B81-2-5/28/29 + B81-2-13 + B81-2-24/31/40) Rim and body, seven joining, preserving neck and shoulder. D. 0.22, Th. 0.007. Semicoarse; quartz and some lime inclusions, no volcanic; evenly fired, 5YR 6/6 (reddish yellow). Insloping neck, flaring rim; groove at junction of neck and shoulder? Exterior slipped red; burnishing preserved on exterior only.
Early Helladic I.

134 JAR WITH FLARING RIM   Fig. 8
(A33-1-50) Rim. D. 0.15, Max. pres. W. 0.04, Th. 0.006. Semicoarse fabric; quartz inclusions, much lime, no volcanic; evenly fired, 5YR 4/6 (yellowish red). Insloping neck, flaring rim, rounded lip. Plain.
Early Helladic I.

135 JAR WITH FLARING RIM   Fig. 8
(A6/9-B-41) Rim. D. 0.006. Medium fabric; quartz inclusions, little lime, no volcanic; unevenly fired, 5YR 3/4 (dark reddish brown) to 5YR 3/2 (dark reddish brown) [core]. Insloping neck, outturned rim. Slipped black and burnished.
Early Helladic I.

136 JAR WITH FLARING RIM   Fig. 8
(A33-81-1-11+26) Rim. D. 0.17, Max. pres. W. 0.05, Th. 0.009. Medium fabric; volcanic and quartz inclusions; unevenly fired, 5YR 5/6 (yellowish red) to 5YR 4/6 (yellowish red) [core]. Flaring rim. Slipped red and burnished (to gloss).
Early Helladic I.

137 JAR WITH FLARING RIM   Fig. 9
(C11-NE-25) Rim. D. 0.22, Max. pres. W. 0.08, Th. 0.013. Semicoarse fabric; quartz and silver inclusions, no lime, no volcanic; unevenly fired, 2.5YR 4/8 (red) to 5YR 4/3 (reddish brown) [core]. Slightly flaring rim. Exterior slipped red-brown and burnished; lip and interior worn.
Early Helladic I.

138 JAR WITH FLARING RIM   Fig. 9
(B24-94) Rim. D. 0.22, Max. pres. W. 0.08, Th. 0.015. Semicoarse fabric; quartz inclusions; unevenly fired, 5YR 5/6 (yellowish red) to 5YR 4/2 (dark reddish gray) [core]. Flaring rim. Slipped red and burnished.
Early Helladic I.

139 JAR WITH FLARING RIM   Fig. 9
(A6-72-18) Rim. D. 0.22, Max. pres. W. 0.05, Th. 0.013. Semicoarse fabric; volcanic and quartz inclusions; evenly fired, 5YR 5/4 (reddish brown). Flaring rim. Slipped red and burnished (to luster).
Early Helladic I.

140 JAR WITH FLARING RIM   Fig. 9
(A9-3-2) Rim. D. 0.24, Max. pres. W. 0.07, Th. 0.009. Medium fabric; volcanic and quartz inclusions; evenly fired, 5YR 4/4 (reddish brown). Flaring rim. Slipped red (mottled to black in spots) and burnished (to gloss).
Early Helladic I.

141 JAR WITH FLARING RIM   Fig. 9
(A6/9-B-40) Rim. D. 0.25, Max. pres. W. 0.08, Th. 0.009. Medium fabric; volcanic and quartz inclusions; evenly fired, 5YR 2.5/1 (black). Flaring rim. Slipped orange and burnished.
Early Helladic I.

142 JAR WITH FLARING RIM   Fig. 9
(G9-13) Rim. D. 0.28, Max. pres. W. 0.05, Th. 0.009. Medium fabric; quartz inclusions; evenly fired, 2.5YR 4/6 (red). Flaring rim. Slipped red and burnished (to gloss).
Early Helladic I.

143 JAR WITH FLARING RIM   Fig. 9
(A6-72-8) Rim. D. 0.32, Max. pres. W. 0.05, Th. 0.009. Semicoarse fabric; volcanic? and quartz inclusions; evenly fired, 2.5YR 5/6 (red). Flaring rim. Slipped red and burnished.
Early Helladic I.

144 JAR WITH FLARING RIM   Fig. 9
(A9-5-5) Rim. D. 0.35, Max. pres. W. 0.075, Th. 0.012. Semicoarse fabric; volcanic and quartz inclusions; evenly fired, 5YR 4/4 (reddish brown). Flaring rim. Slipped red (poorly preserved).
Early Helladic I.

145 JAR WITH FLARING RIM   Fig. 9
(A6/9-C-1) Rim. D. indet., Max. pres. W. 0.04, Th. 0.012. Medium fabric; volcanic? and quartz inclusions; unevenly fired, 5YR 4/6 (yellowish red) to 5YR 4/4 (reddish brown) [core]. Flaring rim. Slipped red and burnished (to luster).
Early Helladic I.

146 JAR WITH FLARING RIM   Fig. 9
(A9-6-8) Rim. D. indet., Max. pres. W. 0.02, Th. 0.010. Semicoarse fabric; volcanic and quartz inclusions; evenly fired, 5YR 5/6 (yellowish red). Flaring rim. Slipped red and burnished (to gloss).
Early Helladic I.

147 JAR WITH FLARING RIM   Fig. 9
(A6-74-9) Rim. D. indet., Max. pres. W. 0.025, Th. 0.009. Medium fabric; volcanic and quartz inclusions; unevenly fired, 5YR 6/6 (reddish yellow) to 5YR 5/2 (reddish gray) [core]. Flaring rim. Slipped red-orange and burnished to luster.
Early Helladic I.

148 JAR WITH FLARING RIM   Fig. 9
(C11-NE-6) Rim. D. indet., Max. pres. W. 0.05, Th. 0.007. Semicoarse fabric; quartz inclusions, no volcanic?; unevenly fired, 7.5YR 5/4 (brown) to 2.5YR 4/8 (red) [core]. Flaring rim, rounded lip. Slipped red and burnished.
Early Helladic I.

149 JAR WITH INSLOPING NECK   Fig. 9
(A6-1-4) Rim. D. 0.19, Max. pres. W. 0.055, Th. 0.011. Medium fabric; volcanic and quartz inclusions; unevenly fired, 2.5YR 4/6 (red) to 5YR 3/3 (dark reddish brown) [core]. Insloping neck, rim thickened to exterior. Exterior slipped red;

not preserved on lip and interior, but originally slipped?
Early Helladic I.

150 JAR WITH INSLOPING NECK   Fig. 9
(B24-ALL-3) Rim. D. 0.25, Max. pres. W. 0.07, Th.
0.010. Semicoarse fabric; volcanic and quartz inclusions; evenly
fired, 5YR 5/8 (yellowish red). Insloping neck, rim thickened to
exterior. Exterior and lip slipped red (originally burnished?);
interior burnished only.
Early Helladic I.

151 JAR WITH INSLOPING NECK   Fig. 10
(A6-74-16) Rim. D. 0.26, Max. pres. W. 0.04, Th. 0.010.
Medium fabric; volcanic and quartz inclusions; evenly fired, 5YR
4/6 (yellowish red). Insloping neck, rim thickened to exterior.
Exterior and lip slipped red and burnished; traces of red slip on
interior.
Early Helladic I.

152 JAR WITH INSLOPING NECK   Fig. 10
(A9-8-2) Rim. D. 0.29, Max. pres. W. 0.09, Th. 0.012.
Semicoarse fabric; quartz inclusions, no volcanic, no lime;
unevenly fired, 5YR 5/8 (yellowish red) to 5YR 5/1 (gray) [core].
Insloping neck, rim thickened to exterior. Exterior and lip slipped
red-brown and burnished; interior worn?
Early Helladic I.

153 JAR WITH INSLOPING NECK   Fig. 10
(A6-65-3) Rim. D. 0.37, Max. pres. W. 0.09, Th. 0.009.
Semicoarse fabric; quartz and much lime inclusions; unevenly
fired, 5YR 6/6 (reddish yellow) to 5YR 5/4 (reddish brown) [core].
Insloping neck, rim thickened to exterior, lip flat. Plain.
Early Helladic I.

154 JAR WITH INSLOPING NECK   Fig. 10
(A9-1-1) Rim. D. 0.38, Max. pres. W. 0.05, Th. 0.012.
Semicoarse fabric; volcanic and quartz inclusions; evenly fired,
7.5YR 4/6 (strong brown). Insloping neck, rim thickened to
exterior, lip rounded. Traces of red slip on exterior, lip, and
interior.
Early Helladic I.

155 JAR WITH INSLOPING NECK   Fig. 10
(A6-72-13) Rim. D. indet., Max. pres. W. 0.03, Th. 0.012.
Semicoarse fabric; volcanic and quartz inclusions; evenly fired,
2.5YR 4/6 (red). Insloping neck, rim thickened to exterior.
Exterior and lip sipped red and burnished; interior worn.
Early Helladic I.

156 JAR   Fig. 10
(C11-C19-14) Neck and shoulder. D. at junction 0.15, Max.
pres. W. 0.03, Th. 0.006. Medium fabric; silver inclusions,
some lime, no volcanic; unevenly fired, 2.5YR 5/8 (red) to 7.5YR
4/6 (strong brown) [core]. Flaring neck. Exterior slipped red;
interior neck slipped red.
Early Helladic I.

157 JAR WITH INCISED SHOULDER   Fig. 10
(G9-B-1) Neck and shoulder. D. at junction 0.10, Th. 0.007.
Fabric not determined. Groove at junction of neck and shoulder;
two pair of shallow grooves meet at neck junction. Exterior
slipped red.
Early Helladic I.

158 JAR WITH INCISED SHOULDER   Fig. 10
(A9-5-4) Incised body, preserving junction of neck and
shoulder. D. at junction 0.16/0.17, Th. 0.011. Semicoarse
fabric; quartz inclusions; unevenly fired, 5YR 4/6 (yellowish red)
to 5YR 3/4 (dark reddish brown) [core]. Deep, sharp-edged groove
at junction of neck and shoulder. Exterior slipped red and
burnished.
Early Helladic I.

159 JAR WITH INCISED SHOULDER   Fig. 10
(B24-92) Incised body, preserving junction of neck and
shoulder. D. at junction 0.20, Max. pres. W. 0.07, shoulder Th.
0.007, neck Th. 0.011. Medium fabric; quartz inclusions, little
lime; unevenly fired, 2.5YR 5/8 (red) to 5YR 4/3 (reddish brown)
[core]. Groove at junction of neck and shoulder, diagonal slashes
on shoulder. Exterior and neck interior slipped red and burnished.
Early Helladic I.

160 JAR WITH INCISED SHOULDER   Fig. 10
(F32-N-166) Incised body, preserving neck/ shoulder
junction. D. at junction 0.25, Max. pres. W. 0.07, neck Th.
0.014, shoulder Th. 0.012. Semicoarse fabric; volcanic (silver)
inclusions, no lime; unevenly fired, 2.5YR 5/8 (red) to 5YR 4/1
(dark gray) [core]. Grooves at junction of neck/shoulder, diagonal
slashes to left on shoulder. Exterior red slipped.
Early Helladic I.

161 JAR WITH INCISED SHOULDER   Figs. 11, 118
(A6-72-17) Incised body, preserving junction of neck and
shoulder. D. at junction 0.40, Max. pres. W. 0.12, neck Th.
0.12, shoulder Th. 0.009. Volcanic inclusions; color not
determined. Groove at junction of neck and shoulder, vertical
slashes on shoulder. Exterior slipped red and burnished.
Early Helladic I.

162 JAR WITH INCISED SHOULDER   Fig. 11
(A6-1-16) Incised body, preserving neck/ shoulder junction.
Max. pres. W. 0.115, Th. 0.009. Volcanic and quartz inclusions;
evenly fired, 5YR 3/2-3 (dark reddish brown). Groove at junction
neck/shoulder, two diagonal grooves on shoulder. Exterior slipped
red and burnished.
Early Helladic I.

163 CLOSED? VESSEL WITH STAMPED SPIRAL
          Figs. 11, 118
(E16-17) Stamped and incised body. Max. pres. W. 0.035,
Th. 0.009. Medium fabric; volcanic and quartz inclusions;
unevenly fired, 5YR 4/6 (yellowish red) to 5YR 4/4 (reddish
brown) [core]. Stamped spiral, flanked by shallow incised groove.
Exterior slipped red and burnished; interior plain.
Early Helladic I.

164 CLOSED? VESSEL WITH STAMPED SPIRAL
          Figs. 11, 118
(A9-6-23*) Incised and stamped body. Max. pres. W. 0.065,
Th. 0.012. Semicoarse fabric; quartz and little volcanic
inclusions; unevenly fired, 5YR 4/6 (yellowish red) to 5YR 3/3
(dark reddish brown) [core]. Central groove flanked by two sets of
diagonal grooves; portion of stamped spiral between two diagonal
grooves. Exterior slipped red and burnished; interior plain. *may
be A9-9-23.
Early Helladic I.

165   CLOSED VESSEL WITH INCISED BAND
                                         Figs. 11, 118
(F9-ALL-5) Incised body. Max. pres. W. 0.06, Th. 0.007.
Semicoarse fabric; volcanic and quartz inclusions; evenly fired,
5YR 4/6 (yellowish red). Raised band at least 0.033 wide and
0.002 high incised with irregular herringbone. Exterior body (not
on band) slipped red; interior plain.
   Early Helladic I.

166   CLOSED VESSEL WITH INCISION   Fig. 11
(F32-S-128) Incised body. Max. pres. W. 0.06, Th. 0.009.
Medium fabric; volcanic and quartz inclusions; evenly fired, 5YR
4/6 (yellowish red). Shallow groove flanked by alternating
diagonal slashes. Exterior slipped red and burnished; interior
plain.
   Early Helladic I.

167   CLOSED VESSEL WITH INCISION   Fig. 11
(F17-11) Incised body. Max. Pres. W. 0.03, Th. 0.008.
Volcanic inclusions. Groove, diagonal slashes. Exterior slipped
and burnished; interior plain.
   Early Helladic I.

168   CLOSED VESSEL WITH INCISION   Fig. 11
(A6-74-7) Incised body. Max. pres. W. 0.04, Th. 0.007.
Volcanic inclusions. Three converging? grooves, diagonal slash.
Exterior slipped red and burnished.
   Early Helladic I.

169   CLOSED VESSEL WITH INCISION   Fig. 11
(B24-111) Incised body. Max. pres. W. 0.045, Th. 0.008.
Quartz inclusions, no lime. Two sets of parallel grooves at
different orientations, forming hatched triangles? Plain. Could be
fragment of a handle.
   Early Helladic I.

170   CLOSED VESSEL WITH INCISION   Fig. 11
(A33-1-74) Incised body. Max. pres. W. 0.035, Th. 0.003-
0.005. Volcanic inclusions. Two parallel grooves. Exterior
slipped red and burnished.
   Early Helladic I.

171   CLOSED VESSEL WITH INCISION   Fig. 11
(A6-75-20) Incised body. Max. pres. W. 0.03, Th. 0.013.
Quartz inclusions. Two converging grooves, two diagonal
slashes. Exterior slipped red and burnished.
   Early Helladic I.

172   CLOSED VESSEL WITH INCISION   Fig. 11
(A6-72-3) Incised body. Max. pres. W. 0.085, Th. 0.012.
Volcanic and quartz inclusions. At least five parallel grooves.
Exterior slipped red and burnished.
   Early Helladic I.

173   CLOSED VESSEL WITH INCISION   Fig. 11
(A6-72-4) Incised body. Max. pres. W. 0.09, Th. 0.006-
0.007. Volcanic inclusions. Four converging grooves. Exterior
slipped red and burnished.
   Early Helladic I.

174   LARGE OPEN VESSEL WITH INCISION   Fig. 11
(E9-275) Body preserving handle attachment. Max. pres.
W. 0.16, Th. 0.014. Semicoarse fabric; volcanic and quartz
inclusions, no lime; color not determined. Attachment for large

horizontal(?) handle with dowel set into round hole; remnant of
dowel in hole; below attachment, three grooves. Exterior slipped
red.
   Early Helladic I.

175   ASKOS? HANDLE   Fig. 11
(C11-SW-24) Handle fragment. Max. pres. W. 0.045, Max.
pres. L. 0.035. Semifine fabric; little lime; unevenly fired,
2.5YR 6/8 (light red) to 5YR 5/4 (reddish brown) [core]. Wide
vertical strap handle, one end curving to attachment; underside
poorly finished; on top, two parallel longitudinal grooves at each
side, two parallel diagonal grooves between. Slipped red. cf.
Blegen's AII.
   Early Helladic I [Blegen].

176   CLOSED? VESSEL WITH HANDLE   Fig. 11
(C11-C28-15) Handle fragment. Max. pres. W. of handle
0.065, Th. 0.007. Semicoarse fabric; quartz inclusions, much
lime; unevenly fired, 2.5YR 4/6 (red) to 5YR 4/4 (reddish brown)
[core]. Horizontal handle, wide and flat in section; on outer
surface five diagonal lines converging at lower left corner of
handle, vertical groove on wall at handle attachment. Slipped red.
   Early Helladic I.

177   CLOSED? VESSEL WITH HANDLE   Fig. 11
(A6-74-12) Body with handle. Max. pres. W. 0.08, Th.
0.008. Semicoarse fabric; volcanic (black and gold) and quartz
inclusions, no lime; evenly fired 2.5YR 4/6 (red). Horizontal
loop handle, oval in section; three longitudinal grooves on handle
with one continuing onto wall, vertical groove on wall at handle
attachment. Exterior slipped red and burnished.
   Early Helladic I.

178   CLOSED VESSEL WITH HANDLE   Fig. 11
(A6/9-B-5) Body with handle. Max. pres. W. 0.08, Th.
0.006. Medium fabric; quartz inclusions, much lime; evenly
fired, 5YR 5/6 (yellowish red). Horizontal loop handle, oval in
section with flattened ends. Exterior slipped red (almost urfirnis);
interior plain.
   Early Helladic I (to Early Helladic II).

179   CLOSED? VESSEL WITH HANDLE   Fig. 11
(A6-65-2) Body with handle attachments. Max. pres. W.
0.075, Th. 0.007. Medium to semicoarse fabric; quartz and
volcanic (black and gold) inclusions, no lime; evenly fired, 2.5YR
4/6 (red). Tubular handle, vertical orientation. Exterior slipped
red; interior unfinished? (or worn?).
   Early Helladic I.

180   OPEN VESSEL WITH HANDLE   Fig. 11
(E16-16) Body with handle. Max. pres. W. 0.065, Th.
0.006. Medium fabric; volcanic and quartz inclusions, no lime;
evenly fired, 2.5YR 4/8 (red). Tubular handle, vertical
orientation. Exterior slipped red; interior plain.
   Early Helladic I.

181   CLOSED VESSEL WITH LUG   Figs. 11, 119
(A6/9-B-7) Body with pierced lug. Max. pres. W. 0.055,
Th. 0.007, H. of lug 0.035, W. 0.017. Semicoarse fabric; quartz
inclusions, much lime; unevenly fired, 2.5YR 5/8 (red) to 5YR
5/6 (yellowish red) [core]. Vertical? lug pierced horizontally; on
body two parallel grooves at angle to lug. Exterior slipped red and
burnished.
   Early Helladic I.

182 VESSEL WITH LUG Fig. 11
(E13-81-1-63) Body with lug. Max. pres. W. 0.04, Th. 0.005. Medium fabric; quartz inclusions, no lime; evenly fired, 2.5YR 5/8 (red). Lug in shape of rectangular section handle stub, pierced horizontally. Plain.
Early Helladic I.

183 VESSEL WITH LUG Fig. 11
(E74-15-8) Body with lug. Max. pres. W. 0.025, Th. 0.003. Medium fabric; quartz inclusions, no lime; evenly fired, color indet. Small half-round lug, pierced.
Early Helladic I.

184 CLOSED VESSEL WITH KNOB Fig. 11
(C11-SE-22) Body with rounded knob. Max. pres. W. 0.06, Th. 0.010, H. of knob 0.024, D. of knob 0.024. Semicoarse fabric; quartz inclusions, no lime; evenly fired 2.5YR 4/8 (red). Rounded knob on angled constricted stem; perhaps from pithos? Burnished.
Early Helladic I.

185 VESSEL WITH KNOB Fig. 11
(A6/9-A-34) Body with knob. Max. pres. W. 0.06, Th. 0.009, H. of knob 0.02. Semicoarse fabric; quartz inclusions, some lime; unevenly fired, 2.5YR 4/8 (red) to 2.5YR-N3/0 (very dark gray) [core]. Rounded conical knob. Plain.
Early Helladic I.

186 VESSEL WITH SMALL KNOB Fig. 11
(E13-2-18) Body with small knob or pellet. Max. pres. W. 0.045, Th. 0.009, H. of knob 0.006. Semicoarse fabric; volcanic and quartz inclusions, some lime; evenly fired, 5YR 5/4 (reddish brown). Small knob or pellet on exterior. Surfaces not preserved.
Early Helladic I.

187 KNOB Fig. 11
(E4-B-17) Knob. 0.034 x 0.038, H. 0.021. Medium fabric; volcanic and quartz inclusions, no lime; evenly fired, 2.5YR 4/6 (red). Truncated conical knob (broken off from wall?). Plain.
Early Helladic I.

188 CLOSED VESSEL WITH RIDGES Fig. 12
(B9-18) Body. Max. pres. W. 0.095, Th. 0.009-0.011. Semicoarse fabric; quartz inclusions; unevenly fired, 2.5YR 5/8 (red) to 7.5YR 4/4 (brown-dark brown) [core]. Two parallel (vertical?) ridges. Exterior slipped red (almost urfirnis). cf. Blegen's AI.
Early Helladic I (to Early Helladic II).

189 OPEN VESSEL WITH HOLLOW BASE Fig. 12
(A33-1-12) Base. D. 0.12, Max. pres. W. 0.075, Th. 0.008. Semicoarse fabric; volcanic (black) inclusions, little lime; unevenly fired, 5YR 5/4 (reddish brown) to 2.5YR 4/8 (red) to 2.5YR-N4/0 (dark gray) [core]. Slightly hollow base, straight wall. Exterior slipped red (mottling to black) and burnished; interior slipped red and burnished.
Early Helladic I.

190 VESSEL WITH HOLLOW BASE Fig. 12
(B81-2-27) Base. D. 0.07, Max. pres. W. 0.055, Th. 0.005; very worn. Coarse fabric; quartz inclusions, no lime; evenly fired, 5YR 5/1 (gray). Slightly hollow base. Surfaces not preserved.
Early Helladic I.

191 VESSEL WITH HOLLOW BASE Fig. 12
(A33-1-14) Base. D. 0.09, Max. pres. W. 0.075, Th. 0.009. Coarse fabric; quartz inclusions, no lime; unevenly fired, 2.5YR 4/8 (red) to 2.5YR-N3/0 (very dark gray) [core]. Slightly hollow base, steep straight wall. Plain.
Early Helladic I.

192 OPEN VESSEL WITH FLAT BASE Fig. 12
(A6-75-4) Base. D. 0.06, Max. pres. W. 0.045, Th. 0.007. Coarse fabric; quartz inclusions, no lime; unevenly fired, 2.5YR 4/6 (red) to 2.5YR-N4/0 (dark gray) [core]. Flat base, concave then curving wall as if base formed by added disc. Burnished.
Early Helladic I?

193 OPEN VESSEL WITH FLAT BASE Fig. 12
(C11-SW-7) Base. D. 0.06, Max. pres. W. 0.055, Th. 0.007. Medium fabric; quartz inclusions, no lime; evenly fired, 2.5YR 3/4 (dark reddish brown). Flat base. Exterior and bottom slipped red and burnished; interior burnished.
Early Helladic I.

194 OPEN VESSEL WITH FLAT BASE Fig. 12
(A6-72-153) Base, three joining. D. 0.15, Th. 0.009. Coarse fabric; medium to very large inclusions, little lime; evenly fired, 5YR 4/6 (yellowish red). Flat base, wall begins concave then continues convex. Heavily burnished.
Early Helladic I?

195 CLOSED? VESSEL WITH FLAT BASE Fig. 12
(B39-64) Base. D. 0.05, Max. pres. W. 0.035, Th. 0.006. Semicoarse fabric; quartz inclusions, much lime; unevenly fired, 5YR 5/6 (yellowish red) to 5YR 5/3 (reddish brown) [core]. Flat base. Exterior and bottom slipped red and burnished.
Early Helladic I.

196 CLOSED? VESSEL WITH FLAT BASE Fig. 12
(E13-81-1-76) Base. D. 0.09, Max. pres. W. 0.10, Th. 0.009; bottom worn. Medium fabric; quartz and some lime inclusions; unevenly fired, 5YR 6/6 (reddish yellow) to 7.5YR 6/2 (pinkish gray) [core]. Flat base. Exterior slipped red and burnished (almost urfirnis); interior unfinished?
Early Helladic I (late).

197 CLOSED VESSEL WITH FLAT BASE Fig. 12
(E13-11) Base. D. 0.14, Max. pres. W. 0.09, Th. 0.007. Medium fabric; quartz and "silver" inclusions, no lime; unevenly fired, 5YR 5/4 (reddish brown) to 7.5YR 5/2 (brown) [core]. Flat base. Exterior and bottom slipped red and burnished; interior unfinished.
Early Helladic I.

198 CLOSED VESSEL WITH FLAT BASE Fig. 12
(A33-1-31) Base. D. indet., Max. pres. W. 0.09, Th. 0.007. Medium fabric; quartz and some black volcanic minerals, no lime; unevenly fired, 2.5YR 4/8 (red) to 5YR 3/3 (dark reddish brown) [core]. Flat base, straight wall. Exterior slipped red; interior plain.
Early Helladic I.

199 CLOSED VESSEL WITH FLAT BASE Fig. 12
(A33-1-32) Base. D. indet., Max. pres. W. 0.045, Th. 0.006. Semicoarse fabric; volcanic minerals, no lime; unevenly fired, 2.5YR 4/6 (red) to 5YR 4/2 (dark reddish gray) [core]. Flat base. Exterior and bottom slipped red and burnished; interior unfinished?
Early Helladic I.

200 VESSEL WITH FLAT BASE   Fig. 12
(A6-65-6) Base. D. 0.06, Max. pres. W. 0.06, Th. 0.005;
worn. Semicoarse fabric; quartz inclusions, some lime; unevenly
fired, 5YR 5/6 (yellowish red) to 5YR 4/2 (dark reddish gray)
[core]. Flat bottom, concave wall at base then convex as if base
formed by disc. Surfaces not preserved.
Early Helladic I.

201 VESSEL WITH FLAT BASE   Fig. 12
(A33-1-27) Base. D. 0.08, Max. pres. W. 0.05, Th. 0.007.
Medium fabric; silver mica, quartz, some lime inclusions; evenly
fired, 2.5YR-N4/0 (dark gray). Flat base. Plain.
Early Helladic I [Blegen].

202 VESSEL WITH FLAT BASE   Fig. 12
(B81-2-30) Base. D. 0.11, Max. pres. W. 0.09, Th. 0.006;
very worn. Coarse fabric; quartz inclusions, no lime; evenly
fired, 2.5YR 4/8 (red). Flat base. Surfaces not preserved.
Early Helladic I.

203 VESSEL WITH FLAT BASE   Fig. 12
(A9-3-12) Base. D. 0.12, Max. pres. W. 0.06, Th. 0.010.
Semicoarse fabric; volcanic minerals (black) and quartz, no lime;
unevenly fired, 2.5YR 4/6 (red) to 2.5YR-N2.5/0 (black) [core].
Flat base. Plain.
Early Helladic I.

204 VESSEL WITH FLAT BASE   Fig. 12
(E74-8-5) Base. D. 0.18, Max. pres. W. 0.105, Th. 0.009.
Semicoarse fabric; volcanic (black) and quartz inclusions, no lime;
unevenly fired, 5YR 3/3 (dark reddish brown) to 5YR 2.5/1
(black) [core]. Flat base. Plain.
Early Helladic I.

205 MAT IMPRESSED FLAT BASE   Fig. 12
(A6-74-65) Base with mat impression. D. 0.09, Max. pres.
W. 0.10, Th. 0.009. Semicoarse fabric; volcanic minerals (black
and gold), no lime; unevenly fired, 2.5YR 4/8 (red) to 2.5YR-
N2.5/0 (black) [core]. Flat base; deep impression of mat. Plain.
Early Helladic I.

206 FRYING PAN?   Fig. 119
(F9-2) Body. Max. pres. W. 0.04, Th. 0.006. Medium
fabric; volcanic inclusions; evenly fired, 5YR 3/2 (dark reddish
brown). Very flat sherd. Portions of two stamped spirals (or
circles) with tangential shallow groove. Slipped red and
burnished.
Early Helladic I.

207 KNOB TO STAND
(A6-74-13) Knob fragment. Max. pres. H. 0.06, Max. pres.
D. 0.065. Solid stem circular to triangular in section. Slipped
red. cf. Blegen's AII.
Early Helladic I [Blegen].

208 KNOB TO STAND
(B53-3-3) Knob fragment. Max. pres. H. 0.06, Max. pres.
D. 0.058. Coarse fabric, volcanic (black and gold) inclusions.
Solid circular stem.
Early Helladic I.

209 WEIGHT?   Fig. 12
(E9-168) Body. Max. pres. W. 0.04, Th. 0.011. Medium
fabric; volcanic and quartz inclusions; color not determined.

Early Helladic I closed red slipped and burnished body sherd
reused as weight by drilling hole through it. Reuse date not
determined, but Early Helladic I?

210 SPINDLE WHORL   Fig. 12
(F9-ALL-6) Whorl, ca. one-half preserved. D. 0.055, H.
0.020, D. of hole ca. 0.010. Semicoarse fabric; volcanic (black
and gold) and quartz inclusions, no lime; evenly fired, 5YR 3/1
(very dark gray). Truncated conical whorl, slightly concave on
bottom. Plain.
Early Helladic I.

211 SPINDLE WHORL   Fig. 12
(C25--) Whorl, ca. one-half preserved. D. 0.055, Ht. 0.018,
D. of hole ca. 0.009. Semicoarse fabric; quartz inclusions, no
lime; evenly fired, 5YR 3/2 (dark reddish brown). Surfaces worn.
Early Helladic I.

212 SPINDLE WHORL   Fig. 12
(C25-M) Complete conical whorl, D. at top 0.061, D. at
bottom 0.013, D. perf. 0.009, Ht. 0.018. Coarse, color not
determined. Plain.
Early Helladic I.

EARLY HELLADIC II

213 SAUCEBOAT   Fig. 13
(A6-65-20) Spout. Max. pres. L. 0.075, Th. 0.004.
Semifine fabric; unevenly fired, 7.5YR 5/4 (brown) to 5YR 4/1
(dark gray) [core]. Slipped (self slip?). Type II (Caskey
1960:290; Fahy 1964:25).
Early Helladic II.

214 SAUCEBOAT   Fig. 13
(A6-2-2) Rim and handle. Semifine fabric; evenly fired,
7.5YR-N6/0 (gray-light gray). Pointed rim; horizontal handle.
Exterior slipped yellow and polished, no reserve below handle;
interior slipped blue and polished. Typical profile for AEP
sauceboats.
Early Helladic II.

215 SAUCEBOAT   Fig. 13
(A6-72-22) Rim. Semifine fabric; evenly fired, 10YR 5/1
(gray). Pointed lip. Slipped yellow-blue and polished.
Early Helladic II.

216 SAUCEBOAT   Figs. 13, 119
(A6-65-21) Rim. Semifine fabric; unevenly fired, 5YR 6/6
(reddish yellow) to 7.5YR 5/2 (brown) [core]. Pointed lip.
Exterior painted red (urfirnis?) and scribble burnished; interior
painted red. Blegen's AII? and therefore early?
Early Helladic II.

217 SAUCEBOAT   Figs. 13, 119
(C11-NE-15) Rim. Semifine fabric; evenly fired, 7.5YR 6/6
(reddish yellow). Lip bevelled to interior (ridge at lip). Painted
mottled red-black (urfirnis), metallic luster in spots.
Early Helladic II.

218 SAUCEBOAT   Fig. 13
(A6-74-100) Rim. Fine fabric; unevenly fired, 7.5YR 7/6
(reddish yellow) to 7.5YR 7/4 (pink) [core]. Slightly flaring rim,
pointed lip. Painted black (urfirnis).
Early Helladic II.

219 SAUCEBOAT Fig. 13
(A6/9-B-27) Rim. Fine fabric; unevenly fired, 5YR 6/8 (reddish yellow) to 7.5YR-N5/0 (gray) [core]. Rim carinated; lip pointed. Painted black (urfirnis).
Early Helladic II.

220 SAUCEBOAT Fig. 13
(F32-E-47) Rim. Fine fabric; evenly fired, 10YR 7/4 (very pale brown). Groove at lip. Painted black (urfirnis).
Early Helladic II.

221 SAUCEBOAT Figs. 13, 119
(A33-81-1-1) Rim. Semifine fabric; evenly fired, 7.5YR 7/6 (reddish yellow). Lip tapering to rounded. Painted black (urfirnis).
Early Helladic II.

222 SAUCEBOAT Fig. 13
(E13-2-56) Rim. Semifine fabric; small silver inclusions, some lime; evenly fired, 2.5YR 5/8 (red). Flattened lip. Exterior painted red (urfirnis); interior plain. Not local fabric.
Early Helladic II.

223 SAUCEBOAT Fig. 13
(F32-N-214) Rim and handle. Fine fabric; unevenly fired, 5YR 5/6 (yellowish red) to 5YR 6/3 (light reddish brown) [core]. Flattened rim; horizontal slightly upswung handle, subrectangular in section. Painted black (urfirnis).
Early Helladic II.

224 SAUCEBOAT Fig. 13
(F32-S-183) Body (near rim) and handle. Semifine fabric; evenly fired, 7.5YR 4/2 (dark brown-brown). Horizontal upswung handle, subrectangular in section. Painted black (urfirnis), reserved area under handle.
Early Helladic II.

225 SMALL INCURVING BOWL Fig. 13
(A6-65-16) Rim. D. 0.07, Max. pres. W. 0.03, Th. 0.004. Semifine fabric; evenly fired, 7.5YR 7/6 (reddish yellow). Curving wall, pointed lip. Exterior painted black mottled to red (urfirnis); interior painted black (urfirnis).
Early Helladic II.

226 SMALL INCURVING BOWL Fig. 13
(C11-ALL-5) Rim. D. 0.13, Max. pres. W. 0.05, Th. 0.005. Semifine fabric; no lime; evenly fired, 10YR 7/3 (very pale brown). Incurving wall, bevelled lip. Painted black (urfirnis). "Corinthian" fabric.
Early Helladic II.

227 SHALLOW INCURVING BOWL Fig. 13
(F29-7) Rim. D. 0.15, Max. pres. W. 0.095, Th. 0.004. Medium fabric; some lime; unevenly fired, 7.5YR 6/6 (reddish yellow) to 7.5YR 5/2 (brown) [core]. Incurved rim, pointed lip. Plain.
Early Helladic II.

228 SHALLOW INCURVING BOWL Fig. 13
(E4-A-1) Rim. D. 0.15, one-quarter circumference preserved, Th. 0.003. Semifine fabric; unevenly fired, 5YR 5/8 (yellowish red) to 5YR 4/1 (dark gray) [core]. Curving wall, pointed lip. Painted black (urfirnis).
Early Helladic II.

229 SMALL INCURVING BOWL Fig. 13
(E5-2-25) Rim. D. 0.16, Max. pres. W. 0.04. Medium fabric; some silver inclusions, some lime; unevenly fired, 5YR 5/6 (yellowish red) to 5YR 4/2 (dark reddish gray) [core]. Incurving wall, slightly thickened rim, flattened lip. Traces of slip.
Early Helladic I to Early Helladic II.

230 SMALL INCURVING BOWL Fig. 13
(A6-65-15) Rim. D. 0.19, Max. pres. W. 0.065, Th. 0.004. Semifine fabric; little lime; evenly fired, 5YR 4/6 (yellowish red). Incurving rim, rounded lip. Painted black (urfirnis).
Early Helladic II.

231 SMALL INCURVING BOWL Fig. 13
(F5-75-11) Rim. D. 0.20, Max. pres. W. 0.045, Th. 0.007. Semifine fabric; some lime; unevenly fired, 7.5YR 6/6 (reddish yellow) to 7.5YR-N6/0 (gray-light gray) [core]. Incurving wall, rim bevelled to interior and exterior. Exterior painted red-black mottled (urfirnis); interior painted black (urfirnis).
Early Helladic II.

232 SMALL INCURVING BOWL Fig. 13
(E5-A-10) Rim. D. 0.22, Max. pres. W. 0.06, Th. 0.006. Medium fabric; some lime; evenly fired, 5YR 5/4 (reddish brown). Incurving rim, rounded lip. Painted red and burnished?
Early Helladic I to Early Helladic II.

233 SMALL INCURVING BOWL Fig. 13
(A6/9-A-4) Rim. D. 0.23, Max. pres. W. 0.06, Th. 0.005. Semicoarse fabric; no lime; unevenly fired, 5YR 5/6 (yellowish red) to 5YR 5/1 (gray) [core]. Incurving wall, slightly thickened rim, flattened lip. Plain.
Early Helladic II.

234 SMALL BOWL WITH INTURNED RIM Fig. 13
(F32-A9-2) Rim. D. 0.20, Max. pres. W. 0.05, Th. 0.005. Medium fabric; little lime; evenly fired, 7.5YR 5/6 (strong brown). Rim inturned to horizontal, rounded lip. Exterior worn?; interior painted red (urfirnis). cf. **235, 236, 237**; import from Boiotia?
Early Helladic II.

235 SMALL BOWL WITH INTURNED RIM Fig. 13
(A6/9-B-14) Rim. D. 0.20, Max. pres. W. 0.04, Th. 0.004. Semifine fabric; some lime; unevenly fired, 5YR 4/4 (reddish brown) to 5YR 5/1 (gray) [core]. Curving wall, inturned to horizontal rim. Slipped (mottled black to 2.5Y 5/4 [light olive brown]) and burnished to high gloss. cf. **234, 236, 237**; import from Boiotia?
Early Helladic II.

236 SMALL BOWL WITH INTURNED RIM Fig. 13
(F32-C5-2) Rim. D. 0.20, Max. pres. W. 0.04, Th. 0.005. Semifine fabric; some lime; unevenly fired, 5YR 5/4 (reddish brown) to 5YR 5/1 (gray) [core]. Curving wall, inturned to horizontal rim. Painted red (urfirnis) and burnished? cf. **234, 235, 237**; import from Boiotia?
Early Helladic II.

237 SMALL BOWL WITH INTURNED RIM Fig. 13
(A6-72-158) Rim. D. 0.20, Max. pres. W. 0.05, Th. 0.006. Semifine fabric; much lime; unevenly fired 2.5YR 4/8 (red) to 5YR 4/4 (reddish brown) [core]. Curving wall, inturned to

horizontal rim. Mottled green slip (ca. 10YR 4-5/3 [brown]) and burnished to high gloss. cf. **234, 235, 236**; import from Boiotia?
Early Helladic II.

238   SMALL INTURNED BOWL   Fig. 13
(F20-ALL-16) Complete profile of joining rim and foot. D. rim 0.15, D. foot 0.05, Max. pres. W. 0.08, Th. 0.006. Semifine fabric; unevenly fired, 7.5YR 7/6 (reddish yellow) to 5YR 4/1 (dark gray) [core]. Splayed ring foot, curving wall, inturned rim, rounded lip. Exterior painted red-brown (urfirnis); interior plain?
Early Helladic II.

239   SMALL INTURNED BOWL   Fig. 13
(E13-2-49) Rim. D. 0.13, Max. pres. W. 0.065, Th. 0.004. Semifine fabric; little lime; unevenly fired, 5YR 5/6 (yellowish red) to 5YR 6/1 (gray-light gray) [core]. Curving wall, inturned rim, pointed lip. Painted brown (urfirnis).
Early Helladic II.

240   SMALL INTURNED BOWL   Fig. 13
(B43-80-2-9) Rim. D. 0.13, Max. pres. W. 0.07, Th. 0.006. Medium fabric; some lime; unevenly fired, 7.5YR 6/6 (reddish yellow) to 5YR 5/1 (gray) [core]. Curving wall, inturned rim, pointed lip. Exterior painted black (urfirnis); interior surface not preserved.
Early Helladic II.

241   SMALL INTURNED BOWL   Fig. 13
(E5-B-4) Rim. D. 0.14, Max. pres. W. 0.07, Th. 0.005. Semifine fabric; little lime; unevenly fired, 7.5YR 6/6 (reddish yellow) to 10YR 5/2 (grayish brown) [core]. Curving wall, inturned to vertical rim, rounded lip. Slipped (cream) and burnished (yellow-blue slip and polish?).
Early Helladic II.

242   SMALL INTURNED BOWL   Fig. 13
(A6-74-56) Rim. D. 0.15, Max. pres. W. 0.03, Th. 0.005. Semifine fabric; unevenly fired, 5YR 6/6 (reddish yellow) to 5YR 5/2 (reddish gray) [core]. Curving wall, inturned rim, pointed lip. Slipped yellow and polished.
Early Helladic II.

243   SMALL INTURNED BOWL WITH TAENIA   Fig. 13
(E9-264) Rim. D. 0.15, Max. pres. W. 0.045, Th. 0.005. Semifine fabric; unevenly fired, 5YR 6/6 (reddish yellow) to 5YR 5/1 (gray) [core]. Incurving wall, flattened lip; below lip, taenia (impressed band) ending. Exterior band, interior, lip painted brown (urfirnis).
Early Helladic II.

244   FLARING BOWL   Fig. 13
(B7-11) Rim. D. 0.14, Max. pres. W. 0.055, Th. 0.004. Medium fabric; evenly fired, 5YR 6/6 (reddish yellow). Painted red (urfirnis).
Early Helladic II.

245   SMALL SPREADING BOWL   Fig. 14
(F20-18) Rim. D. 0.15, Max. pres. W. 0.065, Th. 0.005. Semifine fabric; some lime; unevenly fired, 5YR 5/6 (yellowish red) to 5YR 5/1 (gray) [core]. Straight splayed wall, slightly rounded lip. Exterior plain; interior painted thin wash (urfirnis).
Early Helladic II.

246   MEDIUM SPREADING BOWL   Fig. 14
(B24-60) Rim. D. 0.29, Max. pres. W. 0.06, Th. 0.004. Medium fabric; little lime; unevenly fired, 5YR 5/8 (yellowish red) to 5YR 5/2 (reddish gray) [core]. Curving wall, rim slightly thickened to exterior. Exterior slipped?; interior painted black (urfirnis).
Early Helladic II.

247   MEDIUM BASIN   Fig. 14
(A6-72-57) Rim. D. 0.30, Max. pres. W. 0.06, Th. 0.008. Semicoarse fabric; little lime; unevenly fired, 5YR 5/6 (yellowish red) to 5YR 5/1 (gray) [core]. Splayed, straight wall; lip thickened to exterior. Exterior painted streaky brown-black (urfirnis wash).
Early Helladic II.

248   MEDIUM SPREADING BOWL   Fig. 14
(F32-S-104) Rim. D. 0.30, Max. pres. W. 0.065, Th. 0.009. Semicoarse fabric; silver inclusions, some lime; unevenly fired, 5YR 5/6 (yellowish red) to 5YR 3/1 (very dark gray) [core]. Curving wall, rim thickened to exterior. Plain?
(Early Helladic I to) Early Helladic II.

249   MEDIUM BASIN   Fig. 14
(B24-51) Rim. D. 0.32, Max. pres. W. 0.08, Th. 0.010. Medium fabric, some lime; unevenly fired, 7.5YR 6/6 (reddish yellow) to 10YR 5/1 (gray) [core]. Splayed straight wall, slightly thickened rim. Slipped red.
Early Helladic I? or Early Helladic II.

250   MEDIUM BASIN   Fig. 14
(B43-B-2) Rim. D. 0.32, Max. pres. W. 0.08, Th. 0.010. Semicoarse fabric; much lime; unevenly fired, 2.5YR 5/8 (red) to 5YR 4/3 (reddish brown) [core]. Slightly curving wall, rim slightly thickened to exterior. Surfaces not preserved.
Early Helladic II.

251   MEDIUM BASIN   Fig. 14
(F20-17) Rim. D. 0.33, Max. pres. W. 0.115, Th. 0.007. Semicoarse fabric; some lime; unevenly fired, 2.5YR 5/8 (red) to 7.5YR 5/2 (brown) [core]. Splayed wall, slightly thickened rim, rounded lip. Exterior painted thin black wash (urfirnis); interior and lip painted black (urfirnis).
Early Helladic II.

252   LARGE BASIN   Fig. 14
(F32-N-124) Rim. D. 0.38, Max. pres. W. 0.08, Th. 0.006. Semicoarse fabric; no lime; unevenly fired, 5YR 4/4 (reddish brown) to 2.5YR 5/8 (red) [core]. Straight wall, slightly incurving and slightly thickened rim, flat lip overhanging to interior. Exterior band painted thin urfirnis.
Early Helladic II.

253   LARGE BASIN WITH TAENIA   Fig. 14
(E4-B-1) Rim. D. 0.40, Max. pres. W. 0.065, Th. 0.009. Medium fabric; some lime; unevenly fired, 5YR 6/6 (reddish yellow) to 5YR 4/1 (dark gray) [core]. Spreading wall, slightly thickened rim, round lip; below rim, taenia band of overlapping discs to left (i.e., backwards from majority). Surfaces not preserved.
Early Helladic II.

254 LARGE BASIN WITH TAENIA   Fig. 14
(F32-7) Rim. D. 0.46, Max. pres. W. 0.13, Th. 0.011.
Semicoarse fabric; much lime; unevenly fired, 5YR 5/6
(yellowish red) to 5YR 5/2 (reddish gray) [core]. Spreading
straight wall, rim thickened to exterior, rounded lip bevelled to
exterior; below rim, taenia band of overlapping discs to right.
Plain?
Early Helladic II.

255 LARGE BOWL WITH TAENIA   Figs. 15, 119
(C11-C19-2) Rim. D. 0.46, Max. pres. W. 0.07, Th.
0.008. Semicoarse fabric; some lime; unevenly fired, 5YR 5/6
(yellowish red) to 7.5YR-N3/0 (very dark gray) [core]. Incurving
wall, rim very thickened to "T", lip flattened; below rim, taenia
band of impressions on high pointed ridge. Exterior slipped (self
slip), interior and lip painted? red (urfirnis).
Early Helladic II.

256 LARGE BOWL WITH TAENIA   Figs. 15, 119
(E16-10) Rim. D. 0.47, Max. pres. W. 0.12, Th. 0.009.
Semicoarse fabric; no lime; evenly fired, 5YR 3/4 (dark reddish
brown). Curving wall, rim thickened to interior forming incurve,
flat lip bevelled to interior; below lip, taenia band of finger
impressions on ridge. Plain.
Early Helladic II.

257 LARGE BOWL WITH TAENIA   Figs. 15, 119
(F32-N-68) Rim. D. 0.058, Max. pres. W. 0.075, Th.
0.011. Coarse fabric; little lime; unevenly fired, 5YR 3/3 (dark
reddish brown) to 5YR 3/1 (very dark gray) [core]. Vertical? wall,
rim thickened, flat horizontal lip; below lip, very wide taenia of
overlapping discs to left (or impressions on ridge resembling
overlapping discs?). Plain.
Early Helladic II.

258 LARGE BASIN or BOWL WITH TAENIA   Fig. 15
(B43-80-2-3) Rim. D. 0.62, Max. pres. W. 0.155, Th.
0.013. Coarse fabric; very much lime; unevenly fired, 2.5YR 4/6
(red) to 5YR 3/4 (dark reddish brown) [core]. Spreading wall,
thickened rim, rounded lip; below rim, taenia band of overlapping
discs to right. Plain.
Early Helladic II.

259 LARGE BOWL or BASIN WITH TAENIA
        Figs. 15, 119
(A6-72-82) Rim. D. 0.65-0.66, Max. pres. W. 0.10, Th.
0.007. Semicoarse fabric; little lime; unevenly fired, 2.5YR 4/6
(red) to 5YR 4/4 (reddish brown) [core]. Curving wall, rim very
thickened to exterior to form wide slightly rounded lip; below rim,
taenia band with impressions from bottom of ridge forming
scallop or wave pattern (originally widely spaced overlapping discs
to left?). Exterior band, interior band, and lip painted black.
Early Helladic II.

260 LARGE BOWL or BASIN WITH TAENIA   Fig. 15
(A6-7-2) Rim. D. 0.72, Max. pres. W. 0.08, Th. 0.016.
Coarse fabric; much lime; unevenly fired, 2.5YR 4/8 (red) to
2.5YR 4/6 (red) [core]. Spreading wall, rim thickened to triangle,
rounded lip; below rim, taenia band of overlapping discs to right.
Plain.
Early Helladic II.

261 LARGE BOWL or BASIN WITH TAENIA   Fig. 15
(F15-2) Rim. D. indet., Max. pres. W. 0.05, Th. 0.009.
Semicoarse fabric; silver inclusions, little lime; unevenly fired,
2.5YR 5/8 (red) to 5YR 5/1 (gray) [core]. Spreading, slightly
incurving wall, rim thickened to exterior, slightly rounded lip
bevelled to exterior; below rim, taenia band of impressions on low
ridge. Exterior surface not preserved; interior plain.
Early Helladic I to Early Helladic II ?

262 LARGE BOWL or BASIN WITH TAENIA   Fig. 15
(F32-8) Rim. D. indet., Max. pres. W. 0.12, Th. 0.016.
Semicoarse fabric; much lime; unevenly fired, 5YR 6/8 (reddish
yellow) to 7.5YR 5/2 (brown) [core]. Straight? wall, rim
thickened to triangle, round lip; below lip, taenia band of
overlapping discs to left. Surfaces not preserved.
Early Helladic II.

263 LARGE SPREADING BOWL WITH INCISION Fig. 15
(F32-N-41) Rim. D. indet., Max. pres. W. 0.035, Th.
0.006; worn. Incurving wall, outturned rim; below rim, row of
small triangles.
Early Helladic II.

264 MEDIUM DEEP BOWL   Fig. 15
(A6-74-85) Rim. D. est. 0.32, Max. pres. W. 0.05, Th.
0.005. Semicoarse fabric; some lime; unevenly fired, 5YR 3/2
(dark reddish brown) to 5YR 4/4 (reddish brown) [core]. Straight
wall, slightly splayed, slightly thickened rim, flattened lip. Plain.
Early Helladic II ?

265 MEDIUM DEEP BOWL   Fig. 15
(F6-12) Rim. D. 0.32, Max. pres. W. 0.06, Th. 0.008.
Medium fabric; some lime; unevenly fired, 5YR 5/8 (yellowish
red) to 7.5YR 5/2 (brown) [core]. Slightly incurving wall, rim
thickened to exterior. Slipped (self slip).
Early Helladic II.

266 LARGE DEEP BOWL WITH TAENIA   Figs. 15, 119
(F6-1) Rim. D. indet., Max. pres. W. 0.13, Th. 0.010.
Coarse fabric; very much lime; evenly fired, 2.5YR 4/6 (red).
Vertical wall, rim thickened especially to exterior, rounded lip; on
rim, taenia band of two separate sets of impressions on ridge.
Slipped (self).
Early Helladic II.

267 LARGE DEEP BOWL WITH TAENIA   Fig. 15
(F15-5) Rim. D. indet., Max. pres. W. 0.04, Th. 0.011.
Slightly thickening rim, round lip. Below lip, taenia band of
slashes to right.
Early Helladic II.

268 MEDIUM SHALLOW BOWL   Fig. 16
(A6/9-B-19) Rim. D. 0.25, Max. pres. W. 0.045, Th.
0.006. Medium fabric; little lime; unevenly fired, 2.5YR 4/8
(red) to 5YR 4/4 (reddish brown) [core]. Curving sides, slightly
thickened rim, flattened lip. Slipped (self slip); lip painted red
(urfirnis).
Early Helladic II.

269 MEDIUM SHALLOW BOWL   Fig. 16
(F32-S-45) Rim. D. 0.26, Max. pres. W. 0.05, Th. 0.008.
Medium fabric; some lime; unevenly fired, 7.5YR 6/6 (reddish
yellow) to 5YR 5/1 (gray) [core]. Curving wall, rim thickened to
exterior, flattened lip bevelled to exterior. Surfaces not preserved.
Early Helladic II.

270 MEDIUM SHALLOW BOWL   Fig. 16
(F5-118) Rim. D. 0.26, Max. pres. W. 0.06, Th. 0.005. Medium fabric; silver inclusions, little lime; unevenly fired, 5YR 5/6 (yellowish red) to 10YR 5/1 (gray) [core]. Slightly incurving wall, thickened rim, lip bevelled to interior and exterior. Traces of slip?
Early Helladic II.

271 LARGE SHALLOW BOWL   Fig. 16
(F32-A5-3) Rim. D. est. 0.35, Max. pres. W. 0.07, Th. 0.006. Semicoarse fabric; some lime; unevenly fired, 5YR 6/4 (light reddish brown) to 5YR 5/1 (gray) [core]. Incurving wall, rim thickened to exterior, rounded lip. Exterior painted black (urfirnis)?
Early Helladic II.

272 LARGE SHALLOW BOWL   Fig. 16
(F5-259) Rim. D. 0.35, Max. pres. W. 0.055, Th. 0.009. Semicoarse fabric; few gold inclusions, some lime; evenly fired, 7.5YR 6/6 (reddish yellow). Incurving rim and slightly thickened lip formed by constricting exterior profile with groove; flattened lip. Plain.
Early Helladic I to Early Helladic II.

273 LARGE SHALLOW BOWL   Fig. 16
(B43-3) Rim. D. est. 0.36, Max. pres. W. 0.045, Th. 0.011. Semicoarse fabric; no lime; evenly fired, 2.5YR 4/8 (red). Slightly incurving wall, groove on lip. Plain?
Early Helladic I to Early Helladic II.

274 LARGE SHALLOW BOWL   Fig. 16
(F32-N-16) Rim. D. 0.41, Max. pres. W. 0.06, Th. 0.011. Medium fabric; few very large inclusions, little lime; evenly fired, 7.5YR 6/4 (light brown). Curving wall, rounded lip. Painted black.
Early Helladic II.

275 LARGE SHALLOW BOWL   Fig. 16
(F32-A3-9) Rim. D. indet., Max. pres. W. 0.03, Th. 0.006. Semicoarse fabric; some silver inclusions, some lime; unevenly fired, 2.5YR 5/8 (red) to 7.5YR 5/4 (brown) [core]. Incurving wall, thickened rim, flattened lip. Interior and lip painted red-brown.
(Early Helladic I to) Early Helladic II.

276 MEDIUM SHALLOW BOWL WITH LUG   Fig. 16
(A6-74-29) Rim with lug. D. 0.27, Max. pres. W. 0.04, Th. 0.005. Medium fabric; some lime; unevenly fired, 2.5YR 5/6 (red) to 7.5YR 6/6 (reddish yellow) [core]. Rim extended to exterior forming lug, pierced vertically (lug may extend to right for double pointed lug?). Slipped (self slip).
Early Helladic II?

277 MEDIUM SHALLOW BOWL WITH LUG   Fig. 16
(B43-80-2-4) Rim with lug. D. 0.29, Max. pres. W. 0.05, Th. 0.005. Medium fabric; little lime; unevenly fired, 5YR 6/6 (reddish yellow) to 5YR 4/1 (dark gray) [core]. Splayed sides, thickened rim; rim extended to exterior to form horizontal lug (originally double?), pierced vertically; lug decorated with taenia to right of hole. Plain?
Early Helladic II?

278 MEDIUM SHALLOW BOWL WITH LUG   Fig. 16
(A6-74-69) Rim with lug. D. 0.34, Max. pres. W. 0.06, Th. 0.006. Medium fabric; little lime; unevenly fired, 7.5YR 7/6 (reddish yellow) to 5YR 5/1 (gray) [core]. Incurving wall, rim thickened to exterior forming irregular projecting lug. Plain.
Early Helladic II.

279 LARGE SHALLOW BOWL WITH TRUMPET LUG
                                                Fig. 16
(F32-S-66) Rim. D. 0.36, Max. pres. W. 0.05, Th. 0.009. Semicoarse fabric; some lime; unevenly fired, 5YR 4/4 (reddish brown) to 5YR 3/1 (very dark gray) [core]. Incurving wall, rim thickened to exterior; below rim, horizontal ridge terminating to left in slight thickening (trumpet lug?). Interior and lip slipped red-brown and burnished.
Early Helladic I (to Early Helladic II).

280 LARGE SHALLOW BOWL WITH KNICKED RIM
                                                Fig. 16
(F32-S-68) Rim. D. 0.35-0.45, Th. 0.014. Semicoarse fabric; unevenly fired, 5YR 4/6 (yellowish red) to 5YR 4/4 (reddish brown) [core]. Curving wall, thickened rim, flat horizontal lip; nicks in outer edge of lip. Plain?
Early Helladic II.

281 LARGE SHALLOW BOWL WITH KNICKED RIM
                                                Fig. 16
(F32-SF-15) Rim. D. indet., Th. 0.011. Medium fabric; unevenly fired, 5YR 5/6 (yellowish red) to 5YR 6/1 (gray-light gray) [core]. Curving wall, slightly thickened rim, flattened lip; nicks in outer edge of lip. Painted brown (urfirnis).
Early Helladic II.

282 LARGE HEMISPHERICAL BOWL WITH LUG Fig. 16
(F32-14) Rim. D. est. 0.40, Max. pres W. 0.07, Th. 0.007. Curving wall, flat lip. Horizontal lug 0.007 high ending to right.
Early Helladic II early?

283 MEDIUM BOWL   Fig. 16
(C11-SE-9) Rim. D. est. 0.20, Max. pres. W. 0.03, Th. 0.006. Medium fabric; silver inclusions, little lime; unevenly fired, 5YR 6/6 (reddish yellow) to 5YR 5/2 (reddish gray) [core]. Incurving wall, slightly thickened rim, flattened lip. Slipped (self slip).
Early Helladic II.

284 MEDIUM INCURVING BOWL   Fig. 16
(F32-25) Rim. D. 0.20, Max. pres. W. 0.04, Th. 0.005. Semifine fabric; little lime; evenly fired, 7.5YR 6/4 (light brown). Incurving wall, rim thickened to exterior, flattened lip. Painted black (urfirnis).
Early Helladic II.

285 MEDIUM INCURVING BOWL   Fig. 16
(A6/9-A-8) Rim. D. 0.24, Max. pres. W. 0.045, Th. 0.005. Medium fabric; much lime; evenly fired, 5YR 6/8 (reddish yellow). Incurving wall, rim thickened to exterior, flattened lip. Plain?
Early Helladic II.

286 MEDIUM INCURVING BOWL   Fig. 16
(F32-3) Rim. D. 0.25, Max. pres. W. 0.065, Th. 0.007. Medium fabric; some silver inclusions, some lime; unevenly fired, 7.5YR 5/4 (brown) to 7.5YR-N5/0 (gray) [core]. Incurving wall, slightly thickened rim. Traces of red paint.
Early Helladic II.

287 MEDIUM INCURVING BOWL Fig. 16

(F32-S-22) Rim. D. 0.25, Max. pres. W. 0.065, Th. 0.005. Medium fabric; many silver inclusions, little lime; unevenly fired, 5YR 6/6 (reddish yellow) to 5YR 6/1 (gray-light gray) [core]. Incurving wall, slightly thickened rim, flattened lip. Exterior painted red (urfirnis); interior painted black (urfirnis).

Early Helladic II.

288 MEDIUM INCURVING BOWL Fig. 16

(F5-B-33) Rim. D. 0.25, Max. pres. W. 0.06, Th. 0.005. Semicoarse fabric; some lime; unevenly fired, 5YR 5/6 (yellowish red) to 5YR 5/4 (brown) [core]. Sharply incurving wall, slightly thickened rim, flattened lip. Exterior slipped (self slip) and burnished.

Early Helladic II.

289 MEDIUM INCURVING BOWL Fig. 16

(F32-S-52) Rim. D. 0.27, Max. pres. W. 0.055, Th. 0.005. Medium fabric; some lime; unevenly fired, 7.5YR 6/6 (reddish yellow) to 5YR 6/1 (gray-light gray) [core]. Sharply incurving wall, rim thickened. Slipped yellow-blue and polished.

Early Helladic II.

290 MEDIUM INCURVING BOWL Fig. 16

(F32-N-96) Rim. D. 0.28, Max. pres. W. 0.065, Th. 0.006. Medium fabric; silver inclusions, little lime; unevenly fired, 2.5YR 5/8 (red) to 10YR 5/3 (brown) [core]. Incurving wall, slightly thickened rim, flattened lip. Slipped (self slip).

(Early Helladic I? to) Early Helladic II.

291 MEDIUM INCURVING BOWL Fig. 16

(F20-ALL-12) Rim. D. 0.29, Max. pres. W. 0.08, Th. 0.006. Medium fabric; much lime; unevenly fired, 2.5YR 5/8 (red) to 10YR 5/3 (brown) [core]. Incurving wall, slightly thickened rim, flattened lip. Exterior surface not preserved; interior and lip painted black (urfirnis).

Early Helladic II.

292 MEDIUM INCURVING BOWL Fig. 17

(G9-1) Rim. D. 0.29, Max. pres. W. 0.03, Th. 0.005. Medium fabric; some lime; evenly fired, 2.5YR 4/6 (red). Incurving wall, rim thickened, lip slightly rounded. Plain.

Early Helladic II early.

293 MEDIUM INCURVING BOWL Fig. 17

(G9-1-8) Rim. D. 0.29, Max. pres. W. 0.04, Th. 0.005. Medium fabric; some lime; evenly fired, 2.5YR 5/8 (red). Incurving wall, rim thickened to exterior, flattened lip. Plain.

Early Helladic II early.

294 MEDIUM INCURVING BOWL Fig. 17

(F32-N-83) Rim. D. 0.31, Max. pres. W. 0.075, Th. 0.005. Semicoarse fabric; little lime; evenly fired, 5YR 5/6 (reddish yellow). Incurving wall, rim thickened in and out. Exterior surface not preserved; interior and lip painted brown (urfirnis).

Early Helladic II.

295 LARGE INCURVING BOWL Fig. 17

(A33-81-1-32) Rim. D 0.36, Max. pres. W. 0.045, Th. 0.009. Medium fabric; little lime; unevenly fired, 7.5YR 4/6 (strong brown) to 7.5YR 3/2 (dark brown) [core]. Incurving wall, rounded lip. Plain.

Early Helladic II.

296 LARGE INCURVING BOWL Fig. 17

(F32-1) Rim. D. 0.37, Max. pres. W. 0.12, Th. 0.009. Semicoarse fabric; some lime; unevenly fired, 5YR 6/6 (reddish yellow) to 7.5YR 5/2 (brown) [core]. Incurving wall, rim slightly thickened in and out. Interior painted red (urfirnis).

Early Helladic II.

297 LARGE INCURVING BOWL Fig. 17

(F32-S-103) Rim. D. 0.39, Max. pres. W. 0.06, Th. 0.008. Semicoarse fabric; much lime; unevenly fired, 5YR 5/6 (yellowish red) to 5YR 3/2 (dark reddish brown) [core]. Incurving wall, rim thickened in and out to "T". Plain.

Early Helladic II.

298 LARGE INCURVING BOWL Fig. 17

(B43-80-1-1) Rim. D. est. 0.40, Max. pres. W. 0.055, Th. 0.008. Medium fabric; some lime; unevenly fired, 5YR 5/6-6/8 (yellowish red to reddish yellow) to 7.5YR 5/2 (brown) [core]. Incurving wall, rim thickened in and out. Surfaces not preserved.

Early Helladic II.

299 LARGE INCURVING BOWL Fig. 17

(F32-N-144) Rim. D. est. 0.40, Max. pres. W. 0.85, Th. 0.008. Medium fabric; little lime; unevenly fired, 5YR 6/8 (reddish yellow) to 5YR 6/1 (gray-light gray) [core]. Incurving wall, thickened rim, flattened lip. Surfaces not preserved.

Early Helladic II.

300 LARGE INCURVING BOWL Fig. 17

(F32-A5-1) Rim. D. 0.42, Max. pres. W. 0.075, Th. 0.010. Medium fabric; much lime; unevenly fired, 5YR 5/6 (yellowish red) to 5YR 4/1 (dark gray) [core]. Sharply incurving wall, rim thickened to exterior. Lip painted red-brown (urfirnis).

Early Helladic II.

301 LARGE INCURVING BOWL Fig. 17

(F32-E-7) Rim. D. est. 0.42, Max. pres. W. 0.05, Th. 0.007. Medium fabric; few silver inclusions, little lime; unevenly fired, 5YR 6/6 (reddish yellow) to 10YR 5/2 (grayish brown) [core]. Incurving wall, thickened rim, flattened lip bevelled to interior. Exterior painted thin red-brown (urfirnis).

Early Helladic II.

302 LARGE INCURVING BOWL Fig. 17

(B24-57) Rim. D. est. 0.43, Max. pres. W. 0.075, Th. 0.006. Medium fabric; no lime; evenly fired, 7.5YR 5/4 (brown). Incurving wall, rounded lip. Plain.

Early Helladic II.

303 LARGE INCURVING BOWL Fig. 17

(B81-1-2) Rim. D. 0.46, Max. pres. W. 0.07, Th. 0.009; very worn. Semicoarse fabric; quartz inclusions, little lime; evenly fired, 5YR 5/6 (yellowish red). Incurving wall, constriction below thickened rim. Surfaces not preserved.

Early Helladic II?

304 LARGE INCURVING BOWL Fig. 17

(G9-7) Rim. D. indet., Max. pres. W. 0.045, Th. 0.006. Medium fabric; little lime; unevenly fired, 5YR 3/1 (very dark gray) to 2.5YR 4/6 (red) [core]. Incurving wall, rim thickened to "T", flattened lip. Slipped red-brown and burnished.

Early Helladic II early.

305 LARGE INCURVING BOWL   Fig. 17
(F32-A3-1) Rim. D. est. 0.35-0.45, Max. pres. W. 0.065,
Th. 0.009. Semifine fabric; much lime; unevenly fired, 5YR 5/6
(yellowish red) to 7.5YR 5/2 (brown) [core]. Slightly incurving
wall, rim thickened to exterior, flattened lip. Exterior surface not
preserved; interior and lip painted red-brown (urfirnis).
Early Helladic II.

306 LARGE INCURVING BOWL   Fig. 17
(F32-N-94) Rim. D. > 0.40, Max. pres. W. 0.07, Th.
0.010. Medium fabric; some lime; unevenly fired, 5YR 5/6
(yellowish red) to 5YR 5/1 (gray) [core]. Incurving wall, rim
thickened in and out to "T". Exterior and lip painted brown
(urfirnis); interior slipped (self).
Early Helladic II.

307 LARGE INCURVING BOWL   Fig. 17
(F32-N-147) Rim. D. > 0.48, Max. pres. W. 0.11, Th.
0.010. Coarse fabric; some lime; unevenly fired, 2.5YR 6/6
(light red) to 7.5YR 6/4 (light brown) [core]. Incurving wall, rim
thickened. Exterior plain?; interior surface not preserved; lip
painted brown (urfirnis).
Early Helladic II.

308 LARGE INCURVING BOWL   Fig. 17
(F32-A3-4) Rim. D. indet., Max. pres. W. 0.055, Th.
0.013. Coarse fabric; little lime; evenly fired, 5YR 5/6 (reddish
yellow). Incurving wall, rim thickened to exterior. Painted red
(urfirnis).
Early Helladic II.

309 MEDIUM INCURVING BOWL WITH RIDGE   Fig. 18
(E4-B-8) Rim. D. 0.28, Max. pres. W. 0.04, Th. 0.004.
Semicoarse fabric; no lime; evenly fired, 7.5YR 5/2 (brown).
Incurving wall, thickened rim, flat lip; below rim, horizontal
ridge. Interior and lip slipped blue-yellow?
Early Helladic II.

310 MEDIUM INCURVING BOWL WITH RIDGE   Fig. 18
(F32-N-134) Rim. D. 0.32, Max. pres. W. 0.045, Th.
0.008. Coarse fabric; medium to very large inclusions, no lime;
unevenly fired, 5YR 6/6 (reddish yellow) to 5YR 7/3 (pink)
[core]. Incurving wall, flat lip bevelled to interior; below rim,
horizontal ridge. Plain.
Early Helladic I to Early Helladic II.

311 LARGE INCURVING BOWL WITH RIDGE   Fig. 18
(F32-E-6) Rim. D. est. 0.41, Max. pres. W. 0.065, Th.
0.008. Semicoarse fabric; some lime; unevenly fired, 5YR 5/6
(yellowish red) to 5YR 5/1 (gray) [core]. Incurving wall, slightly
thickened rim; below rim, horizontal ridge. Exterior traces of
black paint? (or blue slip?).
Early Helladic II.

312 LARGE INCURVING BOWL WITH RIDGE   Fig. 18
(B24-52) Rim. D. indet., Max. pres. W. 0.055, Th. 0.010.
Medium fabric; little lime; evenly fired, 5YR 6/6 (reddish yellow).
Incurving wall, thickened rim; below rim, ridge formed by wide
groove incised in thickened rim. Exterior painted black (urfirnis).
Early Helladic II.

313 LARGE INCURVING BOWL WITH RIDGE   Fig. 18
(F32-S-98) Rim. D. indet., Max. pres. W. 0.04, Th. 0.007.
Medium fabric; no lime; unevenly fired, 5YR 6/8 (reddish yellow)
to 5YR 6/1 (gray-light gray) [core]. Incurving wall, flat lip
bevelled to interior; below rim, horizontal ridge. Traces of slip on
exterior.
Early Helladic I to Early Helladic II.

314 LARGE INCURVING BOWL WITH RIDGE   Fig. 18
(F32-SF-13) Rim. D. indet., Max. pres. W. 0.065, Th.
0.010. Semifine fabric; no lime; evenly fired, 7.5YR 7/4 (pink).
Incurving wall, thickened rim; below rim, curving ridge (possibly
bucrania appliqué). Exterior painted black (urfirnis); interior
slipped (self slip?).
Early Helladic II.

315 MEDIUM INCURVING BOWL WITH RIDGE ENDING
                                                   Fig. 18
(A6/9-A-7) Rim. D. 0.23, Max. pres. W. 0.05, Th. 0.004.
Semifine fabric; some lime; unevenly fired, 7.5YR 7/6 (reddish
yellow) to 5YR 5/2 (reddish gray) [core]. Sharply incurving wall,
horizontal flattened lip; below rim, ridge terminating to left.
Slipped (self slip?).
Early Helladic I - Early Helladic II.

316 MEDIUM INCURVING BOWL WITH RIDGE ENDING
                                                   Fig. 18
(A6-74-62) Rim. D. 0.26, Max. pres. W. 0.045, Th. 0.005.
Semicoarse fabric; much lime; evenly fired, 5YR 4/4 (reddish
brown). Incurving wall, slightly thickened rim, flattened lip;
below rim, horizontal ridge terminating to left. Exterior
irregularly burnished; interior plain; lip painted brown (urfirnis).
Early Helladic II.

317 MEDIUM INCURVING BOWL WITH RIDGE ENDING
                                                   Fig. 18
(F32-B6-2) Rim. D. 0.28, Max. pres. W. 0.055, Th. 0.006.
Medium fabric; some lime; evenly fired, 7.5YR 6/4 (light brown).
Incurving bowl, flattened lip; below rim, horizontal ridge,
terminating to left with impression? Painted black (urfirnis).
Early Helladic II.

318 MEDIUM INCURVING BOWL WITH RIDGE ENDING
                                                   Fig. 18
(F32-S-161) Rim. D. 0.33, Max. pres. W. 0.055, Th.
0.009. Incurving wall, rim thickened to exterior and interior
forming "T", flattened lip bevelled to interior. Below rim,
horizontal ridge ending to right.
Early Helladic II.

319 LARGE INCURVING BOWL WITH RIDGE ENDING
                                                   Fig. 18
(A6/9-B-25) Rim. D. 0.41, Max. pres. W., 0.07, Th.
0.007. Semicoarse fabric; little lime; unevenly fired, 5YR 5/4
(reddish brown) to 5YR 4/2 (dark reddish gray) [core]. Incurving
wall, thickened rim, flattened lip; below rim, horizontal ridge
(ledge handle?) ending, to right continued by taenia. Interior and
lip painted black (urfirnis).
Early Helladic II.

320 LARGE INCURVING BOWL WITH RIDGE ENDING
                                                   Fig. 18
(F20-ALL-15) Rim. D. indet., Max. pres. W. 0.045, Th.
0.005. Medium fabric; some lime; unevenly fired, 7.5YR 6/4
(light brown) to 5YR 6/1 (gray-light gray) [core]. Slightly
incurving wall, flattened lip; below lip, horizontal ridge
terminating to left. Traces of slip on interior.
Early Helladic I to Early Helladic II.

321 LARGE INCURVING BOWL WITH RIDGE ENDING
Fig. 18
(C12-ALL-7) Rim. D. indet., Max. pres. W. 0.045, Th. 0.005. Semicoarse fabric; some lime; unevenly fired, 7.5YR 6/4 (light brown) to 5YR 5/1 (gray) [core]. Incurving wall, rim thickened to interior and exterior (exterior folded down); below rim, horizontal ledge lug, 0.04 wide (may continue to right). Surfaces not preserved.
Early Helladic II.

322 LARGE INCURVING BOWL WITH RIDGE ENDING
Fig. 18
(F20-11) Rim. D. indet., Max. pres. W. 0.05, Th. 0.008. Semicoarse fabric; some lime; unevenly fired, 5YR 6/6 (reddish yellow) to 5YR 5/2 (reddish gray) [core]. Incurving wall, rim thickened in and out to "T" and folded down; below rim, horizontal ridge terminating to right. Originally slipped?
Early Helladic I to Early Helladic II.

323 LARGE INCURVING BOWL WITH RIDGE AND IMPRESSION
Fig. 18
(F32-C5-1) Rim. D. indet., Max. pres. W. 0.045, Th. 0.008. Semifine fabric; some silver inclusions, no lime; unevenly fired, 2.5YR 6/8 (light red) to 7.5YR 6/4 (light brown) [core]. Incurving wall, rim thickened in and out to "T"; below rim, horizontal ridge ending? to right with impression. Painted red-brown (urfirnis).
Early Helladic II

324 LARGE INCURVING BOWL WITH RIDGE AND IMPRESSION
Figs. 18, 119
(F21-4) Rim. D. indet., Max. pres. W. 0.04, Th. 0.007. Semicoarse fabric; much lime; evenly fired, 5YR 5/6 (yellowish red). Incurving wall, slightly thickened rim, flattened lip; below rim, horizontal ridge from left ending, line continued by diagonal slashes. Plain.
Early Helladic I to Early Helladic II.

325 LARGE INCURVING BOWL WITH TRUMPET? LUG
Fig. 18
(F32-N-51) Rim. D. indet., Max. pres. W. 0.07, Th. 0.008. Semicoarse fabric; many small to medium, some large inclusions, little lime; evenly fired, 7.5YR 6/6 (reddish yellow). Incurving wall, rim thickened, lip flattened; below rim, horizontal ridge, terminating? to left in a vertical impression (a trumpet?). Painted black (urfirnis).
Early Helladic II.

326 MEDIUM INCURVING BOWL WITH APPLIQUE
Fig. 18
(C11-SW-14) Rim. D. 0.21, Max. pres. W. 0.08, Th. 0.006. Semicoarse fabric; many silver inclusions, some lime; unevenly fired, 5YR 4/6 (yellowish red) to 5YR 3/2 (dark reddish brown) [core]. Incurving rim, slightly thickened; beginning of taenia? Plain.
Early Helladic I? to Early Helladic II.

327 MEDIUM INCURVING BOWL WITH APPLIQUE
Fig. 18
(B43-A-9) Rim with plastic decoration. D. 0.26, Max. pres. W. 0.06, Th. 0.005. Medium fabric; much lime; evenly fired, 7.5YR 7/6 (reddish yellow). Incurving bowl, thickened rim; at maximum diameter two applied buttons (D. est. 0.012). Surfaces not preserved.
Early Helladic II.

328 LARGE INCURVING BOWL WITH LEDGE HANDLE
Figs. 19, 119
(F32-N-139) Rim. D. 0.38, Max. pres. W. 0.14, Th. 0.008. Medium fabric; few lime inclusions; unevenly fired, 2.5YR 5/8 (red) to 2.5YR-N5/0 (gray) [core]. Incurving wall, lip folded over to interior to form thickened rim; below rim, horizontal ledge handle 0.07 wide by up to 0.012 high, flanked by taenia of impressions (forming appearance of overlapping discs). Exterior slipped (self).
Early Helladic II.

329 LARGE INCURVING BOWL WITH LEDGE HANDLE
Figs. 19, 119
(F32-N-140) Rim. D. 0.43, Max. pres. W. 0.09, Th. 0.008. Semicoarse fabric; no lime; unevenly fired, 2.5YR 6/8 (light red) to 7.5YR 5/2 (brown) [core]. Incurving wall, rim thickened to exterior; below rim, part of ledge handle (protruding more at end) to right, row of diagonal slashes to left. Exterior slipped (self slip); interior and lip painted black (urfirnis).
Early Helladic II.

330 LARGE INCURVING BOWL WITH TUBULAR HANDLE
Fig. 19
(F32-A9-4) Rim with tubular handle. D. 0.36, Max. pres. W. 0.10, Th. 0.008. Semicoarse fabric; little lime; unevenly fired, 5YR 6/6 (reddish yellow) to 7.5YR 5/2 (brown) [core]. Incurving wall, thickened rim, flattened lip; wide tubular handle attached just below lip and below maximum diameter of bowl, taenia to left and right of upper attachment, row of diagonal slashes to right of handle opening. Exterior burnished.
(Early Helladic I to) Early Helladic II.

331 LARGE INCURVING BOWL WITH TUBULAR HANDLE
Fig. 19
(F32-C7-2) Rim with tubular handle. D. 0.41, Max. pres. W. 0.085, Th. 0.007. Coarse fabric; some lime; unevenly fired, 5YR 6/8 (reddish yellow) to 5YR 5/2 (reddish gray) [core]. Incurving wall (almost carinated), rim thickened in and out, flat lip; wide tubular handle attached at maximum diameter and below. Surfaces not preserved.
Early Helladic II.

332 LARGE INCURVING BOWL WITH TUBULAR HANDLE
Fig. 19
(A9-6-10) Rim with part of tubular handle. D. 0.41, Max. pres. W. 0.08, Th. 0.007. Coarse fabric; some lime; unevenly fired, 2.5YR 6/8 (light red) to 7.5YR 5/4 (brown) [core]. Incurving wall, slightly thickened rim, flat lip; wide tubular handle attached below rim and below maximum diameter. Surfaces not preserved.
Early Helladic II.

333 LARGE INCURVING BOWL WITH TUBULAR HANDLE
Fig. 19
(F32-N-206) Rim with part of tubular handle. D. 0.42, Max. pres. W. 0.07, Th. 0.007. Semicoarse fabric; some lime; unevenly fired, 5YR 6/6 (reddish yellow) to 5YR 5/2 (reddish gray) [core]. Incurving wall, slightly thickened rim, flattened lip; wide tubular handle attached below rim and below maximum diameter, taenia to left of upper attachment. Exterior slipped (self slip?).
Early Helladic II.

334 LARGE INCURVING BOWL WITH TUBULAR HANDLE   Fig. 19
   (F32-N-207) Rim with tubular handle. D. indet., Max. pres. W. 0.06, Th. 0.008. Coarse fabric; much lime; unevenly fired, 2.5YR 5/8 (red) to 7.5YR 5/2 (brown) [core]. Incurving wall, slightly thickened rim, flattened lip bevelled to interior; wide tubular handle attached at maximum diameter and below. Painted red (urfirnis).
   Early Helladic II.

335 LARGE INCURVING BOWL WITH TUBULAR HANDLE   Fig. 19
   (E36-5-4) Rim with tubular handle. D. indet., Max. pres. W. 0.075, Th. 0.008. Semicoarse fabric; some lime; unevenly fired, 5YR 6/8 (reddish yellow) to 7.5YR 5/2 (brown) [core]. Incurving wall, slightly thickened rim, flattened lip; wide tubular handle attached just below rim and below maximum diameter. Exterior slipped and polished.
   Early Helladic II.

336 LARGE INCURVING BOWL WITH TUBULAR HANDLE   Fig. 19
   (F32-N-208) Rim with part of tubular handle. D. indet., Max. pres. W. 0.05, Th. 0.010. Coarse fabric; much lime; unevenly fired, 5YR 6/6 (reddish yellow) to 5YR 6/1 (gray-light gray) [core]. Straight wall, thickened rim, flattened lip bevelled to interior; wide tubular handle attached below lip and further down. Exterior surface not preserved; interior and lip painted black (urfirnis).
   Early Helladic II.

337 LARGE INCURVING BOWL WITH TUBULAR HANDLE   Fig. 19
   (F17-8) Rim with tubular handle. D. indet., Max. pres. W. 0.08, Th. 0.008. Semicoarse fabric; much lime; unevenly fired, 7.5YR 7/4 (pink) to 7.5YR 5/2 (brown) [core]. Incurving wall, thickened rim, flat lip; wide tubular handle attached at rim and below maximum diameter. Plain?
   Early Helladic II.

338 LARGE INCURVING BOWL WITH TUBULAR HANDLE   Fig. 19
   (A6-9-4) Rim with part of tubular handle. D. indet., Max. pres. W. 0.06, Th. 0.009. Semicoarse fabric; some lime; unevenly fired, 7.5YR 6/4 (light brown) to 7.5YR-N5/0 (gray) [core]. Incurving wall, rim very thickened in and out to "T"; wide tubular handle attached below lip. Interior painted black (urfirnis).
   Early Helladic II.

339 LARGE INCURVING BOWL WITH TUBULAR HANDLE   Fig. 19
   (F32-E-1) Rim with part of tubular handle. D. indet., Max. pres. W. 0.08, Th. 0.007. Medium fabric; little lime; unevenly fired, 7.5YR 6/6 (reddish yellow) to 7.5YR 4/2 (dark brown-brown) [core]. Incurving rim, rim thickened in and out to triangle, flattened lip; wide tubular handle attached below lip and below maximum diameter, impressed taenia band continues to right of upper attachment. Interior and lip burnished.
   Early Helladic II.

340 LARGE INCURVING BOWL WITH HANDLE?   Fig. 19
   (F32-33) Rim. D. indet., Max. pres. W. 0.08, Th. 0.007. Semicoarse fabric; some lime; unevenly fired, 5YR 5/6 (yellowish red) to 5YR 4/2 (dark reddish gray) [core]. Incurving wall,

thickened rim; below rim, from left, taenia (impressed band) terminating in ledge protruding est. 0.02 (perhaps handle?). Painted red (urfirnis).
   Early Helladic II.

341 SMALL INCURVING BOWL WITH TAENIA   Fig. 19
   (A6-74-88) Rim. D. 0.14, Max. pres. W. 0.05, Th. 0.004. Semicoarse fabric, much lime; evenly fired, 7.5YR 6/4 (light brown). Incurving wall, flat horizontal lip; at lip, taenia band of finger impressions forming scallop. Plain.
   Early Helladic II.

342 MEDIUM INCURVING BOWL WITH TAENIA
                                                   Figs. 19, 119
   (F32-19) Rim. D. 0.24, Max. pres. W. 0.055, Th. 0.006. Semicoarse fabric; little lime; unevenly fired, 5YR 7/6 (reddish yellow) to 5YR 5/4 (reddish brown) [core]. Sharply incurving wall, rim thickened with slight groove below round lip; at maximum diameter, taenia band of overlapping discs to right. Surfaces not preserved.
   Early Helladic II.

343 MEDIUM INCURVING BOWL WITH TAENIA   Fig. 19
   (F32-N-44) Rim. D. 0.26, Max. pres. W. 0.055, Th. 0.005; worn. Semicoarse fabric; some lime; evenly fired, 7.5YR 7/4 (pink). Incurving wall with ridge on interior, rim thickened to exterior and impressed to form piecrust decoration, flattened lip; below rim, taenia band of impressions on low ridge. Painted black (urfirnis).
   Early Helladic II.

344 MEDIUM INCURVING BOWL WITH TAENIA
                                                       Fig. 19
   (G1-A-58) Rim. D. 0.28, Max. pres. W. 0.06, Th. 0.005. Medium fabric; little lime; unevenly fired, 5YR 6/8 (reddish yellow) to 5YR 4/2 (dark reddish gray) [core]. Incurving wall, rim thickened, slightly rounded lip bevelled to interior; below rim, taenia band of overlapping discs to right. Surfaces not preserved.
   Early Helladic II.

345 MEDIUM INCURVING BOWL WITH TAENIA
                                                   Figs. 19, 119
   (C11-NE-13) Rim. D. 0.29, Max. pres. W. 0.055, Th. 0.008. Coarse fabric; some lime; unevenly fired, 2.5YR 4/6 (red) to 5YR 4/4 (reddish brown) [core]. Incurving wall, rounded lip; below lip, taenia band of impressions on pointed ridge. Plain.
   Early Helladic II.

346 MEDIUM INCURVING BOWL WITH TAENIA
                                                   Figs. 19, 119
   (F32-S-81) Rim. D. 0.29, Max. pres. W. 0.055, Th. 0.006. Medium fabric; little lime; unevenly fired, 5YR 6/6 (reddish yellow) to 5YR 6/2 (pinkish gray) [core]. Incurving wall, rim thickened especially to exterior, rounded lip; below lip, taenia band of overlapping discs to left. Exterior surface not preserved; interior painted black (urfirnis).
   Early Helladic II.

347 MEDIUM INCURVING BOWL WITH TAENIA ENDING   Fig. 19
   (B81-2-16/22 + B81-2-23/26/29) Rim (two joining) and nonjoining body (of three joining). D. 0.32, Max. pres. W. 0.09, Th. 0.010. Semicoarse fabric; quartz inclusions, some lime; evenly fired, 7.5YR 5/6 (strong brown). Incurving wall, pointed

lip; taenia ending to left. Surfaces not preserved.
(Early Helladic I? to) Early Helladic II.

348   MEDIUM INCURVING BOWL WITH TAENIA   Fig. 20
(F6-4) Rim. D. 0.33-0.34, Max. pres. W. 0.07, Th. 0.007.
Coarse fabric; little lime; unevenly fired, 5YR 6/6 (reddish
yellow) to 5YR 6/1 (gray-light gray) [core]. Incurving wall, rim
thickened to exterior, rounded lip; below lip, wide taenia band of
overlapping discs to right. Surfaces not preserved.
Early Helladic II.

349   LARGE INCURVING BOWL WITH TAENIA   Fig. 20
(F32-C7-4) Rim. D. 0.35, Max. pres. W. 0.045, Th. 0.007.
Medium fabric; no lime; unevenly fired, 5YR 4/6 (yellowish red)
to 5YR 3/3 (dark reddish brown) [core]. Incurving wall, slightly
thickened rim, rounded lip; at lip, taenia band of overlapping discs
to right. Plain?
Early Helladic II.

350   LARGE INCURVING BOWL WITH TAENIA   Fig. 20
(A6-72-191) Rim. D. 0.36, Max. pres. W. 0.08, Th. 0.007.
Semicoarse fabric; little lime; unevenly fired, 2.5YR 4/6 (red) to
5YR 4/3 (reddish brown) [core]. Incurving wall, rounded lip;
below lip, taenia band of finger impressions on ridge. Plain.
Early Helladic II.

351   LARGE INCURVING BOWL WITH TAENIA
Figs. 20, 119
(F32-S-64) Rim. D. 0.36, Max. pres. W. 0.105, Th. 0.009.
Semicoarse fabric; no lime; evenly fired, 5YR 2.5/2 (dark reddish
brown). Sharply incurving wall, rim thickened to "T", slightly
rounded lip bevelled to interior; partly on and below rim, taenia
band of impressions to left on ridge forming twisted rope pattern.
Slipped (self?).
Early Helladic II.

352   LARGE INCURVING BOWL WITH TAENIA   Fig. 20
(F32-C4-6) Rim. D. 0.37, Max. pres. W. 0.055, Th. 0.007.
Medium fabric; no lime; unevenly fired, 5YR 6/8 (reddish yellow)
to 5YR 5/1 (gray) [core]. Incurving wall, slightly thickened rim,
flat lip bevelled to interior; below rim and below maximum
diameter, taenia bands of widely spaced impressions on ridges.
Plain?
Early Helladic II.

353   LARGE INCURVING BOWL WITH TAENIA
Figs. 20, 119
(F32-D6-1) Rim. D. 0.37, Max. pres. W. 0.085, Th. 0.009.
Semicoarse fabric; some lime; unevenly fired, 5YR 5/6 (yellowish
red) to 5YR 4/1 (dark gray) [core]. Incurving wall, rim slightly
thickened to exterior and folded down, rounded lip; below rim,
taenia band of impressions on ridge. Slipped (self).
Early Helladic II.

354   LARGE INCURVING BOWL WITH TAENIA   Fig. 20
(F32-B8-3) Rim. D. 0.38, Max. pres. W. 0.09, Th. 0.009.
Semicoarse fabric; some lime; unevenly fired, 5YR 6/6 (reddish
yellow) to 7.5YR 5/2 (brown) [core]. Very incurving wall, rim
thickened to exterior, flattened lip bevelled to interior; below rim,
taenia band of impressions on ridge. Exterior painted black
(urfirnis); interior surface not preserved. could be F32-C8-3.
Early Helladic II.

355   LARGE INCURVING BOWL WITH TAENIA
Figs. 20, 119
(F32-N-75) Rim. D. 0.38, Max. pres. W. 0.065, Th. 0.011.
Semicoarse fabric; much lime; evenly fired, 2.5YR 5/8 (red).
Incurving wall thickening towards rim, flat lip bevelled to
interior; below rim, taenia band of impressions slanted to left on
ridge forming twisted rope pattern. Lip burnished; other surfaces
worn?
Early Helladic II.

356   LARGE INCURVING BOWL WITH TAENIA
Figs. 20, 120
(F32-65) Rim. D. 0.38, Max. pres. W. 0.07, Th. 0.006.
Semicoarse fabric; some lime; unevenly fired, 5YR 5/8 (yellowish
red) to 7.5YR 5/2 (brown) [core]. Incurving wall, rim slightly
thickened, rounded lip bevelled to interior; below lip, taenia band
of overlapping discs to right. Surfaces not preserved.
Early Helladic II.

357   LARGE INCURVING BOWL WITH TAENIA
Figs. 20, 120
(F32-S-74) Rim. D. 0.38, Max. pres. W. 0.011, Th. 0.013.
Coarse fabric; much lime; unevenly fired, 5YR 5/4 (reddish
brown) to 5YR 3/1 (very dark gray) [core]. Incurving wall, rim
greatly thickened to triangle, flat horizontal lip; at lip, double
taenia band of overlapping discs to right. Plain.
Early Helladic II.

358   LARGE INCURVING BOWL WITH TAENIA   Fig. 20
(A6-74-73) Rim. D. 0.38, Max. pres. W. 0.06, Th. 0.009.
Incurving wall, rim thickened to interior and exterior. Double
taenia band just below lip.
Early Helladic II.

359   LARGE INCURVING BOWL WITH TAENIA   Fig. 20
(C11-C19-3) Rim. D. 0.39, Max. pres. W. 0.065, Th.
0.009. Medium fabric; silver inclusions, much lime; unevenly
fired, 2.5YR 4/8 (red) to 5YR 3/1 (very dark gray) [core].
Curving wall, rim thickened to interior, rounded lip bevelled to
interior; below rim, taenia band of irregular impressions on ridge
ending to left. Exterior plain; interior and lip painted red (urfirnis).
Early Helladic II.

360   LARGE INCURVING BOWL WITH TAENIA   Fig. 20
(F32-26) Rim. D. 0.40, Max. pres. W. 0.09, Th. 0.010.
Semicoarse fabric; little lime; unevenly fired, 2.5YR 4/8 (red) to
5YR 3/2 (dark reddish brown) [core]. Very incurving wall, lip
flattened and bevelled to interior; below lip, taenia band of finger
impressions in high, wide ridge. Slipped (self slip).
Early Helladic II.

361   LARGE INCURVING BOWL WITH TAENIA
Figs. 20, 120
(F32-N-53) Rim. D. 0.40, Max. pres. W. 0.06, Th. 0.009.
Semicoarse fabric; some lime; evenly fired, 5YR 4/6 (yellowish
red). Incurving wall, flat lip bevelled to interior; below lip, taenia
band of deep impressions slanted to left on high ridge forming
"twisted band." Plain.
Early Helladic II.

362   LARGE INCURVING BOWL WITH TAENIA   Fig. 20
(E5-B-1) Rim. D. 0.40, Max. pres. W. 0.085, Th. 0.008.
Semicoarse fabric; no lime; unevenly fired, 7.5YR 6/4 (light
brown) to 7.5YR 6/2 (pinkish gray) [core]. Very incurving wall,

rim thickened to interior and exterior, flattened lip bevelled to interior; below rim, taenia band of deep finger impressions on high ridge forming discs overlapping to right. Painted red-brown (urfirnis).
Early Helladic II.

363 LARGE INCURVING BOWL WITH TAENIA   Fig. 20
(F32-E-2) Rim. D. 0.40, Max. pres. W. 0.09, Th. 0.008. Coarse fabric; some lime; unevenly fired, 5YR 6/8 (reddish yellow) to 5YR 6/1 (gray-light gray) [core]. Incurving wall, rim thickened to triangle, slightly rounded lip bevelled to interior; at lip, taenia band of impressions on high ridge. Plain.
Early Helladic II.

364 LARGE INCURVING BOWL WITH TAENIA   Fig. 20
(F32-A9-1) Rim. D. 0.42, Max. pres. W. 0.08, Th. 0.012. Semicoarse fabric; much lime, evenly fired, 5YR 4/3 (reddish brown). Incurving wall, thickened rim, rounded lip; below lip, taenia band of impressions on small band giving appearance of overlapping discs to right. Surfaces not preserved.
Early Helladic II.

365 LARGE INCURVING BOWL WITH TAENIA
Figs. 20, 120
(A6-74-15) Rim. D. 0.42, Max. pres. W. 0.075, Th. 0.009. Semicoarse fabric; some lime; evenly fired, 7.5YR 6/4 (light brown). Incurving wall, rim slightly thickened, flat lip bevelled to interior; two taenia bands of overlapping discs to right, one just below lip and one at maximum diameter. Exterior plain?; interior and lip painted red (urfirnis).
Early Helladic II.

366 LARGE INCURVING BOWL WITH TAENIA   Fig. 20
(F6-2) Rim. D. 0.42, Max. pres. W. 0.165, Th. 0.011. Coarse fabric; little lime; unevenly fired, 2.5YR 3/6 (dark red) to 5YR 3/3 (dark reddish brown) [core]. Insloping rim thickening towards rounded lip; below lip, wide taenia band of overlapping discs to right. Slipped (self slip).
Early Helladic II.

367 LARGE INCURVING BOWL WITH TAENIA   Fig. 20
(F32-A3-5) Rim. D. 0.43, Max. pres. W. 0.085, Th. 0.008. Medium fabric; some lime; unevenly fired, 5YR 5/8 (yellowish red) to 5YR 5/1 (gray) [core]. Incurving wall, rim thickened to "T", rounded lip bevelled to interior; below rim, taenia band of impressions on ridge; lower edge of taenia band smoothed forming carination ridge. Plain.
Early Helladic II.

368 LARGE INCURVING BOWL WITH TAENIA   Fig. 20
(F32-S-89) Rim. D. 0.45, Max. pres. W. 0.065, Th. 0.007. Coarse fabric; much lime; unevenly fired, 2.5YR 4/8 (red) to 5YR 5/2 (reddish gray) [core]. Very incurving wall, rim thickened to exterior, flat horizontal lip; at lip, taenia band of narrow vertical impressions on low ridge. Exterior slipped (self?); interior surface not preserved.
Early Helladic II.

369 LARGE INCURVING BOWL WITH TAENIA
Figs. 21, 120
(F32-N-59) Rim. D. 0.47, Max. pres. W. 0.13, Th. 0.009. Semicoarse fabric; no lime; unevenly fired, 5YR 5/6 (yellowish red) to 5YR 5/1 (gray) [core]. Incurving wall, rim thickened to triangle, flattened lip bevelled to interior; below rim, taenia band

of finger impressions slanted to right on ridge forming rope pattern. Slipped (self).
Early Helladic II.

370 LARGE INCURVING BOWL WITH TAENIA   Fig. 21
(B49-1-1) Rim. D. 0.48, Max. pres. W. 0.10, Th. 0.008. Semicoarse fabric; little lime; unevenly fired, 5YR 5/8 (yellowish red) to 5YR 5/1 (gray) [core]. Incurving wall, thickened rim; below rim, taenia band of slanted finger impressions on ridge. Exterior worn; interior and lip painted red (urfirnis).
Early Helladic II.

371 LARGE INCURVING BOWL WITH TAENIA   Fig. 21
(F32-S-43) Rim. D. 0.48, Max. pres. W. 0.07, Th. 0.009. Medium fabric; little lime; unevenly fired, 5YR 5/8 (yellowish red) to 5YR 5/1 (gray) [core]. Incurving wall, rim thickened to interior and exterior, rounded lip bevelled to interior; below rim, taenia band of impressions on ridge; ridge sharply demarcated at bottom. Interior and lip slipped (self).
Early Helladic II.

372 LARGE INCURVING BOWL WITH TAENIA
Figs. 21, 120
(F32-S-88) Rim. D. 0.52, Max. pres. W. 0.12, Th. 0.009. Coarse fabric; some lime; unevenly fired, 2.5YR 5/8 (red) to 5YR 5/3 (reddish brown) [core]. Very incurving wall, rim thickened to "T", slightly rounded lip bevelled to interior; below rim, taenia band of overlapping discs to right. Exterior and lip painted red (urfirnis); interior surface not preserved.
Early Helladic II.

373 LARGE INCURVING BOWL WITH TAENIA
Figs. 21, 120
(A6-74-18) Rim. D. 0.58, Max. pres. W. 0.11, Th. 0.009. Semicoarse fabric; some lime; evenly fired, 2.5YR 4/8 (red). Incurving wall, rim thickened to "T", rounded below rim, taenia band of overlapping discs to right; on outer edge of lip, row of slashes to right. Plain.
Early Helladic II.

374 LARGE INCURVING BOWL WITH TAENIA
Figs. 21, 120
(F32-S-67) Rim. D. 0.62, Max. pres. W. 0.115, Th. 0.009. Coarse fabric; silver inclusions, little lime; unevenly fired, 2.5YR 5/8 (red) to 7.5YR 5/2 (brown) [core]. Incurving wall, rim thickened especially to exterior, slightly rounded lip; below rim, taenia band of irregular overlapping discs to right. Exterior burnished; interior surface not preserved.
Early Helladic II.

375 LARGE INCURVING BOWL WITH TAENIA
Figs. 21, 120
(F6-ALL-2) Rim. D. est. 0.67, Max. pres. W. 0.65, Th. 0.012. Incurving wall, thickened rim. Below rim, taenia of overlapping discs.
Early Helladic II.

376 LARGE INCURVING BOWL WITH TAENIA   Fig. 21
(F32-S-85*) Rim. D. indet., Max. pres. W. 0.055, Th. 0.014. Semicoarse fabric; little lime; unevenly fired, 5YR 5/8 (yellowish red) to 5YR 6/1 (gray-light gray) [core]. Incurving wall, slightly thickened rim; at rim, taenia band of impressions on low ridge. Surfaces worn. May be F32-S-95.
Early Helladic II.

377 LARGE INCURVING BOWL WITH TAENIA
Figs. 21, 120
(F32-N-50) Rim. D. indet., Max. pres. W. 0.05; interior very worn. Semicoarse fabric; little lime; evenly fired, 5YR 3/1 (very dark gray). Incurving wall, thickened rim, flattened lip; below rim, taenia band of impressions on low ridge giving appearance of overlapping discs to left. Plain?
Early Helladic II.

378 LARGE INCURVING BOWL WITH TAENIA Fig. 21
(F32-N-74) Rim. D. indet., Max. pres. W. 0.055, Th. 0.011. Coarse fabric; much lime; unevenly fired, 2.5YR 4/8 (red) to 5YR 3/2 (dark reddish brown) [core]. Incurving wall, thickened rim, rounded lip; below lip, taenia band of deep impressions on ridge. Plain; lip burnished.
Early Helladic II.

379 INCURVING BOWL WITH TAENIA Figs. 21, 120
(B46-18) Rim. D. indet., Max. pres. W. 0.06, Th. 0.005, worn. Medium fabric; some lime; unevenly fired, 2.5YR 5/8 (red) to 2.5YR 3/2 (dusky red) [core]. Incurving wall, rim thickened to exterior, lip flattened; below rim, taenia band of impressions on small ridge. Surfaces not preserved .
Early Helladic II.

380 INCURVING BOWL WITH TAENIA Figs. 21, 120
(F32-S-93) Rim. D. indet., Max. pres. W. 0.065, Th. 0.007. Medium fabric; no lime; unevenly fired, 5YR 5/8 (yellowish red) to 5YR 5/1 (gray) [core]. Incurving wall, rim thickened, flattened lip bevelled to interior; below rim and below maximum diameter, taenia bands of finger impressions on ridges; upper band appearing scalloped or twisted. Exterior surface not preserved; interior slipped? red-brown (or painted?).
Early Helladic II.

381 LARGE INCURVING BOWL WITH TAENIA
Figs. 21, 120
(F32-28) Rim. D. indet., Max. pres. W. 0.12, Th. 0.007. Medium fabric; no lime; unevenly fired, 5YR 5/4 (reddish brown) to 5YR 6/1 (gray-light gray) [core]. Very incurving wall, rim thickened to exterior forming ridge, rounded lip; below rim, taenia band of deep narrow impressions on high ridge giving appearance of overlapping discs to left. Exterior plain; interior and lip painted black (urfirnis).
Early Helladic II.

382 LARGE INCURVING BOWL WITH TAENIA Fig. 21
(F32-N-73) Rim. D. indet., Max. pres. W. 0.09, Th. 0.013. Semicoarse fabric; some lime; unevenly fired, 5YR 5/6 (yellowish red) to 5YR 5/1 (gray) [core]. Incurving wall, slightly thickened rim, rounded lip; below rim, taenia band of irregular impressions on high wide ridge. Slipped (self).
Early Helladic II.

383 LARGE INCURVING BOWL WITH TAENIA
Figs. 21, 120
(F32-D4-3) Rim. D. indet., Max. pres. W. 0.08, Th. 0.012. Semicoarse fabric; much lime; unevenly fired, 7.5YR 5/4 (reddish brown) to 5YR 5/1 (gray) [core]. Incurving wall, thickened rim, slightly rounded lip; at lip and below, taenia bands of deep impressions on high ridges forming scallop on upper and overlapping discs to right on lower. Plain?
Early Helladic II.

384 LARGE INCURVING BOWL WITH TAENIA Fig. 21
(F32-S-79) Rim. D. indet., Max. pres. W. 0.06, Th. 0.008. Medium fabric; silver inclusions, little lime; unevenly fired, 5YR 5/6 (yellowish red) to 5YR 4/1 (dark gray) [core]. Incurving wall (interior carinated), rim thickened, lip bevelled to interior and exterior; below lip and below maximum diameter, taenia bands of impressions (forming scallop on upper ridge; lower worn). Exterior plain?; interior slipped red-brown.
Early Helladic I to Early Helladic II ?

385 LARGE INCURVING BOWL WITH TAENIA Fig. 21
(F32-4) Rim. D. indet., Max. pres. W. 0.075, Th. 0.009. Semicoarse fabric; little lime; unevenly fired, 7.5YR 6/6 (reddish yellow) to 5YR 5/2 (reddish gray) [core]. Incurving wall, rim thickened especially to exterior, flat lip bevelled to interior; below rim, taenia band of impressions on ridge. Surfaces not preserved.
Early Helladic II.

386 LARGE INCURVING BOWL WITH TAENIA Fig. 21
(F32-N-76) Rim. D. indet., Max. pres. W. 0.085, Th. est. 0.016. Coarse fabric; much lime; evenly fired, est. 7.5YR 5/4 (brown). Slightly incurving wall, rim thickened to exterior, flattened horizontal lip; two taenia bands, one just below thickening of rim, other below that. Surfaces not preserved.
Early Helladic II.

387 LARGE INCURVING BOWL WITH TAENIA Fig. 21
(F32-N-64) Rim. D. indet., Max. pres. W. 0.055, Th. 0.010. Semicoarse fabric; no lime; unevenly fired, 5YR 4/4 (reddish brown) to 5YR 4/2 (dark reddish gray) [core]. Incurving wall, rim thickened to "T", round lip; below rim, taenia band of overlapping discs to right. Surfaces not preserved.
Early Helladic II.

388 LARGE INCURVING BOWL WITH TAENIA
Figs. 21, 120
(F32-S-87) Rim. D. indet., Max. pres. W. 0.09, Th. 0.012. Coarse fabric; some lime; unevenly fired, 2.5YR 5/8 (red) to 7.5YR 5/2 (brown) [core]. Incurving wall, rim slightly thickened, lip rounded; at lip and at maximum diameter, taenia bands of overlapping discs to right. Exterior and lip slipped (self slip); interior worn.
Early Helladic II.

389 MEDIUM INCURVING BOWL WITH IMPRESSIONS
Fig. 21
(F32-A5-6) Rim. D. 0.24, Max. pres. W. 0.04, Th. 0.006. Incurving wall, thickened rim, flattened lip; below rim, row of slightly diagonal slashes to left. Surfaces not preserved.
Early Helladic II.

390 MEDIUM INCURVING BOWL WITH IMPRESSIONS
Fig. 21
(C11-C19-5) Rim. D. 0.24, Max. pres. W. 0.035, Th. 0.007. Incurving wall, rim thickened to exterior; below rim, row of diagonal slashes to right. Surfaces not preserved.
Early Helladic II.

391 MEDIUM INCURVING BOWL WITH IMPRESSIONS
Fig. 21
(B43-A-5) Rim. D. 0.25, Max. pres. W. 0.055, Th. 0.005. Incurving wall, thickened rim; below rim, row of small triangles. Interior slipped yellow-blue and polished.
Early Helladic II.

392   MEDIUM INCURVING BOWL WITH IMPRESSIONS
Fig. 21

(E5-A-11) Rim. D. 0.25, Max. pres. W. 0.05, Th. 0.007. Incurving wall, thickened rim, rounded lip; below rim, row of diagonal slashes to right. Surfaces not preserved.
Early Helladic II.

393   MEDIUM INCURVING BOWL WITH IMPRESSIONS
Fig. 21

(F32-34) Rim. D. 0.25, Max. pres. W. 0.05, Th. 0.007; worn. Incurving wall, rim thickened to exterior; below rim, row of diagonal slashes to right.
Early Helladic II.

394   MEDIUM INCURVING BOWL WITH IMPRESSIONS
Fig. 21

(A6-75-26) Rim. D. 0.26, Max. pres. W. 0.055, Th. 0.005. Incurving wall, thickened rim; below rim, row of diagonal slashes to right. Lip painted black (urfirnis).
Early Helladic II.

395   MEDIUM INCURVING BOWL WITH IMPRESSIONS
Fig. 22

(C11-11-2) Rim. D. 0.27, Max. pres. W. 0.035, Th. 0.006; worn. Incurving wall, thickened rim; below rim, row of diagonal slashes to right.
Early Helladic II.

396   MEDIUM INCURVING BOWL WITH IMPRESSIONS
Fig. 22

(F32-E-16) Rim. D. 0.27, Max. pres. W. 0.45, Th. 0.006; worn. Incurving wall, rim thickened to exterior; below rim, row of vertical strokes.
Early Helladic II.

397   MEDIUM INCURVING BOWL WITH IMPRESSIONS
Fig. 22

(C11-SW-2) Rim. D. 0.28, Max. pres. W. 0.095, Th. 0.007. Incurving wall, thickened rim, flat lip bevelled to exterior; below rim, row of diagonal slashes to right. Slipped (self slip).
Early Helladic II.

398   MEDIUM INCURVING BOWL WITH IMPRESSIONS
Fig. 22

(A6/9-B-26) Rim. D. 0.28, Max. pres. W. 0.04, Th. 0.006. Incurving wall, thickened rim, flat lip; below rim, row of narrow oblique slashes to right. Interior painted brown.
Early Helladic II.

399   MEDIUM INCURVING BOWL WITH IMPRESSIONS
Fig. 22

(E5-B-2) Rim. D. 0.28, Max. pres. W. 0.04, Th. 0.006. Incurving wall, rim thickened to interior, flat lip; below rim, row of diagonal slashes to right. Exterior slipped?; interior plain.
Early Helladic II.

400   MEDIUM INCURVING BOWL WITH IMPRESSIONS
Fig. 22

(F32-N-47) Rim. D. 0.29, Max. pres. W. 0.06, Th. 0.007. Sharply incurving wall, thickened rim, flattened lip; below rim, row of diagonal triangular slashes to right. Surfaces not preserved.
Early Helladic II.

401   MEDIUM INCURVING BOWL WITH IMPRESSIONS
Fig. 22

(B43-2-1) Rim. D. 0.30, Max. pres. W. 0.065, Th. 0.005. Incurving wall, thickened rim, flat lip; below rim, row of small triangles. Interior painted?
Early Helladic II.

402   MEDIUM INCURVING BOWL WITH IMPRESSIONS
Fig. 22

(F32-S-90) Rim. D. 0.30, Max. pres. W. 0.04, Th. 0.006. Incurving wall, thickened rim; below rim, two rows of diagonal slashes to right. Surfaces not preserved.
Early Helladic II.

403   MEDIUM INCURVING BOWL WITH IMPRESSIONS
Fig. 22

(F32-N-40) Rim. D. 0.31, Max. pres. W. 0.045, Th. 0.006. Incurving wall, thickened rim; below rim, row of diagonal triangular slashes to right. Exterior surface not preserved; interior slipped (self).
Early Helladic II.

404   MEDIUM INCURVING BOWL WITH IMPRESSIONS
Figs. 22, 120

(B43-ALL-2-2) Rim. D. 0.32, Max. pres. W. 0.08, Th. 0.006. Medium fabric; much lime; unevenly fired, 5YR 6/6 (reddish yellow) to 5YR 5/1 (gray) [core]. Incurving wall, rim thickened to exterior, flattened lip bevelled to interior; at maximum diameter, row of deep vertical slashes. Painted black (urfirnis).
Early Helladic II.

405   MEDIUM INCURVING BOWL WITH IMPRESSIONS
Fig. 22

(F32-18) Rim. D. est. 0.32, Max. pres. W. 0.045, Th. 0.007. Carinated wall, thickened rim; below rim, row of triangles. Surfaces not preserved.
Early Helladic II.

406   MEDIUM INCURVING BOWL WITH IMPRESSIONS
Fig. 22

(F32-N-49) Rim. D. 0.32, Max. pres. W. 0.06, Th. 0.007. Incurving wall, thickened rim, flattened horizontal lip; below rim, row of diagonal slashes to right. Lip painted red (urfirnis).
Early Helladic II.

407   LARGE INCURVING BOWL WITH IMPRESSIONS
Fig. 22

(F32-N-48) Rim. D. 0.35, Max. pres. W. 0.09, Th. 0.007. Incurving wall, thickened rim curves out slightly; below rim, row of diagonal triangular slashes to right. Plain.
Early Helladic II.

408   LARGE INCURVING BOWL WITH IMPRESSIONS
Fig. 22

(F32-N-42) Rim. D. 0.35, Max. pres. W. 0.045, Th. 0.005; worn. Incurving wall, rim thickened to exterior, flattened lip; below rim, row of diagonal slashes to right.
Early Helladic II.

409   LARGE INCURVING BOWL WITH IMPRESSIONS
Fig. 22

(A6-75-21) Rim. D. 0.36, Max. pres. W. 0.055, Th. 0.006. Sharply incurving wall, thickened rim; below rim, row of

diagonal slashes to right.   Slipped yellow-brown, some burnishing.
Early Helladic II.

410 LARGE INCURVING BOWL WITH IMPRESSIONS
                                          Fig. 22
(C11-SE-2) Rim. D. 0.37, Max. pres. W. 0.07, Th. 0.009. Incurving wall, thickened rim, flat lip; below rim, row of diagonal triangular slashes to right. Slipped light brown (self?).
Early Helladic II.

411 LARGE INCURVING BOWL WITH IMPRESSIONS
                                          Fig. 22
(F32-N-46) Rim. D. 0.37, Max. pres. W. 0.04, Th. 0.005. Sharply incurving wall, thickened rim, flattened lip; below rim, row of diagonal slashes to right. Surfaces not preserved.
Early Helladic II.

412 LARGE INCURVING BOWL WITH IMPRESSIONS
                                          Fig. 22
(B24-43) Rim. D. 0.38, Max. pres. W. 0.06, Th. 0.008. Incurving wall, thickened rim especially to interior; below rim, row of triangles. Exterior worn; interior painted black (urfirnis).
Early Helladic II.

413 LARGE INCURVING BOWL WITH IMPRESSIONS
                                          Fig. 22
(F32-N-43) Rim. D. 0.38, Max. pres. W. 0.055, Th. 0.007. Incurving wall, thickened rim, flattened lip; below rim, row of diagonal slashes to right. Surfaces not preserved.
Early Helladic II.

414 LARGE INCURVING BOWL WITH IMPRESSIONS
                                          Fig. 22
(C11-SW-34) Rim. D. 0.38, Max. pres. W. 0.05, Th. 0.008. Incurving wall, thickened rim, flattened lip; below rim, row of diagonal slashes to right. Painted red-brown (urfirnis).
Early Helladic II.

415 LARGE INCURVING BOWL WITH IMPRESSIONS
                                          Fig. 22
(B43-ALL-3-1) Rim. D. 0.38, Max. pres. W. 0.06, Th. 0.006; worn. Sharply incurving wall, thickened rim; below rim, row of diagonal triangular slashes to right.
Early Helladic II.

416 LARGE INCURVING BOWL WITH IMPRESSIONS
                                          Fig. 22
(C11-SE-3) Rim. D. 0.38, Max. pres. W. 0.045, Th. 0.008. Incurving wall, rim thickened to exterior; below rim, row of diagonal triangular slashes to right. Burnished.
Early Helladic II.

417 LARGE INCURVING BOWL WITH IMPRESSIONS
                                          Fig. 23
(F32-N-77) Rim. D. 0.39, Max. pres. W. 0.055, Th. 0.006. Incurving wall, rim thickened to exterior; below rim, row of oblique slashes to right. Exterior painted red-brown (urfirnis); interior surface not preserved.
Early Helladic II.

418 LARGE INCURVING BOWL WITH IMPRESSIONS
                                          Figs. 23, 120
(F32-9) Rim. D. 0.43, Max. pres. W. 0.11, Th. 0.009.

Semicoarse fabric; some lime; unevenly fired, 5YR 5/6 (yellowish red) to 7.5YR-N5/0 (gray) [core]. Incurving wall, thickened rim, flattened lip; below rim, diagonal slashes to right. Painted brown (urfirnis).
Early Helladic II.

419 LARGE INCURVING BOWL WITH IMPRESSIONS
                                          Fig. 23
(F32-D12-1) Rim. D. 0.43, Max. pres. W. 0.055, Th. 0.007. Incurving wall, thickened rim; below rim, row of oblique slashes to right. Surfaces not preserved.
Early Helladic II.

420 LARGE INCURVING BOWL WITH IMPRESSIONS
                                          Fig. 23
(F6-ALL-4) Rim. D. indet., Max. pres. W. 0.07, Th. 0.007. Incurving wall, thickened rim; below rim, row of small triangles. Interior slipped (self slip) and burnished.
Early Helladic II.

421 LARGE INCURVING BOWL WITH IMPRESSIONS
                                          Fig. 23
(B9-1) Rim. D. indet., Max. pres. W. 0.08, Th. 0.009. Incurving wall, rim thickened to "T", flattened lip; below rim, row of irregular triangles. Slipped blue? and burnished.
Early Helladic II.

422 LARGE INCURVING BOWL WITH IMPRESSIONS
                                          Fig. 23
(F19-4) Rim. D. indet., Max. pres. W. 0.045, Th. 0.008; worn. Incurving wall, thickened rim; below rim, row of irregular slightly diagonal to left slashes.
Early Helladic II.

423 LARGE INCURVING SHALLOW BOWL WITH IMPRESSIONS   Fig. 23
(B43-80-2-2) Rim. D. indet., Max. pres. W. 0.09, Th. 0.009. Incurving wall, thickened rim; below rim, row of diagonal slashes to right. Exterior painted?
Early Helladic II.

424 LARGE INCURVING BOWL WITH IMPRESSIONS
                                          Fig. 23
(F32-N-84) Rim. D. indet., Max. pres. W. 0.06, Th. 0.008. Incurving wall, thickened rim; below rim, row of diagonal slashes to right. Painted red-brown (urfirnis).
Early Helladic II.

425 LARGE INCURVING BOWL WITH IMPRESSIONS
                                          Fig. 23
(F32-N-45) Rim. D. indet., Max. pres. W. 0.06, Th. 0.006. Incurving wall, rim thickened to triangle; below rim, row of diagonal slashes to right. Surfaces not preserved.
Early Helladic II.

426 SPOUTED BOWL   Fig. 23
(F32-24) Rim with part of spout. D. 0.28, Max. pres. W. 0.05, Th. 0.008. Coarse fabric; several very large inclusions, some lime; unevenly fired, 5YR 6/4 (light reddish brown) to 5YR 5/2 (reddish gray) [core]. Incurving wall, thickened rim, flattened lip; oval spout hole, spout oval in section continues right as ridge; to right of spout and below ridge, taenia band. Surfaces not preserved.
Early Helladic II.

427 SPOUTED BOWL   Fig. 23
(F32-N-141) Rim with part of spout. D. est. 0.26, Max. pres. W. 0.06, Th. 0.005. Semicoarse fabric; some lime; unevenly fired, 5YR 5/6 (yellowish red) to 7.5YR 5/2 (brown) [core]. Flaring rim, rounded lip; below rim, part of U-shaped spout; below rim, horizontal groove (row of slashes?). Exterior and band at interior rim slipped yellow-orange (yellow slip and polish?).
Early Helladic II.

428 MEDIUM OUTTURNED BOWL WITH IMPRESSIONS
Fig. 23
(F32-A7-5) Rim. D. 0.22, Max. pres. W. 0.035, Th. 0.004; worn. Incurving wall, outturned rim; below rim, row of oblique slashes to right.
Early Helladic II.

429 MEDIUM OUTTURNED BOWL WITH IMPRESSIONS
Fig. 23
(C11-32-5) Rim. D. 0.22, Max. pres. W. 0.04, Th. 0.004. Incurving wall, outturned rim; below rim, row of diagonal slashes to right. Interior and lip painted black (urfirnis).
Early Helladic II.

430 MEDIUM OUTTURNED BOWL WITH IMPRESSIONS
Fig. 23
(A6/9-A-6) Rim. D. 0.25, Max. pres. W. 0.03, Th. 0.006. Incurving wall, outturned rim; below rim, row of diagonal triangular slashes to right. Painted black-brown (urfirnis).
Early Helladic II.

431 MEDIUM OUTTURNED BOWL WITH IMPRESSIONS
Fig. 23
(C11-SW-25) Rim. D. 0.28, Max. pres. W. 0.06, Th. 0.005. Incurving wall, outturned rim; below rim, row of narrow triangles. Painted black (urfirnis).
Early Helladic II.

432 MEDIUM OUTTURNED BOWL WITH IMPRESSIONS
Fig. 23
(A6-72-14) Rim. D. 0.28, Max. pres. W. 0.045, Th. 0.008. Incurving wall, rim turned out, lip bevelled to interior. On lip, two rows impressed triangles, apices to interior.
Early Helladic II.

433 MEDIUM OUTTURNED BOWL WITH IMPRESSIONS
Fig. 23
(F32-N-39) Rim. D. 0.29, Max. pres. W. 0.035, Th. 0.007. Incurving wall, outturned rim; below rim, row of narrow diagonal slashes to left. Surfaces not preserved.
Early Helladic II.

434 MEDIUM OUTTURNED BOWL WITH IMPRESSIONS
Fig. 23
(B43-80-2-11) Rim. D. 0.29, Max. pres. W. 0.05, Th. 0.0045. Incurving wall, outturned rim; below rim, row of triangles. Painted? (urfirnis?).
Early Helladic II.

435 MEDIUM OUTTURNED BOWL WITH IMPRESSIONS
Fig. 23
(F32-N-146) Rim. D. 0.32, Max. pres. W. 0.065, Th. 0.011. Incurving wall, outturned rim; below rim, row of irregular

triangles. Lip painted black (urfirnis); other surfaces not preserved.
Early Helladic II.

436 LARGE OUTTURNED BOWL WITH IMPRESSIONS
Fig. 24
(B24-49) Rim. D. est. 0.35, Max. pres. W. 0.05, Th. 0.007. Incurving wall, outturned rim; below rim, row of triangles. Surfaces not preserved.
Early Helladic II.

437 LARGE OUTTURNED BOWL WITH IMPRESSIONS
Figs. 24, 121
(A6-72-149) Rim. D. 0.35, Max. pres. W. 0.08, Th. 0.008. Medium fabric; many small to medium inclusions, little lime; unevenly fired, 5YR 6/6 (reddish yellow) to 5YR 5/1 (gray) [core]. Incurving wall, outturned rim; below rim, row of irregular triangular impressions, deeper at upper left. Slipped light brown and burnished.
Early Helladic II.

438 LARGE OUTTURNED BOWL WITH IMPRESSIONS
Fig. 24
(F32-32) Rim, two joining. D. 0.40, Max. pres. W. 0.11, Th. 0.008. Incurving wall, outturned rim; below rim, row of triangles. Painted black (urfirnis).
Early Helladic II.

439 LARGE OUTTURNED BOWL WITH IMPRESSIONS
Fig. 24
(B24-53) Rim. D. 0.42, Max. pres. W. 0.055, Th. 0.011. Incurving wall, outturned rim; below rim, row of irregular triangles. Surfaces not preserved.
Early Helladic II.

440 LARGE OUTTURNED BOWL WITH IMPRESSIONS
Figs. 24, 121
(F32-A3-6 + 12) Rim and two joining body. D. 0.43, Max. pres. W. 0.10, Th. 0.007. Medium fabric; no lime; unevenly fired, 5YR 5/4 (reddish brown) to 5YR 5/1 (gray) [core]. Incurving wall, outturned rim; below rim, irregular row of impressed triangles, deeper at top. Painted black (urfirnis).
Early Helladic II.

441 LARGE OUTTURNED BOWL WITH IMPRESSIONS
Fig. 24
(F17-2) Rim. D. 0.43, Max. pres. W. 0.065, Th. 0.009. Incurving wall, outturned rim; below rim, row of oblique slashes to right. Exterior and lip painted brown (urfirnis), interior worn.
Early Helladic II.

442 LARGE OUTTURNED BOWL WITH IMPRESSIONS
AND RIDGE   Figs. 24, 121
(A6-83-1) Rim. D. 0.64, Max. pres. W. 0.08, Th. 0.008. Semicoarse fabric; no lime; unevenly fired, 7.5YR 6/6 (reddish yellow) to 7.5YR 5/2 (brown) [core]. Incurving wall, outturned rim; below rim, row of diagonal impressed slashes with pronounced corners (poor triangles?); below slashes, curving ridge appliqué. Traces of paint on interior.
Early Helladic II.

443 OUTTURNED BOWL WITH IMPRESSIONS   Fig. 24
(F32-C2-1) Rim. D. indet., Max. pres. W. 0.03, Th. 0.004. Incurving wall, outturned rim; below rim, row of oblique slashes

to right. Exterior painted red-brown (urfirnis?).
Early Helladic II.

444 LARGE OUTTURNED BOWL WITH IMPRESSIONS
Fig. 24
(F20-ALL-10) Rim. D. indet., Max. pres. W. 0.05, Th.
0.009. Insloping wall, outturned rim; below rim, row of
triangles. Exterior painted black (urfirnis); interior worn.
Early Helladic II.

445 LARGE BOWL WITH IMPRESSIONS   Figs. 24, 121
(B24-64) Rim. D. indet., Max. pres. W. 0.07. Coarse
fabric. Rim thickened to exterior, flattened lip; on rim, incised
herringbone. Painted red (urfirnis).
Early Helladic II.

446 LARGE SHALLOW BOWL WITH IMPRESSIONS
Fig. 24
(A6-65-27) Rim. D. indet., Max. pres. W. 0.055.
Semicoarse fabric; some lime; evenly fired, 2.5YR 4/6 (red).
Flaring wall, rim turned out and down, curved sloping lip; on lip,
three rows of alternating diagonal slashes (herringbone?). Fabric
very different, many small "burnt out" vacuoles.
Early Helladic II (early?) or Early Helladic I?.

447 LARGE BOWL or PITHOS   Fig. 24
(E5-A-1) Rim. D. 0.45, Max. pres. W. 0.12, Th. 0.008.
Medium fabric; little lime; unevenly fired (secondary firing?),
5YR 4/1 (dark gray) to 5YR 4/4 (reddish brown) [core]. Incurving
wall, rim outturned and thickened to triangular section, flat lip;
below rim, two rows of impressed triangles; on lip, two rows of
impressed triangles with apices facing each other, forming
kerbschnitt. Painted black (urfirnis).
Early Helladic II.

448 SMALL JAR or PITHOS WITH IMPRESSIONS Fig. 24
(F32-D6-5) Rim. D. indet., Max. pres. W. 0.035, Th.
0.007. Medium fabric; no lime; unevenly fired, 5YR 5/6
(yellowish red) to 5YR 5/2 (reddish gray) [core]. Incurving wall,
thickened rim, flattened lip; below rim, slight ridge, small
impressed triangles; on lip, two rows of small impressed triangles
with apices facing each other forming raised zigzag. Painted?
Early Helladic II.

449 JAR or SMALL PITHOS   Fig. 25
(F32-C11-1) Rim. D. 0.17, Max. pres. W. 0.065, Th.
0.008. Semicoarse fabric; no lime; unevenly fired, 2.5YR 4/4
(reddish brown) to 2.5YR-N5/0 (gray) [core]. Insloping wall, rim
turned out and bevelled to interior. Burnished?
Early Helladic II?

450 PITHOS   Fig. 25
(A6-9-7) Rim. D. 0.26, Max. pres. W. 0.09, Th. 0.008.
Semicoarse fabric; some lime; evenly fired, est. 7.5YR 6/4 (light
brown). Rim turned out, outer edge of rim flattened, flat lip
bevelled to interior; below rim, taenia band of slashes on shallow
ridge. Exterior and lip painted red wash.
Early Helladic II.

451 JAR or PITHOS   Fig. 25
(E5-2-30) Rim. D. 0.27, Max. pres. W. 0.13, Th. 0.009.
Semicoarse fabric; medium inclusions, some lime; unevenly fired,
7.5YR 5/4 (brown) to 10YR 5/2 (grayish brown) [core]. Convex

curving shoulder; rim thickened out, lip bevelled to interior.
Plain.
Early Helladic II.

452 PITHOS   Fig. 25
(F20-28) Rim. D. 0.32, Max. pres. W. 0.15, Th. 0.008.
Coarse fabric; some lime; unevenly fired, 2.5YR 5/8 (red) to 5YR
5/4 (reddish brown) [core]. Straight insloping shoulder, rim
thickened to exterior to triangle, slightly rounded lip bevelled to
interior. Exterior painted irregular red-brown (urfirnis) "bands";
lip painted red-brown wash.
Early Helladic II.

453 PITHOS   Fig. 25
(A6-65-26) Rim. D. 0.34, Max. pres. W. 0.115, Th. 0.007.
Semicoarse fabric; little lime; evenly fired, 5YR 4/3 (reddish
brown). Incurving shoulder, rim thickened and turned out, outer
edge of rim flat, flattened lip bevelled to interior; below rim,
taenia band of diagonal slashes to right on shallow ridge. Surfaces
not preserved.
Early Helladic II.

454 PITHOS   Fig. 25
(A6-74-61) Rim. D. 0.34, Max. pres. W. 0.125, Th. 0.005.
Medium fabric; small to medium inclusions, little lime; unevenly
fired, 2.5YR 5/8 (red) to 2.5YR 5/4 (reddish brown) [core]. Lip
turned out, bevelled on interior. Exterior and top of lip painted
black (urfirnis?). Cf. **807**.
Early Helladic II (or later, but pre-Mycenaean).

455 PITHOS or LARGE JAR   Fig. 25
(B5-9) Rim. D. 0.35, Max. pres. W. 0.14, Th. 0.012.
Coarse fabric; medium to large inclusions, some lime; unevenly
fired, 2.5YR 4/8 (red) to 7.5YR 4/6 (strong brown) [core]. Very
flaring neck; lip slightly thickened on exterior, flattened on
interior. Exterior irregular horizontal burnishing.
Early Helladic II? (or later?).

456 PITHOS   Fig. 25
(A33-1-62) Rim. D. 0.36, Max. pres. W. 0.105, Th. 0.012.
Coarse fabric; some lime; unevenly fired, 5YR 6/6 (reddish
yellow) to 7.5YR 7/4 (pink) [core]. Incurving shoulder, rim
thickened to exterior to triangle, flat lip bevelled to interior.
Surfaces not preserved.
Early Helladic II.

457 PITHOS   Fig. 25
(F32-N-150) Rim. D. 0.36, Max. pres. W. 0.090, Th.
0.016. Semicoarse fabric; little lime; unevenly fired, 2.5YR 4/6
(red) to 5YR 3/3 (dark reddish brown) [core]. Incurving shoulder,
rim thickened and turned out, flat lip bevelled to interior. Plain.
Early Helladic II.

458 PITHOS   Fig. 25
(E4-1-17) Rim. D. 0.38, Max. pres. W. 0.075, Th. 0.008.
Semicoarse fabric; little lime; unevenly fired, 7.5YR 5/2 (brown)
to 5YR 5/4 (reddish brown) [core]. Rim turned out, flat lip
bevelled to interior; below rim, taenia band of overlapping discs to
right. Exterior painted thin black wash.
Early Helladic II.

459 PITHOS   Fig. 26
(F20-ALL-22) Rim, two joining. D. 0.41, Max. pres. W.
0.255, Th. 0.010. Coarse fabric; some lime; evenly fired, 10YR

6/3 (pale brown). Insloping shoulder, rim thickened and turned to exterior, slightly rounded lip bevelled to interior. Exterior and lip painted irregular thin wash.
Early Helladic II.

460 PITHOS   Fig. 26
(F20-31) Rim. D. 0.42, Max. pres. W. 0.15, Th. 0.010. Coarse fabric; much lime; evenly fired, 5YR 5/1 (gray). Incurving wall, rim turned out, flat lip bevelled to interior. Traces of thin wash.
Early Helladic II.

461 PITHOS   Fig. 27
(A9-3-13) Rim. D. 0.42, Max. pres. W. 0.09, Th. 0.010. Semicoarse fabric; some silver inclusions, little lime; unevenly fired, 5YR 6/6 (reddish yellow) to 7.5YR 6/2 (pinkish gray) [core]. Incurving shoulder, rim thickened to exterior to triangle, flat lip bevelled to interior. Surfaces not preserved. Cf. **1096**.
Early Helladic II (or Geometric?).

462 PITHOS WITH IMPRESSIONS   Fig. 26
(A9-8-1) Rim. D. 0.44, Max. pres. W. 0.11, Th. 0.008. Coarse fabric; some lime; unevenly fired, 2.5YR 5/8 (red) to 5YR 5/1 (gray) [core]. Incurving wall, wide outturned rim, flat lip; below rim, taenia (impressed band); below, row of diagonal triangular slashes to right; on lip, three rows of impressed triangles. Exterior and lip painted black (urfirnis); interior worn (but plain?).
Early Helladic II.

463 PITHOS   Fig. 27
(F6-10) Rim. D. 0.45, Max. pres. W. 0.10, Th. 0.010. Coarse fabric; much lime; unevenly fired, 5YR 4/8 (yellowish red) to 5YR 4/2 (dark reddish gray) [core]. Incurving shoulder, rim thickened and turned out, flat lip bevelled to interior. Surfaces not preserved.
Early Helladic II.

464 PITHOS   Fig. 27
(F20-30) Rim. D. 0.47, Max. pres. W. 0.18, Th. 0.010. Coarse fabric; little lime; evenly fired, 7.5YR 6/2 (pinkish gray). Insloping shoulder, rim thickened to exterior to triangle, flattened lip bevelled to interior. Plain.
Early Helladic II.

465 PITHOS   Fig. 27
(F20-29) Rim. D. 0.48, Max. pres. W. 0.14, Th. 0.011. Coarse fabric; some lime; evenly fired, 5YR 4/2 (dark reddish gray). Insloping shoulder, rim thickened and turned out, flat lip bevelled to interior and exterior. Exterior and lip painted irregular thin wash.
Early Helladic II.

466 PITHOS WITH HANDLE?   Fig. 26
(A33-1-60) Rim. D. 0.53, Max. pres. W. 0.09, Th. 0.012. Coarse fabric; some lime; unevenly fired, 2.5YR 5/8 (red) to 5YR 5/4 (reddish brown) [core]. Incurving shoulder, rim thickened to exterior and turned out, flat lip bevelled to interior; below rim, taenia (or wide tubular handle attachment). Surfaces not preserved (traces of red paint on exterior?).
Early Helladic II.

467 PITHOS   Fig. 28
(E5-2-31) Rim. D. 0.54, Max. pres. W. 0.09, Th. 0.010.

Coarse fabric; some lime; unevenly fired, 2.5YR 5/8 (red) to 7.5YR 5/2 (brown) [core]. Incurving shoulder, rim thickened to interior and to exterior to triangle, flattened lip bevelled to interior. Exterior surface not preserved; interior burnished.
Early Helladic II.

468 PITHOS   Fig. 28
(F20-27) Rim. D. est. 0.54, Max. pres. W. 0.19, Th. 0.012. Coarse fabric; much lime; evenly fired, 5YR 4/1 (dark gray). Incurving wall, rim turned out, slightly rounded lip bevelled to interior. Exterior band below rim painted thin wash; burnished along outer edge of lip/rim.
Early Helladic II.

469 PITHOS   Fig. 26
(E5-2-34) Rim. D. est. 0.58, Max. pres. W. 0.10, Th. 0.013. Coarse fabric; some lime; unevenly fired, 5YR 5/4 (reddish brown) to 2.5YR 5/6 (red) [core]. Incurving? shoulder, rim thickened to interior and turned out, slightly rounded lip bevelled to interior. Plain?
Early Helladic II.

470 PITHOS   Fig. 28
(F20-ALL-8) Rim. D. 0.58, Max. pres. W. 0.12, Th. 0.013. Coarse fabric; some lime; unevenly fired, 5YR 5/3 (reddish brown) to 5YR 4/1 (dark gray) [core]. Incurving shoulder, rim thickened to exterior to triangle, slightly rounded lip bevelled to interior. Exterior and lip painted thin wash, including part of loop on exterior.
Early Helladic II.

471 PITHOS   Fig. 28
(A33-1-63) Rim. D. 0.61, Max. pres. W. 0.075, Th. 0.011. Coarse fabric; little lime; evenly fired, 2.5YR 4/6 (red). Rim thickened, rounded lip; traces of taenia below rim. Surfaces not preserved.
Early Helladic II.

472 PITHOS   Fig. 28
(F32-B12-2) Rim. D. 0.63, Max. pres. W. 0.145, Th. 0.010. Coarse fabric; little lime; unevenly fired, 5YR 6/4 (light reddish brown) to 7.5YR 5/2 (brown) [core]. Incurving shoulder, rim thickened to exterior to triangle, slightly rounded lip bevelled to interior. Exterior surface not preserved; interior painted black (urfirnis).
Early Helladic II.

473 PITHOS   Fig. 29
(F32-N-151) Rim. D. 0.70, Max. pres. W. 0.135, Th. 0.012. Coarse fabric; much lime; evenly fired, 7.5YR 5/4 (brown). Incurving shoulder, rim thickened to "T", slightly rounded lip bevelled to interior; below rim, beginning of appliqué (taenia?). Lip painted red-brown (urfirnis).
Early Helladic II.

474 PITHOS WITH RIDGE   Fig. 29
(F32-D8-1) Rim. D. > 0.70, Max. pres. W. 0.16, Th. 0.013. Semicoarse fabric; many small inclusions; unevenly fired, 5YR 5/4 (reddish brown) to mottled dark core. Incurving wall, lip thickened to exterior (triangular in section); below rim, horizontal ridge ending to right. Surfaces not preserved.
Early Helladic II.

475 PITHOS   Fig. 29
(A9-9-1) Rim. D. indet., Max. pres. W. 0.06, Th. 0.010.
Coarse fabric; some lime; unevenly fired, 7.5YR 6/4 (light
brown) to 7.5YR 5/2 (brown) [core]. Incurving shoulder, rim
thickened to exterior to triangle, flattened lip bevelled to interior.
Surfaces not preserved.
Early Helladic II.

476 PITHOS   Fig. 29
(F17-3) Rim. D. 0.40-0.50, Max. pres. W. 0.105, Th.
0.010. Coarse fabric; little lime; unevenly fired, 5YR 4/1 (dark
gray) to 2.5YR 4/6 (red) [core]. Incurving shoulder, rim thickened
to exterior, flattened lip bevelled to interior. Surfaces not
preserved.
Early Helladic II.

477 PITHOS WITH TAENIA   Fig. 29
(F32-N-79) Rim. D. indet., Max. pres. W. 0.105, Th.
0.012. Coarse fabric; some lime; evenly fired, 2.5YR 5/8 (red).
Rim thickened and turned out, flat lip bevelled to interior; below
rim, taenia band of overlapping discs to right. Exterior painted red
(urfirnis); interior and lip surfaces not preserved.
Early Helladic II.

478 PITHOS   Fig. 29
(A6-1-15) Rim. D. indet. (>0.40), Max. pres. W. 0.07, Th.
0.009. Coarse fabric; large to very large inclusions, some lime;
unevenly fired, 2.5YR 6/8 (light red) to 5YR 6/2 (pinkish gray)
[core]. Insloping wall, rim turned out and bevelled to interior.
Painted red (urfirnis) and burnished irregularly to luster.
Early Helladic II.

479 PITHOS? WITH IMPRESSIONS   Figs. 29, 121
(F6-ALL-5) Rim. D. est. 0.40-0.50, Max. pres. W. 0.09.
Coarse fabric. Insloping wall, thickened rim, flattened lip
bevelled to interior; on lip, incised hatched triangles.
Early Helladic II.

480 PITHOS WITH IMPRESSIONS   Figs. 29, 121
(F32-N-269) Rim. D. indet., Max. pres. W. 0.065. Coarse
fabric. Insloping wall, rim thickened to triangle on exterior, flat
lip; on lip, stamped herringbone.
Early Helladic II.

481 PITHOS WITH IMPRESSIONS   Figs. 29, 121
(A6-2-7) Rim. D. indet., Max. pres. W. 0.055. Coarse
fabric. Insloping wall, rim thickened to exterior, flat lip; on lip,
stamped herringbone.
Early Helladic II.

482 PITHOS WITH IMPRESSIONS   Fig. 29
(E5-2-35) Rim. D. indet., Max. pres. W. 0.06. Coarse
fabric. Rim thickened to exterior, flattened lip; on lip, rows of
alternating triangles, deeper at one apex, forming kerbschnitt.
Early Helladic II.

483 PITHOS   Fig. 121
(F20-34) Body. Max. pres. W. 0.23, Max. pres. H. 0.21,
Th. 0.010-0.011. Medium fabric; some lime; evenly fired, color
indet., est. 10YR 5/1-2 (gray-grayish brown). Straight wall.
Exterior painted with two wide tangential loops of thin urfirnis
wash on irregularly scored surface.
Early Helladic II.

484 PITHOS   Figs. 29, 121
(F32-A11-6) Rim. D. 0.40, Max. pres. W. 0.08, Th. 0.007.
Coarse fabric; little lime; unevenly fired, 2.5YR 6/8 (light red) to
5YR 5/2 (reddish gray) [core]. Flaring wall, rim thickened to
exterior, lip flattened. Exterior black wash (urfirnis) below rim;
interior plain.
Early Helladic II.

485 PITHOS   Fig. 29
(E5-2-32) Rim. D. 0.48, Max. pres. W. 0.11, Th. 0.008.
Semicoarse fabric; little lime; evenly fired, 2.5YR 4/8 (red).
Vertical wall, rim thickened to exterior with slight thickening to
interior forming hollow on interior of rim. Exterior thin black
paint (urfirnis).
Early Helladic II.

486 JAR   Fig. 30
(C11-NE-17) Rim. D. 0.10, Max. pres. W. 0.07, Th.
0.007. Medium fabric; no lime; unevenly fired, 5YR 6/6-8
(reddish yellow) to 2.5YR-N4/0 (dark gray) [core]. Neck/shoulder
sloping in; slightly flaring rim; rounded lip. Burnished.
Early Helladic II.

487 JAR WITH SPLAYED NECK   Fig. 30
(F32-S-115) Rim. D. 0.11, Max. pres. W. 0.085. Medium
fabric; little lime; unevenly fired, 7.5YR 4/4 (brown-dark brown)
to 7.5YR-N5/0 (gray) [core]. Offset splayed neck, rounded lip.
Exterior painted black? (urfirnis?).
Early Helladic II.

488 JAR WITH SPLAYED NECK   Fig. 30
(F32-S-121) Rim. D. 0.12, Max. pres. W. 0.07. Semifine
fabric; little lime; evenly fired, 5YR 6/8 (reddish yellow). Offset
splayed neck; lip slightly thickened to exterior. Slipped (self
slip).
Early Helladic II.

489 JAR WITH SPLAYED NECK   Fig. 30
(A6/9-A-3) Rim. D. 0.12, Max. pres. W. 0.11, Th. 0.006.
Semicoarse fabric; much lime; evenly fired, 7.5YR 5/4 (brown).
Splayed, offset neck; rim rounded to exterior, flattened to interior.
Exterior burnished; interior of neck burnished.
Early Helladic II.

490 JAR WITH SPLAYED NECK   Fig. 30
(A6/9-A-9) Rim. D. 0.13, Max. pres. W. 0.085, Th. 0.009.
Medium fabric; much lime; unevenly fired, 5YR 5/4 (reddish
brown) to 7.5YR-N5/0 (gray) [core]. Offset, flaring neck, rounded
lip. Exterior burnished; interior of neck burnished.
Early Helladic II.

491 JAR WITH SPLAYED NECK   Fig. 30
(F32-N-129) Rim. D. 0.13, Th. 0.005. Semifine fabric;
evenly fired, 7.5YR 7/4 (pink). Painted black (urfirnis).
Early Helladic II.

492 JAR WITH SPLAYED NECK   Fig. 30
(C11-SW-15) Rim. D. 0.14, Max. pres. W. 0.12, Th.
0.007. Medium fabric; some lime; evenly fired, 5YR 3/2 (dark
reddish brown). Offset, flaring neck; everted lip. Plain.
Early Helladic II.

493 JAR WITH SPLAYED NECK   Fig. 30
(C11-NE-27) Rim. D. 0.14, Max. pres. W. 0.055, Th.
0.004. Semifine fabric; much lime; unevenly fired, 7.5YR 6/4
(light brown) to 7.5YR 5/2 (brown) [core]. Offset splayed neck,
rounded lip. Plain?
Early Helladic II.

494 JAR WITH SPLAYED NECK   Fig. 30
(C11-SE-19) Rim. D. 0.14, Th. 0.007. Semicoarse fabric;
some lime; unevenly fired, 7.5YR 6/6 (reddish yellow) to 10YR
5/1 (gray) [core]. Offset, flaring neck; rounded lip. Plain.
Early Helladic II.

495 JAR WITH SPLAYED NECK   Fig. 30
(F6-28 + 29) Rim, two joining. D. 0.14, Th. 0.006.
Semicoarse fabric; some lime; unevenly fired, 7.5YR 6/4 (light
brown) to 7.5YR-N4/0 (dark gray) [core]. Offset, flaring neck;
rounded lip. Plain.
Early Helladic II.

496 JAR WITH SPLAYED NECK   Fig. 30
(B43-80-2-1) Rim. D. 0.14, Th. 0.009. Semicoarse fabric;
much lime; evenly fired, 7.5YR 6/4 (light brown). Offset,
splayed neck; rounded lip. Plain.
Early Helladic II.

497 JAR WITH SPLAYED NECK   Fig. 30
(F32-N-81) Rim. D. 0.16, Max. pres. W. 0.095, Th. 0.007.
Semicoarse fabric; much lime; unevenly fired, 7.5YR 6/4 (light
brown) to 10YR 5/2 (grayish brown) [core]. Offset, flaring neck;
rounded lip. Plain.
Early Helladic II.

498 JAR WITH SPLAYED NECK   Fig. 30
(A6-72-147) Rim. D. 0.18, Max. pres. W. 0.07, Th. 0.008.
Semicoarse fabric; some lime; evenly fired, 2.5YR 5/8 (red).
Very flaring neck, rounded lip. Slipped?
Early Helladic II.

499 JAR WITH SPLAYED NECK   Fig. 30
(F32-S-110) Rim. D. 0.18, Max. pres. W. 0.11, Th. 0.007.
Semicoarse fabric; small to medium inclusions, little lime;
unevenly fired, 5YR 5/8 (yellowish red) on interior and 5YR 6/6
(reddish yellow) on exterior to 5YR 5/1 (gray) [core]. Curving
shoulder, flaring neck, slightly thickened lip. Exterior slipped
(self slip); interior of lip slipped (self slip).
Early Helladic II

500 JAR WITH SPLAYED NECK   Fig. 30
(F32-N-95) Rim. D. 0.20, Max. pres. W. 0.08, Th. 0.009.
Coarse fabric; large inclusions, some lime; unevenly fired, 5YR
6/6 (reddish yellow) to 5YR 5/4 (reddish brown) [core]. Splayed
neck; rounded lip. Plain?
Early Helladic II.

501 LARGE JAR WITH SPLAYED NECK   Fig. 30
(A6-72-67) Rim. D. 0.22, Max. pres. W. 0.08, Th. 0.009.
Semicoarse fabric; little lime; unevenly fired, 7.5YR 6/4 (light
brown) to 5YR 5/3 (reddish brown) [core]. Offset, tall flaring
neck; rounded lip. Exterior painted brown (urfirnis).
Early Helladic II.

502 JAR WITH FLARING NECK   Fig. 31
(E13-10 + E13-2-45) Rim, two joining. D. 0.11, Th.

0.005. Semicoarse fabric; much lime; unevenly fired, 7.5YR 6/4
(light brown) to 7.5YR-N3/0 (very dark gray) [core]. Offset,
splayed neck; flaring rim; rounded lip. Exterior painted red-brown
(urfirnis).
Early Helladic II.

503 JAR WITH FLARING NECK   Fig. 31
(B43-A-10) Rim, three joining. D. 0.13, Th. 0.006.
Medium fabric; little lime; unevenly fired, 7.5YR 5/6 (strong
brown) to 7.5YR 5/2 (brown) [core]. Offset, flaring neck; rounded
lip. Plain.
Early Helladic II.

504 JAR WITH FLARING NECK   Fig. 31
(C11-SE-4) Rim. D. 0.13, Max. pres. W. 0.07, Th. 0.005.
Medium fabric; some lime; evenly fired, 5YR 4/3 (reddish brown).
Offset, flaring neck; rounded lip. Plain.
Early Helladic II.

505 JAR WITH FLARING NECK   Fig. 31
(A6/9-A-16) Rim. D. 0.14, Max. pres. W. 0.055, Th.
0.007. Semifine fabric; some lime; unevenly fired, 5YR 6/6
(reddish yellow) to 10YR 7/4 (very pale brown) [core]. Offset,
tall straight neck; flaring rim; rounded lip. Plain?
Early Helladic II.

506 JAR WITH FLARING NECK   Fig. 31
(F32-S-111) Rim. D. 0.15, Max. pres. W. 0.09, Th. 0.009.
Semicoarse fabric; some lime; unevenly fired, 7.5YR 5/4 (brown)
to 7.5YR-N5/0 (gray) [core]. Offset, flaring neck; rounded lip.
Plain.
Early Helladic II.

507 JAR WITH FLARING NECK   Fig. 31
(C11-C19-10) Rim. D. 0.18, Max. pres. W. 0.055, Th.
0.006. Semicoarse fabric; small to large inclusions, some lime;
unevenly fired, 2.5YR 4/8 (red) to 7.5YR 4/2 (dark brown-brown)
[core]. Offset, flaring neck; rim thickened to exterior, flat on
interior. Exterior burnished in spots.
Early Helladic II.

508 JAR WITH FLARING RIM   Fig. 31
(F20-ALL-9) Rim. D. 0.18, Max. pres. W. 0.075, Th.
0.007. Semicoarse fabric; little lime; unevenly fired, 5YR 6/6
(reddish yellow) to 10YR 6/1 (gray-light gray) [core]. Splayed
wall, slightly flaring rim, rounded lip. Exterior and band at
interior painted thin black (urfirnis).
Early Helladic II.

509 COLLARED JAR   Fig. 31
(F32-E-33) Rim. D. 0.12, Max. pres. W. 0.05, Th. 0.007.
Semicoarse fabric; some lime; evenly fired, 2.5YR 5/8 (red).
Sloping shoulder, short vertical collar, rounded lip. Exterior
painted (urfirnis).
Early Helladic II.

510 COLLARED JAR   Fig. 31
(F32-S-41) Rim. D. 0.12, est. one-fourth of diameter. pres.,
Th. 0.007. Semicoarse fabric; medium to large inclusions, some
lime; unevenly fired, 5YR 6/6 (reddish yellow) to 5YR 5/2
(reddish gray) [core]. Curving shoulder; short, splayed neck;
rounded lip. Exterior painted mottled red to brown (urfirnis);
interior of lip painted mottled red to brown (urfirnis).
Early Helladic II.

511 COLLARED JAR Fig. 31
(F32-E-19) Rim. D. 0.14, Max. pres. W. 0.05, Th. 0.005. Medium fabric; much lime; unevenly fired, 7.5YR 5/4 (brown) to 7.5YR-N5/0 (gray) [core]. Offset splayed neck, lip rounded. Exterior painted red-brown (urfirnis); interior of neck painted red-brown (urfirnis).
Early Helladic II.

512 COLLARED JAR Fig. 31
(F32-S-61) Rim. D. 0.20, Max. pres. W. 0.07, Th. 0.007. Semicoarse fabric; little lime; evenly fired, 2.5YR 5/8 (red). Flat shoulder, short vertical collar, flat lip; raised ridge 0.010 wide, 0.007 tall, on shoulder approx. 0.014 from neck. Exterior: band at lip and below ridge painted black (urfirnis); interior of neck painted black (urfirnis).
Early Helladic II.

513 COLLARED JAR Fig. 31
(A33-1-40) Rim. D. 0.21, Max. pres. W. 0.07, Th. 0.007. Medium fabric; little lime; evenly fired, 7.5YR 6/4 (light brown). Slightly offset, splayed neck; rim slightly thickened; lip rounded. Exterior painted black (urfirnis); interior band painted black (urfirnis).
Early Helladic II.

514 JAR SHOULDER WITH TAENIA Fig. 31
(F32-B8-6) Shoulder. D. (interior) at junction est. 0.12, Th. 0.006. Semicoarse fabric; much lime; evenly fired, 7.5YR-N4/0 (dark gray). Sharply offset neck, fairly flat shoulder; narrow taenia band 0.006-0.007 wide on shoulder around neck. Plain.
Early Helladic II.

515 JAR NECK WITH RIDGES Figs. 31, 121
(F32-S-97) Neck/shoulder. D. (interior) at junction 0.09, Th. 0.006. Semicoarse fabric; some lime; unevenly fired, 5YR 6/8 (reddish yellow) to 5YR 3/2 (dark reddish brown) [core]. Neck offset from shoulder and insloping; ridge, square in section, applied at junction of neck and shoulder; second ridge, square in section, extends vertically from first ridge down shoulder. Exterior: traces of red-brown slip.
(Early Helladic I?) to Early Helladic II.

516 JUG Fig. 31
(F32-D2-1) Rim and spout. D. 0.055, Th. 0.005. Semicoarse fabric; many small to medium inclusions, some lime; unevenly fired, 7.5YR 5/6 (strong brown) to 5YR 6/1 (gray-light gray) [core]. Slightly flaring neck, rising to "cut-away" spout. Exterior painted black (urfirnis); interior rim painted black (urfirnis).
Early Helladic II.

517 BOWL (or SAUCEBOAT) Fig. 32
(F32-S-176) Ring foot. D. 0.025, Th. 0.005. Semicoarse fabric; no lime; evenly fired, 5YR 5/3 (reddish brown). Small vertical ring (formed by depressing a disc?). Exterior plain; interior painted red (urfirnis).
Early Helladic II.

518 BOWL (or SAUCEBOAT) Fig. 32
(F32-N-223) Ring foot. D. 0.03, Th. 0.003. Medium fabric; no lime; evenly fired, 5YR 6/6 (reddish yellow). Small vertical ring foot, curving wall. Surfaces not preserved.
Early Helladic II.

519 (BOWL or) SAUCEBOAT Fig. 32
(F5-31) Ring foot. D. 0.045, Th. 0.005. Semifine fabric; much lime; unevenly fired, 5YR 6/8 (reddish yellow) to 5YR 6/2 (pinkish gray) [core]. Splayed, offset ring foot with pontile bottom. Painted red (urfirnis).
Early Helladic II.

520 BOWL or SAUCEBOAT Fig. 32
(B43-A-12) Ring foot. D. 0.04, Th. 0.009. Medium to semicoarse fabric; some lime; unevenly fired, 5YR 5/6 (yellowish red) to 5YR 4/3 (reddish brown) [core]. Splayed ring foot. Surfaces worn.
Early Helladic II.

521 BOWL Fig. 32
(F32-N-243) Ring foot. D. 0.04, Th. 0.008. Semicoarse fabric; some lime; unevenly fired 5YR 5/6 (yellowish red) to 5YR 4/4 (reddish brown) [core]. Splayed ring foot, steeply curving wall. Exterior plain; interior painted red (urfirnis?).
Early Helladic II.

522 BOWL Fig. 32
(A6-72-69) Ring foot. D. 0.04, Th. 0.005. Semifine fabric; unevenly fired, 5YR 6/8 (reddish yellow) to 5YR 5/2 (reddish gray) [core]. Splayed ring base, incurving wall. Painted thin brown-black (urfirnis).
Early Helladic II.

523 BOWL or SAUCEBOAT Fig. 32
(F32-S-170) Ring foot. D. 0.05, Th. 0.005. Medium fabric; little lime; evenly fired, 5YR 4/3 (reddish brown). Vertical ring foot. Painted black (urfirnis).
Early Helladic II.

524 BOWL or SAUCEBOAT Fig. 32
(E5-B-9) Ring foot. D. 0.05, Th. 0.004. Medium fabric; some small to occasional large inclusions, little lime; unevenly fired, 5YR 6/6 (reddish yellow) to 7.5YR-N5/0 (gray) [core]. Splayed ring base, curving wall. Plain.
Early Helladic II.

525 BOWL or SAUCEBOAT Fig. 32
(F32-N-245) Ring foot. D. 0.05, Th. 0.004. Semifine fabric; little lime; evenly fired, 2.5YR 6/6 (light red). Vertical ring foot. Painted black (urfirnis).
Early Helladic II.

526 BOWL or SAUCEBOAT Fig. 32
(F32-N-212) Ring foot. D. 0.05, Th. 0.004. Semifine fabric; no lime; unevenly fired, 2.5Y 7/2 (light gray) to 5YR 7/4 (pink) [core]. Splayed ring foot. Exterior painted black (urfirnis); interior painted brown (urfirnis). "Corinthian green" fabric.
Early Helladic II.

527 BOWL or SAUCEBOAT Fig. 32
(F32-42) Ring foot. D. 0.055, Th. 0.006. Medium fabric; little lime; unevenly fired, 5YR 6/6 (reddish yellow) to 5YR 5/1 (gray) [core]. Vertical ring foot, gently curving wall. Plain?
Early Helladic II.

528 BOWL or SAUCEBOAT Fig. 32
(A33-3-6) Ring foot. D. 0.055, Th. 0.005. Medium fabric; small to medium inclusions, little lime; unevenly fired, 5YR 6/6 (reddish yellow) to 5YR 6/1 (gray-light gray) [core]. Splayed ring foot, curving wall. Surfaces not preserved.
Early Helladic II.

529 BOWL or SAUCEBOAT   Fig. 32
(F32-S-172) Ring foot. D. 0.055, Th. 0.004. Semicoarse fabric; no lime; unevenly fired, 5YR 5/6 (yellowish red) to 5YR 5/4 (reddish brown) [core]. Splayed ring foot. Exterior slipped blue; interior worn.
Early Helladic II.

530 BOWL   Fig. 32
(F32-D4-16) Ring foot. D. 0.06, Th. 0.008; worn. Semicoarse fabric; small to large inclusions, much lime; unevenly fired, 5YR 6/6 (reddish yellow) to 5YR 3/1 (very dark gray) [core]. Vertical ring foot (almost hollow base), steeply curving wall. Surfaces not preserved.
Early Helladic II.

531 BOWL or SAUCEBOAT   Fig. 32
(F32-A1-7) Ring foot. D. 0.06, Th. 0.006. Medium fabric; no lime; evenly fired, 5Y 7/3 (pale yellow). Splayed ring foot, curving wall. Plain. "Corinthian green" fabric.
Early Helladic II.

532 BOWL or SAUCEBOAT   Fig. 32
(B9-28) Ring foot. D. 0.06, Th. 0.005. Medium fabric; small to medium inclusions, some lime; unevenly fired, 5YR 6/6 (reddish yellow) to 5YR 4/3 (reddish brown) [core]. Splayed ring foot, curving wall. Plain? Method of attaching ring foot preserved: slashes on bottom and extra clay added to join.
Early Helladic II.

533 BOWL or SAUCEBOAT   Fig. 32
(F32-N-224) Ring foot. D. 0.065, Th. 0.004. Semifine fabric; no lime; unevenly fired (secondary burning?), 2.5YR 3/4 (dark reddish brown) to 5YR 4/2 (dark reddish gray) [core]. Vertical ring foot, curving wall. Painted black (urfirnis).
Early Helladic II.

534 BOWL   Fig. 32
(F32-E-45) Ring foot. D. 0.065, Th. 0.008. Semicoarse fabric; medium to large inclusions, some lime; unevenly fired, 7.5YR 7/4 (pink) to 7.5YR 5/4 (brown) [core]. Vertical ring foot. Plain.
Early Helladic II.

535 BOWL or SAUCEBOAT   Fig. 32
(E4-1-33) Ring foot. D. 0.065, Th. 0.004. Semifine fabric; no lime; unevenly fired, 5YR 6/6 (reddish yellow) to 5YR 5/3 (reddish brown) [core]. Splayed ring foot. Exterior slipped yellow (and polished).
Early Helladic II.

536 BOWL or SAUCEBOAT   Fig. 32
(F32-S-175) Ring foot. D. 0.07. Semifine fabric; no lime; unevenly fired, 5YR 5/6 (yellowish red) to 5YR 3/2 (dark reddish brown) [core]. Splayed ring foot. Slipped yellow [10YR 8/6 (yellow)] and polished.
Early Helladic II.

537 BOWL or SAUCEBOAT   Fig. 32
(F32-N-234) Ring foot. D. 0.08, Th. 0.008. Medium fabric; little lime; evenly fired, 2.5YR 6/6 (light red). Splayed ring foot, steeply curving wall. Exterior painted red (urfirnis); interior plain?
Early Helladic II.

538 BOWL   Fig. 32
(B24-14) Ring foot. D. 0.09. Semicoarse fabric; much lime; unevenly fired, 7.5YR 6/6 (reddish yellow) to 7.5YR 4/2 (brown-dark brown) [core]. Splayed ring foot, sharply curving wall. Plain.
Early Helladic II.

539 BOWL or SAUCEBOAT   Fig. 32
(A6-2-17) Ring foot. D. 0.10, Th. 0.009. Semicoarse fabric; medium to large inclusions, no lime; unevenly fired, 5YR 6/8 (reddish yellow) to 5YR 5/2 (reddish gray) [core]. Splayed ring foot, curving wall. Plain.
Early Helladic II.

540 BOWL   Fig. 32
(F32-N-253) Ring foot. D. 0.10, Th. 0.007. Semicoarse fabric; some lime; unevenly fired, 2.5YR 5/8 (red) to 2.5YR-N6/0 (gray-light gray) [core]. Splayed ring foot (almost pedestal foot). Exterior painted black (urfirnis).
Early Helladic II.

541 BOWL or SAUCEBOAT   Fig. 32
(A6-75-6) Ring foot. D. 0.10, Th. 0.005. Medium fabric; much lime; unevenly fired, 5YR 7/4 (pink) to 2.5YR-N5/0 (gray) [core]. Splayed ring foot. Exterior plain; interior painted red (urfirnis).
Early Helladic II.

542 OPEN VESSEL   Fig. 32
(F23-41) Ring foot. D. est. 0.06, Th. 0.006. Medium fabric; some lime; unevenly fired, 7.5YR 6/6 (reddish yellow) to 5YR 3/1 (very dark gray) [core]. Flaring ring foot. Exterior and bottom slipped red and partially burnished; interior slipped red-brown and burnished to luster. cf. Blegen's AI.
Early Helladic II early.

543 OPEN VESSEL   Fig. 32
(F32-S-173) Ring foot. D. 0.065, Th. 0.005. Medium fabric; much lime; unevenly fired, 2.5YR 5/8 (red) to 7.5YR 5/2 (brown) [core]. Flaring ring foot. Exterior, interior, and bottom slipped red (urfirnis?) and burnished. cf. Blegen's AI.
Early Helladic II early.

544 OPEN VESSEL   Fig. 32
(F32-39) Ring foot. D. 0.07, Th. 0.010. Medium fabric; small to occasional large lime inclusions; unevenly fired, 2.5YR 5/8 (red) to 2.5YR-N5/0 (gray) [core]. Splayed ring foot, curving walls. Painted black (urfirnis).
Early Helladic II.

545 OPEN VESSEL   Fig. 32
(A6-74-35) Ring foot. D. 0.08, Th. 0.006. Medium fabric; little lime; evenly fired, 7.5YR 6/4 (light brown). Flaring ring foot. Slipped red and burnished; bottom slipped red (not burnished). cf. Blegen's AI.
Early Helladic II early.

546 OPEN VESSEL   Fig. 32
(A6/9-A-1) Ring foot, two joining. D. 0.09, Th. 0.007. Coarse fabric; large to very large inclusions, no lime; unevenly fired, 7.5YR 6/4 (light brown) to 5YR 5/2 (reddish gray) [core]. Splayed ring foot; gently curving wall. Surfaces not preserved?
Early Helladic II.

547 OPEN VESSEL   Fig. 32
(F32-E-28) Ring foot. D. 0.09, Th. 0.008. Semicoarse fabric; small to medium inclusions, some lime; unevenly fired, 2.5YR 5/8 (red) to 7.5YR 5/4 (brown) [core]. Splayed ring foot. Slipped (self-slip).
Early Helladic II.

548 CLOSED VESSEL   Fig. 32
(F32-38) Ring foot. D. 0.09-0.10, Th. 0.006. Semicoarse fabric; small to medium inclusions, little lime; unevenly fired, 5YR 6/6 (reddish yellow) to 5YR 5/1 (gray) [core]. Splayed ring foot, steeply curving wall. Exterior slipped (self slip); interior plain.
Early Helladic II.

549 CLOSED VESSEL   Fig. 32
(F32-N-226) Ring foot. D. 0.10, Th. 0.006. Semicoarse fabric; medium to large inclusions, no lime; unevenly fired, 2.5YR 4/8 (red) to 5YR 3/3 (dark reddish brown) [core]. Splayed ring foot; steeply curving wall. Exterior slipped; interior plain.
Early Helladic II.

550 OPEN? VESSEL   Fig. 32
(F32-N-262) Ring foot. D. 0.10, Th. 0.007. Semicoarse fabric; many small to medium inclusions, some lime; unevenly fired, 7.5YR 6/6 (reddish yellow) to 5YR 5/1 (gray) [core]. Slightly splayed ring foot, steeply curving wall. Plain.
Early Helladic II.

551 OPEN? VESSEL   Fig. 32
(F32-B12-6) Ring foot. D. 0.10, Th. 0.007. Coarse fabric; medium to large inclusions, no lime; unevenly fired, 2.5YR 6/8 (light red) to 7.5YR 6/2 (pinkish gray) [core]. Splayed ring base, steeply curving wall. Plain.
Early Helladic II.

552 OPEN VESSEL   Fig. 32
(F20-21) Ring foot. D. 0.10, Th. 0.010. Coarse fabric; large to very large inclusions, some lime; unevenly fired, 2.5YR 3/6 (dark red) to 5YR 4/4 (reddish brown) [core]. Splayed ring foot; steeply curving wall. Exterior plain; interior smoothed and slipped.
Early Helladic II.

553 OPEN? VESSEL   Fig. 32
(B24-5) Ring foot. D. 0.10, Th. 0.011; worn. Semicoarse fabric; little lime; unevenly fired, 5YR 6-7/6-8 (reddish yellow) to 5YR 4/2 (dark reddish gray) [core]. Vertical ring foot; steeply curving wall. Surfaces not preserved.
Early Helladic II.

554 OPEN VESSEL   Fig. 32
(F32-N-255) Ring foot. D. 0.11, Th. 0.006. Semicoarse fabric; volcanic and quartz inclusions, no lime; evenly fired, 2.5YR 4/6 (red). Ring foot to large open vessel. Plain.
Early Helladic II.

555 OPEN? VESSEL   Fig. 32
(A6-65-7) Ring foot. D. 0.11, Th. 0.009. Semicoarse fabric; volcanic (gold) inclusions, some lime; evenly fired, 5YR 6/8 (reddish yellow). Ring foot. Plain.
Early Helladic II.

556 OPEN? VESSEL   Fig. 32
(F32-N-249) Ring foot. D. 0.11, Th. 0.009. Coarse fabric; medium to large inclusions, some lime; unevenly fired, 5YR 6/8 (reddish yellow) to 5YR 5/3 (reddish brown) [core]. Splayed ring foot, thickened towards resting surface; curving wall. Plain.
Early Helladic II.

557 CLOSED VESSEL   Fig. 32
(F32-N-257) Ring foot. D. 0.11, Th. 0.008. Semicoarse fabric; medium to large inclusions, little lime; unevenly fired, 5YR 5/6 (yellowish red) to 5YR 4/3 (reddish brown) [core]. Splayed ring foot; curving wall. Exterior slipped (self?).
Early Helladic II.

558 OPEN VESSEL   Fig. 32
(C11-SE-28) Ring foot. D. 0.11, Th. 0.008. Semicoarse fabric; small to large inclusions, much lime; unevenly fired, 5YR 5/6 (yellowish red) to 5YR 5/2 (reddish gray) [core]. Splayed ring foot, steeply curving wall. Exterior plain; interior black paint (urfirnis). Preserves evidence for method of attaching ring foot to vessel: slashes on bottom of foot attached, clay added to smooth and strengthen join.
Early Helladic II.

559 OPEN VESSEL   Fig. 32
(F32-S-184) Ring foot. D. 0.12, Th. 0.011. Semicoarse fabric; quartz inclusions, no lime; unevenly fired, 5YR 5/6 (yellowish red) to 5YR 4/2 (dark reddish gray) [core]. Ring foot to large open vessel. Plain.
Early Helladic II.

560 CLOSED VESSEL?   Fig. 32
(F32-C9-9) Ring foot. D. 0.12, Th. 0.013. Coarse fabric; large to very large inclusions, some lime; unevenly fired, 7.5YR 5/4 (brown) to 7.5YR 4/2 (brown-dark brown) [core]. Vertical ring foot; steeply curving wall. Exterior plain; interior very rough (surface not preserved?).
Early Helladic II.

561 CLOSED VESSEL?   Fig. 32
(B39-34) Ring foot. D. 0.12, Th. 0.008. Medium fabric; small to medium inclusions, little lime; unevenly fired, 7.5YR 4/6 (strong brown) to 7.5YR 4/2 (brown-dark brown) [core]. Splayed ring foot, curving wall; bottom curves down to level of foot resting surface. Exterior plain; interior rough (not preserved?).
Early Helladic II.

562 OPEN? VESSEL   Fig. 32
(F32-41) Ring foot. D. 0.12, Th. 0.007. Semicoarse fabric; medium to large inclusions, some lime; unevenly fired, 5YR 6/6 (reddish yellow) to 5YR 4/1 (dark gray) [core]. Splayed ring foot; bottom of vessel curves down to level of foot resting surface; wall curves up. Plain.
Early Helladic II.

563 OPEN? VESSEL   Fig. 32
(A6-75-100) Ring foot. D. 0.11, Th. 0.006. Semicoarse fabric; small to large inclusions, some lime; unevenly fired, 7.5YR 7/4 (pink) to 5YR 6/3 (light reddish brown) [core]. Splayed ring foot; gently curving wall. Plain.
Early Helladic II.

564   OPEN? VESSEL   Fig. 33
   (A33-1-65) Ring foot. D. est. 0.12, Th. 0.011. Semicoarse fabric; small to medium inclusions, some lime; evenly fired, 2.5YR 4/8 (red). Splayed ring foot; curving wall. Plain.
   Early Helladic II.

565   OPEN? VESSEL   Fig. 33
   (F32-A7-4) Ring foot. D. 0.12, Th. 0.008. Coarse fabric; many medium to large inclusions, some lime; evenly fired, 2.5YR 4/8 (red). Vertical ring foot, curving wall; junction of wall and foot smoothed over. Surfaces not preserved.
   Early Helladic II.

566   OPEN VESSEL   Fig. 33
   (F32-B6-6) Ring foot. D. 0.12, Th. 0.007. Semicoarse fabric; medium to large inclusions, no lime; unevenly fired, 2.5YR 5/8 (red) to 5YR 3/2 (dark reddish brown) [core]. Splayed ring foot, steeply curving wall. Slipped (self slip).
   Early Helladic II.

567   OPEN? VESSEL   Fig. 33
   (C11-C28-2) Ring foot. D. 0.12. Semicoarse fabric; medium inclusions, some lime; unevenly fired, 5YR 5/6 (yellowish red) to 5YR 5/2 (reddish gray) [core]. Splayed ring foot. Plain.
   Early Helladic II.

568   OPEN? VESSEL   Fig. 33
   (F32-D4-14) Ring foot. D. 0.12, Th. 0.007. Medium fabric; small to medium inclusions, no lime; unevenly fired, 5YR 5/8 (yellowish red) to 7.5YR-N5/0 (gray) [core]. Splayed ring foot, thickening toward resting surface. Surfaces not preserved.
   Early Helladic II.

569   OPEN VESSEL   Fig. 33
   (F32-S-53) Foot. D. 0.12, Th. 0.006. Medium fabric; small to medium inclusions, no lime; unevenly fired, 5YR 6/6 (reddish yellow) to 5YR 5/2 (reddish gray) [core]. Splayed ring foot, steeply curving wall. Exterior plain; interior black paint (urfirnis).
   Early Helladic II.

570   OPEN? VESSEL   Fig. 33
   (F32-N-251) Ring foot. D. 0.13, Th. 0.012. Semicoarse fabric; volcanic (gold and black) and quartz inclusions, no lime; unevenly fired, 5YR 4/4 (reddish brown) to 2.5YR 4/6 (red) [core]. Ring foot to large open? vessel. Plain.
   Early Helladic II.

571   OPEN VESSEL   Fig. 33
   (F32-C9-10) Ring foot. D. 0.13. Coarse fabric; small to large inclusions, no lime; evenly fired, 2.5YR 4/8 (red). Splayed ring foot. Slipped (self-slipped).
   Early Helladic II.

572   LARGE CLOSED? VESSEL   Fig. 33
   (C11-C19-57) Ring foot. D. 0.14, Th. 0.009. Coarse fabric; some very large (0.013) inclusions, much lime; unevenly fired, 2.5YR 4/8 (red) to 5YR 3/2 (dark reddish brown) [core]. Rounded bottom protrudes below added ring foot. Exterior plain; interior very rough.
   Early Helladic II.

573   LARGE CLOSED VESSEL   Fig. 33
   (F32-N-229) Ring foot. D. 0.15, Th. 0.009. Medium fabric; small to medium inclusions, much lime; unevenly fired, 5YR 6/6 (reddish yellow) to 5YR 5/2 (reddish gray) [core]. Splayed ring foot. Exterior slipped orange (5YR 7/6 [reddish yellow]).
   Early Helladic II.

574   CLOSED? VESSEL   Fig. 33
   (A6-4-4) Ring foot. D. 0.16, Th. 0.011. Coarse fabric; volcanic and quartz inclusions, no lime; unevenly fired, 5YR 4/3 (reddish brown) to 2.5YR 4/6 (red) [core]. Added ring flattened to disc base. Plain.
   Early Helladic II?

575   OPEN? VESSEL   Fig. 33
   (F6-64) Ring foot. D. 0.16, Th. 0.007. Coarse fabric; large inclusions, some lime; unevenly fired, 7.5YR 7/4 (pink) to 7.5YR 5/2 (brown) [core]. Vertical ring foot. Surfaces rough.
   Early Helladic II.

576   OPEN? VESSEL   Fig. 33
   (F32-E-34) Ring foot. D. 0.16, Th. 0.007. Semicoarse fabric; medium to large inclusions, much lime; unevenly fired, 5YR 6/8 (reddish yellow) to 5YR 4/2 (dark reddish gray) [core]. Splayed ring foot, thickening towards resting surface. Plain.
   Early Helladic II.

577   OPEN? VESSEL   Fig. 33
   (F32-B8-10) Ring foot. D. 0.18, Th. 0.010. Semicoarse fabric; small to medium inclusions, no lime; unevenly fired, 2.5YR 5/8 (red) to 2.5YR 5/2 (weak red) [core]. Vertical ring foot; curving wall. Plain.
   Early Helladic II.

578   OPEN? VESSEL   Fig. 33
   (F32-N-261) Ring foot. D. 0.19, Th. 0.008. Semicoarse fabric; small to medium inclusions, some lime; unevenly fired, 5YR 6/8 (reddish yellow) to 5YR 5/1 (gray) [core]. High, splayed ring foot; bottom of vessel curves down; wall curves up sharply. Surfaces not preserved.
   Early Helladic II.

579   PEDESTALLED BOWL or SAUCEBOAT   Fig. 33
   (A6/9-B-33) Pedestal. D. 0.04, Th. 0.005. Medium fabric; small to medium inclusions, little lime; unevenly fired, 7.5YR 7/4 (pink) to 10YR 6/3 (pale brown) [core]. Splayed pedestal foot; curving wall. Plain?
   Early Helladic II.

580   PEDESTALLED BOWL or SAUCEBOAT   Fig. 33
   (B24-ALL-7) Pedestal. D. 0.045, Th. 0.007. Semifine fabric; some lime; unevenly fired, 5YR 6/8 (reddish yellow) to 5YR 6/1 (light gray-gray) [core]. Splayed pedestal foot. Exterior traces of yellow-blue slip.
   Early Helladic II.

581   PEDESTALLED BOWL or SAUCEBOAT   Fig. 33
   (F6-60) Pedestal. D. 0.05, Th. 0.009. Semifine fabric; small to few medium inclusions, little lime; unevenly fired, 5YR 6/8 (reddish yellow) to 5YR 5/1 (gray) [core]. Splayed pedestal foot. Surfaces worn.
   Early Helladic II.

582 PEDESTALLED BOWL or SAUCEBOAT   Fig. 33
(B24-9) Pedestal. D. 0.05, Th. 0.004. Medium fabric; small inclusions, little lime; unevenly fired, 5YR 5/6 (yellowish red) to 5YR 4/3 (reddish brown) [core]. Short flaring pedestal foot. Exterior? and interior painted black (urfirnis).
Early Helladic II.

583 PEDESTALLED BOWL or SAUCEBOAT   Fig. 33
(F32-N-237) Pedestal. D. 0.05, Th. 0.006. Medium fabric; some lime; unevenly fired, 7.5YR 6/4 (light brown) to 7.5YR 6/2 (pinkish gray) [core]. Splayed pedestal foot. Exterior slipped red-orange and burnished.
Early Helladic II.

584 PEDESTALLED BOWL or SAUCEBOAT   Fig. 33
(E5-B-12) Pedestal. D. 0.06. Semifine fabric; small inclusions, little lime; unevenly fired, 5YR 7/8 (reddish yellow) to 7.5YR-N6/0 (gray-light gray) [core]. Splayed pedestal foot. Slipped yellow-blue and polished.
Early Helladic II.

585 PEDESTALLED BOWL or SAUCEBOAT   Fig. 33
(F6-71) Pedestal. D. 0.06, Th. 0.006. Medium fabric; little lime; evenly fired, 7.5YR 5/4 (brown). Convex pedestal foot. Exterior painted black (urfirnis).
Early Helladic II.

586 PEDESTALLED BOWL or SAUCEBOAT   Fig. 33
(F32-A11-8) Pedestal. D. 0.065, Th. 0.006. Semifine fabric; small inclusions, little lime; unevenly fired, 7.5YR 7/4 (pink) to 5YR 6/1 (gray-light gray) [core]. Splayed pedestal foot. Surfaces worn.
Early Helladic II.

587 PEDESTALLED BOWL or SAUCEBOAT   Fig. 33
(F32-S-171) Pedestal. D. 0.065, Th. 0.004. Semifine fabric; some lime; unevenly fired, 7.5YR 7/6 (reddish yellow) to 7.5YR-N4/0 (dark gray) [core]. Splayed pedestal foot. Exterior traces of paint; interior worn?
Early Helladic II.

588 PEDESTALLED BOWL or SAUCEBOAT   Fig. 33
(F58-2-2) Pedestal. D. 0.07, Th. 0.007. Semifine to medium fabric; much lime; unevenly fired, 7.5YR 6/4 (light brown) to 7.5YR-N5/0 (gray) [core]. Splayed pedestal foot. Painted red (urfirnis).
Early Helladic II.

589 PEDESTALLED BOWL or SAUCEBOAT   Fig. 33
(F32-E-31) Pedestal. D. 0.075, Th. 0.008. Semicoarse fabric; small to medium inclusions, some lime; evenly fired, 2.5YR 5/6 (red). Splayed pedestal foot. Plain.
Early Helladic II.

590 LARGE PEDESTALLED BOWL   Fig. 33
(F32-N-258) Pedestal. D. 0.08, Th. 0.006. Semicoarse fabric; small to medium inclusions, much lime; unevenly fired, 7.5YR 7/4 (pink) to 5YR 4/1 (dark gray) [core]. Convex pedestal foot. Exterior and interior surfaces not preserved?; bottom painted black (urfirnis).
Early Helladic II.

591 PEDESTALLED BOWL or SAUCEBOAT   Fig. 33
(F32-N-222) Pedestal. D. 0.08, Th. 0.006. Medium fabric; small to medium inclusions, little lime; unevenly fired, 2.5YR 4/8 (red) to 2.5YR-N5/0 (gray) [core]. Splayed pedestal foot. Slipped red?
Early Helladic II.

592 PEDESTALLED BOWL or SAUCEBOAT   Fig. 33
(B24-ALL-5) Pedestal. D. 0.085, Th. 0.006. Medium fabric; small to occasional large inclusions, some lime; unevenly fired, 5YR 6/6 (reddish yellow) to 5YR 6/2 (pinkish gray) [core]. Short, splayed pedestal foot, sharply curving wall. Surfaces worn.
Early Helladic II.

593 LARGE PEDESTALLED BOWL   Fig. 33
(F32-N-252) Pedestal. D. 0.09, Th. 0.007. Semicoarse fabric; large inclusions, little lime; unevenly fired, 5YR 5/8 (yellowish red) to 5YR 4/1 (dark gray) [core]. Splayed pedestal foot. Plain.
Early Helladic II.

594 PEDESTALLED BOWL   Fig. 33
(F32-N-236) Pedestal. D. 0.11. Medium fabric; some lime; evenly fired, 7.5YR 4/2 (brown-dark brown). Pedestal foot. Exterior and bottom slipped red-brown and burnished; interior slipped red-brown (perhaps urfirnis?). cf. Blegen's AI.
Early Helladic II early.

595 LARGE PEDESTALLED BOWL   Fig. 33
(B24-12) Pedestal. D. 0.12, Th. 0.008; worn. Semicoarse fabric; medium to large inclusions, some lime; evenly fired, 5YR 6/6 (reddish yellow). Splayed pedestal foot. Surfaces not preserved.
Early Helladic II.

596 LARGE PEDESTALLED BOWL?   Fig. 33
(C11-SW-37) Pedestal. D. 0.12. Medium fabric; small to medium inclusions, much lime; unevenly fired, 5YR 4/3 (reddish brown) to 7.5YR-N6/0 (gray-light gray) [core]. Splayed pedestal foot. Plain.
Early Helladic II.

597 LARGE PEDESTALLED BOWL   Fig. 33
(B24-15) Pedestal. D. est. 0.16-0.18, Th. 0.009. Medium fabric; small to large inclusions, some lime; evenly fired, 5YR 6/6 (reddish yellow). Splayed pedestal foot. Surfaces not preserved.
Early Helladic II.

598 LARGE PEDESTALLED BOWL   Fig. 33
(F32-SF-1) Pedestal. D. 0.20, Th. 0.008. Coarse fabric; medium to large inclusions, no lime; unevenly fired, 5YR 6/6 (reddish yellow) to 5YR 6/1 (gray-light gray) [core]. Splayed pedestal foot, curving wall. Exterior surface not preserved; interior of bowl: black paint (urfirnis) [poorly preserved].
Early Helladic II.

599 LARGE PEDESTALLED BOWL   Fig. 33
(F32-N-263) Pedestal. D. 0.25, Th. 0.006. Semicoarse fabric; medium to large inclusions, much lime; unevenly fired, 5YR 6/6 (reddish yellow) to 5YR 5/1 (gray) [core]. Splayed pedestal foot. Exterior slipped thin red-brown; interior plain.
Early Helladic II.

600   LARGE PEDESTALLED BOWL   Fig. 34
(F32-N-248) Pedestal. D. indet., Th. 0.009. Semicoarse fabric; small to medium inclusions, some lime; unevenly fired, 5YR 5/6 (yellowish red) to 5YR 5/1 (gray) [core]. Splayed pedestal foot. Exterior plain; interior surface not preserved.
Early Helladic II.

601   PEDESTALLED BOWL or SAUCEBOAT   Fig. 34
(F32-C9-8) Pedestal. D. 0.06, Th. 0.003. Semifine fabric; no lime; unevenly fired, 5YR 5/6 (yellowish red) to 5YR 5/1 (gray) [core]. Splayed pedestal foot. Slipped yellow.
Early Helladic II.

602   PEDESTALLED BOWL or SAUCEBOAT   Fig. 34
(F32-N-230) Pedestal. D. 0.07, Th. 0.005. Semifine fabric; little lime; evenly fired, 7.5YR 6/4 (light brown). Splayed pedestal foot. Slipped (yellow- blue (worn).
Early Helladic II.

603   PEDESTALLED BOWL?   Fig. 34
(F32-S-180) Pedestal. Minimum D. 0.05. Medium fabric; small to medium inclusions, little lime; unevenly fired, 5YR 6/6 (reddish yellow) to 7.5YR 5/4 (brown) [core]. Splayed pedestal, gently curving wall. Exterior painted mottled red-black (urfirnis); interior plain.
Early Helladic II.

604   PEDESTALLED BOWL   Fig. 34
(A6-75-102) Pedestal. Minimum D. 0.06. Semicoarse fabric; medium to large inclusions, much lime; unevenly fired, 2.5YR 4/6 (red) to 5YR 4/3 (reddish brown) [core]. Splayed pedestal. Exterior slipped (self slip); interior painted? (or slipped?).
Early Helladic II.

605   LARGE PEDESTALLED BOWL   Fig. 34
(F32-N-260) Pedestal (foot not preserved). Minimum D. 0.007, Th. 0.015. Semicoarse fabric; small to occasional very large inclusions, no lime; unevenly fired, 2.5YR 4/8 (red) to black core. Splayed pedestal foot. Exterior slipped (urfirnis)?; interior slipped; bottom painted black (urfirnis?).
Early Helladic II?

606   PEDESTALLED BOWL   Fig. 34
(F32-N-247) Pedestal. Minimum D. 0.10, Th. 0.008. Medium fabric; medium inclusions, some lime; unevenly fired, 5YR 6/8 (reddish yellow) to 5YR 6/1 (gray-light gray) [core]. Splayed pedestal, gently curving wall. Painted black (urfirnis).
Early Helladic II.

607   LARGE PEDESTALLED BOWL   Fig. 34
(A6-72-201) Pedestal. Minimum D. est. 0.16, Th. 0.007. Semicoarse fabric; medium to large inclusions, much lime; unevenly fired, 5YR 6/8 (reddish yellow) to 5YR 5/2 (reddish gray) [core]. Splayed pedestal. Exterior plain; interior slipped (self slip).
Early Helladic II.

608   OPEN? VESSEL   Fig. 34
(B43-80-2-14) Base. D. 0.07, Th. 0.006. Medium fabric; little lime; unevenly fired, 5YR 5/6 (yellowish red) to 5YR 5/4 (reddish brown) [core]. Hollow base formed by depressing flat bottom. Surfaces not preserved.
Early Helladic.

609   CLOSED VESSEL   Fig. 34
(F32-D4-18) Base. D. 0.09, Th. 0.008. Medium fabric; no lime; evenly fired, 5YR 6/6 (reddish yellow). Hollow base, gently curving wall. Surfaces not preserved?
Early Helladic II.

610   CLOSED? VESSEL   Fig. 34
(F32-48) Base. D. 0.10, Th. 0.007. Medium fabric; some lime; unevenly fired, 5YR 5/4 (reddish brown) to 5YR 5/1 (gray) [core]. Hollow base, curving wall. Exterior painted?
Early Helladic II.

611   OPEN? VESSEL   Fig. 34
(A6-74-89) Base. D. 0.09, Th. 0.011. Medium fabric; some lime; evenly fired, 5YR 3/2 (dark reddish brown). Flat base, sharply curving walls. Plain.
Early Helladic II (?).

612   LARGE BOWL?   Fig. 34
(F5-235) Base. D. 0.10, Th. 0.008. Medium fabric; some lime; unevenly fired, 5YR 6/8 (reddish yellow) to 5YR 5/2 (reddish gray) [core]. Flat, almost disc-like base, curving wall; two shallow grooves near bottom. Exterior plain; interior painted red (urfirnis).
Early Helladic II.

613   LARGE BOWL   Fig. 34
(A6-74-21) Base. D. 0.12, Th. 0.010. Semicoarse fabric; some lime; unevenly fired, 2.5YR 5/6 (red) to indet. gray [core]. Flat disc base; taenia on wall above base. Interior slipped and burnished.
(Early Helladic I to) Early Helladic II.

614   LARGE BOWL   Figs. 34, 121
(A6-83-4) Base. D. 0.12, Th. 0.010. Medium fabric; little lime; unevenly fired, 2.5YR 5/8 (red) to 2.5YR-N5/0 (gray) [core]. Flat base, impressed by mat, then covered up by thin layer of clay to form flat resting surface; ridge at base with impressions; at least two rows of taenia preserved around bottom of wall; post-firing drill hole in wall. Interior slipped (self).
Early Helladic II.

615   MAT IMPRESSED BASE   Figs. 34, 122
(C11-NE-48) Base. D. 0.12. Coarse fabric; secondary burning. Flat base; mat impression.
Early Helladic II ?

616   MAT IMPRESSED BASE?   Fig. 122
(C11-W-20) Base? Secondary burning.
Early Helladic II ?

617   PLATE   Fig. 34
(B24-112) Rim. D. est. 0.25, Max. pres. W. 0.065, Th. 0.009. Medium fabric; some lime; unevenly fired, 5YR 6/8 (reddish yellow) to 7.5YR 5/2 (brown) [core]. Shallow plate, thickened rim. Interior painted thin black (urfirnis).
Early Helladic II.

618   PAN
(A6/9-A-15) Rim. D. indet., Max. pres. W. 0.065, Th. 0.008. Semicoarse fabric; some lime; unevenly fired, 5YR 5/6 (yellowish red) to 5YR 4/2 (dark reddish gray) [core]. Part of bottom (slightly rounded?), straight wall rising to tab handle. Plain.
Early Helladic II.

619 ASKOS or JUG HANDLE   Fig. 34

(F32-S-194) Handle fragment. Max. pres. L. 0.045. Semifine fabric; no lime; evenly fired, 5YR 3/2 (dark reddish brown). Irregular handle, subrectangular in section, narrowing towards upper end; near top, two diagonal slashes and one added button preserved. Painted black? Secondary burning?

Early Helladic II.

620 ASKOS? HANDLE   Fig. 34

(C11-NE-18) Handle fragment. Max. pres. W. 0.06, Max. pres. L. 0.045. Semicoarse fabric; some lime; evenly fired, 7.5YR 5/4 (brown). Base of wide vertical strap handle; two parallel diagonal grooves between two parallel longitudinal grooves (towards center) and one longitudinal groove near margin. Traces of red paint? (or slip?).

Early Helladic I to Early Helladic II.

621 ASKOS? HANDLE   Fig. 34

(F32-N-188) Body with base of handle. Th. 0.007, Max. pres. L. of handle 0.05, W. of handle base 0.075. Semicoarse fabric; some lime; evenly fired, 7.5YR 4/2 (brown to dark brown). Vertical? wide strap handle; two pairs of diagonal shallow grooves meeting at base. Slipped (self slip).

Early Helladic I to Early Helladic II.

622 ASKOS? HANDLE   Fig. 34

(F32-D8-15) Body with base of handle. Th. 0.005, Max. pres. L. of handle 0.06, W. of handle base 0.068. Medium fabric; little lime; unevenly fired, 7.5YR 6/6 (reddish yellow) to 7.5YR-N6/0 (gray -light gray) [core]. Wide vertical strap handle; three deep longitudinal grooves. Surfaces not preserved.

Early Helladic II.

623 LARGE CLOSED? VESSEL   Fig. 34

(E5-B-15) Body with part of tubular handle. Max. pres. W. 0.09, Th. 0.007. Semicoarse fabric; many medium (some gold) inclusions, much lime; evenly fired, 5YR 5/6 (yellowish red). Wide tubular handle sloping down (indicates closed vessel?). Plain.

(Early Helladic I? to) Early Helladic II.

624 LARGE CLOSED? VESSEL   Fig. 34

(F32-N-209) Body with part of tubular handle. Max. pres. W. 0.095, Th. 0.007. Semicoarse fabric; some lime; unevenly fired, 5YR 6/8 (reddish yellow) to 5YR 5/1 (gray) [core]. Wide tubular handle sloping down (indicates closed vessel?). Plain.

Early Helladic II.

625 HORIZONTAL HANDLE   Fig. 34

(C11-SE-21) Body with base of handle. Th. 0.005. Medium fabric; little lime; evenly fired, 2.5YR 5/8 (red). Horizontal upswung handle, raised margins. Painted red (urfirnis).

Early Helladic II.

626 LUG   Fig. 34

(F1-7) Body with lug. Max. pres. W. 0.02, Th. 0.004. Medium fabric; inclusions indet.; evenly fired, 5YR 6/6 (reddish yellow). Trumpet lug, pierced longitudinally. Yellow slipped and polished?

Early Helladic II?

627 KNOB   Fig. 35

(B24-78) Body with knob. Max. pres. W. 0.06. Semicoarse

fabric; some lime; evenly fired, 10YR 4/2 (dark grayish brown). Slightly narrow necked knob (D. 0.037-0.039, H. 0.016-0.019) set at slight angle on wall; top of knob convex. Surfaces not preserved.

Early Helladic II (?).

628 SPOON   Fig. 35

(B9-X) Handle and part of bowl. Max. pres. L. 0.04. Medium fabric; little lime; unevenly fired, 5YR 6/6 (reddish yellow) to 5YR 5/1 (gray) [core]. Flattened handle, widening towards end; very shallow bowl. Plain?

Early Helladic II.

629 SPOON   Figs. 35, 122

(B24-90) Handle and part of bowl. Max. pres. L. 0.055. Medium fabric; little lime; unevenly fired, 5YR 6/6 (reddish yellow) to 5YR 6/3 (light reddish brown) [core]. Flattened handle, widening towards end; shallow bowl. Painted black (urfirnis).

Early Helladic II.

630 SCOOP   Fig. 35

(F32-S-190) Part of handle and bowl. Max. pres. L. 0.11. Semifine fabric; no lime; unevenly fired, 5YR 5/2 (reddish gray) to 5YR 6/4 (light reddish brown) [core]. Wide thin (0.042 x 0.011), slightly concave handle, shallow bowl. Painted black (urfirnis).

Early Helladic II.

631 LADLE   Fig. 35

(F32-S-199) Handle, two joining fragments. Max. pres. L. 0.18. Semicoarse fabric; much lime; unevenly fired, 5YR 7/6 (reddish yellow) to 7.5YR 5/2 (brown) [core]. Handle subrectangular in section near junction with bowl narrowing to round in section, terminating in large loop which joins underside of handle. Plain?

Early Helladic II.

632 SEAL? or PLUG   Figs. 35, 122

(F16-29) Complete cone. H. 0.033. D. at base 0.025; worn. Semicoarse fabric; color not determined. Concave cone, rounded bottom (due to wear?); three vertical grooves, unevenly spaced.

Early Helladic II.

633 SADDLE-TYPE STAND   Figs. 35, 122

(F32-E-35) Leg. Max. pres. H. 0.13, Max. pres. W. 0.12. Coarse fabric; much lime; secondary burning. Right leg arching up and back, outer edge nicked; bottom of mid section curled back under for internal support; upper mid section arches back to form saddle between legs; vertical taenia along midsection.

Early Helladic II.

634 SADDLE-TYPE STAND   Figs. 35, 122

(F32-N-268) Leg. Max. pres. H. 0.12, Max. pres. W. 0.085. Coarse fabric. Left leg arching up and back, outer edge nicked; internal support curving out from back side of leg; mat impression on bottom of leg.

Early Helladic II.

635 SADDLE-TYPE STAND   Figs. 35, 122

(F32-N-267) Mid section and leg fragment. Max. pres. W. 0.11. Coarse fabric. Part of leg arching back with mid section preserving lower part curled back under for internal support and upper part arching back into saddle; stubs from small vertical

tubular handle in place of usual vertical taenia.
Early Helladic II.

636   SADDLE-TYPE STAND   Fig. 123
(F32-B12-5) Leg. Max. pres. H. 0.10. Coarse fabric. Oval section leg, spreading at top to triangular (to form mid section and arch).
Early Helladic II.

637   SADDLE-TYPE STAND   Fig. 123
(F32-N-266) Mid section and leg fragment. Coarse fabric. Part of mid section with vertical tubular handle.
Early Helladic II.

638   KNOB TO STAND   Fig. 35
(C11-NE-58) Knob. Max. pres. H. 0.065, Max. D. 0.088. Coarse fabric; some silver inclusions; color not determined. Rounded knob on constricted hollow stem roughly triangular in section. Plain.
Early Helladic II.

639   KNOB TO STAND   Fig. 35
(F32-S-204) Knob. Max. D. 0.071, Min. D. 0.058 x 0.047, Max. pres. H. 0.08. Coarse fabric; color not determined. Rounded knob on constricted oval section stem, attached to thick wall (interior of which is curved). Plain.
Early Helladic II.

640   KNOB TO STAND   Figs. 35, 123
(B24-2) Knob. Max. pres. H. 0.07, Max. pres. D. 0.058. Coarse fabric. Solid circular stem, slightly constricted, attached at oblique angle. Slipped red (urfirnis?).
Early Helladic II.

641   STAND   Fig. 35
(C15-A-38) Leg. Max. pres. H. 0.06. Coarse fabric. Leg fragment, pear shape (almost triangular) in section; leg bending to side slightly.
Early Helladic II.

642   STAND   Fig. 35
(B9-B11-11) Leg. Max. pres. H. 0.085. Coarse fabric. Leg, oval in section; leg bending to side as it rises; ridges running down leg.
Early Helladic II.

643   STAND   Fig. 35
(F32-B2-1) Leg. Max. pres. H. 0.06. Coarse fabric. Leg, oval in section, curves to one side.
Early Helladic II.

644   STAND   Fig. 35
(B2-B28-91) Leg. Max. pres. H. 0.03. Coarse fabric. Small leg, oval in section, curves to one side.
Early Helladic II.

645   STAND   Fig. 123
(A6-74-105) Corner. Max. pres. H. 0.07, Max. pres. W. 0.06. Coarse fabric. Corner of stand, flattened resting surface (but open at bottom); part of rectangular cutout on both sides.
Early Helladic II.

646   STAND   Fig. 123
(A6-74-106) Corner. Max. pres. L. 0.10, Max. pres. W. 0.06. Coarse fabric. Corner of stand formed by folding flat slab of clay to 90° and pinching exterior of fold to ridge; rounded finished edge (not flattened for resting).
Early Helladic II.

647   TABLE   Figs. 36, 123
(A33-3-5) Top and leg fragment. Max. pres. H. 0.09. Coarse fabric. Subtriangular section leg rises up to corner of table; slightly raised edge to upper surface; slashes around edge of upper surface and at top of sides. Originally slipped.
Early Helladic II.

648   TABLE?   Fig. 36
(B39-33) Leg. Max. pres. H. 0.12. Coarse fabric. Leg, subtriangular in section, rises to very triangular in section (for corner of table?).
Early Helladic II.

649   ROUND HEARTH RIM   Fig. 36
(F32-N-273) Rim. Max. pres. W. 0.09. Coarse fabric; unevenly fired, 5YR 5/2 (reddish gray) to 5YR 5/4 (reddish brown) [core]. Flaring rim, rounded lip bevelled to exterior; on lip, traces of stamped herringbone.
Early Helladic II.

650   ROUND HEARTH RIM   Figs. 36, 123
(F32-N-271) Rim. Max. pres. W. 0.07. Coarse fabric; evenly fired, 5YR 4/2 (dark reddish gray). Flaring rim, flat lip; on lip, stamped curvilinear design (spirals or concentric circles?).
Early Helladic II.

651   ROUND HEARTH RIM   Figs. 36, 123
(F32-S-207) Rim. Max. pres. W. 0.06. Semicoarse fabric; unevenly fired, 5YR 6/8 (reddish yellow) to 5YR 4/2 (dark reddish gray) [core]. Thickened, flat lip; on lip, stamped design of interlocking connected diamonds.
Early Helladic II.

652   ROUND HEARTH RIM   Fig. 36
(F32-N-275) Rim. Max. pres. W. 0.06. Coarse fabric; evenly fired, 5YR 4/2 (dark reddish gray). Flat lip; on lip, stamped herringbone.
Early Helladic II.

653   ROUND HEARTH RIM   Figs. 36, 123
(F32-S-206) Rim. Max. pres. W. 0.07. Coarse fabric; unevenly fired, 7.5YR 5/4 (brown) to 7.5YR 5/2 (brown) [core]. Wide flat lip; on lip, stamped herringbone.
Early Helladic II.

654   ROUND HEARTH RIM   Fig. 36
(F32-D8-17) Rim. Max. pres. W. 0.065, H. 0.07. Coarse fabric; unevenly fired, 7.5YR 7/6 (reddish yellow) to 7.5YR 5/2 (brown) [core]. Vertical straight rim, flat lip; on lip, row of large impressed triangles.
Early Helladic II.

655   ROUND HEARTH RIM   Figs. 36, 123
(F32-N-274) Rim. Max. pres. W. 0.07, Th. 0.035. Coarse fabric; unevenly fired, 7.5YR 6/6 (reddish yellow) to 7.5YR 5/4 (brown) [core]. Round hearth; on lip, incised herringbone (worn). Interior of basin painted red and burnished.
Early Helladic II.

656 ROUND HEARTH RIM   Fig. 36
(F32-N-272) Rim. Max. pres. W. 0.12; worn. Coarse fabric; unevenly fired, 5YR 5/8 (yellowish red) to 2.5YR-N4/0 (dark gray) [core]. Slightly splayed rim, thickening to rounded lip; on lip, traces of large impressed triangles.
Early Helladic II.

657 ROUND HEARTH RIM   Figs. 36, 123
(F32-68) Rim. Max. pres. W. 0.11. Coarse fabric; unevenly fired, 5YR 5/6 (yellowish red) to 5YR 6/1 (gray-light gray) [core]. Wide flat lip; on lip, incised hatched triangles.
Early Helladic II.

658 ROUND HEARTH RIM   Fig. 36
(F32-N-276) Rim. Max. pres. W. 0.075. Coarse fabric; unevenly fired, 5YR 6/8 (reddish yellow) to 5YR 5/3 (reddish brown) [core]. On lip, incised hatched triangles.
Early Helladic II.

659 ROUND HEARTH RIM   Figs. 36, 123
(F32-69) Rim. Max. pres. W. 0.185. Coarse fabric; unevenly fired, 2.5YR 5/8 (red) to 7.5YR 5/4 (brown) [core]. Wide flat lip; on lip, incised hatched triangles.
Early Helladic II.

660 ROUND HEARTH RIM   Fig. 36
(F32-X) Rim. Max. pres. W. 0.125. Coarse fabric; unevenly fired, 2.5YR 6/8 (light red) to 10YR 5/2 (grayish brown) [core]. Wide, flat lip; on lip, incised hatched triangles.
Early Helladic II.

661 ROUND HEARTH RIM   Fig. 36
(F32-S-209) Rim. Max. pres. W. 0.07. Coarse fabric; evenly fired, 5YR 3/2 (dark reddish brown). Flat lip; on lip, incised hatched triangles.
Early Helladic II.

662 ROUND HEARTH RIM   Figs. 37, 124
(F32-B10-4) Rim, two joining. Max. pres. W. 0.23. Coarse fabric; unevenly fired, 2.5YR 6/8 (light red) to 7.5YR 5/2 (brown) [core]. Two stepped rim; on lower lip, row of alternating impressed triangles; upper lip worn.
Early Helladic II.

663 KEYHOLE HEARTH RIM   Fig. 37
(B39-66) Corner. 0.06 x 0.06, Max pres. H. 0.065. Semicoarse fabric; evenly fired, 7.5YR 5/4 (brown). Corner to keyhole shaped hearth, preserving outer and inner corners; on lip, incised hatching (hatched triangles?).
Early Helladic II.

664 SHIELD SHAPED HEARTH RIM   Figs. 37, 124
(F32-S-208) Rim. Max pres. W. 0.011. Coarse fabric; unevenly fired, 7.5YR 5/6 (strong brown) to 7.5YR 4/2 (dark brown-brown) [core]. Figure "eight" shaped hearth fragment preserving reverse curve of constricted area; rim curves up into thickened, flattened lip; on lip, stamped? hatched triangles. Traces of slip on interior.
Early Helladic II.

665 HEARTH?   Fig. 37
(F20-26) Profile. Max. pres. W. 0.055, H. 0.10. Coarse fabric; unevenly fired, 5YR 5/1 (gray) to 5YR 5/6 (yellowish red).

Flat base, rim curves in slightly, lip bevelled. Traces of slip on interior bottom?
Early Helladic II.

666 ROOFTILE   Figs. 37, 124
(A6-72-219) Rim. Max. pres. L. 0.14, Max. pres. W. 0.085, Th. 0.012-0.018. Semicoarse fabric; quartz inclusions, some lime; unevenly fired, 7.5YR 6/6 (reddish yellow) to 2.5YR 6/6 (light red) [core].
Early Helladic II.

667 ROOFTILE   Fig. 37
(A6-5-8) Rim. Max. pres. L. 0.070, Max. pres. W. 0.060, Th. 0.011-0.013. Coarse fabric; little lime?; color indeterminate (ca. 10YR).
Early Helladic II.

668 ROOFTILE   Fig. 37
(A6-5-7) Rim. Max. pres. L. 0.070, Max. pres. W. 0.070, Th. 0.009-0.011. Coarse fabric; quartz inclusions, little lime; unevenly fired, 7.5YR 7/4 (pink) to 5YR 6/6 (reddish yellow) [core].
Early Helladic II.

669 ROOFTILE   Fig. 37
(B24-124) Rim. Max. pres. L. 0.12, Max. pres. W. 0.11, Th. 0.010-0.015. Semicoarse fabric; some lime; unevenly fired, 2.5YR 6/8 (light red) to 7.5YR 7/4 (pink) [core].
Early Helladic II.

670 ROOFTILE   Fig. 37
(A6-5-9) Rim. Max. pres. L. 0.105, Max. pres. W. 0.13, Th. 0.013-0.017. Coarse fabric; little lime; evenly fired, 5YR 7/4 (pink).
Early Helladic II.

671 ROOFTILE   Fig. 37
(A6-8-17) Rim. Max. pres. L. 0.12, Max. pres. W. 0.095, Th. 0.012-0.016. Semicoarse fabric; quartz inclusions, little lime; evenly fired, 7.5YR 6/4 (light brown).
Early Helladic II.

672 ROOFTILE   Fig. 37
(A6-8-16) Corner. Max. pres. L. 0.115, Max. pres. W. 0.10, Th. 0.010-0.017. Coarse fabric; some lime; evenly fired, 7.5YR 7/4 (pink).
Early Helladic II.

673 ROOFTILE   Fig. 37
(A6-72-217) Corner. Max. pres. L. 0.080, Max. pres. W. 0.075, Th. 0.013-0.015. Semicoarse fabric; some lime; evenly fired, 5YR 6/4 (light reddish brown).
Early Helladic II.

674 ROOFTILE   Fig. 37
(A6-8-15) Rim. Max. pres. L. 0.155, Max. pres. W. 0.145, Th. 0.013-0.018. Coarse fabric; some lime; evenly fired, 10YR 6/2 (light brownish gray).
Early Helladic II.

675 ROOFTILE   Fig. 37
(A33-81-1-X) Rim. Max. pres. L. 0.060, Max. pres. W. 0.065, Th. 0.013-0.016. Semicoarse fabric; little lime; evenly fired, 10YR 8/3 (very pale brown).
Early Helladic II.

676 ROOFTILE   Fig. 37
(F20-3) Corner. Max. pres. L. 0.040, Max. pres. W. 0.050, Th. 0.008-0.010. Medium fabric; some lime; evenly fired, 2.5YR 5/6 (red).
Early Helladic II.

677 ROOFTILE   Fig. 37
(A6-72-220) Rim. Max. pres. L. 0.055, Max. pres. W. 0.050, Th. 0.010-0.011. Coarse fabric; some lime; 10YR 6/2 (light brownish gray).
Early Helladic II.

EARLY HELLADIC III

678 NARROW-NECKED JAR   Fig. 38
(A6-65-32) Body with handle. H. 0.05, Th. 0.009. Handmade. Semifine, softish clay; small to medium round grey, angular white inclusions, occasional mica; biscuit 7.5YR 7/4 (pink), core 5YR 6/4 (light reddish brown). Curved body, horizontal trianguloid handle. Exterior painted 7.5YR N3/ (very dark grey), interior smooth, unpainted. Probably Rutter's type XVII.1.
Early Helladic III.

679 NARROW-NECKED JAR   Figs. 38, 125
(E13-81-1-56) Body with handle. H. 0.072, Th. 0.008. Handmade. Semifine hard clay; small white, large round grey inclusions, little mica; biscuit 5YR 6-5/4 (light reddish brown to reddish brown), core 10YR 5/1 (grey). Carinated body, horizontal trianguloid handle. Exterior painted 7.5YR 6/4 - 5YR 4/3 (light brown to reddish brown). Upper surface of handle smoothed, lower surface rough, interior uneven, unpainted. Probably Rutter's type XVII.1.
Early Helladic III.

680 NARROW-NECKED JAR   Fig. 38
(E13-81-1-55) Body with handle. H. 0.09, Th. 0.006-0.008. Handmade; worn. Semifine hard clay; small to medium white, brown, grey inclusions, occasional mica; biscuit 5YR 6/4-6 (light reddish brown to reddish yellow), core 7.5YR N5/ (grey). Rounded body, horizontal trianguloid handle. Exterior painted, 5YR 5/6 (yellowish red), interior smooth, unpainted. Probably Rutter's type XVII.1.
Early Helladic III.

681 NARROW-NECKED JAR (?)   Figs. 38, 125
(E13-36) Body with handle. D. est. 0.40, H. 0.044, Th. 0.007-0.012. Handmade. Semifine hard well fired clay; small to medium grey, black, white inclusions, little mica; biscuit 5YR 6/6 (reddish yellow), core 7.5YR 5/2 (brown). Slightly curved body, horizontal trianguloid handle. Exterior painted 7.5YR 3/4-5/6 (dark brown to strong brown), interior uneven, unpainted. Probably Rutter's type XVII.1.
Early Helladic III.

682 BOWL WITH HORIZONTAL HANDLES   Fig. 38
(A6-74-67) Rim. D. est. 0.35, H. 0.06, Th. 0.010-0.012. Handmade. Semifine fairly soft clay; small to medium white, black, grey inclusions, little mica; biscuit 5YR 6/4 (light reddish brown), core 10YR 5/1 (grey). Flaring neck, thickened rim. Exterior painted, 5YR 3/2-5/6 (dark reddish brown to yellowish red), interior uneven, unpainted. Rutter's type XII.4.
Early Helladic III.

683 CLOSED VESSEL   Fig. 125
(A6-83-2) Body. Max. pres. W. 0.06, Max pres H. 0.025. Handmade. Semicoarse hard clay; small red, medium to large grey, black inclusions; biscuit 7.5YR 6/4 (light brown), core 10YR 6/2 (brownish grey). Exterior painted, dull 10YR 4-3/1 (dark to very dark grey), horizontally applied bands with impressed rope pattern, interior unpainted.
Early Helladic III.

684 CLOSED VESSEL
(A6-72-159) Body. Max. pres. W. 0.053, Max. pres. H. 0.05. Handmade. Semicoarse hard clay; small red, medium to large grey, black inclusions; biscuit 7.5YR 6/4 (light brown), core 10YR 6/2 (brownish grey). Exterior painted, dull 7.5YR 6/2-4 (pinkish grey to light brown), horizontally applied bands with impressed rope pattern, interior smoothed, unpainted.
Early Helladic III.

685 NARROW-NECKED JAR   Fig. 38
(E13-81-1-38) Body. Max. pres. W. 0.04 , Max. pres. H. 0.05, Th. 0.001. Handmade. Semicoarse clay; white, grey, black inclusions; biscuit 7.5YR 5/4 (dark brown), core 10YR 4/1 (dark grey). Horizontal trianguloid handle. Exterior painted, dull 5YR 4/1-3 to 5YR 5/6 (grey or reddish brown to yellowish red). Probably Rutter's type XVII.1.
Early Helladic III.

686 PITHOS (?)
(E13-81-1-52) Body. Max. pres. H. 0.121, Th. 0.018-.021. Handmade. Coarse hard clay; small to large white, small to medium grey, black inclusions, straw temper; exterior biscuit 2.5YR 5/8 (red), interior 7.5YR 5/4 (brown), core 10YR 6/1-2 (light grey to light brownish grey). Exterior painted 2.5YR 4/6-8 (red), interior unpainted.
Early Helladic III?

687 BOWL WITH HORIZONTAL HANDLES (?)   Fig. 38
(A6-72-66) Neck and shoulder. Max. pres. H. 0.067, Th. 0.010-0.014. Handmade; very worn. Semicoarse well fired clay; small grey, white inclusions; 7.5YR 2-5/4 (light to very dark brown). Rounded shoulder, flaring neck. Exterior and interior neck painted 7.5YR 3/2-4 (dark brown). Probably Rutter's type XIII.3.
Early Helladic III.

688 BOWL WITH HORIZONTAL HANDLES (?)   Fig. 38
(A6-7-3) Rim. D. 0.29, Max. pres. H. 0.075, Th. 0.006-0.010. Handmade; very worn. Semifine clay; small grey, red, white inclusions; biscuit 5YR 6/4 (light reddish brown), core 10YR N1/ (grey). Flaring rim. Exterior and interior rim painted 2.5YR 5/8 - 5YR 5/2 (dark reddish brown to black). Probably Rutter's type XIII.3.
Early Helladic III.

689 NARROW-NECKED JAR (?)   Fig. 38
(E9-88) Body with handle. Max. pres. H. 0.09, Th. 0.06-0.09. Handmade. Semifine hard clay; small to medium white, small black inclusions, very little mica; 7.5YR 4/2 (pinkish grey) in core and biscuit, 2.5YR 6/6 (light red) in between. Rounded body, horizontal trianguloid handle just below rim. Painted exterior 7.5YR 3/2-4/4 (dark brown to brown), interior 2.5YR 4/6 (red). Probably Rutter's type XVII.1.
Early Helladic III.

690 BOWL WITH HORIZONTAL HANDLES (?)   Fig. 38
(F32-N-82) Rim. D. est. 0.20, Max. pres. H. 0.055, Th. 0.008-0.010. Handmade, very worn. Semifine, softish clay; small to medium white, grey, medium black inclusions, little mica, possibly gold mica; 10YR 6/2 (light brownish grey). Offset rim. Painted exterior and interior rim. Either Rutter's type XII.2 or type XIII.3.
Early Helladic III.

691 OPEN VESSEL   Fig. 38
(E13-2-2/E13-2-3) Body, two joining and one non-joining. Max. pres. H. 0.109, Th. 0.007-0.011. Handmade. Semicoarse clay; small to large white, small to medium red, grey inclusions, little mica; biscuit 5YR 5/6 (yellowish red), core 7.5YR 6/2 (pinkish grey). Exterior and interior painted, dull 7.5YR 3/2-5/6 (dark brownish to strong brown).
Early Helladic III.

692 BOWL WITH HORIZONTAL HANDLES (?)   Fig. 38
(A6-72-168) Rim. D. est. 0.30, Max. pres. H. 0.058, Th. 0.007-0.012. Handmade. Semicoarse clay; small to medium white, grey, large black inclusions, very little mica; biscuit 10YR 4/3 (brown), core 10YR 3/1 (grey). Everted rim. Exterior and interior painted 2.5YR 5/4-3/4 (brown to dark brown). Probably Rutter's type XIII.3.
Early Helladic III.

693 BOWL WITH HORIZONTAL HANDLES (?)   Fig. 38
(F-6-31) Rim, two sherds from same or similar vase. D. est. 0.30, Max. pres. H. 0.032, Th. 0.007. Handmade. Semifine clay; small red, white, black inclusions, little mica; biscuit 7.5YR 7/4 - 5YR 7/4 (reddish), core 10YR 6/1 (grey). Offset rim, straight shoulder. Exterior and interior painted 2.5YR 5/4 - 5/2 (brown to dark brown). Possibly Rutter's type XIII.3.
Early Helladic III.

694 BOWL WITH HORIZONTAL HANDLES   Fig. 38
(A6-9-2) Rim. D. indet., Max. pres. H. 0.073, Th. 0.009-0.012. Handmade. Semicoarse clay; red, brown, black, small white, grey inclusions, some mica; biscuit 7.5YR 6/4 (red), surface 2.5YR 6/4 (red), core 7.5YR N6/ (grey). Thickened, almost doubly offset rim. Painted exterior and interior 2.5YR 5-4/6-8 (red). Rutter's type XIII.4.
Late Early Helladic III.

695 NARROW-NECKED JAR   Fig. 38
(E13-81-1-54) Body with handle. Max. pres. H. 0.045, Th. 0.007. Handmade. Very hard, gritty semicoarse clay; small to medium grey, red, white inclusions, very little mica; biscuit 5YR 5/6 (yellowish red), core 5YR 6-5/3 (light reddish brown). Angular body, horizontal trianguloid handle. Exterior painted 5YR 5/3-6/6 (red) on the upper burnished handle surface, lower surface uneven and unpainted. Interior smooth, unpainted. Probably Rutter's type XVII.1.
Early Helladic III.

696 NARROW-NECKED JAR   Fig. 38
(E13-2-4) Body with handle. Max. pres. W. 0.11, Th. 0.009. Handmade. Semicoarse hard clay; small to medium, large grey, red, white inclusions, some mica; 7.5YR 7/4-6 (pink to reddish yellow). Slightly curved body, horizontal trianguloid handle. Exterior painted, 5YR 5/4 (reddish brown), slightly burnished, interior smooth, unpainted. Probably Rutter's type XVII.1.
Early Helladic III.

697 NARROW-NECKED JAR   Figs. 38, 125
(E13-2-27) Body with handle. Max. pres. W. 0.105, Th. 0.005-0.007. Handmade. Semifine hard clay; small to medium grey, white, large brown inclusions, very little mica, including gold mica; biscuit 5YR 6/6 (reddish yellow), core 2.5Y N5/ (grey). Slightly curved body, horizontal trianguloid handle. Exterior painted, 2.5YR 5-4/6 (red), slightly burnished, interior uneven, unpainted. Probably Rutter's type XVII.1.
Early Helladic III.

698 NARROW-NECKED JAR?   Figs. 38, 125
(E13-81-1-60) Body with handle. Max. pres. H. 0.056, Th. 0.009-0.010. Handmade. Semifine hard clay; small white, occasional black inclusions, very little mica; biscuit 5YR 6/4 (light reddish brown), core 10YR 5/1 (grey). Horizontal trianguloid handle. On exterior dull thick burnished paint, upper part of handle 2.5YR 4/4 (reddish brown), lower part 2.5YR N2.5/ (black), interior unevenly smoothed. Rutter's type XVII(?).
Early Helladic III.

699 BOWL WITH HORIZONTAL LUGS   Figs. 38, 125
(E13-2-24) Rim with fragment of handle or lug. D. 0.24, Max. pres. H. 0.048, Th. 0.013. Handmade. Semicoarse well fired clay; medium to large, grey, brown, white inclusions, very little mica, including gold mica; 5YR 6-4/6 (light reddish brown to reddish yellow). Spreading rim, horizontal trianguloid handle or crescentic lug. Exterior painted 5YR 4/6 (yellowish red), burnished, interior smooth, unpainted. Rutter's type XIII.2.
Early Helladic III.

700 SHOULDER HANDLED BOWL (BASS BOWL)
     Figs. 38, 125
(E13-2-46) Body with handle. H. without handle 0.094, Th. 0.006, W. of handle 0.033. Handmade. Semicoarse hard clay; small to medium grey, small to large white inclusions, very little mica; biscuit 7.5YR 6/4 (light brown), core 10YR 4/1 (dark grey). Slightly curved body, vertical strap-handle from belly to shoulder. Exterior painted 5YR 5/4 (reddish brown), interior smooth, slightly burnished exterior and interior. Rutter's type XII.2.
Early Helladic III.

701 TANKARD   Figs. 38, 125
(E13-81-1-40) Belly with handle. Max. pres. H. 0.03, Th. 0.006. Handmade. Fine hard clay; small white inclusions, little mica; biscuit 5YR 5/6 (yellowish red), core 7.5YR 6/2 (pinkish grey). Rounded body, strap-handle attachment. Exterior, lower part painted 2.5YR 4/8-5YR 3/1 (red to very dark grey), burnished; interior smooth, unburnished. Rutter's forms I-III.
Early Helladic III.

702 PEDESTAL-FOOTED CUP or BOWL   Figs. 38, 125
(E13-2-20) Pedestal and lower body. D. of pedestal 0.045, Max. pres. H. 0.05, Th. 0.008. Handmade? Semifine hard clay; small to medium grey, black, white inclusions, gold and transparent mica; 5YR 5/4 (reddish brown), core 2.5YR 5/6 (red). Conical lower body, beginning of pedestal. Exterior painted 7.5YR 5/4-2 (brown), burnished, interior smooth and unpainted. Possibly Rutter's form VII or, more likely when solidly painted, from a pedestal-footed Bass bowl, type XII.3.
Early Helladic III.

703 CUP OR KANTHAROS   Figs. 38, 125
(A6-72-120) Rim and shoulder. D. est. 0.10, Max. pres. H. 0.053, Th. 0.005. Wheelmade? Fine clay; small grey inclusions, little mica; 2.5Y 5/6-8 (red). Rounded shoulder, short everted rim. Exterior painted 2.5YR 4/6 - 5YR 3/1 (red to very dark grey), burnished. Interior smooth, unburnished. Either Rutter's cup, type IV.1 or kantharos, form XI, depending on whether it had one or two handles.
Early Helladic III.

704 BOWL WITH HORIZONTAL HANDLES   Fig. 39
(E13-2-98) Rim. D. 0.29, Max. pres. H. 0.04, Th. 0.009-0.014. Handmade. Semicoarse hard clay; small to medium grey, white inclusions, some mica; biscuit 5YR 6/8 (yellowish red), core 10YR 4/1 (grey). Offset, thickened rim. Exterior and interior painted 7.5YR 5/2-4 (brown), filled semicircles on rim. Rutter's type XIII.4.
Late Early Helladic III.

705 BOWL WITH HORIZONTAL HANDLES   Fig. 39
(A6-72-21) Rim. D. 0.28, Max. pres. H. 0.056, Th. 0.007-0.013. Handmade. Semifine clay; small white inclusions, gold mica; biscuit 5YR 6/6 (red), core 7.5YR N4/ (grey). Thickened, almost doubly offset rim. Exterior and interior painted 10YR 5-4/6 (red), filled semicircles on rim. Rutter's type XIII.4.
Late Early Helladic III.

706 BOWL   Figs. 39, 125
(E9-267) Rim and shoulder. D. est. 0.40, Max. pres. H. 0.075, Th. 0.006-0.010. Handmade. Semifine, well fired clay; grey, brown inclusions, little mica; 5YR 5/4-6/6 (reddish brown to reddish yellow). Everted rim, straight shoulder. Exterior painted, dull 5YR 4/2-3 (dark reddish grey to reddish brown), filled semicircles on rim, interior burnished. Rutter's type XIII.3.
Early Helladic III.

707 CUP OR BOWL   Figs. 39, 125
(F5-74) Rim. D. est. 0.14 (very uneven), Max. pres. H. 0.024, Th. 0.008-0.009. Handmade. Semifine, rather hard clay; small to medium white, small grey inclusions, very little mica; 7.5YR 6/2 (pinkish grey). Offset rim. Exterior painted 5YR 3/1 - 4/4 (very dark grey to reddish brown); filled pendant semicircles on rim, interior burnished. Either Rutter's type IV.1 or type XII.2.
Early Helladic III.

708 OPEN VESSEL   Fig. 39
(A6-65-13) Rim. D. indet., Max. pres. H. 0.032, Th. 0.008-0.009. Handmade? Fine soft clay; small white, black inclusions, very little mica; 2.5YR N7-7/3 (light or pinkish grey to light brown). Everted rim. Surface slipped, 7.5YR 3/2-4/6 (dark brown to strong brown), exterior burnished, interior smooth.
Early Helladic III.

709 SHOULDER-HANDLED BOWL (BASS BOWL)
                                                       Figs. 39, 125
(G9-1-6) Body with strap-handle. Max. pres. H. 0.059, Th. 0.007, W. of handle 0.031. Handmade. Hard semifine clay; small angular grey, white inclusions; 4.5YR 4/6 (yellowish red), surface 5YR 3-4/6 (dark reddish brown to yellowish red). Slightly curved body, broad strap-handle. Burnished exterior and interior. Rutter's type XII.1.
Early Early Helladic III.

710 SMALL JAR   Fig. 39
(F5-B-15) Rim, shoulder and belly. Max. pres. H. 0.053, Th. 0.006-0.008. Handmade. Semicoarse clay; small to large grey, white inclusions; outer biscuit 5YR 6/4 (light reddish brown), inner biscuit 10YR 5/2 (grayish brown), core 5YR 6/6 (red). Angular body, short offset rim. Pared exterior, especially in a band around the belly, interior smoothed.
Early Helladic III.

711 DEEP ROUNDED BOWL   Figs. 39, 125
(E9-79-57/E9-79-79) Rim and body with handle attachment, ca. 1/5 of the vessel preserved. D. 0.26, Max. pres. H. 0.12, Th. 0.003-0.005. Handmade. Semicoarse clay; fairly large grey, brown, white inclusions; 5YR 6/6-10YR 5/2 (reddish brown to grayish brown), surface 5YR 5/6 (yellowish red), wet smoothed. Deep rounded bowl, one strap handle from rim to belly, incurving thickened rim. Exterior highly, but unevenly burnished, interior surface gritty, unevenly burnished. Cf. Goldman 1931, fig. 162 (with handle from exterior rim to belly).
Early Helladic III.

MIDDLE HELLADIC

712 SMALL JAR   Figs. 39, 126
(F26-1) Intact. D. 0.54, Max. D. 0.073, H. 0.056, W. of handle 0.015. Handmade. Fine clay; small white and black inclusions, little mica; surface 2.5Y N4/ (dark grey). Burnished exterior and interior rim. Rounded baggy jar, everted rim, strap-handle from both sides of rim to belly. A small depression, made with a finger, on the handle attachment to body. A baggy version of Buck A12. Cf. Eleusis (Mylonas 1975, Pl. 143:766, Pl. 184:880). Zerner's phase 6.
Late Middle Helladic III.

713 BOWL   Fig. 39
(E13-81-1-24) Shoulder. Max. pres. H. 0.053, Th. 0.007-0.010. Handmade. Semifine clay 10YR 5/1 (grey); small to medium white, small black, occasional grey inclusions, very little mica. Straight shoulder, beginning of everted rim. Burnished exterior and interior; parallel horizontal grooves. Zerner's phase 4-5.
Middle Helladic II-III.

714 CUP WITH HIGH HANDLES (?)   Fig. 39
(E13-81-1-39) Rim and shoulder. D. indet., Max. pres. H. 0.042, Th. 0.007. Handmade. Fine clay 7.5YR N6/ (grey); small black inclusions, very little mica. Slightly everted rim. Burnished exterior and interior; three horizontal incised lines. Zerner's phase 5-6.
Middle Helladic III.

715 CUP WITH HIGH HANDLES   Figs. 39, 126
(A6-74-98) Rim with strap handle. D. 0.19, Max. pres. H. without handle 0.035, Th. 0.003-0.005. Wheelmade (?); worn. Fine clay; small black and white inclusions; 2.5Y N5/ (grey). Carinated profile, offset rim, handle from both sides of rim. Burnished exterior and interior. Cf. Deshayes (1966, pl. XIII:5). Zerner's phase 4-5.
Middle Helladic II-III.

716 CUP   Fig. 39
(E9-227) Rim. D. 0.14, Max. pres. H. 0.015, Th. 0.002. Wheelmade. Fine clay; very little mica; 7.5YR 6/1 (pinkish grey). Offset rim. Highly burnished exterior and interior. Zerner's phase 5-6.
Middle Helladic III.

717 BOWL   Fig. 39
(E13-81-1-47) Shoulder with beginning of neck. Max. pres. H. 0.031, Th. 0.0075. Wheelmade(?). Fine clay; 10YR 4/1 (dark grey). Everted rim. Exterior and interior burnished. Zerner's phase 4-5(?).
Middle Helladic II - Middle Helladic III.

718 CUP WITH HIGH HANDLES (?)   Fig. 126
(A6-72-139) Body with handle. Max. pres. H. 0.031, Th. 0.0045-0.0075. Handmade(?); worn. Fine clay 2.5YR N6/ (grey); small white and black inclusions, occasional mica. Fairly straight body, attachment for a vertical strap handle over two horizontal incisions. Burnished. Zerner's phase 5 (?).
Middle Helladic III.

719 BOWL   Fig. 39
(F5-B-1) Shoulder. Max. pres. H. 0.034, Th. 0.007-0.008. Handmade. Fine clay 10YR 6/1 (grey). Slightly rounded shoulder, everted rim. Burnished exterior and interior. Zerner's phase 4-5 (?).
Middle Helladic II - Middle Helladic III.

720 BOWL   Fig. 39
(F5-A-2) Base. D. 0.05, Max. pres. H. 0.03, Th. 0.0074-0.010. Handmade. Semifine clay; medium white, small black and occasional grey inclusions; 10YR 5-4/1 (grey to dark grey). Flat base. Burnished exterior and interior.
Middle Helladic.

721 CLOSED VESSEL   Fig. 39
(B98-5-8) Base. Max. pres. H. 0.33, Th. of wall 0.008-0.010. Handmade. Semicoarse hard clay; small to medium grey, white inclusions, very little mica; core 10YR 3/1-2 (very dark grey to very dark grayish brown), biscuit 7.5YR 5/4 (brown). Burnished exterior.
Middle Helladic.

722 CUP OR SMALL BOWL   Fig. 39
(E13-81-1-1) Rim. D. 0.14, Max. pres. H. 0.029, Th. 0.006. Handmade. Softish semifine clay; small white and black inclusions, very little mica; 7.5YR N6/-6/4 (grey to light brown), exterior 10YR 5/2-3 (greyish brown to brown), interior 2.5YR 5-4/2 (red). Everted rim. Burnished exterior and interior.
Middle Helladic.

723 LARGE BOWL   Figs. 39, 126
(F5-326) Rim. D. est. 0.30, Max. pres. H 0.039, Th. 0.006-0.010. Handmade(?). Fine clay; very little mica; core 5YR 6/3 (light reddish brown), biscuit 10YR 4-3/1 (dark to very dark grey). Broad everted rim, straight grooved shoulder. Burnished exterior and interior. Cf. Deshayes (1966, pl. XIII:12). Zerner's phase 4-5 (?).
Middle Helladic II - Middle Helladic III.

724 BOWL   Fig. 39
(E13-81-1-50) Body. Max. pres. H. 0.039, Th. 0.006-0.007. Handmade. Semifine clay; small white and black inclusions, a little mica; core 7.5YR 5/2-4 (brown), biscuit 10YR 5/2-4 (grey). Burnished exterior and interior.
Middle Helladic.

725 BOWL   Fig. 39
(F5-193) Rim. D. 0.26, Max. pres. H. 0.04, Th. 0.006-0.007. Handmade. Semifine hard clay; small to medium white and grey inclusions; core 5YR 6/4 (light reddish brown), biscuit 10YR 6/1-2 (light grey to light brownish grey), surface strong 7.5YR 4/6 (brown). Flaring rim, handle from exterior rim. Burnished exterior and interior.
Middle Helladic.

726 BOWL   Fig. 39
(A6-65-43) Rim and shoulder. D. 0.24, Max. pres. H. 0.06, Th. 0.008. Handmade; very worn. Fine softish clay; small chalk inclusions, a little mica; core 5YR 5/4-6 (reddish brown to yellowish red), biscuit 10YR 5/1 (grey). Offset rim, straight shoulder. Burnished. Zerner's phase 4-5 (?).
Late middle to late Middle Helladic.

727 BOWL   Fig. 39
(F5-B-9) Rim. D. 0.18, Max. pres. H. 0.037, Th. 0.007-0.008. Handmade. Coarse hard clay; small to large black, grey and white inclusions; 2.5Y 4/8-5YR 5/6 (red to reddish brown), surface 5YR 5/4 (reddish brown). Thick everted rim. Burnished exterior and interior.
Middle Helladic.

728 CLOSED VESSEL   Fig. 40
(F5-370) Base. D. 0.98, Max. pres. H. 0.012, Th. of wall 0.005-0.008. Wheelmade. Fine clay, 5YR 6/6 (reddish yellow). Technical slip, 7.5YR 7/4 (pink). Flat, slightly hollowed base. Burnished exterior.
Middle Helladic III - Late Helladic I.

729 CLOSED VESSEL   Fig. 40
(F5-184) Shoulder. Max. pres. H. 0.03, Th. 0.007-0.008. Handmade. Semifine fairly hard clay; small grey, brown and white inclusions; core 7.5YR N6/-6/2 (grey to pinkish grey), biscuit 5YR 6/6 (reddish yellow), surface yellowish red (5YR 4/6). Burnished exterior and interior neck.
Middle Helladic III?

730 CUP or BOWL   Fig. 40
(E13-81-1-18) Rim. D. 0.15, Max. pres. H. 0.033, Th. 0.003-0.005. Handmade. Fine clay; very little mica; 10YR 7/3-4 (very pale brown). Everted hollowed rim, straight shoulder. Burnished. Cf. Davis (1979: fig.9, 165).
Late Helladic I.

731 CUP or BOWL   Fig. 40
(A6-2-5) Rim. D. 0.12, Max. pres. H. 0.046, Th. 0.004-0.005. Handmade. Fine clay; core 7.5YR 6/4 (light brown), biscuit 5YR 6/6 (reddish yellow). Slip 7.5YR 7/4-6 (pink to reddish yellow). Rounded bowl, everted hollowed rim. Burnished.
Middle Helladic III - Late Helladic I.

732 BOWL   Fig. 40
(A6-72-42) Rim. D. 0.22, Max. pres. H. 0.037, Th. 0.006-0.007. Handmade. Semifine clay; small to medium white, black and grey inclusions; core 7.5YR 6/4 (light brown), biscuit 5YR 6/6 (reddish yellow). Slip(?) 7.5YR 4/5 (pink to reddish yellow). Flaring rim. Burnished. Cf. Davis (1979: fig. 9, 161-162).
Late Helladic I.

733 BOWL   Fig. 40
   (F4-53) Rim. D. 0.16-0.20, Max. pres. H. 0.039, Th. 0.005-0.009. Wheelmade. Semifine clay; small grey inclusions, little mica; core 7.5YR 6/4 (light brown), biscuit 5.YR 6/7 (light reddish brown). Technical slip 7.5YR 7/4 (pink). Thick everted rim. Evenly burnished.
   Middle Helladic III - Late Helladic I.

734 BOWL   Figs. 40, 126
   (E13-81-1-14) Rim. D. est. 0.20, Max. pres. H. 0.04, Th. 0.005. Wheelmade. Fine clay; occasional mica; core 2.5YR 7/2 (pinkish grey), biscuit 7.5YR 7/4 (pink), Surface 10YR 8/3 (very pale brown). Everted hollowed rim. Burnished. Cf. Davis (1979: fig. 9, 169).
   Late Helladic I.

735 BOWL   Fig. 40
   (E9-115) Rim with strap handle. D. 0.25, Max. pres. H. 0.017, Th. 0.0045-0.0055. Wheelmade(?). Fine clay; 7.5YR 7/4 (reddish yellow to pink). Everted rim, vertical strap handle from exterior rim. Highly burnished.
   Middle Helladic III - Late Helladic I.

736 BOWL   Fig. 40
   (F4-48) Rim with handle. D. 0.16, Max. pres. H. 0.019, Th. 0.003, W. of handle 0.017. Wheelmade(?). Fine clay; core 7.5YR 7/4 (pink), biscuit 5YR 6/6 (reddish yellow). Softly everted rim, vertical strap handle from exterior rim. Burnished.
   Middle Helladic III - Late Helladic I.

737 BOWL or CUP   Fig. 40
   (F26-12) Body with handle. Max pres H. 0.028, Th. 0.004, W. of handle 0.022. Wheelmade(?). Fine soft clay; 5YR 7/2-3 (pinkish grey to grey). Technical slip, 7.5YR 7/4-6 (pink to reddish yellow). Angular body, vertical strap handle from belly. Burnished.
   Middle Helladic III - Late Helladic I.

738 BOWL   Fig. 40
   (F5-103) Neck, shoulder and belly. Max. pres. H. 0.035, Th. 0.0045-0.0065. Wheelmade, worn. Fine clay, 7.5YR 7/4 (pink). Angular profile. Burnished.
   Middle Helladic III - Late Helladic I.

739 CUP WITH HIGH HANDLES (?)   Fig. 40
   (F5-107) Strap handle. Max. pres. L. 0.046, W. 0.023, Th. 0.007. Fine clay; little mica; core 10YR 6/3 (pale brown), biscuit 7.5YR 6/4 (light brown). Exterior 7.5YR 4/6 (strong brown), interior 5YR 4/6 (yellowish red). Burnished.
   Middle Helladic III - Late Helladic I.

740 OPEN VESSEL   Fig. 40
   (E13-29) Base. D. 0.045, Max. pres. H. 0.02, Th. of wall 0.004. Wheelmade. Fine clay; core 5YR 6/4-6 (light reddish brown to reddish yellow), biscuit 5YR 5/4 (reddish brown). Surfaces 5YR 5/4 to 2.5YR 6-5/8 (light red to red). Ring base. Burnished.
   Middle Helladic III - Late Helladic I.

741 BOWL ON HIGH FOOT   Fig. 40
   (E13-31) Base. D 0.063, Max. pres. H. 0.031, Th. of wall 0.006. Wheelmade(?). Fine clay; core 5Y 8/2 (reddish pink), biscuits 2.5Y 8/2 (white) and 5Y 8/2; technical slip 5Y 8/2 (white). Flaring wide foot, short stem.
   Middle Helladic III - Late Helladic I.

742 BOWL ON HIGH FOOT   Fig. 40
   (B43-3) Base. D. 0.07, Max. pres. H. 0.033, Th. of wall 0.007. Handmade(?). Fine clay; core 5Y 8/2 (reddish pink), biscuits 2.5Y 8/2 (white) and 5Y 8/2; technical slip, surface uneven, vitrified, 2.5Y 8/2 to 5Y 8/2 (reddish pink). Flaring wide foot, short stem.
   Middle Helladic III - Late Helladic I.

743 BOWL   Fig. 40
   (F5-100) Rim. D. 0.16, Max. pres. H. 0.045, Th. 0.004-0.006. Wheelmade. Fine clay, 10YR 7/3-4 (very pale brown). Offset rim, rounded body. Highly burnished.
   Late Helladic I.

744 CUP   Fig. 40
   (E9-158) Rim and shoulder. D. est. 0.10, Max. pres. H. 0.043, Th. 0.003. Handmade. Fine clay; very little mica; 7.5YR 6/2-4 (pinkish grey to light brown). Straight shoulder, slightly carinated to belly, offset and slightly hollowed rim; technical slip, 10YR 7/3 (very pale brown). Burnished. Cf. Davis (1979; fig. 9, 170).
   Late Helladic I.

745 CUP WITH HIGH HANDLES (?)   Figs. 40, 126
   (F5-B-86) Rim and body. D. indet., Max. pres. H. 0.055, Th. 0.005-0.006. Handmade. Fine clay; small white and black inclusions, very little mica; 5YR 7/4-6 (pink to reddish yellow). Gently curved profile, everted rim, fragment of vertical strap handle. Burnished. Cf. Rutter and Rutter (1976, ill. 10, no. 239), cf. no. 201.
   Middle Helladic III - Late Helladic I.

746 CLOSED VESSEL   Fig. 40
   (E13-81-1-29) Body with handle. Max. pres. H. 0.04, Th. 0.005-0.006, W. of handle 0.023. Handmade. Semicoarse very hard clay; small white and angular black, large black, smaller shiny black inclusions; 10YR 4/1 (dark grey). Rounded profile, vertical strap-handle. Smooth surface, traces of burnishing, but vitrified and full of holes after grits and air bubbles.
   Middle Helladic.

747 CLOSED VESSEL (?)   Fig. 40
   (F5-218) Rim. D. 0.27, Max. pres. H. 0.055, Th. 0.008-0.010. Handmade. Semicoarse hard clay; small to medium white, grey and brown inclusions; core 2.5Y N6/ (grey), biscuit 2.5YR 5/6 (red). Thickened everted rim. Burnished exterior and interior of rim, interior body uneven.
   Middle Helladic.

748 BOWL   Fig. 40
   (F5-296) Shoulder. Max. pres. H. 0.037, Th. 0.006-0.007. Handmade. Semifine clay; small white, black and grey inclusions; 7.5YR 7/4 (pink). Slightly curved shoulder, broad horizontal grooves. Burnished.
   Middle Helladic II.

749 CUP   Fig. 40
   (E5-B-25) Rim to belly. D. 0.08, Max. pres. H. 0.028, Th. 0.005-0.006. Handmade. Semifine clay; small to medium inclusions, very little mica; 7.5YR 5/2 (brown), surface 7.5YR 3/2-4. Slightly curved profile, rounded rim. Burnished.
   Middle Helladic.

750 BOWL   Fig. 40
(A6-7-5) Rim. D. 0.19, Max. pres. H. 0.048, Th. 0.006-0.01. Handmade. Semicoarse well fired clay; small to medium grey, brown and small white inclusions; 10YR 5/1-2 (grey to greyish brown), surface 10YR 6/3-4 (pale brown to light yellowish brown). Offset rim, gently curved shoulder. Burnished.
Middle Helladic.

751 BOWL ON HIGH FOOT   Fig. 40
(F32-N-142) Foot. D. of stem 0.045, Max. pres. H. 0.053. Handmade. Semifine clay; small to medium brown, white inclusions, very little mica; core 7.5YR N5/ (grey), biscuit 5YR 6/4-6 (light reddish brown to reddish yellow), surface 5YR 5/6 (yellowish red). Short grooved stem, flaring foot. Burnished exterior.
Middle Helladic III.

752 BOWL (?)   Fig. 40
(F5-A-3) Rim with handle. Max. pres. H. without handle 0.025, Th. 0.003, W. of handle 0.03. Wheelmade(?). Semifine clay; small white and grey/black inclusions; core 10YR 6/1 (light grey), biscuit 5YR 6/6 (red). Everted rim, vertical strap-handle from both sides of rim. Burnished.
Middle Helladic ?

753 BOWL   Figs. 40, 126
(E13-1-14) Rim with handle. D. 0.32, Max. pres. H. 0.067, W. of handle 0.028. Handmade; worn. Semifine well fired clay; small grey, small to medium white inclusions, very little mica; core 10YR 4/1-2 (dark grey to dark greyish brown), biscuit 7.5YR 5/4 (brown), surface 2.5YR 7/4 (pale yellow), traces of a thin slip, 5YR 4/4 (reddish brown). Everted rim, vertical strap handle from exterior rim, there decorated with three applied flat pellets, to shoulder; burnished.
Middle Helladic III.

754 BOWL ON HIGH FOOT   Fig. 40
(A9-30) Foot. D. of stem 0.05, Max. pres. H. 0.05. Handmade(?); worn. Semifine clay; small white, black, red inclusions, little mica; core 10YR 8/3 (grey), biscuit 5YR 5/6-8 (yellowish red). High foot with horizontal incised lines. Thick white slip, 10YR 8/3 (very pale brown).
Middle Helladic III.

755 BOWL ON HIGH FOOT   Figs. 40, 126
(F5-75-8) Foot. D. of stem 0.05, Max. pres. H. 0.055. Handmade. Semicoarse clay; small to large grey, brown, red and white inclusions, very little mica; 10YR 5/1 (grey). Slip 5YR 5/6 (yellowish red). Short grooved stem, wide foot. Burnished.
Middle Helladic III.

756 JUG/JAR   Figs. 41, 126
(E13-9) Lower body. Max. pres. H. 0.062, Th. 0.004-0.006. Handmade. Hard fine clay; small to medium, black, grey, white inclusions, a little mica; core 7.5YR N6/ (grey), biscuit 7.5YR 6/4-6 (light brown to reddish yellow). Angular profile. Burnished exterior, interior uneven. Paint 2.5YR 3/2 (dusky red): parallel lines, filled pendant semicircles on the belly and zigzag(?) on shoulder.
Middle Helladic III.

757 WIDE-MOUTHED JAR   Figs. 41, 126
(F5-28) Rim. D. ca. 0.18, Max. pres. H. 0.05, Th. 0.005-0.006. Handmade. Fine clay; very little mica; 5YR 6/7 (light

reddish brown); technical slip 10YR 7/3 (very pale brown), slightly burnished exterior. Everted rim, gently curved shoulder, Buck C2. Paint 10YR 3/2 (very dark greyish brown): pendant triple triangles on shoulder (Buck no. 38), horizontal parallel lines on neck, groups of vertical lines on interior neck.
Middle Helladic II.

758 CLOSED VESSEL   Fig. 41
(E13-8) Shoulder. Max. pres. H. 0.042, Th. 0.008. Handmade. Semifine hard clay; small to medium white and small black inclusions, little mica; core 10YR 5/1 (grey), biscuit 5YR 5/4 (reddish brown), surface 10YR 5/2 (greyish brown). Vitrified. Burnished. Paint 7.5YR 3/2-4 (dark brown): horizontal parallel lines on shoulder.
Middle Helladic.

759 CLOSED VESSEL   Fig. 41
(F5-205) Body. Max. pres. W. 0.058, Max. pres. H. 0.05, Th. 0.01. Wheelmade(?). Semifine clay; small white, grey and occasional medium brown inclusions; 7.5YR 7-6/4 (pink to light brown). Burnished exterior. Paint 10YR 6/2 (light brownish grey): parallel lines.
Middle Helladic III ?

760 JAR   Fig. 41
(F5-226) Neck and shoulder. D. of neck ca. 0.96, Max. pres. H. 0.045, Th. 0.008-0.009. Wheelmade. Hard semifine clay; small to medium white, grey inclusions, very little mica; core 7.5YR N7/ (light grey), biscuit 7.5YR 7/6 (reddish yellow). Everted high rim, Buck C5 or C9. Paint 10YR 3/1-4/4 (very dark grey to dark yellowish brown): two parallel lines around neck, a curvilinear motif on shoulder.
Late Helladic I.

761 CLOSED VESSEL   Fig. 41
(E13-7) Body. Max. pres. W. 0.10, Max. pres. H. 0.04, Th. 0.006-0.01. Handmade. Semifine clay; small to medium grey, white and small straw-like white inclusions, traces of vegetable temper, some mica; core 7.5YR N5/ (grey), biscuit 5YR 6/6 (reddish yellow), surface 7.5YR 7/4 (pink). Slightly curved body. Paint 7.5YR 5/2 (brown): three horizontal parallel lines and zigzag(?) on shoulder.
Middle Helladic.

762 CLOSED VESSEL   Figs. 41, 126
(A6-74-96) Shoulder. Max. pres. H. 0.052, Th. 0.0075-0.009. Wheelmade. Semifine clay; small black, brown and white inclusions, very little mica; core 10YR 5/1 (grey), biscuit 5YR 6/4 (light reddish brown), surface 10YR 7/3 (very pale brown). Straight body. Burnished exterior. Paint 10YR 5/3 (brown): plant motif, cf. Buck no. 129.
Middle Helladic III - Late Helladic I.

763 CLOSED VESSEL (?)   Fig. 41
(E13-81-1-75) Foot and lower body. D. of stem 0.055, Max. pres. H. 0.055, Th. of wall 0.006-0.010. Handmade; very worn. Semicoarse fairly hard clay; small to large white, small angular black, red, grey inclusions, very little mica; core 10YR 6/3 (pale brown), biscuit 5YR 6/6 (reddish yellow), surface 7.5YR 7/4 (pink). Flaring foot, conical lower body. For shape, cf. Goldman 1931:fig. 220,1. Exterior smoothed, interior uneven. Paint 2.5YR N2.5/ (black): horizontal ladder band (Buck no. 67).
Middle Helladic.

764 CLOSED VESSEL   Fig. 41
(F5-13) Body. Max. pres. H. 0.04, Th. 0.005, handmade. Fairly soft, fine clay; 5YR 6/6 (reddish yellow). Gritty surface, slipped(?) 10YR 8/2-3 (white to very pale brown). Thin curved body. Paint 10YR 4/1-5/2 (dark grey to greyish brown): linear.
Middle Helladic.

765 SMALL CLOSED VESSEL   Fig. 41
(F5-71) Shoulder. Max. pres. H. 0.033, Th. 0.005-0.007. Handmade. Hard semifine clay; small to medium white, brown and grey inclusions; 5YR 5/6 (yellowish red), surface 10YR 7/4 (very pale brown), wet smoothed, burnished exterior. Flaring neck, straight shoulder. Paint 7.5YR 5/2-4/4 (brown): band around neck, triple zigzag (Buck no. 6A) on shoulder, vertical line on inside neck.
Middle Helladic.

766 CLOSED VESSEL   Fig. 41
(E13-81-1-44) Body. Max. Pres. H. 0.045, Th. 0.005-0.006. Handmade. Semicoarse very hard, gritty clay; small to medium white, brown, red, small grey inclusions, little mica; core 7.5YR 7/2 (pinkish grey), biscuit 7.5YR 7/5 (pink), surface 7.5YR 7/6 - 5YR 7/5 (reddish yellow). Fairly straight body. Slightly burnished exterior. Paint 5YR 6/2 (pinkish grey): pendant triple triangle (Buck no. 38).
Middle Helladic.

767 CLOSED VESSEL   Figs. 41, 126
(F5-101) Body. Max. pres. H. 0.034, Th. 0.006. Wheelmade (?). Semifine clay; small to medium white inclusions, very little mica; 5YR 6/6 (reddish yellow), surface 7.5YR 7/4 (pink). Straight body. Paint 5YR 4-3/3 (dark reddish grey to dark reddish brown): vertical bands, horizontal incised lines.
Middle Helladic.

768 CUP WITH HIGH HANDLES   Fig. 41
(E13-3) Strap-handle. L. 0.049, W. 0.023, Th. 0.01. Fine clay 5YR 7/1-2 (light grey). Burnished. Paint 5YR 3/1 (very dark grey): a line along the handle.
Middle Helladic.

769 CUP WITH HIGH HANDLES   Fig. 41
(E13-81-1-62) Rim with handle frag. D. indet., Max. pres. H. without handle 0.024, Th. 0.006-0.007, W. of handle 0.031. Handmade; worn. Semifine hard clay; small to medium white, occasional black inclusions; core 10YR 5/2 (greyish brown), biscuit 2.5YR 5/6 (red), surface 7.5YR 7/2-3 (pinkish grey to pink). Strap-handle from exterior rim. Burnished; three flat pellets on the attachment to rim. Paint 2.5YR 4/2 (brown): linear.
Middle Helladic.

770 OPEN VESSEL   Fig. 41
(F5-61) Shoulder. Max. pres. H. 0.043, Th. 0.008-0.01. Wheelmade(?). Semifine fairly hard clay; small grey red, white inclusions, a little mica; 5.YR 7/4 - 7.5YR 7/4 (pink). Matt technical slip, 10YR 8-7/3 (very pale brown). Paint 5YR 3/2 (dark reddish brown): two parallel lines around neck.
Middle Helladic.

771 LARGE OPEN VESSEL   Fig. 41
(F5-11) Body. Max. pres. W. 0.074, Max. pres. H. 0.068, Th. 0.007. Handmade. Semifine clay; small white, grey/black inclusions; 2.5Y 7/2 (light grey). Slightly curved body. Burnished(?). Paint 10YR 3/2 (very dark greyish brown): two horizontal parallel lines and zigzag(?).
Middle Helladic

772 WIDE-MOUTHED BOWL   Fig. 41
(F5-75-1) Rim and body. D. ca. 0.16, Max. pres. H. 0.047, Th. 0.005-0.006. Wheelmade; worn. Semifine softish clay; small to medium white inclusions; 5YR 6/6 (reddish yellow). Everted rim, rounded body, Buck A2. Paint 5YR 3/2 (dark reddish brown): band around neck, zigzag on shoulder (Buck no. 5).
Middle Helladic.

773 BOWL   Fig. 41
(E13-81-1-13) Rim. D. ca. 0.21, Max. pres. H. 0.027, Th. 0.007-0.008. Handmade. Semifine softish clay; small white, grey inclusions, little mica; 5YR 6/4 (light reddish brown). Short flaring rim. Paint 5YR 3/2 (dark reddish brown): two parallel horizontal lines below rim.
Middle Helladic.

774 CUP   Figs. 41, 126
(F5-B-6) Lower body. Max. pres. H. 0.046, Th. 0.005. Handmade. Almost fine clay; small and medium white, small grey inclusions, very little mica; core 10YR 7-6/3 (very pale brown to pale brown), biscuit 5YR 6/6 (reddish yellow), surface 10YR 7/3 (very pale brown). Exterior and interior slightly burnished. Paint 7.5YR 3/2 (dark brown): horizontal bands with hanging dots, possibly the start of a panel or spiral. Traces of a finger print on the decoration.
Late Middle Helladic.

775 CUP   Fig. 41
(E13-81-1-36) Body. H 0.029, Th. 0.003-0.0055. Handmade. Semifine hard clay; small white, grey inclusions, very little mica; 7.5YR 7/4-6 (pink to reddish yellow). Slightly curved body. Paint 5YR 3/1-2 (very dark grey to reddish brown): parallel slightly curved bands, part of a multiple semicircle(?), (Buck no. 90).
Late Middle Helladic.

776 CUP WITH HIGH HANDLES   Figs. 41, 126
(E13-2-37) Body with handle frag. Max. pres. H. 0.05, Th. 0.009-0.010. Handmade. Semicoarse hard clay; several small to medium grey, brown, black, white inclusions, very little mica; core 5YR 6/8 (reddish yellow), biscuit 7.5YR 6/4 (light brown), surface 2.5Y 7/4 (pale yellow). Angular belly, vertical strap-handle (Buck A6). Slightly burnished exterior, interior smoothed. Paint 10YR 6/3 (pale brown), linear motif.
Middle Helladic.

777 BOWL   Fig. 41
(F5-320) Body. Max. pres. W. 0.05, Max. pres. H. 0.04, Th. 0.005-0.011. Handmade. Semicoarse clay; small to large white, small to medium grey, brown inclusions; core 10YR 6/2 (light brownish grey), biscuit 7.5YR 6/4 (light brown). Fairly straight body. Burnished. Paint 7.5YR 6/2 (pinkish grey), linear motif.
Middle Helladic.

778 OPEN VESSEL   Fig. 41
(F5-293) Base. D. ca. 0.065, Max. pres. H. 0.018. Handmade. Fine clay, 2.5Y 6/1 (light brownish). Slightly raised base. Exterior and interior burnished. Paint 10YR 6/2 (light

brownish grey): a band around the base, alternating circle sections on bottom, cf. Zerner (1987: 23).
Middle Helladic.

779 SMALL BOWL or CUP   Fig. 41
(B5-3) Body. Max. pres. H. 0.03, Th. 0.005. Handmade. Fine clay; very small white, black, mica inclusions; core 10YR 7/1 (light grey), biscuit 2.5Y 8/4 (pale yellow). Gently curved body. Traces of burnishing. Paint 7.5YR 3/2 (dark brown): one broad band with four parallel lines on one side and one on the other.
Middle Helladic.

780 PANELLED CUP   Figs. 41, 126
(E76-5) Foot and lower body. D. of foot 0.06, Max. pres. H. 0.047, Th. of wall 0.0045. Handmade(?). Semifine fairly soft clay; small to medium grey, black, several small to large white inclusions, very little mica; 5YR 6/6 (reddish yellow), surface 10YR 6/3-4 (pale brown to light reddish brown). Vitrified. Short slightly hollowed out foot, gently curved lower body. Paint 7.5YR 4/2-3 (brown to dark brown): lower panel border extending over half of the surface. Cycladic panelled style? (Davis 1978).
Middle Cycladic (?).

781 PANELLED CUP   Figs. 41, 126
(E13-2-10) Foot and lower body. D. of foot ca. 0.50, Max. pres. H. 0.036, Th. of wall 0.007. Wheelmade; worn. Semifine hard clay; small brown, grey, white inclusions, very little mica; 5YR 6/6 (reddish yellow). Hollowed out foot, conical lower body. Burnished. Paint 5YR 3/1 (very dark grey): a band around the foot, a lower panel border consisting of a band with small pendant semicircles (Buck no. 57). Mainland panelled style (Davis 1978).
Middle Helladic III.

782 PANELLED CUP   Fig. 41
(E13-1-10) Foot and lower body. D. of stem 0.044, Max. pres. H. 0.022. Handmade; worn. Fine to semifine hard clay; small brown, grey, white inclusions, very little mica; core 2.5YR 5/2 (greyish brown), biscuit 7.5YR 6/4 (light brown). Dull surface, 7.5YR 8/4 (pink). Burnished(?). Paint 10YR 3/1-2 (very dark grey to very dark greyish brown): two parallel lines around foot vertical panel border. Mainland panelled style? (Davis 1978).
Middle Helladic III.

783 PANELLED CUP   Fig. 41
(E13-81-1-68) Foot. D. of foot 0.06, Max. pres. H. 0.03, Th. of wall 0.01. Wheelmade(?). Semifine hard clay; small to medium white, occasional red, several small black inclusions, very little mica; core 10YR 5/1 (grey), biscuit 5YR 6/6 (reddish yellow), technical(?) slip 10YR 8/2 (white). Short hollowed out foot, conical lower body. Paint 10YR 8/2 (very dark): a band around stem, vertical panel border. Mainland panelled style? (Davis 1978).
Middle Helladic III.

784 SMALL CLOSED VESSEL (?)   Figs. 42, 127
(F5-145) Body. Max. pres. W. 0.027, Max. pres. H. 0.019, Th. 0.007. Wheelmade. Semifine clay; small white, grey inclusions, very little mica; core 5YR 6/4 (light reddish brown), biscuit 2.5YR 5/6 (red), surface slipped (?), 7.5YR 8/2 (pinkish white). Slightly curved body. Paint 5YR 3/1 (very dark grey) and 2.5YR 4/6 (red): linear motif.
Middle Helladic - Late Helladic I.

785 CLOSED VESSEL (?)   Figs. 42, 127
(E13-81-1-41) Shoulder (?). Max. pres. H. 0.034, Th. 0.006-0.006. Handmade. Semifine hard lay; small to medium white, angular black inclusions, very little mica; 5YR 7/3-7/4 (pink), surface 7.5YR 7/4 (pink); exterior burnished over decoration, interior uneven. Slightly curved body. Paint 7.5YR 3/0-3/2 (very dark grey to dark brown) and 2.5YR 3/6 (dark red): linear motif.
Middle Helladic - Late Helladic I.

786 JAR (?)   Figs. 42, 127
(A6-75-92) Neck and shoulder. D. of neck ca. 0.18, Max. pres. H. 0.045, Th. 0.008-0.01. Handmade. Fine clay 5YR 6/4-6 (light reddish brown to reddish yellow), surface 5YR 7/4 (pink). Everted neck, Buck C5 or C9. Burnished. Paint 5YR 3/1 - 10YR 3/4 (very dark grey to dusky red): bands around neck, zigzag on shoulder.
Middle Helladic.

787 CLOSED VESSEL   Fig. 127
(F5-44) Handle. Max. pres. W. 0.056, Max. pres. H. 0.02, Th. 0.016. Semifine hard clay; several small grey, white and fewer black, brown inclusions; core 7.5YR 5/2 (brown), biscuit 5YR 5/6 (yellowish red). Rounded in section, probably horizontal handle. Coat 5YR 2.5/1 to 4/6-8 (black to red), traces of dull white paint.
Middle Helladic.

788 OPEN VESSEL
(E13-81-1-28) Body. Handmade. Fine clay; small black inclusions; 7.5YR 7/4 (pink). Slightly curved body. Coat 10YR 3/2 to 2.5YR 3/2 (dusky red to dark reddish brown).
Middle Helladic.

789 SMALL BOWL or CUP   Fig. 42
(E13-81-1-16) Base. D. 0.05, Max. pres. H. 0.018, Th. 0.005. Wheelmade. Fine clay; small black inclusions; 7.5YR 7/4 (pink). Flat slightly hollowed base, conical lower body; traces of cutting wire on the bottom. Uneven thin coat on interior and exterior, thicker in the turning grooves, 5YR 3/3 to 7.5YR 5/6-N3/ (dark reddish brown, strong reddish brown to very dark grey).
Middle Bronze Age.

790 CLOSED VESSEL
(E13-81-1-19) Body. Handmade(?). Semifine hard clay; small white, black inclusions, little mica; core 7.5YR 8/2 (pink), biscuit 2.5YR 6/6 (red). Coat 5YR 3/1-2 to 10YR 3/3 (very dark grey, dark reddish brown to dusky red).
Middle Bronze Age.

791 CLOSED VESSEL   Fig. 42
(E13-33) Body. Max. pres. H. 0.069, Max. pres. W. 0.038, Th. 0.007-0.0085. Handmade. Semifine clay; small brown, black, white inclusions, gold and black mica; 5YR 6/4-6 (light reddish brown to reddish brown), surface 10YR 7/4 (very pale brown). Slightly curved body. Paint 2.5YR 4/6 (red): double wavy lines.
Very late Middle Helladic - Late Helladic I.

792 WIDE-MOUTHED JAR (?)   Fig. 42
(F5-72) Shoulder. Max. pres. H. 0.05, Th. 0.007-0.009. Handmade. Semifine clay; small to medium white, grey inclusions, gold mica; core 5YR 7/4 (pink), biscuit 10YR 7/3

very pale brown). Straight shoulder, everted neck, Buck C2.
Paint 2.5YR N3/ (very dark grey): horizontal parallel bands around
neck, pendant triple triangles on shoulder, Buck no. 37.
Middle Helladic II - Middle Helladic III.

793 CLOSED VESSEL   Fig. 42
(E13-81-1-51) Body. Max. pres. W. 0.056, Th. 0.006.
Handmade. Semifine clay; small white, black inclusions, little
mica including gold mica; 5YR 6/6 (reddish yellow). Gently
curved body. Paint 5YR 5-4/2 (reddish grey to dark reddish grey):
three parallel horizontal lines.
Middle Helladic.

794 CLOSED VESSEL   Figs. 42, 127
(F5-B-8) Body. Max. pres. H. 0.043, Th. 0.007.
Handmade. Semifine clay; small to medium white, grey
inclusions, little mica including gold mica; 10YR 8/2 (white).
Straight body. Paint 5YR 4-3/2 (light reddish grey): linear.
Middle Helladic.

795 WIDE-MOUTHED JAR   Figs. 42, 127
(F5-10) Rim and shoulder. D. ca. 0.14, Max. pres. H.
0.049, Th. 0.007-0.008. Handmade; worn. Semifine clay; small
white, grey inclusions, little mica including gold mica; 2.5Y 8-
7/2 (white to light grey). Flaring rim, rounded shoulder, Buck
A2. Paint 5YR 3/2 (dark reddish brown): a band around neck,
triple zigzag on shoulder, Buck no. 6A.
Middle Helladic II - Middle Helladic III.

796 JAR   Fig. 42
(E13-81-1-9) Rim. D. 0.28, Max. pres. H. 0.059, Th.
0.008-0.014. Wheelmade(?). Semifine clay; some, mostly small,
white, angular black/grey inclusions, very little mica including
gold and black mica; core 7.5YR 7/6 (reddish yellow), biscuit
10YR 7/4 (very pale brown). Everted rim. Paint 7,5YR N3/ -3/2
(very dark grey to dark brown): three parallel lines around neck.
Middle Helladic.

797 BROAD-RIMMED BOWL   Fig. 42
(F5-3A) Rim. D. 0.46, Max. pres. H. 0.063, Th. 0.01.
Handmade. Semicoarse hard clay; small to medium grey, black,
red, white inclusions, very little mica including gold mica; 5YR
5/4 (reddish brown), surface 10YR 7/4 (very pale brown).
Thickened straight rim, straight shoulder, Buck A1(?). Burnished
exterior and on rim, interior smoothed. Paint 5YR 4/1 (dark
grey): filled semicircles below rim, parallel lines across rim.
Middle Helladic III.

798 BROAD-RIMMED BOWL   Figs. 42, 127
(E13-1) Rim. D. 0.33, Max. pres. H. 0.058, Th. 0.009-
0.017. Handmade(?). Semifine hard clay; small grey, brown,
small to medium white inclusions, very little mica including gold
mica; core 10YR 6/3 (pale brown), biscuit 5YR 6/6 (reddish
yellow). Broad offset rim, thick wall, gently curved profile. Dull
paint 2.5YR 3/4-6 (dark reddish brown to dark red): painted rim,
band below rim, a double wavy line on the shoulder.
Burnished(?).
Late Helladic I.

799 BROAD-RIMMED BOWL   Fig. 42
(E13-2) Rim. D. 0.24, Max. pres. H. 0.057, Th. 0.006.
Wheelmade. Semifine hard clay; a small grey, small to medium
white inclusions, some mica including gold mica; core 10YR 7/2
(light grey), biscuit 7.5YR 7/4 (pink). Straight everted rim. Dull
paint 2.5YR 3/4-6 (dark reddish brown to dark red): painted rim, a
double wavy line on shoulder. Burnished(?).
Late Helladic I.

800 BOWL   Fig. 42
(F5-315) Rim. D. 0.25, Max. pres. H. 0.03, Th. 0.008-
0.010. Wheelmade. Semifine clay; small grey, white inclusions,
very little mica, including gold mica; 7.5YR 6/4 (light brown).
Thickened straight rim. Burnished exterior and interior. Paint
5YR 3/2-3 (dark reddish brown): band below exterior rim.
Middle Helladic.

801 SMALL BOWL   Figs. 42, 127
(B39-58) Rim with handle frag. D. 0.21, Max. pres. H.
0.078, Th. 0.005-0.007, W. of handle 0.023. Handmade.
Semifine well fired clay; small to medium grey, black, white,
large red inclusions, occasional mica including gold mica; 5YR
6/1-3 (light grey to reddish brown), surface 2.5Y7/2-4 (light grey
to pale yellow). Vitrified. Angular profile, everted rim, strap-
handle from exterior rim to shoulder. Burnished exterior and
interior. Paint 2.5Y 3/2 (very dark greyish brown): zigzag on
shoulder.
Middle Helladic III.

802 BOWL   Fig. 42
(E9-86) Rim and handle. D. 0.17, Max. pres. H. 0.037, Th.
0.007-0.008. Wheelmade. Fine soft clay; little mica including
black mica; 10YR 6/4 (light yellowish brown). Fairly straight
shoulder, everted rim, strap-handle from rim to shoulder. Slip on
interior 5YR 3/1-2 to 5/6 (very dark grey, dark reddish brown to
yellowish red), slightly burnished.
Middle Helladic III - Late Helladic I.

803 BOWL
(F26-6) Rim and handle. D. ca. 0.20, Max. pres. H. 0.04,
Th. 0.007-0.008. Handmade(?); very worn. Fine soft clay; little
mica including black mica; 10YR 6/4 (light yellowish brown).
Fairly straight shoulder, everted rim, strap-handle from rim to
shoulder. Slip 7.5YR 7/6 (reddish yellow) to 5YR 4/3 (dark
reddish brown/ reddish brown), slightly burnished.
Middle Helladic III.

804 BROAD-RIMMED BOWL   Fig. 42
(E13-2-63) Rim. D. 0.30, Max. pres. H. 0.047, Th. 0.008-
0.010. Wheelmade. Fine hard clay; small white, grey inclusions,
very little mica including gold mica; core 10YR 6/2 (light
brownish grey), biscuit 5YR 6/4-6 (light reddish brown to reddish
yellow). Broad rim, straight shoulder. Slip 2.5YR 4-3/4 (reddish
to dark reddish brown) on rim and in a line below interior rim,
burnished.
Late Helladic I.

805 BROAD-RIMMED BOWL   Fig. 42
(F5-A-16) Rim. D. 0.31, Max. pres. H. 0.07, Th. 0.006-
0.010. Handmade. Semifine well fired clay; several small grey,
white, black inclusions, mica including gold mica; core 10YR
7/1 (light grey), biscuit 5YR 6/6 (red). Broad rim, straight
shoulder curving into belly. Slip 2.5YR 5-4/6 (red), slightly
burnished.
Middle Helladic III - Late Helladic I.

806 BROAD-RIMMED BOWL   Fig. 42
(B43-B-26) Rim. D. indet., Max. pres. H. 0.027, Th.
0.007. Handmade; worn. Semifine well fired clay; several small

grey, white, black inclusions, some mica including gold mica; core 10YR 7/1 (light grey), biscuit 5YR 6/6 (red). Broad offset rim, straight shoulder. Slip 2.5YR 5/8 (red), slightly burnished. Middle Helladic III.

807 BROAD-RIMMED BOWL   Fig. 42
(A6-74-61) Rim. D. 0.35, Max. pres. H. 0.061, Th. 0.005-0.013. Handmade. Semifine well fired clay; small white, grey, red inclusions, little mica including gold mica; core 10YR 5/1 (grey), biscuit 5YR 5/6-4 (red). Broad everted rim, straight shoulder. Slip 10YR 8/3 - 10YR 4/1-3/3 (red to black) on exterior and on interior rim, slightly burnished. Cf. **454**.
Middle Helladic III.

808 BROAD-RIMMED BOWL   Figs. 42, 127
(A6-74-11) Rim with horizontal handle. D. 0.30, Max. pres. H. 0.045, Th. 0.007, W. of handle 0.019. Wheelmade. Fine well fired clay; small white inclusions, very little mica including gold mica; 5YR 2-6/4 (pink to light reddish brown). Broad everted rim, straight shoulder, thick horizontal strap-handle just below rim. Slip, 2.5YR 4/6 (red), slightly burnished.
Late Helladic I.

809 BOWL   Fig. 42
(F5-B-11) Neck and shoulder, Max. pres. H. 0.033, Th. 0.005-0.008. Wheelmade(?). Fine softish clay; core 10YR 7/2 (light grey), biscuit 5YR 7/4 (pink). Everted rim, slightly carinated body. Thick slip 2.5YR 4/6 (red), slightly burnished.
Middle Helladic III - Late Helladic I.

810 BOWL ON HIGH FOOT   Fig. 42
(F5-39) Foot. D. of stem 0.057, Max. pres. H. 0.038, Th. 0.016. Handmade. Semifine clay; core 7.5YR N7/ (grey), biscuit 7.5YR 7/4 (pink). Short grooved stem, flaring pedestalled foot. Slip 2.5YR 4/6 (red), slightly burnished.
Middle Helladic.

811 BOWL   Fig. 42
(E13-81-1-7) Rim. D. 0.17, Max. pres. H. 0.037, Th. 0.007-0.009. Wheelmade. Hard fine clay; small white inclusions, little mica including gold mica; core 10YR 6/3 (pale brown), biscuit 5YR 6/4 (light reddish brown). Everted rim. Slip 5YR 3/2-4/3 (dark reddish brown to reddish brown) on exterior and interior, burnished.
Middle Helladic III - Late Helladic I.

812 CLOSED VESSEL   Fig. 43
(E9-266) Rim. D 0.14, Max. pres. H. 0.049, Th. 0.006-0.007. Handmade. Hard well fired semicoarse clay; several small to medium grey, white inclusions, a little mica, possibly gold mica; 5YR 5/6 (yellowish red). Flaring rim. Unevenly smoothed on exterior and interior rim.
Middle Helladic.

813 JAR   Fig. 43
(F5-75-9) Rim and handle. D 0.165, Max. pres. H. 0.062, Th. 0.006-0.008. Handmade. Very hard semicoarse clay; small to medium grey, white inclusions, very little mica including gold mica; core 10YR 6/1-2 (light grey), biscuit 2.5YR 5/4-6 (reddish brown to red). Flaring rim, vertical strap-handle from both sides of rim to shoulder. Smoothed exterior and interior of rim; Buck B7(?). For parallels, cf. Grave Circle B (Mylonas 1972 pin. 172 alpha:3, gamma) and Eleusis (Mylonas 1975, pin. 48:357).
Late Middle Helladic III - Late Helladic I.

814 CLOSED VESSEL   Fig. 43, 127
(B5-7-1) Base. D. ca. 0.06, Max. pres. H. 0.021. Handmade. Coarse clay; many small black, red, small to medium grey, much mica including black mica; core 2.5YR N5/ (grey), biscuit 5YR 5/8 (yellowish red). Slightly hollowed, raised base. Potter's mark underneath base.
Late Helladic I.

815 JAR   Figs. 43, 127
(F26-16) Base. D. 0.06, Max. pres. H. 0.035. Handmade. Coarse clay; many small white, fewer small to medium grey, brown inclusions, much mica including gold mica; core 5YR 6/4 (light reddish brown), biscuit 2.5YR 6/6 (light red), surface 10YR 8-7/3 (very pale brown). Flat raised base. Potter's mark underneath base.
Late Helladic I.

816 JAR   Figs. 43, 127
(F23-47) Base. D 0.064, Max. pres. H. 0.021. Handmade. Coarse clay; several small to medium red, black, brown, white inclusions, some mica including gold mica; 7.5YR 5/4 (brown). Slightly raised base. Potter's mark underneath base.
Late Helladic I.

817 JAR (?)   Fig. 43
(B83-5) Base. D. 0.07, Max. pres. H. 0.022. Handmade(?). Coarse very hard clay; several small to large white, grey, transparent inclusions, much mica including black mica; core 7.5YR N6/ (grey), biscuit 2.5YR 5/6 (red), surface 7.5YR 6-5/2. Hollowed base.
Late Middle Helladic (?).

818 SMALL PITHOS (?)   Figs. 43, 127
(A6-65-28) Rim. D. 0.35, Max. pres. H. 0.055, Th. 0.02. Handmade. Coarse fairly hard clay; many small to medium grey, black, white, red (burned clay) inclusions, very little mica; 7.5YR 7/4-8/2 (pink to pinkish white). Everted, unevenly thick rim, oblique finger imprints over rim. A thin wash over the edge of the rim, 2.5YR 6/6-5/6 (light red to red).
Middle Helladic?

819 CLOSED VESSEL   Fig. 43
(E9-272) Base. D. 0.076, Max. pres. H. 0.029. Handmade. Coarse clay; several small to medium shiny black, light red, grey, white inclusions, little mica; 2.5YR 4/2-4 (weak red to reddish brown). Matt surface, 5YR 4/1-2 (dark grey to dark reddish grey). Slightly hollowed base. Potter's mark underneath base.
Middle Bronze Age (?).

820 CLOSED VESSEL   Figs. 43, 127
(A6-3-3) Handle. D. 0.023-0.028. Handmade. Coarse clay; several small to large white, small to medium black, red, grey inclusions, very little mica; 7.5YR 5/4 (brown) to 2.5YR 5/8 (red). Round handle with a potter's mark.
Middle Helladic.

821 CLOSED VESSEL   Fig. 43
(A6-65-29) Base. D. 0.09, Max. pres. H. 0.035, Th. 0.009. Handmade. Coarse clay; several small to large red (clay), small white inclusions, little mica; core 10YR 6/2 (light brownish grey), biscuit 2.5YR 5/6 (red). Flat, raised base. Smooth surface.
Middle Helladic.

822   CLOSED VESSEL   Fig. 43
(E74-3-9) Base. D. 0.075, Max. pres. H. 0.042, Th. of wall
0.07. Handmade. Coarse very hard clay; several small to large
white, black, shiny black and transparent inclusions, much mica;
5YR 3/1-2 (very dark grey to dark reddish brown), surface 5YR
4/3-4 to 2.5YR 4/6 (reddish brown to red). Hollowed base.
Probably import.
Middle Bronze Age.

823   TERRACOTTA WHORL   Figs. 43, 127
(E13) Biconical whorl. D. 0.042, Max. pres. H. 0.033, D.
of hole 0.006. Semicoarse clay; white, black inclusions; 7.5YR
6/4 (brown). Slipped (?) 7.5YR 6/2 (pinkish grey). Burnished.
Middle Helladic (?).

824   TERRACOTTA WHORL   Figs. 43, 127
(F5-B) Concave conical whorl. D. est. 0.043, Max. pres. H.
0.030, D. of hole 0.005. Semicoarse clay; white, black
inclusions; 10YR 5/1 (grey), surface 10YR 5/2 (greyish brown).
Burnished.
Middle Helladic (?).

LATE HELLADIC IIA

Piriform jar FS 20 / Bridge-spouted jug FS 103

825   PIRIFORM JAR   Figs. 44, 128
(B95-1) Body. Buff with a few grits and inclusions; black to
brown paint. FM 13, ogival canopy.
Late Helladic IIA.

Squat jug FS 87

826   SQUAT JUG   Figs. 44, 128
(A6-65-45) Body. Pale orange; buff slip, black to brown
paint. FM 63, hatched loop.
Late Helladic IIA.

Bridge-spouted jug FS 103

827   BRIDGE-SPOUTED JUG   Fig. 44
(F5-153) Handle. Buff; shaded-brown paint.
Late Helladic IIA.

Cup, rounded FS 211

828   ROUNDED CUP   Figs. 44, 128
(A6-75-89) Body. Buff; red-brown paint. FM 76, variegated
stone pattern, monochrome interior.
Late Helladic IIA.

Vapheio cup FS 224, Type III

829   VAPHEIO CUP   Fig. 44
(E9-238) Body. Buff; shaded-brown paint. FM 64, foliate
band.
Late Helladic IIA.

Goblet FS 254

830   GOBLET   Fig. 44
(F26-10) Base, D. 0.052. Pale yellow; thin brown wash.
Late Helladic IIA.

831   GOBLET   Fig. 44
(E13-81-1-67) Base, D. 0.082. Pale orange fired buff; brown
wash.
Late Helladic IIA.

LATE HELLADIC IIB

Vapheio cup FS 224 Type III

832   VAPHEIO CUP   Figs. 44, 128
(E9-175) Body. Buff; orange-brown paint. FM 64, foliate
band.
Late Helladic IIB.

Goblet FS 254

833   GOBLET   Figs. 44, 128
(E13-81-1-34) Body. Ephyraean. Buff fired pale orange; buff
slip, orange-brown paint. Chevron under handle.
Late Helladic IIB.

834   GOBLET   Figs. 44, 128
(E13-1-4) Body. Buff; orange-brown paint. FM 9, lily.
Late Helladic IIB.

835   GOBLET   Fig. 44
(E13-1-2) Rim. D. 0.13. Pale orange; buff slip, shaded-
brown paint.
Late Helladic IIB.

836   GOBLET   Fig. 44
(F5-7) Base. D. 0.064. Buff; orange-brown paint.
Late Helladic IIB.

LATE MATT PAINTED

Amphora / hydria

837   AMPHORA or HYDRIA   Fig. 44
(C11-SW-6) Rim. D. 0.126. Pale orange; greenish slip,
orange-brown paint. Handmade.
Late Helladic II - IIIA1.

838   AMPHORA or HYDRIA   Fig. 44
(E23-6) Rim. D. 0.15. Green with small grits; black to
brown paint. Handmade.
Late Helladic II - IIIA1.

839   AMPHORA or HYDRIA   Figs. 44, 128
(C11-SE-12) Body. Green; black paint. Handmade.
Late Helladic II - IIIA1.

840   AMPHORA or HYDRIA   Figs. 44, 128
(A6-83-3) Body. Green; sepia paint. Handmade.
Late Helladic II - IIIA1.

Krater

841   Krater   Fig. 44
(F5-A-8) Base. D. 0.132. Buff; orange-brown matt wash.
Late Helladic II - IIIA1.

LATE HELLADIC IIIA1

Piriform jar FS 19

842 PIRIFORM JAR Figs. 45, 128
(E13-25) Body. Buff with a few small grits fired pink; buff slip, orange-brown paint. Spiral.
Late Helladic IIIA1.

Krater FS 7

843 KRATER Fig. 45
(A6-72-100) Body. Buff; pale yellow slip, fugitive orange paint. Stems.
Late Helladic IIIA1.

Cup FS 213

844 CUP Fig. 45
(E9-165) Rim. D. 0.13. Pale yellow; red-brown paint.
Late Helladic IIIA1.

Cup, shallow FS 219

845 SHALLOW CUP Fig. 45
(E5-A-15) Rim. D. 0.14. Buff; fugitive shaded-brown paint. FM 77, stipple.
Late Helladic IIIA1.

846 SHALLOW CUP Fig. 45
(F4-4-6) Base. D. 0.042. Pale orange; buff slip, orange-brown paint.
Late Helladic IIIA1.

Goblet FS 254

847 GOBLET Figs. 45, 128
(E13-28 + E13-81-1-32) Body. Buff; brown paint. FM 12, ivy with double wavy stems.
Late Helladic IIIA1.

848 GOBLET Figs. 45, 128
(F5-83) Body. Buff fired pinkish; pale yellow slip, orange-brown paint. Stems.
Late Helladic IIIA1.

849 GOBLET Fig. 45
(E13-20) Body. Buff fired pale orange; buff slip, red-brown paint. FM 46, running spiral.
Late Helladic IIIA1.

850 GOBLET Fig. 45
(F5-B-72) Rim. D. 0.19. Buff; orange-brown paint. Edge of decoration.
Late Helladic IIIA1.

851 GOBLET Fig. 45
(B43-B-39) Rim. Pink-buff; pale yellow slip, orange-brown paint.
Late Helladic IIIA1.

852 GOBLET Fig. 45
(E5-B-24) Rim. D. 0.23. Orange; pale yellow slip, worn brown paint. Paint not extant inside.
Late Helladic IIIA1.

853 GOBLET Fig. 45
(F5-73-57) Body. Grey fired buff; black to brown paint.
Late Helladic IIIA1.

854 GOBLET Fig. 45
(C11-SW-3) Base. D. 0.06. Buff; orange-brown paint.
Late Helladic IIIA1.

Krater FS 279

855 KRATER Fig. 45
(F5-2) Rim. D. 0.17. Buff; pale yellow slip, red-brown paint. Beginning of horizontal handle.
Late Helladic IIIA1.

LATE HELLADIC IIIA2

Piriform jar FS 45

856 PIRIFORM JAR Fig. 45
(F17-16) Body. Buff; orange paint. FM 64, foliate band.
Late Helladic IIIA2.

Stirrup jar FS 164

857 STIRRUP JAR Fig. 45
(B2-B28-ALL-3-2) Body. Pale yellow fired pale orange; pale yellow slip, orange paint. FM 21, octopus.
Late Helladic IIIA2.

Mug FS 225

858 MUG Fig. 45
(E9-169) Rim. D. 0.15. Pale orange fired pale yellow; yellow slip, fugitive black paint. Ridged rim. FM 29, trefoil rockwork.
Late Helladic IIIA2.

Kylix FS 256, 257, 264

859 KYLIX Fig. 45
(E5-A-14) FS 257. Rim. Pale yellow; worn black paint. FM 19, tongue.
Late Helladic IIIA2.

860 KYLIX Fig. 45
(E5-B-27) FS 256. Rim. Pink; buff slip, orange-brown paint. Edge of tricurved arch.
Late Helladic IIIA2.

861 KYLIX Fig. 45
(C3-21) FS 257. Rim. D. 0.15. Buff; worn orange paint.
Late Helladic IIIA2.

862 KYLIX Fig. 45
(F5-77) FS 257. Body. Buff; orange-brown paint. FM 18, flower.
Late Helladic IIIA2.

863 KYLIX Fig. 45
(F5-26) FS 256. Stem. Pale orange; orange paint. Worn inside; interior could be monochrome.
Late Helladic IIIA2.

864 KYLIX   Fig. 45
(F5-16) FS 264. Rim and handle. Buff; orange-brown paint.
Late Helladic IIIA2.

865 KYLIX or STEMMED BOWL   Fig. 45
(F5-73-18) FS 264/stemmed bowl FS 304. Rim. D. 0.16.
Buff; orange-brown paint.
Late Helladic IIIA2.

866 KYLIX or STEMMED BOWL   Fig. 45
(E74-8-43) FS 264/stemmed bowl FS 304. Rim. D. 0.13.
Orange; orange paint.
Late Helladic IIIA2.

867 KYLIX or STEMMED BOWL   Fig. 45
(E9-151) FS 264/stemmed bowl FS 304. Rim. D. 0.17.
Greenish; black paint.
Late Helladic IIIA2.

868 KYLIX or STEMMED BOWL   Fig. 45
(A6-75-86) FS 264/stemmed bowl FS 304. Rim. D. 0.15.
Buff; black paint.
Late Helladic IIIA2.

869 KYLIX OR STEMMED BOWL   Fig. 45
(E9-147) FS 264/stemmed bowl FS 304. Base. D. 0.09.
Grey fired pink; orange paint.
Late Helladic IIIA2.

Stemmed bowl FS 304

870 STEMMED BOWL   Figs. 45, 128
(F5-86) Rim. D. 0.17. Pink-buff; buff slip, orange paint.
FM 75, panelled, monochrome interior.
Late Helladic IIIA2.

871 STEMMED BOWL   Fig. 45
(F5-32) Rim. D. 0.15. Buff; pale yellow slip, orange-
brown paint. FM 53, wavy band.
Late Helladic IIIA2.

872 STEMMED BOWL   Fig. 45
(E13-ALL-10) Rim and handle. Pale orange; buff slip,
orange-brown paint. Edge of handle splash.
Late Helladic IIIA2.

873 STEMMED BOWL   Fig. 45
(F32-N-3) Rim. D. 0.15. Pale yellow fired buff; fugitive
orange paint. Monochrome interior.
Late Helladic IIIA2.

874 STEMMED BOWL   Fig. 45
(F4-25) Body. Buff; fugitive brown paint. FM 13, ogival
canopy.
Late Helladic IIIA2.

875 STEMMED BOWL   Figs. 45, 128
(F4-42) Body. Buff; pinkish-buff slip, orange paint. FM
64, foliate band.
Late Helladic IIIA2.

876 STEMMED BOWL   Fig. 45
(B5-33) Body. Buff fired pink; buff slip, orange paint.
Late Helladic IIIA2.

Miscellaneous bowl

877 BOWL   Fig. 45
(F5-73-16) Rim. D. 0.12. Pink-buff; buff slip, red-brown
paint. Monochrome interior.
Late Helladic IIIA2.

LATE HELLADIC IIIB

Piriform jar FS 40

878 PIRIFORM JAR   Fig. 46
(F5-25) Body. Orange; buff slip, orange paint. FM 62,
tricurved arch.
Late Helladic IIIB.

Stirrup jar FS 164

879 STIRRUP JAR   Fig. 46
(C11-SW-32) False mouth. D. 0.059. Buff; orange-brown
paint.
Late Helladic IIIB.

Amphora FS 69 / Hydria FS 128 / Jug FS 105

880 AMPHORA or HYDRIA or JUG   Fig. 46
(F5-B-76) Rim. D. 0.13. Buff with large inclusions; red-
brown paint.
Late Helladic IIIB.

Narrow-necked jug FS 120

881 NARROW-NECKED JUG   Fig. 46
(A6-75-95) Rim. D. 0.06. Buff; fugitive brown paint.
Late Helladic IIIB.

Closed shape

882 CLOSED VESSEL   Fig. 46
(C11-C19-51) Base. D. 0.12. Grey fired orange; buff slip,
orange-brown paint.
Late Helladic IIIB.

Krater FS 9, 281

883 KRATER   Fig. 46
(F5-81) FS 281? Rim. D. 0.28. Buff; shaded-brown paint.
FM 75, panelled.
Late Helladic IIIB.

884 KRATER   Fig. 46
(B9-42) Rim. Orange; pale yellow slip, orange paint.
Late Helladic IIIB.

885 KRATER   Fig. 46
(E13-30) Rim. D. 0.22. Buff; orange-brown paint.
Late Helladic IIIB.

886 KRATER   Fig. 46
(B97-5-15) Rim. D. 0.26. Pale orange; buff slip, fugitive
shaded-brown paint.
Late Helladic IIIB.

887 KRATER   Fig. 46
(F4-56) FS 9. Base. D. 0.137-0.14. Buff; orange-brown paint. Nine holes pierced round inside of base giving rise to bumps on outside. Worn inside, could be closed shape.
Late Helladic IIIB.

888 KRATER   Fig. 46
(C11-SW-42) FS 9. Base. D. 0.12. Buff; black paint.
Late Helladic IIIB.

889 KRATER   Fig. 46
(B43-B-30) FS 9. Base. D. 0.13. Buff; orange-brown paint. Worn in, could be closed shape.
Late Helladic IIIB.

890 KRATER   Fig. 46
(F5-73-42) FS 281. Base. D. ca. 0.11. Buff fired pale orange; orange paint.
Late Helladic IIIB.

Mug FS 226

891 MUG   Fig. 46
(E13-81-1-10) Rim. D. 0.16. Buff with small grits; black paint. Edge of decoration.
Late Helladic IIIB.

892 MUG   Fig. 46
(F4-22) Body. Buff with small white grits; red-brown paint. FM 75, panelled with lozenge fill.
Late Helladic IIIB.

893 MUG   Figs. 46, 128
(F5-73-29) Body. Orange; buff slip, orange paint. FM 62, tricurved arch with fill.
Late Helladic IIIB.

Kylix FS 258, 259

894 KYLIX   Fig. 46
(F5-73-21) Rim. D. 0.17. Buff; orange-brown paint. FM 23, whorl-shell.
Late Helladic IIIB.

895 KYLIX   Fig. 46
(E9-250) Rim. D. 0.12. Greenish; fugitive black paint. Traces of decoration.
Late Helladic IIIB.

896 KYLIX   Fig. 46
(F5-4) Body. Buff; shaded-brown paint. FM 23, whorl-shell body.
Late Helladic IIIB.

897 KYLIX   Fig. 46
(E5-B-26) Body. Greenish; buff slip, fugitive brown paint. FM 19, multiple stem.
Late Helladic IIIB.

898 KYLIX   Fig. 46
(F5-B-83) Stem. Grey fired buff; orange paint. FM 23, whorl-shell tail tip.
Late Helladic IIIB.

899 KYLIX   Fig. 46
(F21-15) Stem. Buff; shaded-brown paint. Panel with ? flower.
Late Helladic IIIB.

900 KYLIX   Fig. 46
(F32-S-1) Zygouries type. Stem. Grey fired buff; orange paint. Panel.
Late Helladic IIIB.

901 KYLIX   Fig. 46
(C3-27) Zygouries type. Stem. Buff; orange paint. Panel.
Late Helladic IIIB.

902 KYLIX   Fig. 46
(F5-1) Stem. Buff fired pale orange; pale yellow slip, red-brown paint.
Late Helladic IIIB.

903 KYLIX   Fig. 46
(F4-1) Base. D. 0.095. Grey fired pale yellow; fugitive brown paint.
Late Helladic IIIB.

Kylix, carinated FS 267

904 CARINATED KYLIX   Fig. 46
(C24-10) Rim. D. 0.14. Buff; orange-brown paint.
Late Helladic IIIB.

Deep bowl FS 284

905 DEEP BOWL   Fig. 47
(B21-1) Rim, base and body. D. of rim 0.16, D. of base 0.062. Buff; fugitive shaded-brown paint. FM 50, antithetic spiral.
Late Helladic IIIB.

906 DEEP BOWL   Fig. 47
(F4-14) Rim. D. 0.115. Buff; pale yellow slip, fugitive orange paint. FM 23, whorl-shell.
Late Helladic IIIB.

907 DEEP BOWL   Fig. 47
(F4-11) Rim. D. 0.15. Buff; orange-brown paint. FM 23, whorl-shell.
Late Helladic IIIB.

908 DEEP BOWL   Fig. 47
(B21-1-1) Rim. D. 0.15. Buff; red-brown paint. Decoration not extant.
Late Helladic IIIB.

909 DEEP BOWL   Fig. 47
(C11-C19-19) Body. Buff; black to shaded-brown paint. FM 62?, tricurved arch.
Late Helladic IIIB.

910 DEEP BOWL   Fig. 47
(E9-188) Body. Buff; shaded-brown paint. Edge of decoration.
Late Helladic IIIB.

911   DEEP BOWL   Fig. 47
(E9-254) Body. Buff; red-brown paint. Edge of decoration.
Late Helladic IIIB.

912   DEEP BOWL   Fig. 47
(F5-27) Base. D. 0.056. Buff; orange paint.
Late Helladic IIIB.

913   DEEP BOWL   Fig. 47
(F4-6) Base. D. 0.06. White; fugitive sepia paint.
Late Helladic IIIB.

914   DEEP BOWL   Fig. 47
(F5-300) Base. D. 0.05. Buff; pale yellow slip; black to
red-brown paint.
Late Helladic IIIB.

915   DEEP BOWL   Fig. 47
(E13-81-1-74) Base. D. 0.054. Buff; orange-brown paint.
Late Helladic IIIB.

916   DEEP BOWL   Figs. 47, 128
(E13-81-1-12) Rim. Pinkish; buff slip, orange-brown paint.
FM 75, panelled, monochrome interior.
Late Helladic IIIB2.

Stemmed bowl FS 305

917   STEMMED BOWL   Fig. 47
(C11-C19-20) Rim. D. 0.15. Buff; yellow buff slip,
orange-brown paint. FM 75, panelled.
Late Helladic IIIB.

918   STEMMED BOWL   Fig. 47
(E13-ALL-5) Rim. D. 0.15. Buff; orange paint.
Late Helladic IIIB.

919   STEMMED BOWL   Fig. 47
(C11-SW-5) Body. Pale orange; buff slip, black to brown
paint.
Late Helladic IIIB.

920   STEMMED BOWL   Fig. 47
(A6-2-6) Handle. Pink with a few grits; buff slip, red-orange
paint.
Late Helladic IIIB.

921   STEMMED BOWL   Fig. 47
(F5-14) Body. Buff; pale yellow-buff slip, shaded-brown
paint.
Late Helladic IIIB.

922   STEMMED BOWL   Fig. 47
(B97-5-4) Base. D. 0.09. Buff fired pink-buff; buff slip,
orange-brown paint.
Late Helladic IIIB.

Conical bowl, spouted FS 300, 301

923   CONICAL BOWL, SPOUTED   Fig. 47
(F5-97) Base. D. 0.09. Pink; buff slip, orange-brown paint.
Late Helladic IIIB.

LATE HELLADIC IIIC EARLY

Collar-necked jar FS 63

924   COLLAR-NECKED JAR   Figs. 48, 128
(E13-81-1-49) Body. Buff; brown paint. FM 25, bivalve.
Late Helladic IIIC.

Amphora / hydria FS 69 / 128

925   AMPHORA or HYDRIA   Fig. 48
(F5-228) Rim. D. 0.14. Grey fired buff; worn brown paint.
Slight hollow lip.
Late Helladic IIIC.

926   AMPHORA or HYDRIA   Fig. 48
(F5-89) Body. Buff; whitish slip, red-brown paint.
Miscellaneous decoration.
Late Helladic IIIC.

Krater FS 281/282

927   KRATER   Fig. 48
(C11-C19-21) Rim. D. ca. 0.34. Pale orange; pale yellow
slip, orange-brown paint. Edge of decoration.
Late Helladic IIIC.

928   KRATER   Fig. 48
(F5-73-17) Rim. D. ca 0.30. Buff; shaded-brown paint.
Monochrome interior.
Late Helladic IIIC.

929   KRATER   Figs. 48, 128
(E13-1-3) Body. Mauve; pale yellow slip, orange-brown
paint. Edge of decoration, monochrome interior.
Late Helladic IIIC.

Kylix FS 274

930   KYLIX   Fig. 48
(F5-B-71) Base. D. 0.084. Buff; black paint. Reserved edge
to base.
Late Helladic IIIC.

Deep bowl FS 284

931   DEEP BOWL   Figs. 48, 128
(F5-B-79) Rim. D. 0.15. Buff; orange paint. FM 75,
panelled with FM 50, antithetic spiral, monochrome interior.
Late Helladic IIIC.

932   DEEP BOWL   Fig. 48
(E3-9) Rim. D. 0.15. Buff; black paint. Edge of splash,
monochrome interior.
Late Helladic IIIC.

933   DEEP BOWL   Fig. 48
(B21-6) Rim. D. 0.15. Buff; worn brown paint. Exterior
surface not extant, monochrome interior.
Late Helladic IIIC.

934   DEEP BOWL   Figs. 48, 128
(F5-B-57) Body. Orange; buff slip, red-brown paint. FM
46, running spiral, monochrome interior.
Late Helladic IIIC.

935 DEEP BOWL   Fig. 48
(F5-3B) Body. Buff with mica; orange paint. Spiral, monochrome interior.
Late Helladic IIIC.

936 DEEP BOWL   Fig. 48
(F5-346 + F5-169) Body. Buff; orange-brown paint. FM 50, loop of antithetic spiral, monochrome interior.
Late Helladic IIIC.

937 DEEP BOWL   Fig. 48
(E13-81-1-46) Body. Buff; red-orange paint. FM 51, stemmed spiral, monochrome interior.
Late Helladic IIIC.

938 DEEP BOWL   Figs. 48, 128
(F5-B-37) Body. Light brown; buff slip, brown paint. FM 61, zigzag, monochrome interior.
Late Helladic IIIC.

939 DEEP BOWL   Figs. 48
(F5-B-51) Body. Buff; orange-brown paint. FM 53, wavy line, monochrome interior.
Late Helladic IIIC.

940 DEEP BOWL   Fig. 48, 128
(F5-20) Body. Orange-buff with fine grits; orange to brown paint. FM 75, panelled, monochrome interior.
Late Helladic IIIC.

941 DEEP BOWL   Fig. 48
(F5-73-45) Base. D. 0.06. Buff; orange paint. Monochrome interior.
Late Helladic IIIC.

942 DEEP BOWL   Fig. 48
(E13-81-1-11) Rim. D. 0.16. Buff; black to brown paint.
Late Helladic IIIC.

943 DEEP BOWL   Figs. 48, 128
(G9-40) Body and handle. Greenish; black paint. Small handle, reserved area between stubs.
Late Helladic IIIC.

944 DEEP BOWL   Fig. 48
(E13-27) Base. D. 0.07. Buff; black paint.
Late Helladic IIIC.

<u>Stemmed bowl FS 306</u>

945 STEMMED BOWL   Figs. 48, 128
(E13-1-9) Stem. Pink-buff; orange-brown paint. Reserved interior base.
Late Helladic IIIC.

COARSE WARES / COOKING POT

<u>Pithos</u>

946 PITHOS   Fig. 49
(B21-53) Rim. D. 0.37. Buff with brown inclusions.
Late Helladic.

<u>Tripod cooking pot</u>

947 TRIPOD COOKING POT   Fig. 49
(E5-A-6) Rim. D. 0.22. Buff with inclusions fired brown. Edge of one leg; very long angular rim.
Late Helladic.

948 TRIPOD COOKING POT   Fig. 49
(B25-22) Rim. D. 0.14. Grey with grits fired brown; pale yellow slip out and over rim. Very long angular rim.
Late Helladic.

949 TRIPOD COOKING POT   Fig. 49
(F4-70) Rim. D. 0.16. Brown with grits. Very long angular rim.
Late Helladic.

950 TRIPOD COOKING POT   Fig. 49
(F4-83) Large oval leg. Pink with fine grits fired orange; brown wash.
Late Helladic.

951 TRIPOD COOKING POT   Fig. 49
(F5-73-66) Medium round leg. Buff with grits and inclusions fired orange; buff wash.
Late Helladic.

952 TRIPOD COOKING POT   Fig. 49
(A6-72-84) Leg, body, and handle. Buff with inclusions fired orange. Medium oval leg, vertical incision on handle stub.
Late Helladic.

<u>Button base cooking pot</u>

953 BUTTON BASE COOKING POT   Fig. 49
(B43-96) Rim. D. 0.14. Orange with grits and inclusions.
Late Helladic.

954 BUTTON BASE COOKING POT   Fig. 49
(A6-74-81) Base. D. 0.089. Pink with grits and inclusions fired orange.
Late Helladic.

955 BUTTON BASE COOKING POT   Fig. 49
(B2-B28-99) Base. D. 0.058. Pink with grits; orange-buff wash.
Late Helladic.

956 BUTTON BASE COOKING POT   Fig. 49
(E74-11-14) Base. D. 0.05. Buff with grits and inclusions fired orange. Pot mark.
Late Helladic.

957 BUTTON BASE COOKING POT   Fig. 49
(F4-11-22) Base. D. 0.071. Grey with small black grits fired orange; buff wash.
Late Helladic.

958 BUTTON BASE COOKING POT   Fig. 49
(F4-60) Base. D. 0.043. Orange with white inclusions; grey surface.
Late Helladic.

Miscellaneous rims and bases

959 COARSE WARE   Fig. 50
(E5-A-4) Rim. D. 0.15. Pink with inclusions; brown
wash. Burnt out.
Late Helladic.

960 COARSE WARE   Fig. 50
(E9-109) Rim. D. 0.15. Grey with small white inclusions;
brown wash.
Late Helladic.

961 COARSE WARE   Fig. 50
(B43-B45-16) Rim. D. 0.15. Grey with inclusions fired
orange; buff slip.
Late Helladic.

962 COARSE WARE   Fig. 50
(F5-190) Rim. D. 0.10. Brown with grits.
Late Helladic.

963 COARSE WARE   Fig. 50
(F4-67) Rim. D. 0.18. Orange with grits, smoothed.
Late Helladic.

964 COARSE WARE   Fig. 50
(F4-55) Base. D. 0.082. Buff with white inclusions fired
brown. One side burnt.
Late Helladic.

965 COARSE WARE   Fig. 50
(A6-72-197) Base. D. 0.091. Buff with fine grits and
inclusions.
Late Helladic.

966 COARSE WARE   Fig. 50
(A6-74-25) Base. D. 0.10. Pink with inclusions; orange-
buff wash.
Late Helladic.

967 COARSE WARE   Fig. 50
(B2-B28-95) Base. D. 0.116. Pink with fine grits; grey-buff
wash.
Late Helladic.

968 COARSE WARE   Fig. 50
(F4-2-10) Base. D. 0.072. Grey with mica fired orange-
buff.
Late Helladic.

969 COARSE WARE   Fig. 50
(F29-1) Base. D. 0.12. Brown with large white and grey
inclusions.
Late Helladic.

970 COARSE WARE   Fig. 50
(F32-D12-4) Base. D. 0.16. Pink with inclusions.
Late Helladic.

971 COARSE WARE   Fig. 50
(B43-B-50) Base. D. 0.067-0.07. Grey with white
inclusions fired orange-buff.
Late Helladic.

972 COARSE WARE   Fig. 50
(B46-10) Base. D. 0.09. Deep pink with white inclusions;
buff wash.
Late Helladic.

UNPAINTED

Jug FS 109

973 JUG   Fig. 50
(E74-8-23 + 47) Rim. D. 0.12. Buff, worn.
Late Helladic IIIB.

974 JUG   Fig. 50
(F5-108) Base. D. 0.06. Buff, smoothed.
Late Helladic III.

975 JUG   Fig. 50
(E74-10-10 + 4) Base. D. 0.087. Buff with inclusions;
greenish slip ? once polished.
Late Helladic III.

Alabastron FS 85

976 ALABASTRON   Fig. 50
(E74-10-24) Rim. D. 0.09. Buff worn. Possibly once
painted.
Late Helladic IIIA2-B.

Krater FS 7, 281

977 KRATER   Fig. 50
(E74-11-1) FS 7. Rim. D. 0.41. Pinkish fired orange-buff;
buff slip, worn.
Late Helladic IIIA1.

978 KRATER   Fig. 50
(E74-14-6) FS 281. Rim. D. ca. 0.44. Buff, worn.
Late Helladic IIIB.

979 KRATER   Fig. 50
(E5-A-17) FS 281. Rim. D. 0.31. Buff; greenish slip.
Late Helladic IIIB.

Lipless bowl FS 204

980 LIPLESS BOWL   Fig. 50
(F5-128) Base. D. 0.03. Buff, rough.
Late Helladic III.

Cup FS 219, 220

981 CUP   Fig. 51
(E74-5-2) Rim. Pale orange; buff slip, worn.
Late Helladic IIIA1.

982 CUP   Fig. 51
(E13-ALL-6) Rim. D. 0.14. Buff, polished.
Late Helladic IIIA1.

983 CUP   Fig. 51
(F5-283) Rim. D. 0.12. Buff, polished.
Late Helladic IIIA2.

984 CUP   Fig. 51
(F5-163) Rim. Pale yellow fired buff, polished.
Late Helladic IIIA2.

985 CUP   Fig. 51
(E13-1-7) Base. D. 0.04. Buff with one or two inclusions,
rough.
Late Helladic IIIB.

Dipper FS 236

986 DIPPER   Fig. 51
(F5-B-74) Rim. D. 0.12. Buff, Polished.
Late Helladic III.

Goblet FS 263

987 GOBLET   Fig. 51
(B43-7) Rim. D. 0.15. Buff, worn.
Late Helladic IIIA1.

988 GOBLET   Fig. 51
(F4-9) Rim. D. ca. 0.17. Pale buff; pale yellow slip,
polished.
Late Helladic IIIA1.

989 GOBLET   Fig. 51
(F5-58) Stem. Buff, polished.
Late Helladic IIIA1.

990 GOBLET   Fig. 51
(F20-7) Stem. Buff; greenish slip, standard.
Late Helladic IIIA1.

Kylix, carinated FS 267

991 CARINATED KYLIX   Fig. 51
(F1-43) Rim. D. 0.12. Pale orange; buff slip, polished.
Late Helladic IIIA1.

992 CARINATED KYLIX   Fig. 51
(F5-171) Rim. D. 0.12. Buff, standard.
Late Helladic IIIA1.

Kylix, rounded FS 265

993 ROUNDED KYLIX   Fig. 51
(C3-24) Body. Buff; pale yellow slip, worn.
Late Helladic III.

994 ROUNDED KYLIX   Fig. 51
(F4-18) Rim. D. ca 0.12. Buff; greenish slip.
Late Helladic III.

995 ROUNDED KYLIX   Fig. 51
(B25-13) Rim. D. ca. 0.13. Pale yellow; surface concreted.
Late Helladic III.

996 ROUNDED KYLIX   Fig. 51
(A6-72-99) Rim. D. 0.12. Greenish, rough.
Late Helladic III.

997 ROUNDED KYLIX   Fig. 51
(F5-A-12) Rim. D. 0.13. Buff, standard.
Late Helladic III.

998 ROUNDED KYLIX   Fig. 51
(B43-B45-10) Rim. D. 0.16. Orange, standard.
Late Helladic III.

Kylix, stems and bases

999 KYLIX   Fig. 51
(F4-50) Stem. Orange fired buff, polished.
Late Helladic III.

1000 KYLIX   Fig. 51
(F5-B-82) Stem. Buff, rough.
Late Helladic III.

1001 KYLIX   Fig. 51
(F32-N-210) Stem. Buff, standard.
Late Helladic III.

1002 KYLIX   Fig. 51
(A6-72-85) Base. D. 0.076. Grey with inclusions fired buff;
thick white slip, standard.
Late Helladic III.

1003 KYLIX   Fig. 51
(E13-1-11) Base. D. 0.054. Buff fired orange; buff slip,
rough.
Late Helladic III.

1004 KYLIX   Fig. 51
(F5-30) Base. D. 0.088. Pink-buff; buff slip, polished.
Late Helladic III.

1005 KYLIX   Fig. 51
(F4-45) Base. D. 0.07. Buff; standard.
Late Helladic III.

Deep bowl FS 284

1006 DEEP BOWL   Fig. 51
(F5-21) Base. D. 0.05. Pale orange-buff; whitish surface.
Late Helladic IIIC Early.

Basin FS 294

1007 BASIN   Fig. 51
(C3-12 + 20) Rim. D. 0.32. Buff fired orange; buff,
polished.
Late Helladic III.

Shallow angular bowl FS 295

1008 SHALLOW ANGULAR BOWL   Fig. 51
(B43-B-27) Rim. D. 0.20. Buff, polished.
Late Helladic IIIA2.

1009 SHALLOW ANGULAR BOWL   Fig. 51
(E13-81-1-17) Rim. D. 0.17. Greenish, rough.
Late Helladic IIIB.

Stemmed bowl FS 304, 305

1010 STEMMED BOWL   Fig. 51
(F5-73-14) Buff, polished.
Late Helladic IIIA2.

1011 STEMMED BOWL   Fig. 51
(B98-5-11) Rim. D. 0.17. Greenish, worn.
Late Helladic IIIB.

FIGURINES

1012 FIGURINE PROTO-PHI   Fig. 129
(E13) Buff fired pale orange; buff slip, orange-brown paint.
Max. pres. H. 0.045, width of body (max.) 0.037. Vertical wavy
lines down stem all round, chequer pattern across back, band of
paint down arms, blobs across chest.
Late Helladic IIIA1.

1013 FIGURINE HOLLOW PSI   Fig. 129
(B21-83) Buff; fugitive brown paint. Max. pres. H. 0.036,
width body (max.) 0.0415. Hollow Psi. Diagonal wavy lines on
body front and back, vertical lines round stem. End of applied
plait, moulded breasts. Hollow stem.
Late Helladic IIIB.

1014 FIGURINE PHI B   Fig. 129
(F4-3-3) Grey fired orange-buff; orange paint. Max. pres. H.
0.058, width (max.) 0.031. ? Phi B. Stem solid, vertical lines
round it. Paint not extant on body. Very worn.
Late Helladic IIIA2.

1015 FIGURINE POLOS HEAD   Fig. 129
(B9-46) Orange; traces of orange paint. Max. pres. H.
0.018, polos diameter 0.026. Polos head, paint not extant.
Late Helladic IIIB.

PROTOGEOMETRIC TO EARLY GEOMETRIC

1016 SKYPHOID KRATER   Figs. 52, 130
(E9-102) Rim. D. 0.29, H. 0.052, W. 0.078, Th. 0.005.
Hard fine pinkish fabric, 5YR 6/6-7/6 (reddish yellow). Solid
black paint inside, now fugitive. Exterior with black rim,
concentric circles flanking vertical cross-hatched panel.
Cf. Desborough 1952: 80 Type IIa, pl. 10 nos. 607, 1091,
pl. 28 no. 9; Frickenhaus *et al.* 1912: pl. 16 no. 9; Wells 1976:
108 fig. 89 no. 178, fig. 126 no. 90; Smithson 1961: pl. 27 no.
46 and Kerameikos Inv. 609.
Protogeometric.

1017 KRATER   Fig. 130
(E9-82) Body. H. 0.062, W. 0.041, Th. 0.012. Fine
pinkish orange fabric, 5YR 6/6 (reddish yellow) with very sparse
white inclusions, mica, and vacuoles. Solid brown interior;
exterior has set of twelve concentric circles with unusual "wheel
spoke" central filling.
Cf. Popham and Sackett 1979: 33 and pl. 16 no. 164, pl. 24
no. 633.
Late Protogeometric.

1018 SKYPHOS   Fig. 52
(E9-160) Rim. D. indet., H. 0.029, W. 0.020. Well
levigated warm buff fabric, 7.5YR 6/6 (reddish yellow) with

sparse white and micaceous inclusions. Strong black interior
with metallic sheen, exterior has horizontal bands on and just
below rim and concentric circles below.
Cf. skyphos from Argos in *BCH* 77 (1953) 262 fig. 55;
Desborough 1952: pl. 28 no. 5; Wells 1976: 196 fig. 144 nos.
245, 248.
Late Protogeometric.

1019 SKYPHOS OR KRATER
(E9-167) Lower body. H. 0.052, W. 0.033. Fine light
grayish brown fabric, 10YR 6/3 (pale brown), well levigated with
sparse gray and white inclusions and micaceous particles. Solid
black interior, exterior black with two widely spaced reserved
bands.
Protogeometric to Early Geometric.

1020 SKYPHOS   Fig. 52
(E9-145) Rim. Est. D. 0.15, H. 0.045, W. 0.028.
Smooth, hard pinkish orange fabric, 5YR 6/6 (reddish yellow)
with tiny inclusions of white, black, mica. Solid black interior
with reserved band at lip; exterior has two bands on rim, preserves
set of concentric circles.
Similar to **1018**. Cf. Wells 1976: 196 no. 245;
Desborough 1952: pl. 10 no. 2032, pl. 28 no. 5.
Protogeometric.

1021 SKYPHOS   Fig. 130
(E9-204) Body. Pres. H. 0.027, W. 0.018, Th. 0.005. Hard
light brownish gray fabric (10YR 6/2), well levigated with sparse
gray inclusions, mica flecks, vacuoles. Surface a light yellowish
buff, 10YR 7/4 (very pale brown), with dark brown paint.
Interior solid lustrous brownish black, 10YR 3/1 (very dark gray).
Exterior has dilute zigzag between double horizontal bands.
Cf. Wells 1976: 200 fig. 148 no. 278, 202 fig. 150 no. 321,
266 fig. 201 nos. 833-837; Desborough 1952: pl. 11 nos. 546,
1072, pl. 27 center; unpublished example from Tiryns; *ArchDelt*
26 (1971) B pl. 75b, EG skyphos from Corinth; Weinberg 1943:
pl. 1 nos. 1, 4, pl. 7 no. 38; Kraiker and Kübler 1939: pl. 38
lower left, pl. 67 inv. 546.
Protogeometric to Early Geometric.

1022 SKYPHOS
(E9-140) Body. H. 0.047, W. 0.038. Fine fabric, 5YR 6/4
(light reddish brown) with tiny vacuoles and inclusions of white,
black, mica. Solid black interior and lower exterior, three black
horizontals above.
Cf. Desborough 1952: pl. 10 nos. 2032, 1091; Wells 1976:
195 no. 231.
Protogeometric.

1023 SKYPHOS OR CUP   Fig. 52
(E9-276 + non-joining 257) Body. (a) H. 0.022, W. 0.030,
Th. 0.003; (b) H. 0.015, W. 0.020, Th. 0.003. Gritty buff
fabric, 7.5YR 7/6 to 5YR 7/6 (reddish yellow) with minute white
and micaceous inclusions. Interior solid brown; exterior preserves
solid lower body, thin verticals flanking cross-hatched panel.
Deep body suggests skyphos. Laconian import or Argive
imitation.
Cf. McDonald *et al.* 1985: 46 fig. 5 no. 143, 50 fig. 7 nos.
185, 186, 200.
Protogeometric.

1024   KANTHAROS (OR SKYPHOS)   Fig. 52
(E9-100) Rim. D. 0.15, H. 0.039, Th. 0.006. Well levigated warm buff fabric, 7.5YR 6/6 (reddish yellow), with sparse white, black, and micaceous inclusions. Solid lustrous black interior and exterior.
Cf. Desborough 1952: pl. 12 no. 919; *ArchDelt* 26 (1971) B pl. 66g.
Protogeometric.

1025   KANTHAROS   Figs. 52, 130
(E9-141) Rim. D. 0.145, H. 0.052, W. 0.042, Th. 0.006. Hard fabric with few inclusions, yellowish in color, 10YR 6/4 (light yellowish brown). Solid lustrous black inside and out; three reserved bands on exterior rim.
Cf. Desborough 1972: 155 pl. 30; Desborough 1952: pl. 12 no. 2026; Frickenhaus *et al.* 1912: 153 fig. 15; Courbin 1953: 324 fig. 1 left; Smithson 1961: skyphos with kantharos decoration, pl. 27 no. 45.
Late Protogeometric.

1026   KANTHAROS (OR SKYPHOS)   Fig. 52
(E9-138) Rim. D. 0.14, H. 0.045, W. 0.041, Th. 0.007. Fine pinkish orange fabric, 5YR 6/6 (reddish yellow), with sparse white and micaceous inclusions. Solid black inside and out; single reserved band under lip.
Cf. Kübler 1954: pl. 15 no. 8; Desborough 1952: pl. 12 no. 202; Courbin 1953: 324 fig. 1 left; *AAA* 1974: 22 fig. 19, from Tiryns.
Late Protogeometric to Early Geometric.

1027   KANTHAROS (OR SKYPHOS)
(E9-177) Rim. H. 0.042, Th. 0.006. Hard-fired fabric with few inclusions, light yellowish brown, 10YR 6/4. Solid black interior and exterior, with single reserved band inside and outside lip. Profile as above.
Cf. Frickenhaus *et al.* 1912: 153 fig. 15; Courbin 1953: 324 fig. 1 left, 3; *AAA* 1974: 22 fig. 19, from Tiryns.
Protogeometric to Early Geometric.

1028   CUP   Figs. 52, 130
(E9-243) Rim. D. 0.10, H. 0.025, W. 0.026, Th. 0.003. Thin, hard fine pinkish orange fabric, 5YR 6/6-6/8 (reddish yellow); well levigated with few inclusions and sparse mica particles. Solid lustrous black inside and out; reserved band inside rim and dilute scribble between horizontal bands in thin red paint on exterior.
Cf. Desborough 1972: 147, pl. 26; Wells 1976: 208, figs. 152, 153; Desborough 1952: pl. 11 nos. 1104, 1082; *BCH* 78 (1954) 176, 177, fig. 34; Kraiker and Kübler 1939: pl. 37 top row.
Protogeometric.

1029   HANDLE   Fig. 130
(E9-54) Handle. W. 0.022, L. 0.094. Fine pinkish buff fabric, 7.5YR 7/4 (pink), with white, brown, red inclusions and sparse mica. Exterior is pale grayish buff, 10YR 8/3 (very pale brown) with thin vertical strokes in two groups of nine strokes. Interior of vessel wall covered in thin brown paint. Flattened horizontal reflex handle of open vessel.
Cf. Popham and Sackett 1979: pl. 92 Tomb 2 no. 5, pl. 181 Tomb 24, 1; from Tiryns, Desborough 1952: pl. 28 no. 6.
Protogeometric.

1030   NECK-HANDLED AMPHORA OR HYDRIA   Figs. 52, 130
(E9-99) Rim. D. 0.23, H. 0.043, W. 0.070, max. Th. 0.010. Rough, sandy textured buff fabric, 7.5YR 7/6 - 5YR 7/6 (reddish yellow), with small inclusions. Outward thickened lip with interior indentation, painted black inside and out.
Cf. Desborough 1952: pl. 2 nos. 522, 2008, 672; Desborough 1972: 149, pl. 27; Smithson 1961: pl. 24 no. 1; Wells 1976: 82 no. 523; Kübler 1954: pl. 57. Slight indentation of lip interior may indicate Late Helladic date; cf. vessels from the Klepsydra, Smithson 1982: pl. 22b, LHIIIC hydria, fig. 3, EPG hydria OA314-7.
Protogeometric or Late Helladic IIIC.

1031   AMPHORA   Fig. 130
(E9-83) Body. H. 0.074, W. 0.09, Th. 0.008. Fine pinkish orange fabric, 5YR 6/8-7/8 (reddish yellow), with frequent small to medium red inclusions, fewer white, gray and mica flecks. Concentric circles on shoulder above solid black band varying red to black.
Cf. Desborough 1952: pl. 4 no. 563.
Protogeometric.

1032   OINOCHOE   Fig. 52
(E9-191) Shoulder. H. 0.03, W. 0.043, Th. 0.004. Fine buff fabric with few inclusions, 7.5YR 7/6 (reddish yellow). Solid brown neck, shoulder reserved with thin concentric circles.
Cf. Smithson 1961: pl. 25 no. 9.
Protogeometric.

1033   OINOCHOE OR AMPHORA   Fig. 130
(E9-84) Neck. D. 0.12, H. 0.052, W. 0.067, Th. 0.004. Hard-fired, fine pale pinkish buff fabric, 2.5YR 6/8 (light red). Solid matt black covers neck and extends a short way down the shoulder.
Cf. Courbin 1966: pl. 17 C.52 (EGI); Coldstream 1968: pl. 16b (Corinthian EG); *BCH* 83 (1959) 763 fig. 19 PG amphora.
Protogeometric to Early Geometric.

1034   OINOCHOE   Fig. 52
(E9-127) Vertical strap handle. W. 0.0165, L. 0.030. Fabric is finely levigated, strong pinkish orange, 5YR 6/6 (reddish yellow). Handle is horizontally banded in lustrous black.
Cf. Wells 1976: 285 fig. 224 no. 10390; Frödin and Persson 1938: 427 fig. 275.
Protogeometric.

1035   JUG   Fig. 52
(E9-76) Rim and handle. D. 0.125, H. 0.032, W. handle 0.021. Coarse, handmade fabric, varies pinkish buff to gray at core. Gray and white inclusions, rough texture, 5YR 8/4-7/6 (pink to reddish yellow). Cylindrical neck with flaring rim; rectangular handle attached at rim.
Cf. Smithson 1961: 170 nos. 52-53, pl. 30; Wells 1976: 217 fig. 162 no. 416, 275 fig. 207 nos. 917, 919.
Protogeometric.

EARLY GEOMETRIC

1036   SKYPHOS   Figs. 52, 130
(E9-1982-2) Rim, body, handle. D. 0.12, H. 0.072, Th. 0.0035. Soft orange buff fabric, 5YR 7/6 (reddish yellow) with small to medium white and gray inclusions, mica particles. Streaky brown paint inside and out, poorly preserved. Reserved rim with single band.

Cf. Weinberg 1943: pl. 11 no. 68; Kübler 1954: pl. 100, Inv. 781, Gr. 89; Courbin 1966: pl. 53 C.299 and C.613 (EGI); Smithson 1961: no. 45 pl. 27 (PG).

Early Geometric I.

1037   CUP   Figs. 52, 130
(E9-215) Rim and handle. D. 0.11, H. 0.022, Th. 0.004. Smooth buff fabric, 7.5YR 7/6 (reddish yellow), with sparse white, red, black inclusions. Interior and exterior covered in olive-brown paint with metallic sheen.

Cf. Verdelis 1963: 78 (1963) pl. 10, 2; Kübler 1954: pl. 105; Courbin 1966: pl. 70 C.164 (EGI).

Late Protogeometric to Early Geometric I.

1038   CUP   Fig. 52
(E9-235) Rim. D. 0.08, H. 0.013, Th. 0.004. Fabric is fine, hard, well levigated and pinkish in color, 5YR 6/6 (reddish yellow). Interior and exterior thickly covered in olive-brown paint with highly metallic sheen.

Cf. Courbin 1966: pl. 70 C.164, C.98 (EGI).

Early Geometric.

1039   CUP   Fig. 52
(E9-236) Rim. D. 0.08, H. 0.022, Th. 0.0033. Fabric is well levigated, hard-fired, and warm buff in color, 7.5YR 7/6 (reddish yellow). Interior and exterior covered in olive-brown paint with metallic sheen; possibly reserved band outside rim.

Cf. Courbin 1966: pl. 70 C.98 (EGI), C.851 (EGII).

Early Geometric.

MIDDLE GEOMETRIC

1040   KRATER   Figs. 53, 130
(B17-A-17) Rim. Est. D. 0.26, H. 0.027, W. 0.026, Th. 0.005. Very dark, hard, fine fabric, 10YR 4/3 (brown). Thick lustrous black paint inside and out. Reserved band inside lip, with two vertical strokes preserved; outside two thin reserved bands. Short everted rim.

Cf. **1041.** Säflund 1965: 86-87, figs. 70-73; Kübler 1954: pl. 84 inv. 930 (EG); Coldstream 1968: pl. 24b, Nauplion 4161, MGI pedestal krater.

Middle Geometric.

1041   KRATER   Figs. 53, 130
(B17-A-5) Rim. Est. D. 0.29, H. 0.021, W. 0.036. Medium brown fabric, 10YR 5/4 (yellowish brown). Purplish black paint, thinly applied. Exterior decoration: three horizontal bands on neck; interior: five vertical strokes on lip made without multiple brush. Short everted rim, somewhat higher than **1040.**

Cf. Säflund 1965: 86-87, figs. 70-73; Kübler 1954: pl. 84 inv. 930 (EG); Coldstream 1968: pl. 24b, Nauplion 4161, MGI pedestal krater.

Middle Geometric.

1042   KRATER   Figs. 53, 130
(B17-A-24) Pedestal. Est. D. 0.15, L. 0.062. Fine, light yellowish brown fabric, 10YR 6/4 (light yellowish brown). Brown-black paint only on exterior of foot, with three reserved bands at edge of foot. Low flaring pedestal with hollow ribbed stem.

Possibly from same krater as **1046, 1047,** and uncatalogued handle B17-A-35. Cf. Coldstream 1968: pl. 24b, Nauplion 4161, MGI; Säflund 1965: 86-87, figs. 70-72.

Middle Geometric (I?).

1043   KRATER   Fig. 53
(B17-A-28) Floor and pedestal fragment. Pres. H. 0.037, W. 0.040, floor Th. 0.007, stem Th. 0.011. Smooth, fine light brown fabric, 10YR 6/4 (light yellowish brown). Somewhat lustrous black paint applied thickly inside and out. Three broad ribs preserved on hollow stem.

Cf. Courbin 1966: pl. 27 C.204 (EGI); pl. 50 C.2665, C.1062, C.4027 (MGI, II); Säflund 1965: 86- 87, figs. 70-72.

Middle Geometric.

1044   KRATER   Figs. 53, 130
(A9-10-14) Pedestal rim. D. 0.17, H. 0.051, W. 0.045, Th. 0.0105-0.009. Fine light brown fabric, 10YR 6/4 (light yellowish brown), with occasional small to medium brown and white inclusions, mica flecks, tiny vacuoles. Outside painted in alternating black and reserved bands. Broadly splayed foot with plain rim.

Cf. Säflund 1965: 86-87, figs. 70-72; Coldstream 1968: pl. 24b (Berbati, MGI).

Middle Geometric.

1045   KRATER   Fig. 53
(B17-A-48) Body. H. 0.027, W. 0.019, Th. 0.005. Fine light grayish brown fabric, 10YR 6/3 (pale brown). Solid black interior, exterior preserves left edge of reserved panel with reserved horizontal band below. Slight curvature suggests krater rather than pyxis or skyphos.

Cf. Coldstream 1968: pl. 22 b, h (EGI).

Early to Middle Geometric.

1046   KRATER   Fig. 53
(B17-B-17) Body. H. 0.048, pres. W. 0.044, Th. 0.005. Smooth light yellowish brown fabric, 10YR 6/4. Brown-black interior. Exterior painted with panel of horizontal zigzags bordered by vertical and horizontal lines.

Possibly same krater as **1042, 1047,** and uncatalogued handle B17-A-35. Cf. Coldstream 1968: pl. 24b (MGI); Säflund 1965: 86-87, figs. 70-72.

Middle Geometric.

1047   KRATER   Figs. 53, 130
(B17-B-19) Body. Pres. H. 0.0485, W. 0.043, Th. 0.005. Fine buff fabric, 7.5YR 7/6 (reddish yellow). Few micaceous particles, small white inclusions, well levigated. Interior painted solid brown; exterior with stacked rows of horizontal zigzags (four preserved) above horizontal bands (five preserved). Deep rounded bowl.

Possibly same vessel as **1046, 1042.** Cf. Coldstream 1968: pl. 24b (MGI).

Middle Geometric.

1048   BODY (KRATER?)   Fig. 53
(C12-C14-82-4) Body. H. 0.033, W. 0.038, Th. 0.006. Semi-fine buff fabric with frequent micaceous particles, small white inclusions and vacuoles. Fabric varies light yellowish buff, 10YR 7/3 (very pale brown) on surface to grayish brown (10YR 5/2) at core. Open shape, probably krater or pyxis. Interior solid brown; exterior preserves dogtooth row between horizontal bands.

Cf. *ArchDelt* 18 (1963) B pl. 72; Courbin 1966: pl. 151 amphora from Argos; *BCH* 85 (1961) 67 fig. 9.

Middle Geometric.

1049   SKYPHOS   Figs. 53, 130
(E9-172) Rim. D. 0.14, H. 0.026, W. 0.042, Th. 0.004.
Hard smooth pinkish orange fabric, 5YR 6/6 (reddish yellow),
some micaceous flecks. Paint is glossy, verging on metallic.
Interior is solid very dark grayish brown (10YR 3/2) with vertical
bars on reserved band at rim. Exterior has banded lip and
horizontal zigzags. Probably Attic.
  Cf. Smithson 1974: pl. 78 a.3, pl. 79c NM 15320, 3;
Säflund 1965: 89 fig. 75; Coldstream 1968: pl. 3b and e (Attic
MGI); Kübler 1954: pls. 89, 90, various.
  Middle Geometric I.

1050   SKYPHOS   Figs. 53, 130
(A9-6-25) Rim. Est. D. 0.18, H. 0.021, W. 0.033, Th.
0.004. Fine smooth orange buff fabric, 5YR 6/8 (reddish
yellow). Interior solid streaky brown with reserved band at top of
rim. Exterior: four horizontal bands, below which is a series of
verticals, six preserved. At right edge near handle zone (?) the
paint is thinner with a red hue. Short everted lip above broad
shoulder.
  Cf. Coldstream 1968: pl. 24g (MGII); Bommelaer 1980: 54
fig. 1.
  Middle Geometric.

1051   SKYPHOS   Figs. 53, 130
(A9-10-5) Rim. Est. D. 0.18, pres. H. 0.025, W. 0.032,
wall Th. 0.004. Smooth, hard pinkish orange fabric, 5YR 6/6
(reddish yellow), with minute white, black, micaceous inclusions
and vacuoles. Lustrous black paint inside and out. Everted lip
reserved both sides with one horizontal band on exterior.
  Cf. Courbin 1966: pl. 56 C.838 (MGI); Coldstream 1968:
pl. 24g (MGII).
  Middle Geometric II.

1052   SKYPHOS OR CUP   Figs. 53, 130
(A9-10-18) Rim. Est. D. 0.11, H. 0.023, W. 0.022, wall
Th. 0.004. Fine, well levigated fabric, pinkish orange in tone,
5YR 6/6 (reddish yellow) with micaceous inclusions. Interior is
solid brownish black; reserved interior of lip has four vertical
strokes. Exterior of lip has two horizontal red bands. Shoulder
features two parallel rows of zigzags, painted by hand, not
multiple brush.
  Similar to **1049**. Cf. Kerameikos 2156 and 867,
Coldstream 1968: pl. 3e and 3b (Attic MGI); also Coldstream
1968: pl. 24g (Argive MGII).
  Middle Geometric.

1053   RING FOOT   Fig. 53
(A9-10-16) Fragment of foot, bottom, and wall. D. 0.11, L.
0.038, wall Th. 0.05. Fine well levigated fabric, reddish yellow
(7.5YR 7/6-6/6). Interior and exterior covered in streaky
brownish black paint, underside reserved. Foot has flattened
bottom and bevelled edge; probably from skyphos.
  Cf. *ArchDelt* 16 (1960) B 93, pl. 71b (MGII skyphos).
  Middle Geometric II.

1054   PYXIS   Fig. 53
(C12-9) Rim. Interior D. 0.18, H. 0.030, W. 0.063, Th.
varies 0.014 to 0.007. Fine, hard-fired pinkish buff fabric, 5YR
6/6 (reddish yellow). Interior rim painted black; exterior has
hatched meander in fugitive paint. Preserves hole for lid
attachment on shoulder.

Shape: Cf. **1055**. Related to Courbin 1966: pl. 78 C.895
(EGI) and C.839 (EGI); Popham and Sackett 1979: pl. 34, 8 Inv.
481, MGII.
  Middle Geometric.

1055   PYXIS   Fig. 53
(A9-10-7) Body near rim. H. 0.037, W. 0.037, Th. varies
0.005 to 0.011. Strong smooth pinkish fabric, 5YR 6/6 to 5/6
(reddish yellow). Interior reserved. Exterior has horizontal bands
alternating black and hatched, probably preserves section of
hatched meander.
  Cf. **1054**. For motif: Courbin 1966: pl. 76 C.2530 (MGI);
Kübler 1954: pl. 73 Inv. 300; Coldstream 1968: pl. 5a (MGII
Attic).
  Middle Geometric.

1056   PYXIS   Figs. 53, 131
(B17-A-25) Lid rim. D. 0.14, H. 0.036, W. 0.064. Pale
yellowish buff fabric, 10YR 7/6 (yellow), with few small
inclusions. Brownish black paint and white slip thinly applied;
exterior black with three white bands near rim. Lid slopes down
to plain edge.
  Cf. Courbin 1966: pl. 79 top (MGI).
  Middle Geometric.

1057   COARSEWARE STORAGE VESSEL   Fig. 54
(B17-A-19) Rim. D. 0.22, H. 0.045, L. 0.069. Coarse
heavy fabric, gray in color with black and dark gray inclusions;
surface smoothed. Heavy vertical neck, splayed rim with
horizontal groove.
  Middle Geometric II.

1058   AMPHORA
(B17-A-40) Neck and handle root. W. at break 0.028.
Orange buff fabric, 5YR 6/8 (reddish yellow). Decoration: three
horizontal reserved bands on neck meet strap handle attachment.
  Cf. Coldstream 1968: pl. 24j (MGII).
  Middle Geometric.

1059   AMPHORA   Fig. 54
(B17-A-7) Lip. Est. D. 0.18, H. 0.02, W. 0.055, max. Th.
0.009. Smooth dark grayish brown fabric, 10YR 5/3 (brown).
Black paint, exterior with vertical strokes, X between one pair.
  Cf. Courbin 1966: pl. 4 C.28, C.30 (MGII); Coldstream
1968: pl. 25a (MGII).
  Middle Geometric.

1060   AMPHORA   Figs. 54, 131
(B17-B-4) Strap handle. H. 0.104, W. 0.056, Th. 0.0175.
Strong grayish brown fabric, 7.5YR 5/2 (brown) to 10YR 6/4
(light yellowish brown), with many tiny vacuoles and sparse
micaceous particles. Long X in fugitive matt black paint above
two groups of three horizontal bands.
  Cf. Courbin 1966: pl. 110 C.30 (MGII).
  Middle Geometric.

1061   AMPHORA OR OINOCHOE
(B17-A-34) Strap handle. H. 0.051, W. 0.043. Strong
brown fabric, 7.5YR 5/4 (brown) with numerous vacuoles, white
and micaceous inclusions. Banding on shoulder below handle;
handle is bisected vertically, each side neatly banded horizontally.
  Cf. Courbin 1966: pl. 18 C.53, C.2435 (MGI); Kübler
1954: pl. 151 inv. nos. 2140, 890, 866 (9th c.).
  Middle Geometric.

1062   AMPHORA   Fig. 54
   (A9-10-1) Body. H. 0.064, W. 0.080, wall Th. 0.008. Fine warm buff fabric, 7.5YR 6/6 (reddish yellow). Decorated with reserved St. George's cross inside concentric circles; vertical dotted lozenge chain.
   Cf. Courbin 1966: pl. 151 MG amphora; *BCH* 79 (1955) 239 fig. 17; Coldstream 1968: pl. 34m.
   Middle Geometric II.

1063   OINOCHOE   Fig. 131
   (A9-10-28) Shoulder. W. 0.052, Th. 0.005. Smooth buff fabric, 7.5YR 7/6-6/6 (reddish yellow). Exterior solid brownish black with group of three thin reserved bands. Shoulder angle suggests plump body.
   Cf. Courbin 1966: pl. 18 C.53 (MGI), C.2435 (MGI); pl. 22 C.65 (MGI).
   Middle Geometric.

1064   OINOCHOE OR AMPHORA
   (A9-10-29) Shoulder. W. 0.082, Th. 0.007. Smooth buff fabric, 7.5YR 7/6 (reddish yellow). Exterior solid black. Broad shoulder preserves ridge and groove at neck junction.
   Cf. Coldstream 1968: pl. 23a (EGII); pl. 24c, d, f (MGI, II); Courbin 1966: pl. 17 C.52; pl. 18 C.53, C.2435 (MGI).
   Early to Middle Geometric.

1065   OINOCHOE   Fig. 131
   (C12-ALL-22) Neck. H. 0.047, W. 0.048, Th. 0.0055. Semi-fine buff fabric, 7.5YR 7/6 (reddish yellow) with some large red and brown inclusions, many small vacuoles, and sparse micaceous particles. Panel on neck with three rows of zigzags between horizontal bands.
   Cf. Coldstream 1968: pl. 23a (EGII), pl. 24c (MGI); Desborough 1955: pl. 49e.
   Early to Middle Geometric.

1066   MASTOS OINOCHOE   Figs. 54, 131
   (B17-B-16) Shoulder. H. 0.037, max. W. 0.029. Fine pinkish fabric, 5YR 6/6 (reddish yellow) rather soft in texture; fine vacuoles and black and micaceous inclusions. Black matt paint on exterior. One reserved band at upper shoulder; below, a reserved panel containing three vertical bands at right, a raised mastos with encircling band and solid center, horizontal zigzags below. Thin-walled closed vessel, probably oinochoe.
   Cf. Coldstream 1968: pl. 2c (EGII), pl. 3m (MGI), pl. 24f (MGII); Courbin 1966: pl. 20 C.830 (MGII); *ArchDelt* 16 (1960) B 93, pl. 71c, MGII; Hägg 1971: 45 figs. 6 a and b.
   Middle Geometric.

1067   STAND   Figs. 54, 131
   (B17-B-1) Rim. D. 0.26, H. 0.047. Fine hard buff fabric, 7.5YR 6/6 (reddish yellow), with few white and black inclusions. Interior reserved. Lustrous dark reddish paint on exterior. Broad horizontal rim with two raised ridges at junction to body.
   Cf. Courbin 1966: pl. 88 C.219 (EGI).
   Middle Geometric.

MIDDLE TO LATE GEOMETRIC

1068   KRATER   Figs. 54, 131
   (A9-6-26) Rim. Est. D. 0.36, H. 0.035, W. 0.060. Hard-fired, fine pinkish orange fabric, 5YR 6/6 (reddish yellow), with few vacuoles and inclusions. Interior streaky black. Exterior has row of dots under band on edge of rim; below, two broad horizontal bands, vertical metope divider with angled lines in corner (hatched meander?). Dogtooth design on top of rim.
   Cf. Bommelaer 1972: 236 fig. 9 C.7375.
   Middle to Late Geometric I.

1069   KRATER   Figs. 54, 131
   (A9-10-26) Pedestal rim. D. 0.17, H. 0.035, W. 0.0425, Th. 0.0075. Well levigated warm buff fabric, 7.5YR 6/6 (reddish yellow) with sparse tiny red and black inclusions, mica particles, small vacuoles. Surface covered in red with two reserved bands at edge. Underside reserved. Rim of flaring pedestal foot.
   Cf. Säflund 1965: 86-87, figs. 70-72; Coldstream 1968: pl. 24b.
   Middle to Late Geometric.

1070   KRATER   Figs. 54, 131
   (G1-B-22) Pedestal. H. 0.049, W. 0.0635. Very hard light brown fabric (7.5YR 6/4) with some medium-sized inclusions; mica not evident. Flaring ribbed pedestal covered in lustrous black paint.
   Cf. Courbin 1966: pl. 50 C.2665, C.1062, C.4027 (MGI, II); Säflund 1965: figs. 70-72.
   Middle to Late Geometric.

1071   KRATER   Figs. 54, 131
   (F5-12) Pedestal. D. 0.113, pres. H. 0.048, wall Th. 0.006. Fine, hard pinkish fabric, 5YR 6/6 (reddish yellow), with few white, black, and micaceous inclusions. Interior reserved. Exterior covered in lustrous black paint with metallic sheen covers exterior except for three reserved bands at rim. Pedestal with flaring foot.
   Cf. Säflund 1965: figs. 70-72; Coldstream 1968: pl. 24b (MG); Brann 1962: pl. 5, nos. 92 P21706, 93 P25633 (LG).
   Middle to Late Geometric.

1072   HANDLE   Fig. 131
   (G1-B-23) Rope handle. D. 0.0235, L. 0.055. Fine hard pinkish buff fabric, 7.5YR 7/4 (pink) with small brown and gray inclusions; mica not evident. Covered with lustrous brownish black paint.
   Cf. Courbin 1966: pls. 30, 31 C.13 (LGIIb).
   Middle to Late Geometric.

1073   KRATER OR PYXIS   Fig. 131
   (E9-107) Body. H. 0.049, W. 0.042, Th. 0.008. Fine, hard deep pinkish fabric, 5YR 6/6 (reddish yellow) with small to medium inclusions of white, orange, gray; sparse micaceous particles. Paint varies reddish to dark brown, 10YR 3/3 (dark brown). Solid black interior, exterior with horizontal bands, one angle-hatched (probably meander), the other with a row of dots. Body fragment of large open vessel. Attic?
   Cf. Courbin 1966: pl. 38 C.878 (MGII), pl. 81 top (MGII).
   Middle to Late Geometric I.

1074   KRATER   Fig. 54
   (C12-C14-82-1) Body. H. 0.026, W. 0.034, Th. 0.005. Well levigated light brown fabric, 10YR 6/4 (light yellowish brown), with micaceous particles, small vacuoles, red and white inclusions. Solid thin black paint covers interior, exterior has hatched quatrefoil with filling motif between leaves.
   Cf. Courbin 1966: pl. 121 C.4654 (MGII), pl. 39 C.423 (MGII).
   Middle II to Late Geometric.

1075   KRATER   Fig. 54

(B2-B28-7) Shoulder at neck junction. Est. D. 0.36, H. 0.035, Pres. W. 0.051. Warm buff fabric, 7.5YR 7/8 (reddish yellow). Interior painted thin brownish black. Exterior with hatched quatrefoil beside vertical lines. Rosette between leaves, the latter with central midrib and angled hatching.

Cf. Hägg 1962: 4 pl. VI, 8 LGI krater.

Middle II to Late Geometric.

1076   KRATER   Fig. 54

(F5-105) Body. H. 0.036, W. 0.033, Th. 0.01. Warm buff fabric, 7.5YR 7/8 (reddish yellow). Interior solid black, exterior preserves double axe between verticals and above horizontals.

Cf. Courbin 1966: pl. 121 C.4646 (MG), C.4405 (LG).

Middle to Late Geometric.

1077   SKYPHOS

(B2-B28-26x) Handle and body. W. 0.068, H. 0.043. Fine, hard-fired pinkish orange fabric, 5YR 6/6 (reddish yellow). Interior is solid black, exterior is cream slipped with black horizontal handle round in section, eight-pointed star above handle attachment. Handle set nearly horizontally on broad, shallow body. Attic?

Cf. Smithson 1974: ARI-9, pl. 70 e-h for motif; Kraiker 1951: pl. 2 nos. 31, 32; Kübler 1954: pl. 89 inv. 2156; pl. 91 inv. 829; pl. 92 inv. 241; Courbin 1966: pl. 57 C.1576 and C.564 for shape.

Middle II to Late Geometric.

1078   SKYPHOS   Fig. 54

(B17-B-7) Ring foot. D. 0.085, W. 0.063. Fine gray fabric, 2.5Y 6/2 (light brownish gray). Solid black paint both inside and out. Very low ring foot, hardly more than disc base; of deep broad bowl shape.

Cf. Courbin 1966: pl. 56 C.2477 (MGI), pl. 60 C.64 (LGI).

Middle to Late Geometric I.

1079   SKYPHOS   Fig. 54

(C12-C14-E-6-1) Foot. D. 0.060, H. 0.014. Very fine hard buff fabric, 7.5YR 7/6 (reddish yellow). Semi-lustrous black paint inside and out. Narrow foot with bevelled edge.

Cf. Courbin 1966: pl. 66 C.2511 (MGII); Courbin 1957: 332 fig. 15.

Middle to Late Geometric.

1080   SKYPHOS   Fig. 54

(C12-C14-C-4-13) Shoulder. H. 0.0335, W. 0.033, Th. 0.0043. Fine pale greenish gray fabric, 5Y 7/1 (light gray). Dark brown solid interior. Exterior with single thick zigzag between horizontal bands.

Cf. Courbin 1966: pl. 59 C.2304 (LGII); Frickenhaus *et al.* 1912: pl. XVIII, 2 and 5 (MGII).

Middle to Late Geometric.

1081   SKYPHOS OR KANTHAROS

(A9-10-21) Shoulder. Th. 0.004. Fine, smooth strong orange fabric, 5YR 6/8 (reddish yellow), with tiny white inclusions and sparse mica. Interior solid red; exterior has parallel vertical wavy lines in dilute paint on shoulder.

Cf. Desborough 1954: pl. 44, nos. 53-321, 322, 325; *Hesperia* 25 (1956) pl. 48c; Coldstream 1968: pl. 25 c-e (MGII); Courbin 1966: pl. 60 C.64 and C.2521.

Middle II to Late Geometric I.

1082   PYXIS OR SKYPHOS   Fig. 54

(A9-10-17) Ring foot. D. 0.09, W. 0.072, wall Th. 0.045. Well levigated yellowish buff fabric, 10YR 7/4 (very pale brown). Thick glossy black interior, thin brownish paint on lower exterior, fugitive near foot.

Cf. Courbin 1966: pl. 79 C.2434 (MGI), pl. 60 C.64 (LGI).

Middle to Late Geometric I.

1083   KOTYLE   Figs. 54, 131

(E9-69) Rim. Est. D. 0.14-15, H. 0.026, W. 0.040, Th. 0.004. Hard smooth warm buff fabric, 7.5YR 7/6 (reddish yellow). Many tiny micaceous particles, small white and dark gray inclusions. Red orange paint, solid interior. Exterior has horizontal chevrons between horizontal bands, flanked by verticals.

Cf. Weinberg 1943: 1 nos. 107, 108, 110 (EPC); Coldstream 1968: pl. 19j (LG); Smithson 1974: 338 AR I-9 (MGII/LGI); Neeft 1975: 108, fig. III, 1; *BSA* 48 (1953) 276 nos. 624, 626 and pl. 41 (MG Corinthian cups at Ithaca).

Middle II to Late Geometric.

1084   KANTHAROS   Fig. 54

(C12-17) Vertical strap handle and body. Total H. 0.063, handle W. 0.022, Th. 0.008, wall Th. 0.005. Fine fabric, strong pinkish orange color, 5YR 6/8 (reddish yellow), vacuoles. Exterior decoration preserves handle banded in fugitive orange-red paint, reserved rectangle below. High-handled kantharos is not common in Argolid; possibly Attic.

Cf. Coldstream 1968: pl. 4d (Attic MGII), pl. 10c (Attic LGI); Kübler 1954: pl. 85 inv. 258, pl. 86 inv. 400, 373; Tiryns Gr. III:7, Verdelis 1963: pl. 23 (LGI).

Middle II to Late Geometric.

1085   PLATE   Fig. 55

(C17-61) Rim and handle. Inner D. 0.33, W. 0.093, Th. 0.08. Pinkish buff fabric, 7.5YR 7/4 (pink), with large white inclusions. Round horizontal handle set at flat rim. Solid black interior, rim reserved with black dots.

Cf. Säflund 1965: 88, no. 9 inv. 3608, fig. 67 (MGI).

Middle to Late Geometric.

1086   STAND

(C12-ALL-2-15) Rim. Outer D. 0.29, W. ca. 0.05. Pale yellowish buff fabric, 10YR 7/4 (very pale brown), with few white, black, and micaceous inclusions. Black paint on all surfaces. Broadly flaring rim preserves part of raised ridge below.

Cf. Courbin 1966: pl. 88 C. 219, C.27; *BCH* 91 (1967) 837 fig. 8.

Middle to Late Geometric.

1087   STAND   Figs. 55, 131

(C12-C14-C-4-11) Rim. D. 0.23, H. 0.040, W. rim 0.0245, L. 0.135. Semi-fine light brown fabric, 10YR 7/4 (very pale brown); inclusions are small to medium white, gray, red; small to medium vacuoles; micaceous particles. Surface feels soft and powdery. Exterior and resting surface in thick reddish brown to maroon paint, 10R 4/4 (weak red). Broadly flaring rim with downturned lip, raised ridge below.

Joins with uncatalogued C12-C14-A-4-1. Cf. stand from Argos, Courbin 1966: pl. 88 C.219; from Argive Heraion, Waldstein 1905: 118 fig. 43.

Middle to Late Geometric.

1088   STAND   Figs. 55, 131
(C12-ALL-1) Rim. Outer D. 0.255, H. 0.051, rim W. 0.02. Hard-fired pinkish fabric, 5YR 7/6 (reddish yellow), finely levigated with few vacuoles or inclusions; mica. Resting surface and exterior solid black to carination, bands above. Possibly from the bottom of the stand because rim is only slightly turned up; raised ridge and carination above rim.
Cf. Courbin 1966: pl. 88 C.219 (EG).
Middle to Late Geometric.

1089   STAND   Figs. 55, 131
(C17-47) Body. D. at carination 0.17, H. 0.055, W. 0.072, Th. 0.07. Fine hard light brown fabric, 7.5YR 6/4. Exterior decoration in black paint: wide horizontal bands, double axe between verticals. Tapering body with carination.
Cf. Courbin 1966: pl. 121 C.4646 (MG).
Middle Geometric II to Late Geometric.

1090   STAND
(C17-60) Rim. D. inner angle 0.165, H. 0.038, W. 0.045. Smooth pale brown fabric, 10YR 6/3. Banded(?) exterior, rim in solid red-brown paint. Rounded flaring rim preserves edge of ridge(?).
Cf. Courbin 1966: pl. 121 C.4646 (MG); *BCH* 91 (1967) 837 fig. 8; Waldstein 1905: 118 fig. 43.
Middle II to Late Geometric.

1091   HANDLE   Fig. 131
(C12-ALL-2-22) Rope handle. D. 0.023, L. 0.075. Fine greenish gray fabric burned to very dark gray, 10YR 5/2 (grayish brown); well levigated with few white inclusions; mica not evident. Covered in lustrous brown to black paint. Apparently vertical orientation, possibly from oinochoe.
Cf. Courbin 1966: pl. 4 C.28, C.31 (MGII).
Middle to Late Geometric.

1092   HYDRIA OR AMPHORA   Figs. 55, 132
(G1-A-80) Neck and handle. Est. D. 0.112, H. 0.070, W. 0.064, Th. 0.010. Coarse fabric with smoothed surface, varies in color from pinkish beige surface, 7.5YR 7/4 (pink), to gray core. Small to medium white, black, brown, and micaceous inclusions. Vertical paring or burnishing lines visible. Cylindrical neck with flaring rim and sloping shoulder, round handle attached at bottom of neck.
Cf. Courbin 1966: pl. 94 C.815 (MGII); pl. 91 C.2426 (LGI).
Middle II to Late Geometric.

1093   AMPHORA OR OINOCHOE   Figs. 55, 132
(A9-6-9) Rim. Est. D. 0.13, W. 0.022, L. 0.033, Th. 0.005. Coarse, gritty medium brown fabric, 10YR 6/4 (light yellowish brown), with abundant small to medium gray and white inclusions and sparse mica flecks. Flaring rim, thickened edge with light groove; top of rim has incised zigzag. Handmade.
Cf. Courbin 1966: pl. 93 C.1420 (EGI) and C.1651 (LGI) for zigzag on lip; Verdelis 1963: pl. 12 no. 6; Desborough 1955: pl. 47b.
Middle to Late Geometric I.

1094   AMPHORA OR HYDRIA   Fig. 55
(C17-80) Rim. D. 0.18, H. 0.062, rim W. 0.03, wall Th. 0.007. Coarse fabric with pinkish buff surface, gray core, sandy texture, many white inclusions. Vertical burnishing marks on

neck. Cylindrical neck with flaring rim and flattened lip. Handmade.
Cf. Weinberg 1943: pl. 13 no. 82; Pfaff 1988: 63 fig. 22 no. 69; 64 fig. 23.
Middle II to Late Geometric.

1095   HANDLE
(F5-311) Twisted strap handle. L.0.041, W.0.013, Th. 0.008. Smooth, well levigated yellowish brown fabric, 10YR 7/4 (very pale brown), with small white and gray inclusions. Half of double twisted handle from small plainware vessel.
Cf. Courbin 1966: pl. 94 C.815 (MGII).
Middle to Late Geometric.

1096   PITHOS   Figs. 55, 132
(A9-3-13) Rim. Est. D. 0.42, H. 0.084, W. 0.092, Th. 0.01. Very coarse fabric with unsmoothed surface, color varies warm buff on surface, 5YR 6/6 (reddish yellow), to darker core; micaceous and white inclusions. Thickened horizontal rim above broad shoulder.
Cf. Courbin 1966: pl. 106 C.3966 (LGI), C.4002 (LGII); *BCH* 81 (1957) 658 fig. 43 (LGI).
Middle II to Late Geometric (or Early Helladic II? cf. **461**).

1097   PITHOS   Figs. 55, 132
(A9-2-1) Rim. D. 0.58, H. 0.079, max. W. rim 0.051, L. 0.17. Hard, coarse fabric of warm buff color, 7.5YR 6/6 (reddish yellow), with abundant red, gray, and white inclusions ranging from small to large. Mica not apparent. Interior wall surface not preserved.
Cf. Frickenhaus *et al.* 1912: 131 fig. 5.
Middle II to Late Geometric.

LATE GEOMETRIC I

1098   KRATER   Figs. 56, 132
(C12-1 and various C12/14 sherds) Rim and body fragments. D. 0.34, wall Th. 0.0085. Semi-fine fabric with small vacuoles, sparse micaceous particles, few white and gray inclusions. Surface is light gray buff, 10YR 7/3 (very pale brown) to darker at core, 10YR 5/2 (grayish brown). Dark grayish brown paint, thick on solid interior with tendency to flake.
(a) C12-1A. Rim. H. 0.0915, W. 0.101. Exterior neck with row of dots between horizontal bands; shoulder with vertical bands, stacked zigzags; gear pattern above metopes with hatched quatrefoil, thin meanders diagonally hatched.
(b) C12-C14-ALL-15 + C12-1C. Body. H. 0.062, W. 0.111. Hatched quatrefoil, stacked zigzags, cross-hatched lozenges in vertical columns.
(c) C12-C14-ALL-5 + C12/14-ALL-2-13. Rim. H. 0.049, W. 0.108. Dots on neck, cross-hatched lozenges, stacked zigzags.
(d) C12-1B. Body. H. 0.052, W. 0.057. Diagonally hatched thin meander below gear pattern.
Cf. Courbin 1966: pl. 39 C.289 (MGII) and C.423 (MGII); Hägg 1962: pl. VI, 8; Desborough 1954: pl. 45, Mycenae T. II.
Late Geometric I.

1099   KRATER   Fig. 56
(C12-C14-82-5) Body. H. 0.044, W. 0.044, Th. 0.0085. Semi-fine fabric with small vacuoles, sparse micaceous particles, few white and gray inclusions. Fabric varies light grayish buff, 10YR 7/3 (very pale brown), on surface to darker gray at core, 10YR 5/2 (grayish brown). Row of cross-hatched lozenges between vertical bands.

Possibly from same krater as **1098**. Cf. Courbin 1966: pl. 39 C.289 (MGII).
Late Geometric I.

1100   KRATER   Fig. 56
(C12-C14-D-2-25) Body. H. 0.052, W. 0.049, Th. 0.0085. Semi-fine fabric with small vacuoles, sparse micaceous particles, few white and gray inclusions. Fabric varies light grayish buff, 10YR 7/3 (very pale brown), on surface to darker gray at core, 10YR 5/2 (grayish brown). Gear pattern above horizontal bands and row of dots.
Possibly from same krater as **1098**. See also LGIIa skyphos from Panoply grave, Argos, Courbin 1957: 332 fig. 14.
Late Geometric I.

1101   KRATER   Fig. 56
(C12-C14-ALL-50) Body. H. 0.054, W. 0.048, Th. 0.009. Semi-fine fabric with small vacuoles, sparse micaceous particles, few white and gray inclusions. Fabric varies light grayish buff 10YR 7/3 (very pale brown), on surface to darker gray at core, 10YR 5/2 (grayish brown). Row of dots above horizontal bands and solid lower body.
Possibly from same krater as **1098**. Cf. Coldstream 1968: pl. 27 a, c, d (LGI).
Late Geometric I.

1102   SMALL KRATER OR SKYPHOS   Fig. 56
(C17-A-1) Rim. D. 0.185, H. 0.050, W. 0.040, wall Th. 0.005. Semi-fine pinkish buff fabric, 7.5YR 7/4 (pink). Interior solid with reserved band and vertical strokes inside rim. Exterior has horizontal bands on rim, one reserved band with row of dots; on shoulder, vertical hatched columns separated by vertical line.
For motif, cf. Coldstream 1968: pl. 10h (LGIb), pl. 15a, f (LGIIa); Pfaff 1988: 41, fig. 3. For shape: Hägg 1978: 97 no. 23, fig. 84.
Late Geometric I.

1103   KRATER OR PYXIS   Figs. 56, 132
(E40-ALL-12) Rim. D. 0.18, H. 0.036, W. 0.045, wall Th. 0.007, rim Th. 0.0069. Semi-fine pinkish fabric, 5 to 7.5YR 7/4 (pink), with no significant inclusions. Exterior with three black bands above vertical squiggles in shoulder zone.
Decoration: Deshayes 1966: pl. LII, 1; Desborough 1954: pl. 44 nos. 321, 322, 333 from outside Grave G.II, Mycenae (LGI); Courbin 1966: pl. 116 C.3615 and C.3057 (LGI).
Late Geometric I(?).

1104   KRATER   Figs. 56, 132
(C12-C14-D-3-29 + E-2-5) Shoulder near rim. H. 0.115, W. 0.0655, max. rim Th. 0.015, avg. body Th. 0.011. Semi-fine warm brown fabric, 7.5YR 6/6 (reddish yellow), with micaceous particles, small white inclusions, and vacuoles (some large). Interior solid streaky black. Exterior neck has row of dots between horizontal bands; shoulder has four rows of horizontal zigzags, horizontal bands, and thin meander with angled hatching.
Cf. combination of zigzags and angle-hatched thin meander on Courbin 1966: pl. 39 C.423 (MGII) but broader shoulder.
Late Geometric I.

1105   KRATER
(B17-B-22) Shoulder. Th. 0.009. Semi-fine medium brown fabric, 7.5YR 6/4 (light brown), with small vacuoles, brown and white inclusions, mica flecks. Interior solid blackish brown;

exterior has horizontal banding, angle-hatched meander, and vertical chevrons.
Cf. Courbin 1966: pl. 126 C.4226, C.4599 (LGI) for chevrons; Coldstream 1968: pl. 27a (LGI).
Late Geometric I.

1106   KRATER   Fig. 56
(B17-B-15) Body. H. 0.055, W. 0.067, Th. 0.0095. Smooth, fine warm buff fabric, 7.5YR 6/6 (reddish yellow). Interior painted brownish black. Exterior has two birds in panel enclosed on left by seven vertical lines; above birds are two horizontal lines, row of connected chevrons.
Possibly from same vessel as **1107**. Cf. Bommelaer 1972: fig. 10 krater C.7747 (LGI); Courbin 1966: pl. 126 C.4226 (LGI).
Late Geometric I.

1107   KRATER   Fig. 56
(B17-B-21) Body. H. 0.057, W. 0.069, Th. 0.0105. Smooth, hard-fired light reddish brown fabric, 5YR 6/4. Interior painted dark brown. Exterior: two-legged bird at right end of panel, bordered by horizontals above and below; eight vertical lines extend down to panel below.
Same vessel type as **1106**. Cf. Courbin 1966: pl. 126 C.4226 (LGI).
Late Geometric I.

1108   KRATER   Fig. 132
(C12-2) Shoulder. H. 0.082, W. 0.063, Th. 0.009. Smooth soft fabric varies yellowish buff at surface, 10YR 7/3 (very pale brown) to pinkish orange, 5YR 7/6 (reddish yellow), with sparse mica and very few inclusions. Interior painted solid black. Exterior has sloppy vertical chain of dotted lozenges beside eight thin verticals and a solid zone.
Cf. Verdelis 1963: pl. 14 no. 3 from Tiryns.
Late Geometric I.

1109   DOUBLE HANDLE   Fig. 133
(B17-B-3) Double handle. H. 0.089, W. 0.075, Th. 0.041. Semi-fine, soft orange buff fabric, 7.5YR 7/6 (reddish yellow), with sparse white and micaceous inclusions, occasional large white and chert inclusions. Brownish black paint applied thickly to outline of handle, thinly for horizontal bands within. Double handle in Attic style from large, probably funerary vessel such as amphora, pyxis, or krater.
Cf. Coldstream 1968: pl. 6, 7a (Attic LGI); Brann 1961a: 117 and pl. 17, K5.
Late Geometric I.

1110   AMPHORA   Figs. 56, 133
(C17-54) Neck. D. 0.16, H. 0.049, W. 0.0695, Th. 0.013. Smooth light brownish gray fabric, 2.5YR 6/2 (pale red) with small black inclusions and sparse micaceous particles. Thin black paint preserves obliquely hatched meander in panel.
Cf. Courbin 1966: pl. 4 C.28 (MGII).
Late Geometric I.

1111   AMPHORA   Figs. 56, 133
(B17-B-20) Neck. H. 0.07, W. 0.083, Th. 0.012. Semi-fine, light grayish brown fabric, 10YR 6/3 (pale brown) with few inclusions. Decoration in brown paint: in reserved zone above horizontal bands, hatched meander in panel bordered by three vertical bands; beneath meander, two hatched vertical leaves with midribs.

Cf. amphora neck in Young 1939: 74 fig. 48, xvi. For leaf and battlement meander combined on Argive skyphos, *ArchDelt* 17 (1961) B pl. 58a.
Late Geometric I.

1112 BODY   Fig. 133
(C12-C14-C-3-13) Body. H. 0.059, W. 0.054, Th. 0.0085. Smooth light brown fabric, 7.5YR 6/4, with small gray and white inclusions, sparse micaceous particles. Surface has greenish tinge. Exterior decorated with hatched thin meander bordered by horizontals and verticals. Body fragment of large vessel with unpainted interior; possibly funerary pyxis or krater.
Cf. Courbin 1966: pl. 79 C.43 (MGII); Coldstream 1968: pl. 26 C209 (LGI) and pl. 27a (LGI).
Late Geometric I.

LATE GEOMETRIC II

1113 KRATER   Fig. 133
(B16-3) Rim. H. 0.048, W. 0.063. Warm buff fabric, 7.5YR 6/6 (reddish yellow), with few vacuoles and minute white, black, red inclusions. Exterior: groups of strokes on top of rim; streaky horizontal band on rim, verticals on shoulder leading down to horizontal band.
Profile similar to **1114** and **1115**.
Late Geometric II.

1114 KRATER   Fig. 57
(C12-C14-D-3-1) Rim. D. 0.28, H. 0.034, W. 0.051, Th. 0.006. Smooth light buff fabric, 10YR 7/4-7/6 (very pale brown to yellow). Lustrous black paint inside and out. Short strokes on rim, horizontal bands on neck, vertical bands on shoulder. Short vertical collar above narrow shoulder.
Profile similar to unpublished krater from Argos C.273.
Late Geometric II.

1115 KRATER   Fig. 57
(B2-B28-ALL-1-11) Rim. D. 0.24, H. 0.036, W. 0.054, Th. 0.0064. Smooth well levigated yellowish buff fabric, 10YR 7/6 (yellow). Traces of black paint inside. Exterior has row of vertical strokes between horizontal bands.
Profile similar to unpublished krater from Argos C.273 and LG krater rim C.4166 (Courbin 1966: pl. 128, profile not illustrated).
Late Geometric II.

1116 KRATER   Figs. 57, 133
(A6/9-B-38) Rim. D. 0.30, W. 0.079, Th. 0.007. Smooth, well levigated buff fabric, 7.5YR 7/6 (reddish yellow). Interior painted streaky brown. Exterior has dots around rim between horizontal bands; on shoulder, stack of horizontal zigzags with perpendicular hatching. Vertical rim, taller than on the three preceding kraters.
For profile, cf. Courbin 1957: 332 fig. 14 skyphos (LGIIa). Decorative scheme, cf. Courbin 1966: pl. 57 C.17 skyphos (LGIIb), pl. 122 various (LGII); Desborough 1954: pl. 45 nos. 53-337 (LGI).
Late Geometric.

1117 KRATER   Fig. 57
(C12-C14-C-3-1) Rim. D. 0.26, H. 0.057, W. 0.060, Th. 0.006. Smooth, fine grayish brown fabric, 10YR 5/3 (brown). Painted solid black interior. Exterior rim has sigmas and horizontal bands; shoulder has verticals beside solid black handle zone. Tall, slightly flaring rim.

For profile, cf. Hägg 1978: 109 no. 62; krater from Tiryns, Verdelis 1963: 78 (1963) pl. 14 no. 3. Scheme, cf. Courbin 1966: pl. 116 C.2775 (LGII), pl. 47 C.2509 (LGIIc); krater from Dendra, Hägg 1965: pl. 3, I:2.
Late Geometric II.

1118 KRATER   Fig. 57
(C12-C14-D-3-30+D-4-2) Rim. D. 0.32, H. 0.067, W. 0.074, Th. 0.007. Light tan fabric, some large white inclusions, 10YR 6/4-5/4 (light yellowish brown). Solid interior. Exterior: short strokes on rim, elongated dots on neck, and shoulder preserves part of panel with cross-hatched triangle and tail of bird. Short outturned rim with flattened top. Possibly imported.
For motif cf. Coldstream 1968: pl. 12g (Attic LGIIa), pl. 37e, 38e and f ("Parian" LG), pl. 44f and h (Boeotian LG); Kübler 1954: pl. 97, inv. 328; pl. 139, inv. 356.
Late Geometric II.

1119 KRATER   Figs. 57, 133
(B2-B28-11) Rim. D. 0.036, H. 0.037, W. 0.047. Smooth, hard fabric varies pinkish, 5YR 6/8 (reddish yellow), to gray at core. Reddish brown paint on exterior and interior body with black zigzag on top of rim; two horizontal bands on reserved neck. Short outturned rim with flattened top.
Cf. Bommelaer 1972: fig. 17 C.26608 (LGII).
Late Geometric.

1120 KRATER   Figs. 57, 133
(G1-A-1) Rim. D. 0.24, H. 0.059, W. 0.062, Th. 0.0055. Smooth light greenish gray fabric, 5Y 7/1-7/2 (light gray), slightly sandy texture; occasional vacuoles and small gray inclusions; mica not evident. Interior black with reddish band around inside neck/shoulder junction. Exterior: group of five strokes on rim, horizontal bands on neck and shoulder; upper shoulder has groups of sigmas. Short vertical rim.
Decorative scheme, cf. Courbin 1966: pl. 64 C.880 (LGIIc).
Late Geometric II.

1121 KRATER   Figs. 58, 133
(B40-1) Rim. D. 0.38, H. 0.108, W. rim 0.139, Th. wall 0.010. Smooth light brown fabric, 7.5YR 6/4-7/4 (light brown to pink), with few inclusions of white, brown, mica. Brown paint covers interior to top of rim. Exterior has blind lozenges on rim, horizontal bands, vertical row of cross-hatched lozenges, verticals framing a panel of horizontal zigzags and bands. Short vertical rim flattened at top.
Cf. Courbin 1966: pl. 114 C.1144 (LGIIc); Frickenhaus *et al.* 1912: 145 fig. 9 and pl. 19 no. 4.
Late Geometric II.

1122 KRATER   Fig. 58
(B16-4) Rim. D. 0.375, H. 0.031, Th. rim 0.015, W. 0.070. Well levigated, semi-fine warm buff fabric, 7.5YR 6/6 (reddish yellow), with tiny vacuoles, few inclusions. Crude triangles painted at intervals on reserved rim, exterior neck covered in black paint. Short vertical rim thickened and flattened at top.
Cf. profiles: Courbin 1966: pl. 113 C.210 (LGIIb); Bommelaer 1972: fig. 17 C.7747.
Late Geometric II.

1123 KRATER   Fig. 58
(C12-C14-D-4-1 + C12-ALL-2-17) Rim. D. 0.25, H. 0.048, W. 0.115. Semi-fine pinkish buff fabric, 7.5YR 6/6 (reddish yellow), with vacuoles and few inclusions. Paint varies

solid red on interior to black on exterior. Short strokes on rim top, sloppy dots turning into squiggles between horizontal bands on neck; wavy line on shoulder.

Shape as Bommelaer 1972: fig. 17 C.26608. Undulating line, Courbin 1966: pl. 14 C.1052 (LGIIb).

Late Geometric II.

1124 KRATER   Figs. 58, 133

(B2-B28-8) Rim. D. 0.31, Th. lip 0.016, pres. W. 0.069. Smooth pinkish fabric with few small inclusions, 7.5YR 7/4-7/6 (pink to reddish yellow). Thinly applied decoration in black paint: top of lip solid with short vertical strokes on outside; below on neck horizontal zigzag.

Shape: Bommelaer 1972: fig. 7 and fig. 17 C.26611. Decoration: Hägg 1978: 107 fig. 100, cat. 62.

Late Geometric II.

1125 KRATER OR KANTHAROS   Figs. 58, 133

(E40-ALL-1-19) Rim. D. 0.18, H. 0.038, W. 0.049. Light yellowish brown fabric, 10YR 6/4, with dark gray surface, apparently burned. Interior solid black, exterior has vertical bands beside solid ringed oval. Tall vertical rim offset from shoulder.

Cf. Dugas and Rhomaios 1943: pl. 32 no. 88; for shape, Courbin 1966: pl. 28 C.1, pl. 29 C.14.

Late Geometric II.

1126 KRATER   Fig. 58

(B16-49) Rim. D. indet., H. 0.028, W.0.015, Th. 0.005. Fine warm buff fabric with few white and occasional micaceous inclusions, 7.5YR 7/6 (reddish yellow). Rim decorated in narrow dotted lozenges below horizontal band. Thin flaring rim.

Cf. Courbin 1966: pl. 31 C.13b (LGIIb); pl. 32 MN 231 (LGIIb); pl. 33 C.3393 (LGII).

Late Geometric II.

1127 SMALL KRATER OR SKYPHOS   Fig. 58

(E9-103) Body of large open shape. H. 0.039, W. 0.021, Th. 0.004. Smooth medium to light tan fabric, 10YR 5/4 (yellowish brown), with occasional white particles. Interior solid black; exterior lower body of vessel solid; legs of two-toed bird facing left preserved above three horizontals. Possibly imported.

Cf. Kübler 1954: pl. 97 inv. 327, 325, 376 (Attic LGIb); Coldstream 1968: pl. 36c (Naxian LG), pl. 38b, e ("Parian" LG), pl. 44f (Boeotian LG).

Late Geometric II.

1128 KRATER   Fig. 133

(F5-B-38) Shoulder. H. 0.042, W. 0.078, Th. 0.010. Smooth light brown fabric, 7.5YR 7/4-6/4 (pink to light brown), with occasional medium white inclusions and sparse micaceous particles. Irregularly preserved black paint: panel framed at left by vertical bands, preserving eight one-legged birds.

Cf. Courbin 1966: pl. 130 C.3312 (LGII), pl. 132 C.3717 (LGII).

Late Geometric II.

1129 KRATER OR PYXIS BODY   Figs. 58, 134

(C17-D-2) Body. H. 0.054, W. 0.069, Th. 0.018 - 0.012. Hard pinkish fabric, 5YR 7/6 (reddish yellow) with black and white inclusions varying small to large, occasional micaceous particles, irregular vacuoles. Interior reserved. Exterior decoration in black: tethered horse in panel below vertical hatched zigzags; filler ornaments of zigzag, rosette, vertical dots, triple framed panel behind horse containing hatched gear pattern. Neat,

uncrowded drawing. Body fragment of large probably closed or semi-closed shape, like large pyxis.

For motifs: panel behind horse, Roes 1953: pl. 29, second row left; Jantzen *et al.* 1975: cat. 89, pl. 83.1, 84.1, 2; Courbin 1966: pl. 135 C.2590, pl. 138 C.4210. Hatched angular lozenges as in Frickenhaus *et al.* 1912: pl. 15, 5 or zigzag as in Courbin 1966: pl. 115 C.4656 (LGII).

Late Geometric II.

1130 KRATER   Fig. 58

(A9-5-16) Body. H. 0.034, W. 0.073, Th. 0.006. Smooth, hard fabric, warm buff in color, 7.5YR (pink) to 6/4 (light brown). Interior painted in streaky dark brown, giving effect of bands. Exterior: four legs and tail of horse facing left, with fish angled up beneath horse. Fish rendered in double outlines connected by short strokes, has short curving "fins." Curving column of vertical chevrons between fish and back leg of horse, shorter column between leg and tail of horse. Panel bordered on right by vertical bands.

Cf. general scheme on krater from Melos, Athens NM 877, Coldstream 1968: pl. 29d; LGIIb kantharos in Nauplion from Mycenae, Coldstream 1968: pl. 29f and Courbin 1966: pl. 62. For fish see Courbin 1966: pls. 28 C.1 (LGIIb) and 48 C.242 (LGIIb).

Late Geometric II.

1131 KRATER   Fig. 58

(A9-6-7) Body. H. 0.037, Th. 0.0065. Finely levigated warm buff fabric, 7.5YR 6/6 (reddish yellow). Interior solid red, exterior preserves leaf in triple outline above horizontal band. Attic or Atticizing.

Cf. Coldstream 1968: pls. 9n, 13b (Attic LG); Bommelaer 1972: 234 fig. 8 C.7393 (Argive LG).

Late Geometric II.

1132 KRATER   Fig. 134

(F32-SF-22) Body. L. 0.070, Th. 0.009. Pinkish fabric, 5YR 6/6 (reddish yellow). Solid streaky brown interior; exterior with horizontal bands, row of short verticals and Xs. Body fragment from large open shape.

Cf. Courbin 1966: pl. 40 C.240 (LGI); Frödin and Persson 1938: 327 no. 6; Bommelaer 1972: 236 fig. 10 C.7747.

Late Geometric II.

1133 BODY   Fig. 134

(G1-A-23) Body. H. 0.07, W. 0.11, Th. 0.01. Strong dark orange color, 2.5YR 6/8 (light red), with small black and medium white inclusions, micaceous particles. Interior solid reddish brown, exterior decoration alternates groups of horizontals with bands of dotted lozenges and zigzags. Fragment of very large open or flat shape, with no detectable curvature.

For motif, cf. *BCH* 95 (1971) 738 fig. 4 C.26608, Argos.

Late Geometric II.

1134 KRATER   Fig. 134

(C12-C14-E-3-6) Body. H. 0.057, W. 0.0265, Th. 0.01. Smooth pale buff fabric, 10YR 8/4-7/4 (very pale brown), contains small to medium vacuoles, small white inclusions, sparse micaceous particles. Interior painted solid brown. Exterior has neatly drawn horizontal multiple hatched zigzags above horizontal bands.

Cf. Courbin 1966: pl. 11 (LGIIb), pl. 31 C.13 (LGIIb), pl. 35 C.286 (LGII), pl. 41 C.210 (LGIIb).

Late Geometric II.

1135   KRATER   Fig. 134
(C12-C14-E-3-19) Handle and body. D. handle 0.019, L. 0.077. Fabric has small to large evenly distributed inclusions of white, brown, brick-red. Fabric varies pinkish, 5YR 7/6 (reddish yellow) to brown at core, 7.5YR 5/4 (brown). Horizontal round handle with vertical strokes between bands. Bands encircle handle end on body in flaking black paint.
Cf. Courbin 1966: pl. 113 C.915 (LGII), pl. 47 (LGIIc).
Late Geometric II.

1136   KRATER   Figs. 58, 134
(B2-B28-ALL-1-28) Pedestal. D. 0.040, H. 0.043. Well levigated pinkish fabric, 2.5YR 6/6 (light red). Decorated in alternating bands of cream slip and reddish brown paint. Underside reserved.
Cf. small krater from Asine inv. 2230, Hägg 1965: pl. 4, II:2 (LGI); 7th-c. pedestal kraters from Phlius, Biers 1971: 405 nos. 15, 16.
Late Geometric II to Subgeometric.

1137   KRATER   Fig. 58
(C12-C14-C-3-5) Stirrup handle fragment. L. 0.033, W. 0.015, Th. 0.003. Smooth, well levigated fabric with few tiny white and micaceous inclusions; warm buff in color, 7.5YR 7/8 (reddish yellow). Small flat vertical section of stirrup handle with vertical wavy band.
Cf. Verdelis 1963: 1963, pl. 14 no. 3 from Tiryns; Courbin 1966: pl. 111 C.15 (LGIIb).
Late Geometric II.

1138   KRATER   Figs. 58, 134
(G1-A-6) Pedestal rim. Outer D. 0.335, inner D. 0.31, H. 0.040, W. 0.061. Fairly smooth warm buff fabric, 7.5YR 6/6 (reddish yellow) with medium white inclusions and micaceous particles. Interior reserved, exterior with streaky, elusive black paint. Outturned rim with small ridge above.
Cf. krater from the Agamemnoneion, Cook 1953: fig. 8, A2.
Late Geometric II.

1139   SKYPHOS OR KANTHAROS   Figs. 59, 134
(G22-5-7) Rim. D. 0.14, H. 0.032, W. 0.032. Hard-fired, finely levigated fabric of warm buff color, 7.5YR 6/6 (reddish yellow), few vacuoles and inclusions. Bands on exterior of lip, top of lozenge chain preserved on shoulder.
Cf. Courbin 1966: pl. 61 C.2466 (LGI).
Late Geometric II.

1140   SKYPHOS OR KANTHAROS
(C17-50) Rim. D. 0.15, H. 0.048, Th. 0.004. Smooth greenish gray fabric with small white and black inclusions, 5Y 7/4 (pale yellow). Interior solid, exterior rim with horizontal bands, shoulder in parallel vertical zigzags. Short flaring rim close to **1139**.
Cf. Courbin 1966: pl. 64 C.880 for decoration (LGIIc); **1140** has shorter rim and neater painting.
Late Geometric II.

1141   SKYPHOS   Fig. 59
(F5-67) Rim. D. 0.18, H. 0.033, W. 0.039. Red interior, exterior rim banded, one dot preserved at shoulder.
Cf. Courbin 1966: pl. 64 C.880, pl. 65 C.269 (LGIIc).
Late Geometric II.

1142   SKYPHOS   Figs. 59, 134
(B2-B28-12) Rim. Est. D. 0.12, H. 0.024, W. 0.028. Smooth, warm light brown fabric, 7.5YR 7/6 (reddish yellow to darker). Solid black interior; exterior of lip banded in thin brown paint. High rim, slightly flaring.
Cf. Courbin 1966: pl. 59 C.2464 (LGI), C.562 (LGII) from Mycenae.
Late Geometric II.

1143   SKYPHOS   Fig. 134
(E9-217) Rim. Est. D. 0.17, H. 0.031, W. 0.036. Smooth, hard pinkish orange fabric, 5YR 7/6 (reddish yellow) with small red, black, cream and micaceous inclusions. Interior painted brownish black with three reserved bands at top. Exterior has bands with two-legged bird file. Bodies of birds are oval, heads set diagonally with "chins." Flaring rim.
For motif cf. Coldstream 1968: 143 with other examples of this style; Waldstein 1905: pl. LVI, 11; Kraiker 1951: pl. 5 no. 68. For shape: Coldstream 1968: pl. 31e; Courbin 1966: pl. 59 C.2465 (LGIIb); Frickenhaus *et al.* 1912: pl. 15 no. 10.
Late Geometric II.

1144   SKYPHOS   Fig. 59
(B2-B28-101) Rim. Est. D. 0.08(?), H. 0.026, W. 0.028. Smooth, warm buff fabric, 7.5YR 7/6 (reddish yellow to darker). Exterior has vertical strokes at top above horizontals and blind lozenges. Thin flaring rim.
Cf. Courbin 1966: pl. 59 C.2541 (LGIIb).
Late Geometric II.

1145   SKYPHOS   Fig. 59
(B2-B28-10) Rim. D. ca. 0.16, H. 0.03, W. 0.031, Th. 0.004. Black painted interior, somewhat fugitive. Exterior horizontally banded with row of dots on a cream slip. Thin flaring rim.
Cf. Courbin 1966: pl. 59 C.2464 (LGI), C.2304 (LGIIb), C.2465 (LGIIb).
Late Geometric II.

1146   SKYPHOS   Fig. 59
(C17-C-4) Rim. D. 0.13, H. 0.024, wall Th. 0.0025. Pinkish orange fabric, 5YR 7/6 (reddish yellow). Reddish brown paint now faint and streaky inside and out. Short offset rim.
Cf. Courbin 1966: pl. 55, C.2467, C.2469, C.1045 (LGIIb), C1049 (LGIIc).
Late Geometric II.

1147   SKYPHOS   Figs. 59, 134
(F5-6) Body. H. 0.035, W. 0.031, wall Th. 0.004. Fine hard smooth pinkish brown fabric, 7.5YR 7/2 - 6/4 (pinkish gray to light brown). Sparse micaceous particles. Interior varies gray to orange. Exterior preserves reserved shoulder panel with two horizontal rows of dots between horizontal bands.
Cf. **1148**. For motif: Roes 1953: pl. 27 top left, bottom left; Frickenhaus *et al.* 1912: pl. 18 no. 13; Courbin 1966: pl. 57 C.17 (LGIIb).
Late Geometric II.

1148   BODY   Fig. 59
(A9-10-8) Body. H. 0.028, W. 0.037, Th. 0.004. Fine buff fabric, 7.5YR 7/6 (reddish yellow). Interior wall paint thick black. Exterior with vertical rows of dots, horizontal band. Body of thin-walled open vessel, possibly cup.

Cf. **1147**. For motif: Roes 1953: pl. 27 top left, bottom
left; Courbin 1966: pl. 57 C.17 (LGIIb).
Late Geometric II.

1149 SKYPHOS   Fig. 59
(B2-B28-32) Base. D. 0.08, pres. H. 0.019, H. fragment
0.042, wall Th. 0.003. Well levigated warm buff fabric, 7.5YR
6/6 (reddish yellow). Solid black inside and out.
Cf. Courbin 1966: pl. 54 C.2430 (LGIIa), pl. 55 C.2468
(LGIIb), C.1045 (LGIIb).
Late Geometric II.

1150 CUP   Figs. 59, 134
(C12-ALL-2) Rim. Est. D. 0.08, H. 0.029, wall Th. 0.005.
Fabric smooth, fine pale brown, 10YR 7/4 (very pale brown)
with tiny white and black inclusions. Solid brown all over with
reserved band inside lip.
Cf. Courbin 1966: pl. 71 C.1575 (LGI).
Late Geometric II.

1151 SKYPHOS   Fig. 59
(B2-B28-41) Base. D. 0.06, pres. H. 0.016, fragment H.
0.035, Th. 0.0045. Smooth, fine pale fabric, 10YR 7/4 (very
pale brown) with tiny white and black inclusions. Solid black
paint inside and out.
Cf. Courbin 1966: pl. 74 C.1578, C.173, C.2457 (LGI-
LGIIc).
Probably Late Geometric II.

1152 SKYPHOS OR CUP   Fig. 59
(B2-B28-ALL-1-25) Base. D. 0.04, pres. H. 0.015, H.
fragment 0.0025, W. 0.0345, Th. 0.004. Fine pinkish brown
fabric, 5YR 6/8 to slightly darker. Thin streaky black paint
inside and out; reserved band at lower foot.
Cf. Brann 1962: 52-53 nos. 180-184, pl. 10 no. 184.
Late Geometric to Subgeometric.

1153 KOTYLE   Fig. 134
(E9-241) Rim. D. 0.11, W. 0.029, Th. 0.003. Thin, hard
fabric of warm orange color, 5YR 6/6 (reddish yellow), very well
levigated with sparse white inclusions and vacuoles; mica not
evident. Paint fired even red, 2.5YR 4/6 (red) inside to 4/8
outside. Solid interior, exterior has three bands on rim, verticals
beside panel, horizontal bands. In panel, tail of bird(?).
Cf. Coldstream 1968: pl. 19k (Corinthian LG), pl. 21e
(EPC); Neeft 1975: 108, fig. III, 4-7.
Late Geometric II to Early Protocorinthian.

1154 KANTHAROS   Figs. 59, 134
(B2-B28-13) Rim. D. 0.19, H. 0.037, W. 0.0645,
Th.0.045. Well levigated pinkish orange fabric, 5YR 6/6 (reddish
yellow). Solid interior. Exterior decorated in cross-hatched
triangles above horizontal bands. Thin vertical pointed rim.
Attic.
Cf. Brann 1962: pl. 10 no. 170, ca. 725 B.C.; Kübler 1954:
pl. 120, inv. 1326.
Late Geometric II.

1155 PYXIS   Fig. 59
(C12-C14-E-3-18 + non-joining D-3-10) Base. D. 0.15, W.
0.031 + 0.030, max. H. 0.020, wall Th. 0.006. Strong fine
pinkish fabric, 5YR 7/8-6/8 (reddish yellow). Exterior has row of
dots between horizontal bands. Attic?

Cf. Courbin 1966: pl. 78, LGIIb Würzburg pyxis;
Coldstream 1968: pl. 10k, Attic LGIb horse pyxis; Courbin
1966: pl. 81, LGIIB Mycenae pyxis.
Late Geometric II.

1156 PYXIS(?)   Fig. 59
(F32-E-49) Foot. D. 0.045, H. 0.025. Well- levigated
pinkish buff fabric, 7.5YR 7/4 (pink). Lustrous black paint
inside and out, center of underside reserved. High conical foot,
probably from footed pyxis.
Cf. Courbin 1966: pl. 77 C.2436 (LGIIc).
Late Geometric II.

1157 GLOBULAR PYXIS   Fig. 134
(B16-ALL-3-6) Body and handle. H. 0.0475, W. 0.080, wall
Th. 0.006. Yellowish buff hard fabric, 7.5YR 7/6-6/6 (reddish
yellow) with few small black and white inclusions; mica not
evident. Brown matt paint on handle and in two horizontal bands
below; interior reserved. Round horizontal handle on shoulder.
Cf. Hägg 1978: no. 37, fig. 92.
Late Geometric II.

1158 PYXIS LID   Figs. 59, 134
(C17-117) Knob and body. Knob D. 0.015, H. 0.034, W.
0.038. Soft yellowish buff fabric, 10YR 8/4 (very pale brown)
with few small gray inclusions, sparse micaceous particles, and
vacuoles. Brownish concentric rings on surface. Knob broken
off.
Cf. Courbin 1966: pl. 86 C.2539 (LGII); pl. 87 C.2707
(LGII).
Late Geometric II.

1159 PLATE   Figs. 59, 134
(C27-4) Body. H. 0.046, W. 0.044, Th. 0.005. Fine warm
pinkish fabric, 5YR 7/8 (reddish yellow). Interior painted red
with slipped cream band; exterior, leaves in triple outline between
bands. Attic or island import.
Cf. Coldstream 1968: pl. 38j, pl. 15k; Brann 1961: O33 and
O34; Brann 1962: pl. 6, 105; Cambitoglou 1981: Cat. 120, inv.
2017, pl. 120; Mussche et al. 1984: 129 fig. 76.
Late Geometric II.

1160 PLATE   Figs. 59, 134
(B2-B28-16) Base. D. 0.09, W. 0.047. Fine warm pinkish
fabric, 5YR 6/6 (reddish yellow). Red painted decoration: interior
solid red, exterior banded; bottom with hatched quatrefoil leaf and
cross-hatched triangle. Attic or island import.
Cf. Coldstream 1968: pl. 38j; Dugas and Rhomaios 1943:
pl. 33 nos. 1-3; Mussche et al. 1984: 129 fig. 76.
Late Geometric II.

1161 BOWL   Figs. 59, 135
(C17-58) Rim. D. O.41, W. 0.084, W. rim 0.030, wall Th.
0.011. Coarse buff fabric, 7.5YR 6/6 (reddish yellow) with
vacuoles, white inclusions, and soft powdery surface. Crackled
black paint on exterior and dogtooth pattern on rim. Mending
hole near break. Bowl with broad horizontal rim.
Cf. Courbin 1966: pl. 68 C.234 (LGII). Decoration as
Dunbabin 1962: pl. 33 no. 737 (different shape).
Late Geometric II.

1162   VOTIVE PLAQUE   Fig. 135
(G1-3129) Body. W. 0.0305, H. 0.0595, Th. 0.005. Sandy fabric, grayish brown, 10YR 6/4 (light yellowish brown), with pinker core; well levigated with occasional micaceous particles, small gray and white inclusions. Painting in dark reddish brown with metallic sheen: file of ducks with hatched bodies, zigzag below bill. Row of dotted lozenges separated from duck file by three horizontal bands. Back of plaque reserved.
Cf. Coldstream 1968: pl. 31h; Kraiker 1951: nos. 67-68, 70, 72; Furtwängler 1906: pl. 125 nos. 31-2, 37; Waldstein 1905: pl. 56, no. 12, pl. 58, nos. 9-11. Unpublished votive plaque in similar style also known from Halieis, HP 2830 A+B.
Late Geometric II.

1163   AMPHORA   Fig. 60
(B2-B28-63) Rim. Est. D. 0.20, H. 0.045. Warm pinkish buff fabric, 5YR 6/6 (reddish yellow). Black paint on rim and fillet. SOS amphora rim rounded with raised ridge below. Attic.
Uncatalogued rim B2-B28-62 is the same type. Cf. Brann 1962: 33 nos. 25-27, pls. 2, 42.
Late Geometric II.

1164   AMPHORA   Fig. 60
(C12-C14-ALL-40) Neck. H. 0.078, W. 0.10, Th. 0.011. Semi-fine fabric, 7.5YR 7/6-6/6 (reddish yellow), with vacuoles, small brown inclusions, mica flecks. Black band around bottom of neck, large cross-hatched triangle; shoulder solid(?).
Cf. Hägg 1978: 100, nos. 29-30; Frödin and Persson 1938: 327, fig. 222 nos. 3 and 7.
Late Geometric II.

1165   AMPHORA   Fig. 60
(C12-C14-C-4-16) Neck. H. 0.056, W. 0.066, Th. 0.01. Well levigated warm buff fabric, 7.5YR 7/4 (pink) with small black and occasional micaceous inclusions. Fragment preserves a "fence" motif above horizontal banding near bottom of neck.
Late Geometric II.

1166   AMPHORA   Fig. 60
(C12-C14-82-3) Neck. H. 0.063, W. 0.095, Th. 0.013. Soft semi-fine powdery fabric of warm pinkish buff color, 7.5Y/R 6/4 (light brown) to 6/6 (reddish yellow), with gray and red inclusions, occasionally large, and micaceous particles. Exterior decorated in large meander with perpendicular hatching. Found together with uncatalogued non-joining fragment probably from same neck.
Cf. Frödin and Persson 1938: 327, fig. 222 no. 4.
Late Geometric II.

1167   AMPHORA   Fig. 60
(C12-C14-82-2) Neck. H. 0.090, W. 0.079. Warm pinkish buff fabric, 5YR 6/6 (reddish yellow) with occasional small black inclusions, micaceous particles. Thin vertical line divides the neck into panels, each with a circle containing a cross.
Cf. Frödin and Persson 1938: fig. 222 no. 7; Hägg 1978: 99, 100 no. 30.
Late Geometric II.

1168   AMPHORA?   Fig. 60
(C12-C14-ALL-7) Body. Max. dim. 0.133, Th. 0.008. Smooth strong pink fabric, 5YR 6/8 (reddish yellow). In left panel, bird facing left with hatched body (2-legged, 2-toed), zigzag behind bird; group of vertical lines, handle zone with hatched leaf, zigzag. Below, cross-hatched metope. Possibly an import.

Cf. Courbin 1966: pl. 151r, amphora from Delos; Dugas and Rhomaios 1943: Aa 1-42, 56, Ab all.
Late Geometric II.

1169   AMPHORA?   Figs. 60, 135
(C17-48) Body. H. 0.060, W. 0.089, Th. 0.008. Fine smooth pinkish orange fabric, 5YR 6/6 (reddish yellow), with small red and gray inclusions and occasional micaceous particles. Exterior has ladder beside concentric circles, horizontal bands below. Ladder pattern is Attic motif, could be Atticizing workshop of Asine.
Cf. Frödin and Persson 1938: fig. 222 nos. 4 and 6; Hägg 1978: no. 50.
Late Geometric II.

1170   AMPHORA
(C12-C14-D-3-32+33) Body. Fine smooth pinkish buff fabric, 5YR 6/6 (reddish yellow), with small red and gray inclusions, occasional micaceous particles. Exterior preserves concentric circles and ladder motif.
Similar to **1169**. Cf. Frödin and Persson 1938: 327, fig. 222 no. 6.
Late Geometric II.

1171   BODY   Fig. 135
(C12-C14-C-3-12) Body. H. 0.039, W. 0.061, Th. 0.01. Well levigated soft brown fabric, 7.5YR 6/6 (reddish yellow) with tiny micaceous particles, occasional white inclusions. Horizontal gear pattern above (or below) panel with concentric circles.
Gear pattern: cf. Courbin 1966: pl. 61 C.171 (LGIIa). Circles: Coldstream 1968: pl. 29d; Hägg 1962: pl. VI, 9.
Late Geometric II.

1172   AMPHORA OR OINOCHOE   Fig. 135
(G1-B-21) Neck. H. 0.064, W. 0.086, Th. 0.0085. Smooth pinkish buff fabric, 7.5YR 7/4 (pink) with small black inclusions and occasional micaceous particles. Exterior has angle-hatched meander above gear pattern.
Cf. gear pattern on amphora neck, Hägg 1978: cat. 81, 109 fig. 102, fig. 103; related scheme Frödin and Persson 1938: 327, fig. 222 no. 6; Coldstream 1968: pl. 15n (Attic LGII).
Late Geometric II.

1173   AMPHORA   Figs. 60, 135
(C12-C14-ALL-29) Foot. D. 0.105, H. 0.050, wall Th. 0.0075. Semi-fine buff fabric, 7.5YR 7/6 (reddish yellow), with scattered medium to large white, brown, red inclusions; a few minute mica flecks. Paint now streaky and fugitive, varies black to reddish brown. Lower body solid black, two bands around foot; underside reserved.
Cf. Courbin 1966: pl. 5 C.12 (LGIIb); Frödin and Persson 1938: 327, fig. 222 no. 6.
Late Geometric II.

1174   AMPHORA   Fig. 60
(B5-18) Foot. D. ca. 0.15, H. 0.037. Streaky black paint covers exterior. Low flaring ring foot.
Cf. Courbin 1966: pl. 7 C.847 (LGIIa), pl. 8 C.480 (7th c.).
Late Geometric II to Subgeometric.

1175   AMPHORA
(F32-N-13) Foot. D. ca. 0.16, Th. 0.018. Warm pinkish orange fabric, 5YR 6/6 (reddish yellow), with tiny vacuoles, inclusions of white, black, red, and mica. Exterior covered in

glossy red paint. High narrow foot, thick in section, preserves none of vessel wall.
Cf. Courbin 1966: pl. 6 C.15 (LGIIb).
Late Geometric II to Subgeometric.

1176   AMPHORA   Fig. 135
(C17-75) Handle. W. 0.044-0.055, H. 0.130, Th. 0.014. Semi-fine pinkish fabric, 5YR 7/6 (reddish yellow), with small to large white, brown, red inclusions; sparse micaceous particles. Strap handle with long X in streaky brown paint.
Cf. Frödin and Persson 1938: 325 fig. 221 no. 4.
Late Geometric.

1177   BODY   Fig. 60
(B17-B-18 + A-45) Body. H. 0.050, W. 0.025, Th. 0.005. Smooth light brown fabric, 10YR 6/4 (light yellowish brown). Exterior decoration in brown paint: horizontal bands on lower body, upper divided into two panels, one with hatched bird.
Cf. Hägg 1971: 42 fig. 1, amphoriskos; Verdelis 1963: pl. 17 no. 3 footed pyxis; oinochoe from Siphnos, *BSA* 44 (1949) 37, 4 and pl. 13, 26.
Late Geometric II.

COARSEWARES

1178   PITHOS   Fig. 60
(C12-C14-A-4-2) Rim. D. 0.40, H. 0.060, W. 0.069, Th. wall 0.095. Coarse fabric, pinkish buff surface to gray core. Decorative lines incised on surface: diagonal in panel(?). Short neck with splayed rim and vertical edge, broad shoulder.
Cf. DeVries 1974: pl. 12b; *ArchDelt* 19 (1964) B 123-125; Frickenhaus *et al.* 1912: 131 fig. 5.
Late Geometric.

1179   PITHOS   Figs. 60, 135
(F5-352) Shoulder. H. 0.080, W. 0.095, wall Th. 0.014. Heavy coarse fabric with well-smoothed surface, varies pinkish tan (5YR 7/6 reddish yellow) at surface to strong brown at core (5YR 6/4 light reddish brown to 7.5YR 6/4 light brown). Small black and white, many medium white and gray inclusions, with sparse micaceous particles. Neck decorated with band of incised diagonal strokes.
Cf. Courbin 1966: pl. 106 C.3967 (MGI); Kübler 1954: pl. 156 inv. 1234 (LGI). For incised decoration, Pfaff 1988: pl. 30 no. 83.
Late Geometric.

1180   PITHOS   Fig. 61
(B2-B28-87) Handle and body. H. 0.160, pres. W. 0.152, handle W. 0.064, Th. wall 0.011. Very coarse fabric with smoothed light buff surface, gray at core. Large grit inclusions. Broad strap handle with plain inset on rounded shoulder of pithos.
Uncatalogued body fragment B2-B28-85 probably from same vessel. Cf. Weinberg 1943: pl. 18 no. 134; Brann 1962: 105, no. 648, pl. 42 no. 222 for pithos handle of different form.
Late Geometric.

1181   AMPHORA OR STORAGE VESSEL   Fig. 135
(C27-2) Handle and body. Handle Th. 0.024, W. 0.047, H. 0.101, wall Th. 0.080. Heavy coarse fabric with gray core (7.5YR 5/2 to 5/4 brown) and pinkish brown surface (7.5YR 6/4) with evenly distributed large white, red, orange, and gray inclusions. Vertical handle contains inset with incised braid pattern.

Brann 1962: 105, no. 648, pl. 41; Blegen *et al.* 1964: pl. 12 no. 69-1.
Late Geometric to Subgeometric.

1182   PITHOS   Fig. 61
(F17-18) Rim. D. 0.42, H. 0.048, rim W. 0.028, wall Th. 0.0074. Coarse fabric varies from gray at core (7.5YR 5/2 brown) to buff surface (7.5YR 7/4 pink) with lime inclusions. Horizontal rim with small ridge below, slightly concave neck.
Cf. Hägg 1974: 145 fig. 41; *BCH* 94 (1970) 457 fig. 48; burial amphora, *BCH* 81 (1957) 658 fig. 43.
Late Geometric to Subgeometric.

1183   AMPHORA?   Fig. 61
(F5-201) Rim. D. 0.18, H. 0.035. Coarse gritty fabric pinkish buff at surface (5YR 7/6 reddish yellow or paler) with darker red core; many white, some brown inclusions. Handmade? Splayed rounded rim with raised ridge below.
Cf. **1184**.
Late Geometric.

1184   AMPHORA   Figs. 61, 135
(G1-A-73) Rim. D. 0.20, H. 0.055. Coarse, rough fabric varying from warm pinkish buff surface to blue-gray core; abundant inclusions of gray, white, brown, and straw, few visible on smoothed surface. Flaring rounded rim above raised ridge.
Cf. profiles of **1183** and **1185**. Similar profile in smaller jar from burial at Mycenae, Desborough 1954: pl. 46 no. 53-330, which is of much finer fabric.
Late Geometric.

1185   STORAGE VESSEL   Figs. 61, 135
(B16-ALL-2-12) Rim. D. 0.315, H. 0.065, W. 0.121. Rough, gritty fabric with white inclusions; varies pinkish buff (darker than 7.5YR 8/6 reddish yellow) to greenish gray at core. Vessel wall splays out to outturned rim above lower raised ridge.
Cf. similar profile to **1183, 1184**.
Late Geometric.

1186   AMPHORA OR OINOCHOE   Figs. 61, 135
(F32-N-24) Handle. H. 0.037, W. 0.022, Th. 0.010. Coarse, sandy texture with small white and brown inclusions, occasionally large; also micaceous particles. Color varies warm pinkish buff surface (7.5YR 7/6 reddish yellow) to blue-gray core (7.5YR N7 light gray). Incised braid pattern.
Cf. **1181**. Also unpublished example, Halieis. Cf. Brann 1962: 105 no. 648, pl. 41; Blegen *et al.* 1964: pl. 12 no. 69-1; Brann 1961: pl. 85 F75.
Late Geometric.

1187   JUG OR OINOCHOE   Fig. 61
(G1-A-70) Base. D. 0.16, H. 0.030, W. 0.053, wall Th. 0.0095. Coarse fabric with many surface vacuoles and white inclusions. Color varies from pinkish buff exterior to gray core. Flat disc base on globular body.
Late Geometric.

1188   JUG OR OINOCHOE   Fig. 61
(G1-A-72) Base. D. 0.10, H. 0.027, W. 0.068, wall Th. 0.0045. Coarse fabric, with small to large white and gray inclusions; varies from warm pinkish buff to blue-gray at core. Flat disc base on globular body.
Late Geometric.

LATE GEOMETRIC II TO SUBGEOMETRIC

1189   KRATER   Figs. 62, 136
   (G1-A-4) Rim. Est. D. 0.375, H. 0.054, W. 0.085.
Smooth fabric with mica flecks, warm buff color, 7.5YR 7/6
(reddish yellow). Interior and top of rim solid black; exterior has
group of sigmas beside horizontal connected dots.
   Cf. Courbin 1966: pl. 37 C.169, pl. 46 C.208 (LGIIc); Roes
1953: pl. 28 top right.
   Late Geometric II to Subgeometric.

1190   KRATER   Fig. 62
   (G1-3130) Rim. Est. D. 0.36, H. 0.045, W. 0.052. Fabric
is strong brick-red, 2.5YR 5/6-5/8 (red), finely levigated with
small white inclusions and micaceous particles. Interior covered
in brownish black thin paint; exterior has groups of vertical
zigzags between horizontal bands.
   Cf. similar rim **1189**. Courbin 1966: pl. 37 C.169, pl. 46
C.208 (LGIIc); Subgeometric krater DV15 from Deiras, Deshayes
1966: pl. 25 no. 1 and pl. 51 no. 7.
   Late Geometric II to Subgeometric.

1191   KRATER   Figs. 62, 136
   (F32-N-1) Rim. H. 0.031, W. 0.043. Soft semi-fine gray-
green fabric, 2.5 Y 6/2 (light brownish gray). Decoration in gray
paint, wavy horizontal lines and sigmas. Rim is straight with a
slight flare.
   Cf. Courbin 1966: pl. 46 C.208 (LGIIc), pl. 47 C.2509
(LGIIc) for motif.
   Late Geometric II to Subgeometric.

1192   KRATER   Fig. 62
   (C17-72) Pedestal. D. 0.24, H. 0.051. Black paint on
exterior only. Pedestal flares broadly to rounded rim with groove.
   Late Geometric to Subgeometric.

1193   KRATER   Fig. 62
   (B2-B28-ALL-1-26) Foot. D. 0.14, H. 0.065. Smooth well
levigated fabric, warm pinkish buff, 5YR 6/8 (reddish yellow).
Resting surface reserved, interior and exterior covered in thick
brown flaking paint.
   Cf. *BCH* 81 (1957) 536 fig. 22a, b; Bommelaer 1972: 237
fig. 12 C.26606 (foot **1193** is somewhat lower).
   Late Geometric II to Subgeometric.

1194   SKYPHOS   Fig. 62
   (B2-B28-19) Rim. D. 0.14, H. 0,025, W. 0.032, Th. 0.003.
Warm buff fabric, 7.5YR 6/6 (reddish yellow). Solid streaky
black paint inside and out.
   Cf. Courbin 1966: pl. 55 C.2467 (LGIIb), C.2468 (LGIIb),
C.1056 (LGIIc).
   Late Geometric to Subgeometric.

1195   PYXIS
   (A6/9-B-39) Foot. H. 0.052. Fairly smooth plainware
fabric with warm buff surface varying to gray at core; few
inclusions of white, red, black, and mica. Stemmed foot of
plainware pyxis, conical at bottom. Too badly preserved to
illustrate.
   Cf. Courbin 1966: pl. 99 C.2437 (LG IIC).
   Late Geometric to Subgeometric.

1196   AMPHORA   Fig. 62
   (B2-B28-ALL-1-10) Rim. H. 0.049, D. 0.17. Strong brick-
red fabric, 2.5YR 6/6-5/6 (light red to red), very pitted surface.
Painted black interior and exterior, very poorly preserved surface.
   Cf. Courbin 1966: pl. 6 C.15 (LGIIb); Brann 1962: 99, no.
590, pl. 42 (7th c.).
   Late Geometric to Subgeometric.

1197   BODY   Fig. 136
   (G1-A-25) Body. H. 0.0525, W. 0.036, Th. 0.009. Strong
pinkish orange fabric, 5YR 6/6 (reddish yellow), with small white
and black inclusions, sparse mica flecks. Exterior decorated in
thick vertical squiggles painted apparently by multiple brush,
bordered by horizontals.
   Cf. Courbin 1966: pl. 8 C.480 (7th c.), pl. 114 C.1144
(LGIIc), pl. 116 C.2775 (LGII).
   Late Geometric II to Subgeometric.

SUBGEOMETRIC

1198   KRATER OR STAMNOS   Figs. 62, 136
   (B16-ALL-2-10) Rim. D. 0.31, H. 0.095, W. 0.115.
Smooth light yellowish fabric with few apparent inclusions,
2.5YR 7/4 (pale yellow). Fugitive black paint covers outside
rim, shoulder has hanging rays above large section of horizontal
wavy parallel lines; below, a row of vertical wavy lines or
sigmas.
   Subgeometric.

1199   STAMNOID KRATER   Fig. 63
   (C17-3130-1) Rim and shoulder. D. 0.15, H. 0.050, W.
0.159, wall Th. 0.011. Semi-fine brown fabric, 7.5YR 5/6
(reddish yellow). Thick red paint preserved on neck and rim;
originally decoration on shoulder?
   Cf. *BCH* 94 (1970) 771 fig. 9.
   Subgeometric.

1200   KRATER   Fig. 136
   (G22-5-5) Rim. H. 0.052, W. 0.073. Row of dots on rim,
neck has "mattress" effect of horizontal wavy lines. Tall vertical
rim with outward thickened lip.
   Profile as in Bommelaer 1972: fig. 17 C.26605 and
C.26611; scheme as in Courbin 1966: pl. 38 C.2428, pl. 63
C.2441 (LGIIc), pl. 114 C.3489 (LGIIc).
   Subgeometric.

1201   KRATER   Figs. 63, 136
   (B2-B28-ALL-1-9) Rim. D. 0.38, H. 0.055, Th. 0.017.
Semi-fine strong red fabric, 2.5YR 5/6-5/8 (red). Creamy beige
slip, red decoration in zigzag around top of rim, pendant dogtooth
above horizontal bands.
   Similar to **1202**. Cf. Bommelaer 1972: fig. 7 and 17
C.26611; Roes 1953: pl. 28 middle row left.
   Subgeometric.

1202   KRATER   Figs. 63, 136
   (C17-55) Rim. D. interior 0.43, H. 0.066, W. 0.078, Th.
rim 0.012. Semi-fine pinkish buff fabric, 5YR 7/6-7/8 (reddish
yellow) with small gray and white inclusions, sparse micaceous
particles, frequent medium-sized vacuoles. Solid brown-painted
interior, exterior has cream-colored slip with thick red paint
(2.5YR 5/6-5/8 red) on top of rim and dogtooth row above
horizontal bands.

Similar to **1201**. Cf. Roes 1953: pl. 28 middle left; Bommelaer 1972: 231 fig. 4, 232 fig. 7, fig. 17 C.26611.
Subgeometric.

1203 KRATER   Fig. 63
(G1-A-7) Rim. Est. D. 0.42, H. 0.054, W. 0.059. Smooth greenish fabric, 10YR 6/4 (light yellowish brown). Streaky black-brown paint, interior solid, exterior horizontally banded. Vertical rim with short horizontal lip.
Similar to profile of **1189**. Cf. Courbin 1966: pl. 36 C.645 (LGIIc).
Subgeometric.

1204 KRATER   Figs. 63, 136
(G1-A-2) Rim. Interior D. 0.45, H. 0.065, W. 0.072, Th. rim 0.021. Semi-fine soft fabric strong orange in color, 5YR 7/6-6/8 (reddish yellow), with few large white inclusions, smaller black and red ones, occasional micaceous particles, vacuoles. Interior solid brown; exterior neck solid, one band at top of shoulder, reserved below. Everted rim with outward thickened lip set above narrow shoulder.
For decorative scheme, cf. kraters from Argos, *BCH* 81 (1957) 536 fig. 22a, b. Shape, cf. miniature krater from the Agamemnoneion, Cook 1953: fig. 15, A34.
Subgeometric.

1205 KRATER   Fig. 63
(F6-99) Rim. D. 0.28, H. 0.035, W. rim 0.024. Smooth light brown fabric, 10YR 6/3 (pale brown). Interior and exterior covered in black paint. Neck tapers in toward horizontal rim, an indicator of 7th-c. date.
Cf. Cook 1953: fig. 16, B1; krater from Argos, *BCH* 81 (1957) 536 fig. 22b.
Subgeometric.

1206 SKYPHOS   Figs. 64, 136
(F5-188) Base. D. 0.08, H. 0.017, W. 0.052, wall Th. 0.005. Semi-fine smooth light buff fabric, 7.5YR 7/6 (reddish yellow). Streaky black paint inside and out. Underside of base reserved with single black ring near edge.
Cf. Brann 1962: 48 nos. 135-42, pl. 8.
Subgeometric.

1207 PLATE OR BOWL   Fig. 64
(E19-B-1) Rim. D. 0.28, H. 0.047, W. 0.078. Semi-fine fabric, 7.5YR 6/6 (reddish yellow). Solid paint inside varies red to black; exterior, strokes on rim in groups, horizontal and wavy bands on side.
Cf. for profile: Brann 1962: pl. 6 no. 107. Cf. for shape and decoration: Young 1938: 415 and figs. 8, D14 and 9, D12, D14; Burr 1933: 585 fig. 46 nos. 185, 188 and fig. 47; unpublished plate fragment in Argos C.3443.
Subgeometric.

1208 BOWL   Fig. 64
(A9-3-15) Rim and handle. D. 0.36, H. 0.070, W. 0.046, W. body 0.071, wall Th. 0.011. Hard-fired semi-fine very dark pink fabric, 2.5YR 5/4- 5/6 (reddish brown to red). Interior paint varies red to brown, thickly applied, extending out to underside of handles; bottom surface slipped. Horizontal handle, round in section, set at level of grooved rim.
Cf. Burr 1933: 585 fig. 46 no. 192 for profile; McDonald *et al.* 1983: cat. P1575, pp. 182, 256, pl. 3159, 3-160.
Subgeometric.

1209 BOWL   Figs. 64, 136
(C17-52) Rim and handle. D. 0.27, H. 0.043, W. 0.078, Th. 0.005. Semi-fine greenish surface, pinker at core, 7.5YR 7/6 (reddish yellow). Thin streaky black paint inside and out. Horizontal handle, round in section, set just below incurving rim.
Subgeometric.

1210 AMPHORA   Figs. 64, 136
(B2-B28-9) Body. H. 0.066, W. 0.081, Th. 0.011. Coarse greenish fabric, 5Y 8/3 (pale yellow), with sandy texture, large white and small brown and gray inclusions, occasional small stones. Matt-painted serpentine creature at possible handle attachment; outline body with eye, teeth, tongue, and loop ear; star behind neck.
Cf. amphora from Exochi, Friis Johansen 1957: 14 fig. 6, 95 fig. 198; Laconian Subgeometric sherd from Mantinea, *ArchDelt* 18 (1963) B pl. 103a.
Subgeometric/Orientalizing.

1211 AMPHORA   Fig. 136
(B16-58) Body. H. 0.0365, W. 0.042, Th. 0.009. Semi-fine warm buff fabric 7.5YR 6/6 (reddish yellow) with few white and gray inclusions, sparse mica flecks. Large cross-hatching or net pattern in paint varying red to black.
Cf. Courbin 1966: pl. 8, Heraion (LGIIc); Polyphemos krater, *BCH* 77 (1953) 265 fig. 58; Courbin 1955: pl. 1.
Subgeometric.

1212 BODY   Fig. 136
(C17-ALL-2-5) Body. H. 0.0235, W. 0.039, Th. 0.006. Soft semi-fine yellowish buff fabric, 10YR 7/6-6/6 (yellow to brownish yellow) with small gray inclusions, sparse micaceous particles, and frequent vacuoles. Thin brownish black decoration of parallel wavy vertical lines beside stack of connected dots.
Cf. Courbin 1966: pl. 124 C.767 (7th c.), pl. 125 C.3846 (7th c.); Foley 1988: pls. 10c, 11b, 13b.
Subgeometric.

FIGURINES

1213 TERRACOTTA ANIMAL FIGURINE   Fig. 136
(F32) Head. L. 0.037, H. neck to ear 0.0225, W. at neck 0.022. Fabric is soft and powdery with small to medium white, red, and gray inclusions, sparse micaceous particles, and vacuoles. Fabric varies from light orange buff at surface (7.5YR 8/6 reddish yellow) to a deeper orange at core (5YR 7/8 reddish yellow). Surface preserves flakes of thick reddish brown paint (2.5YR 5/6 red). The slender head tapers to a muzzle with flattened chin. Deeply impressed eye holes and part of a pointed ear are preserved, the other ear broken off. A thin groove marks the mouth below vertical nostril slits.
Geometric.

1214 TERRACOTTA ANIMAL FIGURINE   Fig. 136
(F32) Torso. L. 0.052, H. 0.037, W. at back 0.028, W. at neck 0.018, W. front legs 0.033. Soft coarse fabric with sandy texture and frequent black, red, white, and micaceous inclusions. Fabric surface is pale warm buff (10YR 7/4 very pale brown). Flakes of thick red paint remain (2.5YR 5/8 red). Torso of quadruped broken at mid-belly and along underside preserves neck and parts of splayed front legs.
Cf. Geometric horse from the Argive Heraion, Waldstein 1905: cat. 76, pl. 48 no. 13.
Geometric.

1215   BRONZE BULL FIGURINE   Fig. 64
(A9) Bull. L. 0.061, H.0.035 at head, 0.029 at rump, W. shoulders 0.019, W. rump 0.018, W. torso 0.006. Intact quadruped with short rounded muzzle, horns (or ears?) rendered as knobs, a broad neck, hind hooves flattened like feet, and a long tail which hangs to the ground.

Cf. Geometric horse and Archaic bull from Kalaureia, Wide and Kjellborg 1895: 308 fig. 25, 309 fig. 26; Zimmermann 1989: pl. 11 no. 134; Argive horses from Olympia and the Argive Heraion, Zimmermann 1989: pl. 1 no. 13, pl. 11 nos. 155, 156.

Geometric to Subgeometric.

Assemblage Tables for Chapters 1–4

The charts in this Appendix comprise all the prehistoric and early Iron Age pottery identified from sites in the Southern Argolid. The charts are organized by chronological period for each site. For each sherd, basic information such as open vs. closed and type of shape, extant portion represented by the sherd, and presence of paint, slip, burnishing, or other decoration is recorded. Catalogue numbers are provided for those sherds individually described elsewhere in this volume. For certain chronological periods, additional information is recorded: for Early Helladic III material, the ware or fabric; for Middle Helladic, the ware or fabric and method of manufacture (hand vs. wheel).

The charts were compiled directly from the survey's object-recording sheets. These sheets were filled out for the preliminary analysis of the material, and were revised with information provided by experts in the various periods. Once the material to be catalogued had been removed from the uncatalogued material, however, the object-recording sheets were not subsequently changed for either catalogued or uncatalogued material. Subsequent study of the material has, however, altered the descriptions of individual objects somewhat, as reflected in the catalogues. The most noticeable difference will be in the shape categories. The categories used in these charts will not always agree with the shape name used in the catalogue for the individual objects, especially with all the varieties of bowls. To identify the shape category of any of the objects in the charts, the reader can consult the catalogue descriptions and illustrations.

The following abbreviations are used in the charts:

Wares (Early Helladic III and Middle Helladic only)

DB	Dark Burnished		
DoL	Dark-on-Light	MCB	Medium Coarse Burnished
DoLP	Dark-on-Light painted	MCU	Medium Coarse Unburnished
FB	Fine Burnished	SP&B	Solidly Painted and Burnished
GM	Gray Minyan	SP&U	Solidly Painted and Unburnished
Goldm	Gold Mica fabric	Unc	unclassified
GoldmC	Gold Mica Coarse fabric	YM	Yellow Minyan

H/W	hand- or wheelmade (Middle Helladic only)

H	handmade
W	wheelmade

O/C	open or closed

O	open (i.e. interior surface finished)
C	closed (i.e. interior surface not finished)
--	not applicable or indeterminate

Shape

Bass bowl	Bass bowl
bowl/basin	bowl or basin
bowl/saucer	bowl or saucer (i.e. small bowl)
C	coarseware
CP	cooking pot ware
fig	figurine
goblet/st.bowl	goblet or stemmed bowl
hemisph.bowl	hemispherical bowl
HFbowl	bowl on high foot
HHcup	high-handled cup
kylix/goblet	kylix or goblet
kylix/st.bowl	kylix or stemmed bowl
lg	large
med	medium
Narrowjar	narrow-mouthed jar
NNjug	narrow-necked jug (FS 120)
pan.cup	panel cup
ped	pedestal foot
ped.bowl	bowl on pedestal foot
r.cup	rounded cup (FS 211)
SAB	shallow angular bowl (FS 267)
sauceboat/bowl	sauceboat or bowl
sm	small
st.bowl	stemmed bowl
st.jar	stirrup jar (FS 164)
widejar	wide-mouthed jar

Extant portion

frag	fragment
H	handle
horiz	horizontal

N	neck
ped	pedestal
rd	round
ring	ring foot
Sh	shoulder
vert	vertical

Paint

bl	black
blue	yellow-blue (blue or gray variety) slip
BR	bichrome
FM	Furumark motif
FP	fine-painted (Late Helladic)
int	interior
Lin	linear painted
LMP	Late Matt-Painted
LoD	light-on-dark
LP	lustrous painted
Mono	monochrome
MP	matt-painted
or	orange
patt	pattern painted
UP	unpainted (Late Helladic)
Urf	Urfirnis
yel	yellow-blue slip and burnish
YM	Yellow Minyan

Other Dec	other decoration

appl	appliqué
burn	burnished
dec	decorated
diag	diagonal
DoL	dark on light
horiz	horizontal
imp	impression/impressed
inc	incision/incised
mat imp	mat impression
MP	matt painted
Pmark	potter's mark
ridge	applied ridge
taenia	applied ridge with impression or incision
triang	triangle
trumpet	trumpet lug

SITE: A6 (Samioti Magoula)   593 collected   583 identified

FINAL NEOLITHIC

O/C	SHAPE	EXTANT PART	PAINT	BURN	OTHER DEC	CATALOGUED
O?	–	1 H horiz		1		47
		1 total				

EARLY HELLADIC

O/C	SHAPE	EXTANT PART	PAINT	BURN	OTHER DEC	CATALOGUED
O	–	7 RIM; 9 Body; 1 Body; 1 R?	6	5; 3?		
C	collar jar	1 R; 1 Body		2		
	pithos	2 Body		1	1 lug; 1 appl	
	–	4 R; 33 Body; 2H; 1 Base	15; 5?	15; 2?	2 appl; 1 drill hole	
O?	–	2 R; 7 Body; 2 Base; 1 H	6; 1?	5		
C?	–	6 Body	3; 1?	1?	1 lug; 1 appl	
		80 total				

EARLY HELLADIC?

O/C	SHAPE	EXTANT PART	PAINT	BURN	OTHER DEC	CATALOGUED
O	–	2 R; 5 Body; 1 H (+ R?)	3	1; 1?		
C	–	9 Body; 2 H	4	1; 2?	1 inc & appl	
O?	–	3 Body; 1 H	1; 1?	1?		
C?	–	9 Body; 3 Base	2; 1?	1		
		35 total				

EARLY HELLADIC I

O/C	SHAPE	EXTANT PART	PAINT	BURN	OTHER DEC	CATALOGUED
O	hem.bowl	4 R	2 red; 2 slip	2; 1?	1 trumpet	84, 88, 90, 94
	bowl	1 R	1	1		
	lg bowl	3 R	3 red	1		85, 91, 106
	lg sh.bowl	1 R				79
	inc.bowl	1 Body	1 red	1		
	sm inc.bowl	1 R	1 red	1		99
	med inc.bowl	1 R	1 red	1		100
	–	6 R; 19 Body; 2 Base	15 red; 8 slip; 1?	23	1 mat imp; 1 crusted?	205
C	jar	7 R; 2 Body	6 red; 2	7	2 inc	139, 143, 147, 149, 151, 153, 155, 161, 162
	–	2 H; 18 Body; 1 Base	18 red; 2 slip	20	1 appl; 3 inc; 3 grooves	168, 171, 172, 173, 177
–	stand	1 knob	1 red			207
–	–	2 Body; 1 Base flat	1 red	1		200
O?	–	1 R; 1 H; 1 Body	2 red	3	1 inc	119
C?	–	1 R; 1 H; 3 Body	3 red; 2	3	1 grooves	179
		81 total				

EARLY HELLADIC I?

O/C	SHAPE	EXTANT PART	PAINT	BURN	OTHER DEC	CATALOGUED
O	lg sh.bowl	1 R			1 inc/imp	446
	–	2 R; 2 Base; 1 H?	1 red; 1	3	1 kerbschnitt	192, 194, 432
O?	–	1 Body	1			
C?	–	1 Body	1			
		8 total				

EARLY HELLADIC I - EARLY HELLADIC II

O/C	SHAPE	EXTANT PART	PAINT	BURN	OTHER DEC	CATALOGUED
O	bowl/basin	1 R	1 red			
–		1 R; 1 Body; 1 Base flat	2; 1 red	3	1 appl	613
O?	–	1 Body	1 red	1		
–	stand	1 knob	1 red	1		
		6 total				

EARLY HELLADIC II

O/C	SHAPE	EXTANT PART	PAINT	BURN	OTHER DEC	CATALOGUED
O	bowl/sauceboat	5 Body; 1 ped; 3 ring	2 red urf; 3 urf; 3 yel	3		242, 522, 539, 541
	sm bowl	2 R	1 urf		1 taenia	225, 341
	sauceboat	11 R; 11 Body; 4 spout; 1 H	15 urf; 11 yel; 1	10		213, 214, 215, 216, 218
	sauceboat?	2 R; 1 Body; 2 H; 1 R + H	5 urf; 1 yel	1		
	sh.saucer	6 R	3 urf	1		
	inc.bowl	6 R; 1 Base flat	5 urf; 1			
	ped.bowl	1 ped	1 urf?			604
	bowl/saucer	8 R; 1 Base hollow	6 urf; 1 yel; 1	2		230, 237
	lg bowl/basin	6 R; 1 R + H	3 urf; 1 red; 1 bl	1	2 slashes; 1 appl; 3 taenia	259, 260, 338, 358, 365, 394, 409
	basin	1 R; 1 Body	2 urf			247
	deep bowl	1 R	1 brown	1	1 slashes	437
	bowl	10 R; 1 Base flat	1 red; 4 urf; 2; 2?	3	1 taenia; 1 ridge; 1 lug	278, 316, 350
	lg bowl	2 R; 1 Body; 1 Base flat	1 urf		2 taenia; 1 slashes; 1 mat imp	373, 442, 614
	pan?	1 R		1		
	–	4 R; 28 Body; 2 H; 1 ped; 1 foot; 3 Base; 5 ring;	32 urf; 4 yel; 1 patt; 1; 2?	6; 1?	3 appl	545, 555, 563, 607, 611
C	collared jar	2 R	1 urf; 1	1		501
	jar	2 R; 1 Body; 1 R + Body	3	1		498
	pithos	4 R; 4 Body	6	1	1 taenia; 1 herringbone; 1 slashes on ridge	450, 453, 454, 478, 481
	pithos?	4 Body	2		1 ridges	
	–	24 Body; 4 H; 1 ring; 2 Base	25 urf; 1?	1; 1?	3 appl	
O?	–	6 Body	5 urf			
C?	–	1 R; 4 Body	3 urf; 1?		1 appl	
–	scoop	1 H	1			
	stand	2 frag				645, 646
	rooftile	15 frags				666, 667, 668, 670, 671, 672, 673, 674, 677
	–	2 H vert; 2 Body	1 red urf			
		215 total				

EARLY HELLADIC II?

O/C	SHAPE	EXTANT PART	PAINT	BURN	OTHER DEC	CATALOGUED
O	bowl	2 R	1		1 lug pierced	264, 276
	–	3 Body	1 urf?; 1	1		
C	jar?	1 R	1			
	pithos?	1 Body			1 ridges	
	–	2 Body; 1 H	2; 1?	2		
O?	–	4 Body	2; 2?	2	1 taenia	
C?	–	1 Body; 1 Base	1			574
–	–	1 Body	1?			
		17 total				

EARLY HELLADIC III

WARE	O/C	SHAPE	EXTANT PART	PAINT	OTHER DEC	CATALOGUED
SP&U	O	bowl	3 R, 1 Body			682, 687, 688, 692, 694
	C	Narrowjar	1 Body			678
	C		2 Body		2 imp	683, 684
SP&B	O	cup/kantharos	1 R			703
DoLP	O	bowl	1 R	PP		705
FB	O		1 R			708
			12 total			

MIDDLE HELLADIC

WARE	O/C	H/W	SHAPE	EXTANT	SLIP	BUR	DEC	CATALOGUED
GM	O	h?	HHcup	1 R, 1 Body		Y		715, 718
DB	O	h	bowl	1 R		Y		726
YM	O	h	bowl?	2 R	Slip	Y		731, 732
	O	w		1 H	Slip	Y		
Bur	O	h	bowl	1 R		Y		750
MP	C	w		1 Sh		Y	MP	762
	C	h?		1 H		Y	?	
	C	h		1 Body		N	MP	
LP	C	h	jar?	1 neck	?	Y	DoL	786
Goldm	O	w?		1 R	Red	Y		807
	O	h		1 R	Red	Y		808
Coarse	C	h	pithos	1 R	Slip	N	imp	818
	C	h		1 H; 1 Base		1?; 1N	Pmark	820, 821
Unc	C	h		1 Body		?		
				17 total				

LATE HELLADIC

O/C	SHAPE	EXTANT PART	PAINT	OTHER DEC	CATALOGUED
O	C: pithos	2 R			
	CP: tripod	1 leg; 1 H + Body + leg			952
	CP	1 Body; 1 Base	1 slip		966
	goblet?	1 H	1 UP (slip)		
	–	6 Body; 1 H	1 FP; 2 Mono; 4 UP (1 slip?)	3 burn	
C	CP	1 H rd; 1 Base			965
	jar	1 Body	1 Lin		
	–	6 Body; 1 H horiz	2 FP; 2 Lin; 1 Mono; 2 UP (1 slip)	1 burn	

O?	CP	1 Base button			954
	–	1 Body;	1 FP; 1 Lin		
		1 Base torus			
–	–	2 H vert	2 Mono		
		29 total			

LATE HELLADIC II - IIIA1

O/C	SHAPE	EXTANT PART	PAINT	OTHER DEC	CATALOGUED
C	amphora	1 Body	1 LMP		840
	–	1 Body	1 LMP Lin		
–	–	2 H vert	2 LMP		
		4 total			

LATE HELLADIC IIA

O/C	SHAPE	EXTANT PART	PAINT	OTHER DEC	CATALOGUED
O	r.cup (FS211)	1 Body	1 FM76 (stone)		828
C	squat jug	1 Body	1 FM13		826
		2 total			

LATE HELLADIC III

O/C	SHAPE	EXTANT PART	PAINT	OTHER DEC	CATALOGUED
O	kylix	1 R; 2 Base; 2 stem	5 UP (2 slip)		996, 1002
	kylix/goblet	1 Base	1 UP		
	goblet	1 stem	1 UP (1 slip)		
C	jug	1 R	1 Lin		
–	–	1 H rd			
		9 total			

LATE HELLADIC IIIA

O/C	SHAPE	EXTANT PART	PAINT	OTHER DEC	CATALOGUED
O	goblet/st.bowl	1 Body	1 Mono		
		1 total			

LATE HELLADIC IIIA1

O/C	SHAPE	EXTANT PART	PAINT	OTHER DEC	CATALOGUED
O	krater	1 Body	1 Patt		843
	goblet	1 H	1 Lin		
		2 total			

LATE HELLADIC IIIA2

O/C	SHAPE	EXTANT PART	PAINT	OTHER DEC	CATALOGUED
O	kylix/st.bowl	1 R; 2 Body	3 Mono		868
	krater	1 Body	1 Mono		
C	–	1 Body	1 Mono		
		5 total			

LATE HELLADIC IIIA2-B

O/C	SHAPE	EXTANT PART	PAINT	OTHER DEC	CATALOGUED
C	–	2 Body	2 Lin		
		2 total			

LATE HELLADIC IIIB

O/C	SHAPE	EXTANT PART	PAINT	OTHER DEC	CATALOGUED
O	st.bowl	1 H	1 Lin		920
C	NNjug (FS120)	1 R	1 Lin		881
		2 total			

LATE HELLADIC?

O/C	SHAPE	EXTANT PART	PAINT	OTHER DEC	CATALOGUED
O	C: tripod CP?	1 leg			
C	C	1 Body	1		
C?	C	1 Body			
–	C	1 H			
		4 total			

LATE GEOMETRIC

O/C	SHAPE	EXTANT PART	PAINT	OTHER DEC	CATALOGUED
O	krater	2 Body; 1 R	pattern		
	skyphos	1 ring	solid		
C	pyxis	1 ring			
		5 total			

SITE: A6/9   91 collected   91 identified

EARLY HELLADIC I

O/C	SHAPE	EXTANT PART	PAINT	BURN	OTHER DEC	CATALOGUED
O	bowl	1 Body	1	1		
	lg inc.bowl	2 R	2 red	2		104, 108
	–	4 Body	2 red; 1	4		
C	jar	3 R	2 red; 1 bl	3		135, 141, 145
	–	1 H; 5 Body; 1 lug	6 red; 1	5	1 grooves	178, 181
O?	–	1 Body	1 red	1		
C?	–	1 H	1 red		1 grooves	
–	–	1 knob				185
		20 total				

EARLY HELLADIC I - EARLY HELLADIC II

O/C	SHAPE	EXTANT PART	PAINT	BURN	OTHER DEC	CATALOGUED
O	–	2 Body	2	2		
		2 total				

EARLY HELLADIC II

O/C	SHAPE	EXTANT PART	PAINT	BURN	OTHER DEC	CATALOGUED
O	inc.bowl	1 R				233
	bowl	4 R; 1 ped; 1 Body	2 urf; 1 bl; 1	2		235, 285
	lg bowl	1 R	1 bl		1 slashes	430
	bowl/saucer	1 R			1 ridge	315
	sh.bowl/saucer	2 R	1 band; 1 urf			268
	sauceboat	6 R	4 black; 1; 1 blue	2		219
	sauceboat?	1 Body	1 urf			
	pan	1 R				618
	lg bowl/basin	2 R	1 urf		1 taenia; 1 diag slashes	319, 398
	bowl/sauceboat	1 ped				579
	–	4 Body; 1 ring	3 urf	2		546
C	jar/jug	1 R		1		489
	jar	3 R	1 ?	1		490, 505
	askos/jug	1 Body + lug	1 urf			
	pithos	1 R			1 taenia	
	pithos?	1 Body	1 urf			
	–	4 H; 1 Body	2 bl		1 grooves	
		39 total				

EARLY HELLADIC II?

O/C	SHAPE	EXTANT PART	PAINT	BURN	OTHER DEC	CATALOGUED
O	–	2 Base				
C	–	1 Body	1 urf?			
		3 total				

LATE HELLADIC

O/C	SHAPE	EXTANT PART	PAINT	OTHER DEC	CATALOGUED
O	CP: tripod	2 leg	1		
C	–	1 H horiz	1 UP		
		3 total			

LATE HELLADIC III

O/C	SHAPE	EXTANT PART	PAINT	OTHER DEC	CATALOGUED
O	goblet	1 stem	1 UP		
		1 total			

LATE HELLADIC IIIA1

O/C	SHAPE	EXTANT PART	PAINT	OTHER DEC	CATALOGUED
O	goblet	1 R	1 Patt		
		1 total			

LATE HELLADIC IIIA2+

O/C	SHAPE	EXTANT PART	PAINT	OTHER DEC	CATALOGUED
O	kylix	1 Body	1 UP		
		1 total			

LATE GEOMETRIC

O/C	SHAPE	EXTANT PART	PAINT	OTHER DEC	CATALOGUED
O	krater	1 R; 2 Body	pattern		1116
	skyphos	1 Base	solid		
C	pyxis	1 ring	solid		1195
		5 total			

SITE: A9 (Flamboura Magoula)   305 collected   266 identified

EARLY HELLADIC

O/C	SHAPE	EXTANT PART	PAINT	BURN	OTHER DEC	CATALOGUED
O	–	1 R; 1 Foot	1			
		2 total				

EARLY HELLADIC?

O/C	SHAPE	EXTANT PART	PAINT	BURN	OTHER DEC	CATALOGUED
O?	–	2 Body	1; 1?	1?		
C?	–	1 Body	1			
?	–	1 R				
		4 total				

EARLY HELLADIC I

O/C	SHAPE	EXTANT PART	PAINT	BURN	OTHER DEC	CATALOGUED
O	bowl/saucer	1 R	1 red			72
	–	1 R; 10 Body; 1 Base	7 red; 1 slip; 1?	7		203
C	jar	5 R; 1 Body	6 red	4	1 grooves	140, 144, 146, 152, 154, 158
	–	6 Body	5 red; 1	5	1 stamped	164

O/C	SHAPE	EXTANT PART	PAINT	BURN	OTHER DEC	CATALOGUED
O?	–	1 R; 2 Body	1 red; 1	2		
C?	–	1 Body	1 red	1		
		29 total				

EARLY HELLADIC I?

O/C	SHAPE	EXTANT PART	PAINT	BURN	OTHER DEC	CATALOGUED
C	–	1 Body	1			
		1 total				

EARLY HELLADIC I - EARLY HELLADIC II

O/C	SHAPE	EXTANT PART	PAINT	BURN	OTHER DEC	CATALOGUED
O	lg bowl/basin	2 R	1 red	1	1 appl	
	–	1 Body	1 red-brown	1		
C	jar	1 R	1 red-brown		1 ledge	
?	–	1 H horiz	1 red	1		
		5 total				

EARLY HELLADIC II

O/C	SHAPE	EXTANT PART	PAINT	BURN	OTHER DEC	CATALOGUED
O	bowl/sauceboat	2 Body	1 bl; 1 yel			
	lg bowl/basin	1 Body + H				332
	bowl	1 ped				
	–	1 ring				
C	pithos	4 R	1 bl		1 slashes + taenia	461, 462, 475
	–	1 Body; 4 H vert	1 urf; 1		1 ridges	
C?	–	2 Body; 1 H vert	1 urf	1		
–	scoop	2 H	2 bl			
	stand	1 knob	1	1		
		20 total				

EARLY HELLADIC II?

O/C	SHAPE	EXTANT PART	PAINT	BURN	OTHER DEC	CATALOGUED
O	–	1 Body	1 red			
C	–	2 H vert				
		3 total				

MIDDLE HELLADIC

WARE	O/C	H/W	SHAPE	EXTANT	SLIP	BUR	OTHER DEC	CATALOGUED
Bur?	O	h?	HFbowl	1 foot	Slip	?	incd	754
				1 total				

LATE HELLADIC

O/C	SHAPE	EXTANT PART	PAINT	OTHER DEC	CATALOGUED
C	–	1 H	1		
		1 total			

LATE HELLADIC III

O/C	SHAPE	EXTANT PART	PAINT	OTHER DEC	CATALOGUED
O	kylix	1 stem	1 slip		
		1 total			

MIDDLE GEOMETRIC

O/C	SHAPE	EXTANT PART	PAINT	OTHER DEC	CATALOGUED
O	krater	1 ring	bands		1044
		1 ring	solid		1053
	skyphos	3 R; 2 Body	pattern		1050, 1051, 1052
		1 H	solid		
C	amphora	1 Body	pattern		1062
		1 Body	solid		1064
	pyxis	1 Body	pattern		1055
	lekythos	1 Shoulder	bands		1063
		12 total			

MIDDLE TO LATE GEOMETRIC

O/C	SHAPE	EXTANT PART	PAINT	OTHER DEC	CATALOGUED
O	krater	1 R	pattern		1068
		1 ring	bands		1069
	skyphos	2 Body; 1 H	pattern		1081
	cup	2 Base	pattern		
	–	2 Body	pattern		
	–	1 Body	solid		
	pithos	2 R			1096, 1097
C	amphora	1 R		inc. zigs	1087
	pyxis	4 ring	solid		1082
	stand?	1 R	solid		
	–	2 Body; 1 ring	solid		
	–	1 Body	pattern		
		22 total			

LATE GEOMETRIC

O/C	SHAPE	EXTANT PART	PAINT	OTHER DEC	CATALOGUED
O	krater	1 Body	pattern		1130
	skyphos	2 R	pattern		
	plate	1 Body	pattern		1131
	cup	1 R; 1 Body	pattern		1148
	–	4 Body	pattern		
C	–	2 Body	pattern		
		12 total			

LATE GEOMETRIC TO SUBGEOMETRIC

O/C	SHAPE	EXTANT PART	PAINT	OTHER DEC	CATALOGUED
O	bowl	1 R	solid		1208
		1 total			

GEOMETRIC

O/C	SHAPE	EXTANT PART	PAINT	OTHER DEC	CATALOGUED
O	krater	1 ring	solid		
	skyphos	4 H	solid		
	cup	1 R	pattern		
		4 base	solid		
	–	1 Body	pattern		
	–	2 Body; 1 ring	solid		
C	jug	2 Base			
	–	9 Body; 2 ring; 2 H; 1 R	solid		
	–	2 Body	pattern		
?	–	21 Body; 1 R; 2 H; 1 ring	solid		
	–	1 R	pattern		
		58 total			

SITE: A32 (Nisi Kheliou #1)

<u>LATE HELLADIC</u>

O/C	SHAPE	EXTANT PART	PAINT	OTHER DEC	CATALOGUED
C	CP: tripod	1 leg			
		1 total			

SITE: A33 (Nisi Kheliou #3)   156 collected   135 identified

<u>FINAL NEOLITHIC</u>

O/C	SHAPE	EXTANT PART	PAINT	BURN	OTHER DEC	CATALOGUED
O	spreading bowl	1 R			1 taenia	14
–		1 Body	1		1 ridges	58
		2 total				

<u>EARLY HELLADIC</u>

O/C	SHAPE	EXTANT PART	PAINT	BURN	OTHER DEC	CATALOGUED
O	–	1 R; 3 Body	1; 1?	1?	1 appl	
C	–	2 Body	1 red		1 inc/imp	
C?	–	5 Body	1; 2?	1; 1?		
?	–	1 H	1?			
		12 total				

<u>EARLY HELLADIC?</u>

O/C	SHAPE	EXTANT PART	PAINT	BURN	OTHER DEC	CATALOGUED
O	–	1 Body		1		
C	pithos	1 R	1?			
		2 total				

<u>EARLY HELLADIC I</u>

O/C	SHAPE	EXTANT PART	PAINT	BURN	OTHER DEC	CATALOGUED
O	inc.bowl	1 R	1 red	1		102
	sm sp.bowl	1 R				80
	sm bowl	2 R				81, 127
	sm inc.bowl	1 R				97
	lg sh.bowl	1 R	1	1		75
	lg hem.bowl	1 R	1			96
	bowl	1 R + H	1	1		89
	–	1 R; 9 Body; 2 Base	2 red; 9; 1 or-brown	9; 2?		189
C	jar	3 R; 2 Body	2 red; 2	4	1 inc	131, 132, 134, 136
	–	13 Body; 1 H; 2 Base	9 red; 3	10	2 appl; 1 inc	170, 198, 199
O?	frying pan?	1 Body	1 red	1		
	–	2 Body; 1 Base	1 red	1	1 appl	191
C?	–	3 Body; 1 Base	2 red; 1	2; 1?		201
		49 total				

<u>EARLY HELLADIC I?</u>

O/C	SHAPE	EXTANT PART	PAINT	BURN	OTHER DEC	CATALOGUED
O	–	1 R; 1 Body	1	1	1 crusted?	
C	–	5 Body				
O?	–	1 R; 2 Body	3	2	1 hole	
		10 total				

EARLY HELLADIC I - EARLY HELLADIC II

O/C	SHAPE	EXTANT PART	PAINT	BURN	OTHER DEC	CATALOGUED
C	–	8 Body	1			
C?	–	1 Body; 1 H				
		10 total				

EARLY HELLADIC II

O/C	SHAPE	EXTANT PART	PAINT	BURN	OTHER DEC	CATALOGUED
O	inc. bowl	1 R	1 urf			
	sauceboat/bowl	2 ring	1 yel			528
	sauceboat	1 R; 2 spout	2 bl; 1?			221
	sauceboat?	1 R; 2 Body	1 bl; 2?			
	bowl	2 R	1	1		295
	lg bowl/basin	1 R			1 taenia	
	–	1 R; 2 Body; 1 ring; 1 Base	2 urf; 1	1	1 ridge	564
C	jar	3 R	1 urf; 1 urf?			513
	pithos	3 R	1?		2 taenia; 1 inc?	456, 466, 471
	–	1 Body	1 urf			
O?	–	1 Body	1 urf			
C?	–	1 Body	1 urf			
–	ladle	1 H	1 red			
	table?	1 foot				647
	rooftile	3 frag				675
		31 total				

EARLY HELLADIC II?

O/C	SHAPE	EXTANT PART	PAINT	BURN	OTHER DEC	CATALOGUED
C?	–	1 H	1 urf?			
–	–	1 R	1 urf			
		2 total				

SITE: A51 (Methokhi tower)   152 collected   69 identified

FINAL NEOLITHIC - EARLY HELLADIC I

O/C	SHAPE	EXTANT PART	PAINT	BURN	OTHER DEC	CATALOGUED
?	–	2 Body	2			
		2 total				

SITE: A65 (Halieis)

FINAL NEOLITHIC
material present

EARLY HELLADIC I
material present

SITE: B2 (Dhouroufi Ridge [Dhroukoulina])   248 collected   240 identified

EARLY HELLADIC I - EARLY HELLADIC II

O/C	SHAPE	EXTANT PART	PAINT	BURN	OTHER DEC	CATALOGUED
?	–	1 Body	1			
		1 total				

EARLY HELLADIC II

O/C	SHAPE	EXTANT PART	PAINT	BURN	OTHER DEC	CATALOGUED
–	stand	1 foot				**644**
		1 total				

EARLY HELLADIC II?

O/C	SHAPE	EXTANT PART	PAINT	BURN	OTHER DEC	CATALOGUED
C	pithos	1 Body			1 taenia	
		1 total				

LATE HELLADIC

O/C	SHAPE	EXTANT PART	PAINT	OTHER DEC	CATALOGUED
O	bowl/krater	1 foot	1 red		
C	CP: jug?	1 Base			
C?	CP	3 Base	2 wash		**955, 967**
–	C	1 H		1 pierced	
		6 total			

LATE HELLADIC III

O/C	SHAPE	EXTANT PART	PAINT	OTHER DEC	CATALOGUED
O	kylix	3 stem; 3 Base	1 Lin		
	SAB (FS267)	1 Body	1 UP		
		7 total			

LATE HELLADIC IIIA

O/C	SHAPE	EXTANT PART	PAINT	OTHER DEC	CATALOGUED
O	kylix	1 stem	1 UP		
		1 total			

LATE HELLADIC IIIA2

O/C	SHAPE	EXTANT PART	PAINT	OTHER DEC	CATALOGUED
C	st.jar (FS164)	1 Body	FM21 Octopus		**857**
		1 total			

LATE HELLADIC?

O/C	SHAPE	EXTANT PART	PAINT	OTHER DEC	CATALOGUED
–	–	1 H			
		1 total			

MIDDLE TO LATE GEOMETRIC

O/C	SHAPE	EXTANT PART	PAINT	OTHER DEC	CATALOGUED
O	krater	1 Body	pattern		1075
	skyphos	1 H	pattern		1077
		2 total			

LATE GEOMETRIC

O/C	SHAPE	EXTANT PART	PAINT	OTHER DEC	CATALOGUED
O	krater	1 Body; 1 R	pattern		1124, 1119
		1 R; 1 ring	bands		1115, 1136
	skyphos	5 H; 3 R	pattern		1144, 1145
		2 R	bands		1142
		2 ring	solid		1149, 1152
	cup	1 Base	solid		1151
	kantharos	1 R	pattern		1154
	plate	1 Base	pattern		1160
	pithos	1 R; 1 H			1180
C	amphora	1 R; 1 Body	solid		1163
–	–	2 H	1 bands	1 twist	
		25 total			

LATE GEOMETRIC TO SUBGEOMETRIC

O/C	SHAPE	EXTANT PART	PAINT	OTHER DEC	CATALOGUED
O	krater	3 R; 2 Base	3 bands; 1 pattern		**1193**
		11 Body	3 solid		
	skyphos	1 H; 3 ring	solid		
		1 R	solid		**1194**
		7 Body	bands		
		1 Body	pattern		
	cup	4 R	bands		
		2 R	pattern		
		1 R	solid		
C	amphora	1 R	solid		**1196**
		1 Body	bands		
	oinochoe	1 Base	solid		
	–	5 Body	solid; pattern		
–	–	1 H	solid		
	–	1 ring	bands		
		46 total			

GEOMETRIC TO ARCHAIC

O/C	SHAPE	EXTANT PART	PAINT	OTHER DEC	CATALOGUED
O	krater	1 R; 3 Body	solid		
	cup/skyphos	1 Base	bands		
		14 Body; 1 H	solid		
	–	1 R; 9 Body;	solid		
		12 Base	solid		
	–	1 R; 2 Body	bands		
C	–	1 Base; 3 Body	solid		
	–	2 Body	bands		
		51 total			

SUBGEOMETRIC

O/C	SHAPE	EXTANT PART	PAINT	OTHER DEC	CATALOGUED
O	krater	1 R	pattern		**1201**
C	amphora	2 Body	pattern		**1210**
		3 total			

SITE: B5 (Melindra) 210 collected   180 identified

FINAL NEOLITHIC?

O/C	SHAPE	EXTANT PART	PAINT	BURN	OTHER DEC	CATALOGUED
C	jar?	1 R				**33**
		1 total				

EARLY HELLADIC

O/C	SHAPE	EXTANT PART	PAINT	BURN	OTHER DEC	CATALOGUED
?	–	2 Body			2 taenia	
		2 total				

EARLY HELLADIC?

O/C	SHAPE	EXTANT PART	PAINT	BURN	OTHER DEC	CATALOGUED
O	bowl	1 Body	1	1		
		1 total				

EARLY HELLADIC I

O/C	SHAPE	EXTANT PART	PAINT	BURN	OTHER DEC	CATALOGUED
O	bowl?	1 Body	1 red	1		
		1 total				

EARLY HELLADIC II

O/C	SHAPE	EXTANT PART	PAINT	BURN	OTHER DEC	CATALOGUED
O	bowl	1 R	1 urf		1 taenia	
C	pithos	1 R		1		455
		2 total				

MIDDLE HELLADIC

WARE	O/C	H/W	SHAPE	EXTANT	SLIP	BUR	OTHER DEC	CATALOGUED
Bur	O	h	bowl?	1 Body		Y	MP	779
GoldmCC		h	jar	1 Base		N	Pmark	814
				2 total				

LATE HELLADIC

O/C	SHAPE	EXTANT PART	PAINT	OTHER DEC	CATALOGUED
O	CP	1 R			
	C basin?	1 H			
C	C jug?	1 H vert rd			
–	CP	1 Base torus;			
		1 Body; 1 H			
		6 total			

LATE HELLADIC II - IIIA1

O/C	SHAPE	EXTANT PART	PAINT	OTHER DEC	CATALOGUED
O	cup	1 R	1 UP		
C	–	1 neck	1 LMP		
		2 total			

LATE HELLADIC III

O/C	SHAPE	EXTANT PART	PAINT	OTHER DEC	CATALOGUED
O	kylix	1 R; 2 stem	3 UP		
C	–	1 H horiz rd	1 UP		
–	–	1 Body	1		
		5 total			

LATE HELLADIC IIIA2

O/C	SHAPE	EXTANT PART	PAINT	OTHER DEC	CATALOGUED
O	st.bowl	1 Body	1 Patt		876
		1 total			

LATE HELLADIC IIIB

O/C	SHAPE	EXTANT PART	PAINT	OTHER DEC	CATALOGUED
O	mug	1 R	1 Patt		
		1 total			

LATE GEOMETRIC TO SUBGEOMETRIC

O/C	SHAPE	EXTANT PART	PAINT	OTHER DEC	CATALOGUED
O	krater	1 Body	pattern		
C	amphora	2 ring	solid		1174
	–	1 Body	pattern		
		4 total			

SITE: B7 (Bardhounia)   16 collected   16 identified

EARLY HELLADIC I

O/C	SHAPE	EXTANT PART	PAINT	BURN	OTHER DEC	CATALOGUED
O	–	4 Body	3 red	1		
C?	–	1 Body	1 red	1		
		5 total				

EARLY HELLADIC I?

O/C	SHAPE	EXTANT PART	PAINT	BURN	OTHER DEC	CATALOGUED
O	bowl?	1 Body	1	1		
	–	3 Body	3	2		
		4 total				

EARLY HELLADIC II

O/C	SHAPE	EXTANT PART	PAINT	BURN	OTHER DEC	CATALOGUED
O	sauceboat/bowl	1 R; 2 ring	2 red; 1 bl			244
	–	1 Body	1 red			
		4 total				

SITE: B8? (Kokkinos Vrakhos)   15 collected   14 identified

FINAL NEOLITHIC

O/C	SHAPE	EXTANT PART	PAINT	BURN	OTHER DEC	CATALOGUED
C	–	1 Body	1 red		1 inc herringbone	65
		1 total				

FINAL NEOLITHIC?

O/C	SHAPE	EXTANT PART	PAINT	BURN	OTHER DEC	CATALOGUED
?	–	1 lug, pierced				50
		1 total				

EARLY HELLADIC I

O/C	SHAPE	EXTANT PART	PAINT	BURN	OTHER DEC	CATALOGUED
O	–	1 Body	1 red	1		
		1 total				

EARLY HELLADIC II

O/C	SHAPE	EXTANT PART	PAINT	BURN	OTHER DEC	CATALOGUED
O	bowl/sauceboat	1 ring				
		1 total				

SITE: B9 (Loutro/ Ayios Andreas)   134 identified   112 collected

FINAL NEOLITHIC

O/C	SHAPE	EXTANT PART	PAINT	BURN	OTHER DEC	CATALOGUED
O	–	1 Body	1?			
		1 total				

FINAL NEOLITHIC - EARLY HELLADIC I

O/C	SHAPE	EXTANT PART	PAINT	BURN	OTHER DEC	CATALOGUED
O	–	1 Body	1	1		
		1 total				

EARLY HELLADIC I

O/C	SHAPE	EXTANT PART	PAINT	BURN	OTHER DEC	CATALOGUED
O	lg sp.bowl	1 R	1 red	1		83
	lg bowl/basin	1 R	1		1 ridge	123
	–	2 Body	2 red	2		
C	–	1 ?	1			
		5 total				

EARLY HELLADIC I - EARLY HELLADIC II

O/C	SHAPE	EXTANT PART	PAINT	BURN	OTHER DEC	CATALOGUED
C	–	1 Body	1 red	1	1 ridges	**188**
		1 total				

EARLY HELLADIC II

O/C	SHAPE	EXTANT PART	PAINT	BURN	OTHER DEC	CATALOGUED
O	lg bowl/basin	3 R	1 bl	1	1 inc; 2 taenia	**421**
	bowl/sauceboat	1 ring	1 yel			**532**
	sauceboat?	1 R				
	–	1 R			1 slashes	
O?	–	1 Body	1			
–	spoon	1 frag				**628**
	stand	1 foot				**642**
		9 total				

EARLY HELLADIC II?

O/C	SHAPE	EXTANT PART	PAINT	BURN	OTHER DEC	CATALOGUED
O	–	3 Body; 1 ring				
		4 total				

LATE HELLADIC

O/C	SHAPE	EXTANT PART	PAINT	OTHER DEC	CATALOGUED
O	lg bowl	1 R	1		
C	C jar	1 Body; 2 H vert	3 Lin		
–	CP	1 Base; 1 Body + H			
–	figurine	1 polos head			**1015**
		7 total			

LATE HELLADIC I - II

O/C	SHAPE	EXTANT PART	PAINT	OTHER DEC	CATALOGUED
O	–	1 stem			
		1 total			

LATE HELLADIC III

O/C	SHAPE	EXTANT PART	PAINT	OTHER DEC	CATALOGUED
O	kylix	1 Body; 3 stem	2; 2 UP		
		4 total			

LATE HELLADIC IIIB

O/C	SHAPE	EXTANT PART	PAINT	OTHER DEC	CATALOGUED
O	deep bowl	1 R; 2 H	2 Lin		
	krater	1 R	1 Lin		**884**
		4 total			

LATE HELLADIC?

O/C	SHAPE	EXTANT PART	PAINT	OTHER DEC	CATALOGUED
O	lg bowl	1 R			
		1 total			

SITE: B16 (Kastro)   186 collected   142 identified

EARLY HELLADIC I

O/C	SHAPE	EXTANT PART	PAINT	BURN	OTHER DEC	CATALOGUED
C	jug	1 Body	1 red	1		
		1 total				

LATE GEOMETRIC

O/C	SHAPE	EXTANT PART	PAINT	OTHER DEC	CATALOGUED
O	krater	4 R	pattern		1113, 1122, 1126
	skyphos	1 H	solid		
		2 Body	pattern		
	basin	1 R			
		8 total			

LATE GEOMETRIC TO SUBGEOMETRIC

O/C	SHAPE	EXTANT PART	PAINT	OTHER DEC	CATALOGUED
O	krater	6 ring; 1 Body; 2 H	2 pattern, 7 solid		
	cup/skyphos	1 Base; 2 Body	solid		
		1 Body	pattern		
	pyxis	1 H	pattern		1157
	pithos	1 R			
	—	26 Body	16 pattern, 10 solid		
C	amphora	4 ring; 4 Body	2 pattern, 6 solid		
	oinochoe?	1 Base	solid		
	jug	2 H			
	—	8 Body	4 pattern, 4 solid		
?	—	1 strap H			
		61 total			

SUBGEOMETRIC

O/C	SHAPE	EXTANT PART	PAINT	OTHER DEC	CATALOGUED
O	Krater	2 R	Pattern		1198
		1 R	solid		
C	amphora	1 ring			
		1 Body	pattern		1121
		5 total			

GEOMETRIC TO ARCHAIC

O/C	SHAPE	EXTANT PART	PAINT	OTHER DEC	CATALOGUED
O	krater	1 R	solid		
	—	13 Body; 1 H	solid		
C	pithos?	1 Body			
	jug	1 H		inset	
—	—	1 H			
		18 total			

SITE: B17 (Roadside)   145 collected   130 identified

EARLY HELLADIC I - EARLY HELLADIC II?

O/C	SHAPE	EXTANT PART	PAINT	BURN	OTHER DEC	CATALOGUED
O?	—	1 Body	1?	1		
		1 total				

EARLY HELLADIC II

O/C	SHAPE	EXTANT PART	PAINT	BURN	OTHER DEC	CATALOGUED
O	lg bowl	1 R				
		1 total				

MIDDLE GEOMETRIC

O/C	SHAPE	EXTANT PART	PAINT	OTHER DEC	CATALOGUED
O	krater	4 R	bands		1041, 1057
		1 Lid R	bands		1056
		3 Body	pattern		1045, 1046, 1047
		5 ped; 1 ring	solid		1042, 1043
		2 H; 3 Body	solid		
		1 R	solid		1040
	skyphos	1 R; 2 Body	solid		
		2 Body	pattern		
C	stand	1 R	solid		1067
	amphora	1 R; 2 H	pattern		1059, 1060, 1061
		1 H; 2 R	solid		1058
		7 Body	solid		
	oinochoe	4 H	bands		
		1 Body	pattern		1066
		3 Body	solid		
		47 total			

MIDDLE TO LATE GEOMETRIC

O/C	SHAPE	EXTANT PART	PAINT	OTHER DEC	CATALOGUED
O	krater	4 Body	pattern		
		3 ring; 1 H	solid		
		7 Body	solid		
		3 Body	bands		
	skyphos	13 Body; 1 ring	solid		1078
	cup	3 Base; 1 R	solid		
C	amphora	1 R	bands		
		7 Body	pattern		
	oinochoe	1 R; 1 Body	solid		
	amphora/oinochoe	6 Body	solid		
	jug	5 Body			
–	–	12 Body	solid		
		69 total			

LATE GEOMETRIC

O/C	SHAPE	EXTANT PART	PAINT	OTHER DEC	CATALOGUED
O	krater	3 Body; 1 H	pattern		1105, 1106, 1107, 1109
		1 Body	solid		
	cup	1 H	band		
C	amphora	1 Body	pattern		1111
		1 Body	bands		
	oinochoe	1 Body	pattern		1177
		9 total			

SITE: B20 (Loutro)   42 collected   42 identified

FINAL NEOLITHIC - EARLY HELLADIC I

O/C	SHAPE	EXTANT PART	PAINT	BURN	OTHER DEC	CATALOGUED
O	bowl	1 R	1 red			
		1 total				

EARLY HELLADIC?

O/C	SHAPE	EXTANT PART	PAINT	BURN	OTHER DEC	CATALOGUED
?	–	1 Body	1	1		
		1 total				

LATE HELLADIC

O/C	SHAPE	EXTANT PART	PAINT	OTHER DEC	CATALOGUED
C?	–	1 Body	1		
		1 total			

GEOMETRIC TO SUBGEOMETRIC

O/C	SHAPE	EXTANT PART	PAINT	OTHER DEC	CATALOGUED
O	–	1 Body	solid		
C	amphora?	1 R	solid		
		2 total			

SITE: B21 (Profitis Ilias Peak #1)   143 collected   129 identified

EARLY HELLADIC?

O/C	SHAPE	EXTANT PART	PAINT	BURN	OTHER DEC	CATALOGUED
C	–	1 Body	1?			
		1 total				

LATE HELLADIC

O/C	SHAPE	EXTANT PART	PAINT	OTHER DEC	CATALOGUED
O	deep bowl?	2 R			
	bowl	1 R; 1 ring	1		
	goblet	1 Body	1?		
	–	1 R; 4 Body	4; 1?		
C	jar	1 H; 1 neck; 1 R + H	1	1 pierced	
	C pithos	3 R; 1 H			946
	–	2 Base			
O?	–	2 Body	1		
C?	–	3 Body	2		
–	CP	1 Base button; 1 H; 1 leg	1	1 pierced	
	figurine	1 frag			1013
	–	5 Body; 3 H	3	1 mend holes	
		36 total			

LATE HELLADIC III

O/C	SHAPE	EXTANT PART	PAINT	OTHER DEC	CATALOGUED
O	kylix	5 stem; 1 Body	3; 1?; 1 UP		
C	jar	1 R; 1 R + H	2		
	C st.jar	1 false mouth			
		9 total			

LATE HELLADIC IIIB

O/C	SHAPE	EXTANT PART	PAINT	OTHER DEC	CATALOGUED
O	deep bowl	3 R; 2 H; 1 Body; 2 Base	3 Lin; 4; 1 Patt (FM50)		905, 908
	st.bowl	1 Body	1 Lin		
		9 total			

LATE HELLADIC IIIC

O/C	SHAPE	EXTANT PART	PAINT	OTHER DEC	CATALOGUED
O	deep bowl	2 R	2 Mono int		933
C	C jug	1 R	1 slip		
		3 total			

LATE HELLADIC?

O/C	SHAPE	EXTANT PART	PAINT	OTHER DEC	CATALOGUED
O	–	8 R; 3 Body; 1 H	2		
C	–	2 Body			
O?	–	1 Base; 1 Body; 1 Base + lug	1 slip		
C?	–	1 Body	1		
–	CP?	2 Body			
	–	2 H	1		
		22 total			

SITE: B24 (Ayios Athanasios)   175 collected   149 identified

EARLY HELLADIC?

O/C	SHAPE	EXTANT PART	PAINT	BURN	OTHER DEC	CATALOGUED
-	plaque	1 Body	1 red			
?	–	1 R	1	1		
		2 total				

EARLY HELLADIC I

O/C	SHAPE	EXTANT PART	PAINT	BURN	OTHER DEC	CATALOGUED
O	lg bowl	1 R	1 red	1	1 grooves	125
	sp.bowl	1 R			1 triangles	87
	–	5 Body	3 red; 2	4; 1?		
C	jar	2 R; 1 Body	3 red	3	1 groove + slashes	138, 150, 159
	–	3 Body	3 red	2; 1?	1 grooves	169
C?	–	1 Body	1 red	1?		
–	–	1 Body	1 red	1		
		14 total				

EARLY HELLADIC I?

O/C	SHAPE	EXTANT PART	PAINT	BURN	OTHER DEC	CATALOGUED
O	bowl	1 R	1	1		
	–	1 Body; 1 Base	2 red			
–	–	5 Body	5	1?		
		8 total				

EARLY HELLADIC I - EARLY HELLADIC II

O/C	SHAPE	EXTANT PART	PAINT	BURN	OTHER DEC	CATALOGUED
O	bowl	1 R			1 imp triangles	
	lg bowl	2 R	2 red	2		
	–	1 Body	1	1		
C?	–	1 Body	1	1?		
?	–	1 R; 1 H				
		7 total				

EARLY HELLADIC II

O/C	SHAPE	EXTANT PART	PAINT	BURN	OTHER DEC	CATALOGUED
O	bowl/sauceboat	8 ring; 4 ped	2 urf; 1 yel; 2			580, 582, 592
	lg bowl	2 R; 1 ring; 1 ped	1 red; 1		1 herringbone	302, 445, 538, 595, 597
	bowl	2 R; 1 Body; 1 ped	1		1 ridge	
	bowl/saucer	1 R	1 bl			
	bowl/basin	17 R	1 urf; 1 red; 1 bl		2 taenia; 2 ridge; 1 slashes; 1 triangles; 1 taenia?	249, 312
	miniature bowl	1 ring				
	sauceboat?	1 R + H	1 urf?			
	sh.bowl/saucer	4 R	2 urf			246
	lg bowl/basin	7 R	3 bl; 2 urf		2 taenia; 3 triangles	412
	deep bowl	4 R			2 triangles	436, 439
	hem.bowl	1 R	1 urf?			
	plate	1 R	1 bl			617
C	jar	2 R; 3 Body	1 ?			
	askos/jug	1 H				
	pithos?	1 knob				627
	–	4 Body			4 ridges	
O?	lg vessel	2 ring	1?			553
C?	–	6 H vert				
–	stand	3 leg; 1 knob	1 red			640
	dipper	1 loop	1 red			
	lg vessel	3 ring	1?			
	scoop	1 H	1 red			
	spoon	1 H	1 bl			629
	rooftile	2 frag				669
	–	1 H vert; 1 H horiz; 7 Body; 1 Base flat	7 urf			
		98 total				

EARLY HELLADIC II?

O/C	SHAPE	EXTANT PART	PAINT	BURN	OTHER DEC	CATALOGUED
O?	–	1 ring				
–	–	5 R				
		6 total				

LATE HELLADIC

O/C	SHAPE	EXTANT PART	PAINT	OTHER DEC	CATALOGUED
O	basin	1 R + H			
	–	1 Body; 1 R?	1		
C	jar	1 R	1 Lin		
C?	–	1 Body	1 Patt		
–	–	1 Body + H	1 Patt		
		6 total			

LATE HELLADIC?

O/C	SHAPE	EXTANT PART	PAINT	OTHER DEC	CATALOGUED
–	–	1 Body?			
		1 total			

SITE: B25 (Loutro northwest) — 108 collected — 94 identified

MIDDLE HELLADIC

WARE	O/C	H/W	SHAPE	EXTANT	SLIP	BUR	OTHER DEC	CATALOGUED
Goldm?	O	h	bowl	1 R	?	N		
				1 total				

LATE HELLADIC

O/C	SHAPE	EXTANT PART	PAINT	OTHER DEC	CATALOGUED
O	bowl	1 R	1?		
	CP tripod	1 R			948
	–	1 Body + H	1		
C	jar	1 R; 2 Body	1 UP; 1 Lin		
O?	–	1 Body	1		
–	C	1 H		1 pierced	
	–	5 Body; 1 Base	5 slip		
		14 total			

LATE HELLADIC III

O/C	SHAPE	EXTANT PART	PAINT	OTHER DEC	CATALOGUED
O	kylix	3 R; 7 stem; 3 Base	8 slip; 1 UP; 1 Patt		995
	goblet	1 Base	1		
	bowl	1 R	1?		
C	jug/jar	1 Body + H vert	1 Lin		
		16 total			

LATE HELLADIC IIIA1

O/C	SHAPE	EXTANT PART	PAINT	OTHER DEC	CATALOGUED
O	cup	1 R	1 Lin		
		1 total			

LATE HELLADIC IIIB

O/C	SHAPE	EXTANT PART	PAINT	OTHER DEC	CATALOGUED
O	st.bowl	1 R	1 Mono		
	deep bowl	1 Base; 1 H	2 Lin?		
		3 total			

SITE: B33 (Moliza #1) — 8 collected — 8 identified

EARLY HELLADIC II

O/C	SHAPE	EXTANT PART	PAINT	BURN	OTHER DEC	CATALOGUED
O	bowl/sauceboat	1 ring	1 urf			
		1 total				

SITE: B38 (Ayios Nikolaos) — 151 collected — 149 identified

EARLY HELLADIC I - EARLY HELLADIC II

O/C	SHAPE	EXTANT PART	PAINT	BURN	OTHER DEC	CATALOGUED
O	lg vessel	1 Body	1 red			
C	lg vessel	1 Body + lug (or H)	1 red			
		2 total				

LATE HELLADIC

O/C	SHAPE	EXTANT PART	PAINT	OTHER DEC	CATALOGUED
O	CP	1 Body; 1 Base; 1 leg			
	bowl	1 R			
	basin?	1 R			
C	C: pithos	2 R			
	–	5 Body	2; 1 UP; 2 Mono		
C?	C	1 foot			
–	–	6 Body; 3 H lg rd	6 UP; 1 Lin; 1; 1?		
		22 total			

LATE HELLADIC III

O/C	SHAPE	EXTANT PART	PAINT	OTHER DEC	CATALOGUED
O	krater (1 FS9)	2 Base; 1 stem	2 Lin		
	bowl/cup	2 R	1 Mono		
C	–	1 Body	1 Lin		
		6 total			

LATE HELLADIC IIIA1

O/C	SHAPE	EXTANT PART	PAINT	OTHER DEC	CATALOGUED
O	cup	2 R + H	2 UP		
		2 total			

LATE HELLADIC IIIB

O/C	SHAPE	EXTANT PART	PAINT	OTHER DEC	CATALOGUED
O	deep bowl	3 Body; 1 H	1 Lin; 3 Mono		
	deep/st.bowl	1 Body	1 Mono		
		5 total			

SITE: B39 (To Milo) 77 collected 67 identified

FINAL NEOLITHIC

O/C	SHAPE	EXTANT PART	PAINT	BURN	OTHER DEC	CATALOGUED
O	deep bowl (jar?)	1 R		1	1 taenia	30
		1 total				

EARLY HELLADIC I

O/C	SHAPE	EXTANT PART	PAINT	BURN	OTHER DEC	CATALOGUED
O	bowl/basin	1 R + lug				118
	bowl	2 Body	2 red	2		
	fruitstand	1 R	1	1	1 grooves	69
	–	5 Body	4 red; 1	5		
C	beaked jug	1 Body	1 red	1		
	–	3 Body; 1 Base	3 red	3		195
–	–	1 ?	1?	1		
		15 total				

EARLY HELLADIC I - EARLY HELLADIC II

O/C	SHAPE	EXTANT PART	PAINT	BURN	OTHER DEC	CATALOGUED
O	deep bowl	1 R				
	–	2 Body	1	2		
C	jug/jar	1 R	1 red	1		
		4 total				

EARLY HELLADIC II

O/C	SHAPE	EXTANT PART	PAINT	BURN	OTHER DEC	CATALOGUED
O	sauceboat/bowl	1 R; 1 ring	1; 1?	1		
	sh.bowl	1 R				
	bowl/basin	4 R	1 urf	1		
	sauceboat	1 H horiz				
	bowl	2 R	2 urf			
	–	2 Body	2 red			
C	pithos	1 R			1 slashes	
	–	3 Body; 1 H	1	1		
C?	lg vessel	1 ring	1 urf			561
–	stand	1 leg			1 slashes	
	table	1 foot				648
	hearth	1 R			1 hatching	663
	–	1 ?				
		22 total				

EARLY HELLADIC II?

O/C	SHAPE	EXTANT PART	PAINT	BURN	OTHER DEC	CATALOGUED
C	–	1 Body				
		1 total				

MIDDLE HELLADIC

WARE	O/C	H/W	SHAPE	EXTANT	SLIP	BUR	OTHER DEC	CATALOGUED
Goldm	O	h	bowl	1 R		Y	MP	801
				1 total				

SITE: B40

LATE GEOMETRIC

O/C	SHAPE	EXTANT PART	PAINT	OTHER DEC	CATALOGUED
O	krater	1 R; 2 Body	pattern		1121
	cup	1 ring	solid		
		4 total			

LATE GEOMETRIC TO ARCHAIC

O/C	SHAPE	EXTANT PART	PAINT	OTHER DEC	CATALOGUED
C	amphora?	1 Body	solid		
?	–	1 ring	solid		
		2 total			

SITE: B41 (Pandeleika)   244 collected   206 identified

FINAL NEOLITHIC

O/C	SHAPE	EXTANT PART	PAINT	BURN	OTHER DEC	CATALOGUED
O	lg bowl	1 R			1 taenia	16
		1 total				

EARLY HELLADIC

O/C	SHAPE	EXTANT PART	PAINT	BURN	OTHER DEC	CATALOGUED
O	–	1 R				
?	–	6 Body				
		7 total				

EARLY HELLADIC?

O/C	SHAPE	EXTANT PART	PAINT	BURN	OTHER DEC	CATALOGUED
O	–	1 Body	1	1		
?	–	2 Body	2	1		
		3 total				

EARLY HELLADIC I

O/C	SHAPE	EXTANT PART	PAINT	BURN	OTHER DEC	CATALOGUED
O	lg bowl	1 R	1 red	1		78
	bowl	1 R	1?	1		
	bowl/basin	1 R	1 red			77
	–	4 Body	2 red; 2?	3; 1?		
O?	–	1 Body; 1 R?	1?	1; 1?		
C?	–	1 Body	1?	1		
–	–	1 Body				
		11 total				

EARLY HELLADIC I?

O/C	SHAPE	EXTANT PART	PAINT	BURN	OTHER DEC	CATALOGUED
O	–	2 Body		2		
		2 total				

EARLY HELLADIC I - EARLY HELLADIC II

O/C	SHAPE	EXTANT PART	PAINT	BURN	OTHER DEC	CATALOGUED
O	bowl	1 R	1?			273
C	–	1 Base		1		
C?	–	2 R; 1 Body; 1 H vert				
?	–	1 Base flat; 1 Base?	1 red	1		
		9 total				

EARLY HELLADIC I - EARLY HELLADIC II?

O/C	SHAPE	EXTANT PART	PAINT	BURN	OTHER DEC	CATALOGUED
?	–	1 H horiz	1	1		
		1 total				

EARLY HELLADIC II

O/C	SHAPE	EXTANT PART	PAINT	BURN	OTHER DEC	CATALOGUED
O	bowl/sauceboat	1 Body; 4 ring	1 red; 1 yel; 1 urf			520
	sauceboat	2 R; 1 H; 2 R + H; 1 ring	2 yel; 3	1		
	lg bowl/basin	9 R	1 yel; 2 urf; 1		1 triangles; 2 slashes; 2 taenia; 1 button	258, 298, 327, 391, 404, 423
	bowl	2 R	1 urf?			250
	lg bowl	2 R	2		1 lug; 1 triangles	277, 434
	bowl/sauceboat	7 R	1 red; 1 bl; 2			240
	–	6 R; 7 Body; 1H;	6; 2?; 1 bl	2	1 inc; 1 triangles;	401, 415, 608

O/C	SHAPE	EXTANT PART	PAINT	BURN	OTHER DEC	CATALOGUED
		1 Base hollow			3 taenia	
C	jug	1 R	1			
	jar	2 R				496, 503
	pithos	1 Body	1 urf			
	–	1 R; 2 H	1	1		
O?	–	2 Body; 1 ped; 1 ring	2	1	1 inc	
C?	–	1 Body	1 red			
–	–	5 Body	5	3	1 appl	
		63 total				

EARLY HELLADIC II?

O/C	SHAPE	EXTANT PART	PAINT	BURN	OTHER DEC	CATALOGUED
O?	–	1 stem				
		1 total				

MIDDLE HELLADIC

WARE	O/C	H/W	SHAPE	EXTANT	SLIP	BUR	OTHER DEC	CATALOGUED
YM	O	h	HFBowl	1 Base	Slip	?		742
Goldm	O	h	bowl	1 R	Red	Y		806
				2 total				

LATE HELLADIC

O/C	SHAPE	EXTANT PART	PAINT	OTHER DEC	CATALOGUED
O	CP tripod	5 leg			
	CP bowl?	2 R	2 slip		961
	CP krater	1 Base			
	krater	1 R	1		
	cup?	1 R; 1 Body	1 UP		
	bowl	1 R + H			
	–	2 Body; 1 Base flat	2 Lin; 1 UP		
C	CP pithos	1 R			
	jar	1 neck	1 Lin		
	–	1 Body; 1 Base flat	1 UP; 1		
C?	–	1 Body	1		
–	CP	1 Base; 2 H; 2 Base button			953, 971
	–	1 Body; 1 H; 5 H horiz			
	figurine animal	1	1	1 pierced	
		33 total			

LATE HELLADIC I

O/C	SHAPE	EXTANT PART	PAINT	OTHER DEC	CATALOGUED
O	vapheio cup	1 Body	1 Patt		
		1 total			

LATE HELLADIC II - IIIA1

O/C	SHAPE	EXTANT PART	PAINT	OTHER DEC	CATALOGUED
C	jug	1 neck	1 LMP		
	jar	1 neck	1 LMP		
		2 total			

LATE HELLADIC III

O/C	SHAPE	EXTANT PART	PAINT	OTHER DEC	CATALOGUED
O	goblet	2 R; 1 Base; 2 stem	3 UP; 1 Lin		
	kylix	3 R; 2 Body; 4 stem; 1 H	7 UP; 1 Mono		998
	krater	1 Body; 1 Base	1 Mono; 1 Lin		
		17 total			

LATE HELLADIC IIIA1

O/C	SHAPE	EXTANT PART	PAINT	OTHER DEC	CATALOGUED
O	goblet (FS254)	1 R	1 Lin		851
		1 total			

LATE HELLADIC IIIA2

O/C	SHAPE	EXTANT PART	PAINT	OTHER DEC	CATALOGUED
O	SAB	1 R	1 UP		1008
	st.bowl	1 stem	1 UP?		
	kylix	2 R; 1 stem	2 UP; 1 Mono		987
	deep bowl/ kylix	1 Body	1 Mono		
	deep/st.bowl	2 Body	2 Mono		
	st.bowl/kylix	1 R	1 Mono		
C	–	1 Body	1 Lin		
		10 total			

LATE HELLADIC IIIB

O/C	SHAPE	EXTANT PART	PAINT	OTHER DEC	CATALOGUED
O	st.bowl	1 R	1 Patt		
	krater (FS59)	1 Base	1 Lin		889
	deep bowl	5 Body	5 Lin		
	deep/st.bowl	1 Body	1 Mono		
		8 total			

LATE HELLADIC IIIC?

O/C	SHAPE	EXTANT PART	PAINT	OTHER DEC	CATALOGUED
O	deep bowl	1 Body	1 Mono		
		1 total			

LATE HELLADIC?

O/C	SHAPE	EXTANT PART	PAINT	OTHER DEC	CATALOGUED
O	–	1 H			
O?	–	1 Base			
–	–	1 H			
		3 total			

SITE: B46 (Korakia promontory) 18 collected 18 identified

FINAL NEOLITHIC

O/C	SHAPE	EXTANT PART	PAINT	BURN	OTHER DEC	CATALOGUED
O	–	1 Body		1		
		1 total				

FINAL NEOLITHIC - EARLY HELLADIC I

O/C	SHAPE	EXTANT PART	PAINT	BURN	OTHER DEC	CATALOGUED
O	–	1 Body		1		
		1 total				

EARLY HELLADIC?

O/C	SHAPE	EXTANT PART	PAINT	BURN	OTHER DEC	CATALOGUED
C	askos?	1 Base	1			
		1 total				

EARLY HELLADIC I - EARLY HELLADIC II

O/C	SHAPE	EXTANT PART	PAINT	BURN	OTHER DEC	CATALOGUED
O	bowl	1 R	1 red			
		1 total				

EARLY HELLADIC II

O/C	SHAPE	EXTANT PART	PAINT	BURN	OTHER DEC	CATALOGUED
O	bowl/sauceboat	1 Body	1 bl			
	lg bowl	1 R			1 taenia	379
		2 total				

EARLY HELLADIC II?

O/C	SHAPE	EXTANT PART	PAINT	BURN	OTHER DEC	CATALOGUED
–	–	1 Body				
		1 total				

LATE HELLADIC

O/C	SHAPE	EXTANT PART	PAINT	OTHER DEC	CATALOGUED
–	CP	1 Base	1 slip		972
	–	1 H rd			
		2 total			

SITE: B49 (Bardhounia #2)

EARLY HELLADIC II

O/C	SHAPE	EXTANT PART	PAINT	BURN	OTHER DEC	CATALOGUED
O	bowl	2 R	1; 1 red	1	1 taenia	370
		2 total				

LATE HELLADIC III

O/C	SHAPE	EXTANT PART	PAINT	OTHER DEC	CATALOGUED
O	kylix	1 stem	1 Lin		
		1 total			

SITE: B53 (Flamboura #2)   67 collected   33 identified

FINAL NEOLITHIC - EARLY HELLADIC I

O/C	SHAPE	EXTANT PART	PAINT	BURN	OTHER DEC	CATALOGUED
O	deep bowl	1 R	1 red	1	1 horiz ridges	18
		1 total				

EARLY HELLADIC I

O/C	SHAPE	EXTANT PART	PAINT	BURN	OTHER DEC	CATALOGUED
–	stand	1 knob				208
		1 total				

SITE: B63 (Flamboura #12)

LATE HELLADIC

O/C	SHAPE	EXTANT PART	PAINT	OTHER DEC	CATALOGUED
–	–	1 Body			
		1 total			

SITE: B81 (Yializa #2)   30 collected   30 identified

EARLY HELLADIC I

O/C	SHAPE	EXTANT PART	PAINT	BURN	OTHER DEC	CATALOGUED
O	bowl	1 Base				
	–	3 R; 1 Base				202
C	jar	1 R; 7 Body	8	8		133
O?	–	1 Body	1	1		
C?	–	1 H; 8 Body	8; 1?	3; 2?		
–	–	1 R; 1 H; 1 Body; 1 Base	2	1; 1?		190
		27 total				

EARLY HELLADIC I - EARLY HELLADIC II

O/C	SHAPE	EXTANT PART	PAINT	BURN	OTHER DEC	CATALOGUED
O	bowl	1 R				98
	–	1 R				303
		2 total				

EARLY HELLADIC II

O/C	SHAPE	EXTANT PART	PAINT	BURN	OTHER DEC	CATALOGUED
O	bowl	1 R			1 taenia	347
		1 total				

SITE: B83 (Yializa #4)

MIDDLE HELLADIC

WARE	O/C	H/W	SHAPE	EXTANT	SLIP	BUR	OTHER DEC	CATALOGUED
GoldmC	C		h?	jar?	1 Base	N		817
				1 total				

LATE HELLADIC

O/C	SHAPE	EXTANT PART	PAINT	OTHER DEC	CATALOGUED
–	CP	1 Base			
		1 total			

LATE HELLADIC III

O/C	SHAPE	EXTANT PART	PAINT	OTHER DEC	CATALOGUED
O	kylix	1 stem	1UP		
		1 total			

SITE: B84 (Yializa #5)   22 collected   15 identified

LATE HELLADIC

O/C	SHAPE	EXTANT PART	PAINT	OTHER DEC	CATALOGUED
–	C	2 H rd	1 UP		
		2 total			

LATE HELLADIC III

O/C	SHAPE	EXTANT PART	PAINT	OTHER DEC	CATALOGUED
O	kylix	1 stem	1 UP		
		1 total			

SITE: B89 (Yializa #10)

LATE HELLADIC

O/C	SHAPE	EXTANT PART	PAINT	OTHER DEC	CATALOGUED
–	CP	1 H lg rd			
		1 total			

LATE HELLADIC II - IIIA1

O/C	SHAPE	EXTANT PART	PAINT	OTHER DEC	CATALOGUED
C	jar	1 neck	1 LMP		
		1 total			

LATE HELLADIC III

O/C	SHAPE	EXTANT PART	PAINT	OTHER DEC	CATALOGUED
O	kylix	1 stem			
		1 total			

SITE: B95/96 (Pikrodhafni #2)   22 collected   15 identified

LATE HELLADIC

O/C	SHAPE	EXTANT PART	PAINT	OTHER DEC	CATALOGUED
C	–	1 Body	1 Lin		
		1 total			

LATE HELLADIC II - IIIA1

O/C	SHAPE	EXTANT PART	PAINT	OTHER DEC	CATALOGUED
C	jar	1 neck	1 LMP		
		1 total			

LATE HELLADIC IIA

O/C	SHAPE	EXTANT PART	PAINT	OTHER DEC	CATALOGUED
C	piriform jar	1 Body	1 Patt		825
		1 total			

SITE: B97 (Pikrodhafni #3)   91 collected   77 identified

EARLY HELLADIC

O/C	SHAPE	EXTANT PART	PAINT	BURN	OTHER DEC	CATALOGUED
C	–	1 R				
-	scoop	1 H				
		2 total				

EARLY HELLADIC I

O/C	SHAPE	EXTANT PART	PAINT	BURN	OTHER DEC	CATALOGUED
O	bowl	1 R			1 taenia w/ herringbone	122
		1 total				

EARLY HELLADIC II

O/C	SHAPE	EXTANT PART	PAINT	BURN	OTHER DEC	CATALOGUED
O	bowl	1 R				
	–	1 ped				
		2 total				

LATE HELLADIC

O/C	SHAPE	EXTANT PART	PAINT		OTHER DEC	CATALOGUED
O	CP tripod	1 leg				
C	–	1 Body	1 slip			
–	CP	1 Body				
	–	3 Body; 1 H lg	1 UP		1 pierced	
		7 total				

LATE HELLADIC III

O/C	SHAPE	EXTANT PART	PAINT		OTHER DEC	CATALOGUED
O	kylix	1 Base; 2 stem	1 Lin; 2 UP			
		3 total				

LATE HELLADIC IIIA2

O/C	SHAPE	EXTANT PART	PAINT		OTHER DEC	CATALOGUED
O	kylix	1 stem	1 Mono			
		1 total				

LATE HELLADIC IIIB

O/C	SHAPE	EXTANT PART	PAINT		OTHER DEC	CATALOGUED
O	st.bowl	1 Base	1 Mono			922
	krater	1 R	1 Lin			886
		2 total				

SITE: B98 (Pikrodhafni #4)   97 collected   52 identified

EARLY HELLADIC

O/C	SHAPE	EXTANT PART	PAINT	BURN	OTHER DEC	CATALOGUED
C	pithos	1 R				
		1 total				

EARLY HELLADIC II

O/C	SHAPE	EXTANT PART	PAINT	BURN	OTHER DEC	CATALOGUED
O	bowl	1 R	1 urf			
	–	1 H	1			
		2 total				

MIDDLE HELLADIC

WARE	O/C	H/W	SHAPE	EXTANT	SLIP	BUR	OTHER DEC	CATALOGUED
Bur	C	h		1 Base		Y		721
				1 total				

LATE HELLADIC

O/C	SHAPE	EXTANT PART	PAINT		OTHER DEC	CATALOGUED
C	–	1 Body	1 slip			
C?	–	1 H			1 pierced	
–	CP	1 Base; 2 H				
	–	1 Body				
		6 total				

LATE HELLADIC III

O/C	SHAPE	EXTANT PART	PAINT	OTHER DEC	CATALOGUED
O	kylix	1 Base	1 slip		
		1 total			

LATE HELLADIC IIIA2

O/C	SHAPE	EXTANT PART	PAINT	OTHER DEC	CATALOGUED
O	kylix	1 R	1 Mono		
	kylix/st.bowl	2 Body	2 Mono		
		3 total			

LATE HELLADIC IIIB

O/C	SHAPE	EXTANT PART	PAINT	OTHER DEC	CATALOGUED
O	deep bowl	1 Body	1 Patt		
	st.bowl	1 R	1 UP		1011
		2 total			

LATE HELLADIC IIIB-IIIC

O/C	SHAPE	EXTANT PART	PAINT	OTHER DEC	CATALOGUED
O	deep bowl	1 H	1 Patt		
		1 total			

SITE: B100 (Pikrodhafni #5)   207 collected   52 identified

EARLY HELLADIC I?

O/C	SHAPE	EXTANT PART	PAINT	BURN	OTHER DEC	CATALOGUED
–	–	1 Body				
		1 total				

EARLY HELLADIC II

O/C	SHAPE	EXTANT PART	PAINT	BURN	OTHER DEC	CATALOGUED
O	bowl	1 R	1	1		
	bowl/sauceboat	1 ring				
	lg bowl	1 R				
	sauceboat?	1 R				
–	–	1 H horiz				
		5 total				

SITE: B101 (Pikrodhafni #6)

EARLY HELLADIC II

O/C	SHAPE	EXTANT PART	PAINT	BURN	OTHER DEC	CATALOGUED
O	sauceboat	1 rim				
		1 total				

SITE: C1 (Ayios Spiridon)   72 collected   40 identified

LATE HELLADIC

O/C	SHAPE	EXTANT PART	PAINT	OTHER DEC	CATALOGUED
O	–	1 Body			
C	jar	1 Body			
–	CP	1 R; 1 H vert			
		4 total			

LATE HELLADIC III

O/C	SHAPE	EXTANT PART	PAINT	OTHER DEC	CATALOGUED
O	kylix	1 Base			
		1 total			

LATE HELLADIC IIIA

O/C	SHAPE	EXTANT PART	PAINT	OTHER DEC	CATALOGUED
O	kylix	1 stem			
		1 total			

SITE: C2 (Lepitsa #1)   20 collected   15 identified

FINAL NEOLITHIC - EARLY HELLADIC I

O/C	SHAPE	EXTANT PART	PAINT	BURN	OTHER DEC	CATALOGUED
O	bowl	1 R				
O?	–	1 Body	1 red	1		
		2 total				

EARLY HELLADIC I?

O/C	SHAPE	EXTANT PART	PAINT	BURN	OTHER DEC	CATALOGUED
–	–	1 Body				
		1 total				

SITE: C3 (Lepitsa #2)   36 collected   35 identified

LATE HELLADIC

O/C	SHAPE	EXTANT PART	PAINT	OTHER DEC	CATALOGUED
O	CP tripod	1 leg			
	sm bowl	1 R	1 Lin		
	basin	1 R	1		1007
	–	1 Body			
–	CP	2 Body; 2 H			
		8 total			

LATE HELLADIC III

O/C	SHAPE	EXTANT PART	PAINT	OTHER DEC	CATALOGUED
O	kylix	1 R; 1 Base	1 Lin; 1 UP		993
	st.bowl	1 R			
		3 total			

LATE HELLADIC IIIA2

O/C	SHAPE	EXTANT PART	PAINT	OTHER DEC	CATALOGUED
O	kylix	1 R	1 Lin		861
	st. bowl/kylix	1 R	1 Mono		
		2 total			

LATE HELLADIC IIIB

O/C	SHAPE	EXTANT PART	PAINT	OTHER DEC	CATALOGUED
O	kylix	1 stem	1 Patt		901
	deep bowl	5 Body	2 Mono; 1 Lin; 2 Patt		
		6 total			

LATE HELLADIC?

O/C	SHAPE	EXTANT PART	PAINT	OTHER DEC	CATALOGUED
O	bowl?	1 R			
		1 total			

LATE GEOMETRIC TO SUBGEOMETRIC

O/C	SHAPE	EXTANT PART	PAINT	OTHER DEC	CATALOGUED
O	krater	1 ring	solid		
C	amphora	1 Body	pattern		
	jug/oinochoe	1 H	solid		
		3 total			

SITE: C8 (Windmill Ridge)   16 collected   16 identified

FINAL NEOLITHIC

O/C	SHAPE	EXTANT PART	PAINT	BURN	OTHER DEC	CATALOGUED
O	–	3 Body	1	1		
C	–	1 Body + H				
		4 total				

EARLY HELLADIC I

O/C	SHAPE	EXTANT PART	PAINT	BURN	OTHER DEC	CATALOGUED
O	–	1 Body		1		
O?	–	1 Body		1		
–	–	1 H				
		3 total				

GEOMETRIC

O/C	SHAPE	EXTANT PART	PAINT	OTHER DEC	CATALOGUED
O	krater	1 Body	bands		
		1 total			

SITE: C11 (Magoula Efstratiou / Mases)   1102 collected   542 identified

FINAL NEOLITHIC

O/C	SHAPE	EXTANT PART	PAINT	BURN	OTHER DEC	CATALOGUED
C	lg vessel	1 Body			1 taenia	62
		1 total				

EARLY HELLADIC

O/C	SHAPE	EXTANT PART	PAINT	BURN	OTHER DEC	CATALOGUED
O	–	2 R	2	2		
C	–	1 Body	1	1		
C?	–	1 Body	1	1		
		4 total				

EARLY HELLADIC?

O/C	SHAPE	EXTANT PART	PAINT	BURN	OTHER DEC	CATALOGUED
O?	–	1 R + H				
		1 total				

EARLY HELLADIC

O/C	SHAPE	EXTANT PART	PAINT	BURN	OTHER DEC	CATALOGUED
O	bowl	3 R; 1 Body	4 red	4		
	lg inc.bowl	1 R	1 red	1	1 trumpet	114
	lg bowl	1 R + H	1	1?		86
	bowl/basin	2 R	2	1; 1?	1 trumpet	112
	sm sh.bowl	1 R	1	1		71
	inc.bowl	1 Body	1 red	1		
	–	6 Body; 1 Base	5 red; 1	5		193

O/C	SHAPE	EXTANT PART	PAINT	BURN	OTHER DEC	CATALOGUED
C	jar	5 R	4	3		130, 137, 148, 156
	–	2 H; 1 knob	3	2	1 grooves	175, 184
O?	–	1 Body				
C?	–	2 H; 1 Base	2 red	1	1 grooves	176
–	–	20 Body	20	some		
		48 total				

EARLY HELLADIC I?

O/C	SHAPE	EXTANT PART	PAINT	BURN	OTHER DEC	CATALOGUED
O	lg vessel	1 Body	1 red			
–	–	3 Body; 1 H				
		5 total				

EARLY HELLADIC I - EARLY HELLADIC II

O/C	SHAPE	EXTANT PART	PAINT	BURN	OTHER DEC	CATALOGUED
O	bowl	1 R	1?		1 taenia?	326
	lg bowl/basin	2 R	1		1 ridge	124
	deep bowl	1 R				126
	–	2 Body	1?			
C	pithos?	1 Body	1		1 ridge	
	–	1 H				
O?	–	1 Body	1	1		
C?	–	1 H	1 red			
?	–	19 Body; 1 H	1 red?		1 grooves	620
		30 total				

EARLY HELLADIC I - EARLY HELLADIC II?

O/C	SHAPE	EXTANT PART	PAINT	BURN	OTHER DEC	CATALOGUED
?	–	1 R				
		1 total				

EARLY HELLADIC II

O/C	SHAPE	EXTANT PART	PAINT	BURN	OTHER DEC	CATALOGUED
O	sauceboat	4 R; 2 H; 2 spout	5 bl; 1 red; 1 yel; 1	3		217
	inc.bowl	4 R; 1 Body	1; 1?; 1 bl			226, 283
	bowl/basin	5 R	2		1 taenia; 2 slashes	390, 395
	lg bowl/basin	1 R	1		1 slashes	414
	lg bowl	6 R; 1 Body; 2 R + H vert; 1 ring	2; 3 red; 2 bl	2?	1 triangle; 3 taenia; 1 slashes	255, 429, 558
	bowl/sauceboat	2 ped	1 yel			
	deep bowl	2 R	1 bl	1	1 grooves	431
	bowl	6 R	2; 1 red; 1 bl	2	1 taenia; 4 inc	345, 397, 410, 416
	hem.bowl	1 R	1 red		1 taenia	359
	basin	1 R			1 taenia	
	sh.bowl	1 R				
	–	1 R; 1 Body; 1 ring; 1 Base round	1; 1 urf		1 taenia; 1 inc	
C	askos	1 R				
	jug	1 R + H				
	jar	8 R; 1 H	1?	2		486, 492, 493, 494, 504, 507

O/C	SHAPE	EXTANT PART	PAINT	BURN	OTHER DEC	CATALOGUED
	jar?	1 Body			1 ridge	
	–	3 Body; 1 H vert; 1 H horiz; 1 ring	1; 1?; 2 red	1		572
O?	–	4 Body; 1 ped; 1 ring; 2 H horiz	1 red; 1 blue		2 taenia	567, 596
C?	–	2 Body 1 H vert; 1 H horiz	1 red			625
–	stand	1 knob; 1 leg				638
	dipper	2 H	1 bl			
	scoop	1 H	1 red			
	–	1 R; 3 Body; 1 ring; 2 H; 1 H vert	1 urf; 2 bl		1 ridge	
		88 total				

EARLY HELLADIC II?

O/C	SHAPE	EXTANT PART	PAINT	BURN	OTHER DEC	CATALOGUED
O	–	1 R; 1 Body; 1 Base	1 urf?; 1 brown	1		
C	pithos	1 knob				
	–	1 Base flat			1 mat imp	615
C?	–	1 Body				
–	–	8 Body			1 mat imp	616
		14 total				

LATE HELLADIC

O/C	SHAPE	EXTANT PART	PAINT	OTHER DEC	CATALOGUED
O	CP tripod	1 leg			
	C bowl	1 R			
	–	1 Body; 1 stem	2		
C	jar	1 Body; 1 neck	1 Lin; 1 UP		
–	CP	1 R; 3 Body; 2 H			
	–	1 foot; 1 Base			
		14 total			

LATE HELLADIC I

O/C	SHAPE	EXTANT PART	PAINT	OTHER DEC	CATALOGUED
O	goblet	1 Base	1 Mono		
		1 total			

LATE HELLADIC II - IIIA1

O/C	SHAPE	EXTANT PART	PAINT	OTHER DEC	CATALOGUED
C	amphora/hydria	1 R; 1 Body	2 LMP		837, 839
–	–	1 H	1 LMP		
		3 total			

LATE HELLADIC III

O/C	SHAPE	EXTANT PART	PAINT	OTHER DEC	CATALOGUED
O	kylix	3 stem; 2 Base	4 UP; 1 Mono		
		5 total			

LATE HELLADIC IIIA

O/C	SHAPE	EXTANT PART	PAINT	OTHER DEC	CATALOGUED
O	kylix	1 Base	1 UP		
		1 total			

LATE HELLADIC IIIA1

O/C	SHAPE	EXTANT PART	PAINT	OTHER DEC	CATALOGUED
O	goblet	1 Base	1 Lin		**854**
		1 total			

LATE HELLADIC IIIA2

O/C	SHAPE	EXTANT PART	PAINT	OTHER DEC	CATALOGUED
O	kylix/st.bowl	1 Body	1 Mono		
		1 total			

LATE HELLADIC IIIB

O/C	SHAPE	EXTANT PART	PAINT	OTHER DEC	CATALOGUED
O	deep bowl	1 Body	1 Patt		**909**
	st.bowl	2 R; 2 Body; 1 stem	2 Patt; 1 Lin; 2 Mono		**917, 919**
	krater	2 Base	2 Lin		**888**
C	st.jar	1 falsemouth	1 Lin		**879**
C	jar?	1 Base	1 Mono		**882**
		10 total			

LATE HELLADIC IIIC

O/C	SHAPE	EXTANT PART	PAINT	OTHER DEC	CATALOGUED
O	krater	1 R	1 Patt		**927**
		1 total			

LATE HELLADIC?

O/C	SHAPE	EXTANT PART	PAINT	OTHER DEC	CATALOGUED
C	–	1 R	1 slip		
		1 total			

LATE GEOMETRIC

O/C	SHAPE	EXTANT PART	PAINT	OTHER DEC	CATALOGUED
O	krater	4 Body	bands		
	skyphos	1 Body	bands		
C	oinochoe	1 Body	solid		
		6 total			

GEOMETRIC TO SUBGEOMETRIC

O/C	SHAPE	EXTANT PART	PAINT	OTHER DEC	CATALOGUED
O	krater	1 R; 1 Body; 1 H	solid		
	skyphos	1 Base	solid		
C	amphora	1 R	solid		
		1 Body	bands		
–	–	3 ring	solid		
		9 total			

SITE: C12 (Vista)   2964 collected   517 identified

EARLY HELLADIC

O/C	SHAPE	EXTANT PART	PAINT	BURN	OTHER DEC	CATALOGUED
O	bowl	1 Base				
		1 total				

EARLY HELLADIC?

O/C	SHAPE	EXTANT PART	PAINT	BURN	OTHER DEC	CATALOGUED
C	–	1 R + H				
		1 total				

EARLY HELLADIC I?

O/C	SHAPE	EXTANT PART	PAINT	BURN	OTHER DEC	CATALOGUED
O	–	1 Body	1	1		
		1 total				

EARLY HELLADIC II

O/C	SHAPE	EXTANT PART	PAINT	BURN	OTHER DEC	CATALOGUED
O	lg bowl	1 R + lug				321
C	jug/askos	1 H				
	askos?	1 R + H				
–	–	1 H				
		4 total				

EARLY HELLADIC II?

O/C	SHAPE	EXTANT PART	PAINT	BURN	OTHER DEC	CATALOGUED
–	–	2 H				
		2 total				

MIDDLE GEOMETRIC

O/C	SHAPE	EXTANT PART	PAINT	OTHER DEC	CATALOGUED
O	krater	1 Body	pattern		1048
	pyxis	1 R	pattern	pierced	1054
C	oinochoe	1 Body	pattern		1065
		3 total			

MIDDLE TO LATE GEOMETRIC

O/C	SHAPE	EXTANT PART	PAINT	OTHER DEC	CATALOGUED
O	krater	1 Body	pattern		1074
	skyphos	1 Body	pattern		1080
		1 ring	solid		1079
	kantharos	1 H	pattern		1084
C	stand	2 R	solid		1091, 1092
		1 R	bands		1093
	oinochoe	1 H	solid	twist	1089
		8 total			

LATE GEOMETRIC

O/C	SHAPE	EXTANT PART	PAINT	OTHER DEC	CATALOGUED
O	krater	9 R; 23 Body	pattern		1098, 1099, 1100, 1101, 1104, 1108, 1114, 1117, 1118, 1123, 1134
		1 H	pattern		1137
		3 H; 2 Body	bands		1135
		2 ring	solid		
	skyphos	1 Base; 2 R	solid		
		3 R; 2 Body	pattern		
	cup	2 R	solid		1150
	kantharos?	1 R	solid		
	pyxis	2 Base	pattern		1155
	–	1 Body; 1 R	solid		

O/C	SHAPE	EXTANT PART	PAINT	OTHER DEC	CATALOGUED
C	amphora	1 H		double	
		1 ring	solid		
		23 Body	pattern		1112, 1165, 1166, 1167, 1168, 1170, 1171
		1 H	pattern		
		1 ring; 1 Body	bands		1164, 1173
	stand	5 R	solid		
	pithos	1 R	solid		1178
	—	4 Body	pattern		
		2 H	solid		
—	lid?	1 R	pattern		
		95 total			

LATE GEOMETRIC TO SUBGEOMETRIC

O/C	SHAPE	EXTANT PART	PAINT	OTHER DEC	CATALOGUED
O	krater	9 R; 11 ring	solid		
		10 H; 9 Body	solid		
		2 Body; 1 R	bands		
		2 R	pattern		
	skyphos	15 H; 6 ring	solid		
		5 R; 2 Body	solid		
		2 Body; 1 R	bands		
		4 R	pattern		
	cup/skyphos	16 Base; 1 Body	solid		
		4 R	pattern		
		2 R	bands		
		6 R; 3 H	solid		
	pyxis?	2 R; 1 Base	solid	pierced	
	—	1 ring; 2 Body	solid		
		1 R; 1 H	solid		
		1 Base			
C	amphora	8 R; 10 ring	solid		
		11 H; 15 Body	solid		
		2 R; 4 Body	pattern		
		11 Body; 1 H	bands		
	oinochoe	1 R	bands		
	oinochoe?	7 H	solid		
	stand?	2 R	solid		
	jug	4 R; 7 Base			
	—	3 ring; 4 Body	solid		
		1 body	bands		
—	—	2 Body; 4 ring	solid		
		3 H; 1 R	solid		
		1 Body; 2 H	bands		
		224 total			

SUBGEOMETRIC

O/C	SHAPE	EXTANT PART	PAINT	OTHER DEC	CATALOGUED
O	krater	1 R	bands		
	skyphos	2 R	pattern		
		3 total			

SITE: C13 (FRANCHTHI CAVE)

<u>EARLY NEOLITHIC</u>
material present

<u>MIDDLE NEOLITHIC</u>
material present

<u>LATE NEOLITHIC</u>
material present

<u>FINAL NEOLITHIC</u>
material present   **29**

SITE: C15 (Prehistoric Site)   121 collected   61 identified

<u>FINAL NEOLITHIC</u>

O/C	SHAPE	EXTANT PART	PAINT	BURN	OTHER DEC	CATALOGUED
O	bowl	1 Base		1		35
	carinated bowl	1 R		1		15
O	–	5 Body	3; 1?	1		
O?	–	1?	1			
		8 total				

<u>FINAL NEOLITHIC - EARLY HELLADIC I</u>

O/C	SHAPE	EXTANT PART	PAINT	BURN	OTHER DEC	CATALOGUED
O	lg bowl/basin	1 R				
	spouted bowl	1 R				
	–	1 R; 4 Body	1			
C	jar	1 Body	1	1		
	–	2 Body	1	1		
?	–	4 Body				
		14 total				

<u>FINAL NEOLITHIC - EARLY HELLADIC I?</u>

O/C	SHAPE	EXTANT PART	PAINT	BURN	OTHER DEC	CATALOGUED
C	–	1 R		1		32
?	–	1 Body; 1?	1	2		
		3 total				

<u>EARLY HELLADIC I</u>

O/C	SHAPE	EXTANT PART	PAINT	BURN	OTHER DEC	CATALOGUED
O	lg hem.bowl	1 R	1 red			93
	Talioti bowl	1 ped			1 taenia	
	–	4 Body	3 red; 1	2		
C	–	2 Body	1 red; 1	2		
O?	–	3 Body	2 red	2	1 drill holes	
C?	–	2 Body	2 red	1		
–	–	1 H			1 grooves	
		14 total				

<u>EARLY HELLADIC I - EARLY HELLADIC II</u>

O/C	SHAPE	EXTANT PART	PAINT	BURN	OTHER DEC	CATALOGUED
O?	–	2 Body				
		2 total				

EARLY HELLADIC II

O/C	SHAPE	EXTANT PART	PAINT	BURN	OTHER DEC	CATALOGUED
O	bowl/sauceboat	1 ring	1 bl			
	sauceboat	1 R	1 red			
	lg bowl/basin	2 R			1?	
C	–	1 H vert	1?			
–	stand	1 leg				641
		6 total				

SITE: C17 (Temple Terrace / Mases)   498 collected   255 identified

EARLY HELLADIC?

O/C	SHAPE	EXTANT PART	PAINT	BURN	OTHER DEC	CATALOGUED
?	–	1 Body				
		1 total				

EARLY HELLADIC I

O/C	SHAPE	EXTANT PART	PAINT	BURN	OTHER DEC	CATALOGUED
O	bowl?	1 R	1	1		82
	–	1 R; 1 Base?; 1 R + H;	2	2	1 perforated	
C	–	1 Body		1		
O?	–	2 Body	1	2		
C?	–	2 Body		1?		
–	–	1 H; 1 Body	1	2		
		11 total				

EARLY HELLADIC I?

O/C	SHAPE	EXTANT PART	PAINT	BURN	OTHER DEC	CATALOGUED
O?	–	3 Body; 1 R?				
		4 total				

EARLY HELLADIC II?

O/C	SHAPE	EXTANT PART	PAINT	BURN	OTHER DEC	CATALOGUED
O?	–	1 R				
		1 total				

MIDDLE TO LATE GEOMETRIC

O/C	SHAPE	EXTANT PART	PAINT	OTHER DEC	CATALOGUED
O	krater	1 R	pattern		1102
	plate	1 H	pattern		1085
C	stand	2 Bd	pattern		1089
		1 R	solid		1090
	amphora	1 R		burnish	1094
		6 total			

LATE GEOMETRIC

O/C	SHAPE	EXTANT PART	PAINT	OTHER DEC	CATALOGUED
O	krater	1 R; 2 Bd	pattern		1129
		4 ring	solid		
O	skyphos	1 R, 1 ring	solid		1146
		1 R	pattern		1140
O	pyxis	1 Bd	pattern		1158
O	bowl	1 R	pattern		1161
C	amphora	4 Bd	pattern		1169, 1110
		1 H	pattern		1176
		17 total			

LATE GEOMETRIC TO SUBGEOMETRIC

O/C	SHAPE	EXTANT PART	PAINT	OTHER DEC	CATALOGUED
O	krater	3 R	pattern		
		4 R; 2 ring	solid		1192
		1 H	solid		
		1 Bd/H	bands		
	skyphos	3 ring; 1 R	solid		
	pyxis?	1 R	solid		
	basin	1 H			
	–	1 Bd	solid		
C	amphora	1 Bs; 3 Bd	bands		
		1 ring; 3 Bd	solid		
	jug	7 R; 6 Bs			
		2 H; 1 Bd			
	oinochoe	2 H	pattern		
		1 Bd; 2 ring	solid		
		1 Bd	bands		
–	pedestal?	2 R	solid		
	–	1 H; 1 ring	solid		
	–	1 Bd	pattern		
		53 total			

SUBGEOMETRIC

O/C	SHAPE	EXTANT PART	PAINT	OTHER DEC	CATALOGUED
O	krater	5 R	solid		
		2 R; 2 Bd	pattern		1202
	stamnos	1 R	solid		1199
	bowl	1 R	solid		1209
C	amphora	1 Bd	pattern		1212
		12 total			

SUBGEOMETRIC TO ARCHAIC

O/C	SHAPE	EXTANT PART	PAINT	OTHER DEC	CATALOGUED
O	krater	1 R	solid		
		2 Bd; 1 R	bands		
		1 ring	bands		
	skyphos	3 Bd; 2 H	solid		
C	amphora	1 ring	solid		
	oinochoe?	1 Bd	solid		
		12 total			

SITE: C20/C21 (Ayios Dhimitrios)

EARLY HELLADIC II?

O/C	SHAPE	EXTANT PART	PAINT	BURN	OTHER DEC	CATALOGUED
O	lg bowl/basin	1 ?			1 taenia	
		1 total				

SITE: C24 (Koukoudhi West)   36 collected   36 identified

FINAL NEOLITHIC

O/C	SHAPE	EXTANT PART	PAINT	BURN	OTHER DEC	CATALOGUED
C?	–	2 Body	1; 1 red	1		
?	–	1 H?				
		3 total				

FINAL NEOLITHIC - EARLY HELLADIC I

O/C	SHAPE	EXTANT PART	PAINT	BURN	OTHER DEC	CATALOGUED
O	–	1 Body	1			
?	–	4 Body				
		5 total				

EARLY HELLADIC I

O/C	SHAPE	EXTANT PART	PAINT	BURN	OTHER DEC	CATALOGUED
O	–	1 Body	1 red	1		
		1 total				

LATE HELLADIC

O/C	SHAPE	EXTANT PART	PAINT	OTHER DEC	CATALOGUED
O	basin	1 R + H	1		
	–	1 Body; 1 ring			
C	jar	1 Body + H	1 Lin		
	–	1 Body			
–	–	1 base ring	1 Lin		
		6 total			

LATE HELLADIC III

O/C	SHAPE	EXTANT PART	PAINT	OTHER DEC	CATALOGUED
O	krater	1 Body			
	basin	1 R + H	1		
		2 total			

LATE HELLADIC IIIB

O/C	SHAPE	EXTANT PART	PAINT	OTHER DEC	CATALOGUED
O	spouted bowl	1 R + spout	1		
	deep bowl	1 Body; 1 H	1 Mono		
	carinated kylix	1 R	1 Mono		904
		4 total			

SITE: C25 (Koukoudhi)   22 collected   22 identified

FINAL NEOLITHIC

O/C	SHAPE	EXTANT PART	PAINT	BURN	OTHER DEC	CATALOGUED
O?	–	1 Body; 2 Base	1; 1?	1		36, 37
		3 total				

FINAL NEOLITHIC?

O/C	SHAPE	EXTANT PART	PAINT	BURN	OTHER DEC	CATALOGUED
?	–	8 Body				
		8 total				

FINAL NEOLITHIC - EARLY HELLADIC I

O/C	SHAPE	EXTANT PART	PAINT	BURN	OTHER DEC	CATALOGUED
O	–	1 Base	1	1		41
		1 total				

EARLY HELLADIC I

O/C	SHAPE	EXTANT PART	PAINT	BURN	OTHER DEC	CATALOGUED
-	spindle whorl	2				211, 212
		2 total				

SITE: C27

<u>LATE GEOMETRIC</u>

O/C	SHAPE	EXTANT PART	PAINT	OTHER DEC	CATALOGUED
O	krater	1 Bd	pattern		
		1 H	solid		
	plate	1 Bd	pattern		1159
	cup/sky	1 Bs	solid		
C	amphora	1 Bd	solid		
	pithos	1 H		incised	1181
		1 R			
	jug	2 Bs			
		9 total			

<u>GEOMETRIC TO ARCHAIC</u>

O/C	SHAPE	EXTANT PART	PAINT	OTHER DEC	CATALOGUED
O	krater	2 Bd	solid		
	–	1 Bs	solid		
C	amphora?	2 Bd	solid		
	jug	2 Hdl			
		7 total			

SITE: C29 (Celt Site)   72 collected   44 identified

<u>FINAL NEOLITHIC</u>

O/C	SHAPE	EXTANT PART	PAINT	BURN	OTHER DEC	CATALOGUED
O	deep bowl	1 R	1 red			
	stopper or burnisher	1 Body	1 red		1 taenia	61
	–	2 Body	1 red	1		
C	–	1 Body; 1 H; 1 knob;	1 red; 1?			56
C?	–	1 Body				
?	–	10 Body; 1 H?				
		19 total				

<u>FINAL NEOLITHIC?</u>

O/C	SHAPE	EXTANT PART	PAINT	BURN	OTHER DEC	CATALOGUED
O	bowl	1 R	1?			
C	–	1 Body; 1 H	1 red; 1			44
C?	–	1 H				46
		4 total				

<u>EARLY HELLADIC?</u>

O/C	SHAPE	EXTANT PART	PAINT	BURN	OTHER DEC	CATALOGUED
O	lg bowl	1 R			1 taenia + slashes	
		1 total				

SITE: C30 (Monastiriaka #1)   85 collected   26 identified

<u>LATE HELLADIC?</u>

O/C	SHAPE	EXTANT PART	PAINT	OTHER DEC	CATALOGUED
–	C	1 Base			
		1 total			

SITE: C36 (Dhouroufi Road #4)

LATE HELLADIC II

O/C	SHAPE	EXTANT PART	PAINT	OTHER DEC	CATALOGUED
O	goblet	1 stem			
		1 total			

SITE: C37 (Kesari)   215 collected   117 identified

FINAL NEOLITHIC - EARLY HELLADIC I

O/C	SHAPE	EXTANT PART	PAINT	BURN	OTHER DEC	CATALOGUED
?	–	1 Body + lug				
		1 total				

FINAL NEOLITHIC - EARLY HELLADIC I?

O/C	SHAPE	EXTANT PART	PAINT	BURN	OTHER DEC	CATALOGUED
?	–	1 Body				
		1 total				

EARLY HELLADIC?

O/C	SHAPE	EXTANT PART	PAINT	BURN	OTHER DEC	CATALOGUED
?	–	1 pedestal				
		1 total				

EARLY HELLADIC II

O/C	SHAPE	EXTANT PART	PAINT	BURN	OTHER DEC	CATALOGUED
O	bowl/sauceboat	1 ring				
		1 total				

LATE HELLADIC

O/C	SHAPE	EXTANT PART	PAINT	OTHER DEC	CATALOGUED
C	C	1 Base	1 ?		
		1 total			

LATE HELLADIC III

O/C	SHAPE	EXTANT PART	PAINT	OTHER DEC	CATALOGUED
O	kylix	1 stem	1 UP		
		1 total			

SITE: C39 (Bayside)

LATE HELLADIC?

O/C	SHAPE	EXTANT PART	PAINT	OTHER DEC	CATALOGUED
–	C	1 ?			
		1 total			

LATE GEOMETRIC

O/C	SHAPE	EXTANT PART	PAINT	OTHER DEC	CATALOGUED
O	krater	1 R	pattern		
		1 total			

SITE: C43

LATE GEOMETRIC

O/C	SHAPE	EXTANT PART	PAINT	OTHER DEC	CATALOGUED
O	krater	2 R, 4 Bd	pattern		
		1 Bd	bands		
		7 total			

SITE: D3 (Dhidhima Cave)   70 collected   50 identified

MIDDLE NEOLITHIC

O/C	SHAPE	EXTANT PART	PAINT	BURN	OTHER DEC	CATALOGUED
O	–	2 Bd	2 urf	2		
		2 total				

MIDDLE NEOLITHIC? - LATE NEOLITHIC?

O/C	SHAPE	EXTANT PART	PAINT	BURN	OTHER DEC	CATALOGUED
O	deep bowl	1 R	1 slip & poly-chrome dots			8
		1 total				

LATE NEOLITHIC

O/C	SHAPE	EXTANT PART	PAINT	BURN	OTHER DEC	CATALOGUED
O	carinated shallow bowl	1 R		1		7
	–	5 Bd	1; 1 bl; 1 matt	3; 1?		10
C	–	3 Bd	1; 1 matt	1		
O?	–	2 Bd	1 cream	1		
		11 total				

FINAL NEOLITHIC

O/C	SHAPE	EXTANT PART	PAINT	BURN	OTHER DEC	CATALOGUED
O	–	3 Bd	1; 1 red; cream	1; 1?	1 appl; 1 inc	63
		3 total				

FINAL NEOLITHIC?

O/C	SHAPE	EXTANT PART	PAINT	BURN	OTHER DEC	CATALOGUED
O	deep bowl	1 R		1	1 finger imp	21
	–	1 Bd		1		
C	–	1 Bd	1	1		
?	–	22 Bd				
		25 total				

EARLY HELLADIC I?

O/C	SHAPE	EXTANT PART	PAINT	BURN	OTHER DEC	CATALOGUED
O	–	1 Bd	1	1		
		1 total				

SITE: D4 (Field #1)   14 collected   14 identified

EARLY HELLADIC I

O/C	SHAPE	EXTANT PART	PAINT	BURN	OTHER DEC	CATALOGUED
O	deep bowl	1 R	1?	1?		
	–	1 Bs				
C	–	1 Bd	1 red			
		3 total				

EARLY HELLADIC II

O/C	SHAPE	EXTANT PART	PAINT	BURN	OTHER DEC	CATALOGUED
O	bowl / basin	1 R			1 taenia	
		1 total				

SITE: D9 (Ayios Ioannis Karteris)

EARLY HELLADIC I

O/C	SHAPE	EXTANT PART	PAINT	BURN	OTHER DEC	CATALOGUED
–	–	1 Bd				
		1 total				

LATE HELLADIC IIIB

O/C	SHAPE	EXTANT PART	PAINT	OTHER DEC	CATALOGUED
O	krater	1 R	1		
		1 total			

SITE: E3 (Thermisi Kastro)   85 collected   81 identified

LATE HELLADIC

O/C	SHAPE	EXTANT PART	PAINT	OTHER DEC	CATALOGUED
C	jar	1 Body	1 Lin		
		1 total			

LATE HELLADIC I - II

O/C	SHAPE	EXTANT PART	PAINT	OTHER DEC	CATALOGUED
O	goblet	1 stem	1 Mono		
		1 total			

LATE HELLADIC IIIA2

O/C	SHAPE	EXTANT PART	PAINT	OTHER DEC	CATALOGUED
O	bowl	1 Body	1 Mono		
		1 total			

LATE HELLADIC IIIC

O/C	SHAPE	EXTANT PART	PAINT	OTHER DEC	CATALOGUED
O	deep bowl	1 R	1 Mono int		932
		1 total			

GEOMETRIC

O/C	SHAPE	EXTANT PART	PAINT	OTHER DEC	CATALOGUED
O	skyphos	1 Base	solid		
		2 R; 1 H	pattern		
	plate	1 R	pattern		
	–	1 Body	solid		
	–	1 H	pattern		
C	–	1 Body	pattern		
		8 total			

GEOMETRIC TO ARCHAIC

O/C	SHAPE	EXTANT PART	PAINT	OTHER DEC	CATALOGUED
O	cup	1 Body	solid		
	plate	1 R	pattern		
	krater?	1 H	solid		
	–	1 Body	pattern		
C	–	1 Body	pattern		
	coarse jug	1 H			
		6 total			

SITE: E4 (Kinetta)   172 collected   86 identified

FINAL NEOLITHIC

O/C	SHAPE	EXTANT PART	PAINT	BURN	OTHER DEC	CATALOGUED
C	collared jar	1 R		1		28
		1 total				

EARLY HELLADIC

O/C	SHAPE	EXTANT PART	PAINT	BURN	OTHER DEC	CATALOGUED
O	–	1 Body	1	1		
C	jar	1 R				
	–	4 Body	1	2		
		6 total				

EARLY HELLADIC?

O/C	SHAPE	EXTANT PART	PAINT	BURN	OTHER DEC	CATALOGUED
O	–	1 Body				
C	–	1 Base flat				
		2 total				

EARLY HELLADIC I

O/C	SHAPE	EXTANT PART	PAINT	BURN	OTHER DEC	CATALOGUED
O	lg bowl	1 R				101
	–	2 Body	1 red	1		
C	–	2 Body	1 red; 1?	1		
O?	–	1 Body	1 red	1		
–	–	1 knob				187
		7 total				

EARLY HELLADIC I - EARLY HELLADIC II

O/C	SHAPE	EXTANT PART	PAINT	BURN	OTHER DEC	CATALOGUED
C	–	1 Body	1 red			
		1 total				

EARLY HELLADIC II

O/C	SHAPE	EXTANT PART	PAINT	BURN	OTHER DEC	CATALOGUED
O	sh.bowl	1 R	1 bl			228
	pithos/lg bowl	1 Body	1 streaks			
	bowl/saucer	2 R; 1 Body	3 urf			
	bowl/sauceboat	2 Body; 3 ring	3 urf; 1 yel; 1 yel?	2		535
	basin/hem.bowl	1 R			1 taenia	253
	bowl	1 R; 1 Body	2		1 ridge	309
	lg bowl/basin	1 R; 1 ring	2	1		
C	jar	2 R	2	1		
	pithos	2 R; 6 Body	7		1 taenia	458
	–	1 Body; 1 H	2	1	1 appl	
O?	–	1 Body			1 appl	
–	–	9 Body	9			
		37 total				

EARLY HELLADIC II?

O/C	SHAPE	EXTANT PART	PAINT	BURN	OTHER DEC	CATALOGUED
O	–	1 R	1			
C	pithos	1 Body	1 red	1?		
	–	1 Body	1	1		
–	–	1 ped				
		4 total				

SITE: E5 (Kouverta)   130 collected   117 identified

LATE NEOLITHIC

O/C	SHAPE	EXTANT PART	PAINT	BURN	OTHER DEC	CATALOGUED
O	–	1 Body	1 urf?			
		1 total				

FINAL NEOLITHIC

O/C	SHAPE	EXTANT PART	PAINT	BURN	OTHER DEC	CATALOGUED
C	deep bowl (or jar)	1 R				31
		1 total				

FINAL NEOLITHIC - EARLY HELLADIC I

O/C	SHAPE	EXTANT PART	PAINT	BURN	OTHER DEC	CATALOGUED
O	–	1 Body	1 red	1		
		1 total				

EARLY HELLADIC

O/C	SHAPE	EXTANT PART	PAINT	BURN	OTHER DEC	CATALOGUED
O	–	1 R; 1 Body; 2 Base	2		1 appl	
C	–	3 Body	1		1 appl	
O?	–	1 foot	1			
?	–	2 Body	1		1 appl	
		10 total				

EARLY HELLADIC?

O/C	SHAPE	EXTANT PART	PAINT	BURN	OTHER DEC	CATALOGUED
O	–	1 Body		1		
?	–	1 Body				
		2 total				

EARLY HELLADIC I

O/C	SHAPE	EXTANT PART	PAINT	BURN	OTHER DEC	CATALOGUED
O	lg hem.bowl	2 R	1 red; 1			92, 95
	–	2 Body	1 red; 1	2		
O?	–	1 Body	1 red	1		
		5 total				

EARLY HELLADIC I - EARLY HELLADIC II

O/C	SHAPE	EXTANT PART	PAINT	BURN	OTHER DEC	CATALOGUED
O	bowl	3 R	2 red; 1?	1		229, 232
C	lg vessel	1 H vert				623
C?	–	1 H vert	1?			
		5 total				

EARLY HELLADIC II

O/C	SHAPE	EXTANT PART	PAINT	BURN	OTHER DEC	CATALOGUED
O	bowl	2 R; 1 ring	1?		2 slashes	392, 399
	sauceboat	2 R; 2 spout	3 urf; 1 bl	1		
	lg bowl	1 R	1 urf		1 taenia	362
	bowl/saucer	2 R	1 urf			
	sh. bowl	1 R	1	1		241
	deep bowl	1 R			1 triangles	
	bowl/sauceboat	2 R; 1 ped	2 blue	1		524, 584
	–	1 R; 1 Body	1 urf			

O/C	SHAPE	EXTANT PART	PAINT		OTHER DEC	CATALOGUED
		1 H vert				
C	pithos	5 R	1; 1 bl		1 triangle; 1 kerbschnitt	447, 467, 469, 482
	jar/pithos	2 R	1			451, 485
	jar	3 R; 1 Body	1; 2 urf			
	pithos?	2 Body				
	–	4 Body; 1 H	2			
–	–	1 H vert				
		37 total				

EARLY HELLADIC II?

O/C	SHAPE	EXTANT PART	PAINT	BURN	OTHER DEC	CATALOGUED
O	sh.bowl?	1 R				
	bowl/basin	1 R	1			
		2 total				

MIDDLE HELLADIC

WARE	O/C	H/W	SHAPE	EXTANT	SLIP	BUR	OTHER DEC	CATALOGUED
Bur	O	h	cup	1 R		Y		749
MP	C	h		1 Body			MP	
Goldm	O	h?	bowl	1 R	Red			
				3 total				

LATE HELLADIC

O/C	SHAPE	EXTANT PART	PAINT	OTHER DEC	CATALOGUED
O	CP tripod	1 R; 2 leg			947
	bowl	1 R			
	goblet	1 R	1 UP		
	CP	2 R			
C	CP jar	1 R			959
–	CP	1 Base			
	–	4 H; 1 Base ring	1		
		14 total			

LATE HELLADIC II

O/C	SHAPE	EXTANT PART	PAINT	OTHER DEC	CATALOGUED
C	–	1 Base	1 Lin		
		1 total			

LATE HELLADIC III

O/C	SHAPE	EXTANT PART	PAINT	OTHER DEC	CATALOGUED
O	kylix	1 Body	1?		
	goblet	1 Base + stem			
	–	1 Body			
		3 total			

LATE HELLADIC IIIA1

O/C	SHAPE	EXTANT PART	PAINT	OTHER DEC	CATALOGUED
O	sh.cup	1 R	1 Patt		845
	goblet	1 R	1 Lin		852
		2 total			

LATE HELLADIC IIIA2

O/C	SHAPE	EXTANT PART	PAINT	OTHER DEC	CATALOGUED
O	kylix	2 R	2 Patt		859, 860
		2 total			

LATE HELLADIC IIIB

O/C	SHAPE	EXTANT PART	PAINT	OTHER DEC	CATALOGUED
O	krater	1 R	1 UP		**979**
	kylix	1 Body	1 Patt		**897**
	deep bowl	1 Body	1 Mono		
		3 total			

LATE HELLADIC?

O/C	SHAPE	EXTANT PART	PAINT	OTHER DEC	CATALOGUED
–	–	2 H	1		
		2 total			

LATE GEOMETRIC

O/C	SHAPE	EXTANT PART	PAINT	OTHER DEC	CATALOGUED
O	krater	1 Body	pattern		
		1 total			

SITE: E7 (Kipraiou / Petrothalassa)   302 collected   146 identified

FINAL NEOLITHIC

O/C	SHAPE	EXTANT PART	PAINT	BURN	OTHER DEC	CATALOGUED
C	jar	1 R		1		23
		1 total				

EARLY HELLADIC I

O/C	SHAPE	EXTANT PART	PAINT	BURN	OTHER DEC	CATALOGUED
O	lg bowl	1 Body	1 red	1		
	–	2 Body	2 red	2		
C	–	1 Body	1 red	1?		
–	–	8 Body	7 red	4		
		12 total				

EARLY HELLADIC I - EARLY HELLADIC II

O/C	SHAPE	EXTANT PART	PAINT	BURN	OTHER DEC	CATALOGUED
O	–	1 H	1 red			
?	–	3 Body; 1 H	1 red			
		5 total				

EARLY HELLADIC II

O/C	SHAPE	EXTANT PART	PAINT	BURN	OTHER DEC	CATALOGUED
C	–	1 Body				
		1 total				

SITE: E8 (Ghiafa / Latovouni)

EARLY HELLADIC II

O/C	SHAPE	EXTANT PART	PAINT	BURN	OTHER DEC	CATALOGUED
O	bowl/sauceboat	1 ring	1 urf			
		1 total				

SITE: E9 (Sambariza Magoula)   274 collected   256 identified

FINAL NEOLITHIC - EARLY HELLADIC I

O/C	SHAPE	EXTANT PART	PAINT	BURN	OTHER DEC	CATALOGUED
O	–	1 Body + lug	1	1		
		1 total				

EARLY HELLADIC?

O/C	SHAPE	EXTANT PART	PAINT	BURN	OTHER DEC	CATALOGUED
O	–	1 Body	1?	1		
C	–	1 H	1 brown			
?	–	1 Body				
		3 total				

EARLY HELLADIC I

O/C	SHAPE	EXTANT PART	PAINT	BURN	OTHER DEC	CATALOGUED
O	bowl	1 R	1 red	1	1 lug	73
	–	5 Body	4 red; 1	3	1 taenia; 1 grooves	174
C	jar	1 R				
	weight?	1 Body	1 red	1	pierced	209
–	–	1 Body	1 red	1		
		9 total				

EARLY HELLADIC I?

O/C	SHAPE	EXTANT PART	PAINT	BURN	OTHER DEC	CATALOGUED
O	–	1 Body	1?	1		
		1 total				

EARLY HELLADIC I - EARLY HELLADIC II

O/C	SHAPE	EXTANT PART	PAINT	BURN	OTHER DEC	CATALOGUED
O	bowl	1 R		1		
	–	1 Body	1	1		
C?	–	1 Body		1		
		3 total				

EARLY HELLADIC II

O/C	SHAPE	EXTANT PART	PAINT	BURN	OTHER DEC	CATALOGUED
O	bowl/sauceboat	3 Body	1 red; 1 bl; 1 urf?			
	bowl/saucer	1 R	1 urf			
	bowl	2 R	1 urf		1 taenia	243
C	–	1 Body	1 urf			
		7 total				

EARLY HELLADIC III

WARE	O/C	SHAPE	EXTANT PART	PAINT	OTHER DEC	CATALOGUED SP
	C		1 Body			
	C	Narrowjar	1 H			689
DoLP	O	bowl	1 R	PP		706
FB	O	bowl	1 R			
	C		1 Body			
MCU	O	bowl	1 R		burn	711
	C	jar	1 R		burn	
			7 total			

MIDDLE HELLADIC

WARE	O/C	H/W	SHAPE	EXTANT	SLIP	BUR	OTHER DEC	CATALOGUED
GM	O	w	cup	1 R		Y		716
	O	h		1 Body		Y		
	C	h		1 Body		Y		
DB	C	h		1 R		Y		
YM	O	w?	bowl	1 R		Y		735
	O	h	cup	1 R	slip	Y		744
	O	h?		2 H		Y		
	O	w?		1 Body, 1 foot		Y		
	C	w		2 Body		Y		
	?	w?		1 Body		Y		
MP	O	w?	bowl	1 H		N	?	
	C	w?		1 Body		N	MP	
Goldm	O	h		1 Body, 1 H		N		
	O	w	bowl	1 R, 1 Body	red	Y		802
	C	h	jug?	1 H		N	MP	
	C	h		2 Body, 1 Base	slip	N	1 MP	
	C	h	jar?	1 Sh		N	MP	
	?	h		1 Body		?	MP	
GoldmC	C	h	jar	1 R		N		812
Coarse	O	w?		1 R				
	C	h		2 Base		N	1 Pmark	819
Unc	C	h		1 Body		N		
	C	h?		1 Body	?		MP	
				31 total				

LATE HELLADIC

O/C	SHAPE	EXTANT PART	PAINT	OTHER DEC	CATALOGUED
O	CP	1 R; 1 H			960
	bowl	1 R	1		
	–	1 R; 4 Body	3	1 burnish	
C	–	5 Body	3		
O?	–	1 Body	1		
C?	–	1 Body	1		
–	–	3 H	3		
		18 total			

LATE HELLADIC II

O/C	SHAPE	EXTANT PART	PAINT	OTHER DEC	CATALOGUED
O	cup	1 Base	1		
		1 total			

LATE HELLADIC IIA

O/C	SHAPE	EXTANT PART	PAINT	OTHER DEC	CATALOGUED
O	vapheio cup	1 Body	1 Patt		829
		1 total			

LATE HELLADIC IIB

O/C	SHAPE	EXTANT PART	PAINT	OTHER DEC	CATALOGUED
O	vapheio cup	1 Body	1 Patt		832
		1 total			

LATE HELLADIC III

O/C	SHAPE	EXTANT PART	PAINT	OTHER DEC	CATALOGUED
O	kylix	2 Body; 1 stem; 2 foot			

O/C	SHAPE	EXTANT PART	PAINT	OTHER DEC	CATALOGUED
	bowl	1 R	1		
	st.bowl/kylix	1 Body	1 Mono		
	–	2 Body	2		
C	–	1 Body	1		
		10 total			

LATE HELLADIC IIIA1

O/C	SHAPE	EXTANT PART	PAINT	OTHER DEC	CATALOGUED
O	cup	1 R; 1 Body	1 Lin; 1 Mono		844
		2 total			

LATE HELLADIC IIIA2

O/C	SHAPE	EXTANT PART	PAINT	OTHER DEC	CATALOGUED
O	st.bowl	1 Body; 1 Base	1 Lin		
	st.bowl/kylix	5 R; 1 Base	6 Mono		867
					869
	kylix	1 Body; 1 Base	2 Mono		
	mug	1 R	1 Patt		858
		11 total			

LATE HELLADIC IIIB

O/C	SHAPE	EXTANT PART	PAINT	OTHER DEC	CATALOGUED
O	deep bowl	5 Body; 1 Base	3 Lin; 2 Patt; 1 Mono		910, 911
	kylix	1 R	1		895
		7 total			

LATE HELLADIC?

O/C	SHAPE	EXTANT PART	PAINT	OTHER DEC	CATALOGUED
O	bowl	1 R			
		1 total			

PROTOGEOMETRIC

O/C	SHAPE	EXTANT PART	PAINT	OTHER DEC	CATALOGUED
O	krater	1 R	pattern		1016
		1 Body	pattern		1017
		1 Body	bands		1019
	krater?	1 H	bands		1029
	skyphos	2 R; 1 H	solid		
		4 R; 6 Body	pattern		1018, 1020
					1021, 1022
	cup	1 R	pattern		1028
	kantharos	1 R	solid		1024
		3 R	bands		1025, 1026, 1027
C	amphora	1 Body	pattern		1031
		1 R	solid		1031
	oinochoe	1 shl	pattern		1032
		1 Body	pattern		1033
		1 H	bands		1034
	jug	1 R/H			1035
		28 total			

PROTOGEOMETRIC TO EARLY GEOMETRIC

O/C	SHAPE	EXTANT PART	PAINT	OTHER DEC	CATALOGUED
O	krater	1 H; 2 Body	solid		
	skyphos	5 Body; 2 H	solid		
		1 R	solid		
	cup	1 Base; 2 R	solid		1037
		1 H	bands		
C	amphora	2 Body	solid		
		17 total			

EARLY GEOMETRIC

O/C	SHAPE	EXTANT PART	PAINT	OTHER DEC	CATALOGUED
O	skyphos	1 R	bands		1036
	cup	2 R	solid		1038, 1039
		3 total			

MIDDLE GEOMETRIC

O/C	SHAPE	EXTANT PART	PAINT	OTHER DEC	CATALOGUED
O	krater	1 Body	pattern		
	skyphos	1 R	pattern		1049
		2 total			

MIDDLE TO LATE GEOMETRIC

O/C	SHAPE	EXTANT PART	PAINT	OTHER DEC	CATALOGUED
O	krater	1 Body	pattern		1073
	kotyle	1 R	pattern		1083
		2 total			

LATE GEOMETRIC

O/C	SHAPE	EXTANT PART	PAINT	OTHER DEC	CATALOGUED
O	krater	1 R	pattern		
		2 Body	pattern		1127
	skyphos	1 R	pattern		1142
		1 Body	bands		
	kotyle	1 R	bands		1153
		6 total			

GEOMETRIC

O/C	SHAPE	EXTANT PART	PAINT	OTHER DEC	CATALOGUED
O	krater	1 Body	solid		
	skyphos	1 H; 2 ring	solid		
		7 Body	solid		
		1 Body	pattern		
C	jug/oinochoe	2 Body	solid		
	jug	2 R/H			
		3 Base			
	amphora	1 H; 3 Body	solid		
		3 Body	bands		
	oinochoe?	1 H	solid		
		27 total			

GEOMETRIC TO ARCHAIC

O/C	SHAPE	EXTANT PART	PAINT	OTHER DEC	CATALOGUED
O	krater	1 Body	band		
	skyphos	2 Body	solid		
C	amphora	1 Body	solid		
		1 Body	bands		
	oinochoe	1 H; 1 Body	solid		
		7 total			

SITE: E11 (Ayioi Apostoloi #1)   8 collected   7 identified

EARLY HELLADIC

O/C	SHAPE	EXTANT PART	PAINT	BURN	OTHER DEC	CATALOGUED
?	–	1 R				
		1 total				

EARLY HELLADIC I

O/C	SHAPE	EXTANT PART	PAINT	BURN	OTHER DEC	CATALOGUED
C	–	2 Body	2 red	2		
O?	–	1 Body				
		3 total				

EARLY HELLADIC II

O/C	SHAPE	EXTANT PART	PAINT	BURN	OTHER DEC	CATALOGUED
O	bowl/sauceboat	1 ring	1 bl			
	sauceboat	1 Body	1			
C	pithos	1 R				
	jug, beaked?	1 R				
		4 total				

SITE: E12 (Ayioi Apostoloi #2)   14 collected   12 identified

EARLY HELLADIC I

O/C	SHAPE	EXTANT PART	PAINT	BURN	OTHER DEC	CATALOGUED
–	–	1 H	1 red			
		1 total				

SITE: E13 (Ermioni Magoula)   149 collected   144 identified

FINAL NEOLITHIC

O/C	SHAPE	EXTANT PART	PAINT	BURN	OTHER DEC	CATALOGUED
O	–	1 Body + lug	1			51
		1 total				

FINAL NEOLITHIC - EARLY HELLADIC I

O/C	SHAPE	EXTANT PART	PAINT	BURN	OTHER DEC	CATALOGUED
C	–	1 Body	1 red	1	1 reserved stripes	68
O?	–	1 Body + lug				
		2 total				

EARLY HELLADIC

O/C	SHAPE	EXTANT PART	PAINT	BURN	OTHER DEC	CATALOGUED
O	–	1 Body	1			
C	pithos	1 Body	1 red		1 lug	
	–	1 Body	1			
		3 total				

EARLY HELLADIC?

O/C	SHAPE	EXTANT PART	PAINT	BURN	OTHER DEC	CATALOGUED
O	–	1 R	1			
C	–	2 Body	1 red			
		3 total				

EARLY HELLADIC I

O/C	SHAPE	EXTANT PART	PAINT	BURN	OTHER DEC	CATALOGUED
O	–	4 Body	4 red	4		
C	jar	1 R	1 red	1		129
	–	1 R; 1 Base	2 red	1		197
O?	–	2 Body			1 pellet; 1 lug	182, 186
C?	–	1 Base	1 red	1		196
		10 total				

EARLY HELLADIC I?

O/C	SHAPE	EXTANT PART	PAINT	BURN	OTHER DEC	CATALOGUED
O	bowl?	1 Body		1	1 burned?	
		1 total				

EARLY HELLADIC I - EARLY HELLADIC II

O/C	SHAPE	EXTANT PART	PAINT	BURN	OTHER DEC	CATALOGUED
C	–	2 Body	2 red	1		
		2 total				

EARLY HELLADIC II

O/C	SHAPE	EXTANT PART	PAINT	BURN	OTHER DEC	CATALOGUED
O	bowl	1 R	1			239
	sauceboat	1 R; 1 Body	1; 1 bl			222
C	jar	2 Body	2 red			502
	–	5 Body	1; 4 bl			
		10 total				

EARLY HELLADIC II?

O/C	SHAPE	EXTANT PART	PAINT	BURN	OTHER DEC	CATALOGUED
O	–	1 Base flat	1 yel?	1		
C	jar?	1 R + H	1			
		2 total				

EARLY HELLADIC III

WARE	O/C	SHAPE	EXTANT PART	PAINT	OTHER DEC	CATALOGUED
SP&U	O		1 Body			691
	C	jar	1 Body			685
	C	Narrow jar	1 R, 1 Body, 3 H			679, 680, 681
	C	pithos?	2 Body			686
SP&B	O	tankard	1 Body			701
	O	Bass bowl	1 Body			700
	O	cup/bowl	1 foot			702
	O	bowl	1 R, 1 Body			699

WARE	O/C	SHAPE	EXTANT		CATALOGUED
	C	Narrowjar	4 H		696, 696, 697, 698
	C		1 Body		
DoLP	O	bowl	1 R	PP	704
FB			2 Body		
MCB	O		2 Body		
	C	jar	1 Body		
MCU	O		3 Body		
	C	pithos	2 Body		
			29 total		

MIDDLE HELLADIC

WARE	O/C	H/W	SHAPE	EXTANT	SLIP	BUR	OTHER DEC	CATALOGUED
GM	O	h	bowl	1 R, 1 Sh, 1 Body		Y	inc	713, 714
	O	w?	bowl	1 Sh, 1 Body		Y		717
	C	w		2 Body		Y		
	C	h		1 Body		Y		
DB	O	h	bowl?	1 R, 1 Body		Y		722, 724
YM	O	h	bowl?	1 R, 1 Base		Y		730
	O	w	bowl	1 R	slip	Y		734
	O	h	HHcup	1 H		Y		
	O	h		1 Body	slip	Y		
	O	w?	HFbowl	1 Base	slip	Y		741
	O	w		1 Base		Y		740
	C	w?		1 Base	slip	Y		
Plain	C	h		1 R, 1 H	?	Y		746, 753
MP	O	h	HHcup	1 R, 2 H	?	Y	MP	768, 769, 776
	O	h	bowl	1 R		N	MP	773
	O	h	bowl?	2 Body		Y	MP	
	O	w		1 R, 1 Body		Y	MP	
	O	h	cup?	1 Body	?	N	MP	775
	O	w?	pan.cup	3 foot	slip	Y	MP	781, 782, 783
	O	h		2 Base	?	?	MP	
	C	w		1 neck	slip	Y		
	C	h		1 Sh, 1 Body	?	Y	MP	756, 758
	C	h	jug?	1 Body, 1 foot	?	N	MP	761, 763
	C	h		1 Body		Y	MP	766
	C	w?		1 Body	slip	Y	MP	
BR	C	h		1 Sh	?	Y	BR	785
LP	O	h		1 Body		Y?	LP	788
	O	h?	bowl?	1 Base		Y?	LP	
	O	w		1 Base		Y?	LP	789
	C	h?		1 Body		Y?	LP	790
Goldm	O	h	bowl	1 R, 1 Sh		?	MP	798
	O	w?	bowl	2 R, 1 H	?	Y	MP	799
	O	h?	HHcup	1 H				
	O	w	bowl	2 R	red	Y		804, 811
	C	h		1 H, 3 Body	3 slip?	3 Y	1 MP	791, 793
	C	w?	jar	1 R			MP	796
Coarse	C	h	pithos?	1 Body				
Unc	O	h	bowl?	1 Body	slip			
—	-	h	whorl	1		Y		823
				60 total				

MIDDLE HELLADIC - LATE HELLADIC

O/C	SHAPE	EXTANT PART	PAINT	OTHER DEC	CATALOGUED
C	jar	1 neck	1 Lin		
		1 total			

LATE HELLADIC

O/C	SHAPE	EXTANT PART	PAINT	OTHER DEC	CATALOGUED
O	CP tripod	1 leg			
	goblet?	1 R	1 UP		
	–	5 Body; 1 Base; 1 H		4; 2 UP	
C	piriform jar	1 Body	1 Lin		
	jar	1 H vert	1 Lin		
	–	1 Body; 2 neck	1 LMP; 1; 1 Lin	1 pierced	
–	figurine (proto phi)	1 torso	1 Patt		1012
		15 total			

LATE HELLADIC II

O/C	SHAPE	EXTANT PART	PAINT	OTHER DEC	CATALOGUED
C	jug	1 Body	1 Patt		
		1 total			

LATE HELLADIC II - IIIA1

O/C	SHAPE	EXTANT PART	PAINT	OTHER DEC	CATALOGUED
O	goblet	1 R	1 Lin		
C	jar	1 R	1 LMP		
		1 total			

LATE HELLADIC IIA

O/C	SHAPE	EXTANT PART	PAINT	OTHER DEC	CATALOGUED
O	goblet	1 Base	1 Mono		831
		1 total			

LATE HELLADIC IIB

O/C	SHAPE	EXTANT PART	PAINT	OTHER DEC	CATALOGUED
O	Ephyraean goblet	1 Body	1 Patt		833
	goblet	1 R; 1 Body	1 Patt; 1 Mono		834, 835
		3 total			

LATE HELLADIC III

O/C	SHAPE	EXTANT PART	PAINT	OTHER DEC	CATALOGUED
O	st.bowl/basin	1 Body	1 Mono		
	kylix	8 stem; 1 Base	9 UP		1003
	krater	2 R; 1 Body	2 Lin; 1 Mono		
		13 total			

LATE HELLADIC IIIA

O/C	SHAPE	EXTANT PART	PAINT	OTHER DEC	CATALOGUED
O	kylix	1 R	1 UP		
		1 total			

LATE HELLADIC IIIA1

O/C	SHAPE	EXTANT PART	PAINT	OTHER DEC	CATALOGUED
O	cup	1 R	1 UP		982
	goblet	2 Body	2 Patt		847, 849
C	piriform jar	2 Body	2 Patt		842
		5 total			

LATE HELLADIC IIIA2

O/C	SHAPE	EXTANT PART	PAINT	OTHER DEC	CATALOGUED
O	st.bowl	1 R; 1 Body; 1 R + H	1 Lin; 2 Mono		872
		3 total			

LATE HELLADIC IIIB

O/C	SHAPE	EXTANT PART	PAINT	OTHER DEC	CATALOGUED
O	cup	1 Base	1 UP		985
	deep bowl	2 H; 3 Body; 2 Base		3 Lin; 3 Mono;	915
			1 UP		
	st.bowl	1 R; 2 Body	3 Lin		918
	mug	1 R	1 Lin		891
	SAB	1 R	1 UP		1009
	krater	1 R	1 Lin		885
		14 total			

LATE HELLADIC IIIB2

O/C	SHAPE	EXTANT PART	PAINT	OTHER DEC	CATALOGUED
O	deep bowl	1 Body	1 Patt		916
		1 total			

LATE HELLADIC IIIC

O/C	SHAPE	EXTANT PART	PAINT	OTHER DEC	CATALOGUED
O	krater (FS281/2)	1 Body + H	1 Patt		929
	st.bowl	1 stem	1 Mono		945
	deep bowl	1 R; 2 Base	1 Patt; 2 Mono		937, 942, 944
C	collar neck jar	1 Body	1 Patt		924
		6 total			

LATE HELLADIC?

O/C	SHAPE	EXTANT PART	PAINT	OTHER DEC	CATALOGUED
O	—	2 Body	1	1 burnish	
C	—	3 Body			
C?	—	1 Body; 1 Body + H		1	
—	—	1 H			
		8 total			

SITE: E14 (Mouzaki Cave)   22 collected   22 identified

MIDDLE NEOLITHIC

O/C	SHAPE	EXTANT PART	PAINT	BURN	OTHER DEC	CATALOGUED
O	bowl?	1 Body	1 bl?	1		
	plate	1 R	1 slip			5
	carinated bowl	1 R	1 urf	1		4
	ped.bowl	1 foot	1 urf	1		2
	deep bowl	1 R	1 red urf	1		1
	—	1 Ped; 1 Body	1 urf; 1 bl	2		3
O?	—	1 Body + Base; 1 Body	1 bl	2		
		9 total				

MIDDLE NEOLITHIC?

O/C	SHAPE	EXTANT PART	PAINT	BURN	OTHER DEC	CATALOGUED
O	—	3 Body	2; 1 red	2		
O?	—	1 R		1		
C?	—	1 Body	1			
?	—	1 Body	1			
		6 total				

LATE NEOLITHIC

O/C	SHAPE	EXTANT PART	PAINT	BURN	OTHER DEC	CATALOGUED
C?	—	2 Body		2		
		2 total				

LATE NEOLITHIC?

O/C	SHAPE	EXTANT PART	PAINT	BURN	OTHER DEC	CATALOGUED
O	bowl	1 R		1		**9**
?	–	1 H		1		**11**
		2 total				

FINAL NEOLITHIC

O/C	SHAPE	EXTANT PART	PAINT	BURN	OTHER DEC	CATALOGUED
C?	–	1 Body		1		
		1 total				

SITE: E16 (Ayioi Anaryiroi Graves)   31 collected   31 identified

EARLY HELLADIC?

O/C	SHAPE	EXTANT PART	PAINT	BURN	OTHER DEC	CATALOGUED
C?	–	1 Body				
		1 total				

EARLY HELLADIC I

O/C	SHAPE	EXTANT PART	PAINT	BURN	OTHER DEC	CATALOGUED
O	lg inc.bowl	1 R				103
	–	2 Body; 1 H	1 red; 2	2		180
C?	–	1 Body	1	1	1 stamped spiral	163
		5 total				

EARLY HELLADIC I - EARLY HELLADIC II

O/C	SHAPE	EXTANT PART	PAINT	BURN	OTHER DEC	CATALOGUED
O	–	1 Body	1	1		
		1 total				

EARLY HELLADIC II

O/C	SHAPE	EXTANT PART	PAINT	BURN	OTHER DEC	CATALOGUED
O	hem.bowl	1 R			1 taenia	256
	sauceboat	2 R	2			
		3 total				

LATE HELLADIC IIIA1

O/C	SHAPE	EXTANT PART	PAINT	OTHER DEC	CATALOGUED
O	–	1 R			
		1 total			

GEOMETRIC TO SUBGEOMETRIC

O/C	SHAPE	EXTANT PART	PAINT	OTHER DEC	CATALOGUED
O	krater?	2 Body	solid		
C	–	1 Body	pattern		
		3 total			

SITE: E19

GEOMETRIC

O/C	SHAPE	EXTANT PART	PAINT	OTHER DEC	CATALOGUED
O	plate	1 R	pattern		1207
		1 total			

SITE: E36 (Hilltop West of Kinetta)   79 collected   65 identified

EARLY HELLADIC?

O/C	SHAPE	EXTANT PART	PAINT	BURN	OTHER DEC	CATALOGUED
C?	–	1 Base				
		1 total				

EARLY HELLADIC II

O/C	SHAPE	EXTANT PART	PAINT	BURN	OTHER DEC	CATALOGUED
O	lg bowl	1 R + H vert	1	1		335
	–	1 R				
		2 total				

SITE: E40

LATE GEOMETRIC TO SUBGEOMETRIC

O/C	SHAPE	EXTANT PART	PAINT	OTHER DEC	CATALOGUED
O	krater	1 R; 1 Body	pattern		1103
	krater?	1 R	pattern		1125
	skyphos	1 Body	solid		
	cup	1 R	solid		
	stand	1 R	solid		
	bowl?	1 R	solid		
	–	1 Body	solid		
C	amphora	1 H; 2 Body	solid		
		2 Body; 1 R	pattern		
		14 total			

SITE: E43 (Pikrodhafni #11)   58 collected   44 identified

EARLY HELLADIC II

O/C	SHAPE	EXTANT PART	PAINT	BURN	OTHER DEC	CATALOGUED
C	lg vessel	1 H vert				
		1 total				

SITE: E47

LATE GEOMETRIC

O/C	SHAPE	EXTANT PART	PAINT	OTHER DEC	CATALOGUED
O	stand	1 R	solid		
		1 total			

SITE: E50 (Pikrodhafni #14 / Ayioi Pantoi)   147 collected   121 identified

EARLY HELLADIC I

O/C	SHAPE	EXTANT PART	PAINT	BURN	OTHER DEC	CATALOGUED
O	–	1 Body	1 red	1		
		1 total				

EARLY HELLADIC II

O/C	SHAPE	EXTANT PART	PAINT	BURN	OTHER DEC	CATALOGUED
–	spoon	1	1 red			
		1 total				

EARLY HELLADIC II?

O/C	SHAPE	EXTANT PART	PAINT	BURN	OTHER DEC	CATALOGUED
–	–	1 R				
		1 total				

SITE: E71 (Ermioni Valley #15)   46 collected   20 identified

LATE HELLADIC III

O/C	SHAPE	EXTANT PART	PAINT	OTHER DEC	CATALOGUED
O	krater/deep bowl	1 Base	1		
		1 total			

SITE: E74 (Asprokhoma)   254 collected   188 identified

FINAL NEOLITHIC - EARLY HELLADIC I

O/C	SHAPE	EXTANT PART	PAINT	BURN	OTHER DEC	CATALOGUED
O	–	2 Body	1?			
C?	–	1 H				
		3 total				

FINAL NEOLITHIC - EARLY HELLADIC I?

O/C	SHAPE	EXTANT PART	PAINT	BURN	OTHER DEC	CATALOGUED
C?	–	1 Body	1?			
		1 total				

EARLY HELLADIC I

O/C	SHAPE	EXTANT PART	PAINT	BURN	OTHER DEC	CATALOGUED
C	jar	2 Body				
O?	–	3 Body; 1 Base	1 red			204
–	–	1 Body			1 lug	183
		7 total				

EARLY HELLADIC I - EARLY HELLADIC II

O/C	SHAPE	EXTANT PART	PAINT	BURN	OTHER DEC	CATALOGUED
O	–	1 Ped				
		1 total				

MIDDLE HELLADIC

WARE	O/C	H/W	SHAPE	EXTANT	SLIP	BUR	OTHER DEC	CATALOGUED
YM	O	w?		1 Body		Y		
Goldm	C	w?		1 Sh	red	Y		
Coarse	O	w?		1 R		?		
	C	h		1 Base		N		822
				4 total				

LATE HELLADIC

O/C	SHAPE	EXTANT PART	PAINT	OTHER DEC	CATALOGUED
O	CP	1 R; 2 Body; 4 Base button		1 pot mark	956
	goblet	1 R; 1 H	1 UP		
	CP tripod	4 leg; 1 H			
	–	3 R; 11 Body; 2 Base; 17 H	1 Lin; 2		

O/C	SHAPE	EXTANT PART	PAINT	OTHER DEC	CATALOGUED
C	CP	2 R			
	jar	1 Body			
	–	27 Body; 3 Base			
O?	–	2 H; 1 foot			
C?	–	1 Body; 1 H		1 pierced	
–	–	1 R; 3 Body; 10 H; 1 foot			
		100 total			

LATE HELLADIC I - II

O/C	SHAPE	EXTANT PART	PAINT	OTHER DEC	CATALOGUED
O	goblet	1 Base	1 Lin		
		1 total			

LATE HELLADIC III

O/C	SHAPE	EXTANT PART	PAINT	OTHER DEC	CATALOGUED
O	kylix	8 stem; 2 Base; 3 Body	9 UP; 1		
	basin	1 R; 1 Body	1; 1 UP		
	–	1 R	1		
C	jug	1 Base			975
	–	1 Body			
		18 total			

LATE HELLADIC IIIA1

O/C	SHAPE	EXTANT PART	PAINT	OTHER DEC	CATALOGUED
O	cup	1 R	1 UP		981
	goblet	1 R	1		
	krater	1 R	1		977
		3 total			

LATE HELLADIC IIIA2

O/C	SHAPE	EXTANT PART	PAINT	OTHER DEC	CATALOGUED
O	kylix	2 R	2 Mono		866
	kylix/st.bowl	1 Body	1 Mono		
		3 total			

LATE HELLADIC IIIA2 - B

O/C	SHAPE	EXTANT PART	PAINT	OTHER DEC	CATALOGUED
C	alabastron	1 R	1 ?		976
		1 total			

LATE HELLADIC IIIB

O/C	SHAPE	EXTANT PART	PAINT	OTHER DEC	CATALOGUED
O	deep bowl	4 Body; 2 H; 1 Base		1 Lin; 1 Patt;	
		1 Base	3; 1 Mono		
	st.bowl	1 H	1 Patt		
	krater	1 R	1		978
C	jug	1 R	1 ?		973
		10 total			

LATE HELLADIC?

O/C	SHAPE	EXTANT PART	PAINT	OTHER DEC	CATALOGUED
O	–	1 R; 1 ped			
C	–	2 Body; 2 Base			
C?	–	2 Base			
–	–	5 H; 2 Base	1		
		15 total			

SITE: E76 (Ermioni Magoula Underwater)   12 collected   12 identified

MIDDLE HELLADIC

WARE	O/C	H/W	SHAPE	EXTANT	SLIP	BUR	OTHER DEC	CATALOGUED
Unbur	O	w?	bowl	1 R			?	
	O	h	bowl	1 Sh		?	?	
Goldm	O	h	bowl	2 R				
Cycl?	O	h?	pan.cup	1 foot	?		MP	780
Coarse	C	h	jar?	1 R, 1 Base				
				7 total				

SITE: F1 (Fournoi Public Schoolyard)   73 collected   70 identified

EARLY HELLADIC I - EARLY HELLADIC II

O/C	SHAPE	EXTANT PART	PAINT	BURN	OTHER DEC	CATALOGUED
O	bowl	1 Body		1		
C?	–	1 Body	1	1		
		2 total				

EARLY HELLADIC II

O/C	SHAPE	EXTANT PART	PAINT	BURN	OTHER DEC	CATALOGUED
O	bowl/sauceboat	1 Body; 2 ring	1 red	1		
	sauceboat	1 R; 1 H	1 red; 1 bl			
	lg bowl	1 R; 1 ring	1 urf			
	bowl	2 R	1 bl		1 triangles	
		9 total				

EARLY HELLADIC II?

O/C	SHAPE	EXTANT PART	PAINT	BURN	OTHER DEC	CATALOGUED
–	–	1 Body; 1 H horiz	1; 1 yel	2		626
		2 total				

LATE HELLADIC IIIA1

O/C	SHAPE	EXTANT PART	PAINT	OTHER DEC	CATALOGUED
O	kylix	1 R			991
		1 total			

LATE HELLADIC IIIA2

O/C	SHAPE	EXTANT PART	PAINT	OTHER DEC	CATALOGUED
O	kylix	1 Body	1 Mono		
		1 total			

SITE: F3 (Lambayana Tower)

EARLY HELLADIC II

O/C	SHAPE	EXTANT PART	PAINT	BURN	OTHER DEC	CATALOGUED
O	bowl/sauceboat	1 ped				
		1 total				

SITE: F4 (Ayios Ioannis)   213 collected   160 identified

EARLY HELLADIC II

O/C	SHAPE	EXTANT PART	PAINT	BURN	OTHER DEC	CATALOGUED
O	bowl	2 R				
	lg bowl	2 R			1 taenia	
C	jar/jug	1 Body	1 bl			
–	–	1 Body	1 bl			
		6 total				

MIDDLE HELLADIC

WARE	O/C	H/W	SHAPE	EXTANT	SLIP	BUR	OTHER DEC	CATALOGUED
YM	O	w	Bowl	1 R	Slip	Y		733
	O	w?		1 R		Y		736
				2 total				

LATE HELLADIC

O/C	SHAPE	EXTANT PART	PAINT	OTHER DEC	CATALOGUED
O	CP tripod	1 R; 4 leg			949, 950
	sm bowl	1 R			
	CP	3 R			963
	–	1 R; 3 Body	3; 1 Mono		
C	C	2 Base			964, 968
	jar	2 Body	2 Lin		
	jar/jug	9 Body	9 Lin		
	jug	1 H	1 Lin		
	–	1 Body; 1 H	1 Lin		
C?	–	1 Body	1		
–	CP	4 H;			957, 958
		3 Base button			
	figurine (phi)	1 stem + Body	1		1014
	–	2 H	1		
		40 total			

LATE HELLADIC I - II

O/C	SHAPE	EXTANT PART	PAINT	OTHER DEC	CATALOGUED
O	krater	1 Base	1 Lin		
C	–	1 Base	1 Lin		
		2 total			

LATE HELLADIC III

O/C	SHAPE	EXTANT PART	PAINT	OTHER DEC	CATALOGUED
O	kylix	2 R; 5 stem;			994, 999, 1005
		1 Body; 2 H;			
		2 Base			
	st.bowl?	1 H			
	kylix/st.bowl	3 Body	3 Mono		
	krater	2 R; 1 Body; 2 Base		1; 4 Lin	1 pierced 887
		19 total			

LATE HELLADIC IIIA1

O/C	SHAPE	EXTANT PART	PAINT	OTHER DEC	CATALOGUED
O	sh.cup	1 Base	1 Mono		846
	goblet	2 R			988
		3 total			

LATE HELLADIC IIIA2

O/C	SHAPE	EXTANT PART	PAINT	OTHER DEC	CATALOGUED
O	kylix	3 R; 1 Body; 1 stem	3 Mono; 2 Lin		
	st.bowl	2 Body	1 Mono; 2 Patt		874, 875
	st.bowl/kylix	1 R	1 Mono		
		8 total			

LATE HELLADIC IIIB

O/C	SHAPE	EXTANT PART	PAINT	OTHER DEC	CATALOGUED
O	deep bowl	4 R; 6 Body; 3 H; 3 Base	12 Lin; 2; 2 Patt		906, 907, 913
	kylix	1 R; 1 Base	1 Lin; 1 Mono		903
	mug	1 Body	1 Patt		892
		19 total			

LATE HELLADIC?

O/C	SHAPE	EXTANT PART	PAINT	OTHER DEC	CATALOGUED
O	–	1 R; 1 Body	1 Lin		
		2 total			

SITE: F5 (Profitis Ilias) 542 collected 534 identified

FINAL NEOLITHIC - EARLY HELLADIC I

O/C	SHAPE	EXTANT PART	PAINT	BURN	OTHER DEC	CATALOGUED
O	-	1 Body	1	1		
		1 total				

EARLY HELLADIC?

O/C	SHAPE	EXTANT PART	PAINT	BURN	OTHER DEC	CATALOGUED
O	–	1 R; 2 Body	1 red-brown; 1 black	1		
O?	–	1 Body				
		4 total				

EARLY HELLADIC I

O/C	SHAPE	EXTANT PART	PAINT	BURN	OTHER DEC	CATALOGUED
O	–	2 Body	1 red; 1 ?	2		
C	–	1 Body			1 chevrons	
		3 total				

EARLY HELLADIC I - EARLY HELLADIC II

O/C	SHAPE	EXTANT PART	PAINT	BURN	OTHER DEC	CATALOGUED
O	bowl	2 R; 2 Body	1 red	2; 1?		
C?	–	1 Body	1	1		
		5 total				

EARLY HELLADIC I - EARLY HELLADIC II?

O/C	SHAPE	EXTANT PART	PAINT	BURN	OTHER DEC	CATALOGUED
O	deep bowl	1 R	1	1		
	–	1 Base; 1 Base flat	1	1		
		3 total				

EARLY HELLADIC II

O/C	SHAPE	EXTANT PART	PAINT	BURN	OTHER DEC	CATALOGUED
O	bowl/sauceboat	3 ring	1 red; 1			**519**
	sauceboat	3 R; 1 ring; 1 spout	3 bl; 1 red; 1 blue			
	bowl	4 R; 1 ped	2; 1 bl	1		**231, 270, 272, 288**
	lg bowl	2 R; 1 Base flat	1 red; 1 brown	1 taenia	**612**	
	bowl/saucer	2 R	2	1		
	–	3 body	2 bl; 1 yel			
C	jar	1 R	1 bl			
	hydria	1 H				
	–	5 Body; 1 H vert	2; 1 bl	1		
O?	–	2 Body	1 bl		1 taenia	
–	rooftile	1 frag				
	–	1 H vert	1 urf			
		33 total				

EARLY HELLADIC II?

O/C	SHAPE	EXTANT PART	PAINT	BURN	OTHER DEC	CATALOGUED
O	–	2 Body	1 red; 1?	1	1 ridge	
C	jug/jar	1 R				
	–	2 Body		1		
C?	–	1 Body; 1 ring; 1 H horiz	1; 1 bl; 1 red			
		8 total				

EARLY HELLADIC III

WARE	O/C	SHAPE	EXTANT PART	PAINT	OTHER DEC	CATALOGUED
DoLP	O	cup/bowl	1 R	PP		**707**
FB	O		1 Base			
FU	O	cup?	1 R			
MCU	C	jar	1 R			**710**
			4 total			

MIDDLE HELLADIC

WARE	O/C	H/W	SHAPE	EXTANT	SLIP	BUR	OTHER DEC	CATALOGUED
GM	C	h?		1 neck		?		
	C	h		1 Body		Y		
	O	h?	bowl?	2 R, 1 H		Y		
	O	h	bowl?	1 Sh, 3 Body, 1 Base		Y		**719, 7**
DB	O	h		2 R, 1 Base		Y	1 groove	**723, 725, 727**
	O	w?		1 R	?	Y		
YM	C	w		1 Body		Y		**728**
	C	h		1 Base, 1 Body		Y		**729**
	O	h	HHcup	1 R, 1 H		Y		**739, 745**
	O	w?		3 R, 4 Body		Y		
	O	w	bowl	1 R, 1 Sh, 2 Body		Y		**738, 743**
Bur	C	h		2 R, 1 Sh, 1 Body		Y		**747**
	O	h	bowl	4 R, 1 Sh, 4 Body		Y	1 groove	**748, 752**
	O	h	HFbowl	1 foot		Y		**755**
	O	h?	Cup	1 Body		Y		
	O	h?		3 Body	slip	Y		

Ware	O/C	h/w	Shape	Extant Part	Paint	Other Dec	Dec	Catalogued
MP	C	h	jar	1 R			MP	757
	C	w	jar	1 neck			MP	760
	C	w?		1 Sh, 3 Body		1 Y	MP	759, 767
	C	h		1 Sh, 3 Body	1 ?	3 Y	MP	764, 765
	O	w	bowl?	1 R			MP	772
	O	h	bowl	1 R, 1 Body	slip	1 Y	MP	777
	O	w?		1 Sh	slip		MP	770
	O	h	cup	2 Body		1 Y	MP	774
	O	h	bowl?	1 Body, 1 Base	?	?	MP	771
	O	w		1 Base			MP	778
LP	C			1 H			LoD	787
BR	C	w		1 Body	slip	Y	BR	784
Goldm	C	h	jar?	1 R, 1 neck, 5 Body		Y	MP	792, 7
	C	w?		2 Body			MP	
	C	h		3 Body	slip		MP	
	C	h?		2 Body			MP	
	O	h	bowl	4 R	2 red	3 Y	1 MP	797, 805
	O	w	bowl	1 R		Y	MP	800
	O	w?	bowl	2 Sh, 2 Body	1 red	1 Y	3 MP	809
	O	h?		4 Body			MP	
	O	h		2 Body	1 slip		1 MP	
	O	h	HFbowl	1 foot	red	Y		810
Coarse	C	h	pithos	1 R		?		
	C	h?		1 Body	slip	Y		
GoldmC	C	h	jar	1 R				813
Unc	O	w?		1 R			MP	
—	—	h	whorl	1		Y		824

103 total

LATE HELLADIC

O/C	SHAPE	EXTANT PART	PAINT	OTHER DEC	CATALOGUED
O	bowl	1 R	1 Lin		
	C	1 R			962
	CP tripod	1 leg			951
	—	3 R; 3 Base; 1 H; 25 Body	16 Lin; 13 UP		
C	jar	2 R + H; 5 Body; 1 H	8 Lin		
	—	37 Body; 2 Base	16 Lin; 16 UP; 5 Mono		
C?	—	1 Body; 4 H	1 Mono; 3		
—	—	4 H; 1 ring	4 UP		
	C	1 H	1		

93 total

LATE HELLADIC I - II

O/C	SHAPE	EXTANT PART	PAINT	OTHER DEC	CATALOGUED
O	cup	1 Body	1		
	—	3 Body	3		

4 total

LATE HELLADIC II - IIIA1

O/C	SHAPE	EXTANT PART	PAINT	OTHER DEC	CATALOGUED
O	krater	1 Base	1 LMP		841

1 total

LATE HELLADIC IIA

O/C	SHAPE	EXTANT PART	PAINT	OTHER DEC	CATALOGUED
C	bridge-spouted jug	1 H	1 Patt		827
		1 total			

LATE HELLADIC IIB

O/C	SHAPE	EXTANT PART	PAINT	OTHER DEC	CATALOGUED
O	goblet	1 Base	1 Mono		836
		1 total			

LATE HELLADIC III

O/C	SHAPE	EXTANT PART	PAINT	OTHER DEC	CATALOGUED
O	kylix	3 R; 2 H; 6 Base; 7 stem	8 UP; 1 Mono; 4 Lin	2	997, 1 1004
	krater	1 R; 7 Body	5 Lin; 1; 2 Mono		
	goblet	1 Base; 1 stem	2 UP		989
	st.bowl	4 Body	4 Lin		
	spouted bowl	1 R + spout	1 Lin		
C	st.jar	1 mouth	1 Lin		
	jug	1 Base; 1 H	1 UP; 1 Lin		974
–	dipper	1 R	1 UP		986
		37 total			

LATE HELLADIC IIIA

O/C	SHAPE	EXTANT PART	PAINT	OTHER DEC	CATALOGUED
O	lipless bowl	1 Base			980
		1 total			

LATE HELLADIC IIIA1

O/C	SHAPE	EXTANT PART	PAINT	OTHER DEC	CATALOGUED
O	cup	1 Body	1 Patt		
	kylix	1 R	1 UP		992
	krater	1 R	1 Lin		855
	goblet	1 R; 1 Body; 1 stem	2 Patt; 1 Lin		848, 850, 853
	goblet/kylix	1 R	1 Mono		
		7 total			

LATE HELLADIC IIIA2

O/C	SHAPE	EXTANT PART	PAINT	OTHER DEC	CATALOGUED
O	kylix	2 R; 2 stem; 1 Body; 1 H	3 Mono; 1 Lin; 2 Patt		862, 863, 864
	st.bowl	4 R	2 Patt; 1 UP; 1 UP?		870, 871, 1010
	cup	2 R	2 UP		983, 984
	bowl	1 R	1 Lin		877
	kylix/st.bowl	1 R	1 Mono		865
		14 total			

LATE HELLADIC IIIB

O/C	SHAPE	EXTANT PART	PAINT	OTHER DEC	CATALOGUED
O	kylix	2 R; 3 stem; 1 Body	3 Lin; 3 Patt		894, 896, 898, 902
	deep bowl	2 R; 4 H; 2 Base; 41 Body	32 Mono; 17 Lin		912, 914

O/C	SHAPE	EXTANT PART	PAINT	OTHER DEC	CATALOGUED
	st.bowl	1 Body + H	1 Lin		921
	mug	1 R; 1 Body	1 Lin; 1 Patt		893
	conical bowl	1 Base	1 Lin		923
	krater	1 R; 1 Base	1 Mono; 1 Patt		883, 890
C	piriform jar	1 Body	1 Patt		878
	amphora/jug / hydria	1 R	1 Lin		880
		63 total			

LATE HELLADIC IIIC

O/C	SHAPE	EXTANT PART	PAINT	OTHER DEC	CATALOGUED
O	deep bowl	1 R; 6 Body; 2 Base		7 Patt; 2 UP;	931, 935, 936, 938, 939, 940, 941, 1006
	krater	1 R	1 Lin		928
	kylix	1 Base	1 Lin		930
C	amphora/hydria	1 R; 1 Body	1 Patt; 1 Lin		925, 926
	piriform jar	1 R	1 Lin		
		14 total			

LATE HELLADIC?

O/C	SHAPE	EXTANT PART	PAINT	OTHER DEC	CATALOGUED
O	–	2 R; 3 Body			
C	pithos	2 R; 1 Body		1 taenia	
	–	1 R; 6 Body; 1 Body + H	4		
O?	–	1 Body	1		
C?	–	2 Body; 1 Base	1		
–	–	1 H			
		21 total			

MIDDLE TO LATE GEOMETRIC

O/C	SHAPE	EXTANT PART	PAINT	OTHER DEC	CATALOGUED
O	krater	1 Ped	bands		1071
		2 Body	pattern		1076
C	jug	1 H		twist	1095
		4 total			

LATE GEOMETRIC

O/C	SHAPE	EXTANT PART	PAINT	OTHER DEC	CATALOGUED
O	krater	1 R; 1 H	pattern		
		2 Body	pattern		1128
	skyphos	1 Body; 2 R	pattern		1141, 1147
C	amphora	1 R			1183
	pithos	1 Body		taenia	1179
	—	2 Body	pattern		
		11 total			

GEOMETRIC

O/C	SHAPE	EXTANT PART	PAINT	OTHER DEC	CATALOGUED
O	skyphos	1 Body; 1 ring	solid		
		1 H			
	–	4 Body	solid		
		2 Body	pattern		
C	jug	1 R			
	–	3 Body	solid		
		13 total			

SUBGEOMETRIC

O/C	SHAPE	EXTANT PART	PAINT	OTHER DEC	CATALOGUED
O	skyphos	1 Base	solid		**1206**
		1 total			

GEOMETRIC TO ARCHAIC

O/C	SHAPE	EXTANT PART	PAINT	OTHER DEC	CATALOGUED
O	–	5 Body	solid		
C	amphora	1 R; 1 Body	solid		
		7 total			

SITE: F6 (Fournoi Magoula)   110 collected   110 identified

FINAL NEOLITHIC - EARLY HELLADIC I

O/C	SHAPE	EXTANT PART	PAINT	BURN	OTHER DEC	CATALOGUED
O	–	3 Body; 1 H	2 red	1	1 grooves; 1 appl	**48**
		4 total				

EARLY HELLADIC?

O/C	SHAPE	EXTANT PART	PAINT	BURN	OTHER DEC	CATALOGUED
O	–	1 R				
?	–	1 H	1	1		
		2 total				

EARLY HELLADIC I

O/C	SHAPE	EXTANT PART	PAINT	BURN	OTHER DEC	CATALOGUED
O	lg bowl	1 R			1 taenia	**74**
	sm bowl	1 R		1		**128**
	–	2 Body	2 red	2		
C	–	1 Body	1 red	1		
–	–	1 H	1 red	1		
		6 total				

EARLY HELLADIC I - EARLY HELLADIC II

O/C	SHAPE	EXTANT PART	PAINT	BURN	OTHER DEC	CATALOGUED
O	lg bowl/basin	1 R	1 red	1	1 taenia	**375**
	–	2 Body		1		
		3 total				

EARLY HELLADIC II

O/C	SHAPE	EXTANT PART	PAINT	BURN	OTHER DEC	CATALOGUED
O	bowl	4 R	1 red	1	1 triangles	**420**
	deep bowl	2 R	2		1 taenia	**265, 266**
	lg bowl	9 R; 3 ped	2	2	6 taenia; 2 slashes	**348, 366, 375**
	basin	1 R				
	bowl/saucer	8 R	7		1?	
	sh.bowl	6 R	1 urf			
	sauceboat	4 R; 1 Body; 1 Body + H; 1 R + H; 1 H	6 urf	1?		
	bowl/sauceboat	1 R; 2 Body; 3 ped; 4 ring	1 blue; 4 red; 1 bl	2		**581** **585**
	sauceboat?	1 H horiz				
	–	2 R; 1 Body; 1 ring	3	2	1 taenia	

O/C	SHAPE	EXTANT PART	PAINT	BURN	OTHER DEC	CATALOGUED
C	askos/jug	1 H vert				
	beaked jug	1 spout				
	jar	3 R; 1 H horiz				495
	pithos	1 R				463
	pithos?	1 R			1 hatching	479
	–	1 R; 1 H; 1 Body	1		1 ridge	
O?	–	1 H vert?	1 bl		1 grooves	
–	rooftile	1 frag				
	dipper	2 H				
	stand	1 Body				
	–	2 ring; 1 foot?				575
		74 total				

EARLY HELLADIC II?

O/C	SHAPE	EXTANT PART	PAINT	BURN	OTHER DEC	CATALOGUED
O	–	2 Body	1	1		
–	–	1 Body; 1 Base flat	1			
		4 total				

EARLY HELLADIC III

WARE	O/C	SHAPE	EXTANT PART	PAINT	OTHER DEC	CATALOGUED
SP&B	O	bowl	2 R			693
			2 total			

LATE GEOMETRIC TO SUBGEOMETRIC

O/C	SHAPE	EXTANT PART	PAINT	OTHER DEC	CATALOGUED
O	Krater	3 Body; 1 R	solid		1205
C	–	1 Body	solid		
		5 total			

SITE: F7 (Lambayana Shore)   13 collected   13 identified

EARLY HELLADIC II

O/C	SHAPE	EXTANT PART	PAINT	BURN	OTHER DEC	CATALOGUED
O	bowl/sauceboat	1 ring				
	bowl	1 R			1 taenia	
–	–	1 ped				
		3 total				

SITE: F9 (Korita)   31 collected   26 identified

FINAL NEOLITHIC

O/C	SHAPE	EXTANT PART	PAINT	BURN	OTHER DEC	CATALOGUED
O	–	1 Body	1	1		
C?	–	1 Body	1 red	1		
		2 total				

FINAL NEOLITHIC - EARLY HELLADIC I

O/C	SHAPE	EXTANT PART	PAINT	BURN	OTHER DEC	CATALOGUED
O	–	1 Body	1	1		
C?	–	1 H			1 inc	64
		2 total				

FINAL NEOLITHIC - EARLY HELLADIC I?

O/C	SHAPE	EXTANT PART	PAINT	BURN	OTHER DEC	CATALOGUED
O	–	2 Body		2		
O?	–	1 R				
		3 total				

EARLY HELLADIC I

O/C	SHAPE	EXTANT PART	PAINT	BURN	OTHER DEC	CATALOGUED
O	–	7 Body	6 red; 1 ?	7		
C	jar	1 R	1 red	1		
	–	2 Body	2 red	1	1 inc herringbone	165
–	frying pan	1 Body	1 red	1	1 stamp	206
–	spindle whorl	1 complete				210
O?	–	1 Body	1			
		13 total				

EARLY HELLADIC I?

O/C	SHAPE	EXTANT PART	PAINT	BURN	OTHER DEC	CATALOGUED
–	–	1 Body		1 ?		
		1 total				

EARLY HELLADIC II

O/C	SHAPE	EXTANT PART	PAINT	BURN	OTHER DEC	CATALOGUED
O	lg bowl/basin	1 Body	1?	1	1 taenia	
		1 total				

SITE: F13 (Magoula West Field)   8 collected   8 identified

EARLY HELLADIC II

O/C	SHAPE	EXTANT PART	PAINT	BURN	OTHER DEC	CATALOGUED
O	bowl/sauceboat	1 ring				
	bowl	1 R			1 taenia	
	lg bowl	1 R				
		3 total				

SITE: F14 (Palaiokastro)   5 collected   5 identified

FINAL NEOLITHIC

O/C	SHAPE	EXTANT PART	PAINT	BURN	OTHER DEC	CATALOGUED
O?	–	1 Body			1 inc	66
		1 total				

FINAL NEOLITHIC - EARLY HELLADIC I

O/C	SHAPE	EXTANT PART	PAINT	BURN	OTHER DEC	CATALOGUED
O	–	1 Body		1		
O?	–	1 Body	1 red	1		
		2 total				

FINAL NEOLITHIC - EARLY HELLADIC I?

O/C	SHAPE	EXTANT PART	PAINT	BURN	OTHER DEC	CATALOGUED
O?	–	1 Body				
		1 total				

SITE: F15 (Magoula East)   20 collected   18 identified

EARLY HELLADIC I

O/C	SHAPE	EXTANT PART	PAINT	BURN	OTHER DEC	CATALOGUED
O	lg bowl/basin	1 R	1 ?		taenia	
		1 total				

EARLY HELLADIC II

O/C	SHAPE	EXTANT PART	PAINT	BURN	OTHER DEC	CATALOGUED
O	lg bowl/basin	3 R	1	1	2 taenia	261, 267
	bowl/sauceboat	1 ring	1			
	lg bowl	1 ped				
		5 total				

MIDDLE HELLADIC

WARE	O/C	H/W	SHAPE	EXTANT	SLIP	BUR	OTHER DEC	CATALOGUED
?	O	h	basin	1 R	slip		MP?	
				1 total				

LATE HELLADIC

O/C	SHAPE	EXTANT PART	PAINT	OTHER DEC	CATALOGUED
O	CP	1 H			
		1 total			

LATE HELLADIC III

O/C	SHAPE	EXTANT PART	PAINT	OTHER DEC	CATALOGUED
O	kylix	1 Body; 1 stem	1 UP; 1 Lin		
		2 total			

LATE HELLADIC?

O/C	SHAPE	EXTANT PART	PAINT	OTHER DEC	CATALOGUED
O	cup	1 R	1		
		1 total			

LATE GEOMETRIC TO SUBGEOMETRIC

O/C	SHAPE	EXTANT PART	PAINT	OTHER DEC	CATALOGUED
O	krater	1 H; 1 Body	solid		
		2 Body	banded		
O	skyphos	1 ring; 1 Body	solid		
		6 total			

SITE: F16 (Palaiokastro Orchard)   28 collected   28 identified

EARLY HELLADIC II

O/C	SHAPE	EXTANT PART	PAINT	BURN	OTHER DEC	CATALOGUED
O	large bowl	1 R				
	bowl/basin	2 R			1 ridge	
	bowl	1 R				
	bowl/sauceboat	2 ring				
—	conical seal	1 complete			1 grooves	632
	—	1 Base flat;				
		1 H vert?				
		9 total				

LATE HELLADIC III

O/C	SHAPE	EXTANT PART	PAINT	OTHER DEC	CATALOGUED
O	kylix	2 stem	1 Lin; 1 UP		
		2 total			

LATE HELLADIC?

O/C	SHAPE	EXTANT PART	PAINT	OTHER DEC	CATALOGUED
O?	–	1 Body	1		
		1 total			

SITE: F17 (Fournoi Field)   48 collected   25 identified

EARLY HELLADIC I

O/C	SHAPE	EXTANT PART	PAINT	BURN	OTHER DEC	CATALOGUED
C	–	1 Body	1 red	1	1 groove + slashes	167
		1 total				

EARLY HELLADIC I - EARLY HELLADIC II

O/C	SHAPE	EXTANT PART	PAINT	BURN	OTHER DEC	CATALOGUED
C?	pyxis?	1 Body	1 red-brown	1		
	jug/askos	1 H	1 red			
		2 total				

EARLY HELLADIC II

O/C	SHAPE	EXTANT PART	PAINT	BURN	OTHER DEC	CATALOGUED
O	lg bowl	1 R; 1 ring; 1 R + H	1 bl	1?	1 slashes	441
						337
	bowl/sauceboat	1 ring				
C	pithos	2 R			1 taenia?	476
	jug/askos	1 H vert			1 grooves	
	jar	1?				
–	–	1 Body	1 bl			
		9 total				

LATE HELLADIC III

O/C	SHAPE	EXTANT PART	PAINT	OTHER DEC	CATALOGUED
O	cup	1 Body	1		
	–	1 R	1		
		2 total			

LATE HELLADIC IIIA2

O/C	SHAPE	EXTANT PART	PAINT	OTHER DEC	CATALOGUED
C	piriform jar	1 Body	1 Patt		856
		1 total			

LATE HELLADIC IIIC

O/C	SHAPE	EXTANT PART	PAINT	OTHER DEC	CATALOGUED
O	krater	1 Body	1 Mono		
		1 total			

GEOMETRIC TO SUBGEOMETRIC

O/C	SHAPE	EXTANT PART	PAINT	OTHER DEC	CATALOGUED
O	krater	1 ring	solid		
	skyphos/cup	1 Base	solid		
C	pithos	1 R			1182
		3 total			

SITE: F18 (Oura)   12 collected   10 identified

EARLY HELLADIC I

O/C	SHAPE	EXTANT PART	PAINT	BURN	OTHER DEC	CATALOGUED
O	–	1 Body 1 total	1 red	1		

EARLY HELLADIC II

O/C	SHAPE	EXTANT PART	PAINT	BURN	OTHER DEC	CATALOGUED
O	lg bowl/basin	1 R 1 total				

EARLY HELLADIC II?

O/C	SHAPE	EXTANT PART	PAINT	BURN	OTHER DEC	CATALOGUED
O	–	1 R; 1 stem 2 total				

LATE HELLADIC

O/C	SHAPE	EXTANT PART	PAINT	OTHER DEC	CATALOGUED
C	jar	1 R + H 1 total	1 UP		

LATE HELLADIC?

O/C	SHAPE	EXTANT PART	PAINT	OTHER DEC	CATALOGUED
–	–	1 Body; 1 H 2 total	1 UP		

SITE: F19 (Palaios Milos)   43 collected   40 identified

EARLY HELLADIC I - EARLY HELLADIC II

O/C	SHAPE	EXTANT PART	PAINT	BURN	OTHER DEC	CATALOGUED
O	–	1 Body 1 total	1 red	1		

EARLY HELLADIC II

O/C	SHAPE	EXTANT PART	PAINT	BURN	OTHER DEC	CATALOGUED
O	lg bowl	1 R				
	bowl	1 R			1 slashes	422
C	askos?	2 H vert	1?			
C?	–	1 Base 5 total				

LATE HELLADIC

O/C	SHAPE	EXTANT PART	PAINT	OTHER DEC	CATALOGUED
–	CP	1 H 1 total			

LATE HELLADIC?

O/C	SHAPE	EXTANT PART	PAINT	OTHER DEC	CATALOGUED
–	CP	1 H 1 total			

SITE: F20 (Dhardhitsa) 119 collected 119 identified

<u>FINAL NEOLITHIC?</u>

O/C	SHAPE	EXTANT PART	PAINT	BURN	OTHER DEC	CATALOGUED
C?	pithos	1 Body		1	1 knob	55
		1 total				

<u>EARLY HELLADIC I - EARLY HELLADIC II</u>

O/C	SHAPE	EXTANT PART	PAINT	BURN	OTHER DEC	CATALOGUED
O	lg bowl	1 R	1?		1 ledge	322
	bowl	1 R	1?	1?	1 ledge	320
	–	1 Body	1 red	1		
		3 total				

<u>EARLY HELLADIC II</u>

O/C	SHAPE	EXTANT PART	PAINT	BURN	OTHER DEC	CATALOGUED
O	sauceboat	3 spout	2 yel; 1?	2		
	lg bowl	2 R; 1 ring	1 bl; 1		1 triangles; 1 taenia	444, 552
	bowl/saucer	3 R	1 bl			
	sauceboat?	1 Body	1 polychrome			
	sh.bowl	3 R	1			
	basin	1 R	1 bl			251
	bowl	5 R; 1 Prof	1; 1 band; 1 bl			238, 245, 291
	bowl/sauceboat	1 ring	1 blue			
C	jar/hydria	2 Body	2 urf		2 taenia	
	jar	1 R	1 urf			508
	pithos	7 R; 72 Body	4 bands; 2 irreg; 3 wash; 69 slip; some matt bands			452, 459, 460, 464, 465, 468, 470, 483
–	–	2 Body	1; 1 bl	1	1 taenia	
	dipper	1 H				
	hearth	1 R				665
	rooftile	2 frags				676
		109 total				

<u>LATE HELLADIC IIIA1</u>

O/C	SHAPE	EXTANT PART	PAINT	OTHER DEC	CATALOGUED
O	goblet	1 stem	1 UP		990
		1 total			

SITE: F21 (North Field #1) 43 collected 43 identified

<u>EARLY HELLADIC I - EARLY HELLADIC II</u>

O/C	SHAPE	EXTANT PART	PAINT	BURN	OTHER DEC	CATALOGUED
O	bowl	1 R			1 ledge + slashes	324
		1 total				

<u>EARLY HELLADIC II</u>

O/C	SHAPE	EXTANT PART	PAINT	BURN	OTHER DEC	CATALOGUED
O	lg bowl/basin	4 R			1 lug or ridge; 1 taenia	
	bowl/sauceboat	1 ring	1 blue	1		

C	askos/jug	1 H vert	1		
	lg vessel	1 H horiz			
		7 total			

LATE HELLADIC

O/C	SHAPE	EXTANT PART	PAINT	OTHER DEC	CATALOGUED
O	goblet	1 H	1 Lin		
	CP	1 R			
	–	1 R; 2 Base;	3 Mono; 3 UP;		
		8 Body	2 Lin		
C	–	1 Body	1 Patt		
		14 total			

LATE HELLADIC III

O/C	SHAPE	EXTANT PART	PAINT	OTHER DEC	CATALOGUED
O	krater	1 R	1 Mono		
	kylix/st. bowl	1 Body	1 Lin		
		2 total			

LATE HELLADIC IIIB

O/C	SHAPE	EXTANT PART	PAINT	OTHER DEC	CATALOGUED
O	deep bowl	4 Body; 1 H	5 Lin		
	kylix	1 stem	1 Patt		899
		6 total			

SITE: F23 (Visha)   87 collected   74 identified

EARLY HELLADIC II

O/C	SHAPE	EXTANT PART	PAINT	BURN	OTHER DEC	CATALOGUED
O	bowl	1 ring	1 red	1		542
	–	1 Body	1 urf			
C	askos/jug	1 Body	1 urf			
C?	–	1 Body	1	1		
		4 total				

MIDDLE HELLADIC

WARE	O/C	H/W	SHAPE	EXTANT	SLIP	BUR	OTHER DEC	CATALOGUED
GoldmC	C	h		jar	1 Base		Y	Pmark 816
				1 total				

LATE HELLADIC

O/C	SHAPE	EXTANT PART	PAINT	OTHER DEC	CATALOGUED
C	jar	1 Body	1 Lin		
O?	CP	1 Base			
		2 total			

SITE: F26 (Asprokhoma)   30 collected   26 identified

EARLY HELLADIC?

O/C	SHAPE	EXTANT PART	PAINT	BURN	OTHER DEC	CATALOGUED
O?	–	1 R?				
		1 total				

EARLY HELLADIC II

O/C	SHAPE	EXTANT PART	PAINT	BURN	OTHER DEC	CATALOGUED
O	bowl/saucer	1 R	1 red			
C	–	1 Base flat				
C?	–	1 H vert				
		3 total				

MIDDLE HELLADIC

WARE	O/C	H/W	SHAPE	EXTANT	SLIP	BUR	OTHER DEC	CATALOGUED
GM	C	h	jar	Intact		Y	imp	712
	O	h?	bowl	1 R		Y		
YM	O	w?	bowl	1 Body	slip	Y		737
Goldm	O	h?	bowl	2 R	1 red	1 Y	1 ?	803
GoldmC	C	h		jar	1 Base		Pmark	815
				6 total				

LATE HELLADIC

O/C	SHAPE	EXTANT PART	PAINT	OTHER DEC	CATALOGUED
C	jug	1 H	1 UP		
	–	1 Base			
O?	CP	1 Body			
–	CP	1 H			
	–	6 Body	3 Lin		
		10 total			

LATE HELLADIC IIA

O/C	SHAPE	EXTANT PART	PAINT	OTHER DEC	CATALOGUED
O	goblet	1 Base	1 Mono		830
		1 total			

LATE HELLADIC III

O/C	SHAPE	EXTANT PART	PAINT	OTHER DEC	CATALOGUED
O	kylix	1 stem	1 UP		
	bowl?	1 R	1		
		2 total			

LATE HELLADIC IIIB

O/C	SHAPE	EXTANT PART	PAINT	OTHER DEC	CATALOGUED
O	deep bowl	1 H	1 Lin		
		1 total			

SITE: F29 (House of Dhimitrios Theodhorou)   11 collected   11 identified

EARLY HELLADIC II

O/C	SHAPE	EXTANT PART	PAINT	BURN	OTHER DEC	CATALOGUED
O	bowl/sauceboat	1 R; 1 Body	1 bl			227
		2 total				

EARLY HELLADIC II?

O/C	SHAPE	EXTANT PART	PAINT	BURN	OTHER DEC	CATALOGUED
O	–	1 Body				
–	lg vessel	1 ring				
		2 total				

LATE HELLADIC

O/C	SHAPE	EXTANT PART	PAINT	OTHER DEC	CATALOGUED
O	CP	1 Base			969
	–	1 Body			
C	–	3 Body	3 UP		
		5 total			

LATE HELLADIC IIIA2

O/C	SHAPE	EXTANT PART	PAINT	OTHER DEC	CATALOGUED
O	st.bowl	1 Body	1 Mono		
		1 total			

SITE: F32 (Petres)   902 collected   829 identified

FINAL NEOLITHIC - EARLY HELLADIC I

O/C	SHAPE	EXTANT PART	PAINT	BURN	OTHER DEC	CATALOGUED
O	–	1 Body		1		
		1 total				

EARLY HELLADIC

O/C	SHAPE	EXTANT PART	PAINT	BURN	OTHER DEC	CATALOGUED
S						
O	–	1 Body		1		
		1 total				

EARLY HELLADIC?

O/C	SHAPE	EXTANT PART	PAINT	BURN	OTHER DEC	CATALOGUED
C9						
?	–	1 H horiz rd				
C11						
?	–	1 H horiz				
		2 total				

EARLY HELLADIC I

O/C	SHAPE	EXTANT PART	PAINT	BURN	OTHER DEC	CATALOGUED
E						
C?	–	1 Body	1 red	1?		
N						
O	fruitstand	1 R			1 diag lines	70
	bowl	1 Body	1 red	1		
C	jar	1 Body	1		1 diag slashes	160
	–	1 Body	1 red	1	1 inc	
S						
O	bowl	1 Body			1 taenia	120
	lg bowl/basin	3 R	1 red; 1	2	1 taenia; 1 trumpet; 1 appl	117, 121
	lg bowl	1 R	1		1 trumpet	113
	bowl/saucer	1 Body	1			
	–	5 Body	2 red; 3	5		
C	jar	1 Body	1	1		
	–	1 Body	1 red	1		
O?	–	2 Body	1 red; 1	1		
C?	–	5 Body	4 red	3	1 groove & slashes	166
		25 total				

EARLY HELLADIC I?

O/C	SHAPE	EXTANT PART	PAINT	BURN	OTHER DEC	CATALOGUED
A3						
O	T-rim bowl	1 R	1 ?	1		107

EARLY HELLADIC I - EARLY HELLADIC II

O/C	SHAPE	EXTANT PART	PAINT	BURN	OTHER DEC	CATALOGUED
A3						
O	bowl	1 R	1 red			105
A7						
O	bowl/basin	1 R			1 trumpet	110
B4						
O	bowl	1 R	1 red-brown	1		
D4						
O	lg bowl/basin	1 R				
C	jar/jug	1 R	1 red	1		
1973						
O	bowl	1 R			1 trumpet	111
N						
O	bowl	1 R; 1 R + H	1 red			290, 334
	–	1 Body	1			
C	–	1 Body	1			
O?	–	1 Body	1			
S						
O	lg bowl	1 R			1 trumpet	115
	bowl/saucer	1 R	1 red	1		
	–	6 Body	4 red; 1?	3		
C	–	4 Body	4	2; 1?		
O?	–	2 Body	1; 1 red	1		
C?	–	2 Body	1; 1 red			
		27 total				

EARLY HELLADIC I - EARLY HELLADIC II?

O/C	SHAPE	EXTANT PART	PAINT	BURN	OTHER DEC	CATALOGUED
SF						
O?	–	1 Base flat		1		
		1 total				

EARLY HELLADIC II

O/C	SHAPE	EXTANT PART	PAINT	BURN	OTHER DEC	CATALOGUED
–	hearth	1 rim			1 inc	660
A1						
O	bowl/sauceboat	3 ring	1 urf; 1?			531
	sh.bowl	1 R				
	bowl/basin	2 R	1			
C	jar/jug	1 R				
C?	lg vessel	2 Body			1 taenia	
A3						
O	bowl	1 R	1 red-br			305
	lg bowl	3 R	1 red; 1 bl		1 taenia; 1 triangles	308, 367, 440
	basin	1 R				
	bowl/saucer	4 R	2 bl; 1 red-br			
	sh.bowl	1 R	1 red-br			275
	sauceboat	1 spout	1 bl			
	bowl/sauceboat	1 Body	1 bl			

C	lg vessel	1 H vert	1			
–	stand	1 leg				
	scoop	1 H	1 bl			
	rooftile	1 frag				
O?	–	1 Body			1 taenia	
A5						
O	sh.bowl	2 R	1 red-br; 1 bl			271, 300
	deep bowl basin	1 R			1 taenia	
	bowl/saucer	1 R	1 red-br	1		
	bowl	3 R	1 bl; 1		1 slashes	389
	bowl/sauceboat	1 ring	1?			
	lg bowl	1 R				
C	pithos	1 R	1	1		
–	stand	1 knob				
A7						
O	lg bowl	3 R			1 slashes	428
	bowl/basin	1 R	1 bl			
O?	lg vessel	1 ring				565
A9						
O	lg bowl	3 R; 1 R + H			3 taenia; 1 slashes + taenia	330, 364
	bowl/sauceboat	1 ring				
	bowl	1 R	1 red			234
A11						
O	lg bowl	3 R			1 taenia; 1 slashes	
	bowl/saucer	1 R				
	bowl/sauceboat	1 ped				586
	deep vessel	1 R	1 bl			484
	bowl	1 R				
C	pithos	1 R			1 taenia	
B2						
O	lg bowl/basin	2 R			2 taenia	
	bowl/sauceboat	1 ring	1 bl			
–	stand	1 leg				643
	–	1 ped				
B4						
O	lg bowl/basin	1 R	1 red		1 ridge	
	bowl/saucer	1 R	1?			
	bowl/sauceboat	4 ring	3 red			
–	scoop	1 H	1			
B6						
O	lg bowl	2 R; 1 ring	1			566
	bowl	1 R; 1 ring	1 bl; 1 red		1 ridge	317
–	scoop?	1 H	1			
B8						
O	lg bowl/basin	4 R			2 ridge; 1 taenia	
	lg basin	1 R			1 taenia	354
	lg bowl	1 ring				577
	bowl/sauceboat	3 ring	1 bl			
C	jar	1 Body			1 taenia	514
B10						
O	lg bowl/basin	1 R; 1 Body			1 taenia; 1 trumpet	
	bowl/sauceboat	1 ring	1 yel			

–	hearth	1 R			1 triangles	662
B12						
O	lg bowl/basin	1 R; 1 ring			1 taenia	551
	bowl	1 ped				
C	pithos	1 R	1 bl			472
–	stand	1 leg				636
C1						
O	bowl/sauceboat	2 ring	1 blue			
	lg bowl	1 R				
C2						
O	bowl	1 R			1 slashes	443
C3						
O	lg bowl/basin	2 R				
	bowl/sauceboat	1 ring	1 red			
C	jar	1 Body	1?			
C4						
O	bowl	1 R			1 taenia	352
C5						
O	lg bowl	1 R; 1 Body	1	1	1 ridge; 1 taenia	323
	bowl	1 R	1 red-br	1		236
	bowl/sauceboat	1 ring				
	sauceboat	1 R	1 bl			
C7						
O	bowl	2 R	1 bl		1 taenia	349
	lg bowl	3 R	1 bl		2 taenia	331
C9						
O	lg bowl	2 R; 1 ring; 1 R + H vert			2 taenia	571
	bowl/sauceboat	1 ring; 1 ped	1; 1 bl			601
C?	–	1 ring				560
–	dipper	1 H				
C11						
O	lg bowl	1 R; 1 ring				
C	jar	1 R		1		449
–	stand	1 leg				
	–	1 ped				
D2						
O	lg bowl	1 R			1 triangles	
C	jug	1 spout	1 bl			516
–	dipper	1 H				
D4						
O	lg bowl	8 R	1 bl		1 taenia; 1 ridge	383
	bowl/saucer	2 R	1 red-br	1		
	bowl	1 R	1 bl			
	lg bowl?	1 ring				568
	bowl/sauceboat	1 ring				
O?	–	1 ring				530
C?	–	1 Base flat; 1 Base hollow				609
D6						
O	bowl/sauceboat	1 R; 2 ring	1 bl			
	bowl	1 R			1 taenia	353
C	sm jar/pithos	1 R			1 zigzag	448

D8						
O	lg bowl	4 R			2 taenia	
	bowl/sauceboat	3 ring	1 red; 1?	1?		
	bowl	1 R				
	bowl/saucer	1 R				
	lg vessel	1 ring				
C	pithos	1 R				474
	aksos?	1 Body + H			1 groove	622
C?	lg vessel	1 leg				
—	stand	1 leg				
	stand?	1 corner				
	hearth	1 rim			1 triangles	654
	—	1 Body			1 taenia	
D10						
O	bowl/saucer	2 R	1 bl	1		
	lg bowl	1 R				
C	jar	1 Body				
	lg vessel	1 H vert				
D12						
O	lg bowl	1 R			1 slashes	419
	bowl/saucer	1 R				
SF						
O	lg bowl	1 R; 1 ped	1; 1 bl		1 loop appl	314, 598
	sh.bowl	1 R	1		1 inc	281
	bowl/sauceboat	1 ring				
C	jug/askos	1 H vert	1		1 button	
C?	—	1 Body	1 brown			
—	stand	1 knob				
E						
O	lg bowl	11 R; 1 R + H; 3 ring	4; 2 bl; 1?	1	4 taenia; 1 ledge; 2 ridge	301, 311, 339, 363, 576
	lg bowl?	1 R			1 taenia?	
	basin/lg basin	1 R				
	bowl/saucer	1 R	1 red-br			
	bowl	2 R; 1 ring			1 slashes	396, 534
	bowl/sauceboat	1 Body; 1 ped	1 red			589
	sauceboat	1 R	1 bl			220
	lg vessel	2 ring				
	—	1 ped				
C	jar	2 R; 1 Body	1 urf; 1?; 1 brown			509, 511
	jar/jug	1 Body				
O?	lg vessel	1 ring	1			547
C?	—	1 Base flat; 1 H vert; 1 H hydria				
—	scoop	4 H	1 bl; 1 brown			
	stand	1 leg/foot				633
	—	1 ped; 2 H vert				
1973						
O	lg basin	3 R	1 red		1 taenia; 1 triangles	254, 296, 405
	lg bowl/basin	22 R	1 self; 2 red; 1 bl	1	11 taenia; 4 ridge; 1?; 1 triangles	262, 282

	lg bowl	7 R; 1 ring	1 red; 3 bl; 1; 1 brown		1 slashes; 4 taenia; 1 triangles; 1 lug	282, 340, 356, 360, 381, 418, 438, 544
	bowl	4 R; 1 ped	1; 1 bl	1	2 taenia; 1 slashes	286, 342, 385, 393
	spouted bowl	1 R + spout				426
	sm bowl	1 R	1 bl			284
	lg vessel	1 R; 1 ring			1 taenia	
	bowl/sauceboat	6 ring	1 bl; 1 blue; 1 red-br	1		527
	sauceboat	1 R	1 bl			
	bowl?	1 Body	1 urf			
C	pithos	1 R			1 taenia	
	lg vessel	1 ring	1			548
	askos/jar	2 H vert	1 yel	1		
	jar	2 Body	1			
	jar?	1 Body			1 taenia	
O?	lg vessel	1 ring				562
C?	—	1 Base flat; 1 Base hollow	1 bl			610
—	scoop	2 H				
	hearth	2 R			2 hatched triangles	657, 659
	—	2 H vert			1 taenia	
<u>N</u> O	sauceboat	3 R; 1 Body; 3 spout; 5 H	5 bl; 1 blue; 2			223
	sh.bowl	1 R	1 bl			
	bowl	10 R; 1 ped; 3 ring	1 bl; 2 urf; 1; 1 red	1; 1?	3 slashes; 3 taenia; 1 triangles; 1 ridge; 1 trumpet	109, 274, 294, 310, 343, 355, 387, 400, 403, 433, 435, 521, 540, 594
	lg bowl	25 R; 1 Body; 1 ring; 5 ped	4 red; 1 bl; 6; 1?; 2 red-br; 1 brown	2	1 triangles; 9 slashes; 9 taenia; 2 ledge; 1 trumpet	116, 257, 263, 299, 307, 325, 328, 329, 361, 369, 377, 378, 382, 386, 406, 407, 408, 411, 413, 417, 424, 425, 590, 593, 599, 600, 606
	lg bowl/basin	41 R; 3 R + H vert	3 red; 3 bl; 2; 1?	1	16 taenia; 2 trumpet?; 1 inc; 1?; 2 slashes; 5 ridge	306, 333, 336
	bowl/saucer	5 R	2 red; 1 bl; 2			
	bowl/sauceboat	5 Body; 5 ped; 18 ring; 1 Base	1 red?; 6; 4 red; 3 yel; 7 bl	2		518, 525, 526, 533, 537, 583, 591, 602
	basin	3 R	1 bl; 1			252
	spouted bowl	1 spout	1 yel	1	1 inc?	427
	—	2 Body; 6 ring	2; 1?; 1 bl	1?		550, 554, 578

	askos	1 H vert			1 groove + button	
	askos?	3 H vert; 1 R? + H	1 bl; 1 yel; 2	1	2 groove	621
	pithos?	1 Body	1 bl			
	—	1 Body; 2 ring; 5 H vert	1 bl; 2 urf	1		557, 624
O?	lg bowl?	1 Body			1 appl	
	lg vessel	1 ring				556
	pan?	1 ring				570
	—	2 Body; 1 ped	1 yel		1 taenia	
C?	jar?	1 R	1?			
	—	1 Body; 3 ring; 4 H vert	1; 3 urf			549, 573
—	hearth	6 R			1 stamp; 3 triangles; 2 herringbone	649, 650, 652, 655, 656, 658
	dipper	2 H				
	scoop	6 H	3 bl; 2 red; 1?			
	stand	3 Body; 1 leg			1 taenia; 1 mat imp	634, 635, 637
	—	1 Body; 1 H vert	1 red			
S̲ O	bowl/saucer	9 R	2 bl; 2 red; 3; 2 brown			
	bowl	12 R; 2 ring; 1 foot	4; 1?; 2 yel; 3 red	2	5 taenia; 1 slashes; 2 ridge	269, 287, 289, 313, 318, 346, 351, 357, 380, 384, 402, 543
	sauceboat	1 R; 3 spout; 1 H horiz	2; 2 bl			224
	lg bowl/basin	29 R	3; 6?; 2 red; 1 bl	1	15 taenia; 1 taenia?; 1 trumpet	248
	bowl/sauceboat	1 R; 6 Body; 6 ring; 2 ped	5 red; 3 urf; 5 bl; 1?; 1 yel	1		517, 523, 529, 536, 587
	lg bowl	9 R; 1 ring	3; 1 bl; 1 red	1	6 taenia	297, 368, 371, 372, 374, 376, 388, 569
	lg bowl?	1 R?			1?	
	lg basin	1 R	1 red-br		1 trumpet	279
	sh./hem. bowl	1 R			1 taenia	280
	lg vessel	1 ring				559
	—	7 Body	3; 2?; 2 red	1		
C	jar	8 R; 4 Body; 3 collar	7; 2 red; 2 bl		2 ridge	487, 488, 499, 506, 510, 512, 515
	pithos	3 R			3 taenia	
	lg vessel	1 Base flat; 1 H vert				
	askos?	1 H vert			1 slashes + button	619
	—	1 Body				
O?	lg vessel	2 ring				
	bowl?	1 ped	1 urf			603
	—	2 Body	1?	1		

O/C	SHAPE	EXTANT PART	PAINT	BURN	OTHER DEC	CATALOGUED
C?	–	2 Body; 1 H vert	1		1 taenia	
–	scoop	3 H	2 bl; 1 red			630
	dipper	3 H	1 bl; 1 red			
	ladle	1 H				631
	stand	4 leg; 2 knob				639
	hearth	4 R			1 herringbone; 1 stamped; 2 hatched	651, 653, 661, 664

650 total

EARLY HELLADIC II?

O/C	SHAPE	EXTANT PART	PAINT	BURN	OTHER DEC	CATALOGUED
A3						
O?	–	1 Body	1 red/bl			
A9						
O	bowl	1 R			1 slashes	
B4						
C	med vessel	1 H horiz				
B6						
O	bowl	1 R	1?		1?	
B12						
C	pithos	1 R				
C1						
O	bowl	1 R	1?		1 slashes	
C5						
–	–	1 Body			1 slashes	
C9						
–	scoop?	1 H	1?			
C11						
O?	lg vessel	1 ring?				
D2						
O?	bowl?	1 Body	1 bl		1 slashes	
D10						
O	deep bowl	1 R				
D12						
C	–	1 R				
E						
O?	bowl/sauceboat?	1 ped	1 red			
C?	–	1 H horiz				
–	–	1 H vert; 1 H horiz				
1973						
O	sauceboat?	1 H horiz				
C	–	1 H horiz				
N						
O	pan	1 Prof				
	bowl	1 ped	1			605
C	jar	1 Body			1 taenia	
O?	–	1 ring	1			
C?	–	1 Body	1			
S						
O	–	1 Body	1 bl			
C	jar	1 Body				
	–	3 Body	1; 1?			
C?	–	1 H; 1 H horiz	1 bl			
–	–	1 Body			1 appl	

31 total

EARLY HELLADIC III

WARE	O/C	SHAPE	EXTANT PART	PAINT	OTHER DEC	CATALOGUED
SP&U	O	bowl	1 R			**690**
			1 total			

MIDDLE HELLADIC

WARE	O/C	H/W	SHAPE	EXTANT	SLIP	BUR	OTHER DEC	CATALOGUED
Bur	O	h	HFbowl	1 foot	Y	Y	groove	**751**
				1 total				

LATE HELLADIC

O/C	SHAPE	EXTANT PART	PAINT	OTHER DEC	CATALOGUED
O	CP	1 Base ring			**970**
–	–	1 H	1		
		2 total			

LATE HELLADIC III

O/C	SHAPE	EXTANT PART	PAINT	OTHER DEC	CATALOGUED
O	kylix	1 stem	1 UP		**1001**
	bowl?	1 R	1 Mono		
		2 total			

LATE HELLADIC IIIA2

O/C	SHAPE	EXTANT PART	PAINT	OTHER DEC	CATALOGUED
O	st.bowl	1 R	1 Mono		**873**
		1 total			

LATE HELLADIC IIIB

O/C	SHAPE	EXTANT PART	PAINT	OTHER DEC	CATALOGUED
O	kylix	1 stem	1 Patt		**900**
		1 total			

LATE GEOMETRIC

O/C	SHAPE	EXTANT PART	PAINT	OTHER DEC	CATALOGUED
O	krater	2 R	pattern		**1132**
		1 R; 3 ring	solid		
	skyphos	2 ring	solid		
		1 Body	pattern		
	pyxis	1 ring	solid		**1156**
	–	1 Body	solid		
		2 Body	pattern		
C	amphora	2 R; 2 ring	solid		**1175**
	jug	1 H		braid	**1186**
	–	1 Body	pattern		
		19 total			

LATE GEOMETRIC TO SUBGEOMETRIC

O/C	SHAPE	EXTANT PART	PAINT	OTHER DEC	CATALOGUED
O	krater	1 R	pattern		**1191**
	cup	1 R	solid		
	–	25 Body	solid		
C	–	4 Body	solid		
		31 total			

GEOMETRIC

O/C	SHAPE	EXTANT PART	PAINT	OTHER DEC	CATALOGUED
O	krater	2 H; 1 ring	solid		
	skyphos	1 Body	solid		
	cup/sky	2 Base; 1 H	solid		
	pyxis	1 Base	solid		
	–	3 Body	solid		
	–	1 R	solid		
C	jug	1 Body		burn	
		1 R			
	–	1 ring; 1 Body	solid		
		16 total			

SITE: F45 (Fournoi Valley #6)   21 collected   14 identified

EARLY HELLADIC I

O/C	SHAPE	EXTANT PART	PAINT	BURN	OTHER DEC	CATALOGUED
O	–	1 Body	1 red	1		
C	–	3 Body	3 red	3		
C?	–	1 Body	1 red	1		
–	–	8 Body	some	some		
		13 total				

SITE: F49 (Fournoi Valley #9)   13 collected   10 identified

FINAL NEOLITHIC - EARLY HELLADIC I

O/C	SHAPE	EXTANT PART	PAINT	BURN	OTHER DEC	CATALOGUED
C	–	1 Body	1	1		
C?	–	1 Body	1 red	1		
?	–	1 Body; 1 H				
		4 total				

EARLY HELLADIC I - EARLY HELLADIC II

O/C	SHAPE	EXTANT PART	PAINT	BURN	OTHER DEC	CATALOGUED
O	lg bowl/basin	1 R	1 red			
		1 total				

SITE: F54 (Stonehouse)   16 collected   16 identified

EARLY HELLADIC II

O/C	SHAPE	EXTANT PART	PAINT	BURN	OTHER DEC	CATALOGUED
O	bowl	1 R	1 bl		1 triangles	
		1 total				

SITE: F58 (Fournoi Valley #11)   48 collected   35 identified

EARLY HELLADIC?

O/C	SHAPE	EXTANT PART	PAINT	BURN	OTHER DEC	CATALOGUED
?	–	1 Body	1?			
		1 total				

EARLY HELLADIC I - EARLY HELLADIC II

O/C	SHAPE	EXTANT PART	PAINT	BURN	OTHER DEC	CATALOGUED
O	bowl	1 R; 1 Ped	1; 1?	1	1 lug	
		2 total				

EARLY HELLADIC II

O/C	SHAPE	EXTANT PART	PAINT	BURN	OTHER DEC	CATALOGUED
O	bowl/sauceboat	1 ped;	1 red			588
		1 ring				
	lg bowl/basin	1 R			1 ridge?	
	bowl	1 R	1?		1 lug	
	bowl?	1 R				
C?	–	1 Base flat				
		6 total				

LATE HELLADIC

O/C	SHAPE	EXTANT PART	PAINT	OTHER DEC	CATALOGUED
O	CP	1 R			
		1 total			

LATE HELLADIC III

O/C	SHAPE	EXTANT PART	PAINT	OTHER DEC	CATALOGUED
O	kylix	1 stem	1 UP		
		1 total			

LATE HELLADIC?

O/C	SHAPE	EXTANT PART	PAINT	OTHER DEC	CATALOGUED
C?	–	1 H			
		1 total			

SITE: G1 (Magoula Sta Ilia)   174 collected   164 identified

EARLY HELLADIC?

O/C	SHAPE	EXTANT PART	PAINT	BURN	OTHER DEC	CATALOGUED
?	–	1 ring foot?				
		1 total				

EARLY HELLADIC I

O/C	SHAPE	EXTANT PART	PAINT	BURN	OTHER DEC	CATALOGUED
O	lg sh.bowl	1 R	1 red			76
	bowl	2 Body	2 red	2		
C	jar	1 Body	1 red	1		
		4 total				

EARLY HELLADIC II

O/C	SHAPE	EXTANT PART	PAINT	BURN	OTHER DEC	CATALOGUED
O	sauceboat	1 ring; 1 spout	1 bl			
	lg bowl	1 R			1 taenia	344
	lg bowl/basin	1 R				
C	askos	1 H vert	1 bl			
	jar	1 R; 3 Body				
	–	1 H vert				
		10 total				

EARLY HELLADIC II?

O/C	SHAPE	EXTANT PART	PAINT	BURN	OTHER DEC	CATALOGUED
C	jar	1 Body				
		1 total				

MIDDLE TO LATE GEOMETRIC

O/C	SHAPE	EXTANT PART	PAINT	OTHER DEC	CATALOGUED
O	krater	1 ped; 1 H	solid		1070, 1072
C	amphora	1 H	solid		1092
		3 total			

LATE GEOMETRIC

O/C	SHAPE	EXTANT PART	PAINT	OTHER DEC	CATALOGUED
O	krater	5 R; 1 ring	8 pattern		1120, 1133, 1138
		1 Body; 1 H	4 solid		
	pyxis	1 R	solid		
	skyphos	1 ring	solid		
	plaque	1 R	pattern		1162
	–	1 Base; 1 H	solid		
	–	7 Body	pattern		
	–	4 Body	solid		
C	amphora	1 ring			
	–	3 Body	pattern		1172
	–	7 Body	pattern		
	–	2 Body	solid		
		37 total			

LATE GEOMETRIC TO SUBGEOMETRIC

O/C	SHAPE	EXTANT PART	PAINT	OTHER DEC	CATALOGUED
O	krater	2 R	pattern		1189, 1190
		1 ring	solid		
	–	6 Body	solid		
	–	4 Body	pattern		
C	jug	3 Base			1187, 1188
	amphora	1 R; 1 H			1184
		1 Body	pattern		1197
	–	1 coarse H; 4 Body			
	pithos	1 R			
	–	3 Body	solid		
		28 total			

SUBGEOMETRIC

O/C	SHAPE	EXTANT PART	PAINT	OTHER DEC	CATALOGUED
O	krater	3 R; 1 H	pattern		1203, 1204
	–	1 Body; 1 H	solid		
O?	–	1 Body	solid		
		7 total			

GEOMETRIC TO ARCHAIC

O/C	SHAPE	EXTANT PART	PAINT	OTHER DEC	CATALOGUED
O	krater?	1 Body	solid	groove	
	bowl	1 R		knobs	
C	–	5 Body	pattern		
		7 total			

SITE: G2 (Palaiokastro / Kastro tou Karakashi)

LATE HELLADIC I - II

O/C	SHAPE	EXTANT PART	PAINT	OTHER DEC	CATALOGUED
O	vapheio cup	1 Base	1 Lin		
		1 total			

GEOMETRIC

O/C	SHAPE	EXTANT PART	PAINT	OTHER DEC	CATALOGUED
O	krater	1 ring	solid		
		1 total			

SITE: G6 (Ayios Ioannis)

EARLY HELLADIC III?

WARE	O/C	SHAPE	EXTANT PART	PAINT	OTHER DEC	CATALOGUED
SPoU?	O?		1 Body			
			1 total			

SITE: G9 (Kotena Cave)   227 collected   214 identified

LATE NEOLITHIC

O/C	SHAPE	EXTANT PART	PAINT	BURN	OTHER DEC	CATALOGUED
O	carinated bowl	1 R			1 bl burn	6
	–	1 Body	1 matt			
		2 total				

LATE NEOLITHIC?

O/C	SHAPE	EXTANT PART	PAINT	BURN	OTHER DEC	CATALOGUED
O	–	1 Body		1		
C	–	1 Body		1		
		2 total				

FINAL NEOLITHIC

O/C	SHAPE	EXTANT PART	PAINT	BURN	OTHER DEC	CATALOGUED
O	splayed bowl	1 R	1?	1?		13
	sp.bowl	1 R		1		12
	deep bowl (or jar)	2 R	1?	2		19, 20
	lg bowl	1 R			1 lug	17
	pithos?	1 Body			1 ridges	57
	–	4 R; 12 Body; 1 Base hollow	2 red + cream	12; 2?	1 taenia; 1 pierced	22, 40, 59
C	collared jar	2 R; 1 Body; 1 Body + lug	1 paint	3; 1?		26, 27
	jar?	2 R	1 red + cream (crusted)	2		25, 34
	lg vessel	1 Body			1 knob	54
	hole mouth jar	1 R?				24
	–	11 Body	1; 3 red; 4 red + cream	10		
O?	-- (3 large)	2 Body + lug; 4 Body; 2 Base flat	1 cream; 1 pattern	5; 1?	1 appl; 1 taenia	38, 39, 53, 60, 67
C?	lg vessel	1 Body + lug		1		52
?	–	69 Body; 1 Base; 1 tab; 1 R?	1 red + cream	26		49
		123 total				

FINAL NEOLITHIC?

O/C	SHAPE	EXTANT PART	PAINT	BURN	OTHER DEC	CATALOGUED
O	–	1 H				**45**
O?	vertical sided bowl?	1 R	1?			
?	–	2 H		1		**42, 43**
		4 total				

FINAL NEOLITHIC - EARLY HELLADIC I

O/C	SHAPE	EXTANT PART	PAINT	BURN	OTHER DEC	CATALOGUED
O	–	1 R; 2 Body	1 red; 1 cream + red	3		
O?	–	2 Body	1?	1; 1?		
C?	–	1 Body		1		
		6 total				

EARLY HELLADIC I

O/C	SHAPE	EXTANT PART	PAINT	BURN	OTHER DEC	CATALOGUED
O	–	1 Body	1 red			
C	jar	1 R; 1 Body	2 red	1	1 grooves	**142, 157**
C?	–	1 Body		1		
		4 total				

EARLY HELLADIC II

O/C	SHAPE	EXTANT PART	PAINT	BURN	OTHER DEC	CATALOGUED
O	bowl/sauceboat	1 Body	1 bl			
	lg inc.bowl	3 R	1	1		**292, 293, 304**
–	scoop or dipper	1 H	1 bl			
		5 total				

EARLY HELLADIC III

WARE	O/C	SHAPE	EXTANT PART	PAINT	OTHER DEC	CATALOGUED
FB	O	Bass bowl	1 H			**709**
			1 total			

LATE HELLADIC

O/C	SHAPE	EXTANT PART	PAINT	OTHER DEC	CATALOGUED
C	–	1 ?			
		1 total			

LATE HELLADIC III

O/C	SHAPE	EXTANT PART	PAINT	OTHER DEC	CATALOGUED
O	kylix/goblet	1 Body	1 UP		
		1 total			

LATE HELLADIC IIIB

O/C	SHAPE	EXTANT PART	PAINT	OTHER DEC	CATALOGUED
O	deep bowl	1 Body	1 Mono		
		1 total			

LATE HELLADIC IIIC

O/C	SHAPE	EXTANT PART	PAINT	OTHER DEC	CATALOGUED
O	deep bowl	2 Body	2 Mono		**943**
		2 total			

SITE: G11 (Koufo)   31 collected   29 identified

<u>FINAL NEOLITHIC</u>

O/C	SHAPE	EXTANT PART	PAINT	BURN	OTHER DEC	CATALOGUED
O	–	3 Body	1; 1?	1		
C	jar?	1 Body	1	1		
		4 total				

<u>EARLY HELLADIC</u>

O/C	SHAPE	EXTANT PART	PAINT	BURN	OTHER DEC	CATALOGUED
O	–	1 R + H				
		1 total				

SITE: G13 (Iliokastro Plateau #1)   82 collected   57 identified

<u>LATE HELLADIC</u>

O/C	SHAPE	EXTANT PART	PAINT	OTHER DEC	CATALOGUED
O	CP goblet	1 R			
	basin?	1 Base ring	1 ?		
	–	1 Body			
C	jar	1 Body	1 UP		
	CP	2 Body			
	–	1 Body	1		
–	C	1 Body; 1 H; 1 Base			
	–	1 Base ring	1 UP		
		11 total			

<u>LATE HELLADIC IIIA2</u>

O/C	SHAPE	EXTANT PART	PAINT	OTHER DEC	CATALOGUED
C	alabastron or miniature piriform jar	1 R	1 Mono		
		1 total			

SITE: G15 (Magoula Sta Ilia Area)

<u>LATE HELLADIC</u>

O/C	SHAPE	EXTANT PART	PAINT	OTHER DEC	CATALOGUED
O	CP tripod	1 H		1 incision	
		1 total			

SITE: G22 (Iliokastro Plateau #4)   71 collected   51 identified

<u>LATE HELLADIC</u>

O/C	SHAPE	EXTANT PART	PAINT	OTHER DEC	CATALOGUED
C	–	1 Body	1 Lin		
		1 total			

<u>LATE HELLADIC III</u>

O/C	SHAPE	EXTANT PART	PAINT	OTHER DEC	CATALOGUED
O	kylix	1 stem	1 UP		
		1 total			

LATE GEOMETRIC TO SUBGEOMETRIC

O/C	SHAPE	EXTANT PART	PAINT	OTHER DEC	CATALOGUED
O	krater	1 H; 1 R	pattern		**1200**
		1 ring	solid		
	skyphos?	1 R; 1 Body	solid		
		1 R	pattern		1139
C	oinochoe	1 H	solid		
		7 total			

SITE: G23 (Iliokastro Plateau #5)   111 collected   78 identified

LATE HELLADIC

O/C	SHAPE	EXTANT PART	PAINT	OTHER DEC	CATALOGUED
O	–	2 Body	1 Patt; 1 ?		
–	–	1 H			
		3 total			

LATE HELLADIC III

O/C	SHAPE	EXTANT PART	PAINT	OTHER DEC	CATALOGUED
O	kylix	1 stem	1 UP		
		1 total			

LATE HELLADIC?

O/C	SHAPE	EXTANT PART	PAINT	OTHER DEC	CATALOGUED
O	basin	1 R + H	1 UP		
C	jug	1 Body			
	amphora?	1 H			
–	–	1 H			
		4 total			

SITE: G31 (Iliokastro Plateau #7)

EARLY HELLADIC II?

O/C	SHAPE	EXTANT PART	PAINT	BURN	OTHER DEC	CATALOGUED
C	jug	1 R; 1 Body	2 urf			
		2 total				

Concordance of Catalogue Numbers, Inventory Numbers, and Figure Numbers

The following concordance lists the catalogued pottery according to site and inventory number, to indicate which sherds were found together. The first column lists the number under which the sherd appears in the text and in the pottery catalogue. The second column indicates the site and inventory numbers. Figure numbers and dates appear in the third and fourth columns.

Publ. Cat. No.	AEP Inv. No.	Figure Nos.	Date	Publ. Cat. No.	AEP Inv. No.	Figure Nos.	Date
149	A6-1-4	9	EH I	213	A6-65-20	13	EH II
88	A6-1-14	5	EH I	216	A6-65-21	13, 119	EH II
478	A6-1-15	29	EH II	453	A6-65-26	25	EH II
162	A6-1-16	11	EH I	446	A6-65-27	24	EH II OR EHI
214	A6-2-2	13	EH II	818	A6-65-28	43, 127	MH?
731	A6-2-5	40	MH III-LH I	821	A6-65-29	43	MH
920	A6-2-6	47	LH IIIB	678	A6-65-32	38	EH III
481	A6-2-7	29, 121	EH II	726	A6-65-43	39	MH
90	A6-2-10	5	EH I	826	A6-65-45	44, 128	LH IIA
539	A6-2-17	32	EH II	172	A6-72-3	11	EH I
820	A6-3-3	43, 127	MH	173	A6-72-4	11	EH I
574	A6-4-4	33	EH II	143	A6-72-8	9	EH I
668	A6-5-7	37	EH II	155	A6-72-13	10	EH I
667	A6-5-8	37	EH II	432	A6-72-14	23	EH II
670	A6-5-9	37	EH II	161	A6-72-17	11, 118	EH I
260	A6-7-2	15	EH II	139	A6-72-18	9	EH I
688	A6-7-3	38	EH III	705	A6-72-21	39	EH III
750	A6-7-5	40	MH	215	A6-72-22	13	EH II
674	A6-8-15	37	EH II	732	A6-72-42	40	LH I
672	A6-8-16	37	EH II	247	A6-72-57	14	EH II
671	A6-8-17	37	EH II	687	A6-72-66	38	EH III
694	A6-9-2	38	EH III	501	A6-72-67	30	EH II
338	A6-9-4	19	EH II	522	A6-72-69	32	EH II
450	A6-9-7	25	EH II	259	A6-72-82	15, 119	EH II
179	A6-65-2	11	EH I	952	A6-72-84	49	LH
153	A6-65-3	10	EH I	1002	A6-72-85	51	LH III
84	A6-65-4	5	EH I		A6-72-86	128	LH
106	A6-65-5	6	EH I		A6-72-88	128	LH
200	A6-65-6	12	EH I	996	A6-72-99	51	LH III
555	A6-65-7	32	EH II	843	A6-72-100	45	LH IIIA1
708	A6-65-13	39	EH III	703	A6-72-120	38, 125	EH III
230	A6-65-15	13	EH II	718	A6-72-139	126	MH III
225	A6-65-16	13	EH II	498	A6-72-147	30	EH II

320

Publ. Cat. No.	AEP Inv. No.	Figure Nos.	Date
437	A6-72-149	24, 121	EH II
194	A6-72-153	12	EH I?
237	A6-72-158	13	EH II
684	A6-72-159		EH III
692	A6-72-168	38	EH III
350	A6-72-191	20	EH II
965	A6-72-197	50	LH
607	A6-72-201	34	EH II
673	A6-72-217	37	EH II
666	A6-72-219	37, 124	EH II
677	A6-72-220	37	EH II
94	A6-74-3	6	EH I
168	A6-74-7	11	EH I
99	A6-74-8	6	EH I
147	A6-74-9	9	EH I
808	A6-74-11	42, 127	LH I
177	A6-74-12	11	EH I
207	A6-74-13		EH I
365	A6-74-15	20, 120	EH II
151	A6-74-16	10	EH I
373	A6-74-18	21, 120	EH II
85	A6-74-19	5	EH I
613	A6-74-21	34	EH II
966	A6-74-25	50	LH
91	A6-74-26	5	EH I
100	A6-74-28	6	EH I
276	A6-74-29	16	EH II?
545	A6-74-35	32	EH II
47	A6-74-36	3	FN
242	A6-74-56	13	EH II
454	A6-74-61	25	EH II
807	A6-74-61	42	MH III
316	A6-74-62	18	EH II
205	A6-74-65	12	EH I
682	A6-74-67	38	EH III
278	A6-74-69	16	EH II
358	A6-74-73	20	EH II
954	A6-74-81	49	LH
264	A6-74-85	15	EH II?
341	A6-74-88	19	EH II
611	A6-74-89	34	EH II
762	A6-74-96	41, 126	MH III-LH I
715	A6-74-98	39, 126	MH II-III
218	A6-74-100	13	EH II
645	A6-74-105	123	EH II
646	A6-74-106	123	EH II
192	A6-75-4	12	EH I?
541	A6-75-6	32	EH II
171	A6-75-20	11	EH I
409	A6-75-21	22	EH II
394	A6-75-26	21	EH II
119	A6-75-32	7	EH I
79	A6-75-40	4	EH I
868	A6-75-86	45	LH IIIA2
828	A6-75-89	44, 128	LH IIA
786	A6-75-92	42, 127	MH
881	A6-75-95	46	LH IIIB

Publ. Cat. No.	AEP Inv. No.	Figure Nos.	Date
563	A6-75-100	32	EH II
604	A6-75-102	34	EH II
	A6-83-	124	EH II
442	A6-83-1	24, 121	EH II
683	A6-83-2	125	EH III
840	A6-83-3	44, 128	LH II-IIIA1
614	A6-83-4	34, 121	EH II
546	A6/9-A-1	32	EH II
489	A6/9-A-3	30	EH II
233	A6/9-A-4	13	EH II
430	A6/9-A-6	23	EH II
315	A6/9-A-7	18	EH I-EH II
285	A6/9-A-8	16	EH II
490	A6/9-A-9	30	EH II
618	A6/9-A-15		EH II
505	A6/9-A-16	31	EH II
185	A6/9-A-34	11	EH I
178	A6/9-B-5	11	EH I-EH II
181	A6/9-B-7	11, 119	EH I
108	A6/9-B-13	7	EH I
235	A6/9-B-14	13	EH II
268	A6/9-B-19	16	EH II
104	A6/9-B-20	6	EH I
319	A6/9-B-25	18	EH II
398	A6/9-B-26	22	EH II
219	A6/9-B-27	13	EH II
579	A6/9-B-33	33	EH II
1116	A6/9-B-38	110, 132	GEO
1195	A6/9-B-39		GEO
141	A6/9-B-40	9	EH I
135	A6/9-B-41	8	EH I
145	A6/9-C-1	9	EH I
1215	A9	117	GEO
154	A9-1-1	10	EH I
1097	A9-2-1	108, 132	GEO
140	A9-3-2	9	EH I
203	A9-3-12	12	EH I
461	A9-3-13	27	EH II
1096	A9-3-13	108, 132	GEO
1208	A9-3-15	117	GEO
158	A9-5-4	10	EH I
144	A9-5-5	9	EH I
1130	A9-5-16	111	GEO
72	A9-6-6	4	EH I
1131	A9-6-7	111	GEO
146	A9-6-8	9	EH I
1093	A9-6-9	108, 132	GEO
332	A9-6-10	19	EH II
164	A9-6-23	11, 118	EH I
1050	A9-6-25	106, 130	GEO
1068	A9-6-26	107, 131	GEO
462	A9-8-1	26	EH II
152	A9-8-2	10	EH I
475	A9-9-1	29	EH II
1062	A9-10-1	107	GEO
1051	A9-10-5	106, 130	GEO
1055	A9-10-7	106	GEO

Publ. Cat. No.	AEP Inv. No.	Figure Nos.	Date		Publ. Cat. No.	AEP Inv. No.	Figure Nos.	Date
1148	A9-10-8	112	GEO		1149	B2-B28-32	112	GEO
1044	A9-10-14	106, 130	GEO		1151	B2-B28-41	112	GEO
1053	A9-10-16	106	GEO		1163	B2-B28-63	113	GEO
1082	A9-10-17	107	GEO		1180	B2-B28-87	114	GEO
1052	A9-10-18	106, 130	GEO		644	B2-B28-91	35	EH II
1081	A9-10-21		GEO		967	B2-B28-95	50	LH
1069	A9-10-26	107, 131	GEO		955	B2-B28-99	49	LH
1063	A9-10-28	131	GEO		1144	B2-B28-101	112	GEO
1064	A9-10-29		GEO		779	B5-3	41	MH
754	A9-30	40	MH III		33	B5-8	3	FN?
102	A33-1-3	6	EH I		455	B5-9	25	EH II
131	A33-1-4	8	EH I		1174	B5-18	113	GEO
189	A33-1-12	12	EH I		876	B5-33	45	LH IIIA2
191	A33-1-14	12	EH I		814	B5-7-1	43, 127	LH I
80	A33-1-17	5	EH I		244	B7-11	13	EH II
127	A33-1-18	8	EH I		65	B8?-ALL-4	4	FN
81	A33-1-19	5	EH I		50	B8?-ALL-5	3	FN?
97	A33-1-20	6	EH I		421	B9-1	23	EH II
201	A33-1-27	12	EH I		188	B9-18	12	EH I-EH II
198	A33-1-31	12	EH I		532	B9-28	32	EH II
199	A33-1-32	12	EH I		884	B9-42	46	LH IIIB
513	A33-1-40	31	EH II		1015	B9-46	129	LH
134	A33-1-50	8	EH I		83	B9-63	5	EH I
58	A33-1-55	4	FN		123	B9-B11-10	7	EH I
466	A33-1-60	26	EH II		642	B9-B11-11	35	EH II
456	A33-1-62	25	EH II		628	B9-X	35	EH II
471	A33-1-63	28	EH II		1113	B16-3	133	GEO
564	A33-1-65	33	EH II		1122	B16-4	111	GEO
170	A33-1-74	11	EH I		1126	B16-49	111	GEO
647	A33-3-5	36, 123	EH II		1211	B16-58	136	GEO
528	A33-3-6	32	EH II		1198	B16-ALL2-10	115, 136	GEO
14	A33-3-7	1, 118	FN		1185	B16-ALL2-12	114, 135	GEO
221	A33-81-1-1	13, 119	EH II		1157	B16-ALL3-6	134	GEO
136	A33-81-1-11+	8	EH I		1041	B17-A-5	106, 130	GEO
75	A33-81-1-12	4	EH I		1059	B17-A-7	107	GEO
96	A33-81-1-31	6	EH I		1040	B17-A-17	106, 130	GEO
295	A33-81-1-32	17	EH II		1057	B17-A-19	107	GEO
132	A33-81-1-38	8	EH I		1042	B17-A-24	106, 130	GEO
675	A33-81-1-X	37	EH II		1056	B17-A-25	106, 131	GEO
89	A33-81-2-2	5	EH I		1043	B17-A-28	106	GEO
1201	B2-28-ALL1-9	116, 136	GEO		1061	B17-A-34		GEO
1196	B2-28-ALL1-10	115	GEO		1058	B17-A-40		GEO
1115	B2-28-ALL1-11	110	GEO		1045	B17-A-45	106	GEO
1152	B2-28-ALL1-25	112	GEO		1067	B17-B-1	107, 131	GEO
1193	B2-28-ALL1-26	115	GEO		1109	B17-B-3	133	GEO
1136	B2-28-ALL1-28	111, 134	GEO		1060	B17-B-4	107, 131	GEO
857	B2-28-ALL3-2	45	LH IIIA2		1078	B17-B-7	107	GEO
1075	B2-B28-7	107	GEO		1106	B17-B-15	109	GEO
1124	B2-B28-8	111, 133	GEO		1066	B17-B-16	107, 131	GEO
1210	B2-B28-9	117, 136	GEO		1046	B17-B-17	106	GEO
1145	B2-B28-10	112	GEO		1177	B17-B-18	113	GEO
1119	B2-B28-11	110, 133	GEO		1047	B17-B-19	106, 130	GEO
1142	B2-B28-12	112, 134	GEO		1111	B17-B-20	109, 133	GEO
1154	B2-B28-13	112, 134	GEO		1107	B17-B-21	109	GEO
1160	B2-B28-16	112, 134	GEO		1105	B17-B-22		GEO
1194	B2-B28-19	115	GEO		905	B21-1	47	LH IIIB
1077	B2-B28-26X		GEO		908	B21-1-1	47	LH IIIB

Publ. Cat. No.	AEP Inv. No.	Figure Nos.	Date
933	B21-6	48	LH IIIC
946	B21-53	49	LH
1013	B21-83	129	LH
640	B24-2	35, 123	EH II
553	B24-5	32	EH II
582	B24-9	33	EH II
595	B24-12	33	EH II
538	B24-14	32	EH II
597	B24-15	33	EH II
412	B24-43	22	EH II
436	B24-49	24	EH II
249	B24-51	14	EH I-EH II
312	B24-52	18	EH II
439	B24-53	24	EH II
302	B24-57	17	EH II
246	B24-60	14	EH II
445	B24-64	24, 121	EH II
627	B24-78	35	EH II?
629	B24-90	35, 122	EH II
159	B24-92	10	EH I
138	B24-94	9	EH I
125	B24-96	8	EH I-EH II
169	B24-111	11	EH I
617	B24-112	34	EH II
669	B24-124	37	EH II
87	B24-ALL-2	5	EH I
150	B24-ALL-3	9	EH I
592	B24-ALL-5	33	EH II
580	B24-ALL-7	33	EH II
995	B25-13	51	LH III
948	B25-22	49	LH
118	B39-1	7, 118	EH I
30	B39-2	3, 118	FN
648	B39-33	36	EH II
561	B39-34	32	EH II
801	B39-58	42, 127	MH III
69	B39-62	4	EH I
195	B39-64	12	EH I
663	B39-66	37	EH II
1121	B40-1	110, 133	GEO
273	B43-3	16	EH I-EH II
742	B43-3	40	MH III-LH I
987	B43-7	51	LH IIIA1
401	B43-2-1	22	EH II
298	B43-80-1-1	17	EH II
496	B43-80-2-1	30	EH II
423	B43-80-2-2	23	EH II
258	B43-80-2-3	15	EH II
277	B43-80-2-4	16	EH II?
240	B43-80-2-9	13	EH II
434	B43-80-2-11	23	EH II
608	B43-80-2-14	34	EH II
953	B43-96	49	LH
391	B43-A-5	21	EH II
327	B43-A-9	18	EH II
503	B43-A-10	31	EH II
520	B43-A-12	32	EH II

Publ. Cat. No.	AEP Inv. No.	Figure Nos.	Date
404	B43-ALL-2-2	22, 120	EH II
16	B43-ALL-2-3	1, 118	FN
415	B43-ALL-3-1	22	EH II
78	B43-B-1	4	EH I
250	B43-B-2	14	EH II
806	B43-B-26	42	MH III
1008	B43-B-27	51	LH IIIA2
889	B43-B-30	46	LH IIIB
851	B43-B-39	45	LH IIIA1
971	B43-B-50	50	LH
77	B43-B45-3	4	EH I
998	B43-B45-10	51	LH III
961	B43-B45-16	50	LH
972	B46-10	50	LH
379	B46-18	21, 120	EH II
370	B49-1-1	21	EH II
18	B53-3-1	2	FN-EH I
208	B53-3-3		EH I
303	B81-1-2	17	EH II?
133	B81-2-5/28+	8	EH I
347	B81-2-16/22+	19	EH I?-EH II
190	B81-2-27	12	EH I
202	B81-2-30	12	EH I
98	B81-2-36/37	6	EH I-EH II
817	B83-5	43	MH?
825	B95-1	44, 128	LH IIA
122	B97-1-2	7	EH I
922	B97-5-4	47	LH IIIB
886	B97-5-15	46	LH IIIB
721	B98-5-8	39	MH
1011	B98-5-11	51	LH IIIB
1007	C3-12+20	51	LH III
861	C3-21	45	LH IIIA2
993	C3-24	51	LH III
901	C3-27	46	LH IIIB
395	C11-11-2	22	EH II
429	C11-32-5	23	EH II
226	C11-ALL-5	13	EH II
112	C11-C19-1	7	EH I
255	C11-C19-2	15, 119	EH II
359	C11-C19-3	20	EH II
390	C11-C19-5	21	EH II
507	C11-C19-10	31	EH II
71	C11-C19-12	4	EH I
156	C11-C19-14	10	EH I
909	C11-C19-19	47	LH IIIB
917	C11-C19-20	47	LH IIIB
927	C11-C19-21	48	LH IIIC
882	C11-C19-51	46	LH IIIB
572	C11-C19-57	33	EH II
567	C11-C28-2	33	EH II
62	C11-C28-12	4	FN
176	C11-C28-15	11	EH I
148	C11-NE-6	9	EH I
114	C11-NE-7	7, 118	EH I
345	C11-NE-13	19, 119	EH II
217	C11-NE-15	13, 119	EH II

Publ. Cat. No.	AEP Inv. No.	Figure Nos.	Date
486	C11-NE-17	30	EH II
620	C11-NE-18	34	EH I-EH II
137	C11-NE-25	9	EH I
493	C11-NE-27	30	EH II
615	C11-NE-48	34, 122	EH II?
638	C11-NE-58	35	EH II
86	C11-NW-1	5	EH I
126	C11-NW-2	8	EH I-EH II
410	C11-SE-2	22	EH II
416	C11-SE-3	22	EH II
504	C11-SE-4	31	EH II
130	C11-SE-8	8	EH I
283	C11-SE-9	16	EH II
839	C11-SE-12	44, 128	LH II-IIIA1
494	C11-SE-19	30	EH II
625	C11-SE-21	34	EH II
184	C11-SE-22	11	EH I
558	C11-SE-28	32	EH II
397	C11-SW-2	22	EH II
854	C11-SW-3	45	LH IIIA1
919	C11-SW-5	47	LH IIIB
837	C11-SW-6	44	LH II-IIIA1
193	C11-SW-7	12	EH I
326	C11-SW-14	18	EH I?-EH II
492	C11-SW-15	30	EH II
124	C11-SW-23	7	EH I-EH II
175	C11-SW-24	11	EH I
431	C11-SW-25	23	EH II
879	C11-SW-32	46	LH IIIB
414	C11-SW-34	22	EH II
596	C11-SW-37	33	EH II
888	C11-SW-42	46	LH IIIB
616	C11-W-20	122	EH II?
1098	C12-1	109, 132	GEO
1108	C12-2	132	GEO
1054	C12-9	106	GEO
1084	C12-17	107	GEO
1088	C12-ALL-1	108, 131	GEO
1150	C12-ALL-2	112, 134	GEO
321	C12-ALL-7	18	EH II
1065	C12-ALL-22	131	GEO
1086	C12-ALL2-15		GEO
1091	C12-ALL2-22	131	GEO
1074	C12-C14-82-1	107	GEO
1167	C12-C14-82-2	113	GEO
1166	C12-C14-82-3	113	GEO
1048	C12-C14-82-4	106	GEO
1099	C12-C14-82-5	109	GEO
1168	C12-C14-ALL-7	113	GEO
1173	C12-C14-ALL-29	113, 135	GEO
1164	C12-C14-ALL-40	113	GEO
1101	C12-C14-ALL-50	109	GEO
1178	C12-C14-A4-2	113	GEO
1117	C12-C14-C3-1	110	GEO
1137	C12-C14-C3-5	111	GEO
1171	C12-C14-C3-12	135	GEO
1112	C12-C14-C3-13	133	GEO
1087	C12-C14-C4-11	108, 131	GEO
1080	C12-C14-C4-13	107	GEO
1165	C12-C14-C4-16	113	GEO
1100	C12-C14-D2-25	109	GEO
1114	C12-C14-D3-1	110	GEO
1104	C12-C14-D3-29	109, 132	GEO
1118	C12-C14-D3-30	110	GEO
1170	C12-C14-D3-32		GEO
1123	C12-C14-D4-1	111	GEO
1134	C12-C14-E3-6	134	GEO
1155	C12-C14-E3-18	112	GEO
1135	C12-C14-E3-19	134	GEO
1079	C12-C14-E6-1	107	GEO
29	C13-18	3, 118	FN-EH I?
35	C15-A-4	3	FN
15	C15-A-23	1	FN
93	C15-A-25	5	EH I
641	C15-A-38	35	EH II
32	C15-A-43	3	FN-EH I?
82	C17-26	5	EH I
1089	C17-47	108, 131	GEO
1169	C17-48	113, 135	GEO
1140	C17-50		GEO
1209	C17-52	117, 136	GEO
1110	C17-54	109, 133	GEO
1202	C17-55	116, 136	GEO
1161	C17-58	112, 135	GEO
1090	C17-60		GEO
1085	C17-61	108	GEO
1192	C17-72	115	GEO
1176	C17-75	135	GEO
1094	C17-80	108	GEO
1158	C17-117	112, 134	GEO
1199	C17-3130-1	116	GEO
1102	C17-A-1	109	GEO
1212	C17-ALL-2-5	136	GEO
1146	C17-C-4	112	GEO
1129	C17-D-2	111, 134	GEO
904	C24-10	46	LH IIIB
41	C25-1	3	FN-EH I
37	C25-2	3	FN
36	C25-3	3	FN
211	C25--	12	EH I
212	C25-M	12	EH I
1181	C27-2	135	GEO
1159	C27-4	112, 134	GEO
56	C29-ALL-8	4	FN
61	C29-ALL-13	4	FN (REUSE)
44	C29-ALL-19	3	FN?
46	C29-ALL-23	3	FN?
21	D3-1-1	2	FN?
8	D3-2-6	1, 118	LN?
10	D3-2-10	118	LN
63	D3-2-18	4	FN
7	D3-4-2	1	LN
932	E3-9	48	LH IIIC
458	E4-1-17	25	EH II

Publ. Cat. No.	AEP Inv. No.	Figure Nos.	Date	Publ. Cat. No.	AEP Inv. No.	Figure Nos.	Date
535	E4-1-33	32	EH II	867	E9-151	45	LH IIIA2
228	E4-A-1	13	EH II	744	E9-158	40	LH I
253	E4-B-1	14	EH II	1018	E9-160	105	GEO
101	E4-B-2	6	EH I	844	E9-165	45	LH IIIA1
28	E4-B-7	3	FN	1019	E9-167		GEO
309	E4-B-8	18	EH II	209	E9-168	12	EH I REUSE
187	E4-B-17	11	EH I	858	E9-169	45	LH IIIA2
229	E5-2-25	13	EH I-EH II	1049	E9-172	106, 130	GEO
451	E5-2-30	25	EH II	832	E9-175	44, 128	LH IIB
467	E5-2-31	28	EH II	1027	E9-177		GEO
485	E5-2-32	29	EH II	910	E9-188	47	LH IIIB
469	E5-2-34	26	EH II	1032	E9-191	105	GEO
482	E5-2-35	29	EH II	1021	E9-204	130	GEO
447	E5-A-1	24	EH II	1037	E9-215	105, 130	GEO
95	E5-A-2	6	EH I	1143	E9-217	112, 134	GEO
959	E5-A-4	50	LH	716	E9-227	39	MH III
947	E5-A-6	49	LH	1038	E9-235	105	GEO
232	E5-A-10	13	EH I-EH II	1039	E9-236	105	GEO
392	E5-A-11	21	EH II	829	E9-238	44	LH IIA
859	E5-A-14	45	LH IIIA2	1153	E9-241	134	GEO
845	E5-A-15	45	LH IIIA1	1028	E9-243	105, 130	GEO
979	E5-A-17	50	LH IIIB	895	E9-250	46	LH IIIB
31	E5-A-19	3	FN	911	E9-254	47	LH IIIB
362	E5-B-1	20	EH II	243	E9-264	13	EH II
399	E5-B-2	22	EH II	73	E9-265	4	EH I
241	E5-B-4	13	EH II	812	E9-266	43	MH
524	E5-B-9	32	EH II	706	E9-267	39, 125	EH III
584	E5-B-12	33	EH II	819	E9-272	43	MBA?
623	E5-B-15	34	EH II	174	E9-275	11	EH I
92	E5-B-18	5	EH I	1023	E9-276	105	GEO
852	E5-B-24	45	LH IIIA1	1036	E9-1980-2	105, 130	GEO
749	E5-B-25	40	MH	823	E13-	43, 127	MH?
897	E5-B-26	46	LH IIIB	1012	E13-	129	LH
860	E5-B-27	45	LH IIIA2	798	E13-1	42, 127	LH I
23	E7-48	2	FN	799	E13-2	42	LH I
1029	E9-54	130	GEO	768	E13-3	41	MH
1083	E9-69	107, 131	GEO	761	E13-7	41	MH
1035	E9-76	105	GEO	758	E13-8	41	MH
711	E9-79-57+	39, 125	EH III	756	E13-9	41, 126	MH III
1017	E9-82	130	GEO	502	E13-10+	31	EH II
1031	E9-83	130	GEO	197	E13-11	12	EH I
1033	E9-84	130	GEO	849	E13-20	45	LH IIIA1
802	E9-86	42	MH III-LH I	842	E13-25	45, 128	LH IIIA1
689	E9-88	38	EH III	944	E13-27	48	LH IIIC
1030	E9-99	105, 130	GEO	847	E13-28+	45, 128	LH IIIA1
1024	E9-100	105	GEO	740	E13-29	40	MH III-LH I
1016	E9-102	105, 130	GEO	885	E13-30	46	LH IIIB
1127	E9-103	111	GEO	741	E13-31	40	MH III-LH I
1073	E9-107	131	GEO	791	E13-33	42	MH-LH I
960	E9-109	50	LH	681	E13-36	38, 125	EH III
735	E9-115	40	MH III-LH I	835	E13-1-2	44	LH IIB
1034	E9-127	105	GEO	929	E13-1-3	48, 128	LH IIIC
1026	E9-138	105	GEO	834	E13-1-4	44, 128	LH IIB
1022	E9-140		GEO	985	E13-1-7	51	LH IIIB
1025	E9-141	105, 130	GEO	945	E13-1-9	48, 128	LH IIIC
1020	E9-145	105	GEO	782	E13-1-10	41	MH III
869	E9-147	45	LH IIIA2	1003	E13-1-11	51	LH III

Publ. Cat. No.	AEP Inv. No.	Figure Nos.	Date
753	E13-1-14	40, 126	MH III
691	E13-2-2+	38	EH III
696	E13-2-4	38	EH III
781	E13-2-10	41, 126	MH III
186	E13-2-18	11	EH I
702	E13-2-20	38, 125	EH III
699	E13-2-24	38, 125	EH III
697	E13-2-27	38, 125	EH III
776	E13-2-37	41, 126	MH
51	E13-2-42	3	FN
700	E13-2-46	38, 125	EH III
239	E13-2-49	13	EH II
68	E13-2-50	118	FN-EH I?
222	E13-2-56	13	EH II
804	E13-2-63	42	LH I
704	E13-2-98	39	EH III
722	E13-81-1-1	39	MH
129	E13-81-1-4	8	EH I
811	E13-81-1-7	42	MH III-LH I
796	E13-81-1-9	42	MH
891	E13-81-1-10	46	LH IIIB
942	E13-81-1-11	48	LH IIIC
916	E13-81-1-12	47, 128	LH IIIB
773	E13-81-1-13	41	MH
734	E13-81-1-14	40, 126	LH I
789	E13-81-1-16	42	MBA
1009	E13-81-1-17	51	LH IIIB
730	E13-81-1-18	40	LH I
790	E13-81-1-19		MBA
713	E13-81-1-24	39	MH II-III
788	E13-81-1-28		MH
746	E13-81-1-29	40	MH
833	E13-81-1-34	44, 128	LH IIB
775	E13-81-1-36	41	MH
685	E13-81-1-38	38	EH III
714	E13-81-1-39	39	MH III
701	E13-81-1-40	38, 125	EH III
785	E13-81-1-41	42, 127	MH-LH I
766	E13-81-1-44	41	MH
937	E13-81-1-46	48	LH IIIC
717	E13-81-1-47	39	MH II-III
924	E13-81-1-49	48, 128	LH IIIC
724	E13-81-1-50	39	MH
793	E13-81-1-51	42	MH
686	E13-81-1-52		EH III?
695	E13-81-1-54	38	EH III
680	E13-81-1-55	38	EH III
679	E13-81-1-56	38, 125	EH III
698	E13-81-1-60	38, 125	EH III
769	E13-81-1-62	41	MH
182	E13-81-1-63	11	EH I
831	E13-81-1-67	44	LH IIA
783	E13-81-1-68	41	MH III
915	E13-81-1-74	47	LH IIIB
763	E13-81-1-75	41	MH
196	E13-81-1-76	12	EH I
918	E13-ALL-5	47	LH IIIB
982	E13-ALL-6	51	LH IIIA1
872	E13-ALL-10	45	LH IIIA2
3	E14-1	1, 118	MN
5	E14-7	1	MN
4	E14-9	1	MN
2	E14-11	1	MN
1	E 14-A-1	1	MN
11	E14-A-6	1	LN?
9	E14-A-7	1	LN?
256	E16-10	15, 119	EH II
103	E16-15A	6	EH I
180	E16-16	11	EH I
163	E16-17	11, 118	EH I
1207	E19-B-1	117	GEO
838	E23-6	44	LH II-IIIA1
335	E36-5-4	19	EH II
1125	E40-ALL-1-19	111, 133	GEO
1103	E40-ALL-12	109, 132	GEO
822	E74-3-9	43	MBA
981	E74-5-2	51	LH IIIA1
204	E74-8-5	12	EH I
973	E74-8-23	50	LH IIIB
866	E74-8-43	45	LH IIIA2
975	E74-10-10+	50	LH III
976	E74-10-24	50	LH IIIA2-B
977	E74-11-1	50	LH IIIA1
956	E74-11-14	49	LH
978	E74-14-6	50	LH IIIB
183	E74-15-8	11	EH I
780	E76-5	41, 126	MC
626	F1-7	34	EH II?
991	F1-43	51	LH IIIA1
903	F4-1	46	LH IIIB
913	F4-6	47	LH IIIB
988	F4-9	51	LH IIIA1
907	F4-11	47	LH IIIB
906	F4-14	47	LH IIIB
994	F4-18	51	LH III
892	F4-22	46	LH IIIB
874	F4-25	45	LH IIIA2
875	F4-42	45, 128	LH IIIA2
1005	F4-45	51	LH III
736	F4-48	40	MH III-LH I
999	F4-50	51	LH III
733	F4-53	40	MH III-LH I
964	F4-55	50	LH
887	F4-56	46	LH IIIB
958	F4-60	49	LH
963	F4-67	50	LH
949	F4-70	49	LH
950	F4-83	49	LH
968	F4-2-10	50	LH
1014	F4-3-3	129	LH
846	F4-4-6	45	LH IIIA1
957	F4-11-22	49	LH
902	F5-1	46	LH IIIB
855	F5-2	45	LH IIIA1

Publ. Cat. No.	AEP Inv. No.	Figure Nos.	Date
797	F5-3A	42	MH III
935	F5-3B	48	LH IIIC
896	F5-4	46	LH IIIB
1147	F5-6	112, 134	GEO
836	F5-7	44	LH IIB
795	F5-10	42, 127	MH II-III
771	F5-11	41	MH
1071	F5-12	107, 131	GEO
764	F5-13	41	MH
921	F5-14	47	LH IIIB
864	F5-16	45	LH IIIA2
940	F5-20	48	LH IIIC
1006	F5-21	51	LH IIIC
878	F5-25	46	LH IIIB
863	F5-26	45	LH IIIA2
912	F5-27	47	LH IIIB
757	F5-28	41, 126	MH III
1004	F5-30	51	LH III
519	F5-31	32	EH II
871	F5-32	45	LH IIIA2
810	F5-39	42	MH
787	F5-44	127	MH
989	F5-58	51	LH IIIA1
770	F5-61	41	MH
1141	F5-67	112	GEO
765	F5-71	41	MH
792	F5-72	42	MH II-III
707	F5-74	39, 125	EH III
862	F5-77	45	LH IIIA2
883	F5-81	46	LH IIIB
848	F5-83	45, 128	LH IIIA1
870	F5-86	45, 128	LH IIIA2
926	F5-89	48	LH IIIC
923	F5-97	47	LH IIIB
743	F5-100	40	LH I
767	F5-101	41, 126	MH
738	F5-103	40	MH III-LH I
1076	F5-105	107	GEO
739	F5-107	40	MH III-LH I
974	F5-108	50	LH III
270	F5-118	16	EH II
980	F5-128	50	LH III
784	F5-145	42, 127	MH-LH I
827	F5-153	44	LH IIA
984	F5-163	51	LH IIIA2
992	F5-171	51	LH IIIA1
729	F5-184	40	MH III?
1206	F5-188	117, 136	GEO
962	F5-190	50	LH
725	F5-193	39	MH
1183	F5-201	114	GEO
759	F5-205	41	MH III?
747	F5-218	40	MH
760	F5-226	41	LH I
925	F5-228	48	LH IIIC
612	F5-235	34	EH II
272	F5-259	16	EH I-EH II
983	F5-283	51	LH IIIA2
778	F5-293	41	MH
748	F5-296	40	MH II
914	F5-300	47	LH IIIB
1090	F5-311		GEO
800	F5-315	42	MH
777	F5-320	41	MH
723	F5-326	39, 126	MH II-III
936	F5-346+169	48	LH IIIC
1179	F5-352	113, 135	GEO
728	F5-370	40	MH III-LH I
1010	F5-73-14	51	LH IIIA2
877	F5-73-16	45	LH IIIA2
928	F5-73-17	48	LH IIIC
865	F5-73-18	45	LH IIIA2
894	F5-73-21	46	LH IIIB
893	F5-73-29	46, 128	LH IIIB
890	F5-73-42	46	LH IIIB
941	F5-73-45	48	LH IIIC
853	F5-73-57	45	LH IIIA1
951	F5-73-66	49	LH
772	F5-75-1	41	MH
755	F5-75-8	40, 126	MH III
813	F5-75-9	43	MH III-LH I
231	F5-75-11	13	EH II
720	F5-A-2	39	MH
752	F5-A-3	40	MH?
841	F5-A-8	44	LH II-IIIA1
997	F5-A-12	51	LH III
805	F5-A-16	42	MH III-LH I
824	F5-B-	43, 127	MH?
719	F5-B-1	39	MH II-III
774	F5-B-6	41, 126	MH
794	F5-B-8	42, 127	MH
727	F5-B-9	39	MH
809	F5-B-11	42	MH III-LH I
710	F5-B-15	39	EH III
288	F5-B-33	16	EH II
938	F5-B-37	48, 128	LH IIIC
1128	F5-B-38	133	GEO
939	F5-B-51	48, 128	LH IIIC
934	F5-B-57	48, 128	LH IIIC
930	F5-B-71	48	LH IIIC
850	F5-B-72	45	LH IIIA1
986	F5-B-74	51	LH III
880	F5-B-76	46	LH IIIB
931	F5-B-79	48, 128	LH IIIC
1000	F5-B-82	51	LH III
898	F5-B-83	46	LH IIIB
745	F5-B-86	40, 126	MH III-LH I
266	F6-1	15, 119	EH II
366	F6-2	20	EH II
348	F6-4	20	EH II
74	F6-5	4	EH I
463	F6-10	27	EH II
265	F6-12	15	EH II
128	F6-27	8	EH I?

Publ. Cat. No.	AEP Inv. No.	Figure Nos.	Date	Publ. Cat. No.	AEP Inv. No.	Figure Nos.	Date
495	F6-28+29	30	EH II	1213	F32	138	GEO
693	F6-31	38	EH III	1214	F32	138	GEO
581	F6-60	33	EH II	296	F32-1	17	EH II
575	F6-64	33	EH II	286	F32-3	16	EH II
585	F6-71	33	EH II	385	F32-4	21	EH II
1205	F6-99	116	GEO	254	F32-7	14	EH II
375	F6-ALL-2	21, 120	EH II	262	F32-8	15	EH II
48	F6-ALL-3	3	FN-EH I	418	F32-9	23, 120	EH II
420	F6-ALL-4	23	EH II	282	F32-14	16	EH II
479	F6-ALL-5	29, 121	EH II	405	F32-18	22	EH II
64	F9-1	4, 118	FN-EH I	342	F32-19	19, 119	EH II
206	F9-2	119	EH I	426	F32-24	23	EH II
165	F9-ALL-5	11, 118	EH I	284	F32-25	16	EH II
210	F9-ALL-6	12	EH I	360	F32-26	20	EH II
66	F14-1	4, 118	FN	381	F32-28	21, 120	EH II
261	F15-2	15	EH I-EH II	438	F32-32	24	EH II
267	F15-5	15	EH II	340	F32-33	19	EH II
632	F16-29	35, 122	EH II	393	F32-34	21	EH II
441	F17-2	24	EH II	548	F32-38	32	EH II
476	F17-3	29	EH II	544	F32-39	32	EH II
337	F17-8	19	EH II	562	F32-41	32	EH II
167	F17-11	11	EH I	527	F32-42	32	EH II
856	F17-16	45	LH IIIA2	610	F32-48	34	EH II
1182	F17-18	114	GEO	111	F32-64	7, 118	EH I-EH II
422	F19-4	23	EH II	356	F32-65	20, 120	EH II
676	F20-3	37	EH II	657	F32-68	36, 123	EH II
990	F20-7	51	LH IIIA1	659	F32-69	36, 123	EH II
322	F20-11	18	EH I-EH II	531	F32-A1-7	32	EH II
251	F20-17	14	EH II	305	F32-A3-1	17	EH II
245	F20-18	14	EH II	107	F32-A3-2	7	EH I?
55	F20-20	4	FN?	105	F32-A3-3	6	EH I-EH II
552	F20-21	32	EH II	308	F32-A3-4	17	EH II
665	F20-26	37	EH II	367	F32-A3-5	20	EH II
468	F20-27	28	EH II	440	F32-A3-6+	24, 121	EH II
452	F20-28	25	EH II	275	F32-A3-9	16	EH I-EH II
465	F20-29	27	EH II	300	F32-A5-1	17	EH II
464	F20-30	27	EH II	271	F32-A5-3	16	EH II
460	F20-31	26	EH II	389	F32-A5-6	21	EH II
483	F20-34	121	EH II	110	F32-A7-2	7	EH I-EH II
470	F20-ALL-8	28	EH II	565	F32-A7-4	33	EH II
508	F20-ALL-9	31	EH II	428	F32-A7-5	23	EH II
444	F20-ALL-10	24	EH II	364	F32-A9-1	20	EH II
291	F20-ALL-12	16	EH II	234	F32-A9-2	13	EH II
320	F20-ALL-15	18	EH I-EH II	330	F32-A9-4	19	EH I-EH II
238	F20-ALL-16	13	EH II	484	F32-A11-6	29, 121	EH II
459	F20-ALL-22	26	EH II	586	F32-A11-8	33	EH II
324	F21-4	18, 119	EH I-EH II	643	F32-B2-1	35	EH II
899	F21-15	46	LH IIIB	317	F32-B6-2	18	EH II
542	F23-41	32	EH II	566	F32-B6-6	33	EH II
816	F23-47	43, 127	LH I	354	F32-B8-3	20	EH II
712	F26-1	39, 126	MH III	514	F32-B8-6	31	EH II
803	F26-6		MH III	577	F32-B8-10	33	EH II
830	F26-10	44	LH IIA	662	F32-B10-4	37, 124	EH II
737	F26-12	40	MH III-LH I	472	F32-B12-2	28	EH II
815	F26-16	43, 127	LH I	636	F32-B12-5	123	EH II
969	F29-1	50	LH	551	F32-B12-6	32	EH II
227	F29-7	13	EH II	443	F32-C2-1	24	EH II

Publ. Cat. No.	AEP Inv. No.	Figure Nos.	Date		Publ. Cat. No.	AEP Inv. No.	Figure Nos.	Date
352	F32-C4-6	20	EH II		257	F32-N-68	15, 119	EH II
323	F32-C5-1	18	EH II		382	F32-N-73	21	EH II
236	F32-C5-2	13	EH II		378	F32-N-74	21	EH II
331	F32-C7-2	19	EH II		355	F32-N-75	20, 119	EH II
349	F32-C7-4	20	EH II		386	F32-N-76	21	EH II
601	F32-C9-8	34	EH II		417	F32-N-77	23	EH II
560	F32-C9-9	32	EH II		477	F32-N-79	29	EH II
571	F32-C9-10	33	EH II		497	F32-N-81	30	EH II
449	F32-C11-1	25	EH II		690	F32-N-82	38	EH III
516	F32-D2-1	31	EH II		294	F32-N-83	17	EH II
383	F32-D4-3	21, 120	EH II		424	F32-N-84	23	EH II
568	F32-D4-14	33	EH II		306	F32-N-94	17	EH II
530	F32-D4-16	32	EH II		500	F32-N-95	30	EH II
609	F32-D4-18	34	EH II		290	F32-N-96	16	EH I-EH II
353	F32-D6-1	20, 119	EH II		252	F32-N-124	14	EH II
448	F32-D6-5	24	EH II		491	F32-N-129	30	EH II
474	F32-D8-1	29	EH II		310	F32-N-134	18	EH I-EH II
622	F32-D8-15	34	EH II		109	F32-N-136	7	EH I-EH II
654	F32-D8-17	36	EH II		328	F32-N-139	19, 119	EH II
419	F32-D12-1	23	EH II		329	F32-N-140	19, 119	EH II
970	F32-D12-4	50	LH		427	F32-N-141	23	EH II
339	F32-E-1	19	EH II		751	F32-N-142	40	MH III
363	F32-E-2	20	EH II		299	F32-N-144	17	EH II
311	F32-E-6	18	EH II		435	F32-N-146	23	EH II
301	F32-E-7	17	EH II		307	F32-N-147	17	EH II
396	F32-E-16	22	EH II		457	F32-N-150	25	EH II
511	F32-E-19	31	EH II		473	F32-N-151	29	EH II
547	F32-E-28	32	EH II		70	F32-N-152	4	EH I
589	F32-E-31	33	EH II		160	F32-N-166	10	EH I
509	F32-E-33	31	EH II		621	F32-N-188	34	EH I-EH II
576	F32-E-34	33	EH II		333	F32-N-206	19	EH II
633	F32-E-35	35, 122	EH II		334	F32-N-207	19	EH II
534	F32-E-45	32	EH II		336	F32-N-208	19	EH II
220	F32-E-47	13	EH II		624	F32-N-209	34	EH II
1156	F32-E-49	112	GEO		1001	F32-N-210	51	LH III
1191	F32-N-1	115, 136	GEO		526	F32-N-212	32	EH II
873	F32-N-3	45	LH IIIA2		223	F32-N-214	13	EH II
1175	F32-N-13		GEO		591	F32-N-222	33	EH II
274	F32-N-16	16	EH II		518	F32-N-223	32	EH II
1186	F32-N-24	114, 135	GEO		533	F32-N-224	32	EH II
433	F32-N-39	23	EH II		549	F32-N-226	32	EH II
403	F32-N-40	22	EH II		573	F32-N-229	33	EH II
263	F32-N-41	15	EH II		602	F32-N-230	34	EH II
408	F32-N-42	22	EH II		537	F32-N-234	32	EH II
413	F32-N-43	22	EH II		594	F32-N-236	33	EH II
343	F32-N-44	19	EH II		583	F32-N-237	33	EH II
425	F32-N-45	23	EH II		521	F32-N-243	32	EH II
411	F32-N-46	22	EH II		525	F32-N-245	32	EH II
400	F32-N-47	22	EH II		606	F32-N-247	34	EH II
407	F32-N-48	22	EH II		600	F32-N-248	34	EH II
406	F32-N-49	22	EH II		556	F32-N-249	32	EH II
377	F32-N-50	21, 120	EH II		570	F32-N-251	33	EH II
325	F32-N-51	18	EH II		593	F32-N-252	33	EH II
361	F32-N-53	20, 120	EH II		540	F32-N-253	32	EH II
369	F32-N-59	21, 120	EH II		554	F32-N-255	32	EH II
387	F32-N-64	21	EH II		557	F32-N-257	32	EH II
116	F32-N-65	7	EH I		590	F32-N-258	33	EH II

Publ. Cat. No.	AEP Inv. No.	Figure Nos.	Date
605	F32-N-260	34	EH II
578	F32-N-261	33	EH II
550	F32-N-262	32	EH II
599	F32-N-263	33	EH II
637	F32-N-266	123	EH II
635	F32-N-267	35, 122	EH II
634	F32-N-268	35, 122	EH II
480	F32-N-269	29, 121	EH II
650	F32-N-271	36, 123	EH II
656	F32-N-272	36	EH II
649	F32-N-273	36	EH II
655	F32-N-274	36, 123	EH II
652	F32-N-275	36	EH II
658	F32-N-276	36	EH II
900	F32-S-1	46	LH IIIB
287	F32-S-22	16	EH II
510	F32-S-41	31	EH II
371	F32-S-43	21	EH II
269	F32-S-45	16	EH II
289	F32-S-52	16	EH II
569	F32-S-53	33	EH II
512	F32-S-61	31	EH II
351	F32-S-64	20, 119	EH II
279	F32-S-66	16	EH I-EH II
374	F32-S-67	21, 120	EH II
280	F32-S-68	16	EH II
121	F32-S-73	7	EH I
357	F32-S-74	20, 120	EH II
384	F32-S-79	21	EH II
346	F32-S-81	19, 119	EH II
120	F32-S-82	7	EH I
376	F32-S-85	21	EH II
388	F32-S-87	21, 120	EH II
372	F32-S-88	21, 120	EH II
368	F32-S-89	20	EH II
402	F32-S-90	22	EH II
380	F32-S-93	21, 120	EH II
117	F32-S-96	7, 118	EH I
515	F32-S-97	31, 121	EH I?-EH II
313	F32-S-98	18	EH I-EH II
115	F32-S-99	7	EH I-EH II
297	F32-S-103	17	EH II
248	F32-S-104	14	EH I-EH II
113	F32-S-108	7	EH I
499	F32-S-110	30	EH II
506	F32-S-111	31	EH II
487	F32-S-115	30	EH II
488	F32-S-121	30	EH II
166	F32-S-128	11	EH I
318	F32-S-161	18	EH II
523	F32-S-170	32	EH II
587	F32-S-171	33	EH II
529	F32-S-172	32	EH II
543	F32-S-173	32	EH II
536	F32-S-175	32	EH II
517	F32-S-176	32	EH II
603	F32-S-180	34	EH II

Publ. Cat. No.	AEP Inv. No.	Figure Nos.	Date
224	F32-S-183	13	EH II
559	F32-S-184	32	EH II
630	F32-S-190	35	EH II
619	F32-S-194	34	EH II
631	F32-S-199	35	EH II
639	F32-S-204	35	EH II
653	F32-S-206	36, 123	EH II
651	F32-S-207	36, 123	EH II
664	F32-S-208	37, 124	EH II
661	F32-S-209	36	EH II
598	F32-SF-1	33	EH II
314	F32-SF-13	18	EH II
281	F32-SF-15	16	EH II
1132	F32-SF-22	134	GEO
660	F32-X	36	EH II
588	F58-2-2	33	EH II
1162	G1-3129	135	GEO
1190	G1-3130	115	GEO
1120	G1-A-1	110, 133	GEO
1204	G1-A-2	116, 136	GEO
1189	G1-A-4	115, 136	GEO
1138	G1-A-6	111, 134	GEO
1203	G1-A-7	116	GEO
1133	G1-A-23	134	GEO
1197	G1-A-25	136	GEO
344	G1-A-58	19	EH II
76	G1-A-59	4	EH I
1187	G1-A-70	114	GEO
1188	G1-A-72	114	GEO
1184	G1-A-73	114, 135	GEO
1086	G1-A-80	108, 132	GEO
1172	G1-B-21	135	GEO
1070	G1-B-22	107, 131	GEO
1072	G1-B-23	131	GEO
292	G9-1	17	EH II
19	G9-2	2	FN
17	G9-3	2, 118	FN
38	G9-4	3	FN
304	G9-7	17	EH II
6	G9-10	1	LN
45	G9-11	3	FN?
142	G9-13	9	EH I
22	G9-15	2	FN
67	G9-20	4, 118	FN
40	G9-26	3	FN
39	G9-37	3	FN
943	G9-40	48, 128	LH IIIC
26	G9-1-1+12	2	FN
27	G9-1-2	2	FN
25	G9-1-4	2	FN
709	G9-1-6	39, 125	EH III
34	G9-1-7	3	FN
293	G9-1-8	17	EH II
13	G9-1-17	1	FN
54	G9-1-26	4	FN
49	G9-1-44	3	FN
53	G9-5-13	4	FN

Publ. Cat. No.	AEP Inv. No.	Figure Nos.	Date		Publ. Cat. No.	AEP Inv. No.	Figure Nos.	Date
43	G9-5-14	3	FN?		59	G9-5-29	4	FN
42	G9-5-15	3	FN?		157	G9-B-1	10	EH I
24	G9-5-16	2	FN		52	G9-B-2	4	FN
60	G9-5-18	4, 118	FN		57	G9-B-3	4, 118	FN
12	G9-5-19	1	FN		1200	G22-5-5	136	GEO
20	G9-5-28	2	FN		1139	G22-5-7	112, 134	GEO

Figures

Figures

The illustrations for this volume consist of line drawings (Figs. 1–117) and photographs (Figs. 118–136). The line drawings of ceramics (Figs. 1–64) are reproduced at a scale of 1:3, and the photographs of ceramics (Figs. 118–136) are reproduced at a scale of 1:2; scales appear in all figures of ceramics. Lithic objects (Figs. 65–117) are reproduced at a scale of 1:1 unless otherwise indicated by the presence of a different scale. Figs. 1–64 and 118–136 are arranged by catalogue number so that the reader may move easily between the catalogue entries of Appendix 1 and the illustrations here. Exceptions to the strict catalogue-number ordering of illustrations are due simply to economies of space. Please note that although nearly all objects from Appendix 1 are illustrated by line drawings in Figs. 1–64, some are not illustrated at all, some objects are illustrated only by photographs in Figs. 118–136, and some are illustrated by both line drawings and photographs. In all cases the catalogue entries of Appendix 1 and the concordance of Appendix 3 clearly indicate the figure on which is to be found the illustration(s) for any particular object. Illustrations in Figs. 65–117 (all by Priscilla Murray or Curtis Runnels unless otherwise indicated) are referred to directly in the text of Chapter 5.

We have attempted stylistic consistency among our line drawings of the ceramics, but with such a wide range of materials drawn by so many different artists over a number of years, such consistency has not always been maintained. Within each of the individual chapters, at least, there is a good degree of consistency in the illustrations. Certain conventions, however, have been retained throughout all categories. The profile is always on the right. Where a diameter of the vessel represented by the sherd can be calculated, this is indicated by extending a horizontal line from the profile along the rim or the base to the vertical central axis, whose height reflects the maximum preserved height of the vessel. Where decoration, shape, or size of the sherd warrant, the *exterior* of the vessel is reflected onto the *left* of the axis, occasionally restored to an extent larger than has actually been preserved. Any decoration that appears to the *right* of the central axis when a vessel is shown reflected should be interpreted as appearing on the *interior*. Decoration on the top of a rim or on the bottom of a base is reflected above or below, respectively. Rim and base sherds that cannot be restored to a measurable vessel are indicated by a horizontal line terminating without the vertical central axis.

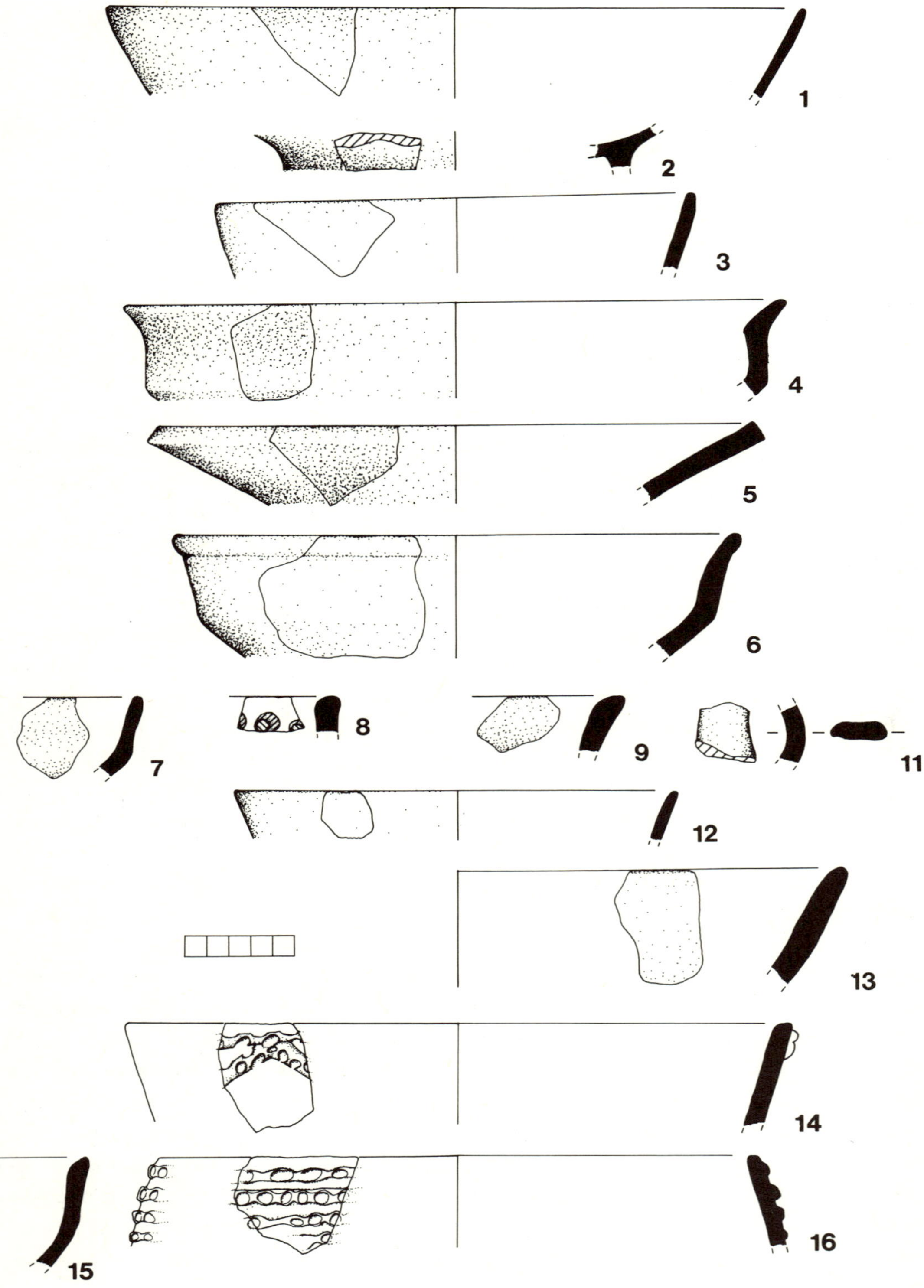

Fig. 1. Middle Neolithic bowls **1–5**; Late Neolithic bowls **6–9**, **11**; Final Neolithic bowls **12–16**.

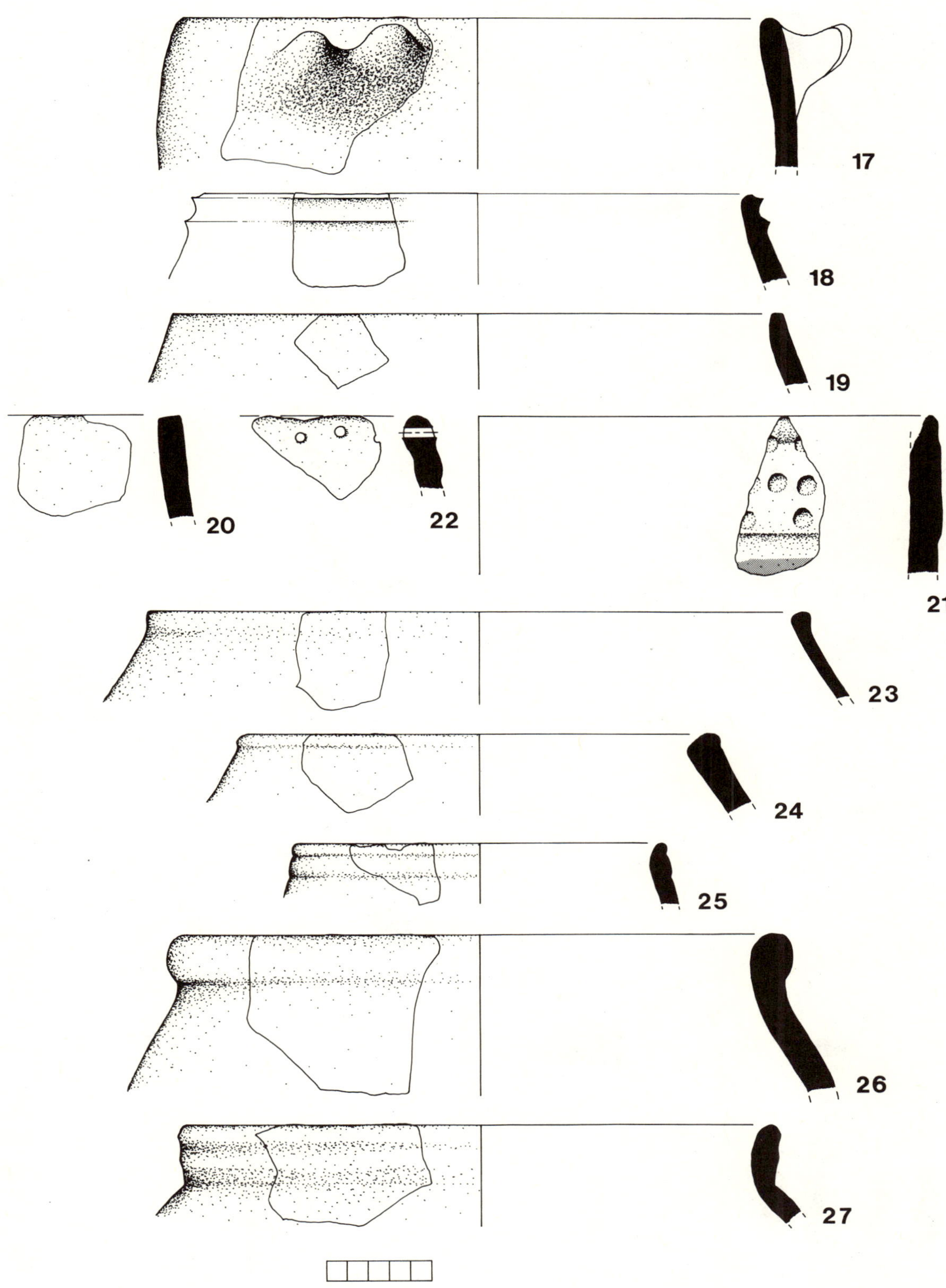

Fig. 2. Final Neolithic bowls **17–22**, jars **23–27**.

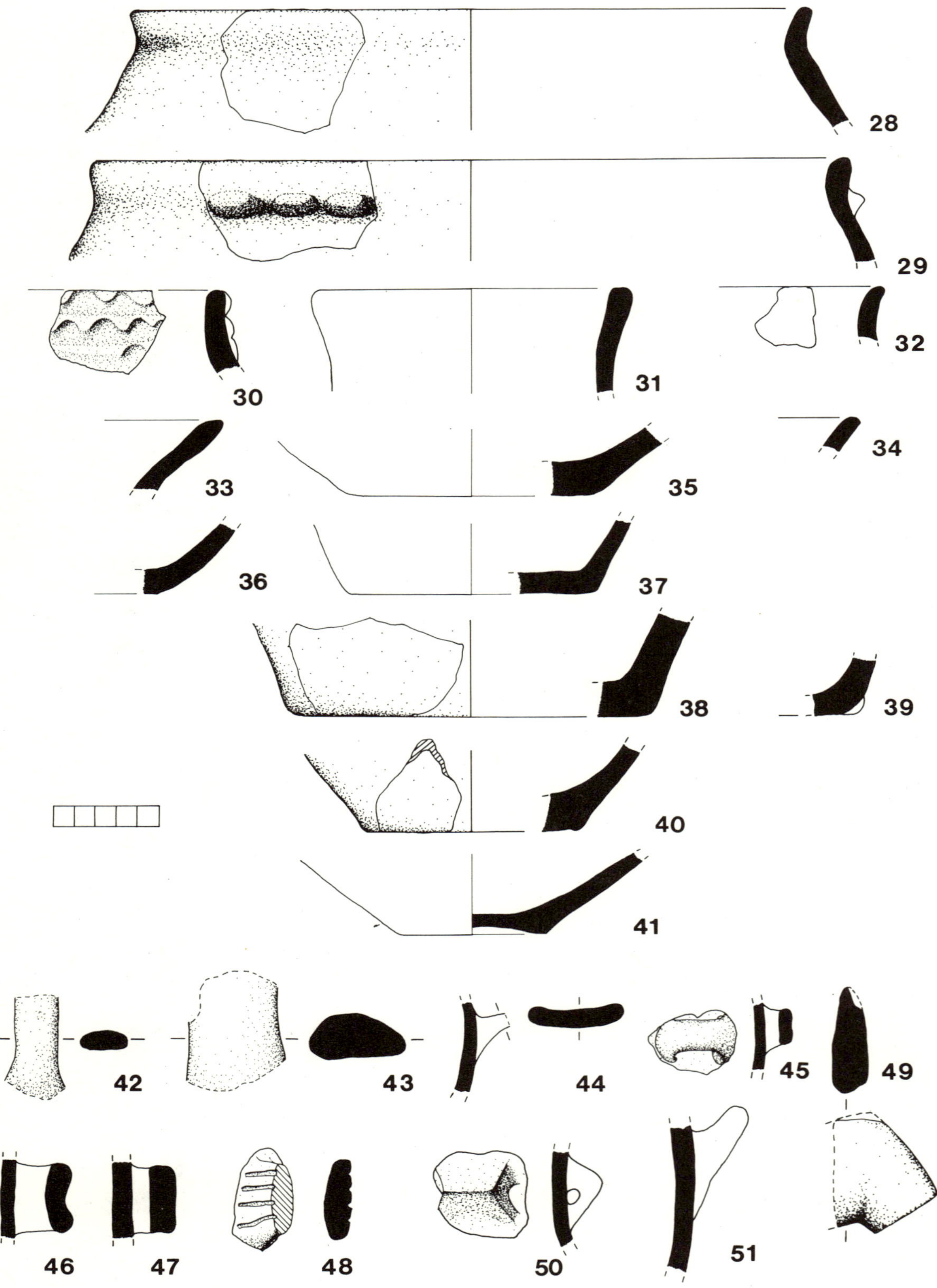

Fig. 3. Final Neolithic jars **28–34**, bases **35–41**, handles **42–49**, lugs **50, 51**.

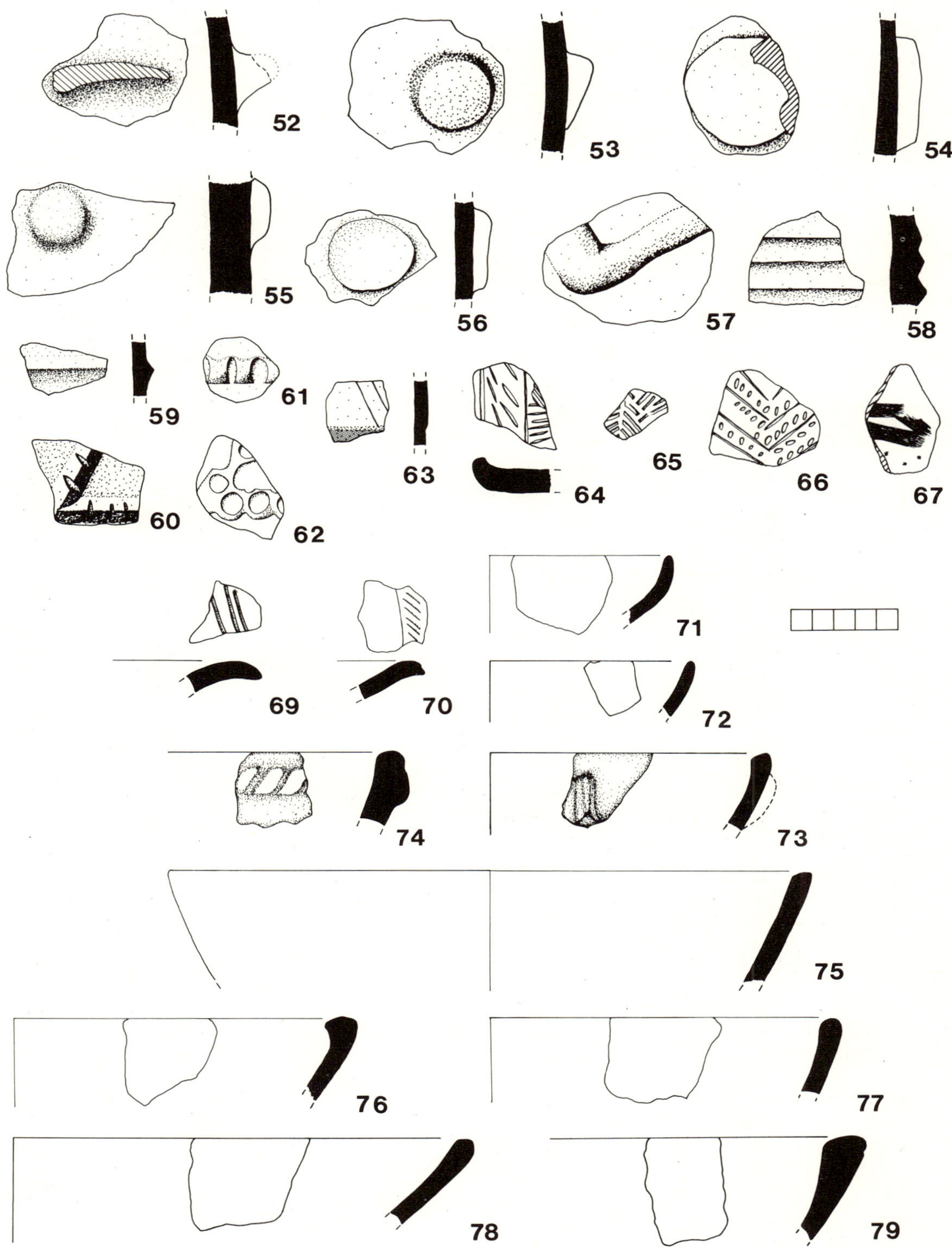

Fig. 4. Final Neolithic lugs **52**, **53**, knobs **54–56**, body **57–67**; Early Helladic I fruitstands **69**, **70**, bowls **71–79**.

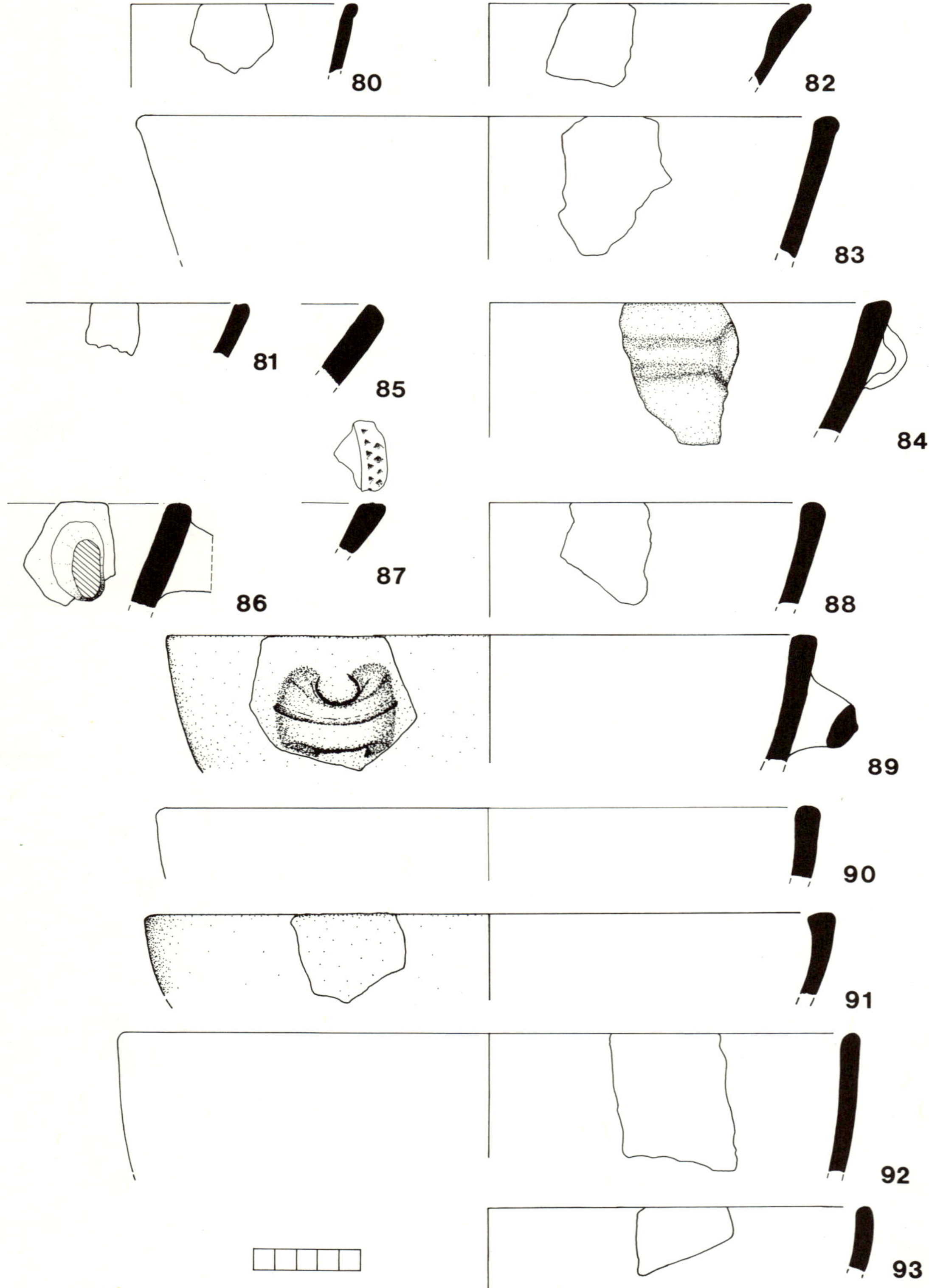

Fig. 5. Early Helladic I bowls **80–93**.

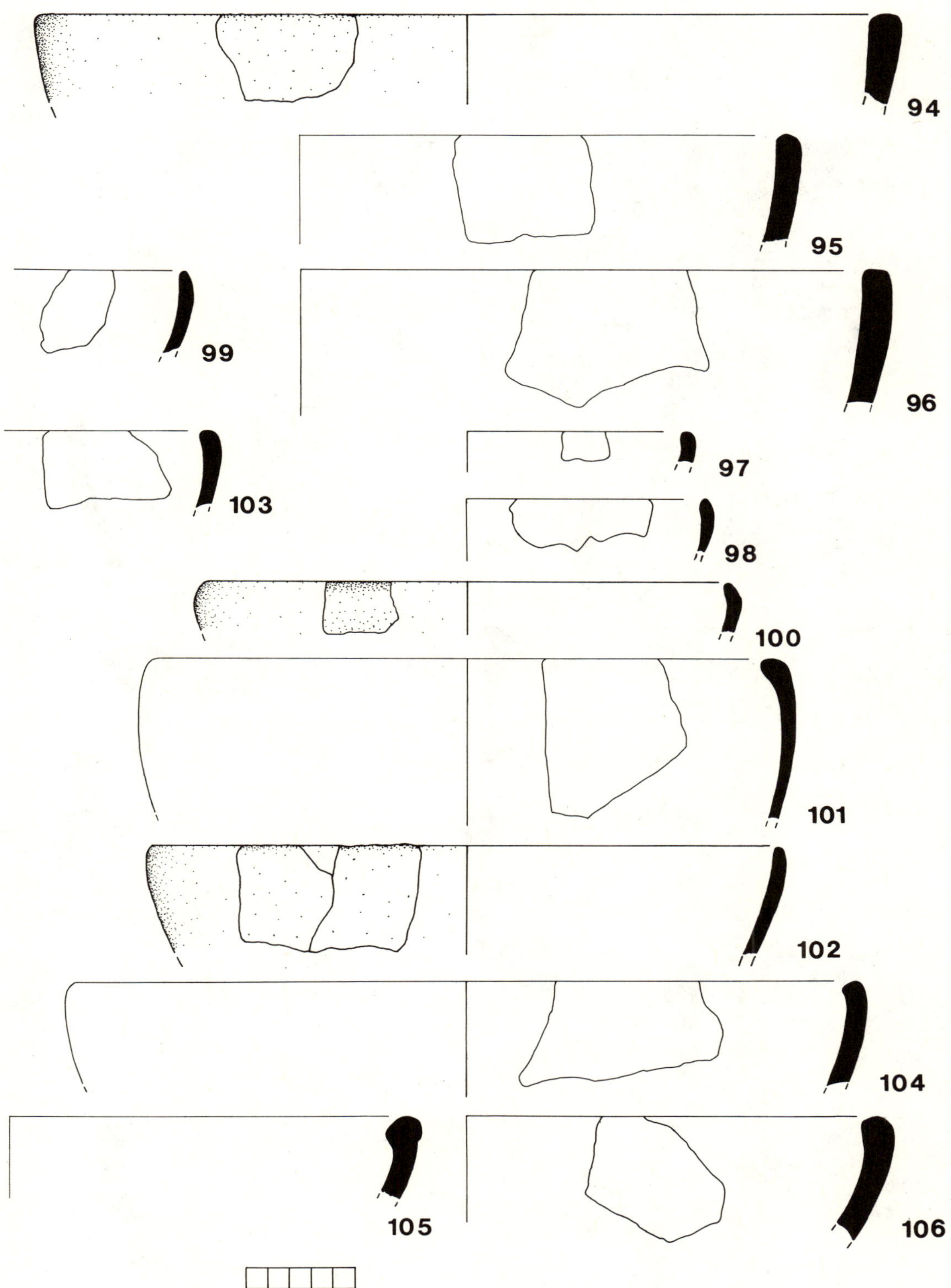

Fig. 6. Early Helladic I bowls **94–106**.

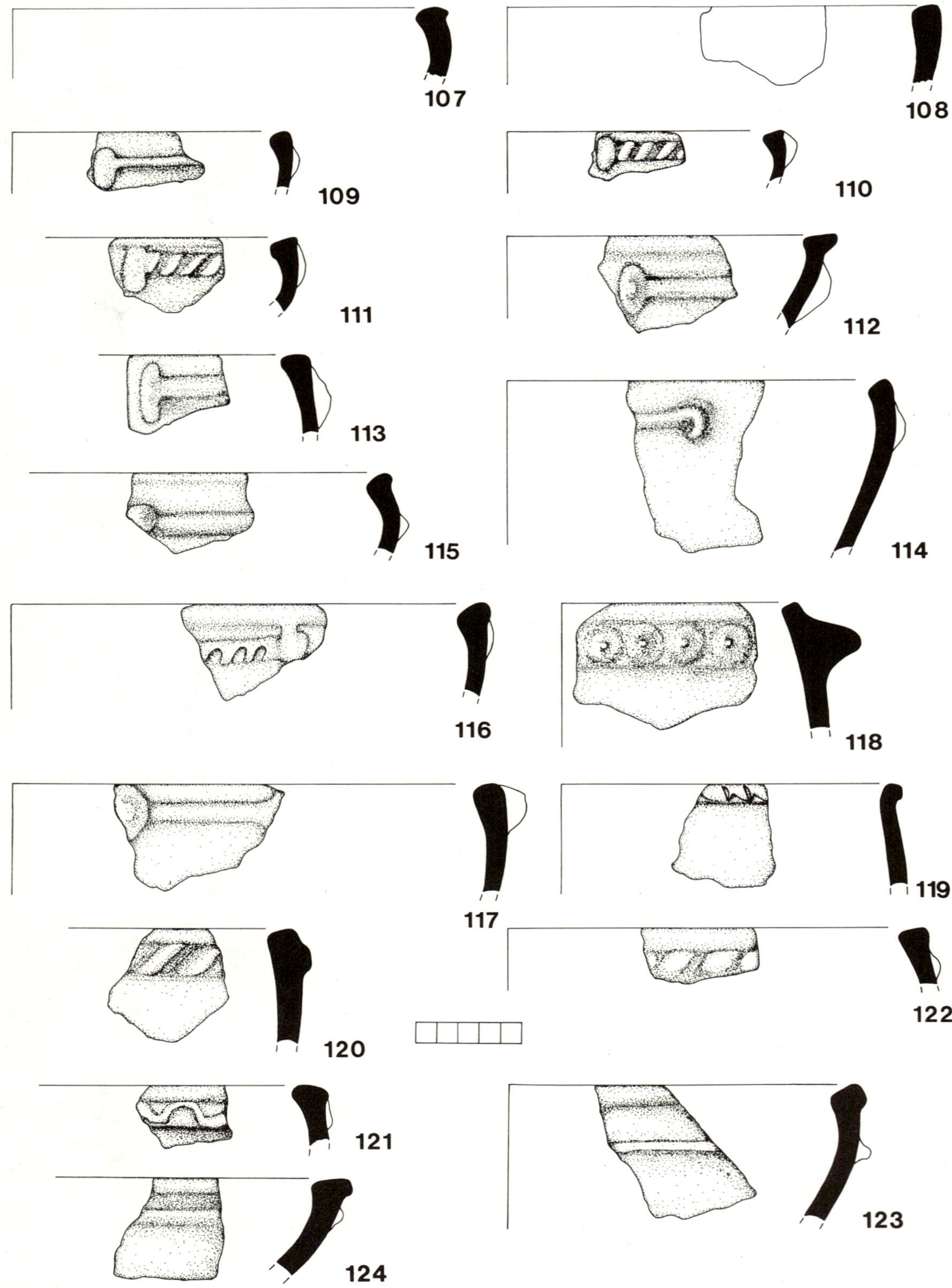

Fig. 7. Early Helladic I bowls **107–124**.

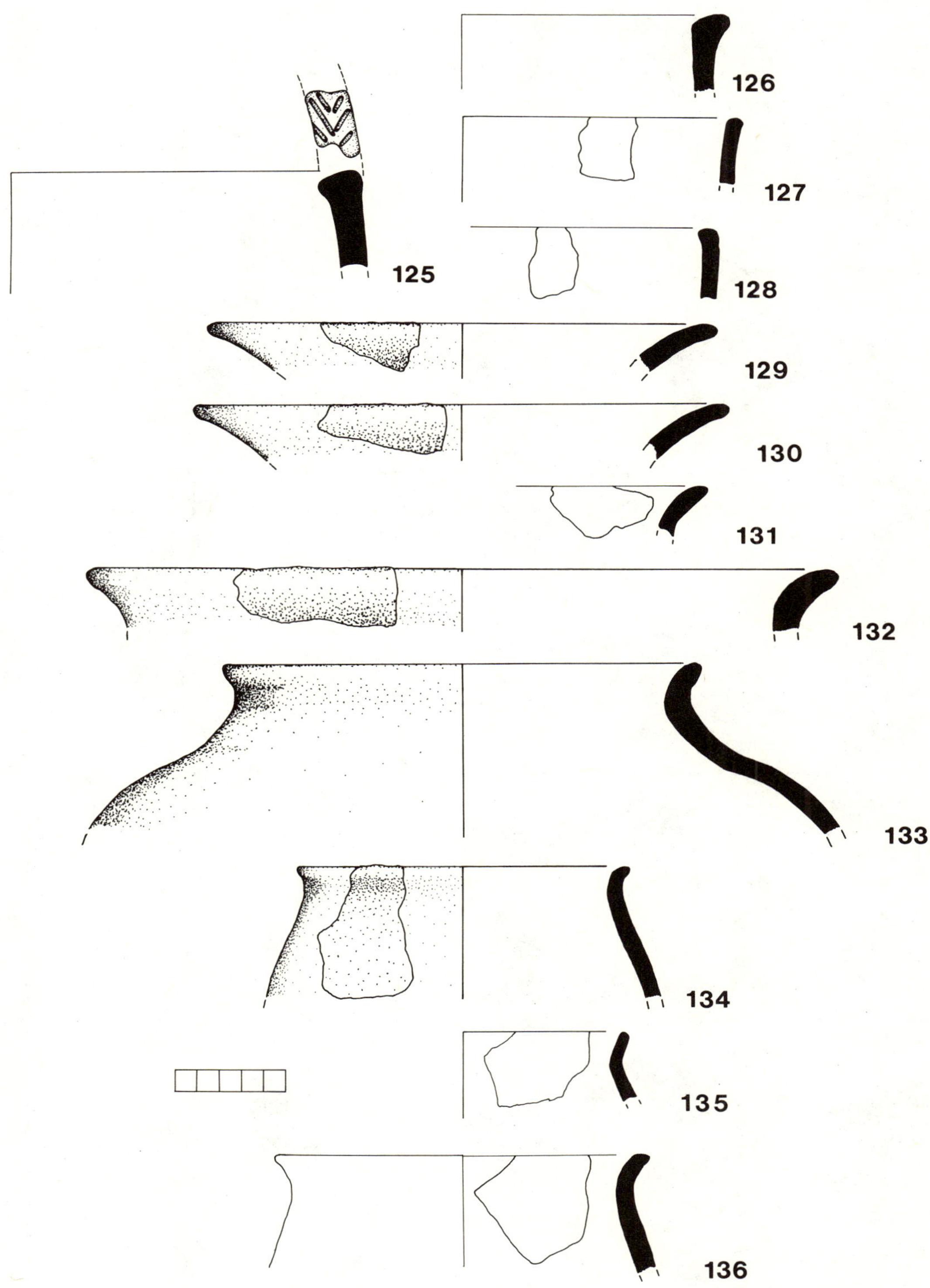

Fig. 8. Early Helladic I bowls **125–128**, jars **129–136**.

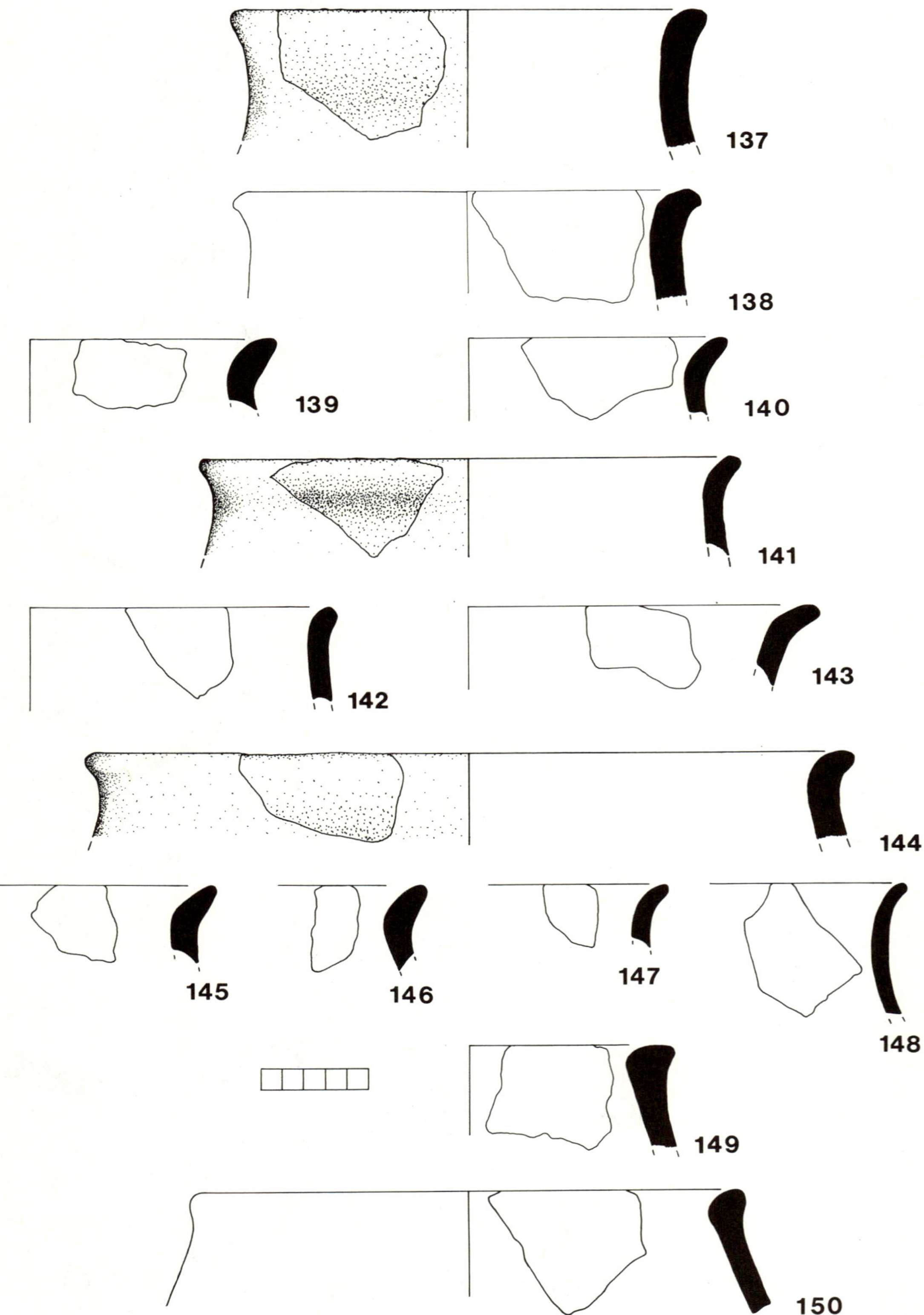

Fig. 9. Early Helladic I jars **137–150**.

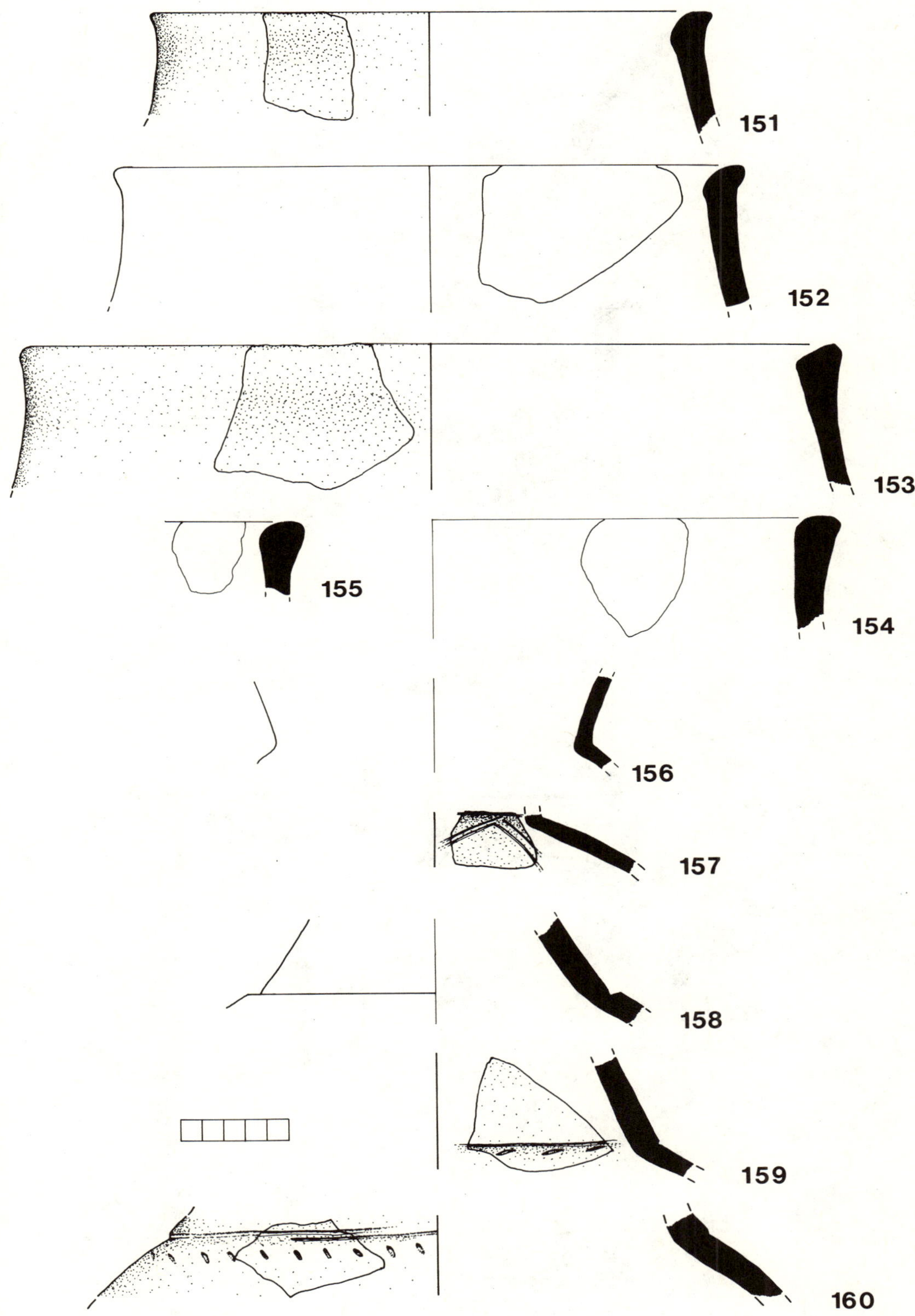

Fig. 10. Early Helladic I jars **151–160**.

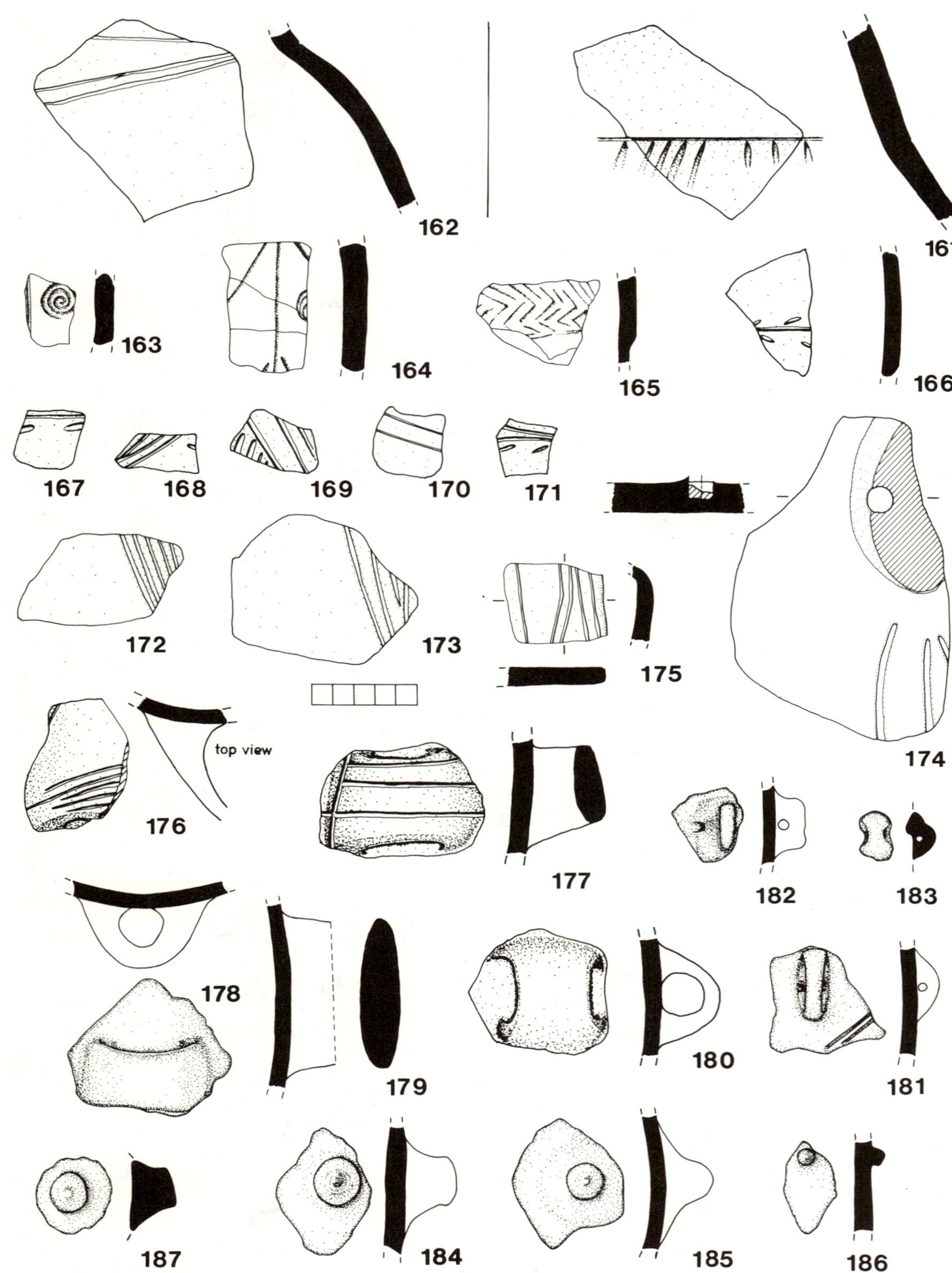

Fig. 11. Early Helladic I jars **161**, **162**, body **163–187**.

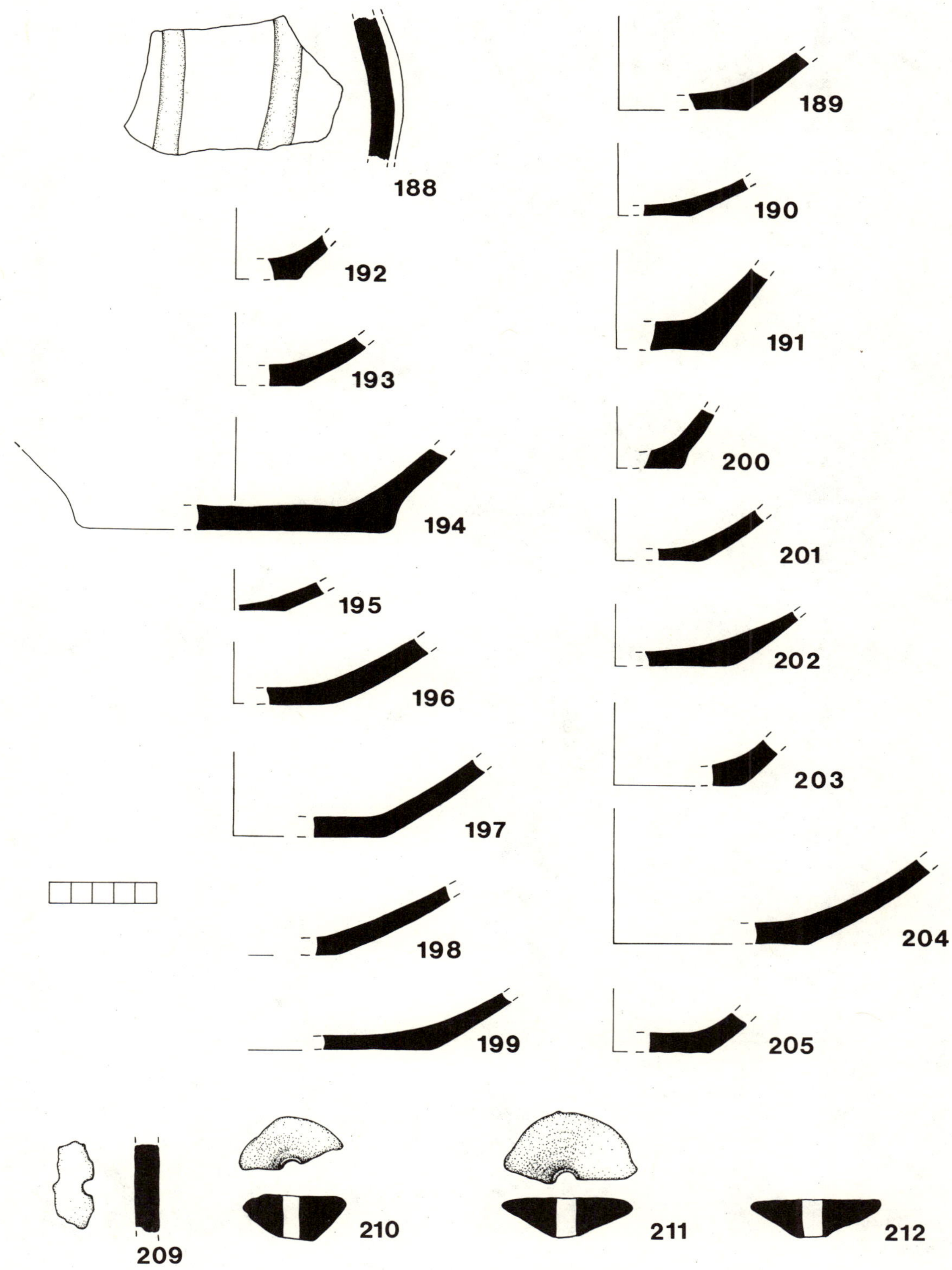

Fig. 12. Early Helladic I body **188**, bases **189–205**, weight **209**, whorls **210–212**.

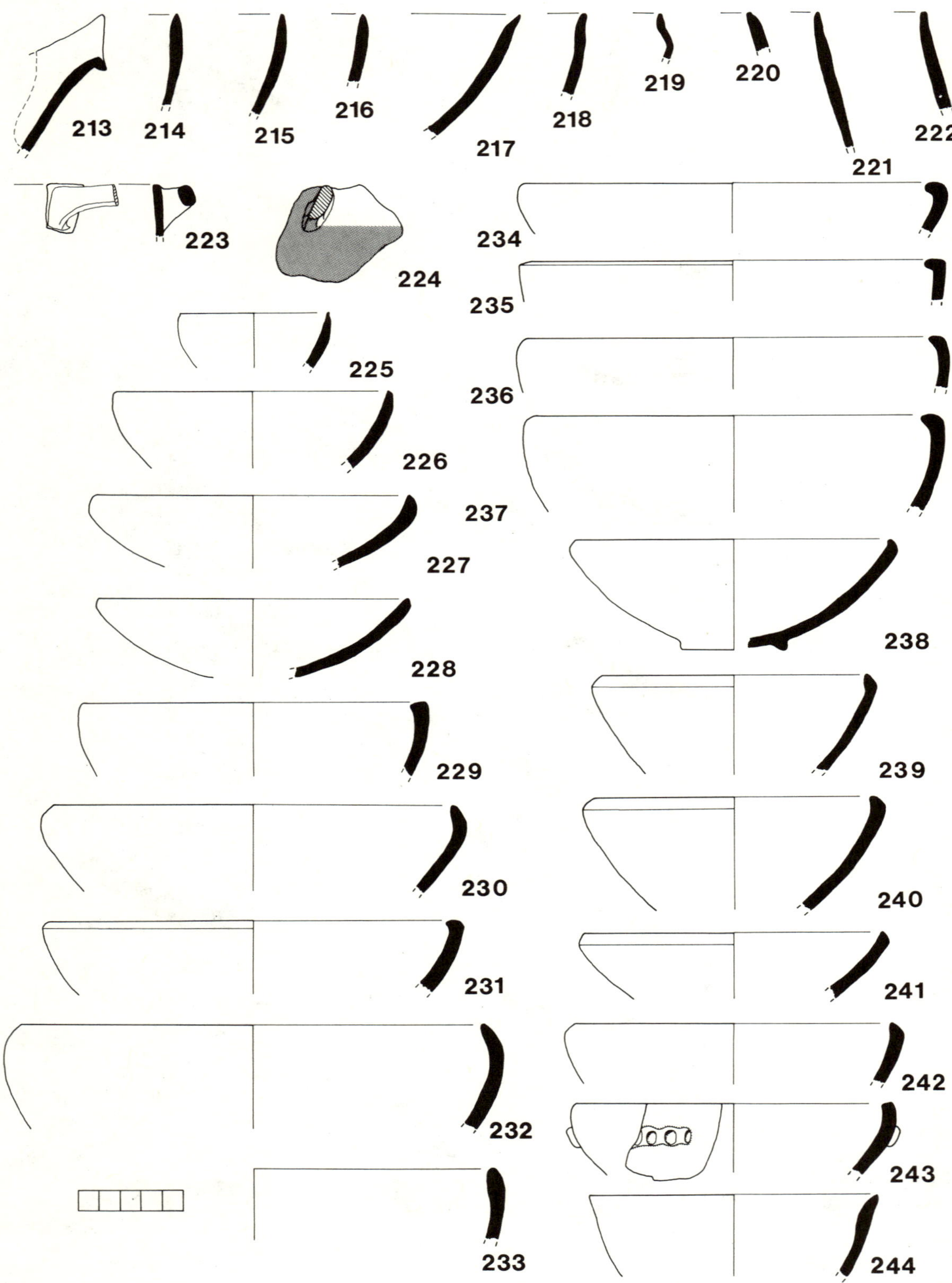

Fig. 13. Early Helladic II sauceboats **213–224**, bowls **225–244**.

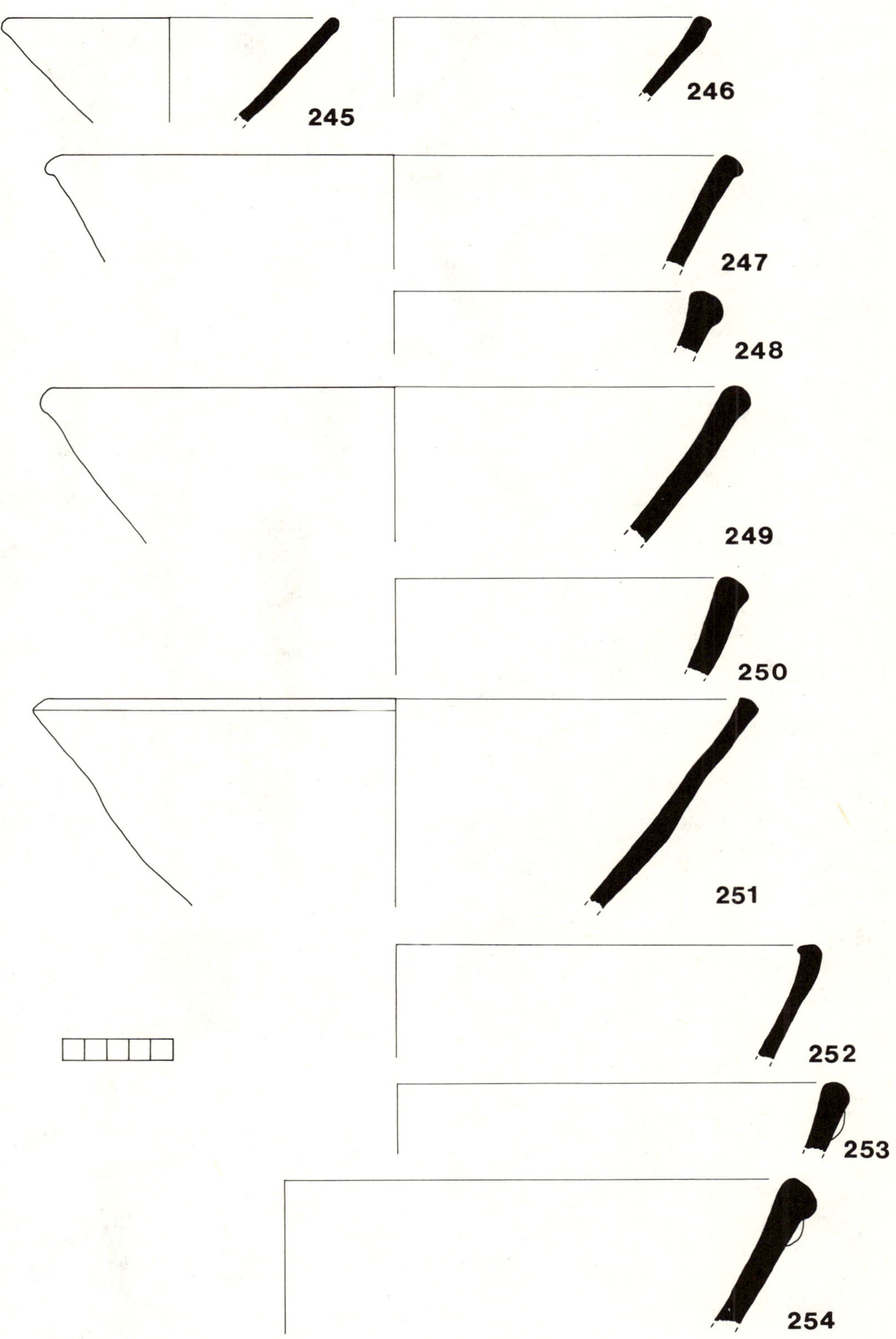

Fig. 14. Early Helladic II bowls **245**, **246**, basins **247–254**.

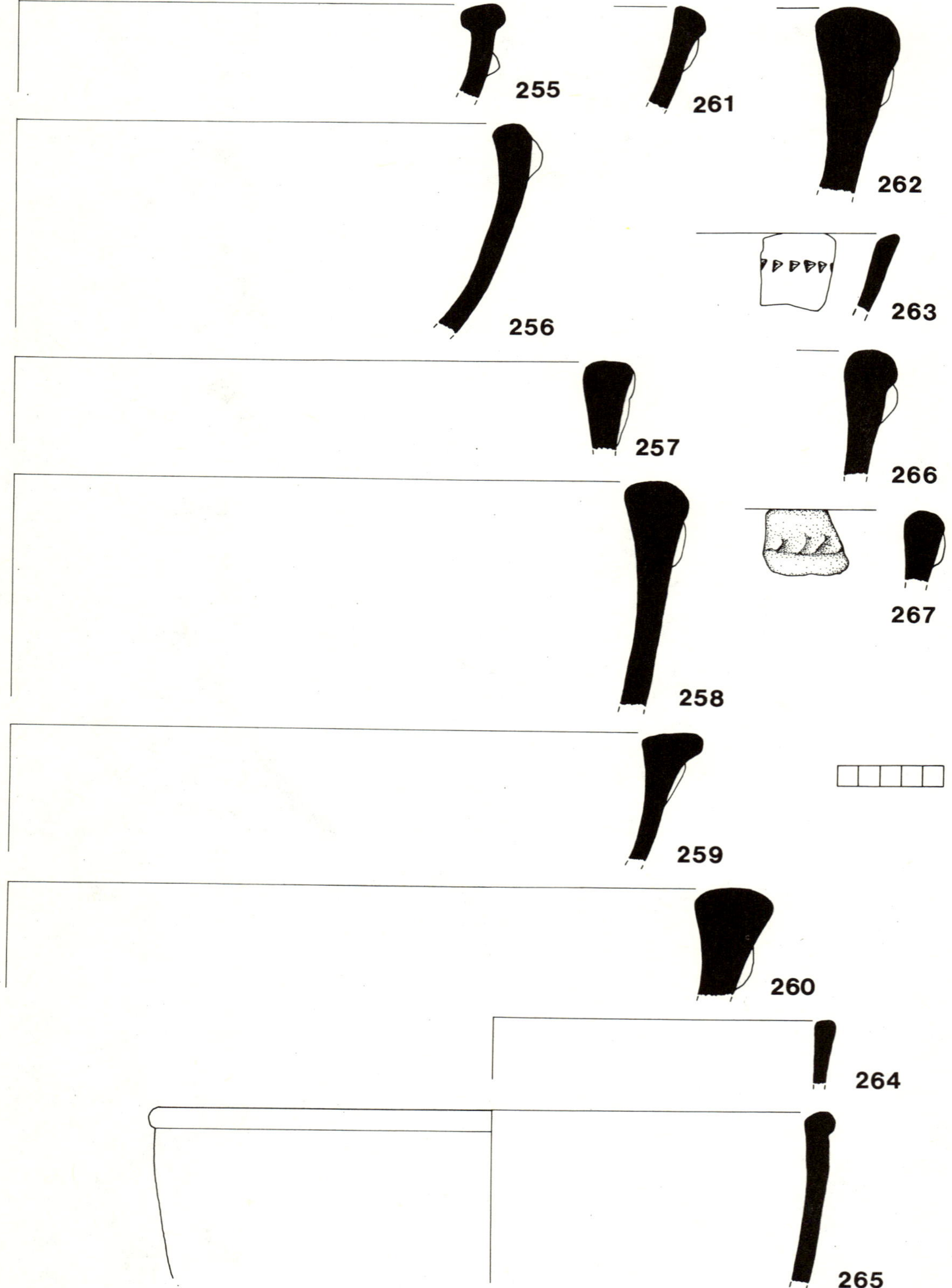

Fig. 15. Early Helladic II large bowls **255–267**.

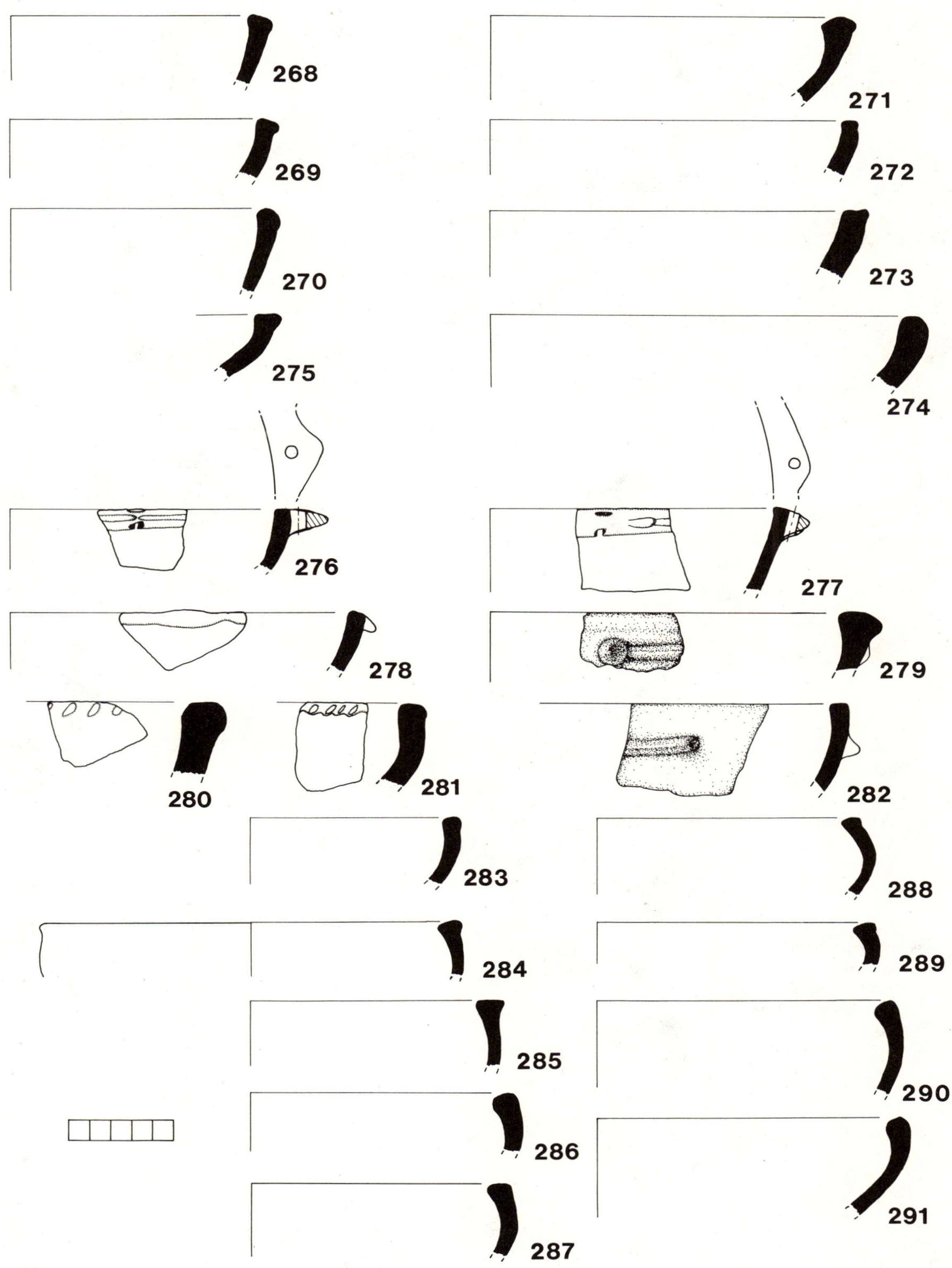

Fig. 16. Early Helladic II bowls **268–291**.

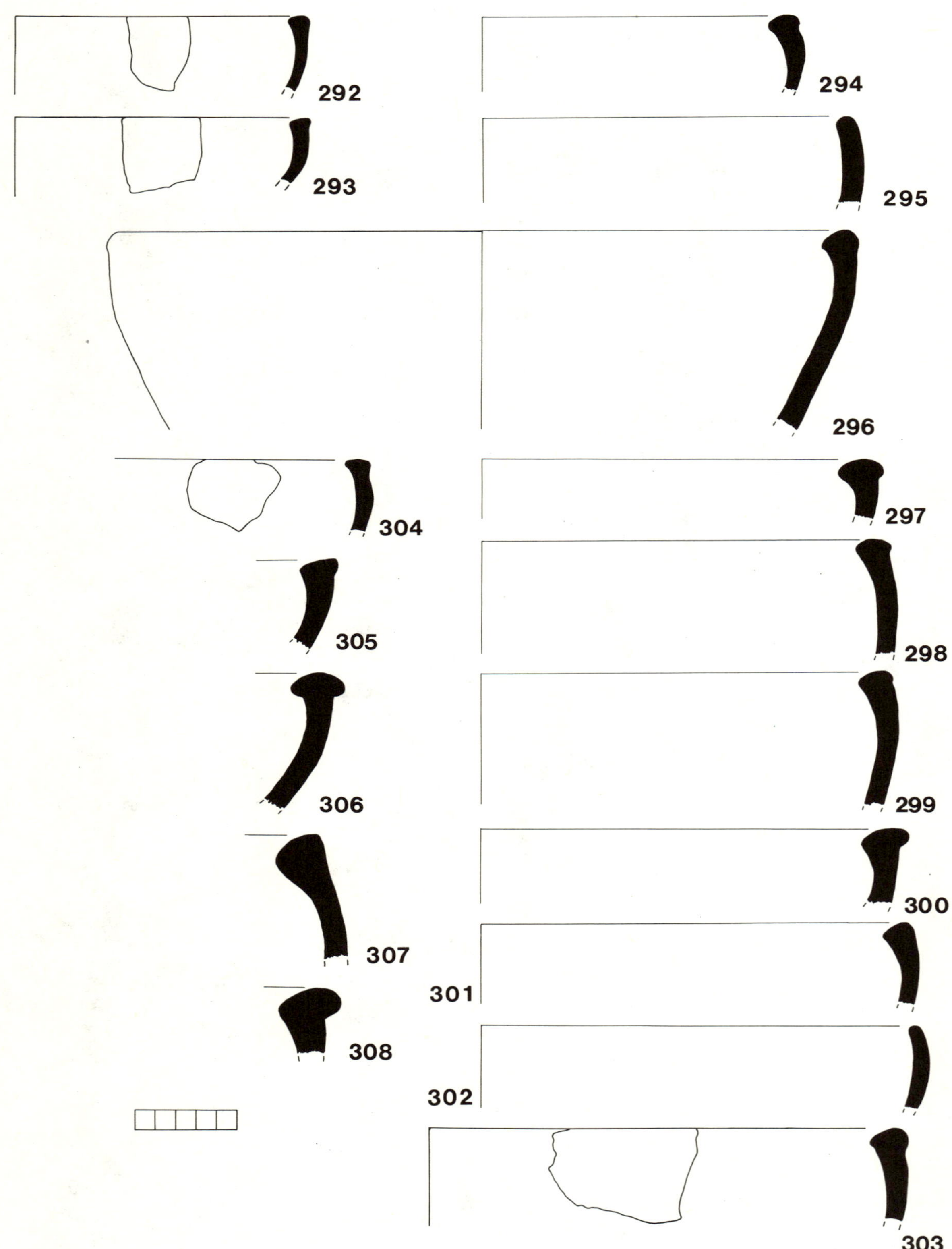

Fig. 17. Early Helladic II incurving bowls **292–308**.

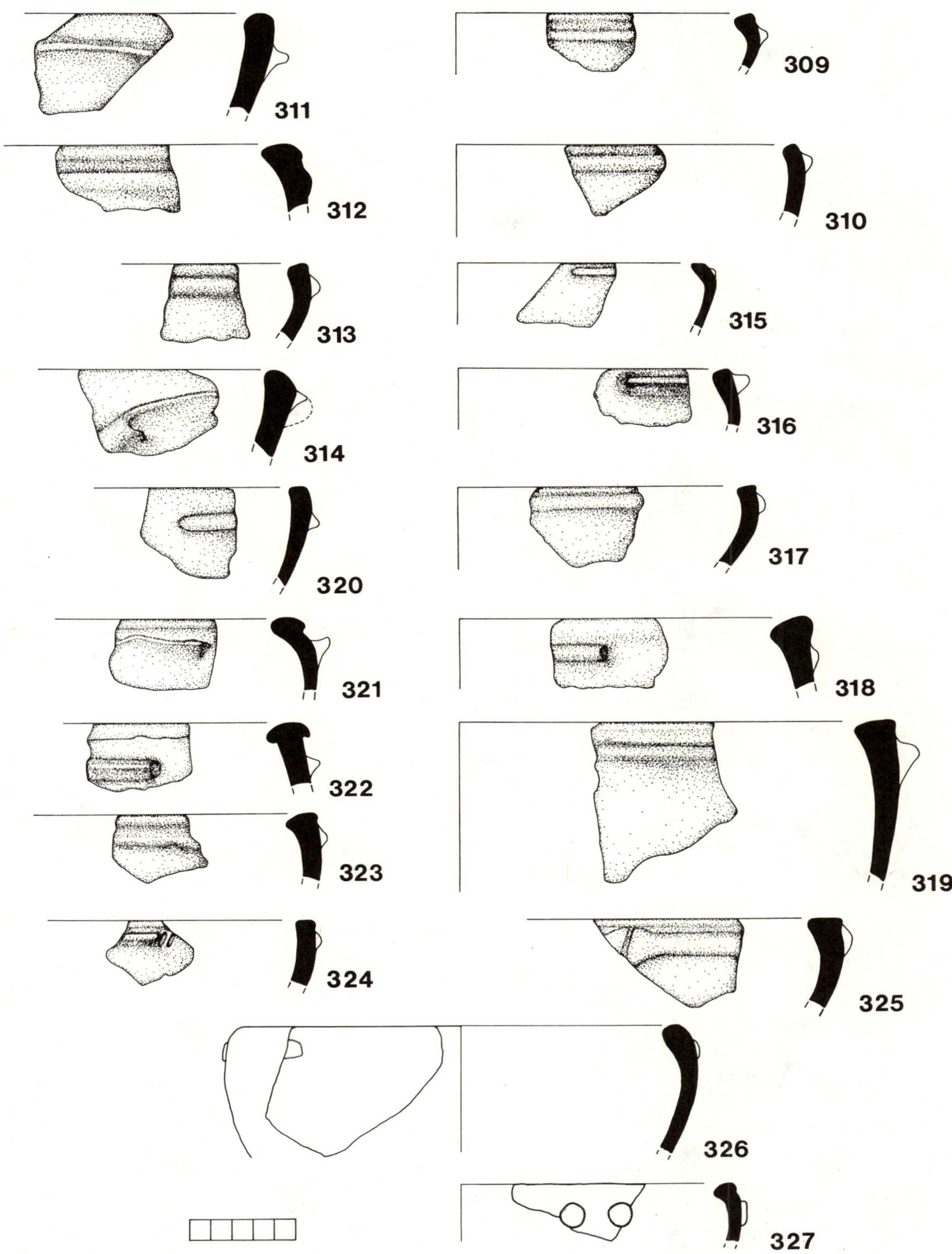

Fig. 18. Early Helladic II incurving bowls **309–327**.

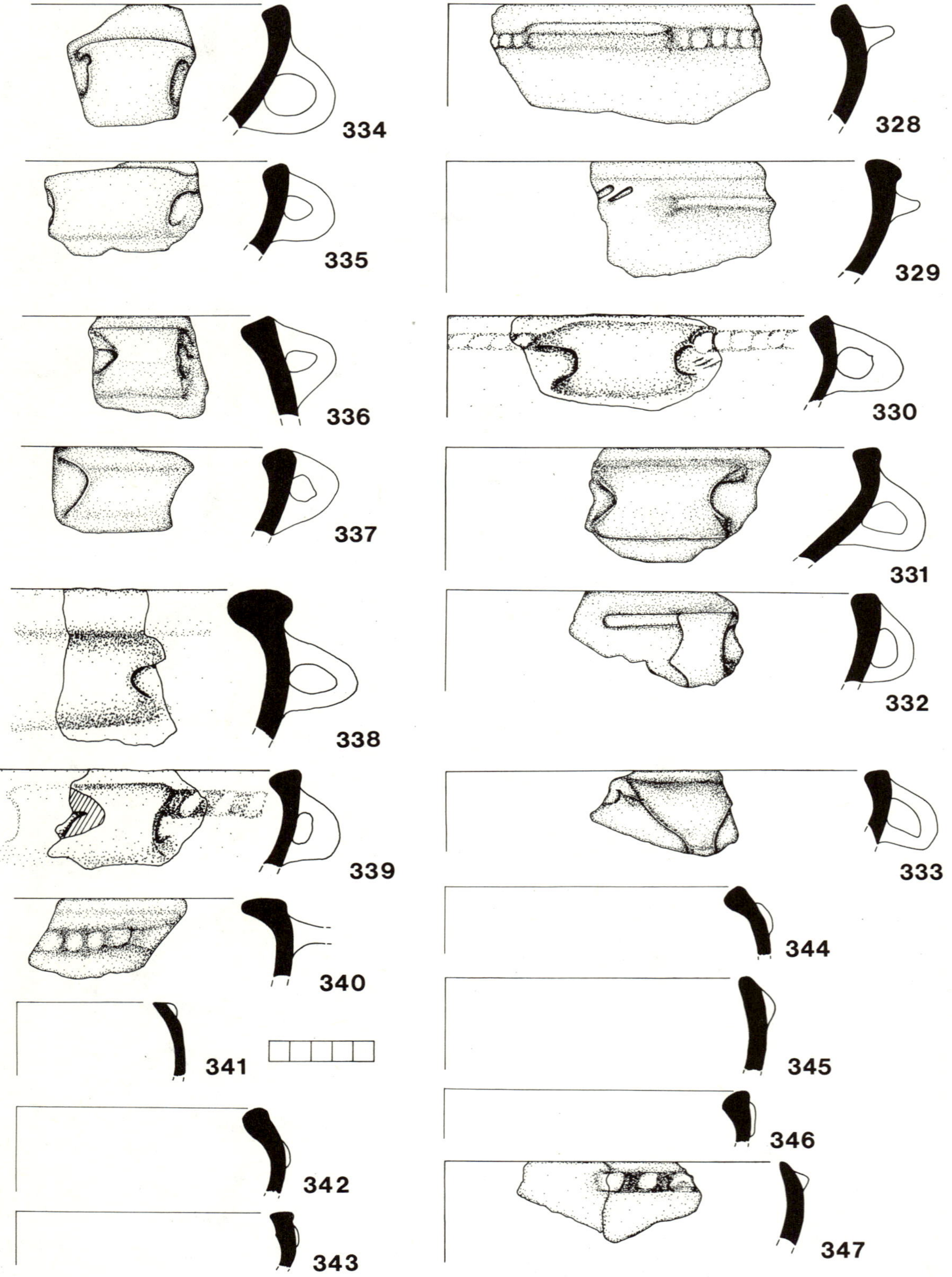

Fig. 19. Early Helladic II incurving bowls **328–347**.

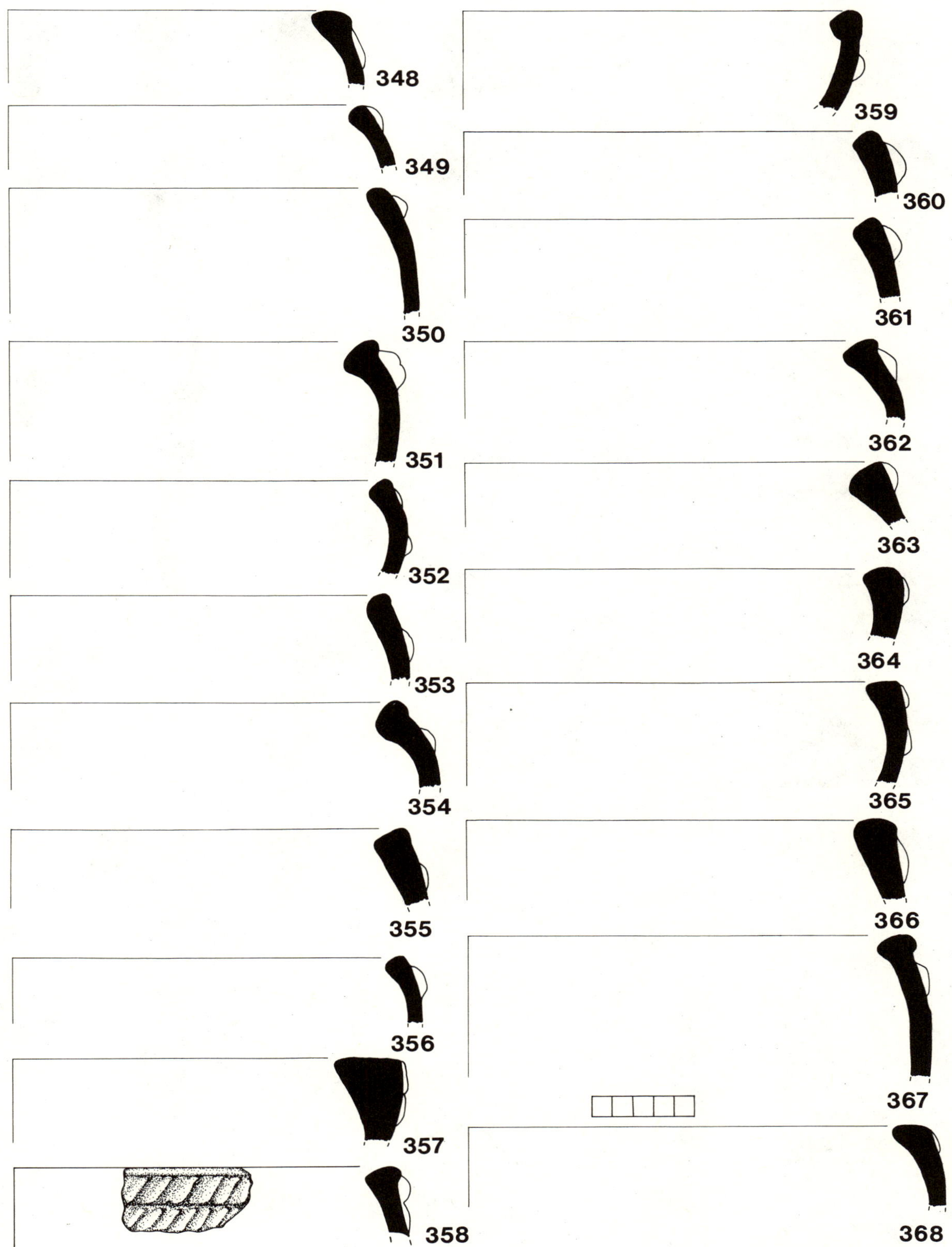

Fig. 20. Early Helladic II incurving bowls **348–368**.

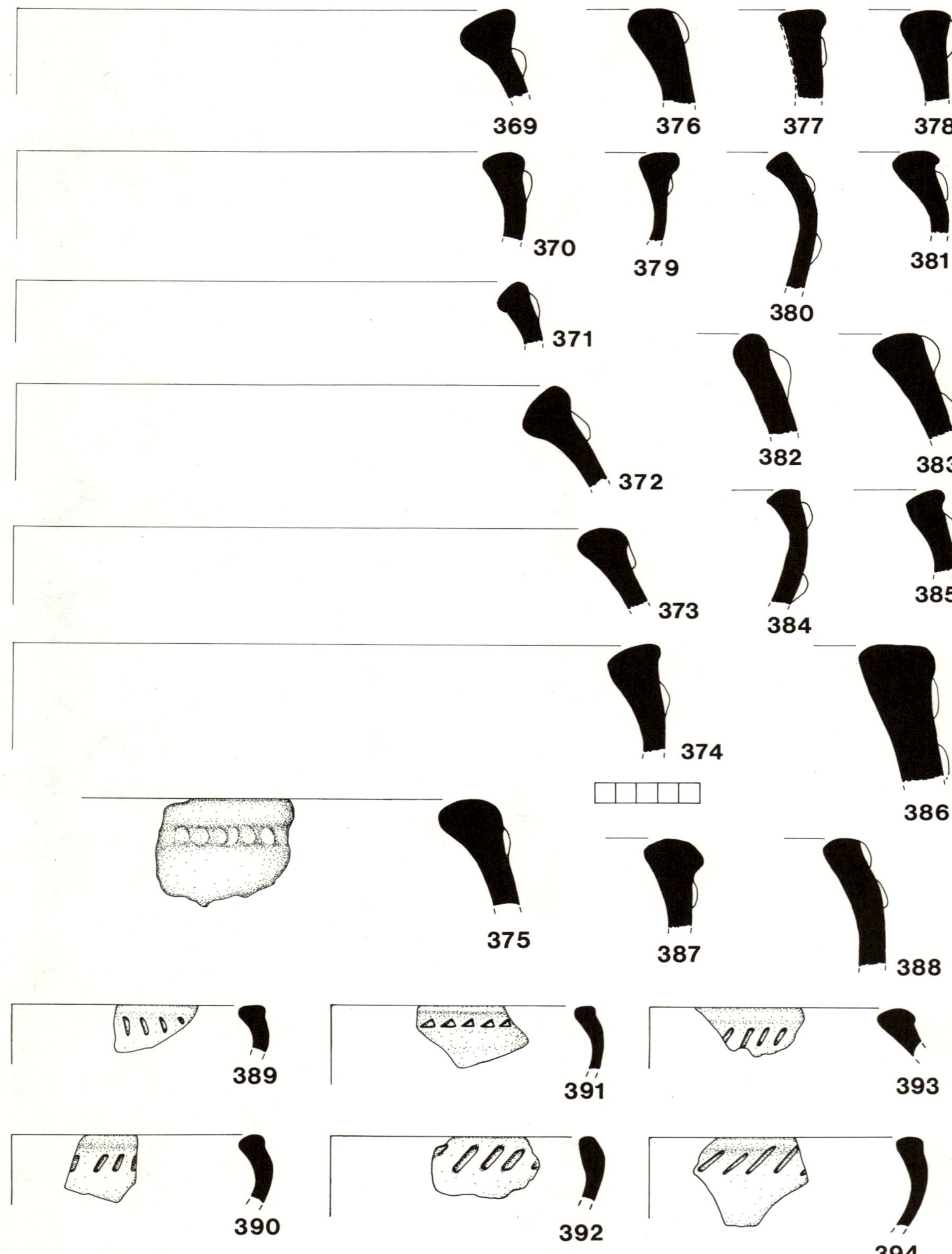

Fig. 21. Early Helladic II incurving bowls **369–394**.

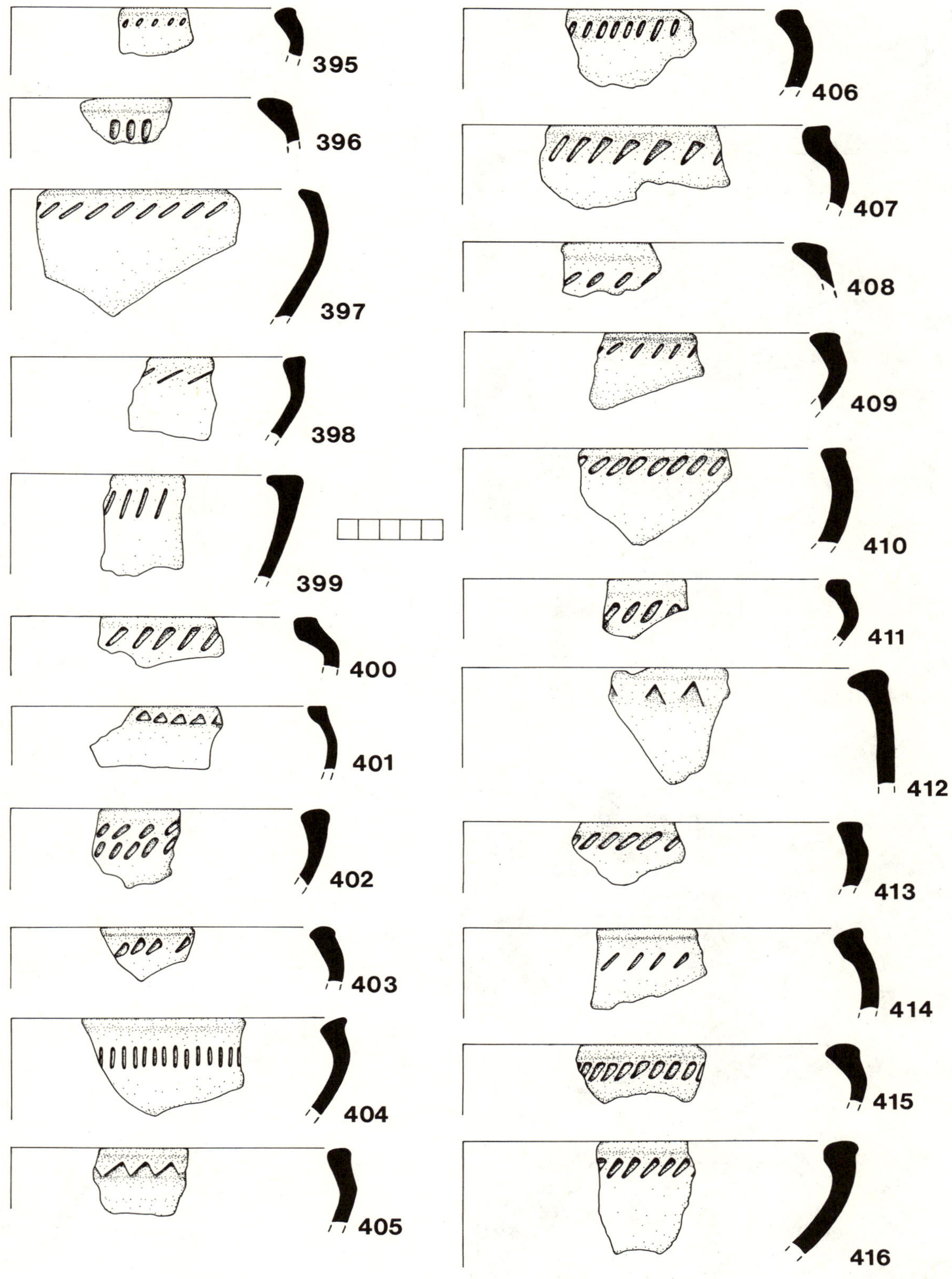

Fig. 22. Early Helladic II incurving bowls **395–416**.

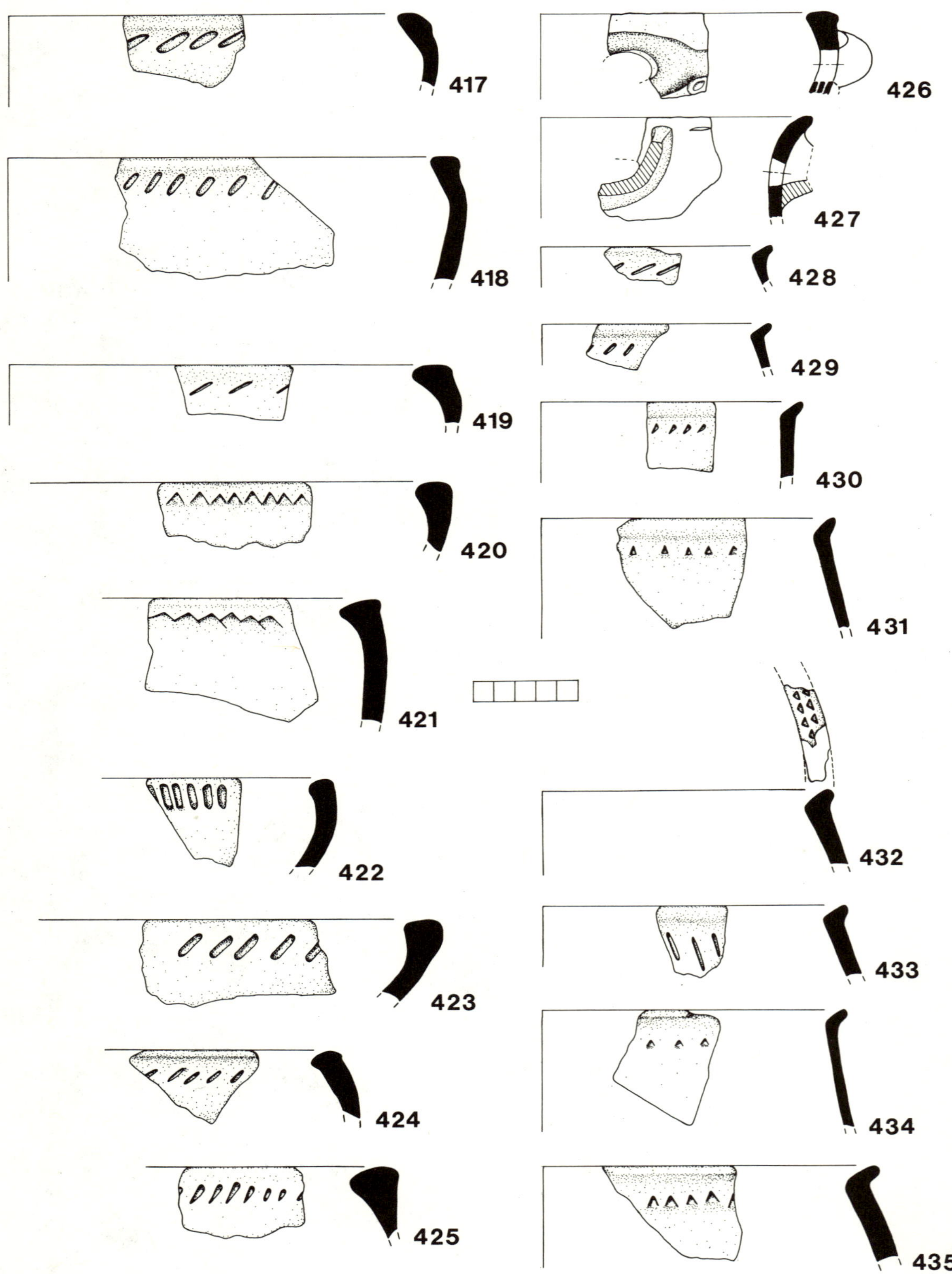

Fig. 23. Early Helladic II incurving bowls **417–425**, spouted bowls **426**, **427**, outturned bowls **428–435**.

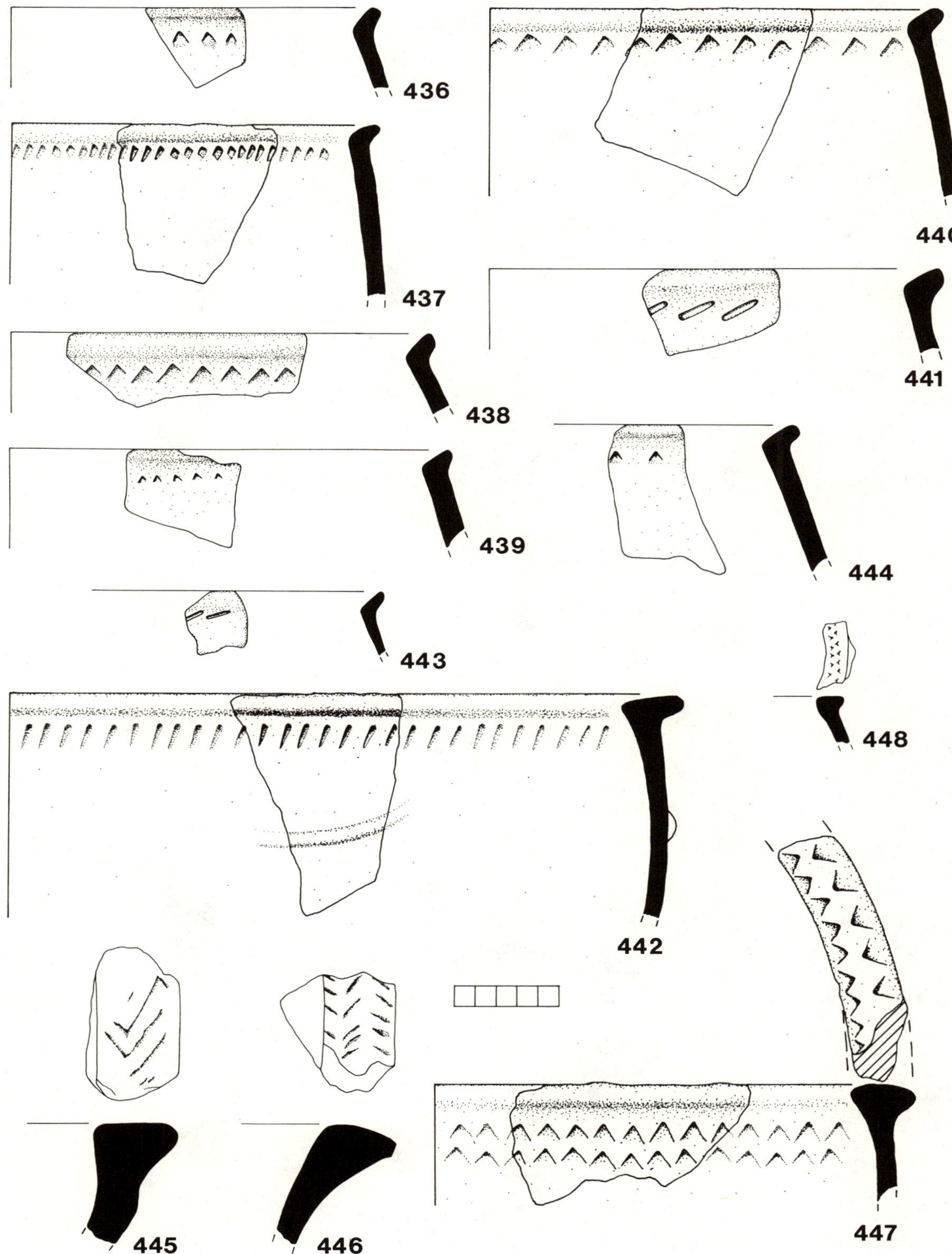

Fig. 24. Early Helladic II outturned bowls **436–444**, large bowls **445–447**, jar **448**.

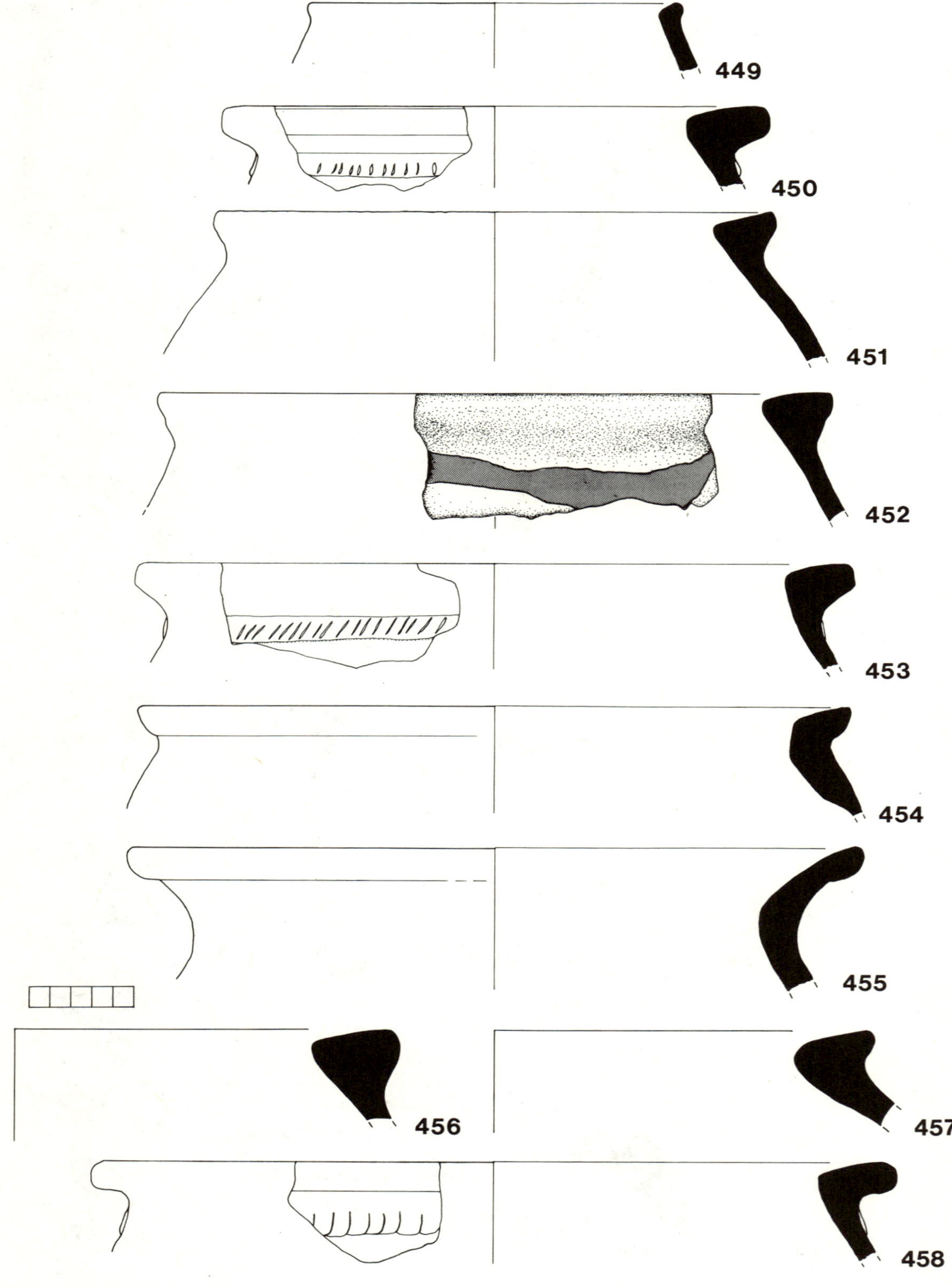

Fig. 25. Early Helladic II pithoi **449–458**.

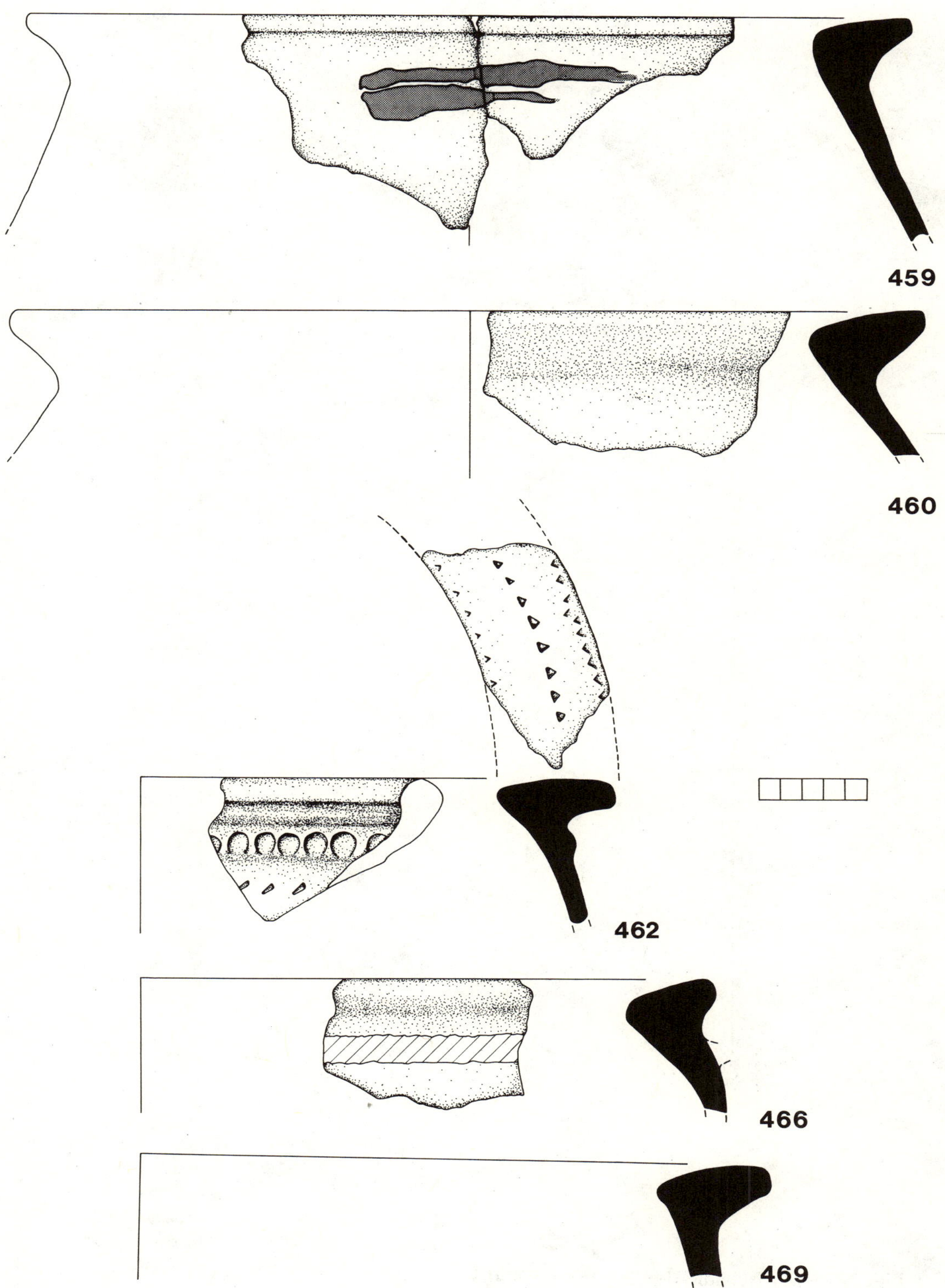

Fig. 26. Early Helladic II pithoi **459**, **460**, **462**, **466**, **469**.

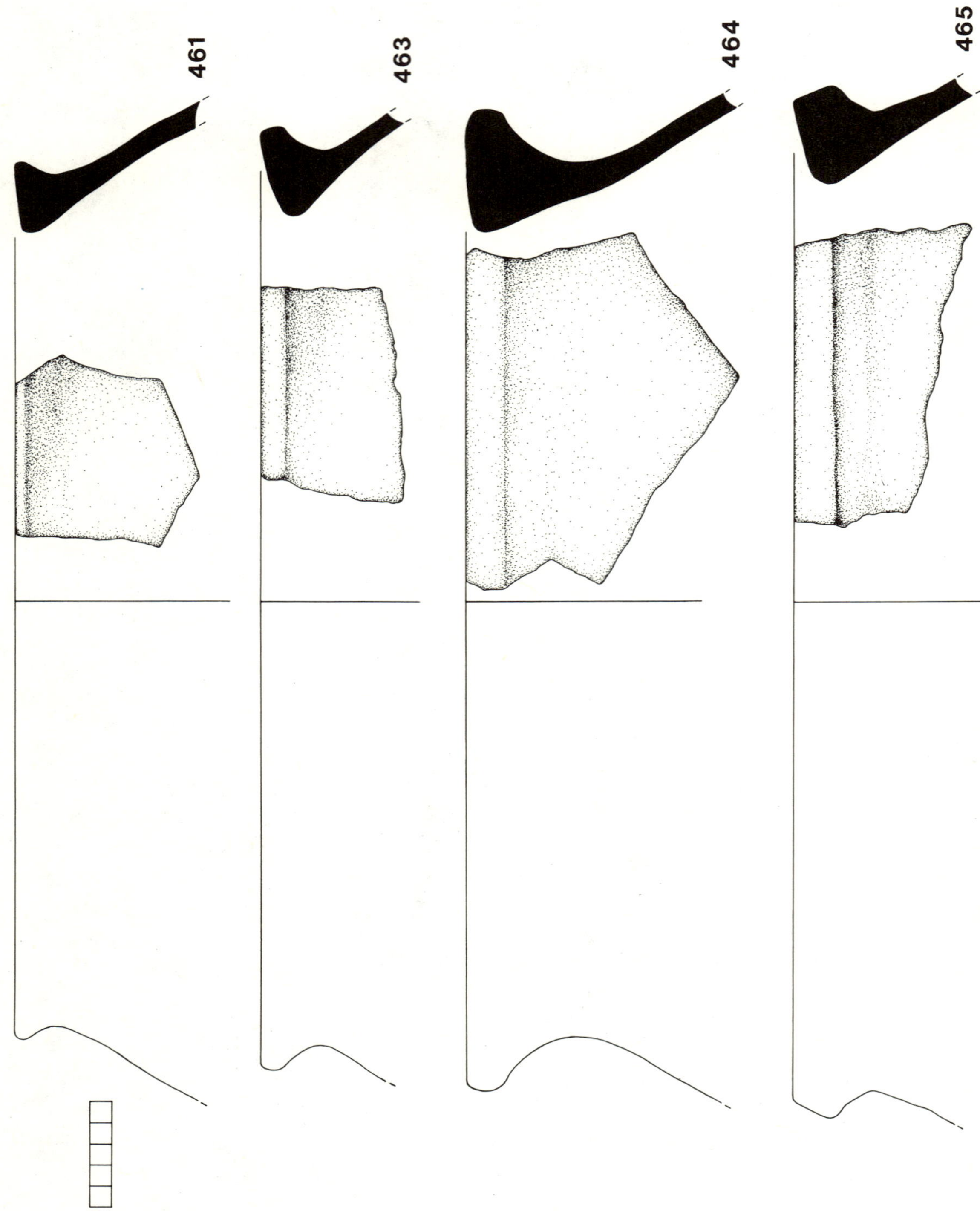

Fig. 27. Early Helladic II pithoi **461**, **463–465**.

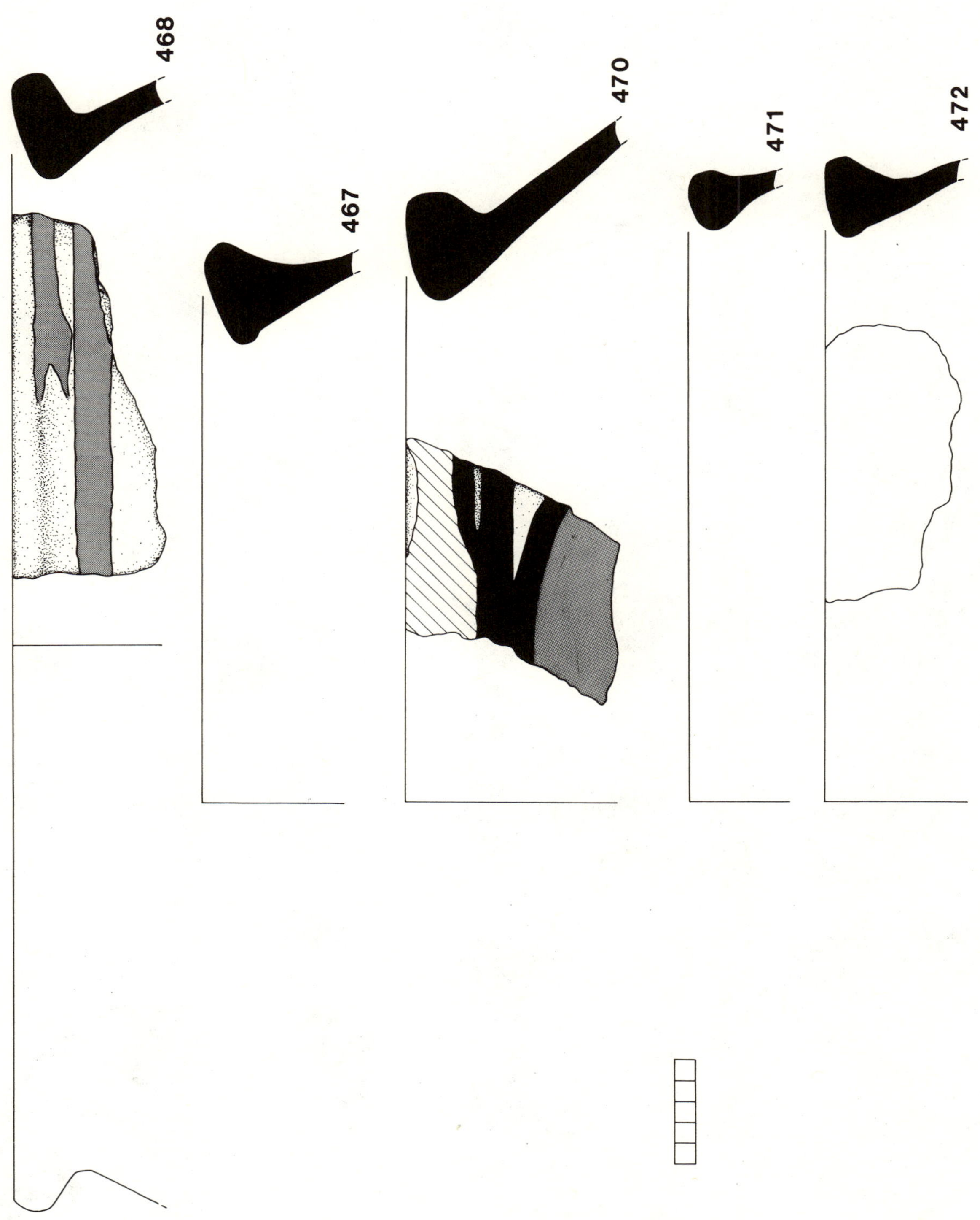

Fig. 28. Early Helladic II pithoi **467**, **468**, **470–472**.

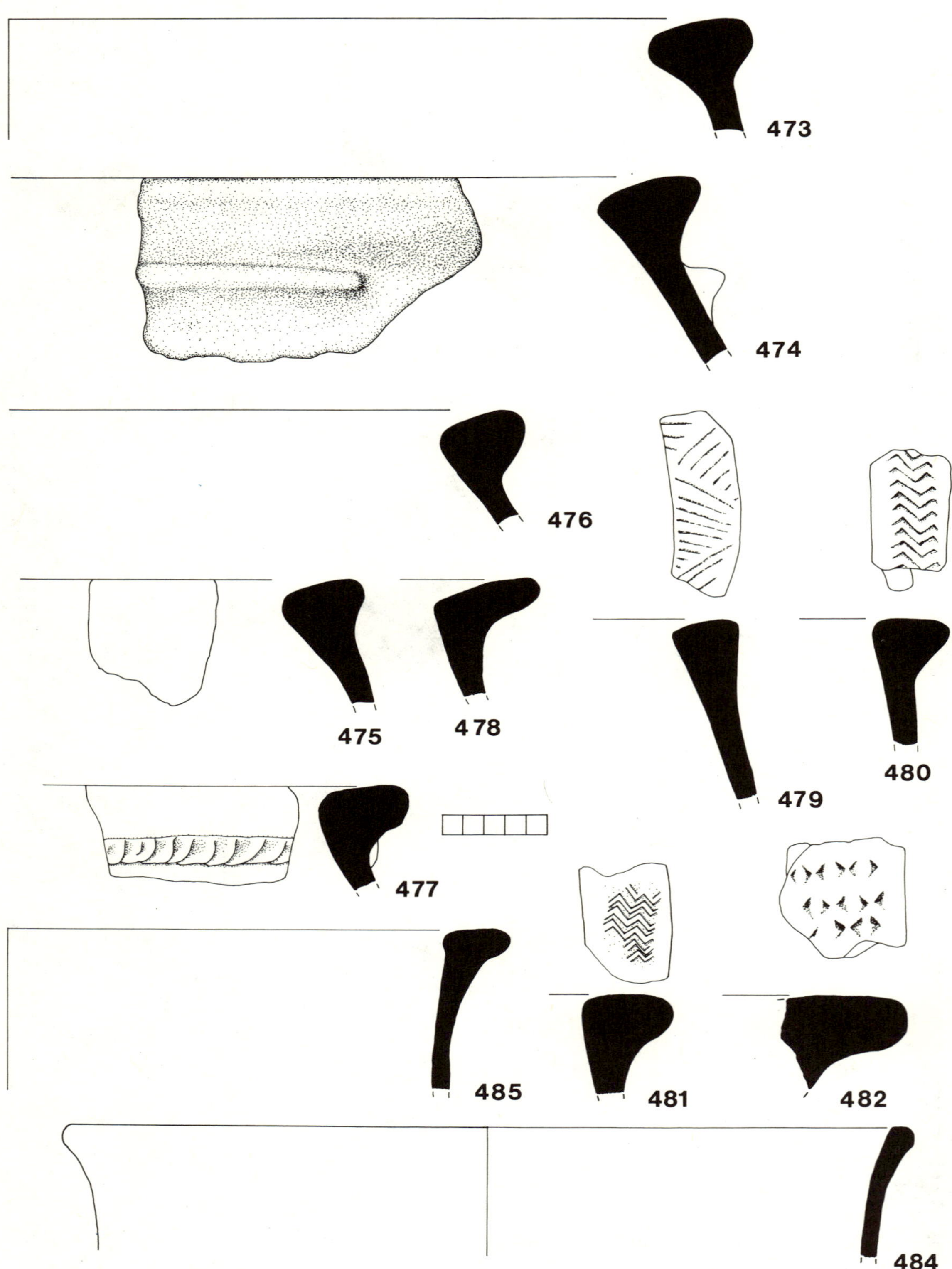

Fig. 29. Early Helladic II pithoi **473–482, 484, 485**.

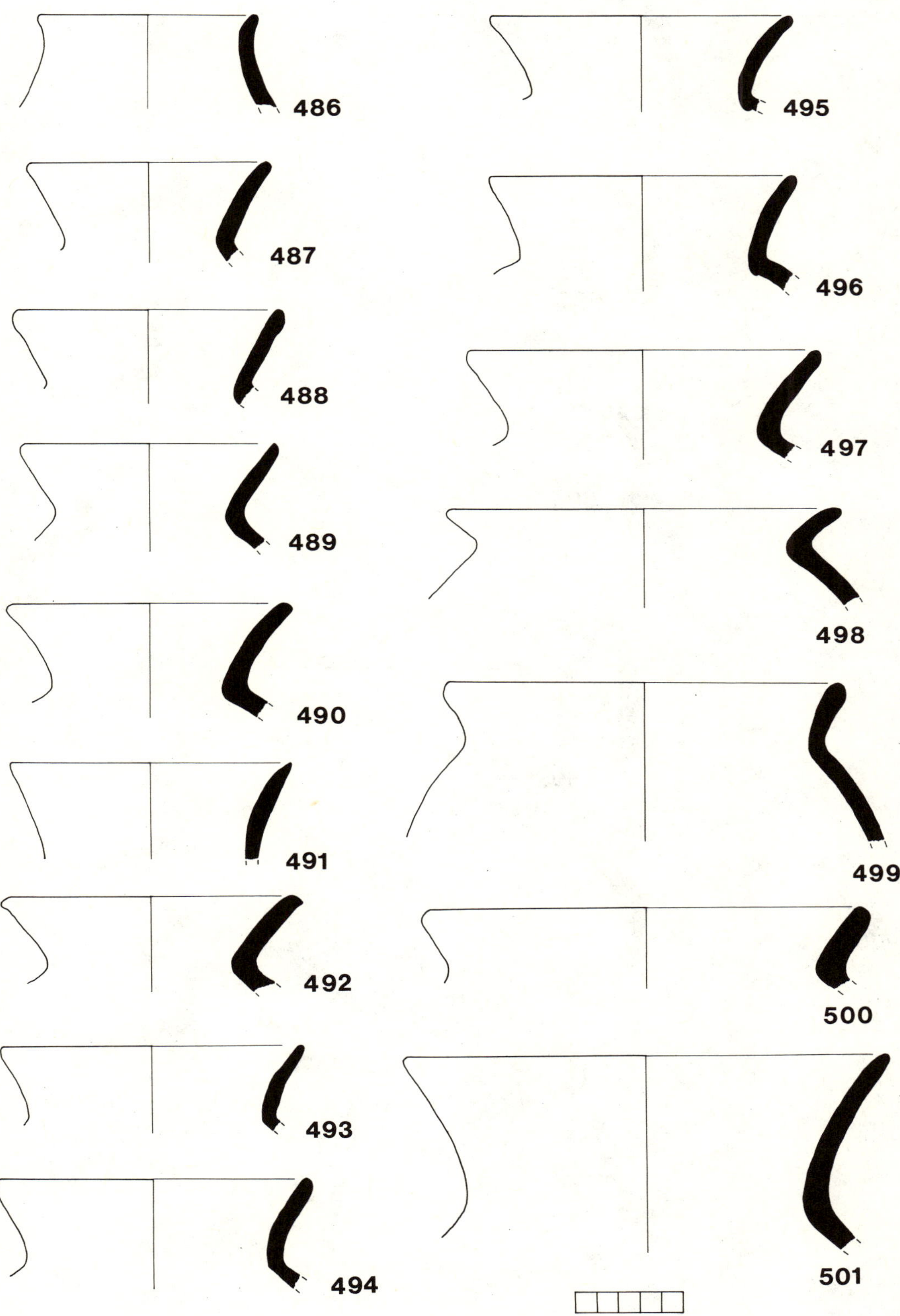

Fig. 30. Early Helladic II jars **486–501**.

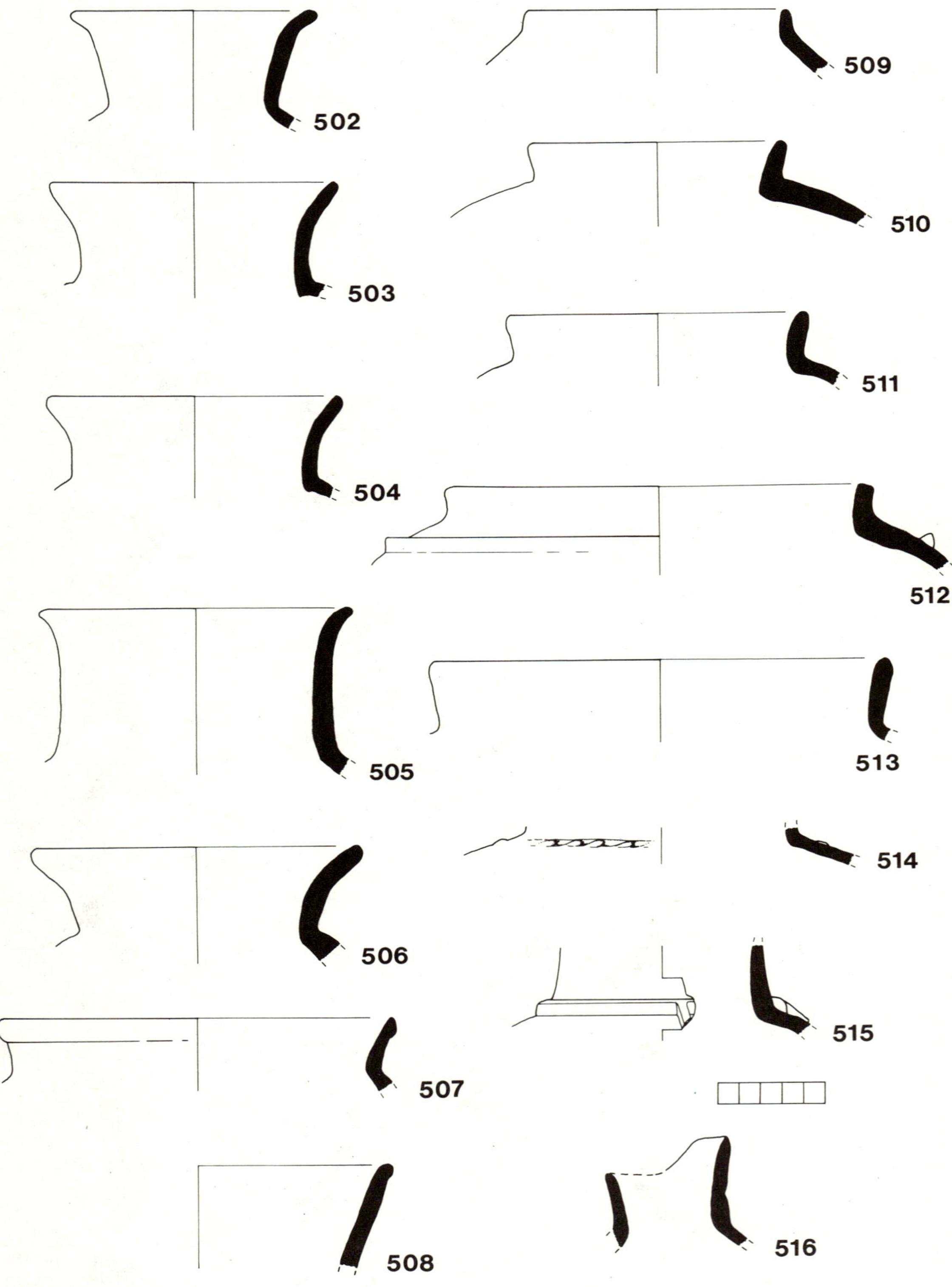

Fig. 31. Early Helladic II jars **502–515**, jug **516**.

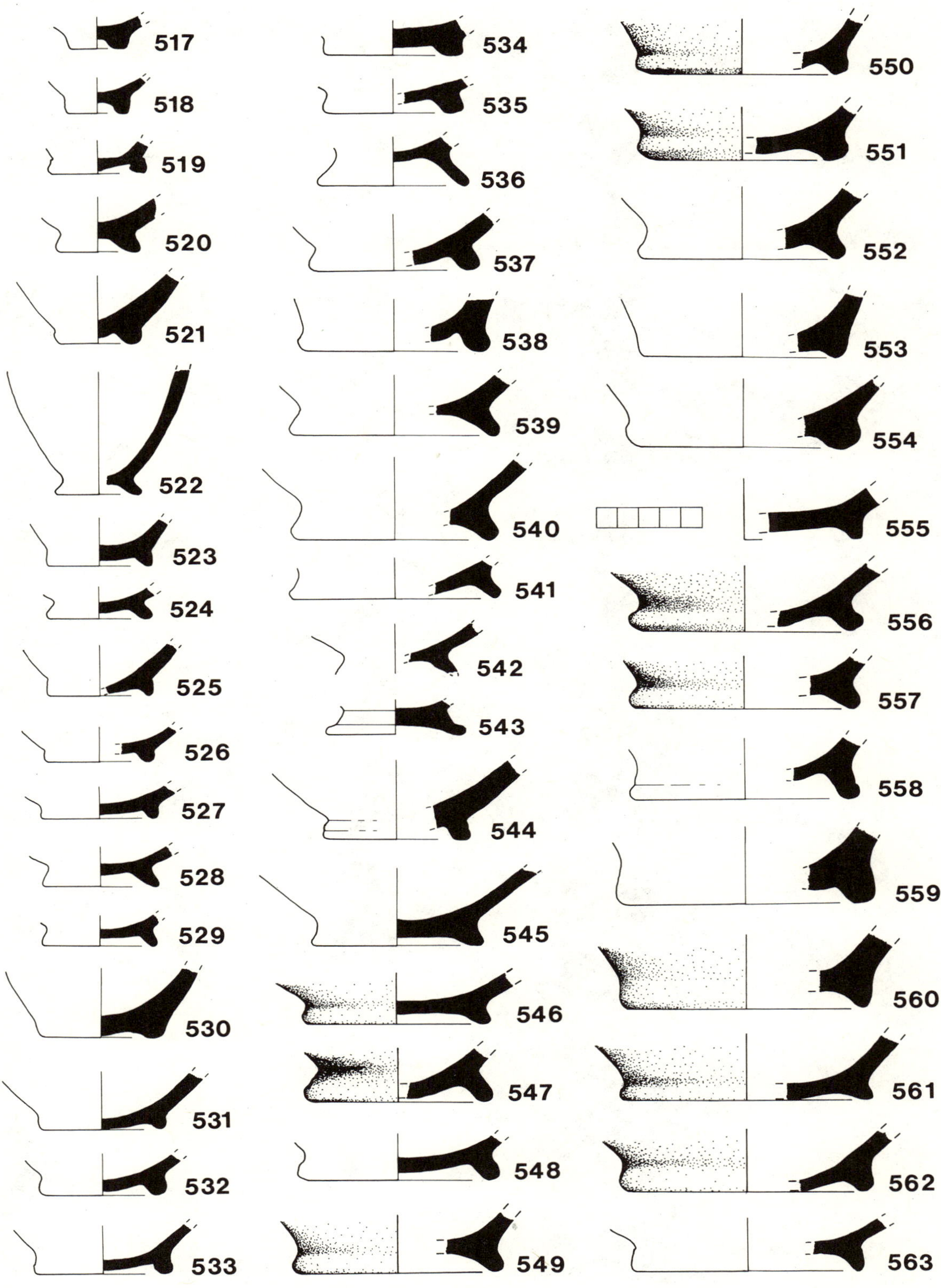

Fig. 32. Early Helladic II bowls or sauceboats **517–541**, ring feet **542–563**.

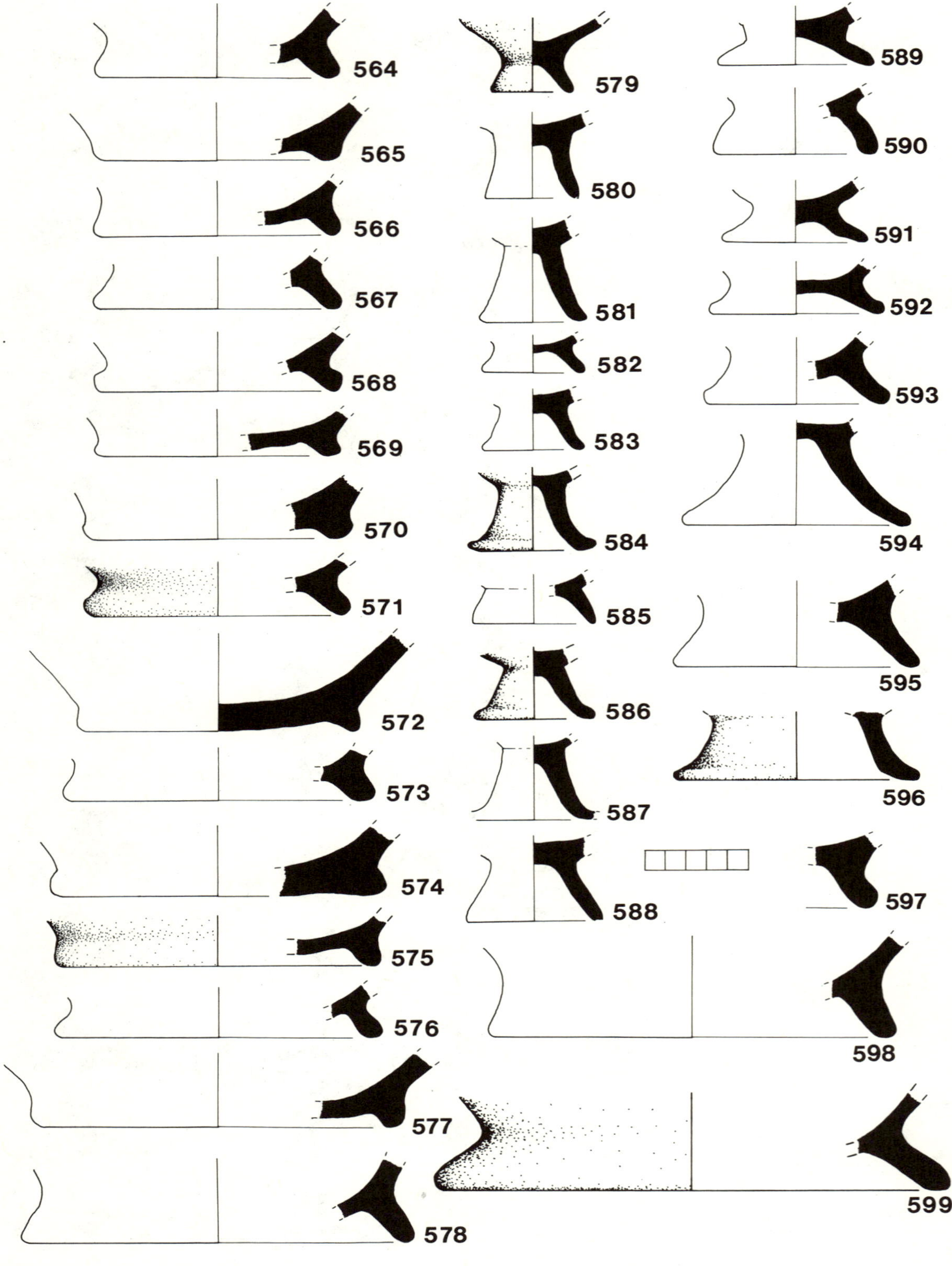

Fig. 33. Early Helladic II ring feet **564–578**, pedestals **579–599**.

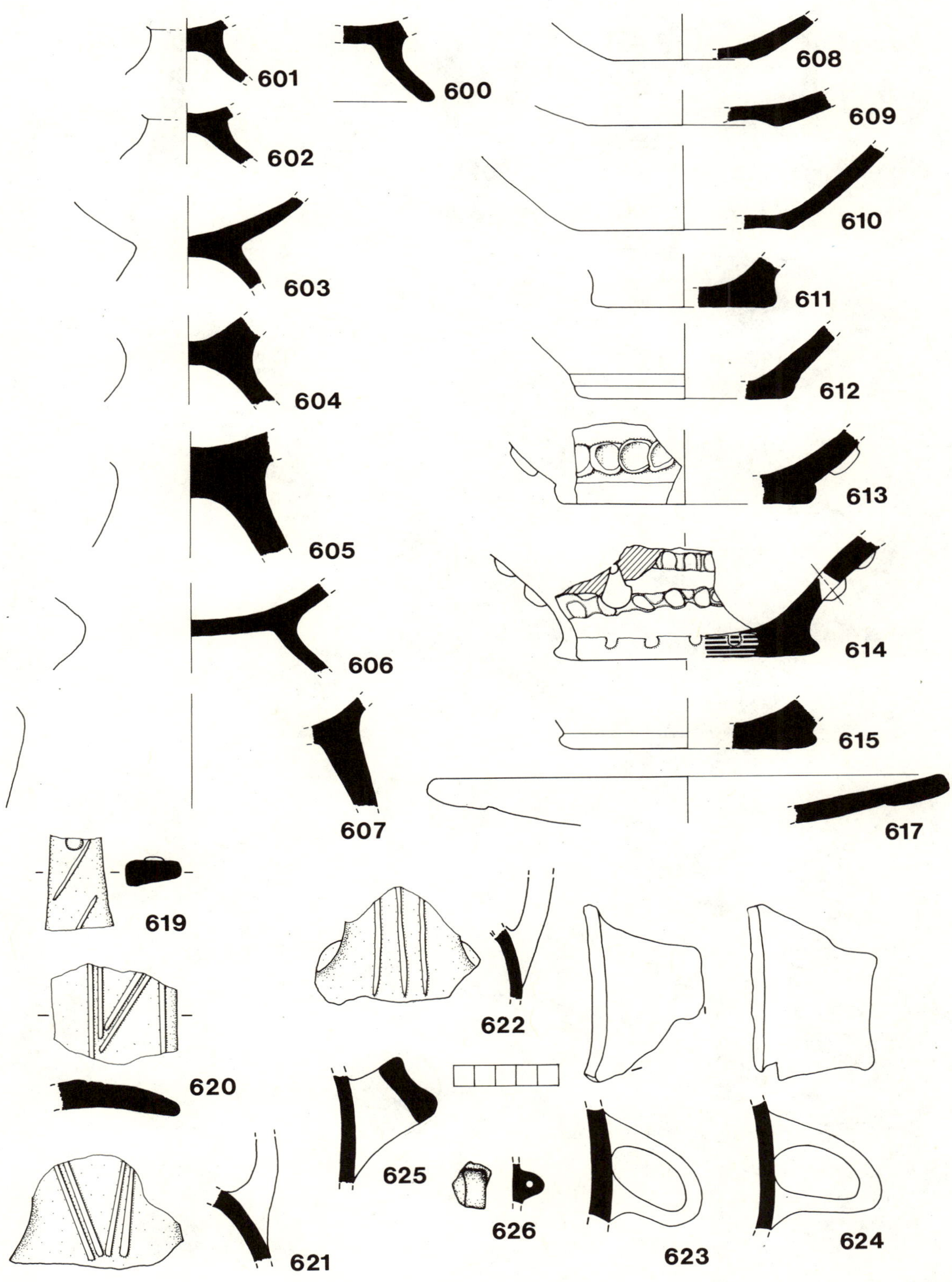

Fig. 34. Early Helladic II pedestalled bowls **600–607**, bases **608–615**, plate **617**, handles **619–626**.

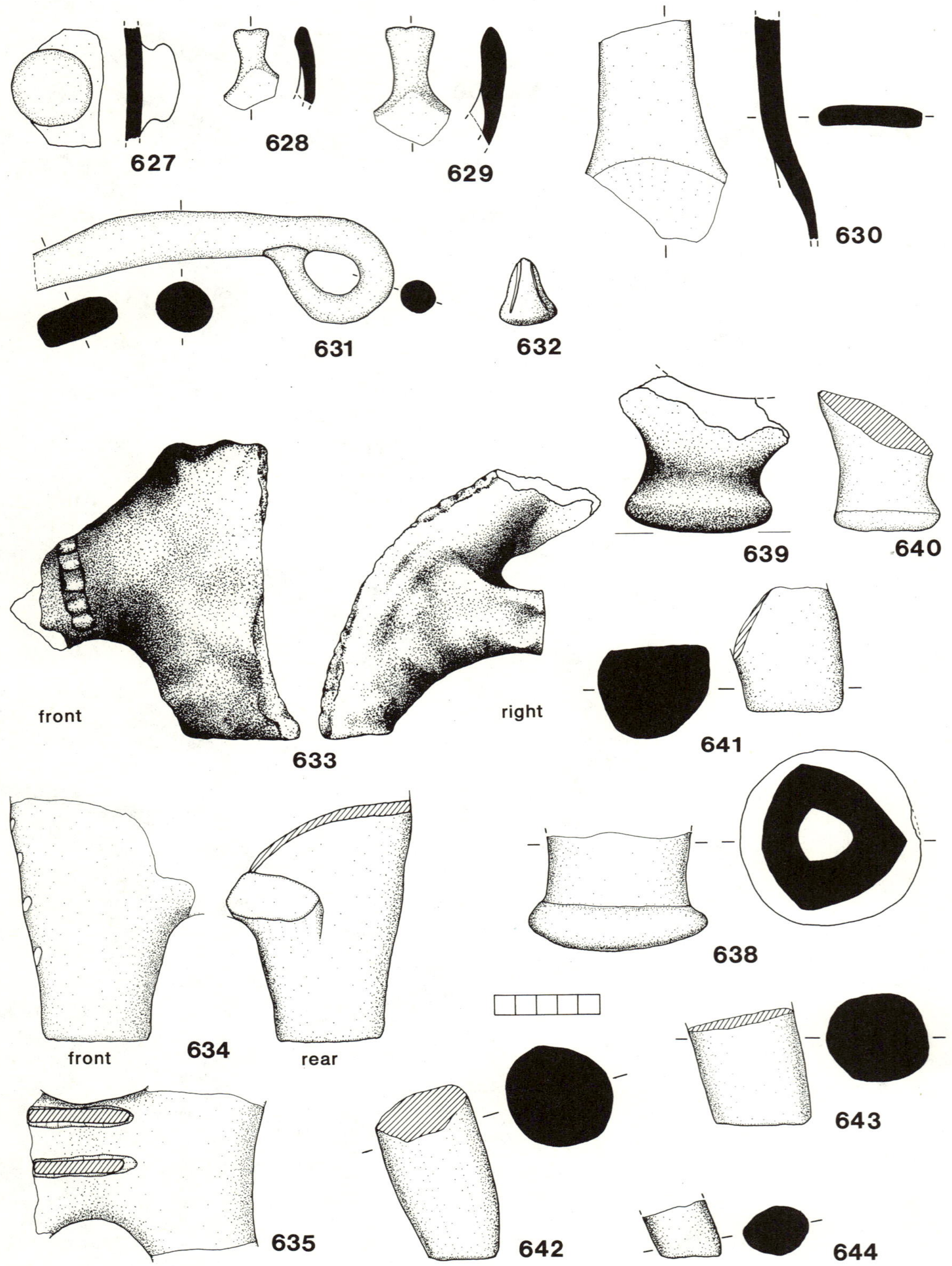

Fig. 35. Early Helladic II knob **627**, spoons **628**, **629**, scoop **630**, ladle **631**, seal **632**, stands **633–635**, **638–644**.

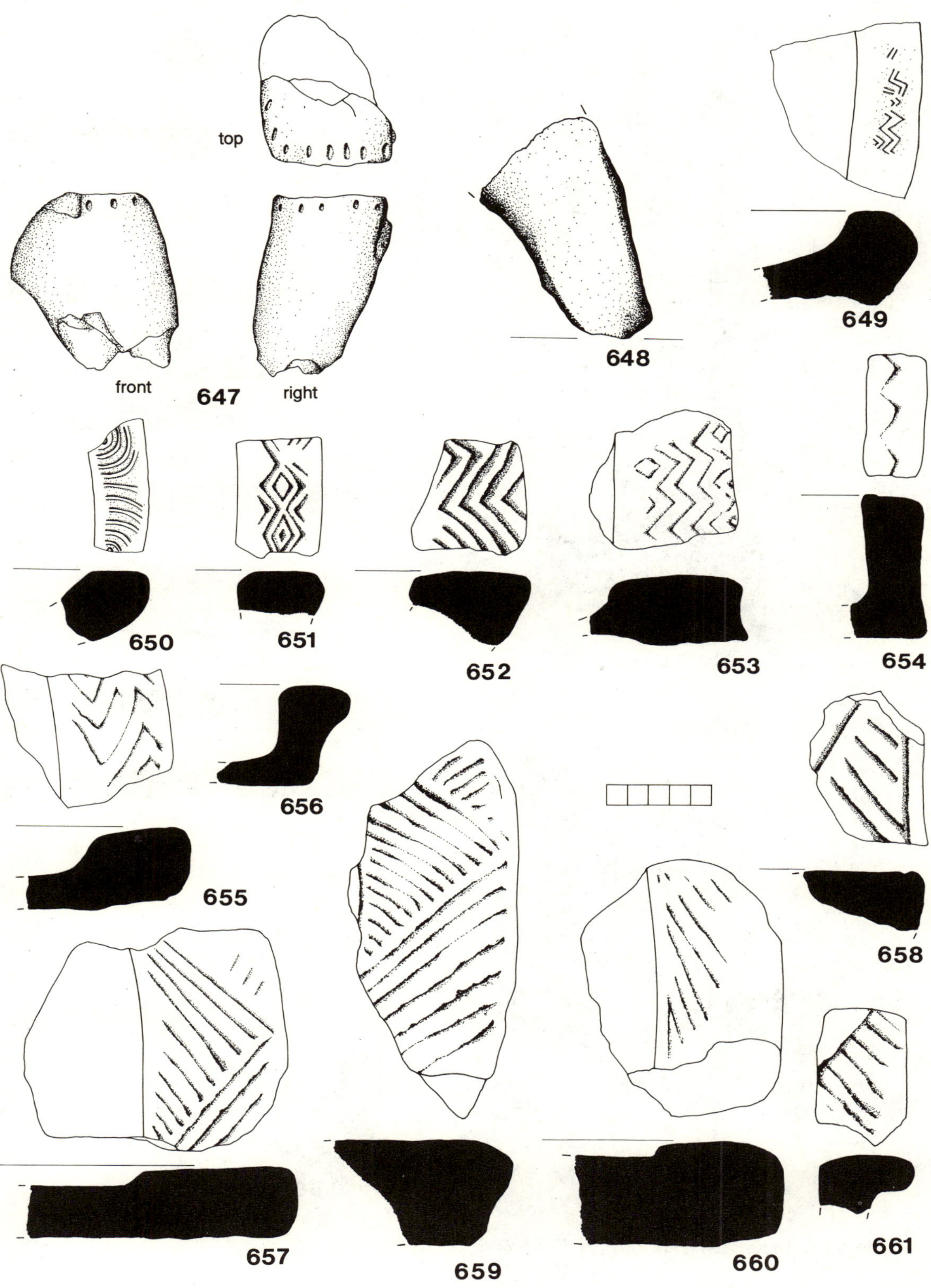

Fig. 36. Early Helladic II tables **647**, **648**, hearth rims **649–661**.

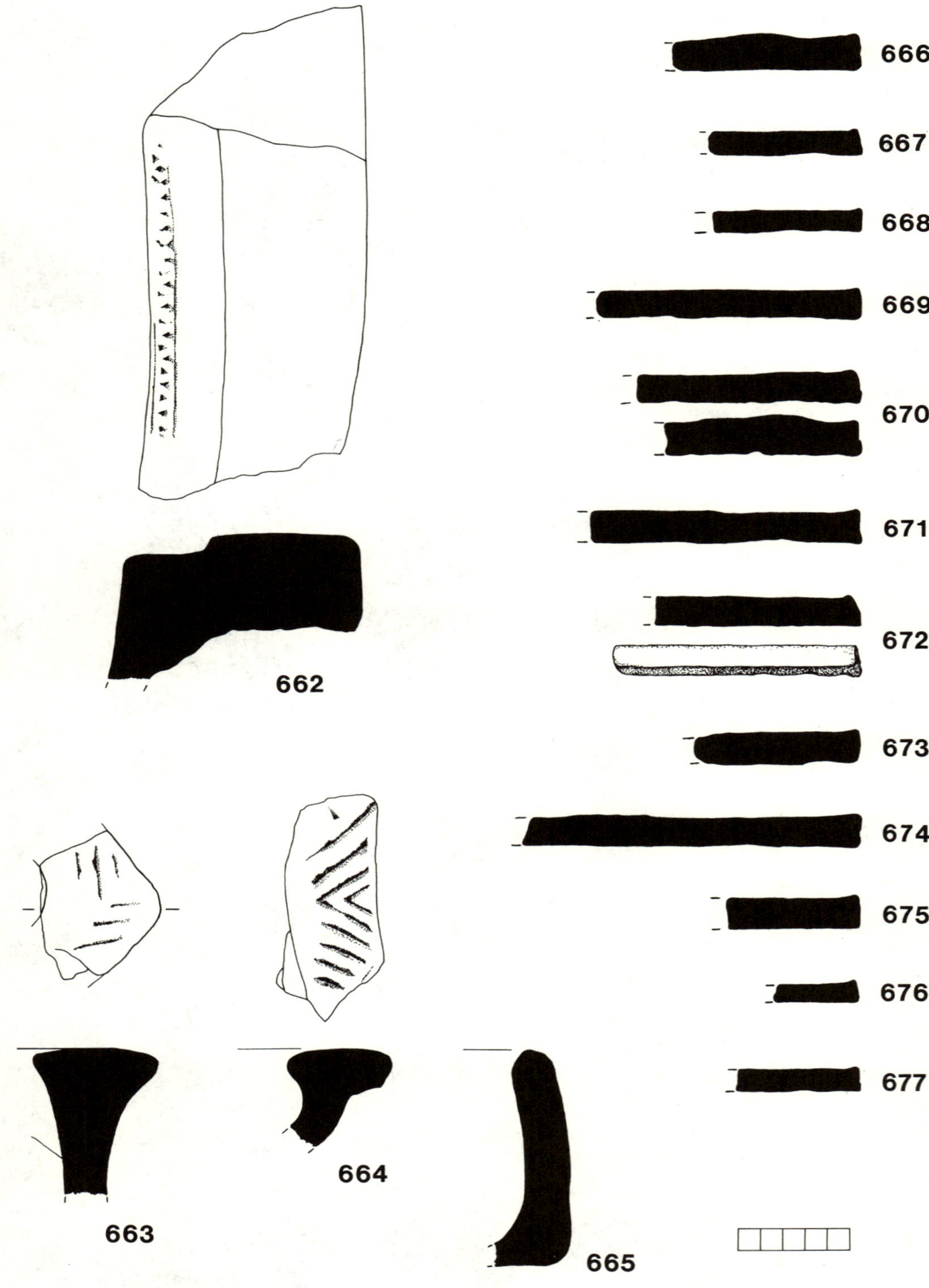

Fig. 37. Early Helladic II hearth rims **662–665**, rooftiles **666–677**.

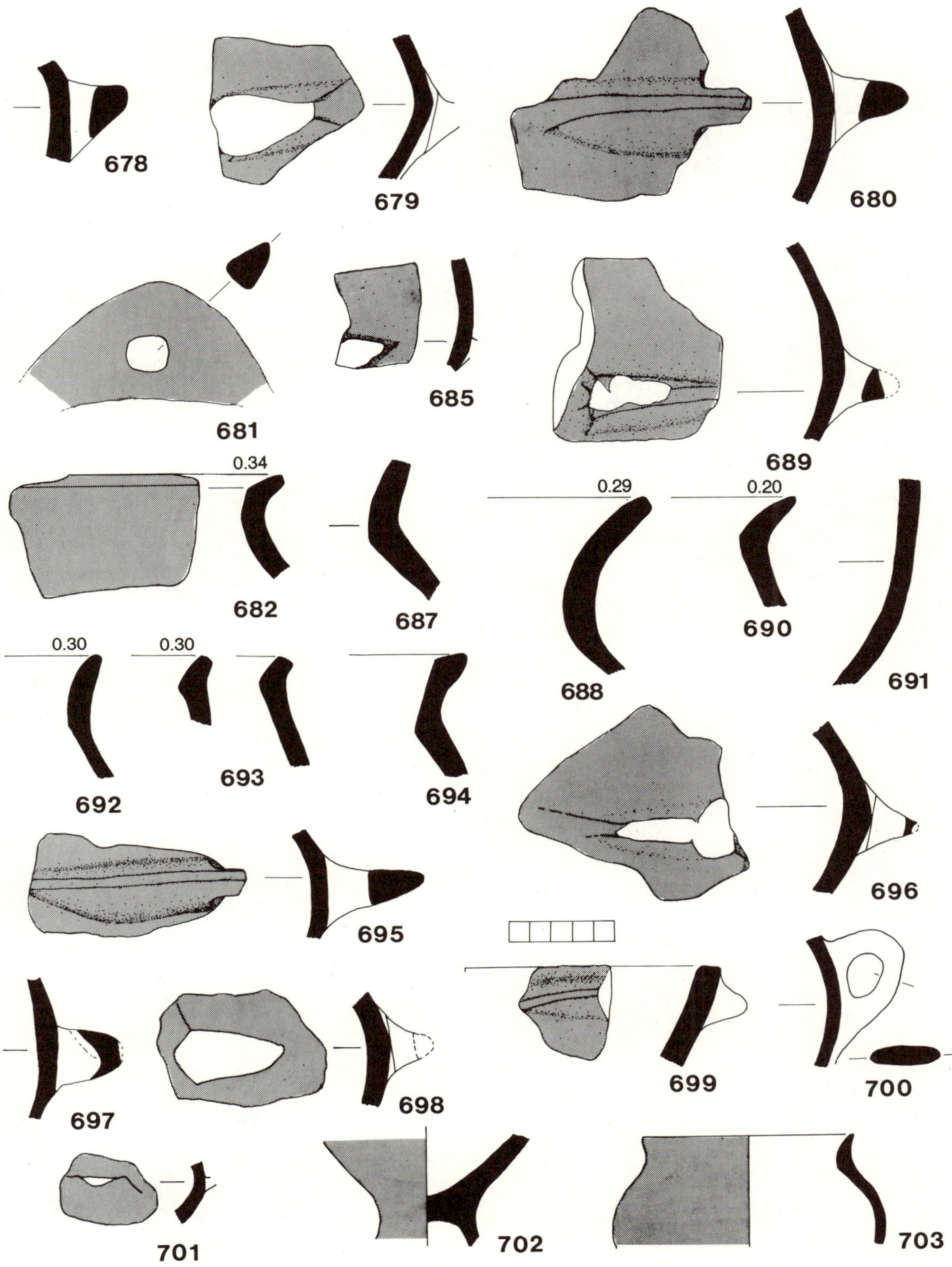

Fig. 38. Early Helladic III jars and bowls **678–682**, **685**, **687–700**, tankard **701**, cups **702**, **703**.

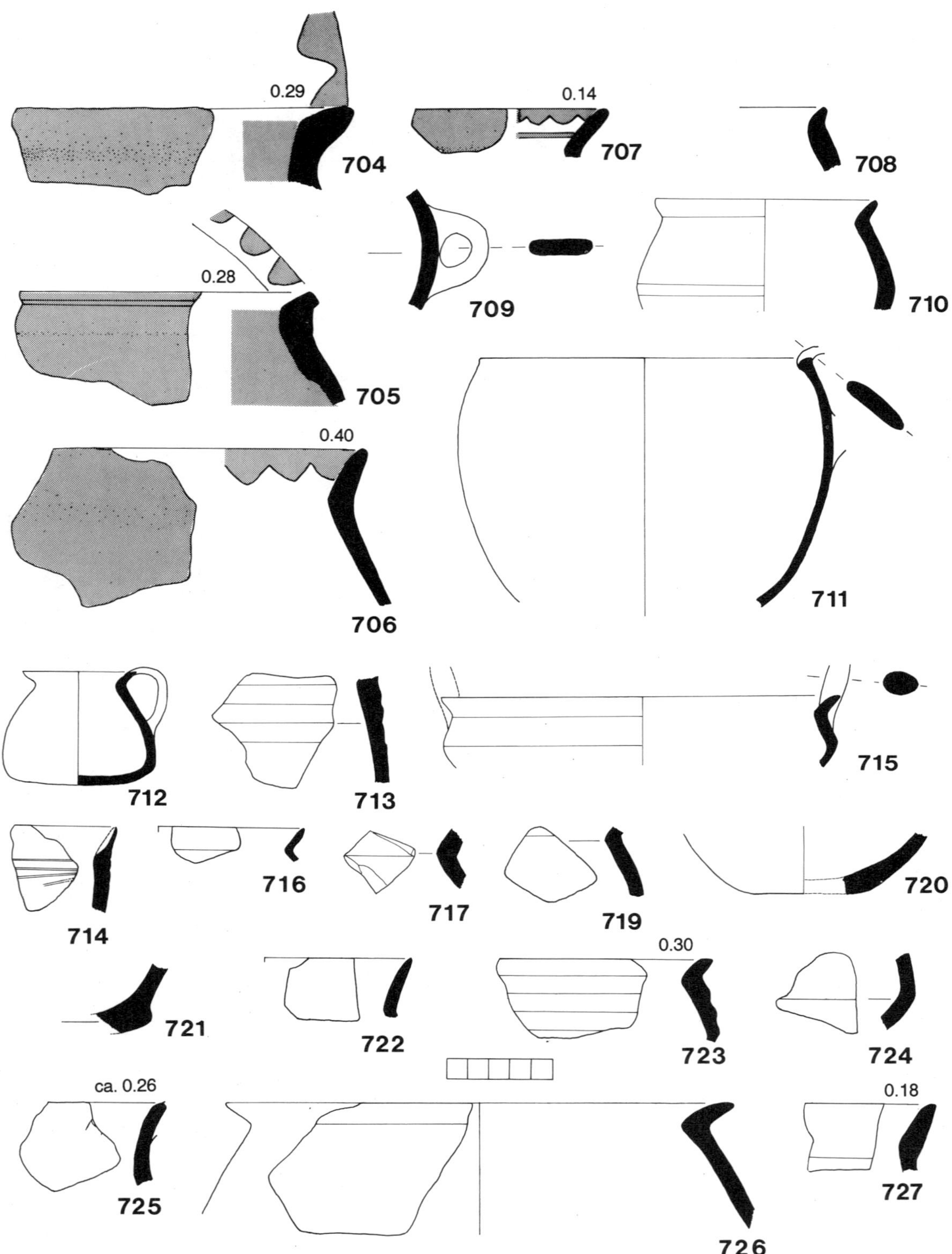

Fig. 39. Early Helladic III vessels **704–711**; Middle Helladic vessels **712–717, 719–727**.

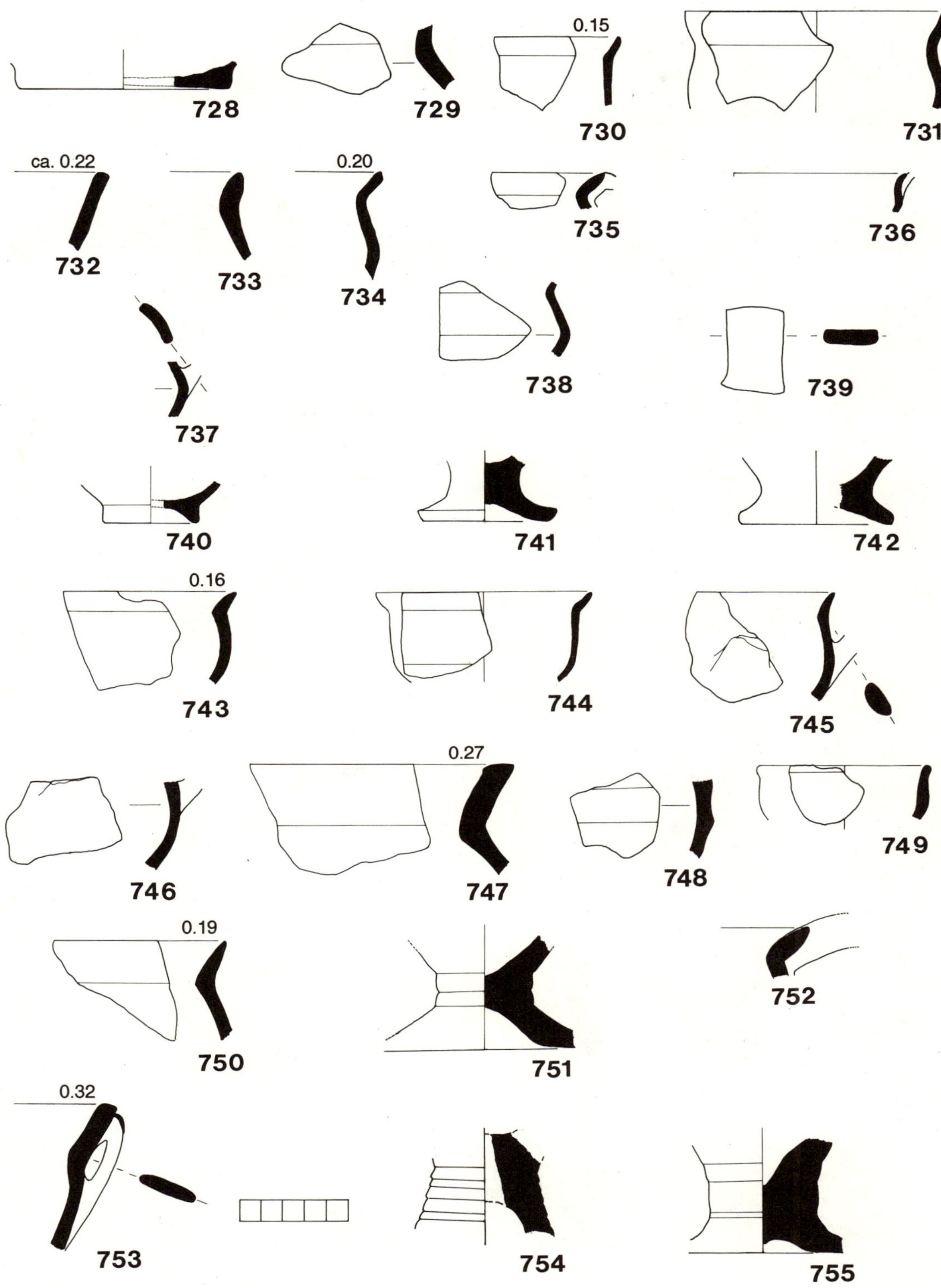

Fig. 40. Middle Helladic II to Late Helladic I vessels **728–755**.

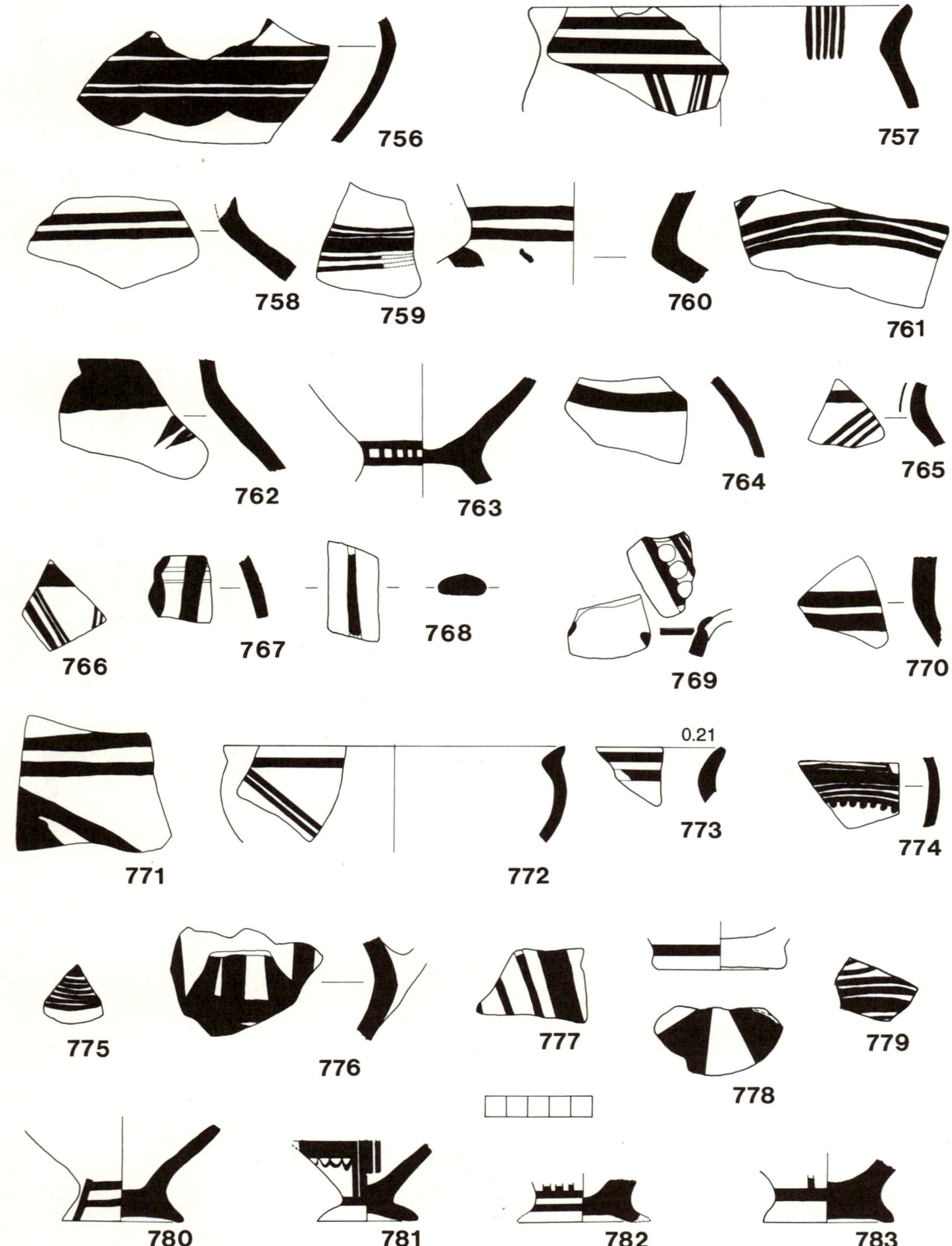

Fig. 41. Middle Helladic II to Late Helladic I vessels **756–783**.

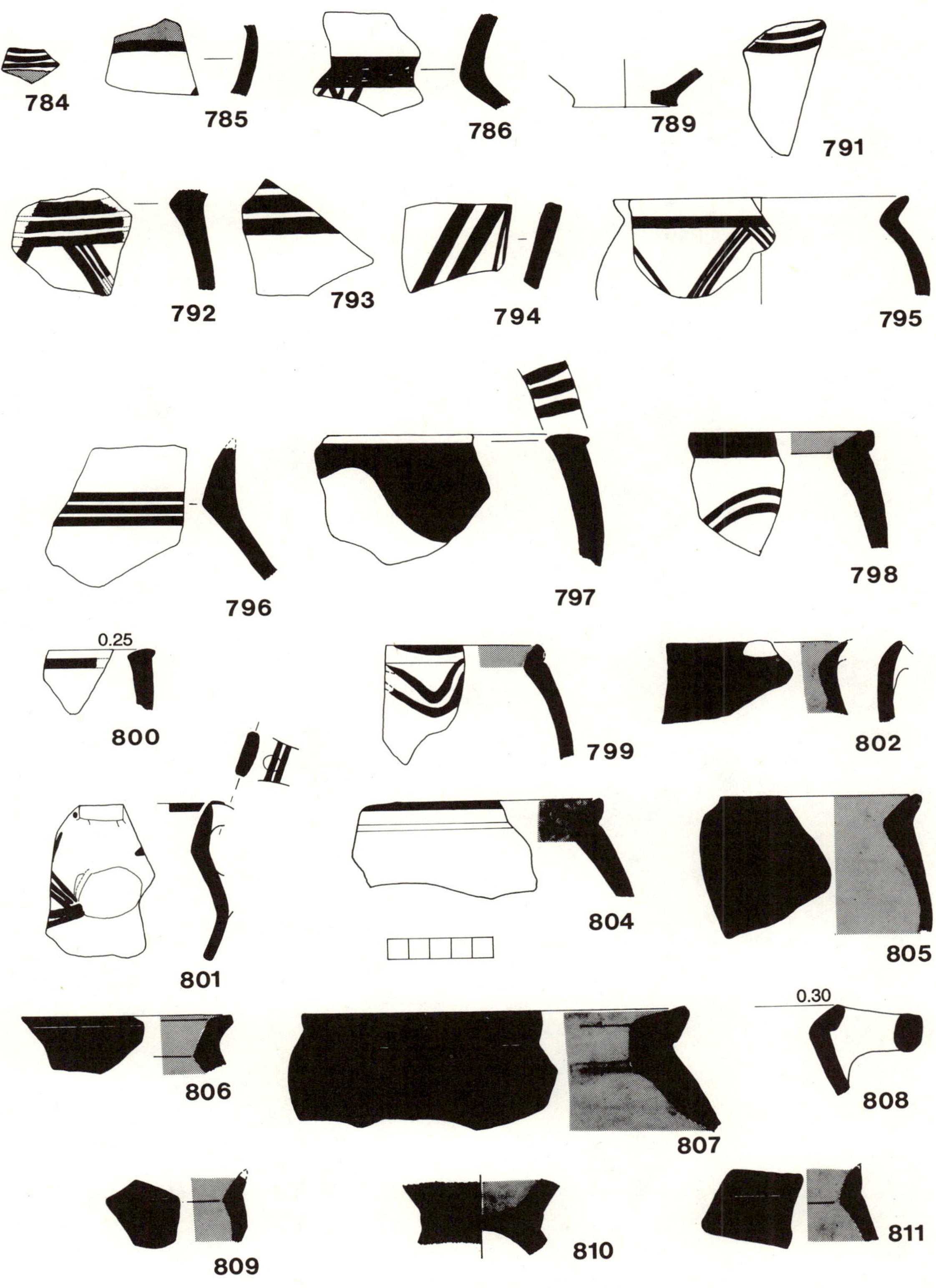

Fig. 42. Middle Helladic II to Late Helladic I vessels **784–786, 789, 791–802, 804–811**.

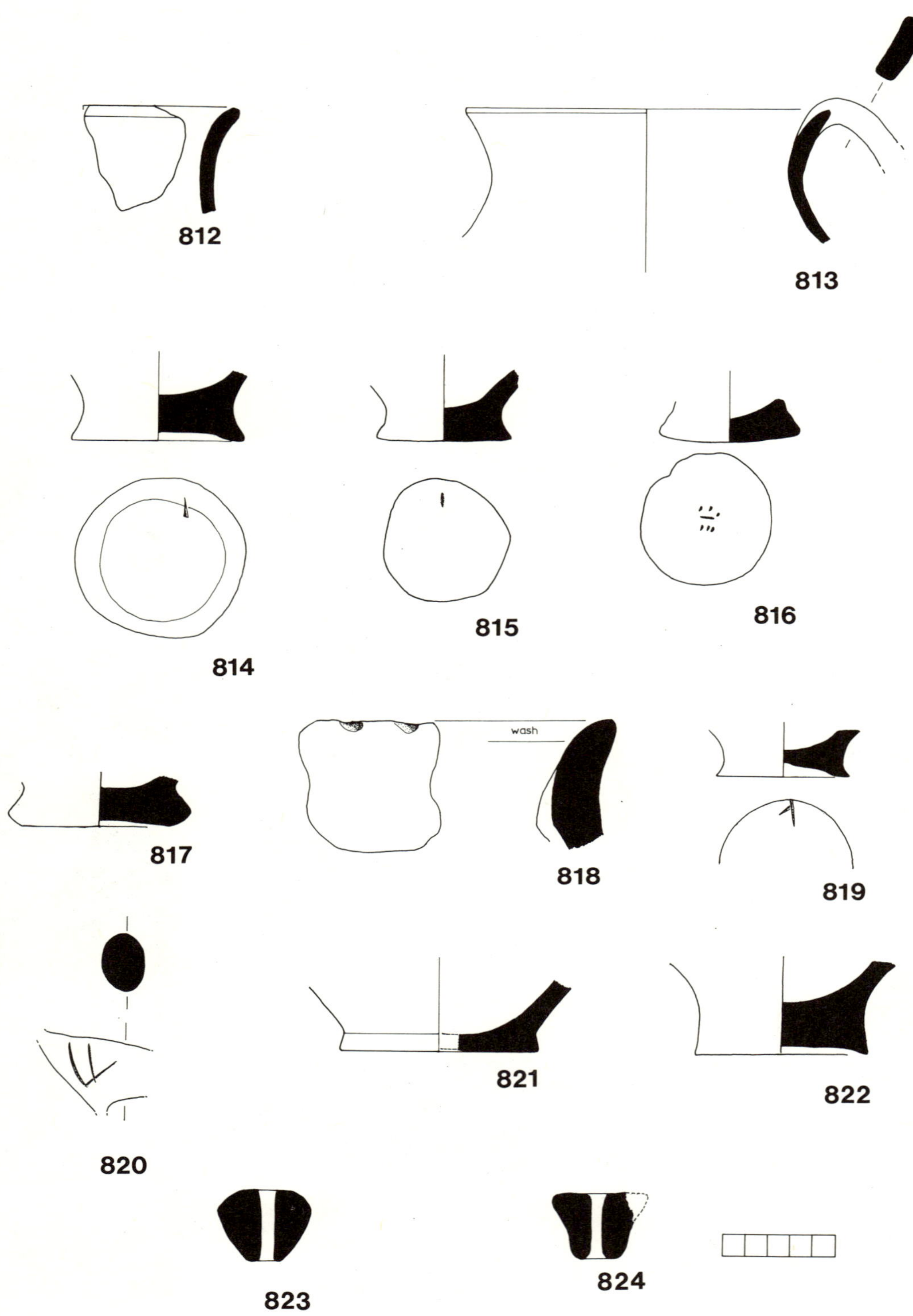

Fig. 43. Middle Helladic to Late Helladic I vessels **812–824**.

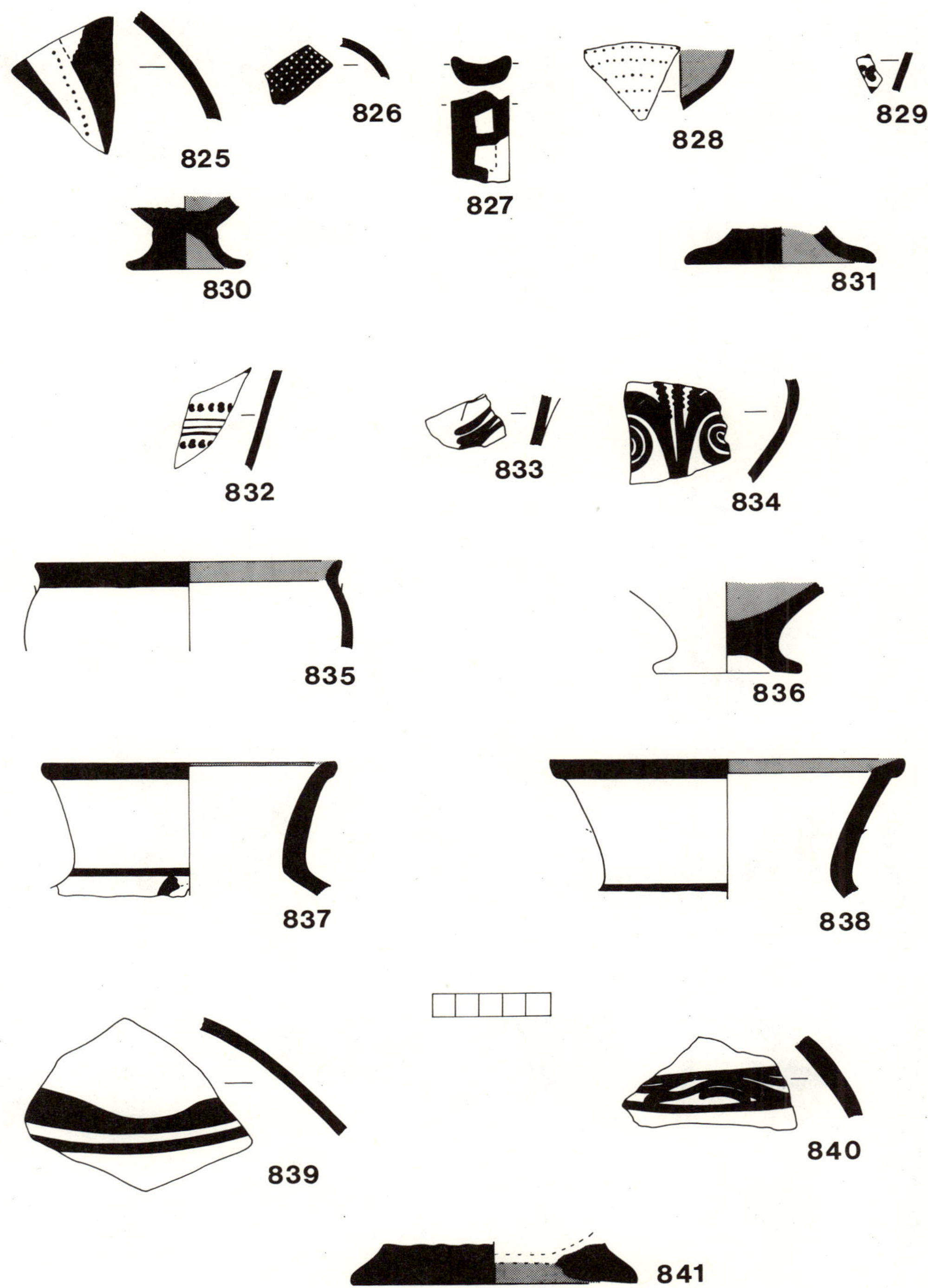

Fig. 44. Late Helladic IIA vessels **825–831**; Late Helladic IIB vessels **832–836**; Late matt painted vessels **837–841**.

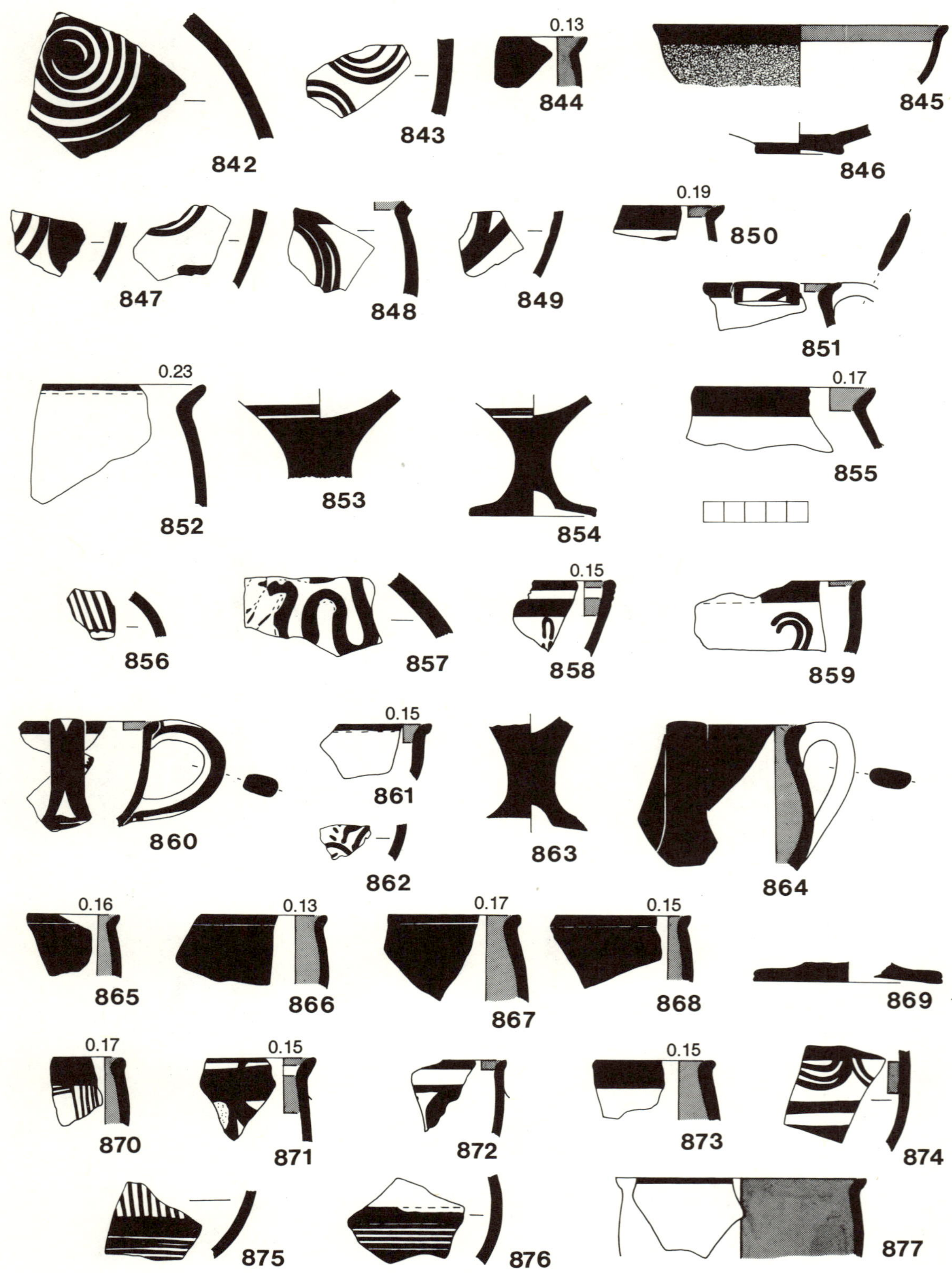

Fig. 45. Late Helladic IIIA1 vessels **842–855**; Late Helladic IIIA2 vessels **856–877**.

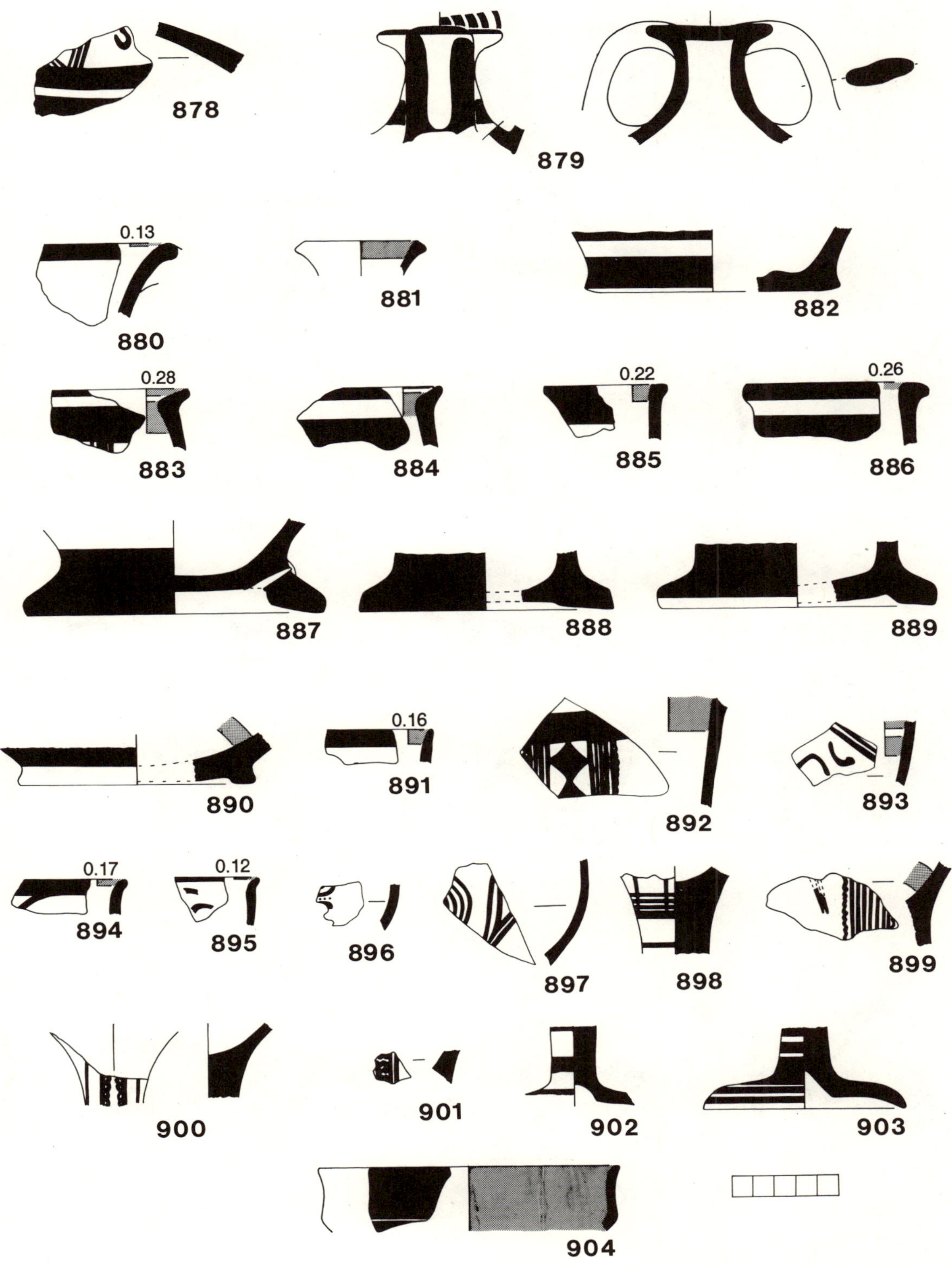

Fig. 46. Late Helladic IIIB vessels **878–904**.

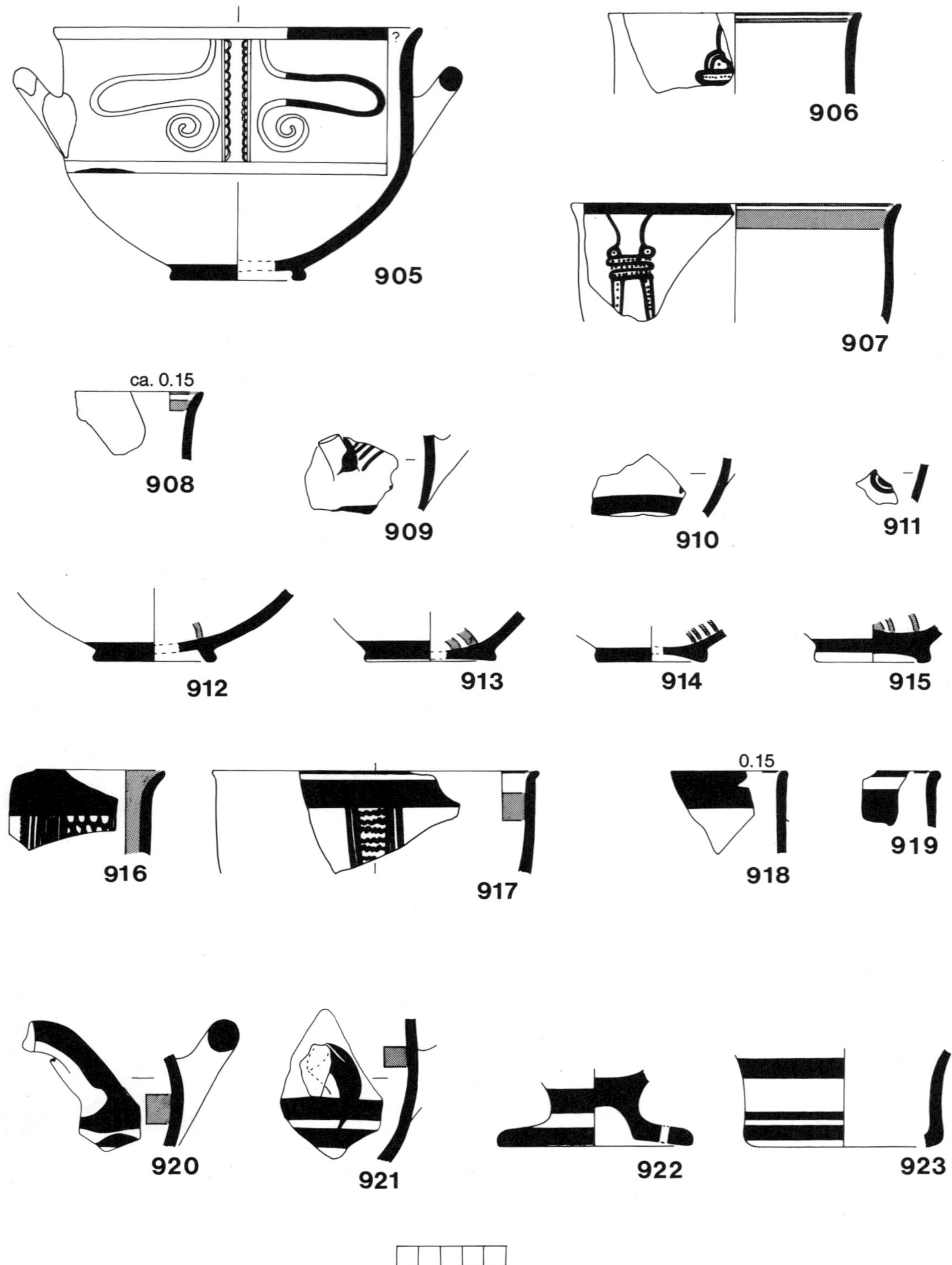

Fig. 47. Late Helladic IIIB vessels **905–923**.

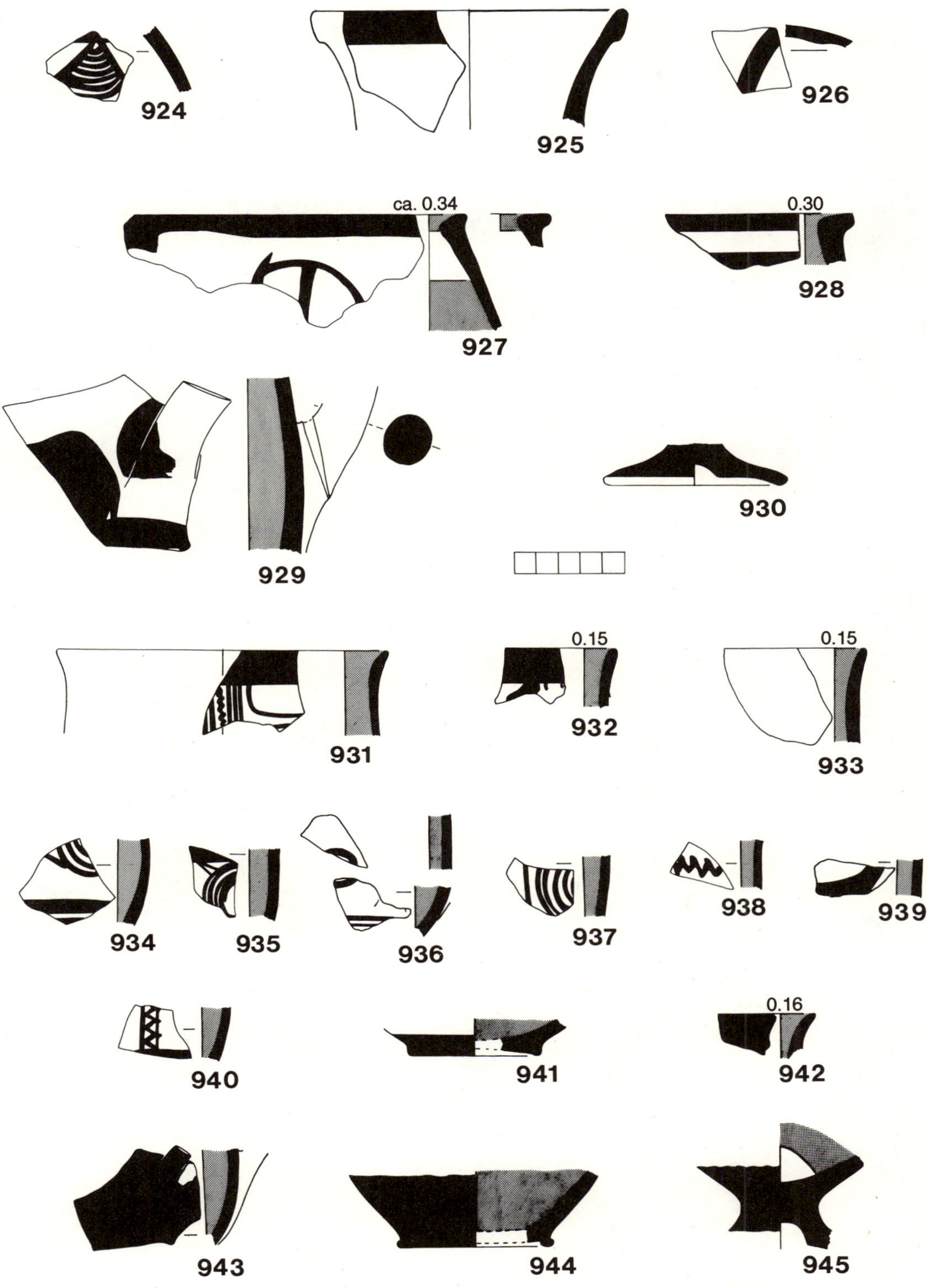

Fig. 48. Late Helladic IIIC vessels **924–945**.

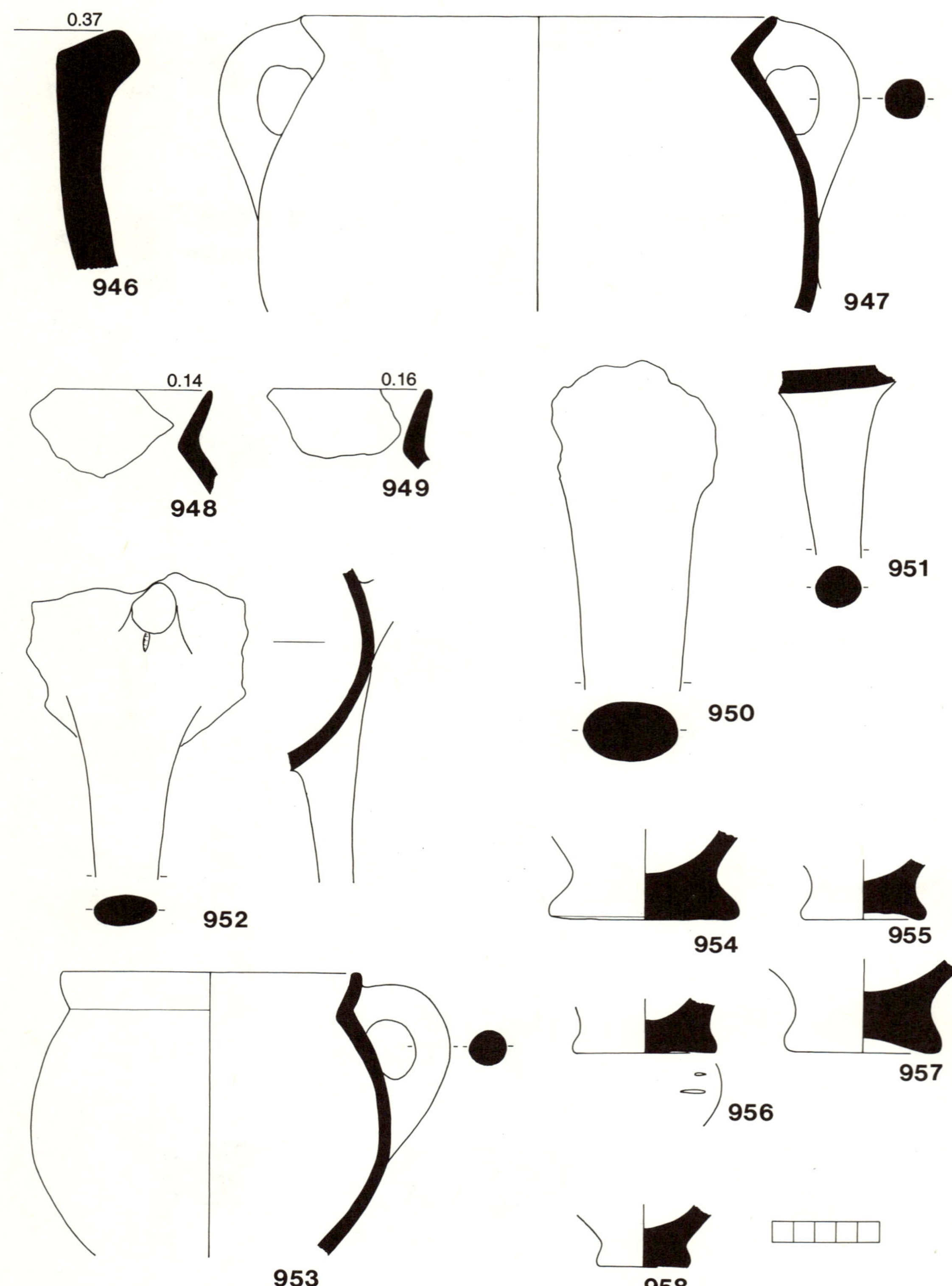

Fig. 49. Late Helladic coarse wares and cooking pots **946–958**.

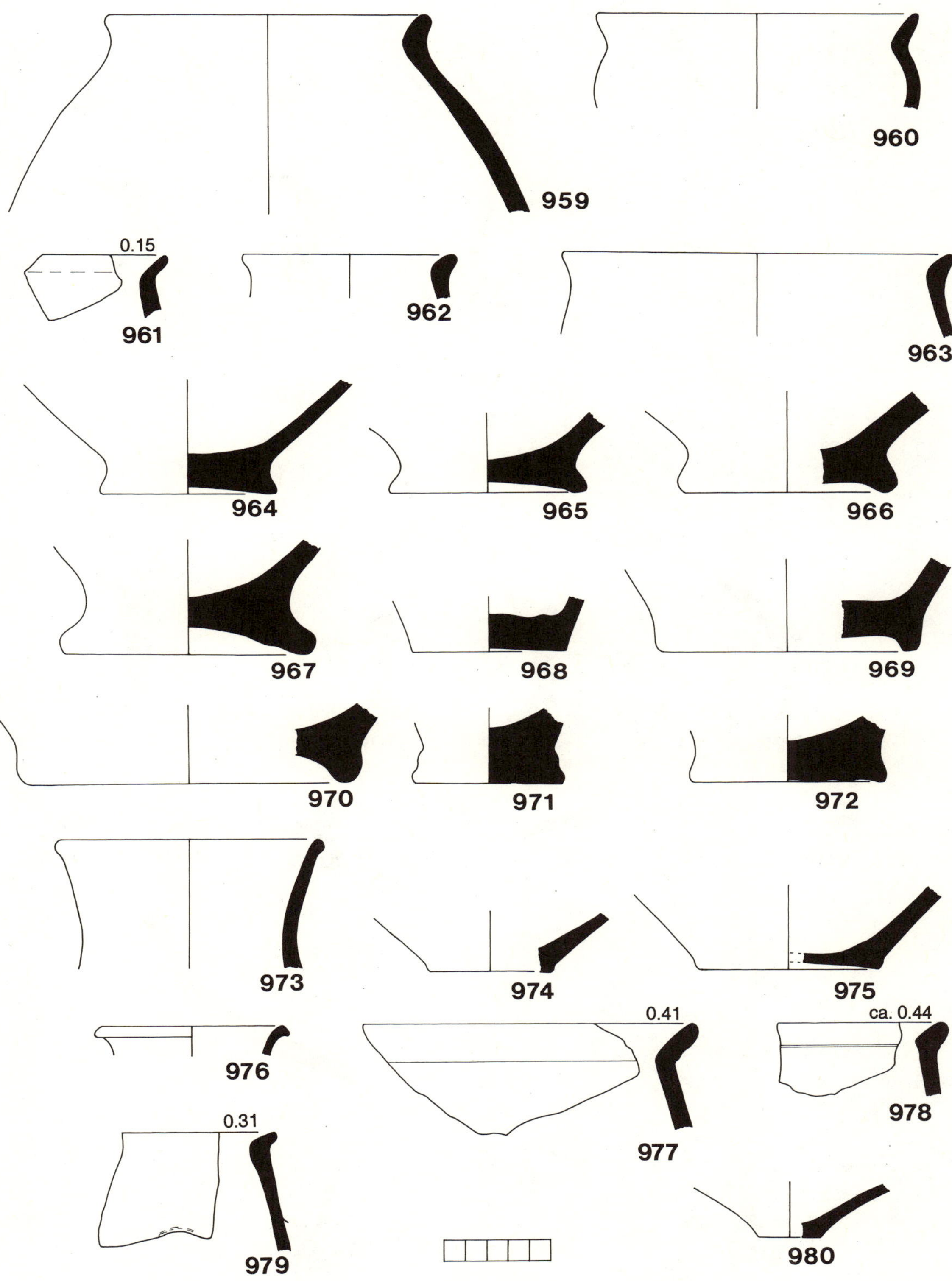

Fig. 50. Late Helladic coarse wares and cooking pots **959–972**; Late Helladic III unpainted vessels **973–980**.

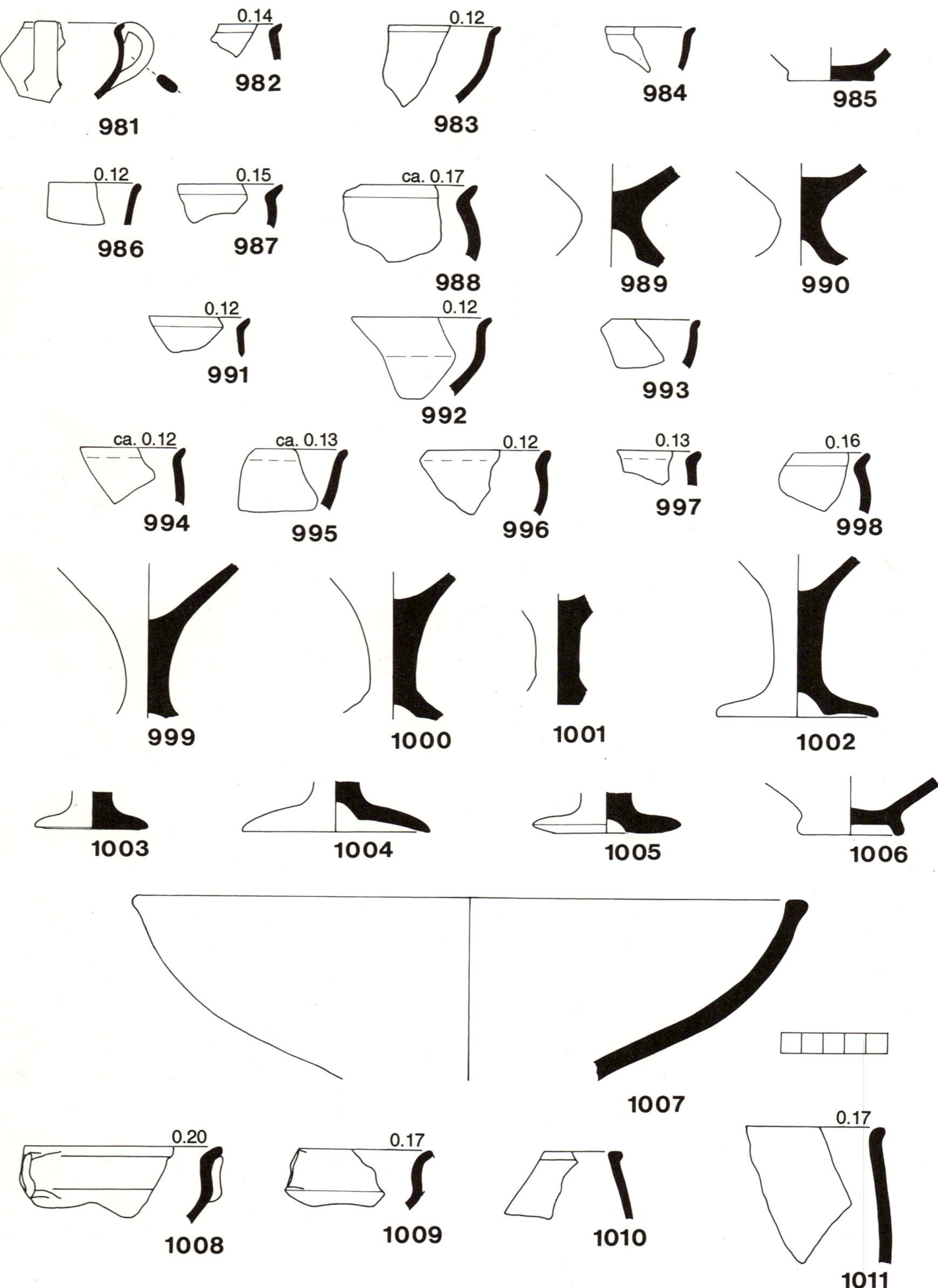

Fig. 51. Late Helladic III unpainted vessels **981–1011**.

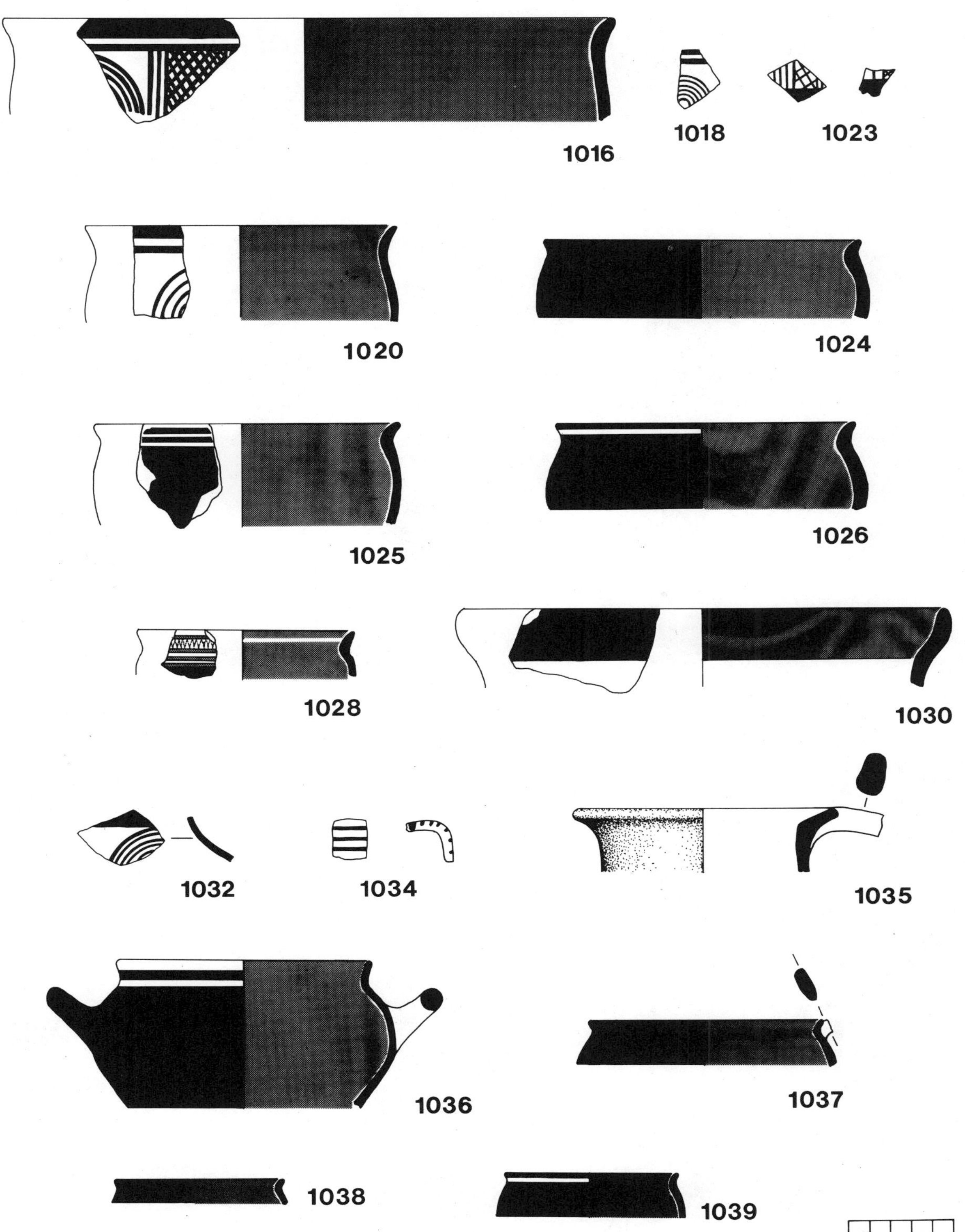

Fig. 52. Protogeometric vessels **1016, 1018, 1020, 1023–1026, 1028, 1030, 1032, 1034, 1035**; Early Geometric vessels **1036–1039**.

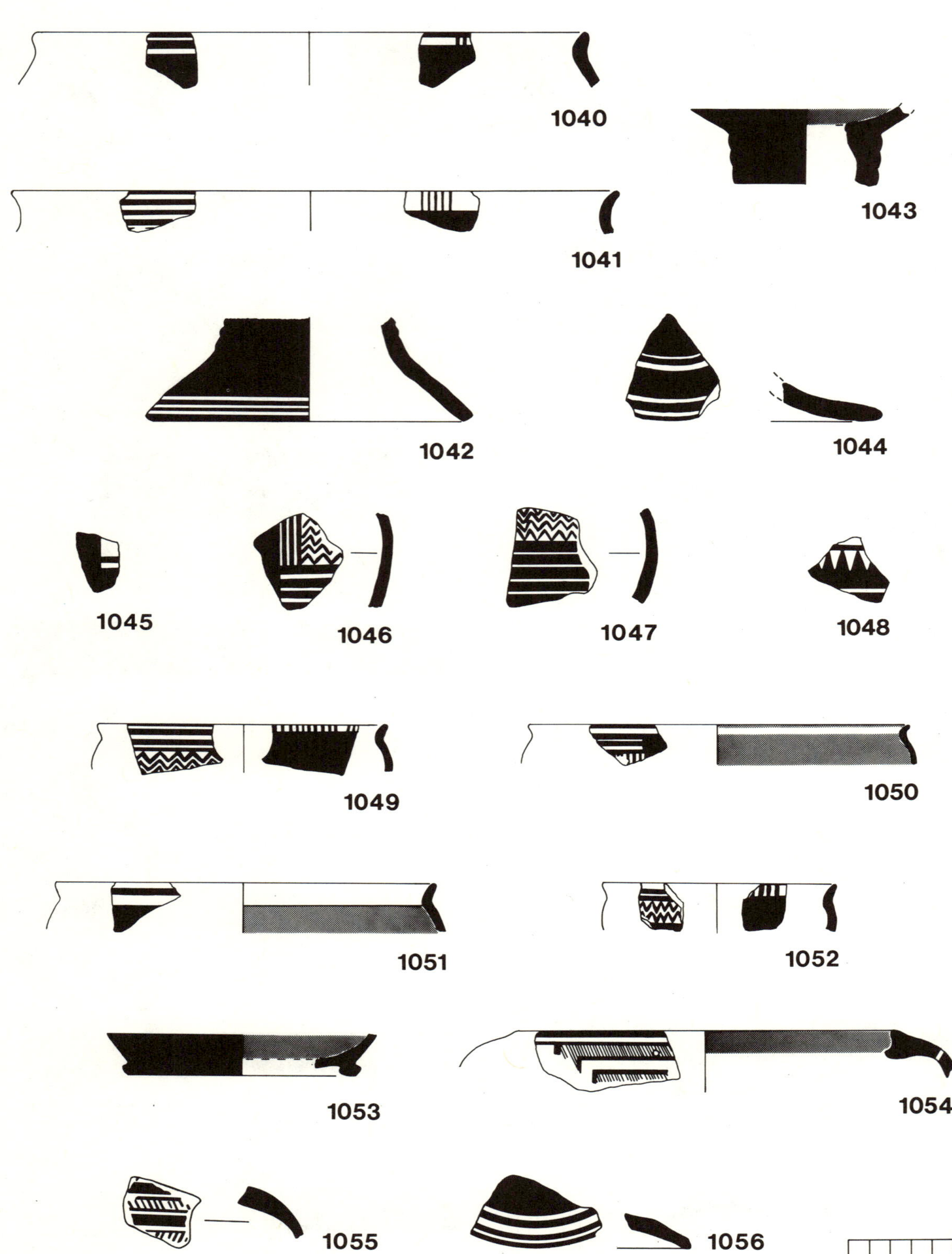

Fig. 53. Middle Geometric kraters **1040–1048**, skyphoi **1049–1053**, pyxides **1054–1056**.

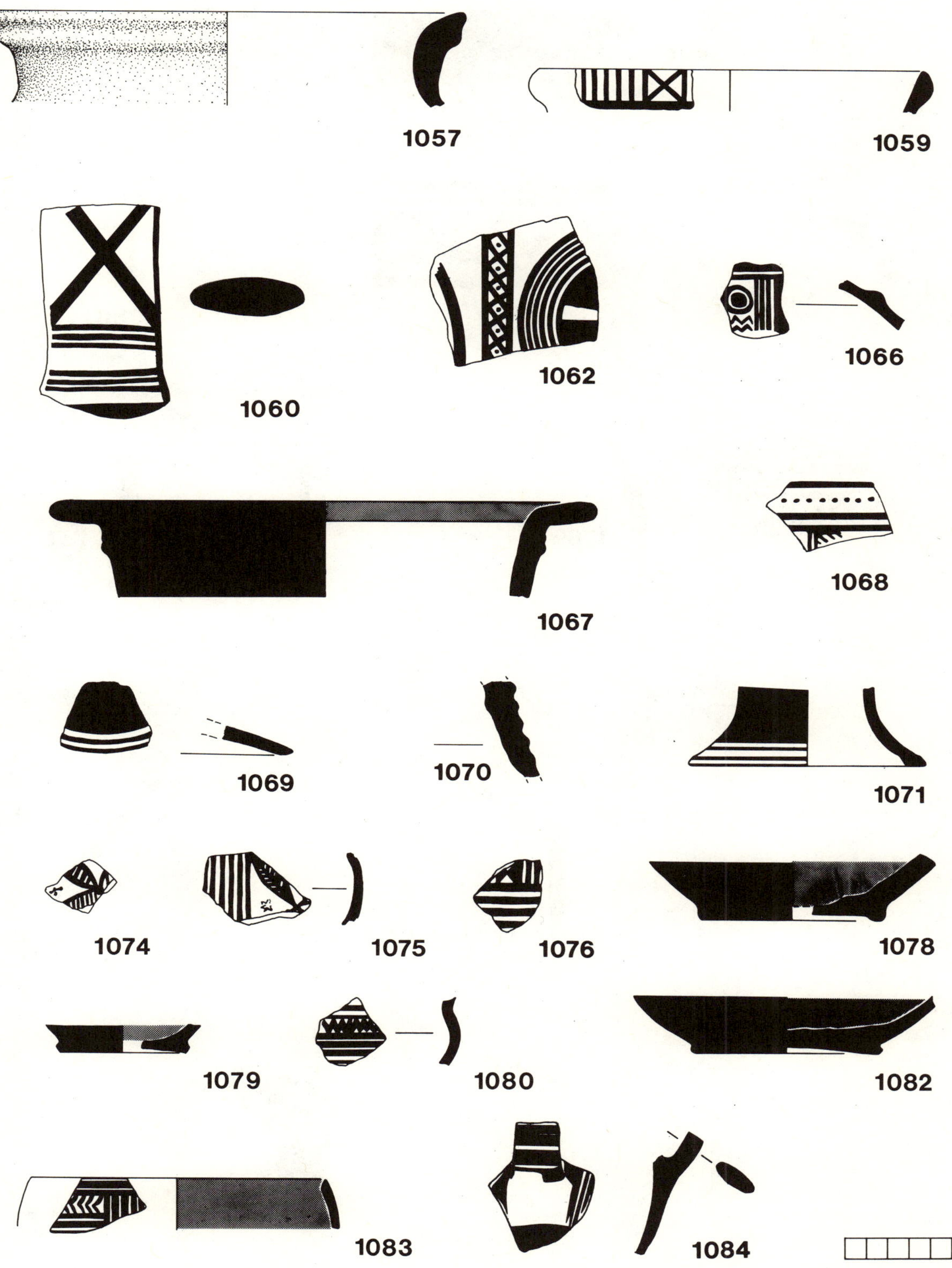

Fig. 54. Middle Geometric closed vessels **1057, 1059, 1060, 1062, 1066, 1067**; Middle to Late Geometric open vessels **1068–1071, 1074–1076, 1078–1080, 1082–1084**.

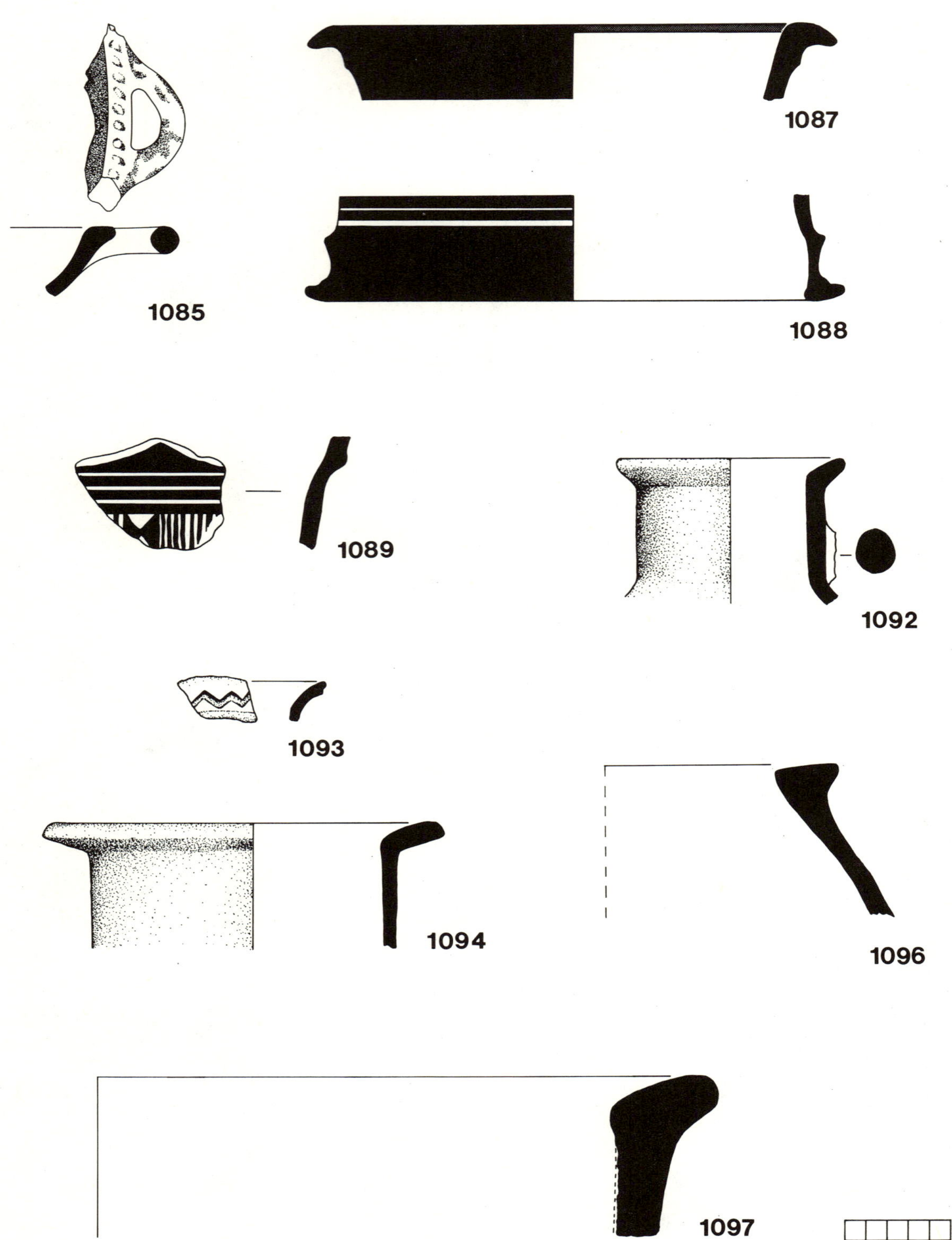

Fig. 55. Middle to Late Geometric vessels **1085**, **1087–1089**, **1092–1094**, **1096**, **1097**.

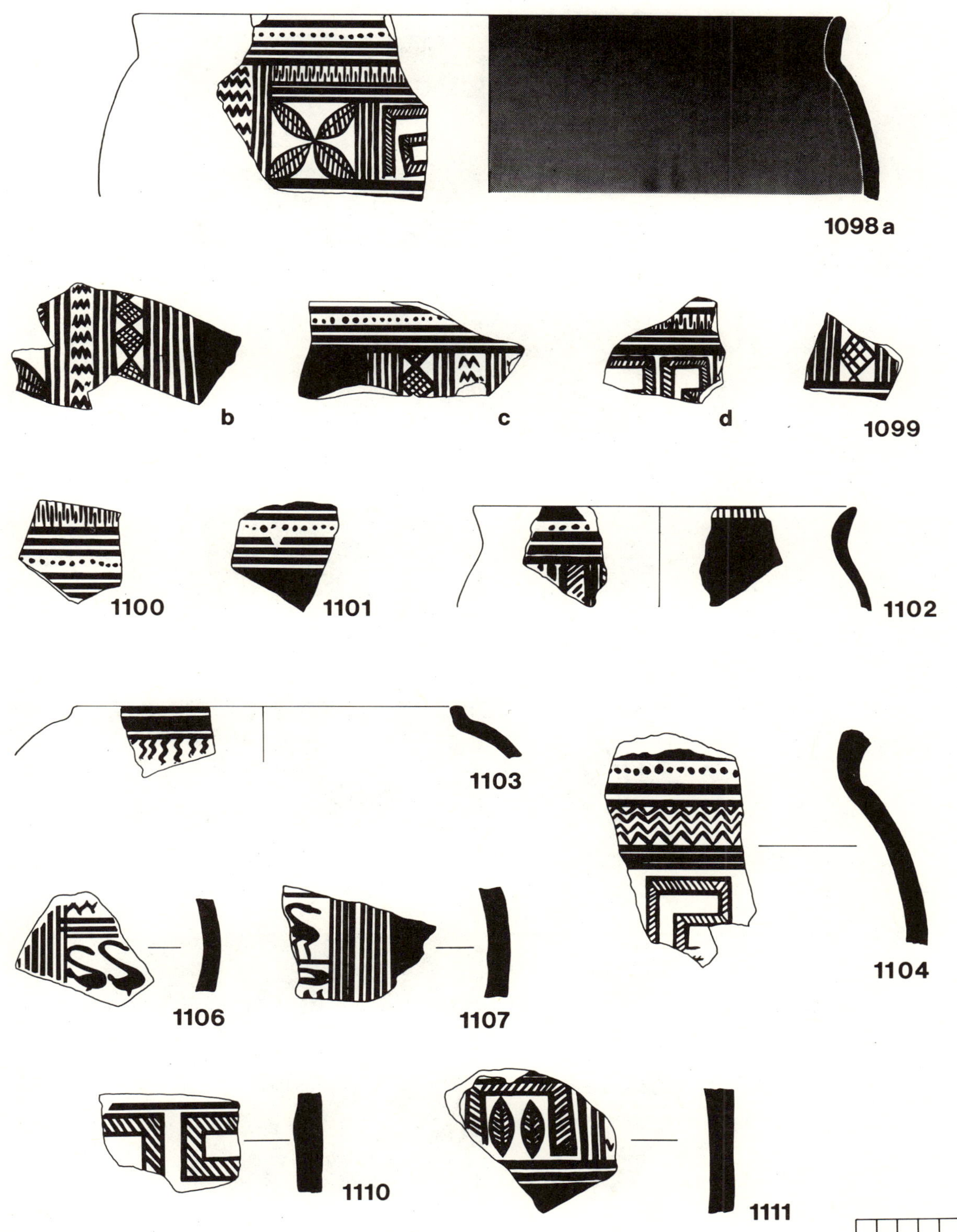

Fig. 56. Late Geometric I kraters **1098a–d–1104**, **1106**, **1107**, amphorae **1110**, **1111**.

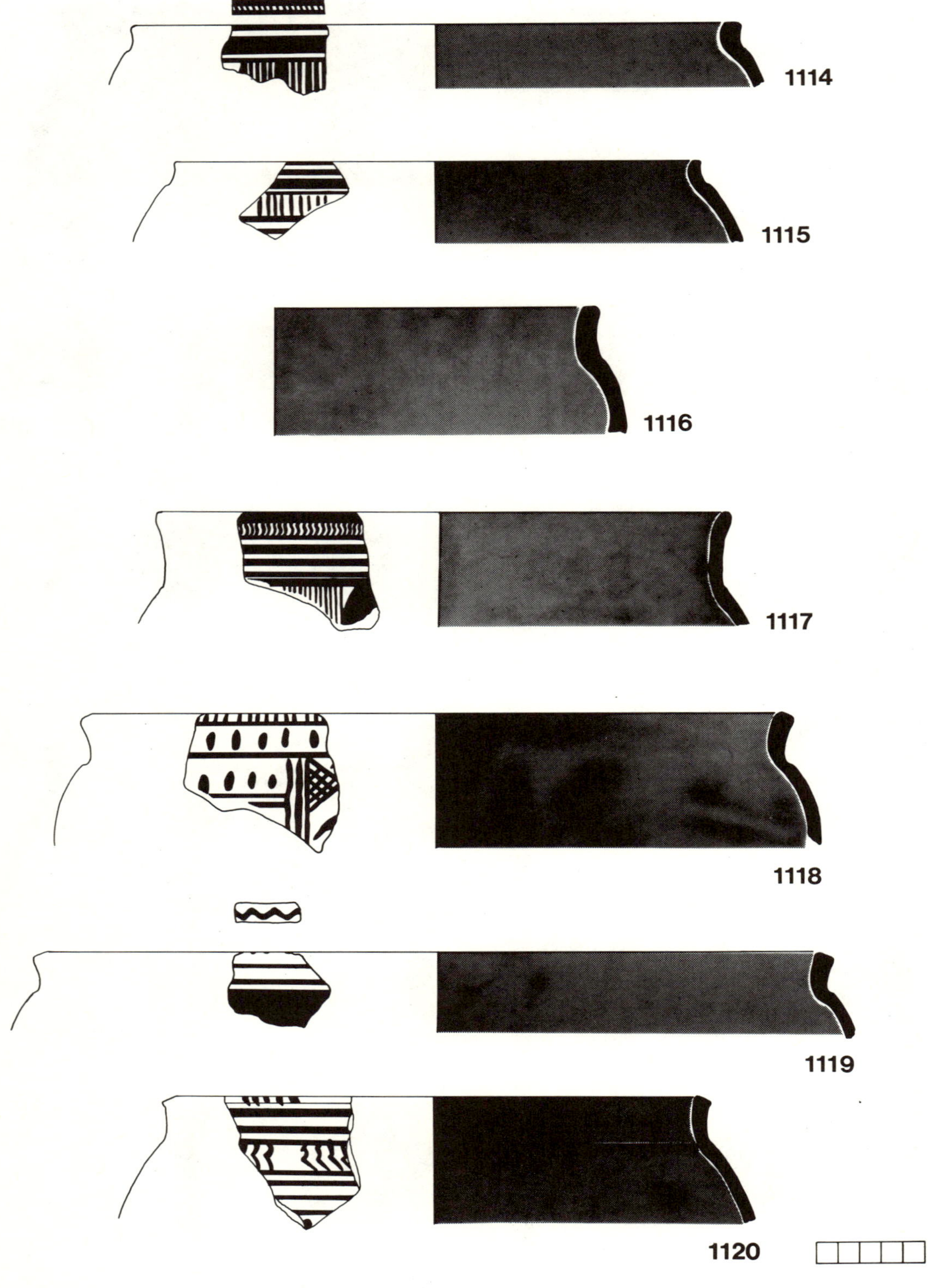

Fig. 57. Late Geometric II kraters **1114–1120**.

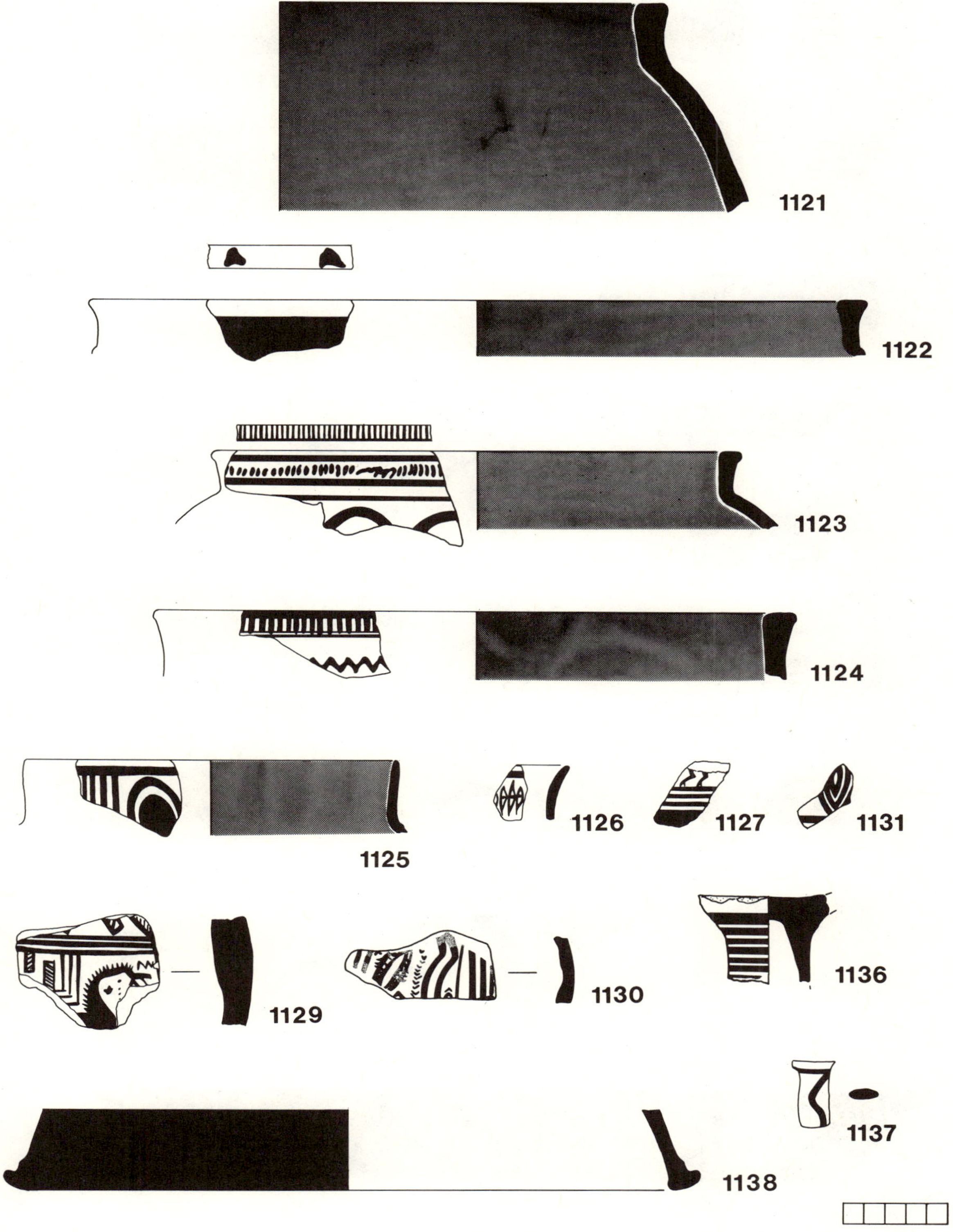

Fig. 58. Late Geometric II kraters **1121–1127**, **1129–1131**, **1136–1138**.

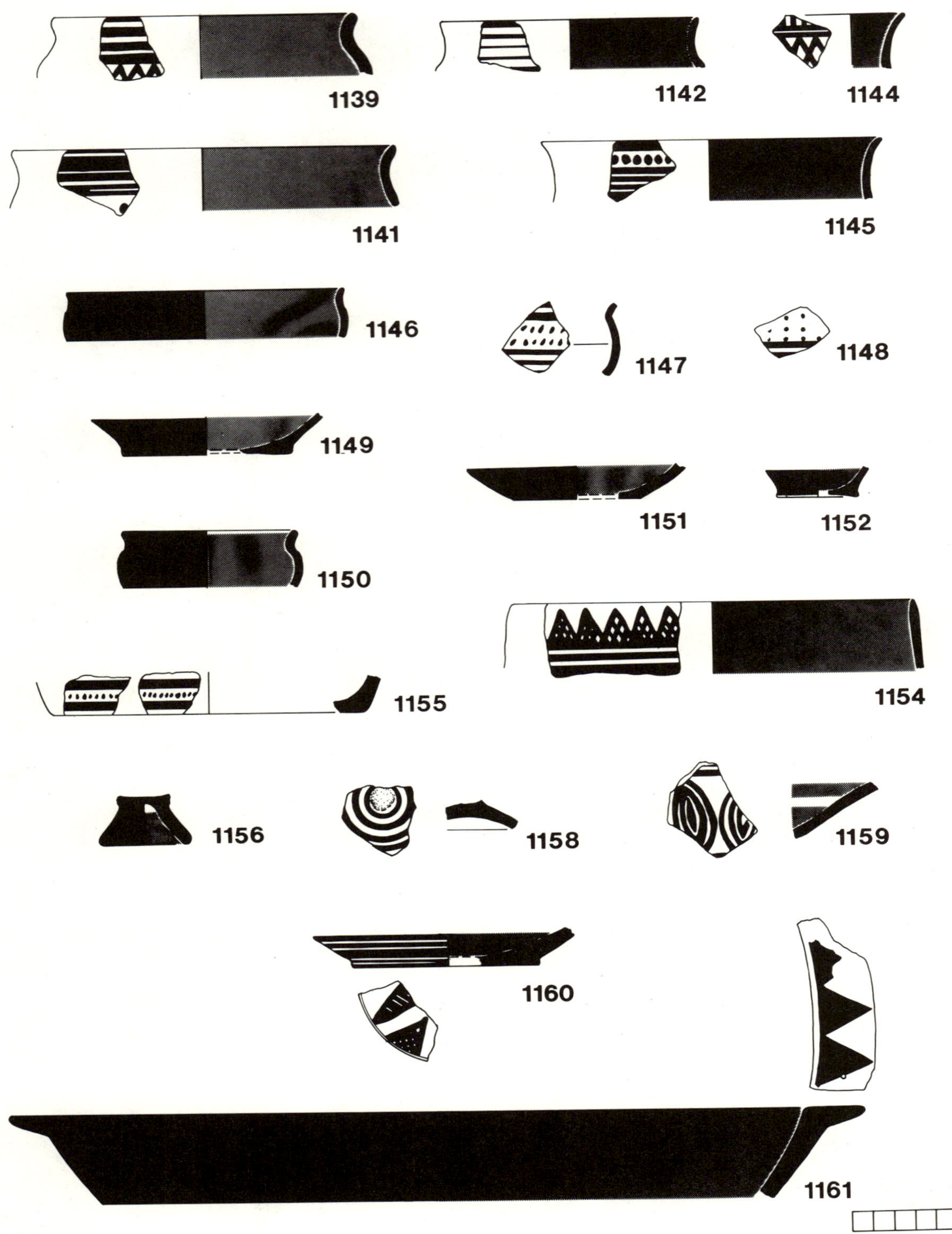

Fig. 59. Late Geometric II skyphoi and cups **1139**, **1141**, **1142**, **1144–1152**, various open vessels **1154–1156**, **1158–1161**.

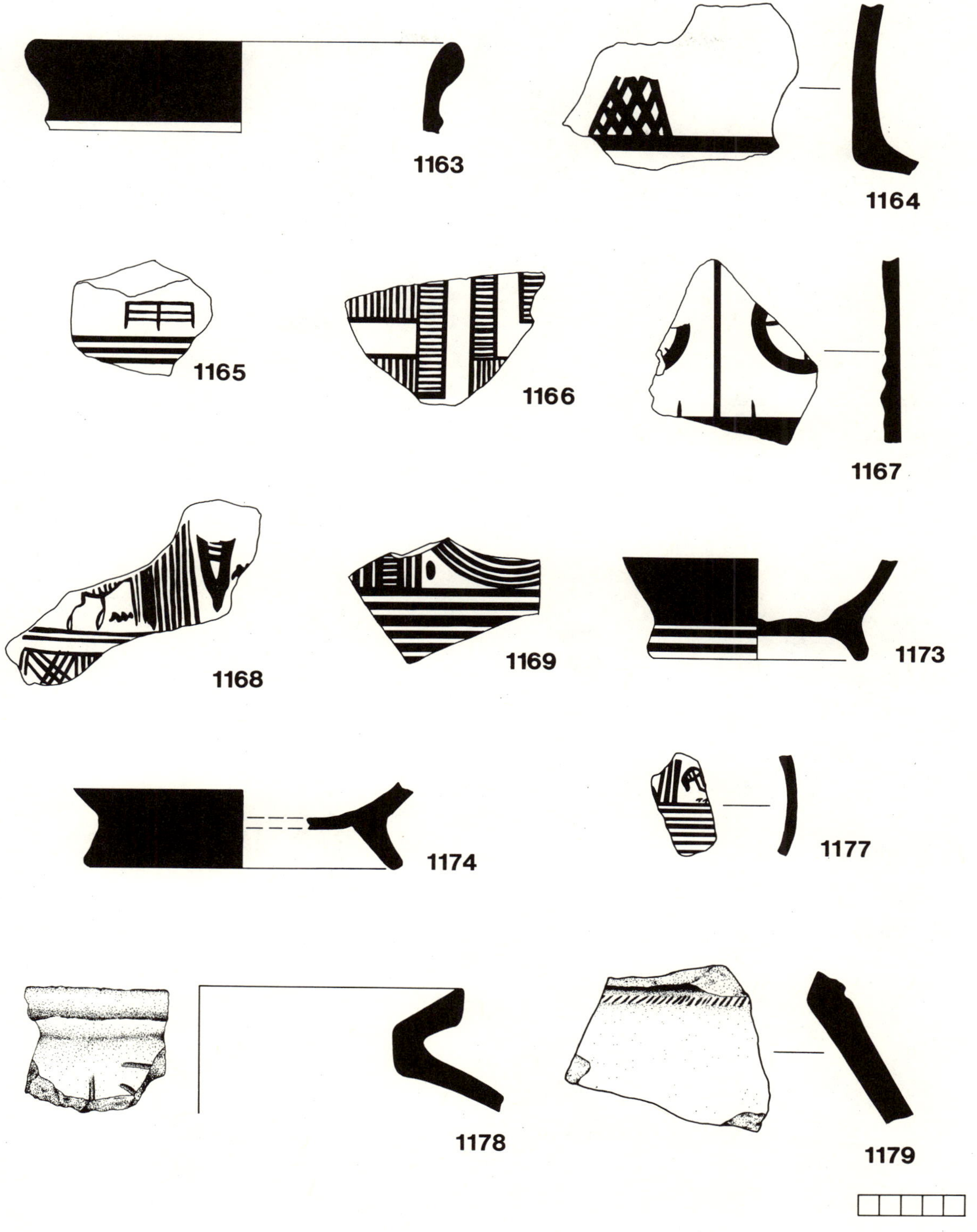

Fig. 60. Late Geometric II amphorae **1163–1169, 1173, 1174, 1177,** pithoi **1178, 1179.**

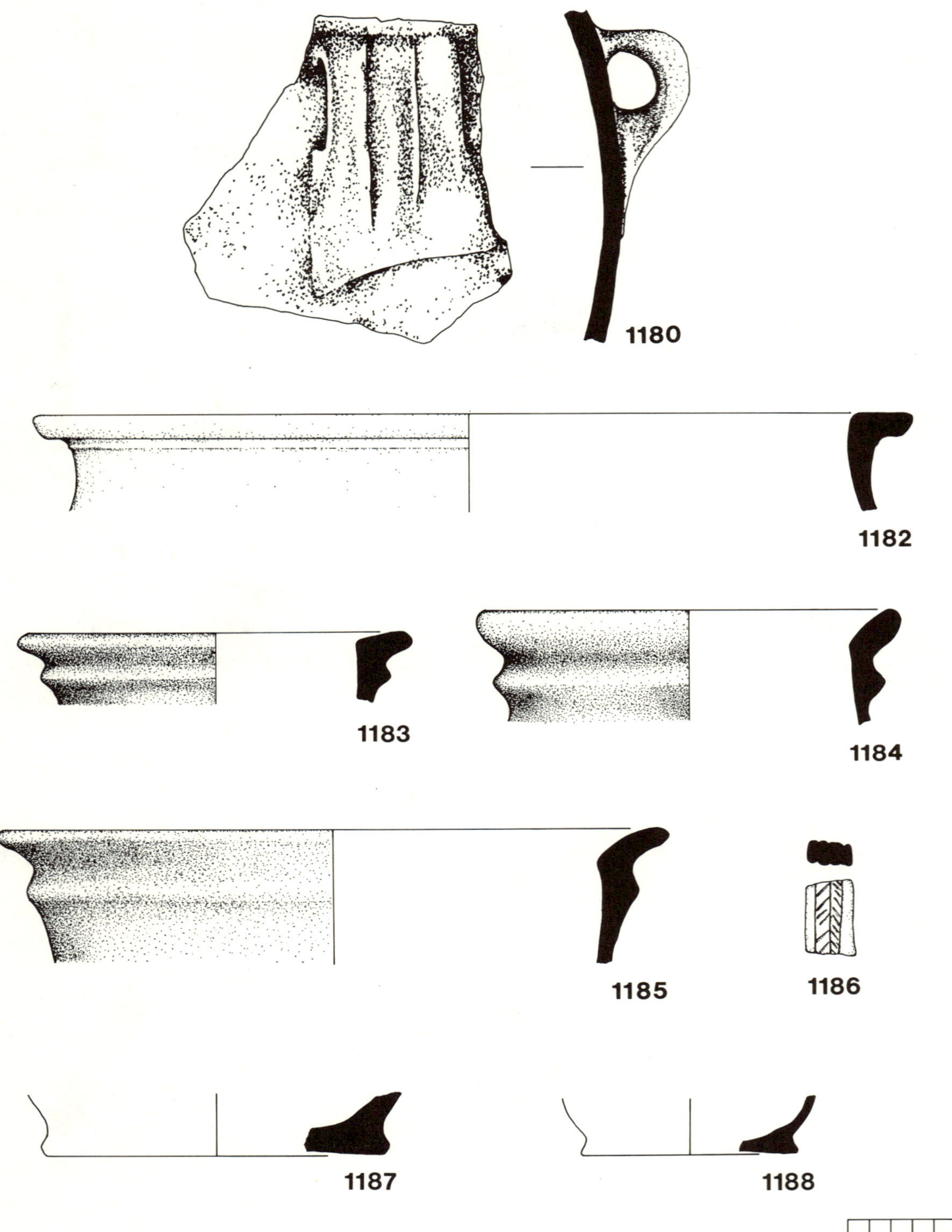

Fig. 61. Late Geometric coarse wares **1180**, **1182–1188**.

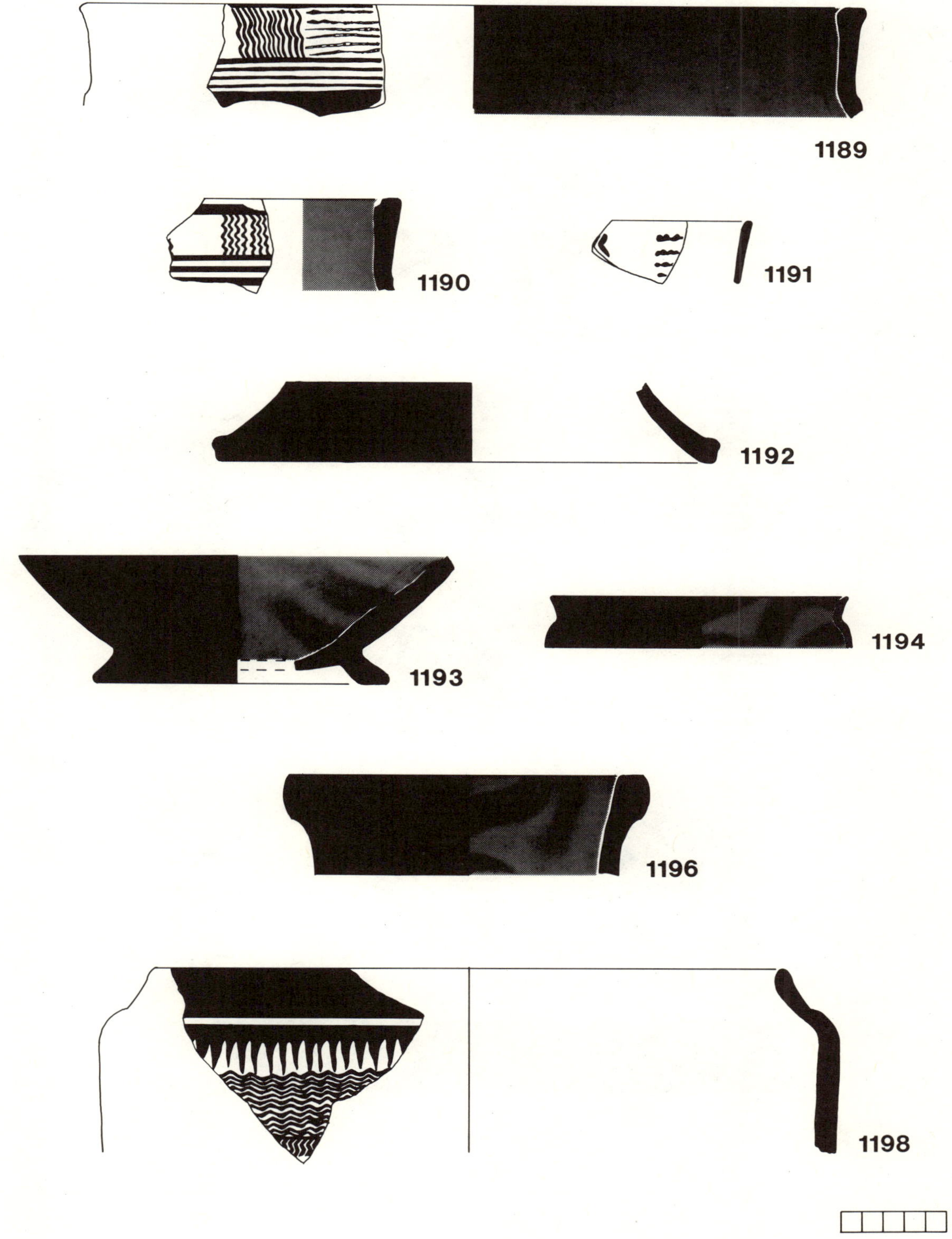

Fig. 62. Late Geometric II to Subgeometric various vessels **1189–1194, 1196, 1198**.

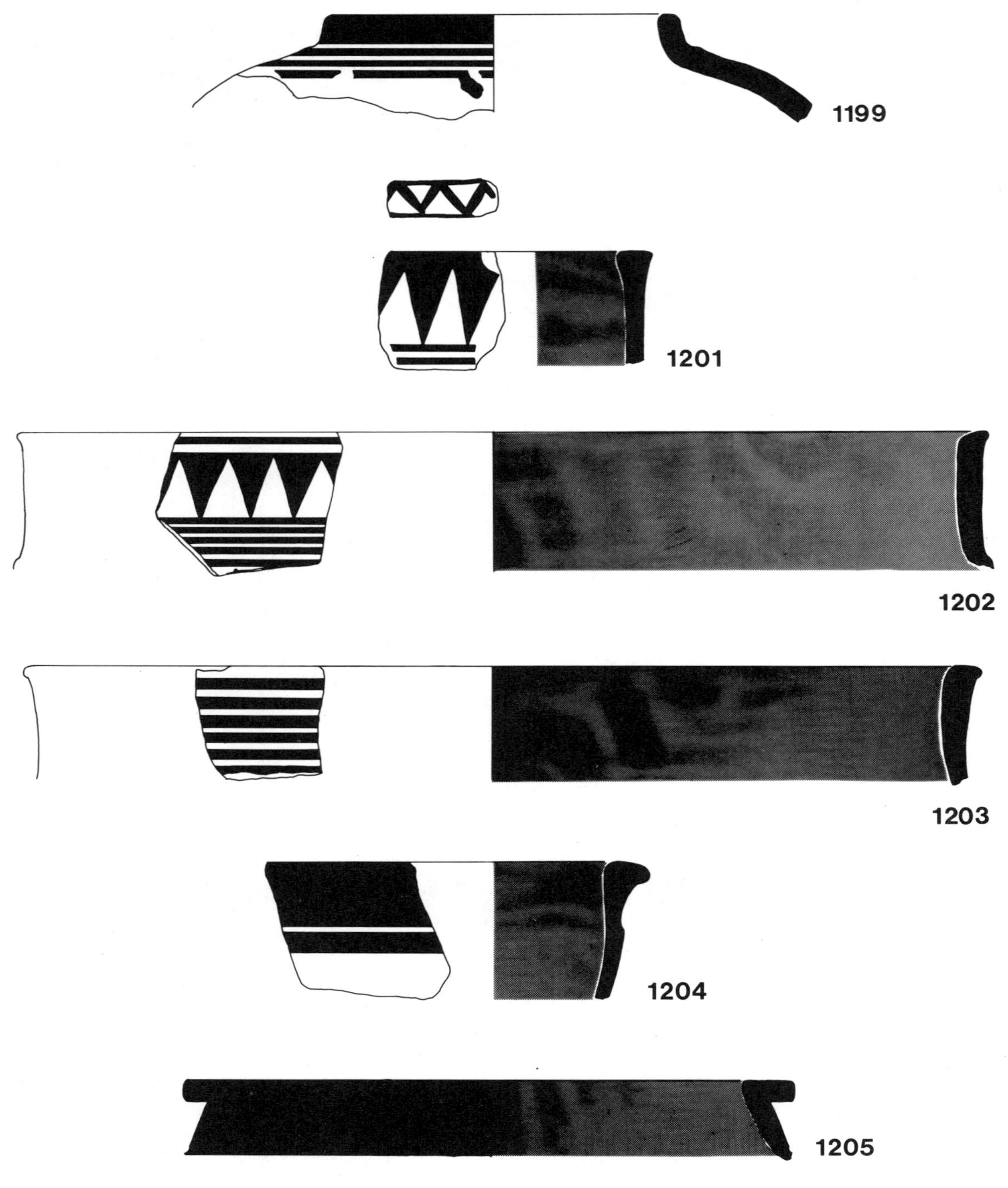

Fig. 63. Subgeometric kraters **1199**, **1201–1205**.

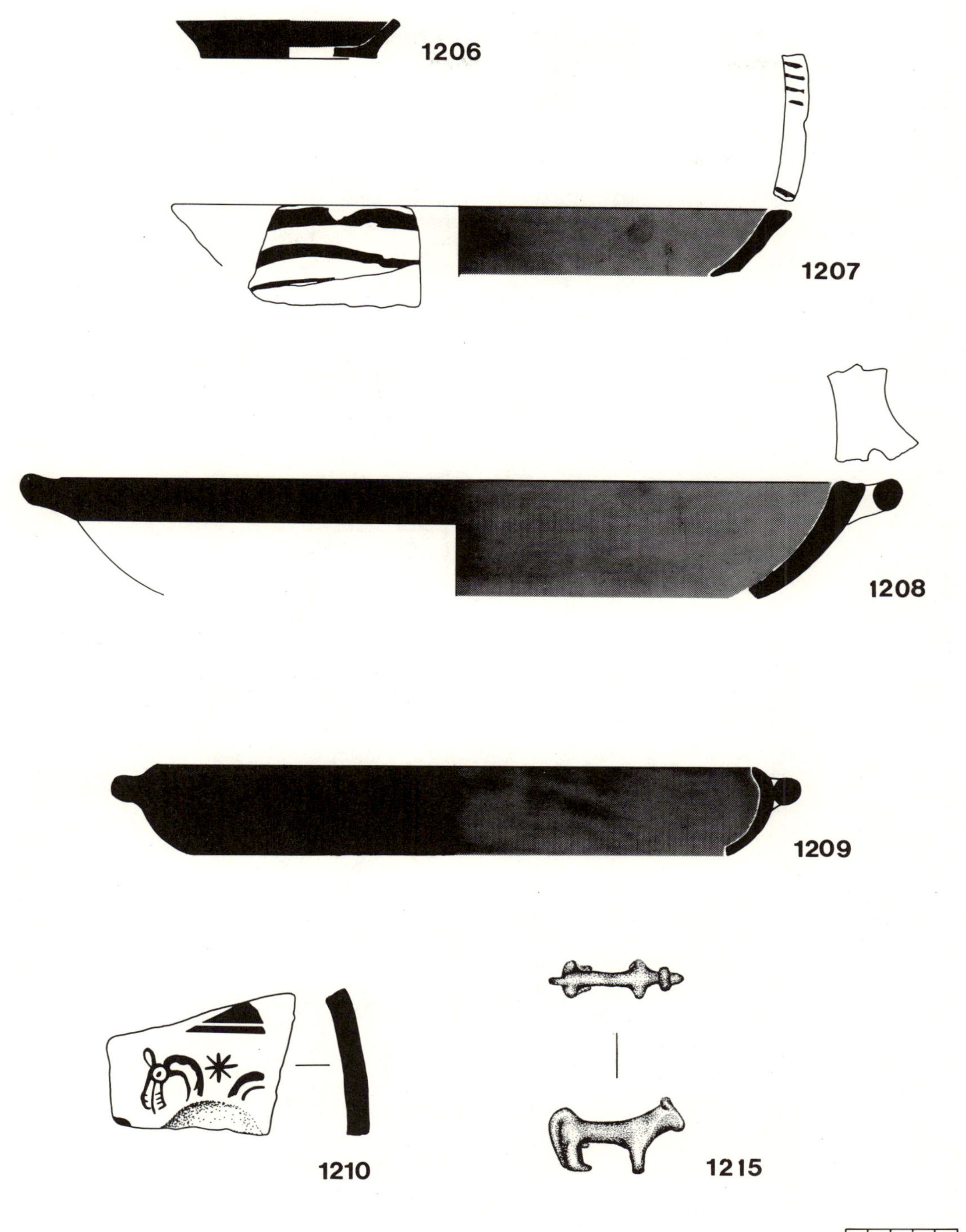

Fig. 64. Subgeometric various vessels **1206–1210**, bronze bull figurine **1215**.

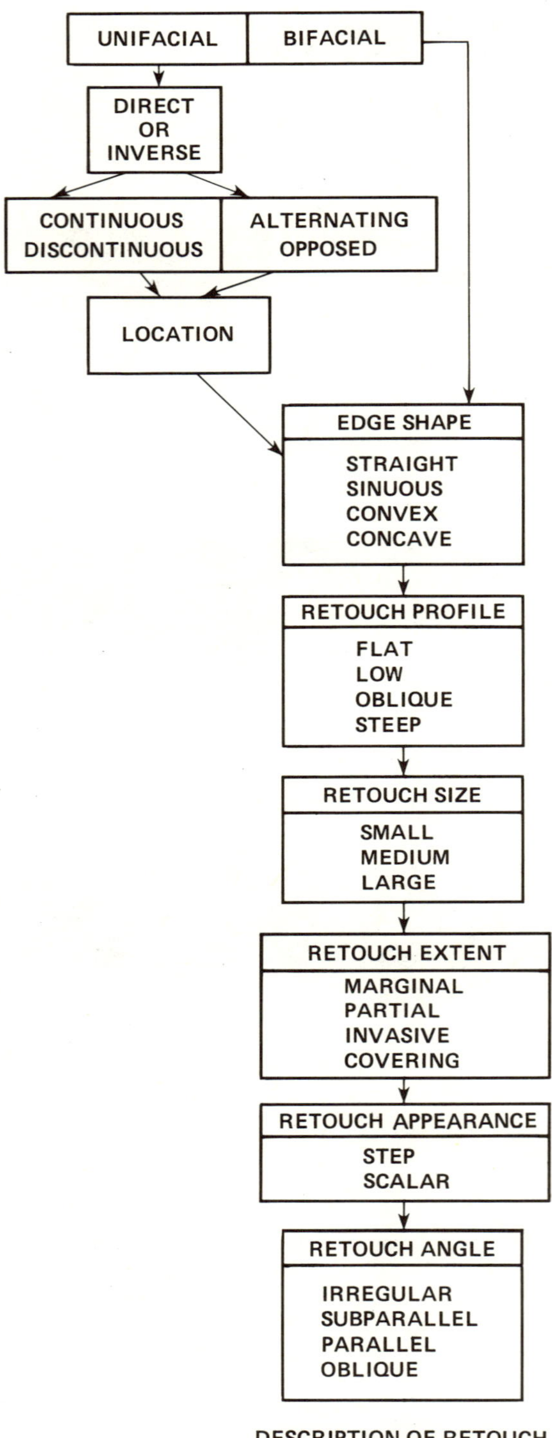

Fig. 65. Flow chart illustrating the procedure followed in describing retouch.

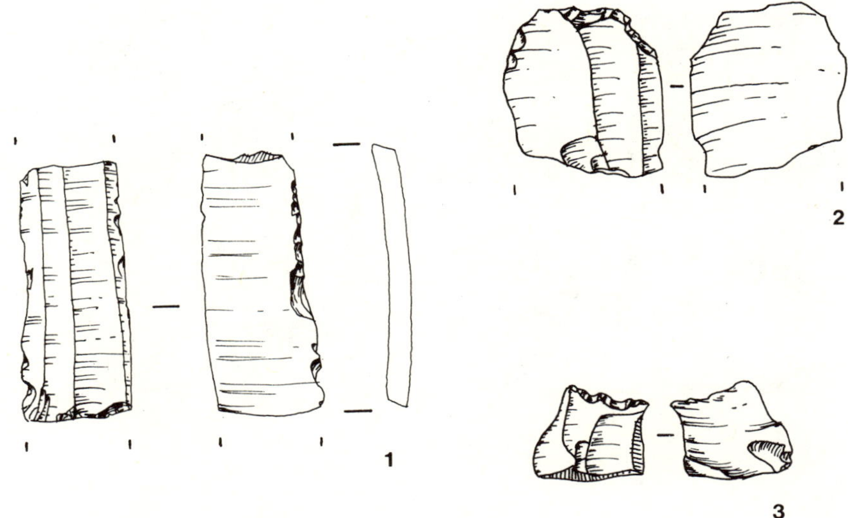

Fig. 66. (1) A6, flint blade with utilization; (2) B81, flint sickle element with continuous gloss on left edge; (3) B106, flint spall with irregular distal truncation, possibly a tinderflint.

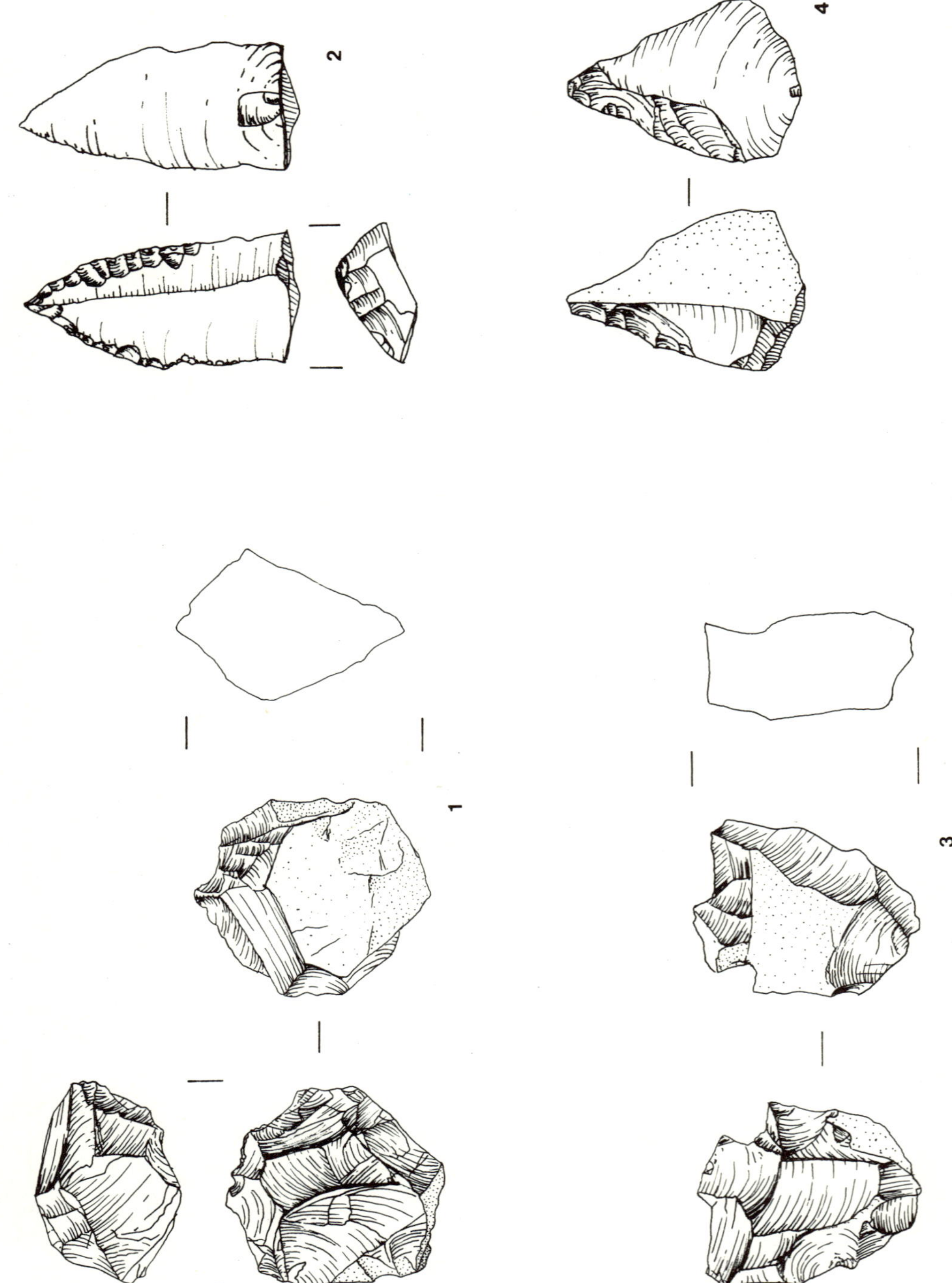

Fig. 67. B27, all flint: (1) core; (2) Mousterian point; (3) core; (4) point with one inverse retouched edge.

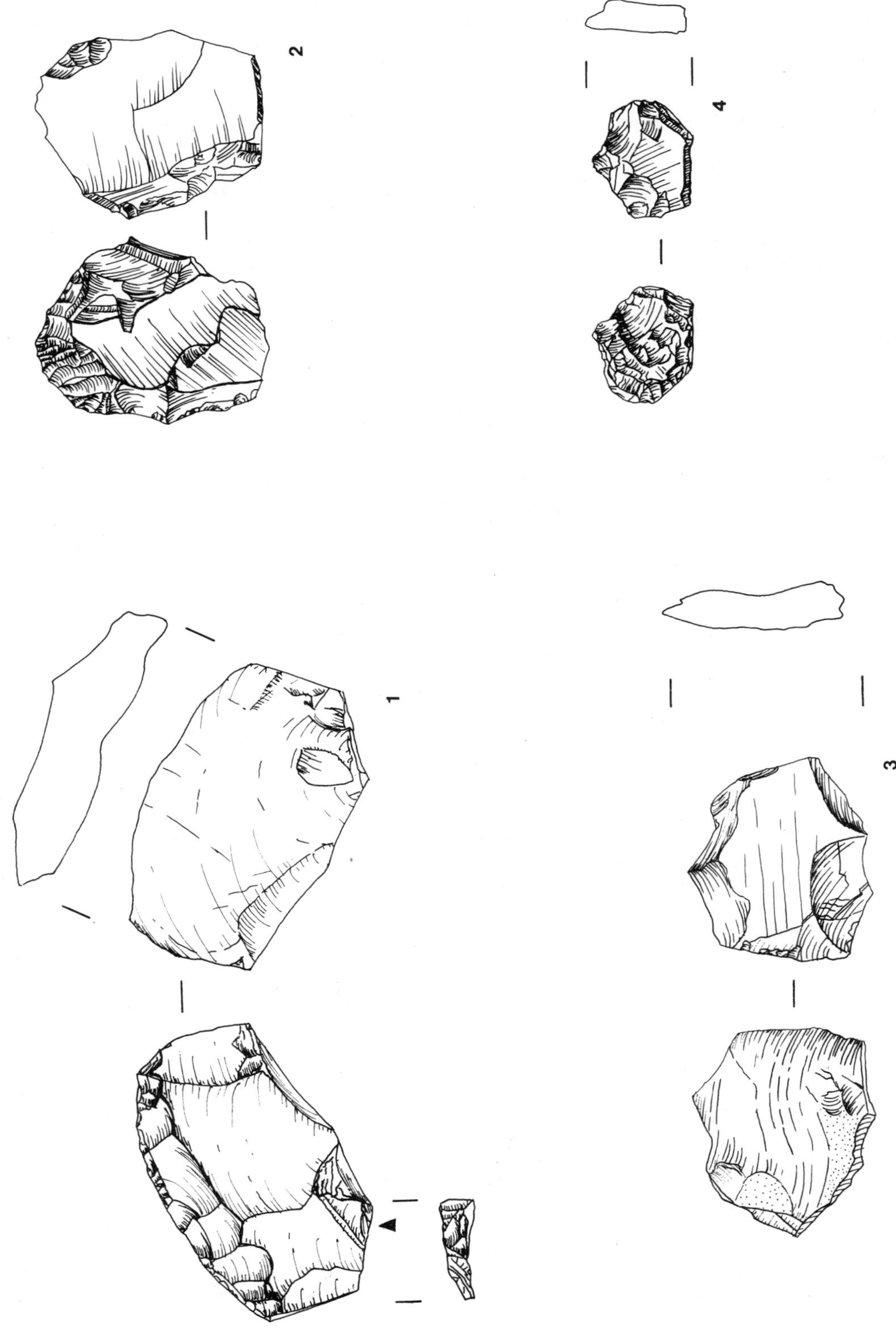

Fig. 68. B27, all flint: (1) sidescraper on a Levallois flake; (2) nosed end scraper on a flake with two retouched edges, one inverse (this piece was collected from the surface and was not in situ); (3) core; (4) bifacially retouched piece (reworked bifacial point?).

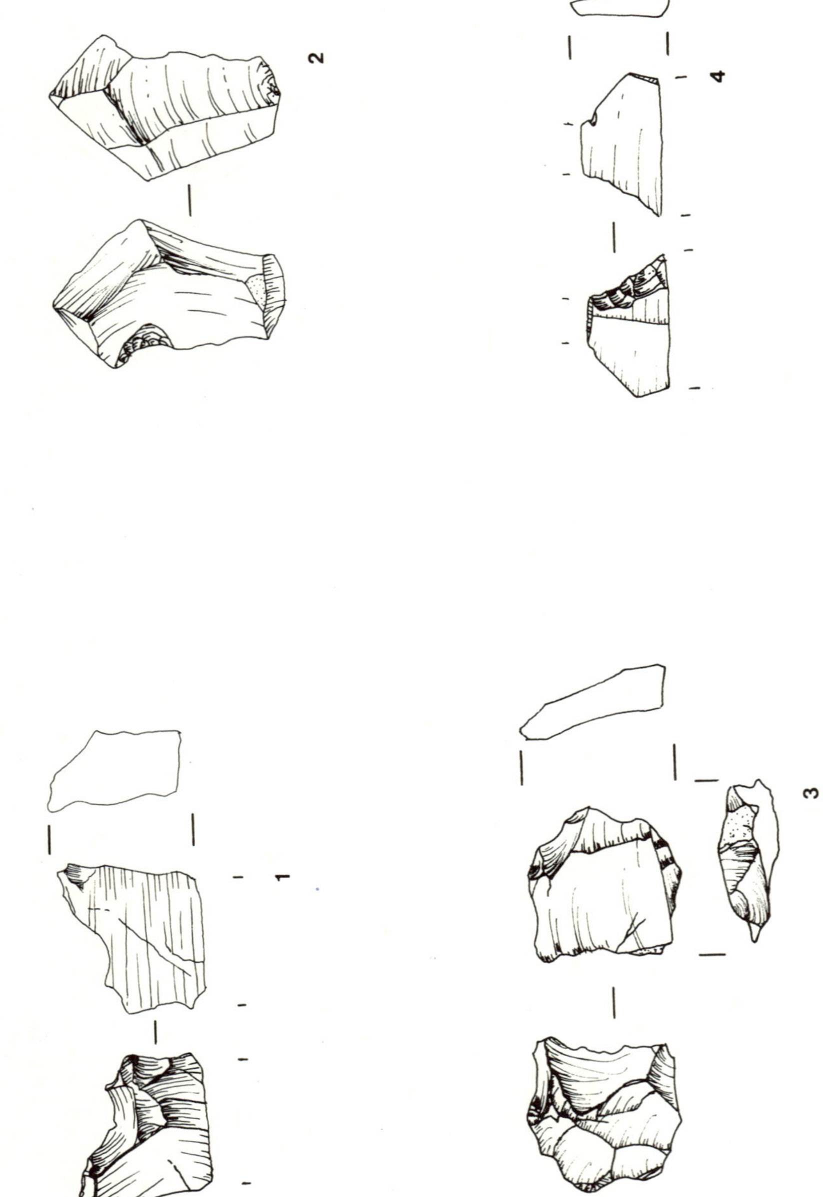

Fig. 69. B27, all flint: (1) notched flake; (2) notched flake; (3) flake with faceted platform; (4) flake with one retouched edge.

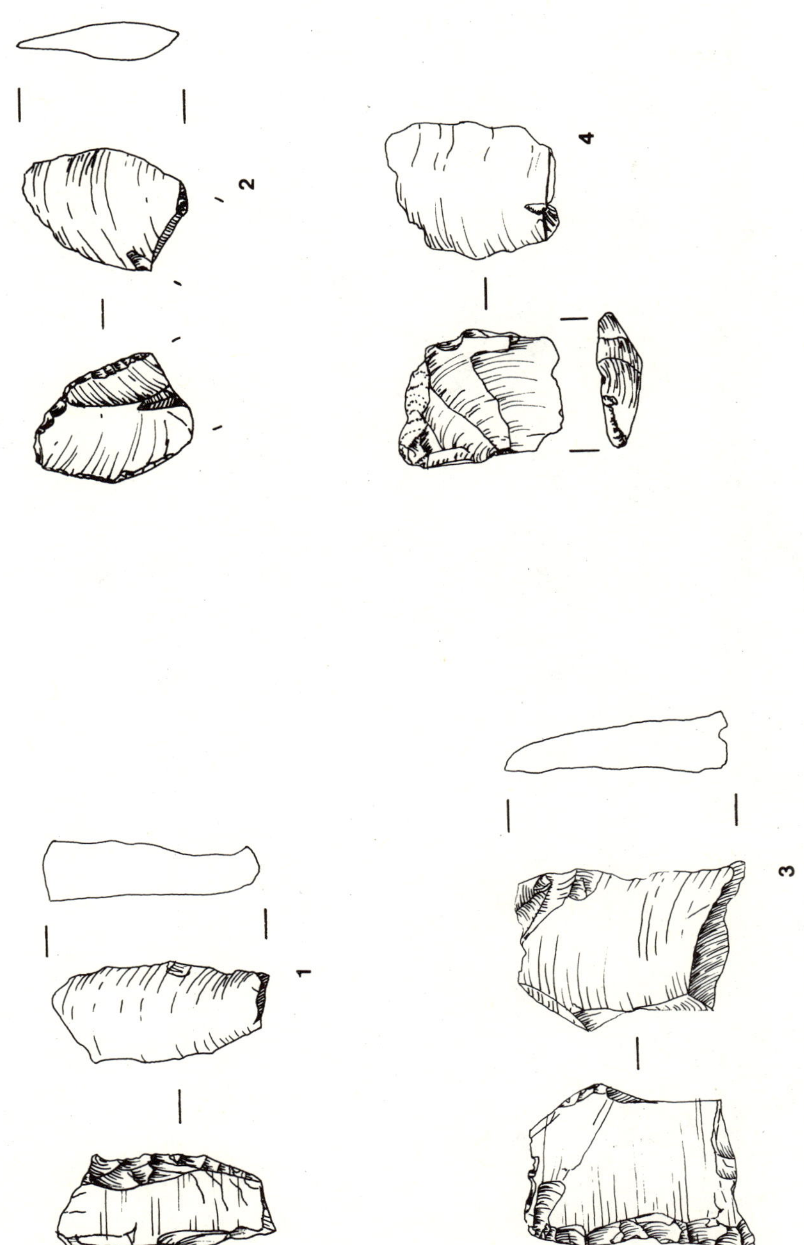

Fig. 70. B27, all flint: (1) flake with one steep retouched edge; (2) flake with continuous fine retouch; (3) flake with one steeply retouched edge; (4) flake with faceted platform.

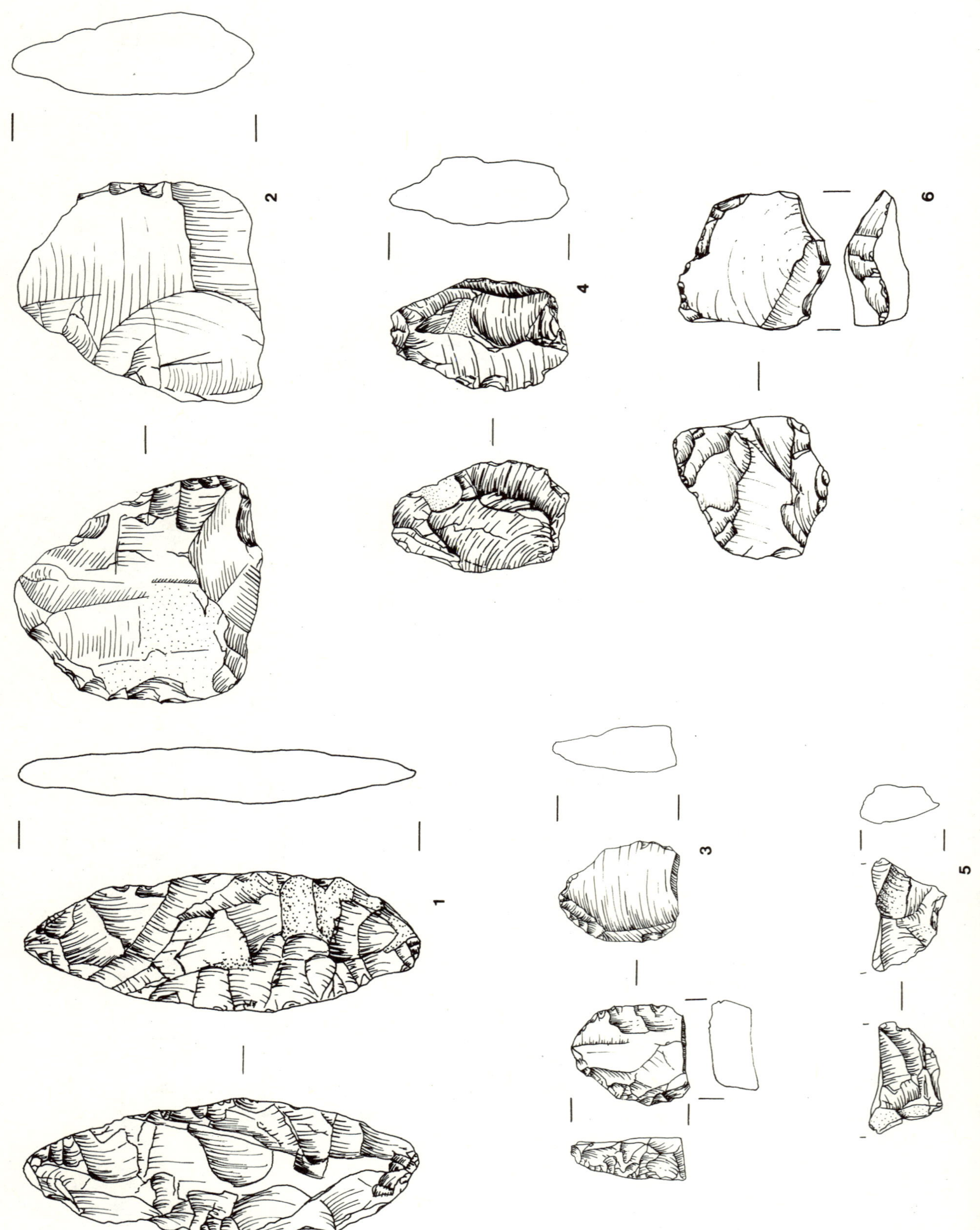

Fig. 71. B85, all flint: (1) bifacial foliate point; (2) sidescraper on a patinated flake (from the same transect, but not found in situ); (3) steeply retouched flake; (4) pièce esquillée or core; (5) fragment of bifacial foliate point? (6) sidescraper on a flake with faceted platform.

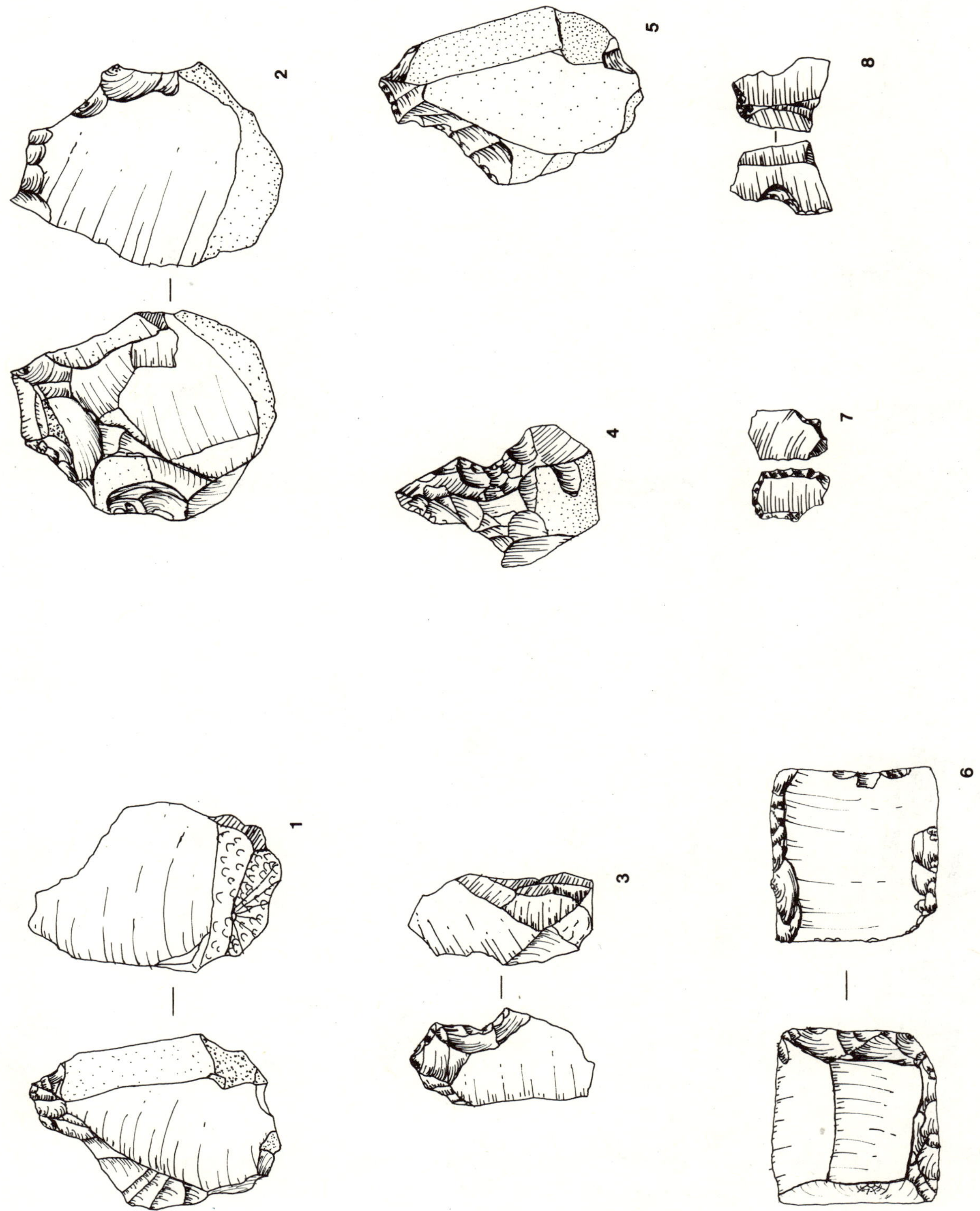

Fig. 72. B102, all flint: (1) nosed end scraper on a flake; (2) chopper; (3) nosed end scraper on a notched flake; (4) strangulated flake; (5) denticulated end scraper on a cortical spall; (6) gunflint; (7) flake with continuous nibbling retouch; (8) notch on a truncated flake.

Fig. 73. C2, all flint: (1) blade core; (2) flake with continuous distal nibbling retouch; (3) flake with proximal truncation; (4) core; (5) flake with continuous retouch on one edge; (6) truncated flake; (7) sidescraper on a flake with one inversely retouched edge; (8) bladelet core; (9) flake with discontinuous retouch on one edge and distal end; (10) flake with continuous abrupt retouch on one edge.

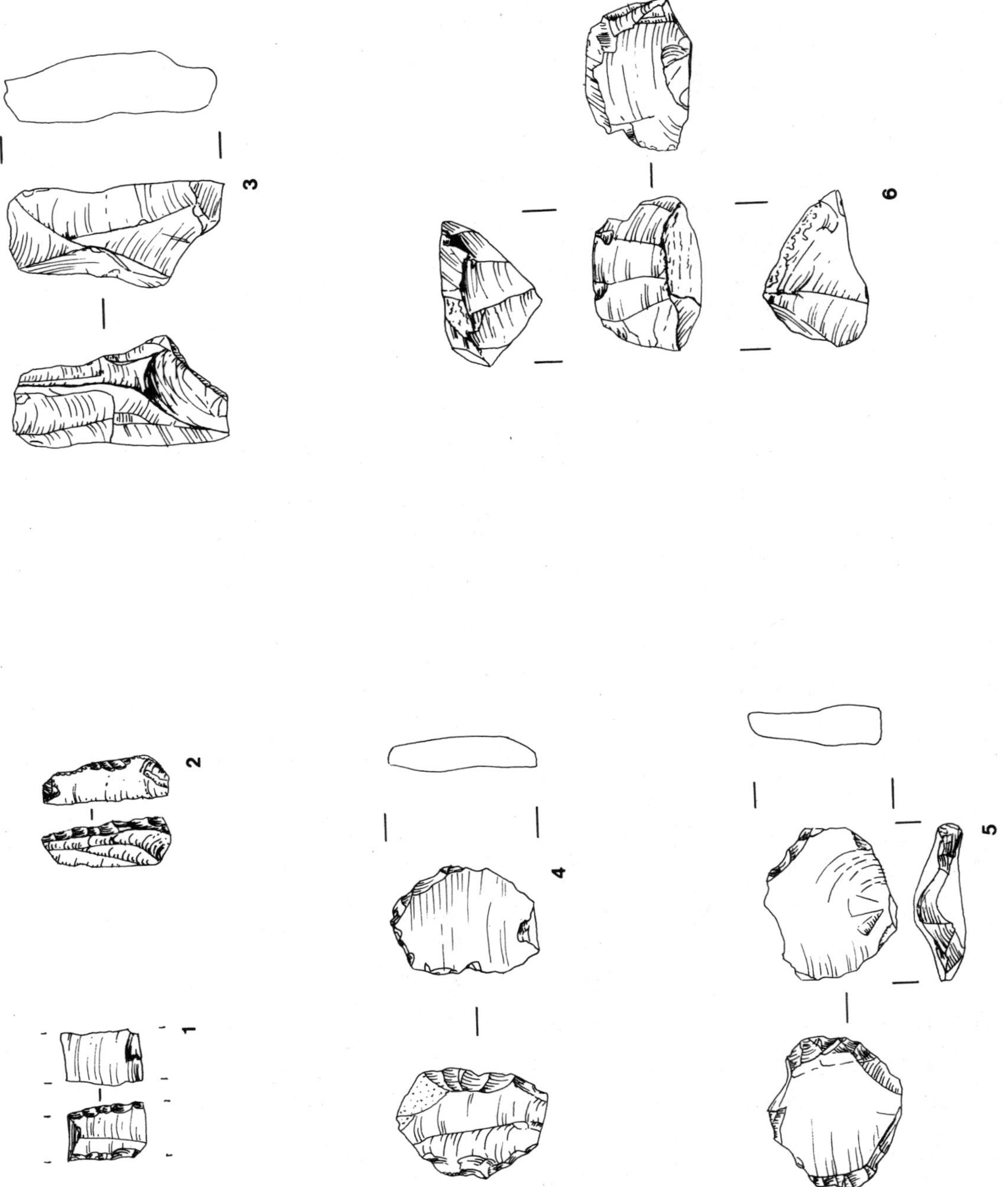

Fig. 74. C6, all flint: (1) bladelet with two backed edges; (2) backed bladelet with distal truncation; (3) blade core; (4) retouched flake; (5) flake with continuous retouch and faceted platform (broken end scraper?); (6) blade core.

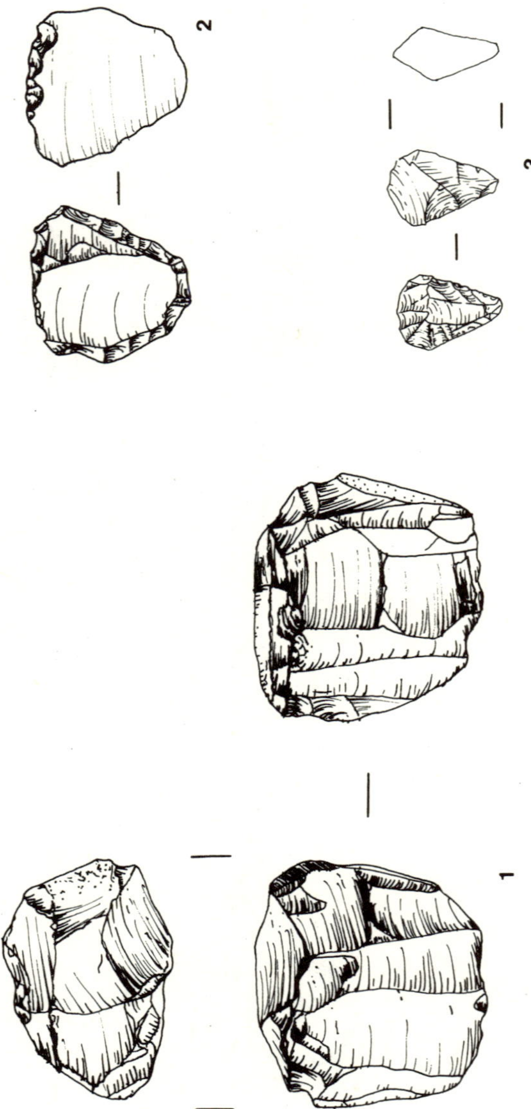

Fig. 75. (1) C17, obsidian blade core; (2) C7, flint sickle element with continuous retouch (traces of gloss on ventral surface); (3) flint end scraper with bifacially retouched tang.

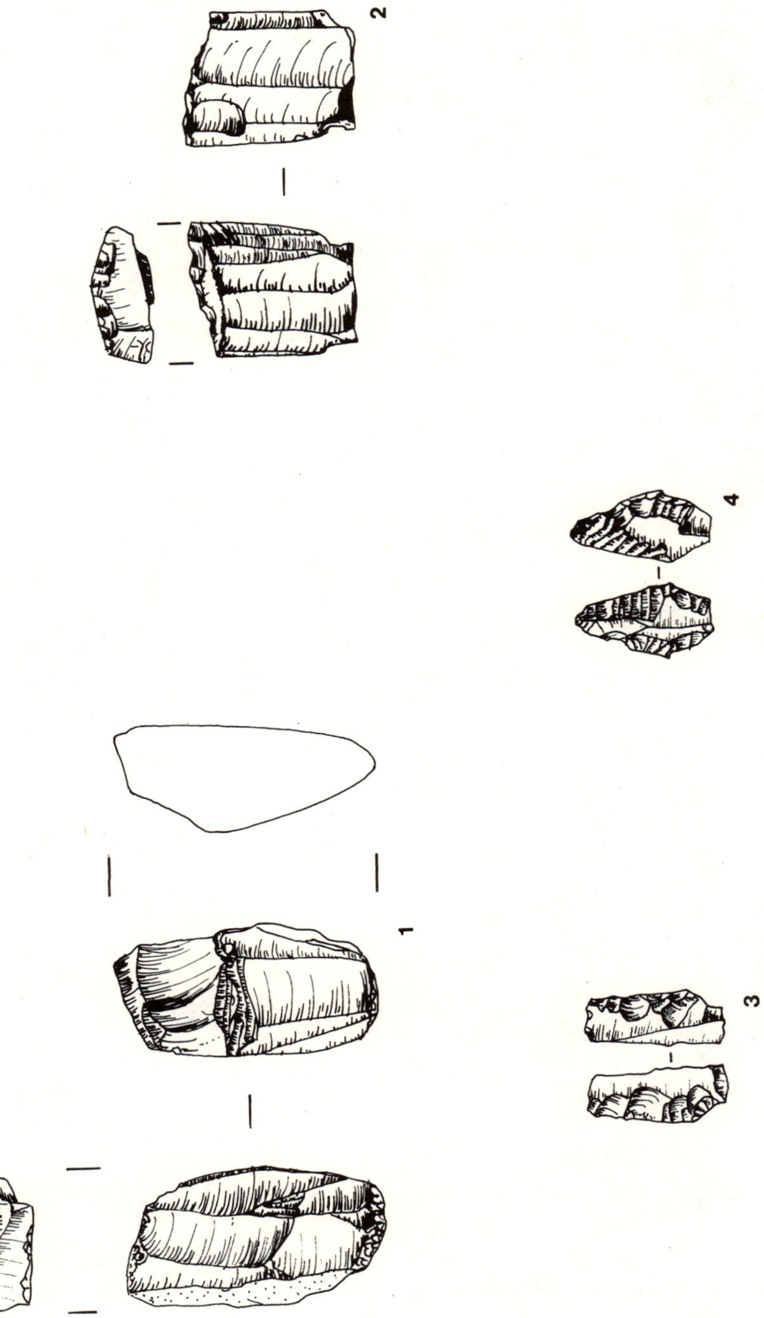

Fig. 76. C29, all obsidian: (1) blade core; (2) blade core; (3) flake with bifacial retouch on one edge; (4) tanged bifacial projectile point.

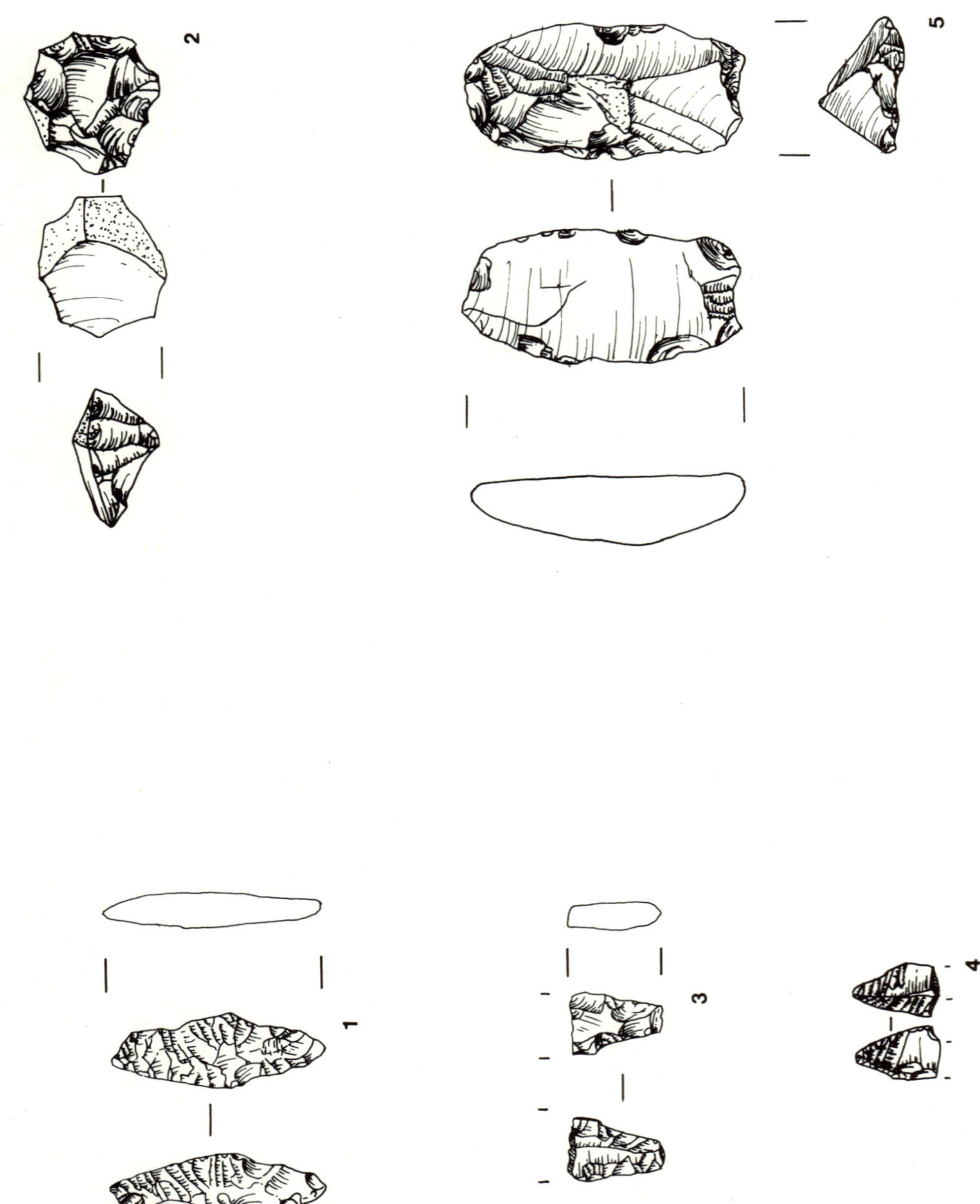

Fig. 77. D3: (1) obsidian tanged bifacial projectile point, the tip repaired by retouched truncation; (2) flint core; (3) obsidian tanged bifacial projectile point; (4) obsidian bifacial projectile point, the tang broken away; (5) flint flake with invasive retouch and splintering.

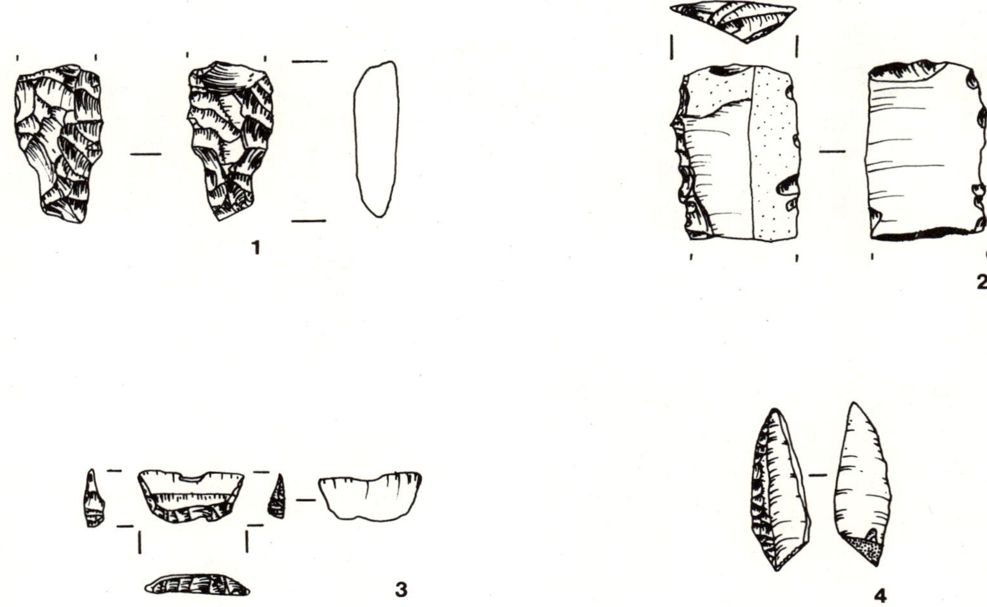

Fig. 78. (1) E3, flint tanged bifacial projectile point; (2) E6, cortical flint sickle element with continuous gloss on left edge and distal truncation; (3) E9, obsidian geometric trapeze with backing and double truncation; (4) E80, flint pointed backed bladelet.

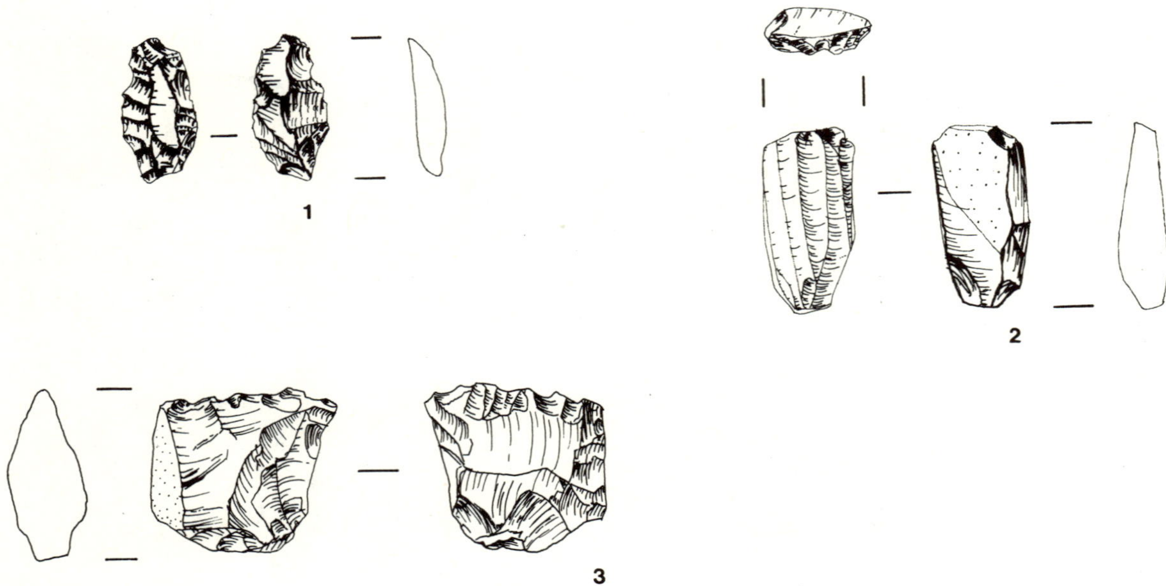

Fig. 79. (1) F4, obsidian bifacially retouched piece; (2) F5, obsidian blade core; (3) F13, flint denticulation on a bifacially retouched piece, probably a sickle element.

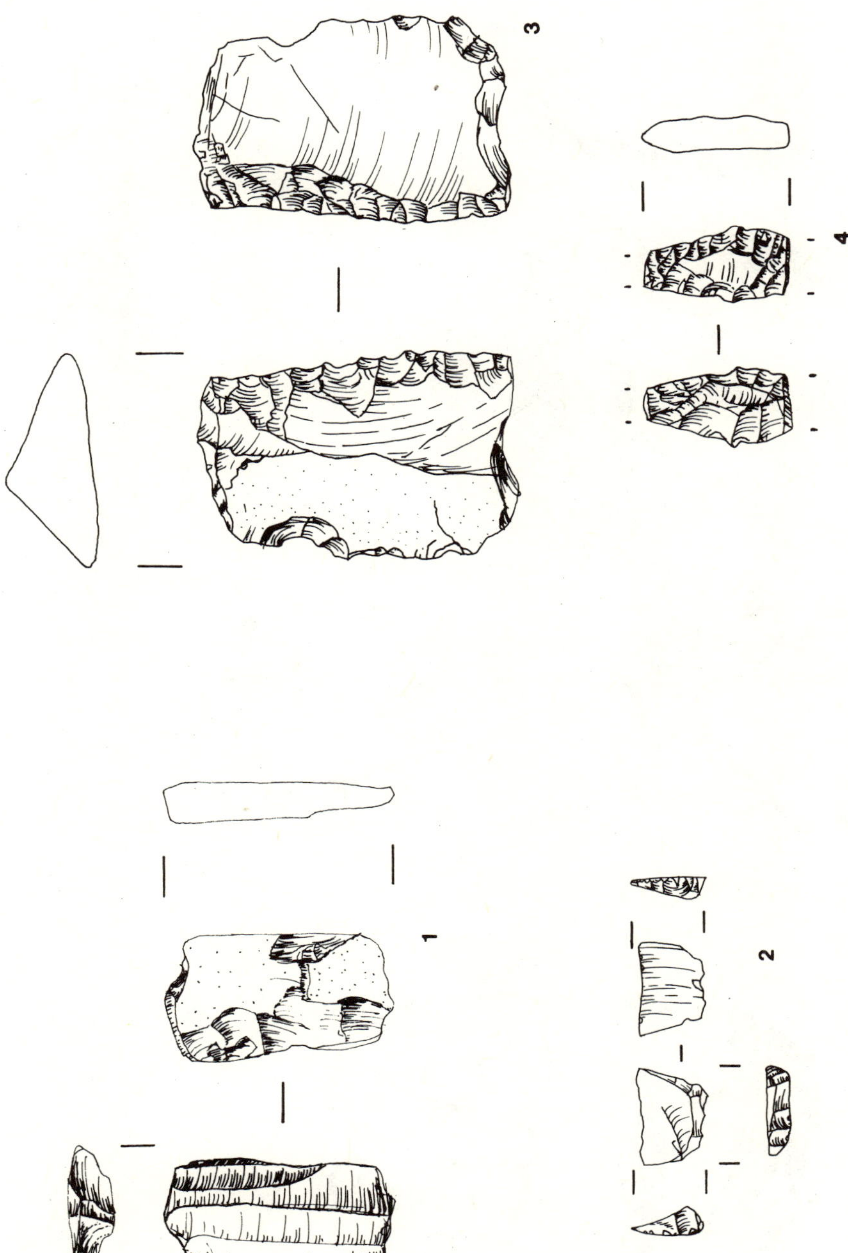

Fig. 80. (1) F20, obsidian blade core; (2) F20, obsidian geometric trapeze with backing and double truncation; (3) F23, cortical flake with continuous denticulation on one edge, a notch, and double truncation: probably a sickle element; (4) obsidian tanged bifacial projectile point.

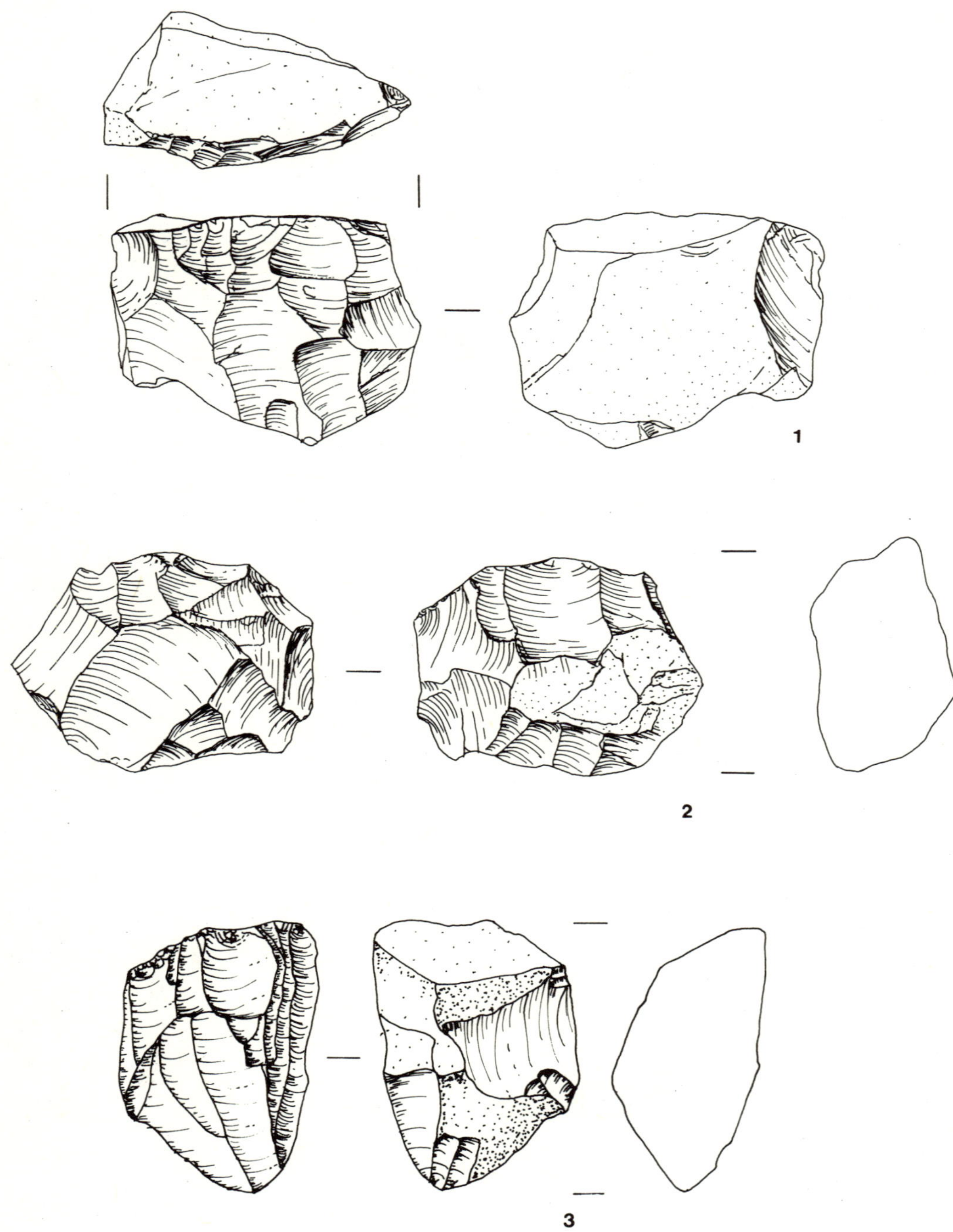

Fig. 81. F25, all flint: (1) core; (2) core; (3) blade core.

Fig. 82. F25, all flint: (1) core; (2) patinated denticulated flake; (3) patinated flake with faceted platform.

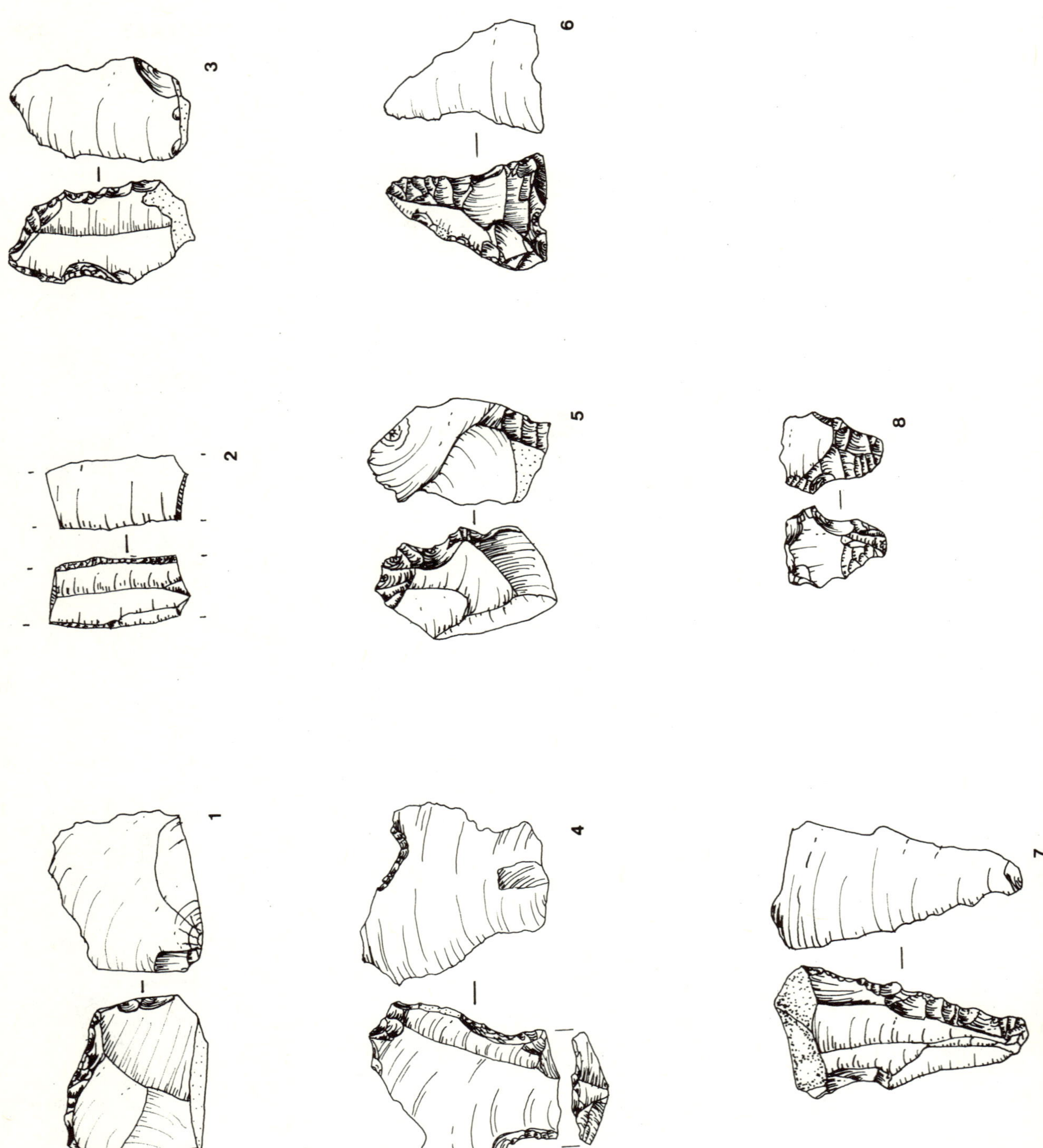

Fig. 83. F25: (1) flint flake with distal retouch; (2) flint backed blade with retouch on one edge; (3) flint denticulated flake; this specimen had a calcium carbonate crust used in dating this site; (4) notched flint flake with faceted platform; (5) flint core with shouldered, nosed end scraper; (6) patinated flint sidescraper on a flake; (7) cortical flint flake with continuous steep retouch on one edge; (8) obsidian tanged piece with bifacial retouch: probably a broken projectile point repaired by distal truncation.

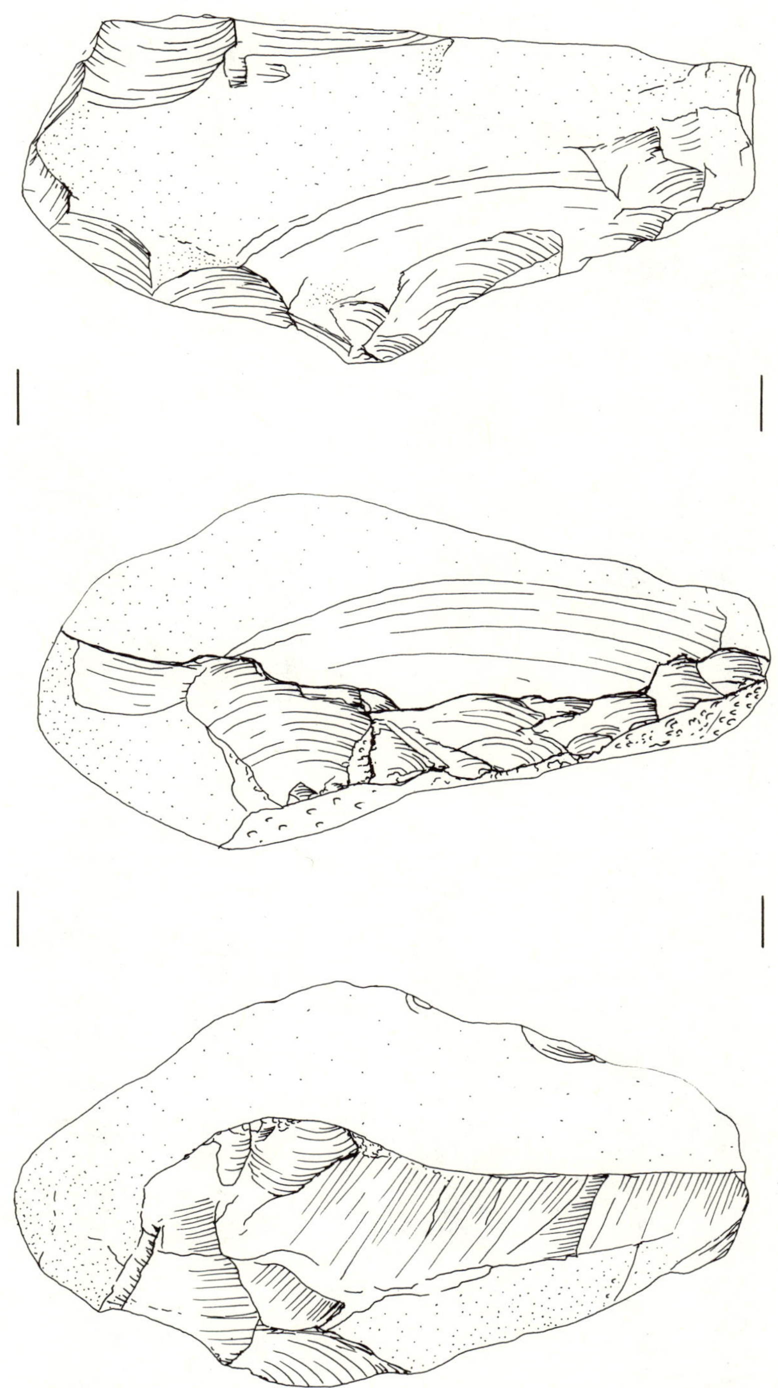

Fig. 84. F25, heavy flint chopping tool.

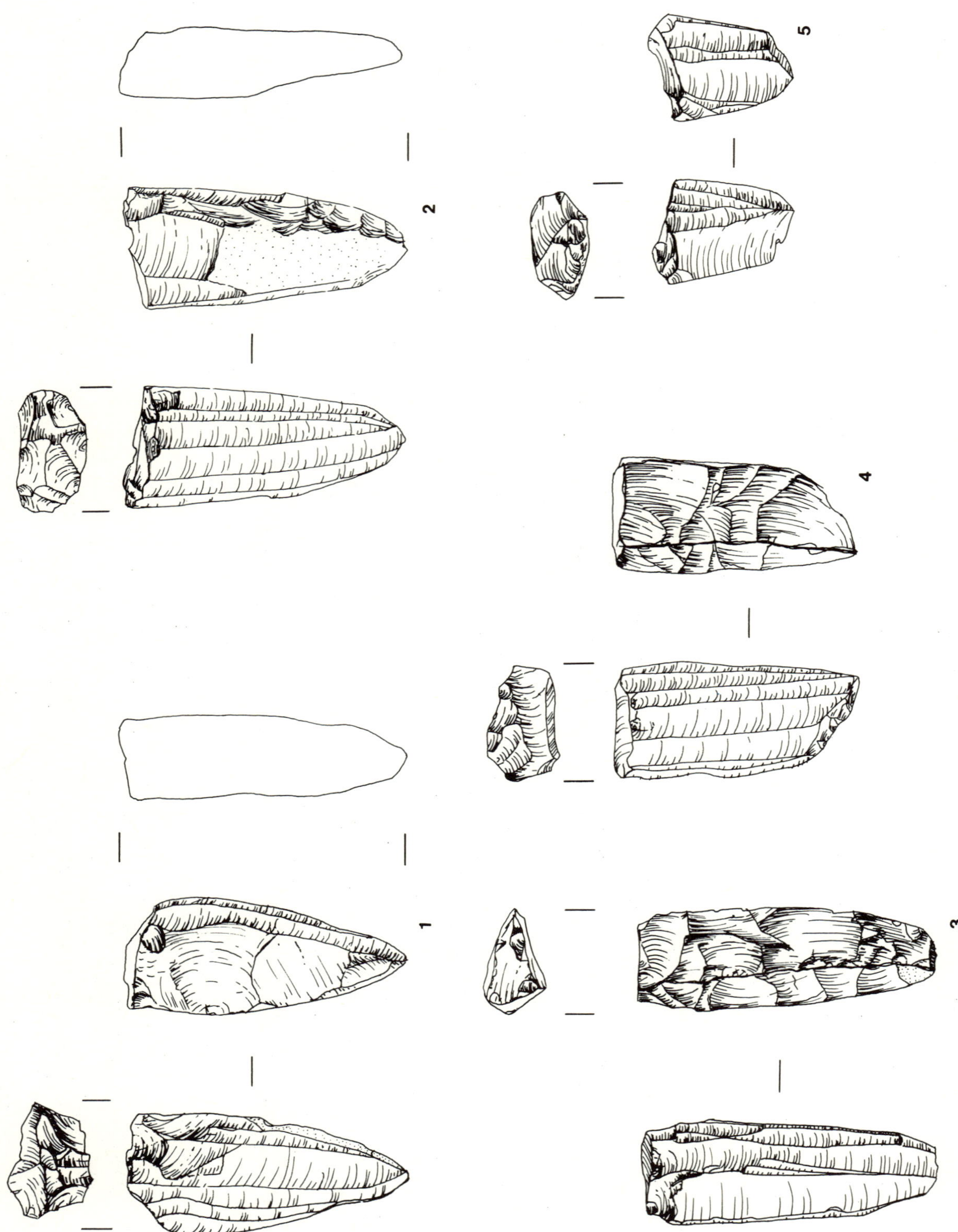

Fig. 85. F32, obsidian blade cores.

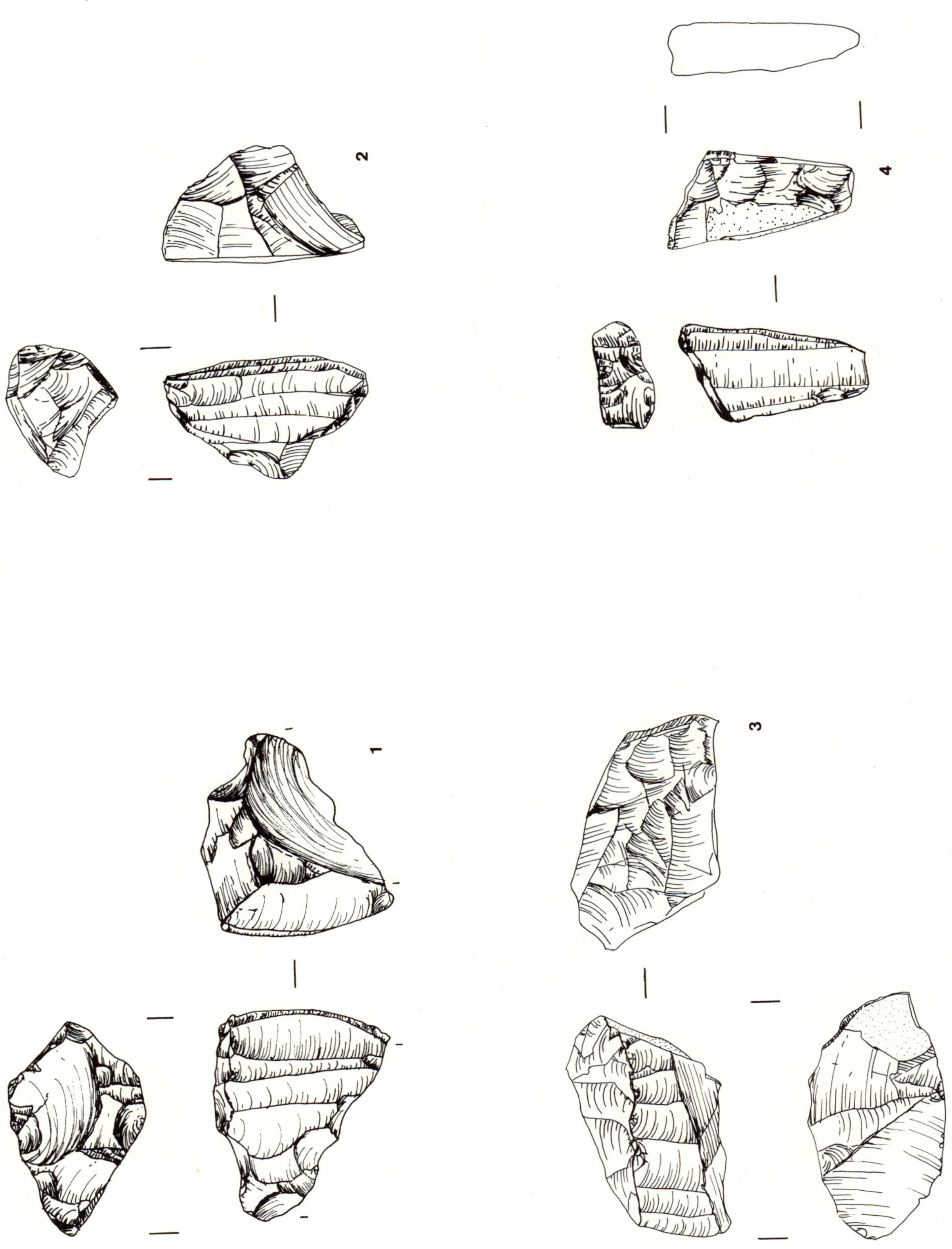

Fig. 86. F32, obsidian blade cores.

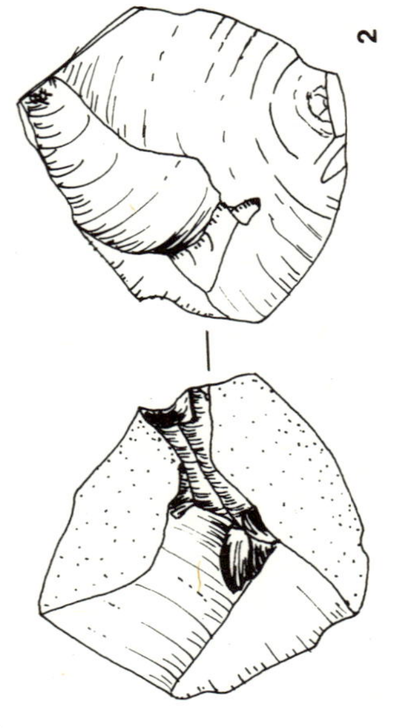

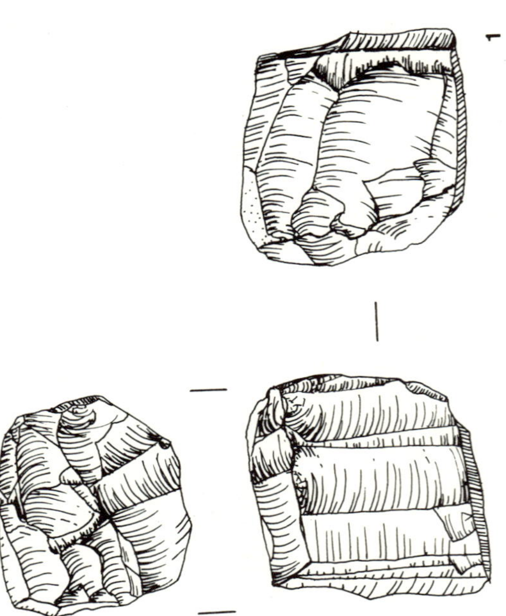

Fig. 87. F32, (1) obsidian blade core; (2) chert cortical flake.

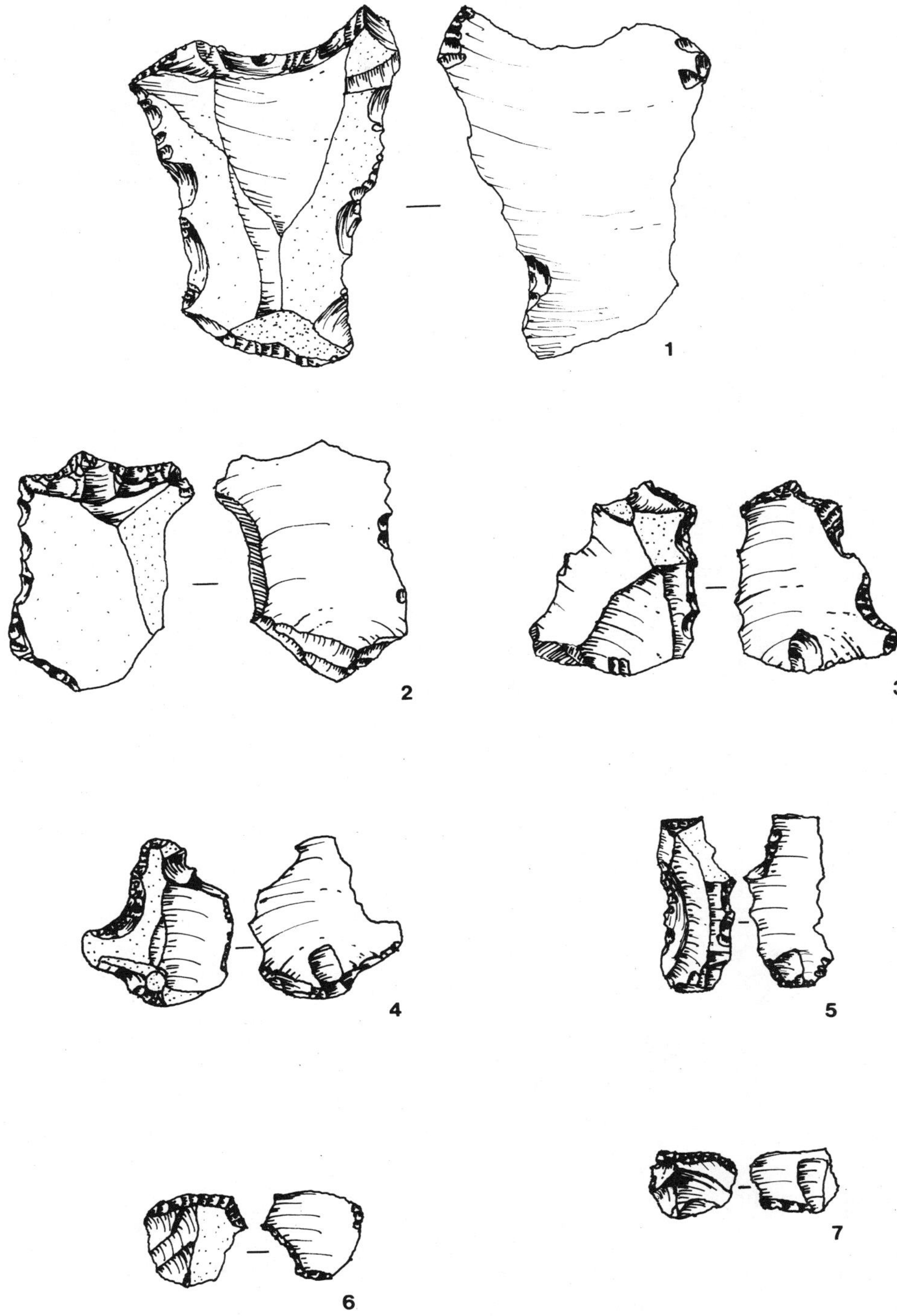

Fig. 88. F32, all obsidian: (1) cortical flake with irregular denticulation; (2) cortical flake with denticulation, perhaps an exhausted perçoir; (3) flake with alternating denticulation on one edge; (4) flake with retouched notch; (5) flake with denticulation and distal truncation; (6) end scraper on a retouched flake; (7) flake with double truncation.

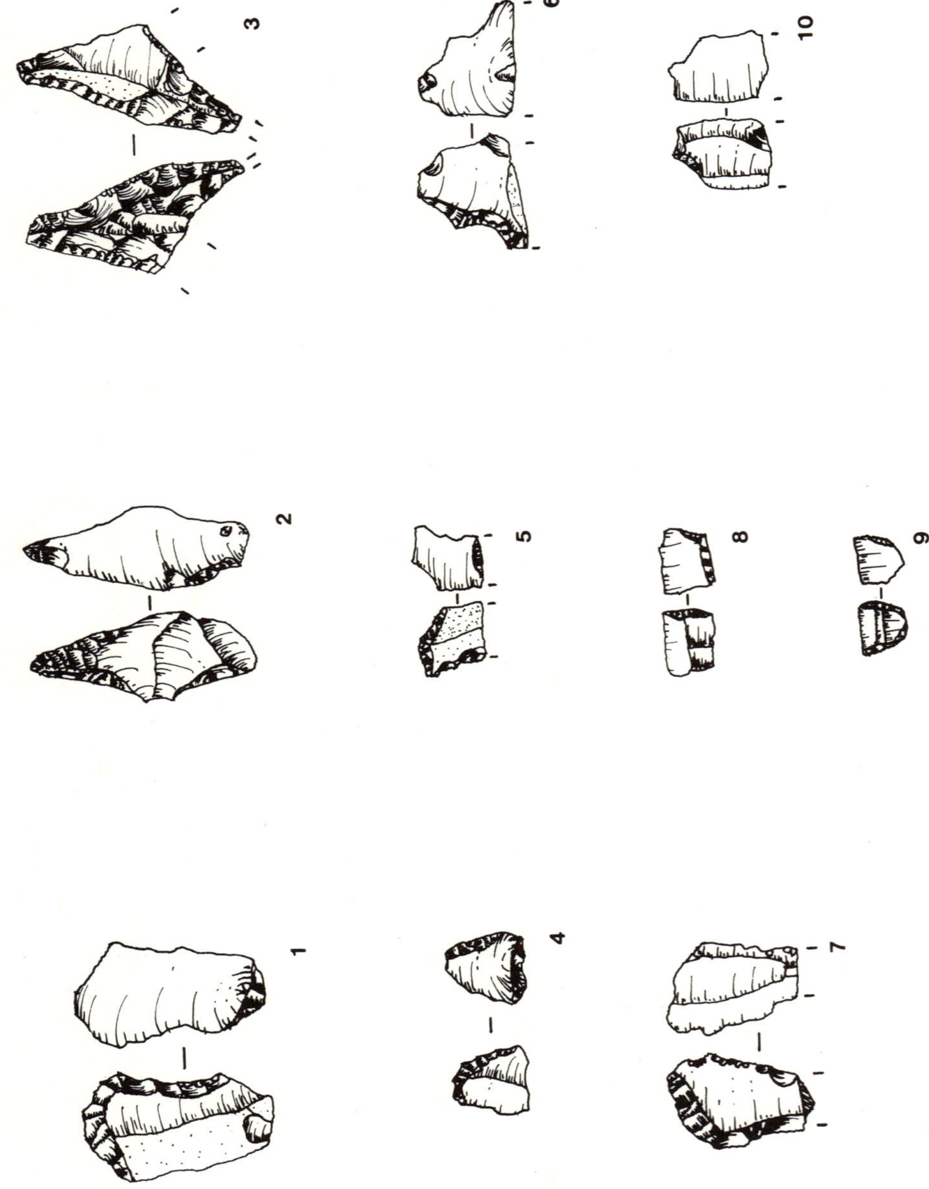

Fig. 89. F32, all obsidian: (1) end scraper on a retouched flake; (2) perçoir on a flake; (3) hollow-based bifacial projectile point; (4) retouched flake; (5) small lateral perçoir on a retouched flake; (6) notched flake; (7) truncated blade; (8) retouched spall (geometric?); (9) geometric with double truncation; (10) small perçoir on a blade.

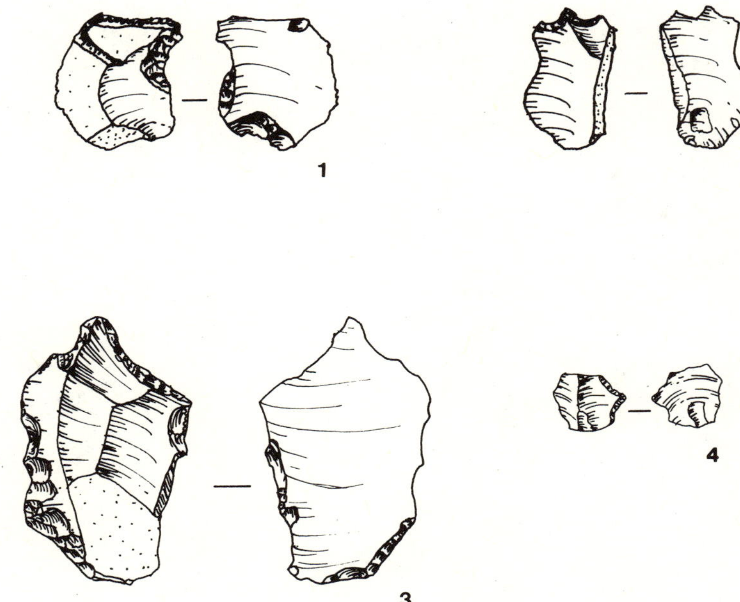

Fig. 90. F32, all obsidian: (1) lateral perçoir on a notched flake; (2) perçoir on a flake; (3) perçoir on a denticulated cortical flake; (4) small lateral perçoir on a flake.

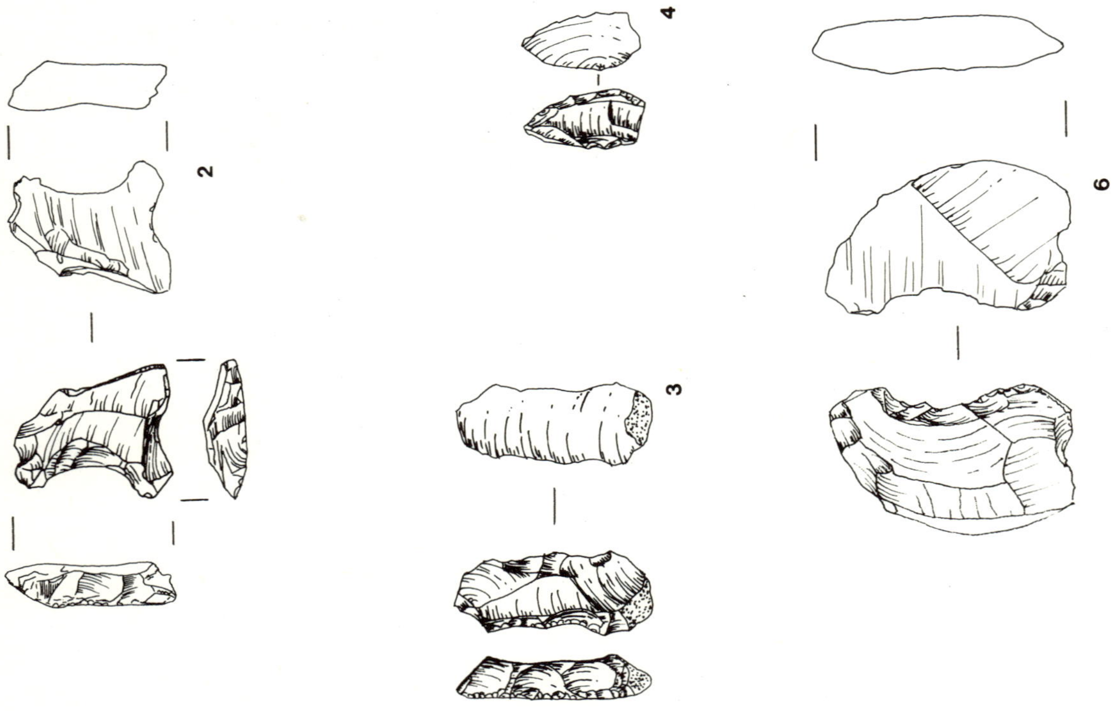

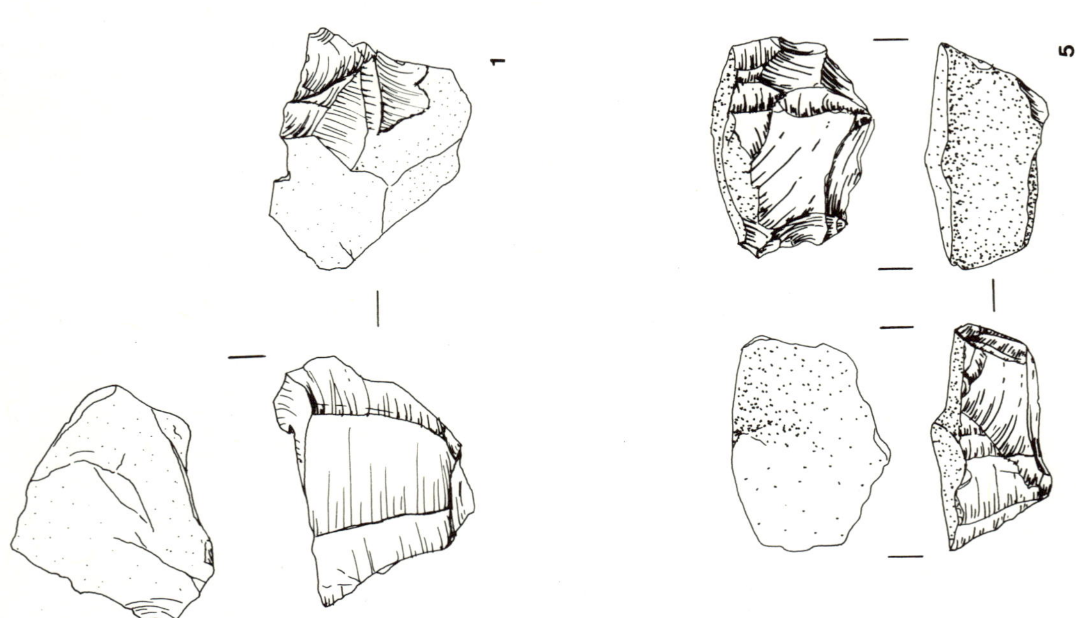

Fig. 91. F35, all flint: (1) core; (2) notch on a faceted flake; (3) backed flake; (4) flake with continuous steep retouch on one edge; (5) core; (6) notched flake.

Fig. 92. (1) G9, flint sickle element with faceted platform, continuous gloss on left edge, and denticulation on right edge; (2) G9, obsidian sickle element with continuous invasive retouch on left edge preserving traces of gloss; (3) sample 2556, a typical example of historical glass sherd with continuous retouch on one edge.

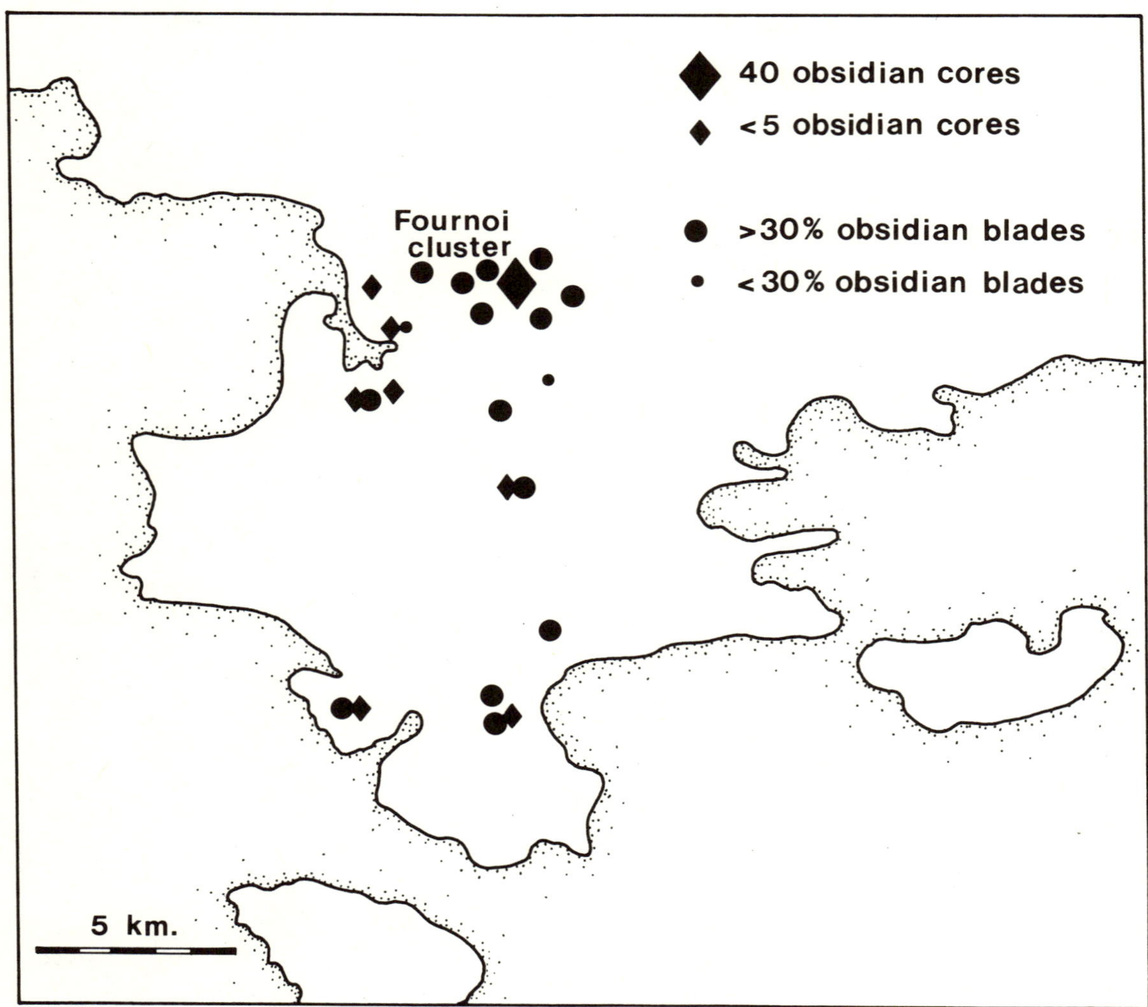

Fig. 93. Map showing the distribution of obsidian cores and obsidian blades in the Southern Argolid.

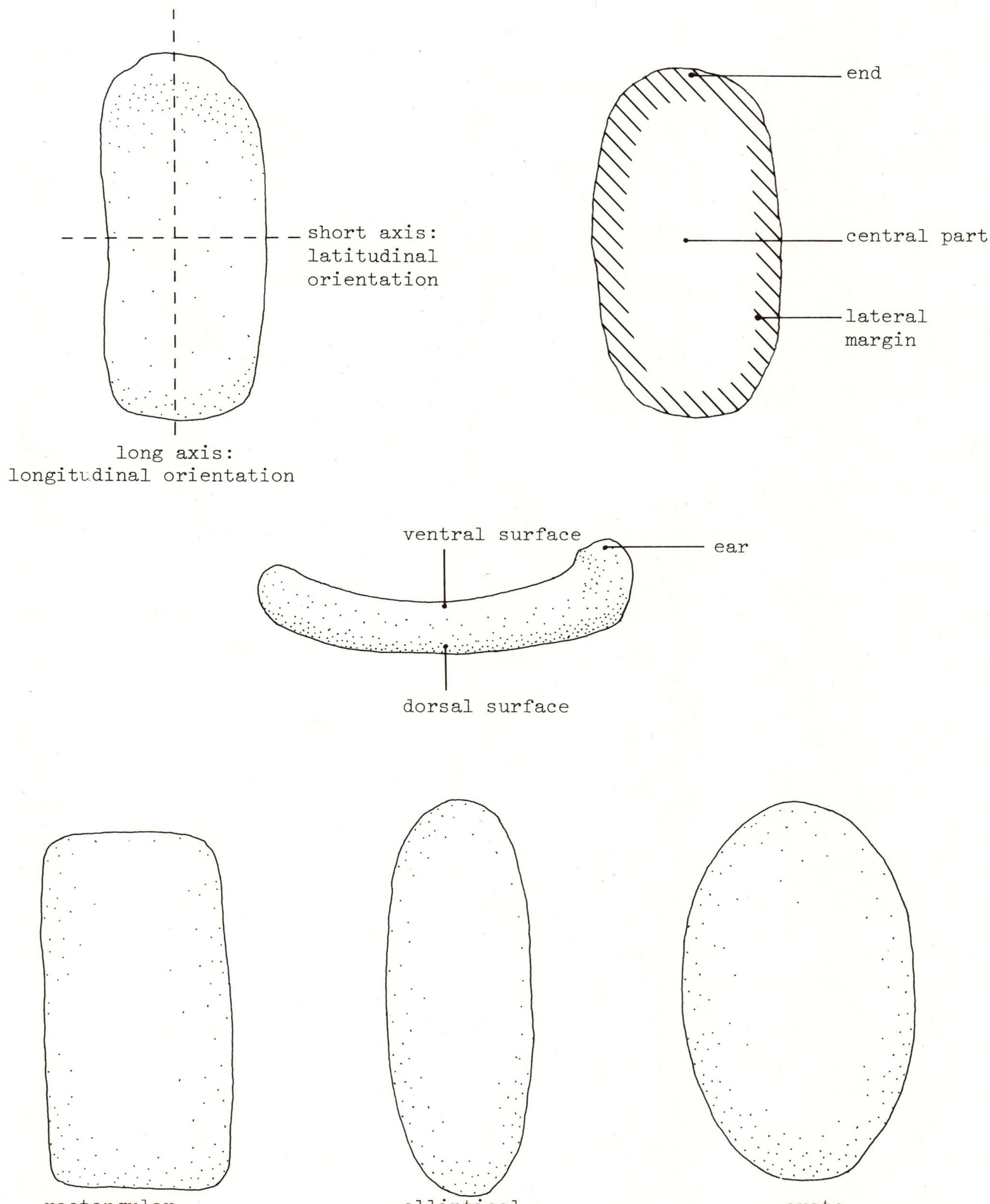

Fig. 94. Glossary of terms used to describe prehistoric saddle querns.

ELLIPTICAL HANDSTONES

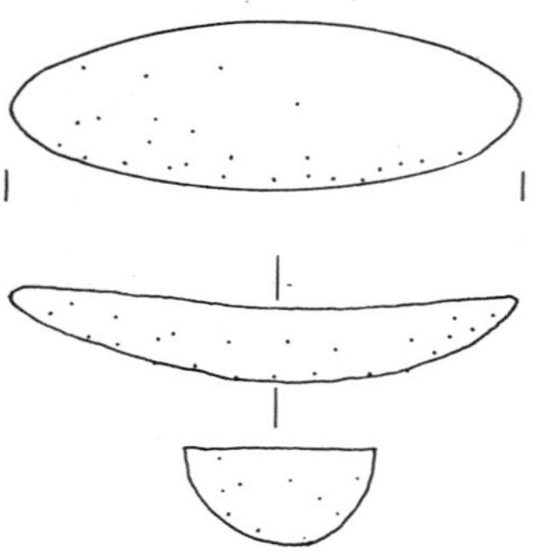

with hemispherical section

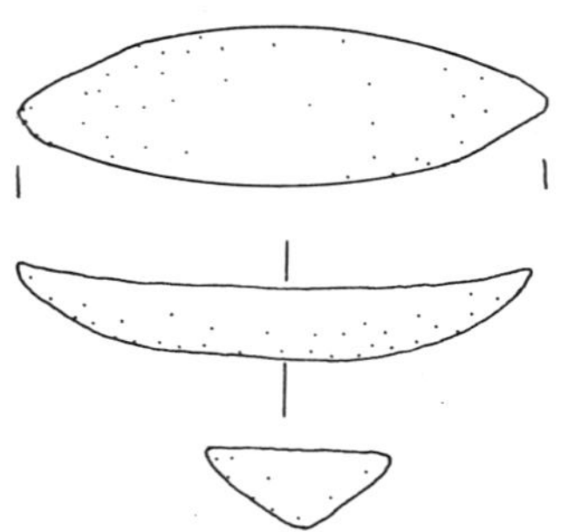

with carinated section

HOPPER MILL

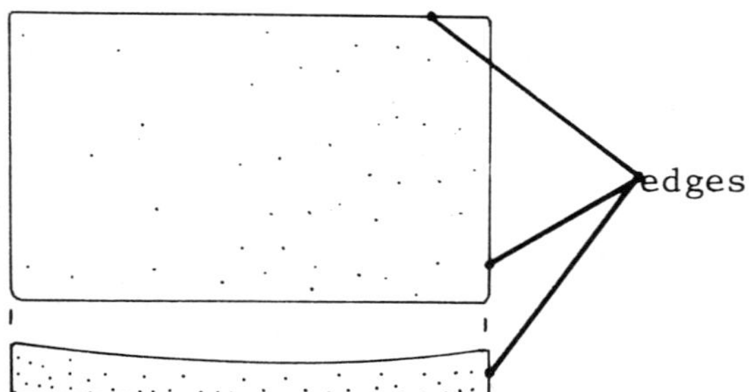

Fig. 95. Glossary of terms used to describe handstones and hopper mills.

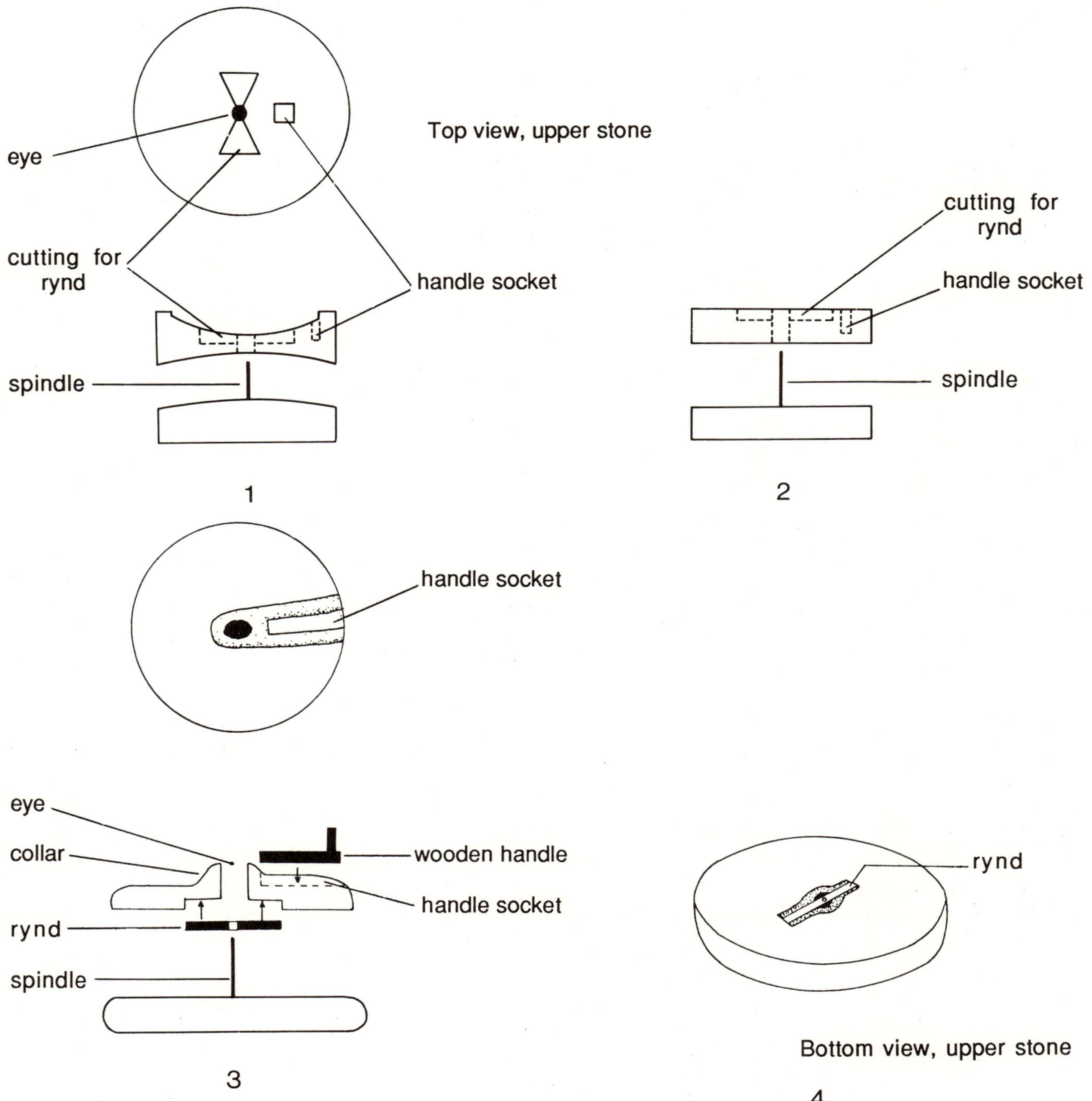

Fig. 96. The topography of the rotary quern. (1) Roman hopper quern. Note that the rynd, typically a small wooden or iron bar with a perforation for the spindle, is located on the top of the upper stone. (2) Roman flat quern with cutting for the rynd on the top of the upper stone. (3) Medieval-Modern flat quern with a raised collar around the eye. Note that the rynd is located on the bottom of the upper stone. (4) Bottom view of the upper stone, showing the placement of the rynd, which is smaller in width than the diameter of the eye. This difference allows the passage of grain through the eye, thus to be ground between the stones. The narrow hole for accommodating the spindle serves to prevent the upper stone from moving too far down the spindle. Thus the upper stone is kept from touching the lower stone, leaving a space for the grain. [Drawing from Runnels 1990.]

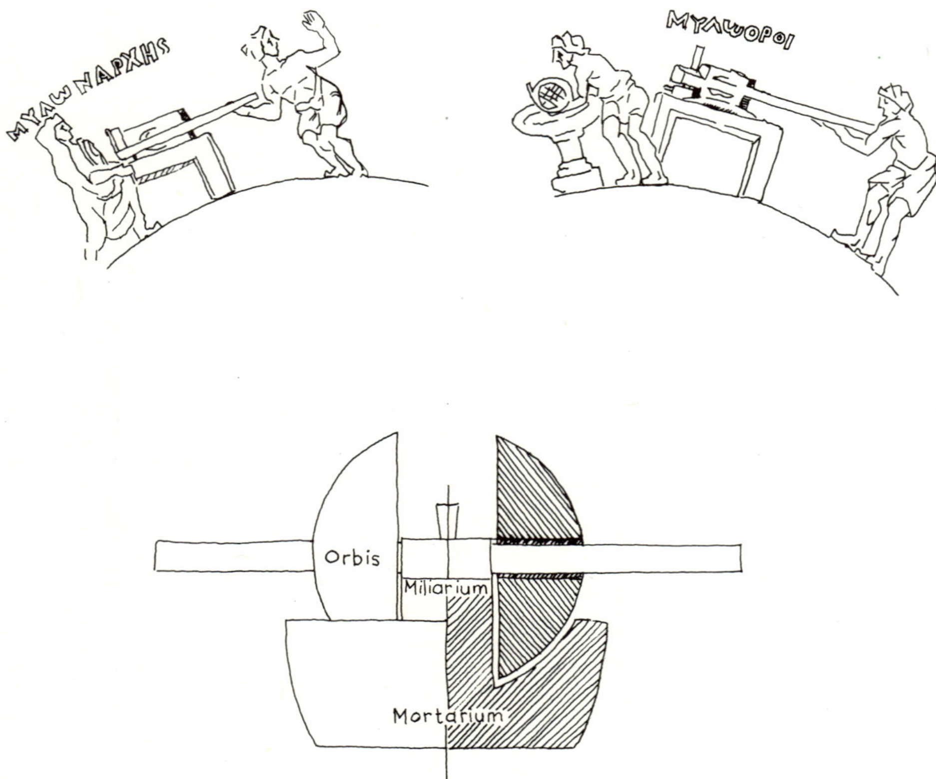

Fig. 97. Drawing (top) from so-called Megarian bowls, showing hopper mill in use. A slave operates the mill with a long handle attached to a pivot on a table. The handle is laid into the handle slots of the upper stone of the mill. The mill is shown from above, in the perspective of the ancient artist, to show the hopper. Drawing (bottom) of a trapetum, or Roman olive mill.

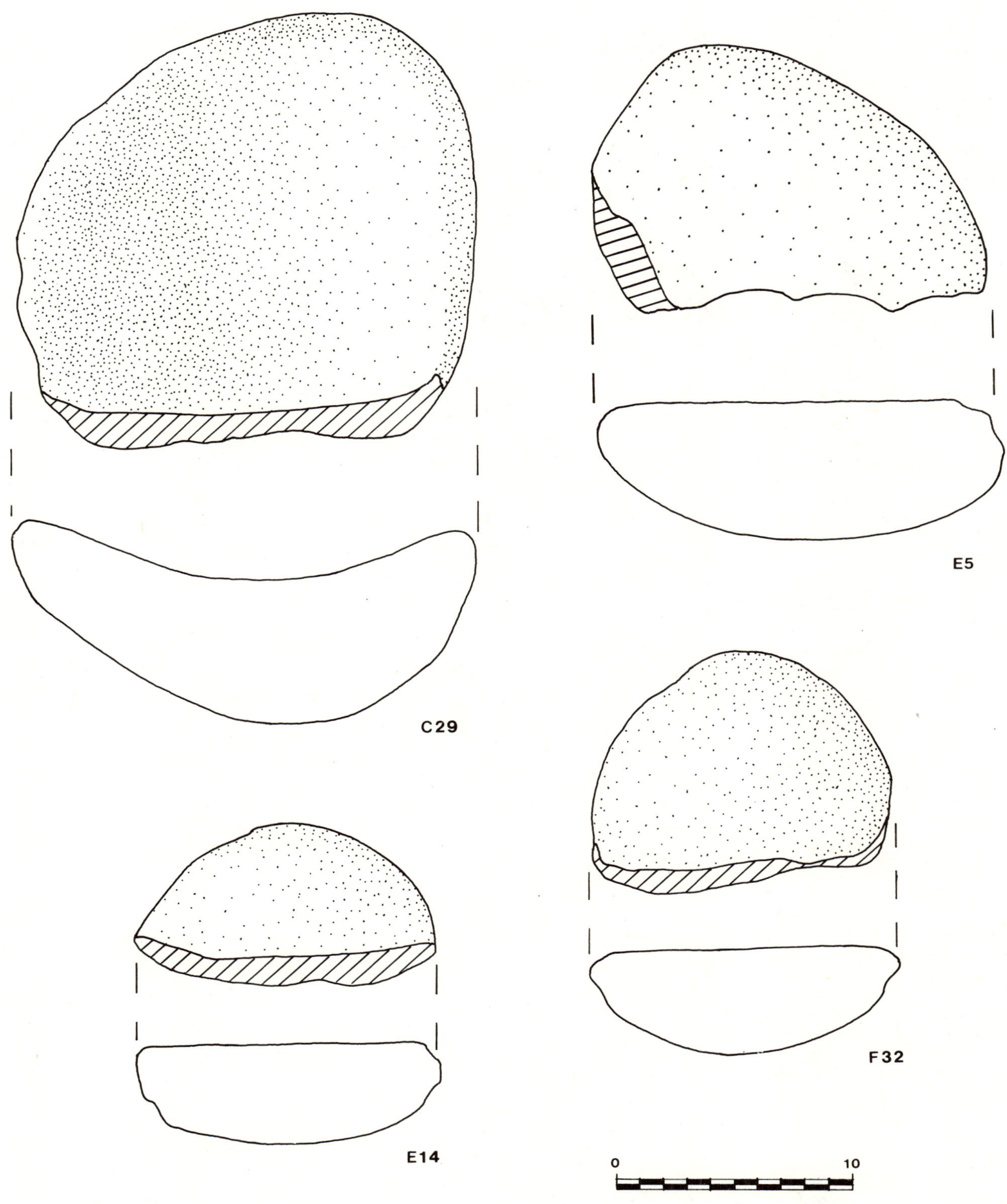

Fig. 98. Neolithic saddle querns: C29, conglomerate, and E14, sandstone. Bronze Age saddle querns: E5, conglomerate, and F32, andesite.

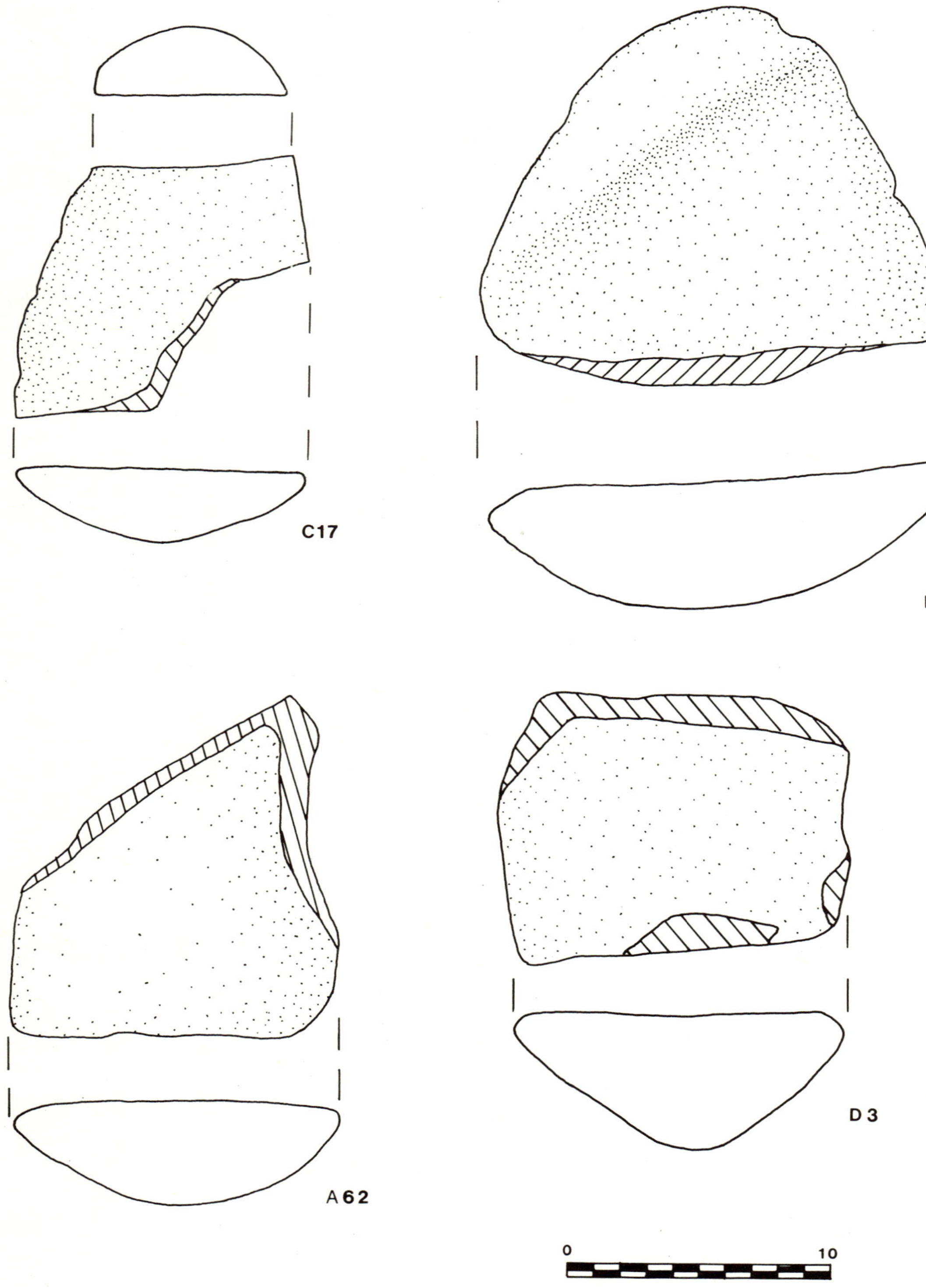

Fig. 99. Handstones: D3, Late or Final Neolithic?, andesite; E74, Late Bronze Age, andesite; A62, Late Classical, andesite; C17, Geometric to Roman, andesite.

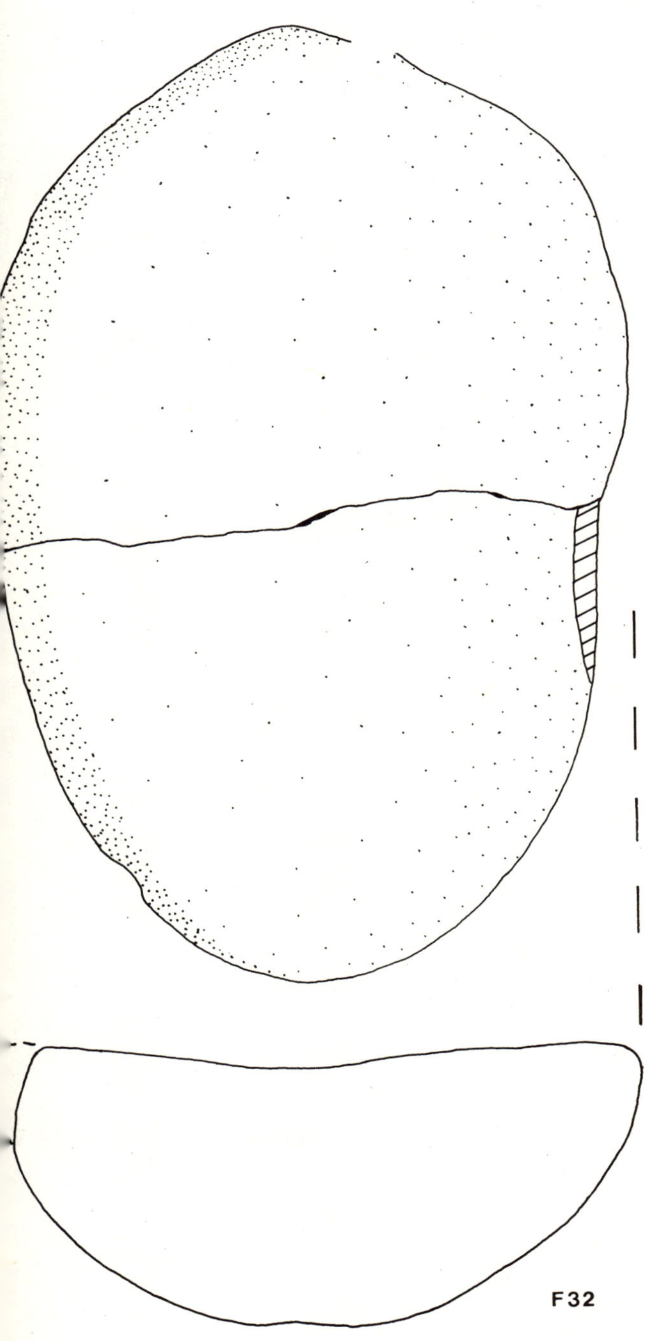

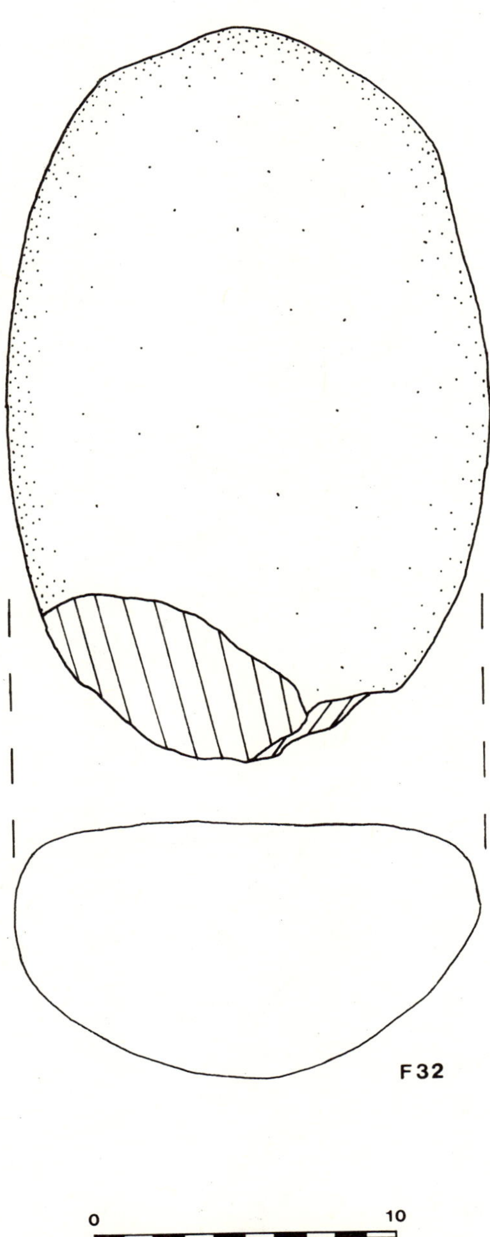

Fig. 100. Early Bronze Age, andesite saddle querns.

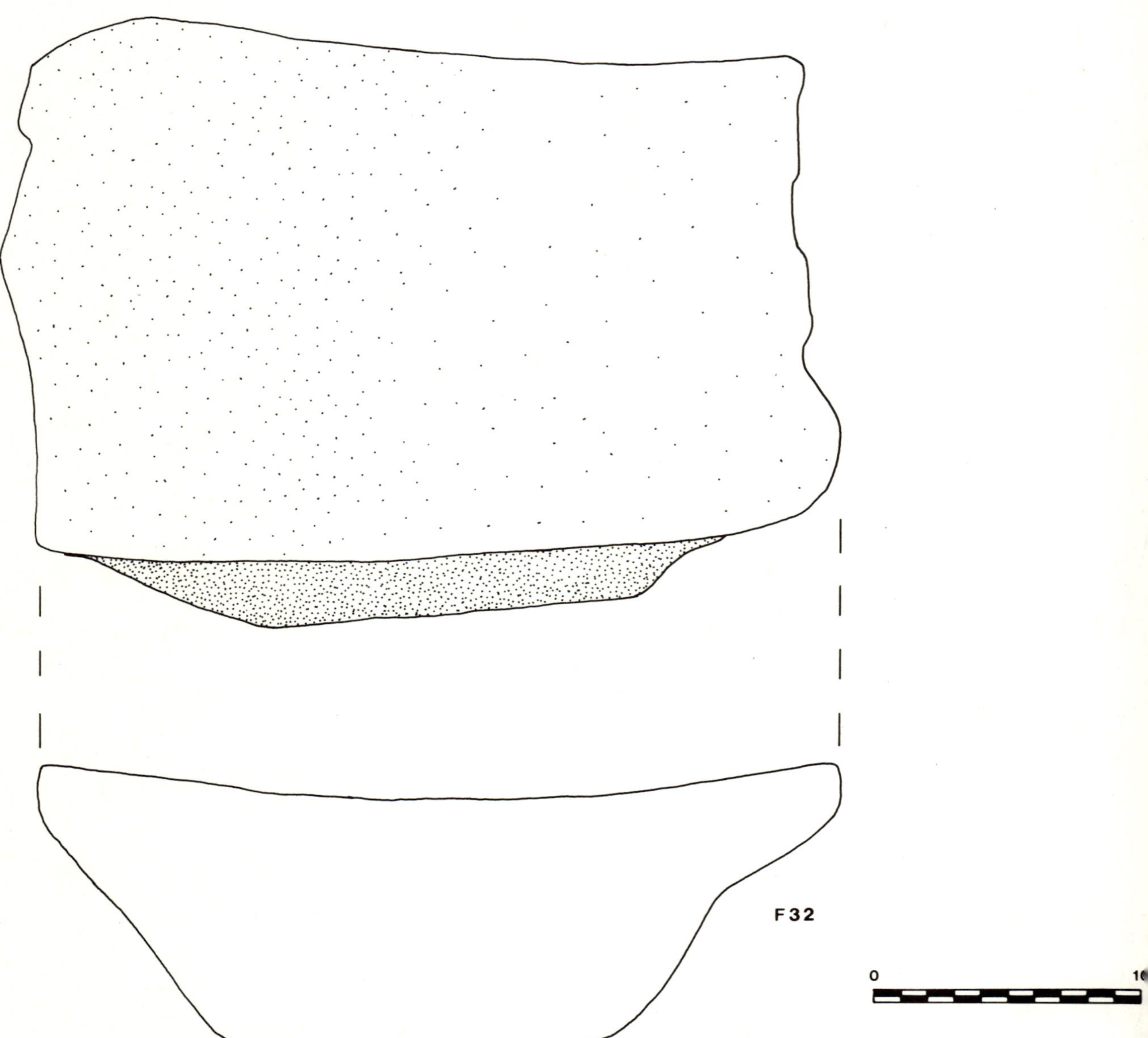

Fig. 101. Early Bronze Age, andesite saddle quern.

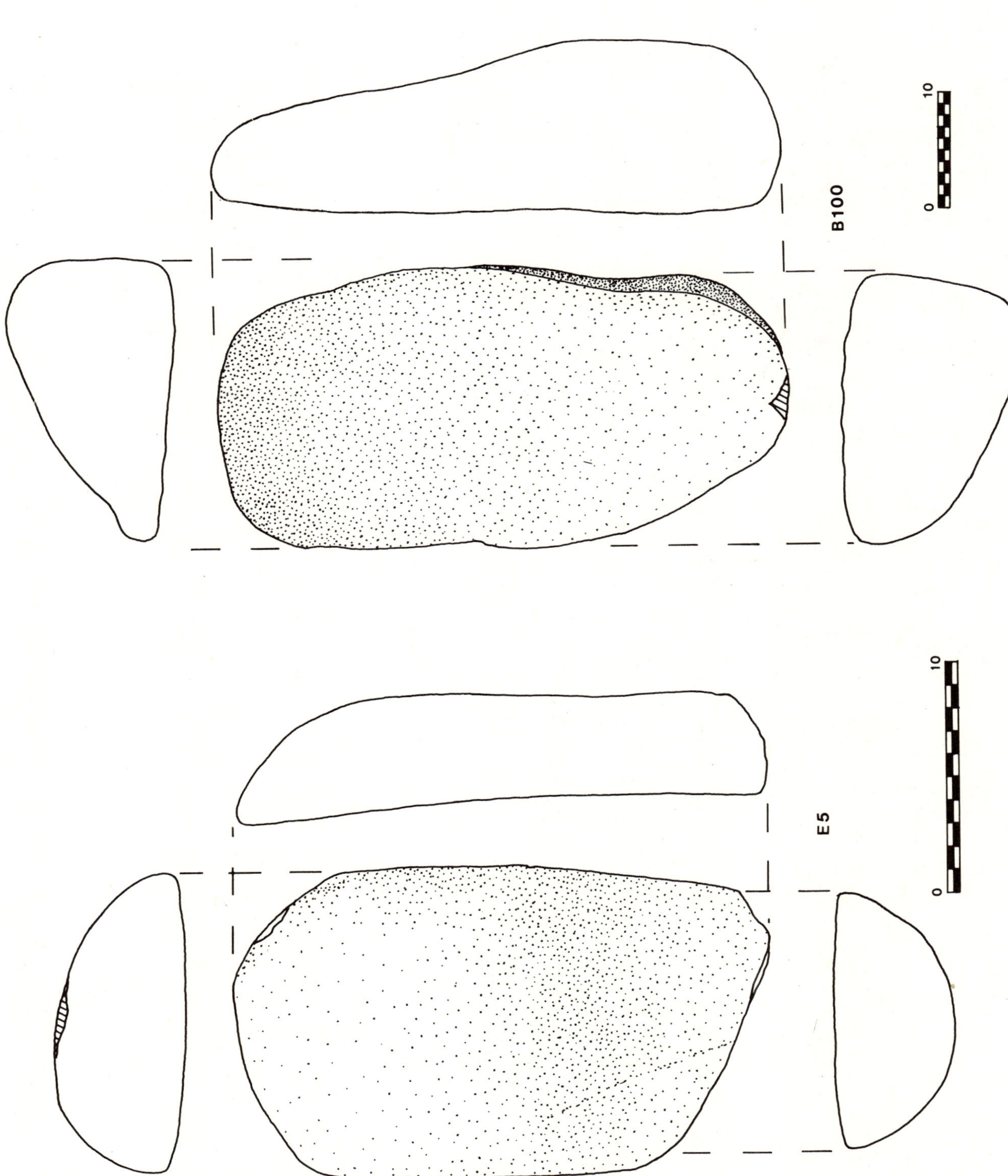

Fig. 102. Bronze Age, andesite saddle querns.

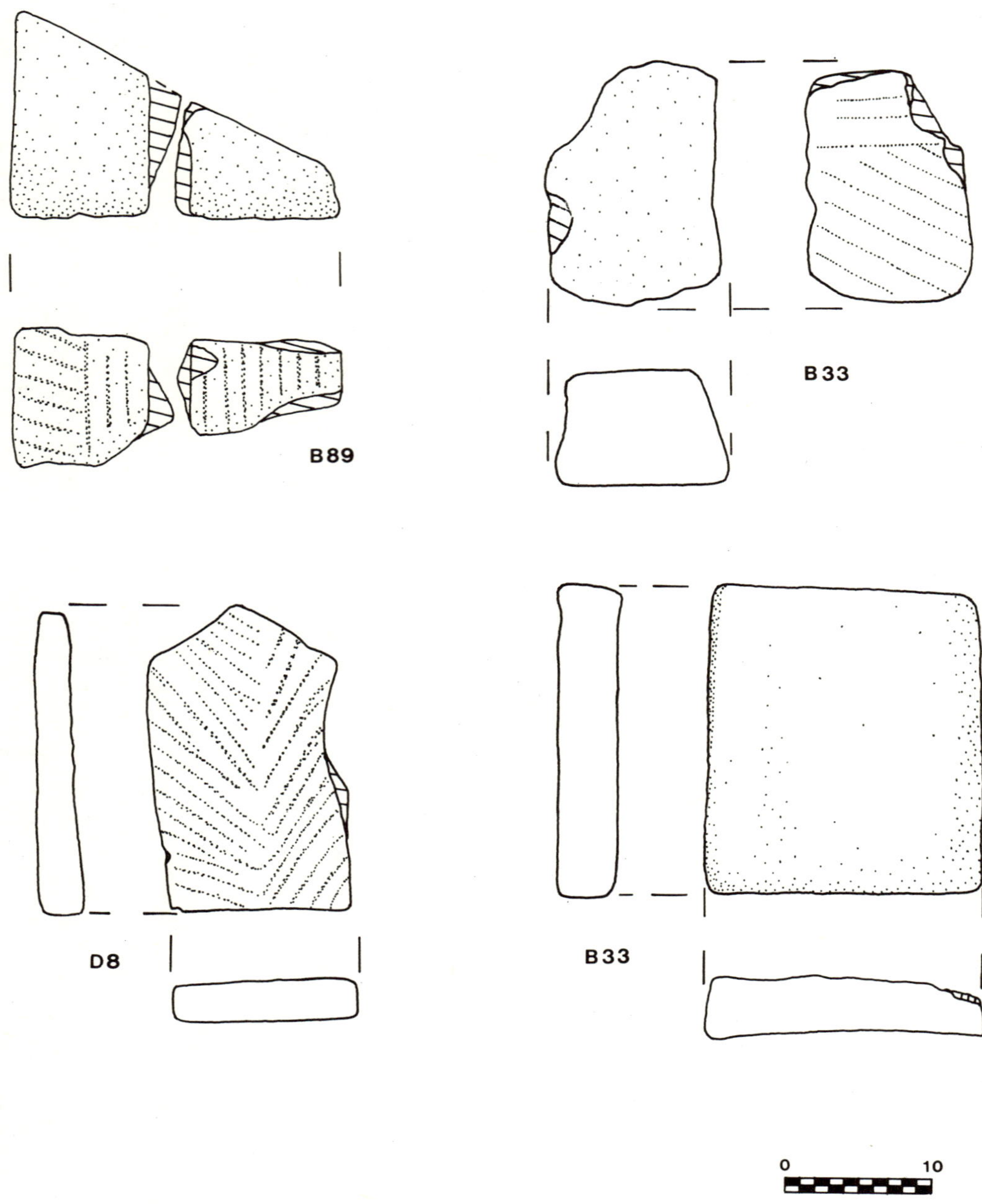

Fig. 103. Late Classical andesite grinding slabs with herringbone furrow patterns (B89, B33, and D8); small, plain andesite grinding slab (B33).

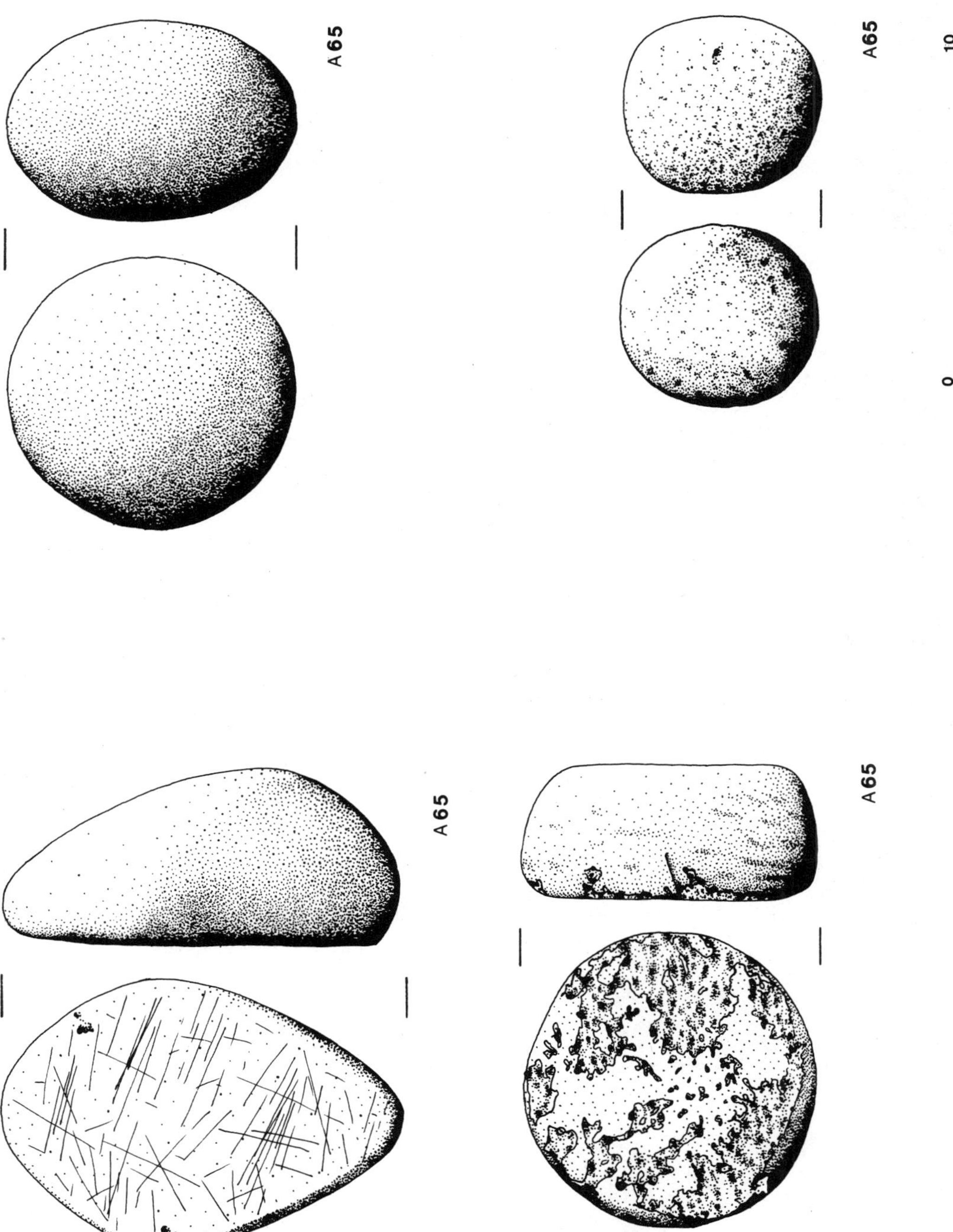

Fig. 104. Late Classical–Early Hellenistic handstones of hard igneous greenstone from Halieis (A65). The example on the left has percussive use-wear, and the example on the right has abrasive use-wear. [Drawings by Martha Breen (1978).]

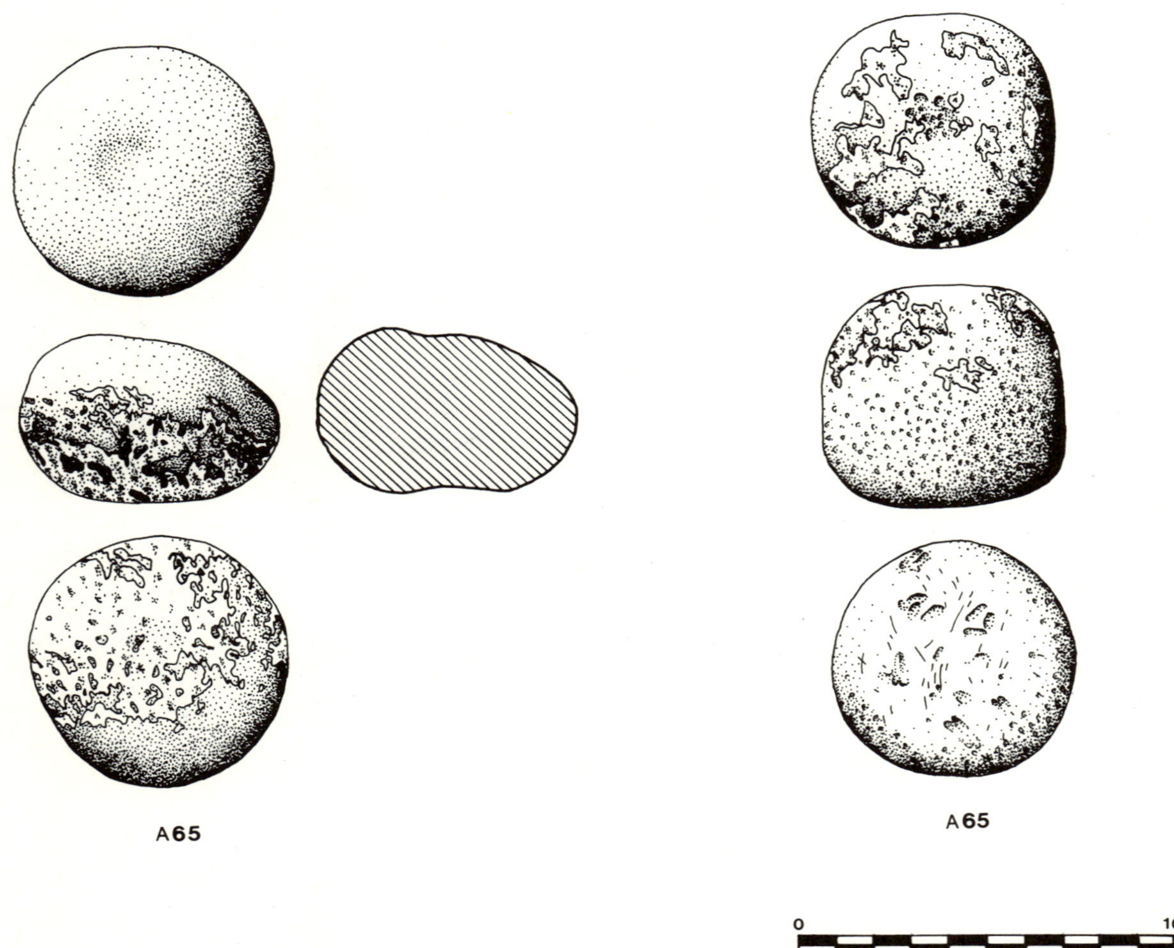

Fig. 105. Late Classical–Early Hellenistic handstones of hard igneous greenstone from Halieis (A65). All show extensive abrasive use-wear. [Drawings by Martha Breen (1978).]

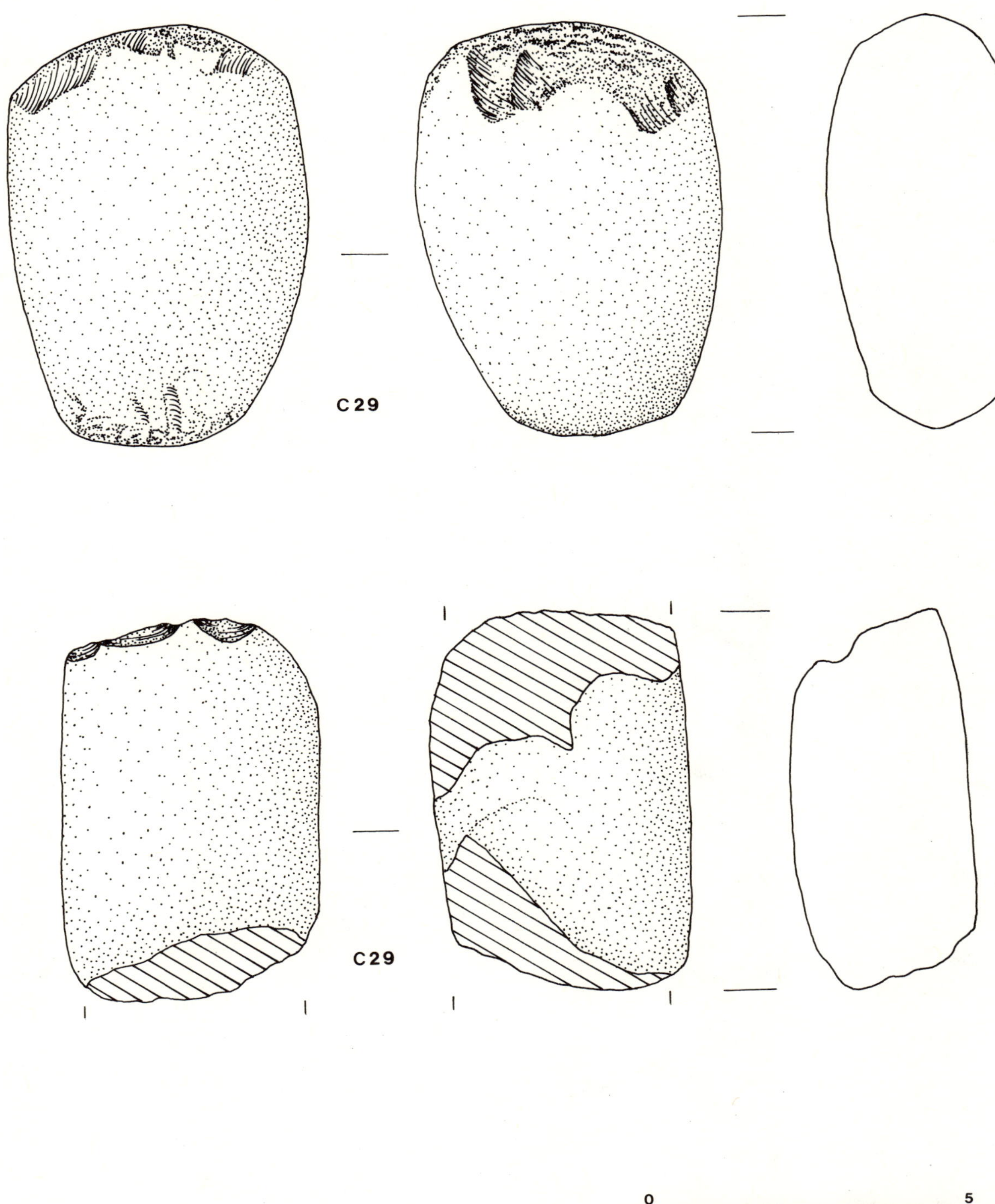

Fig. 106. Final Neolithic handstones or re-used celts of hard igneous greenstone. Both show extensive hard-percussion use-wear.

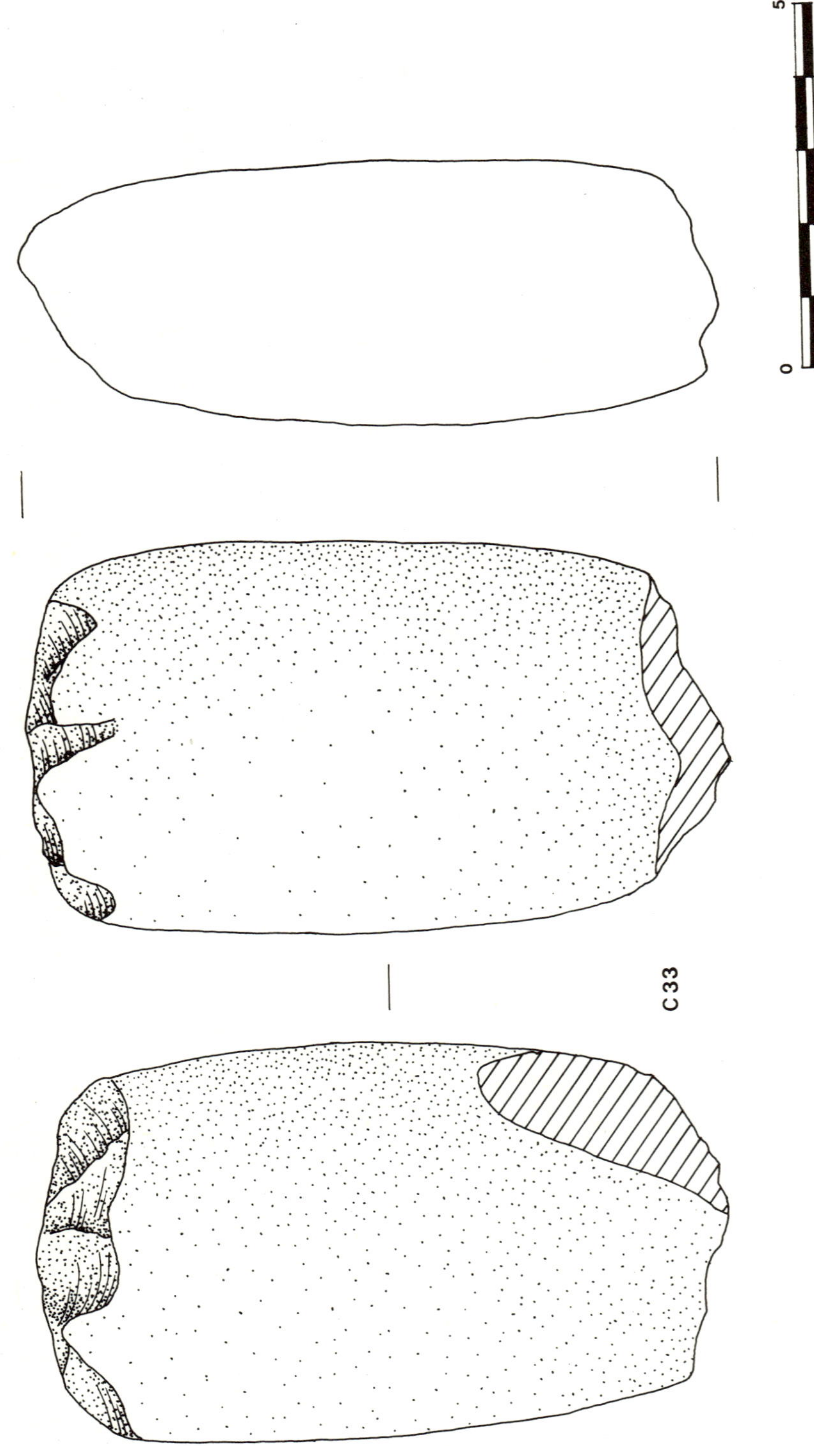

Fig. I07. Probable Neolithic celt of hard igneous greenstone re-used as handstone, showing extensive hard-percussion use-wear.

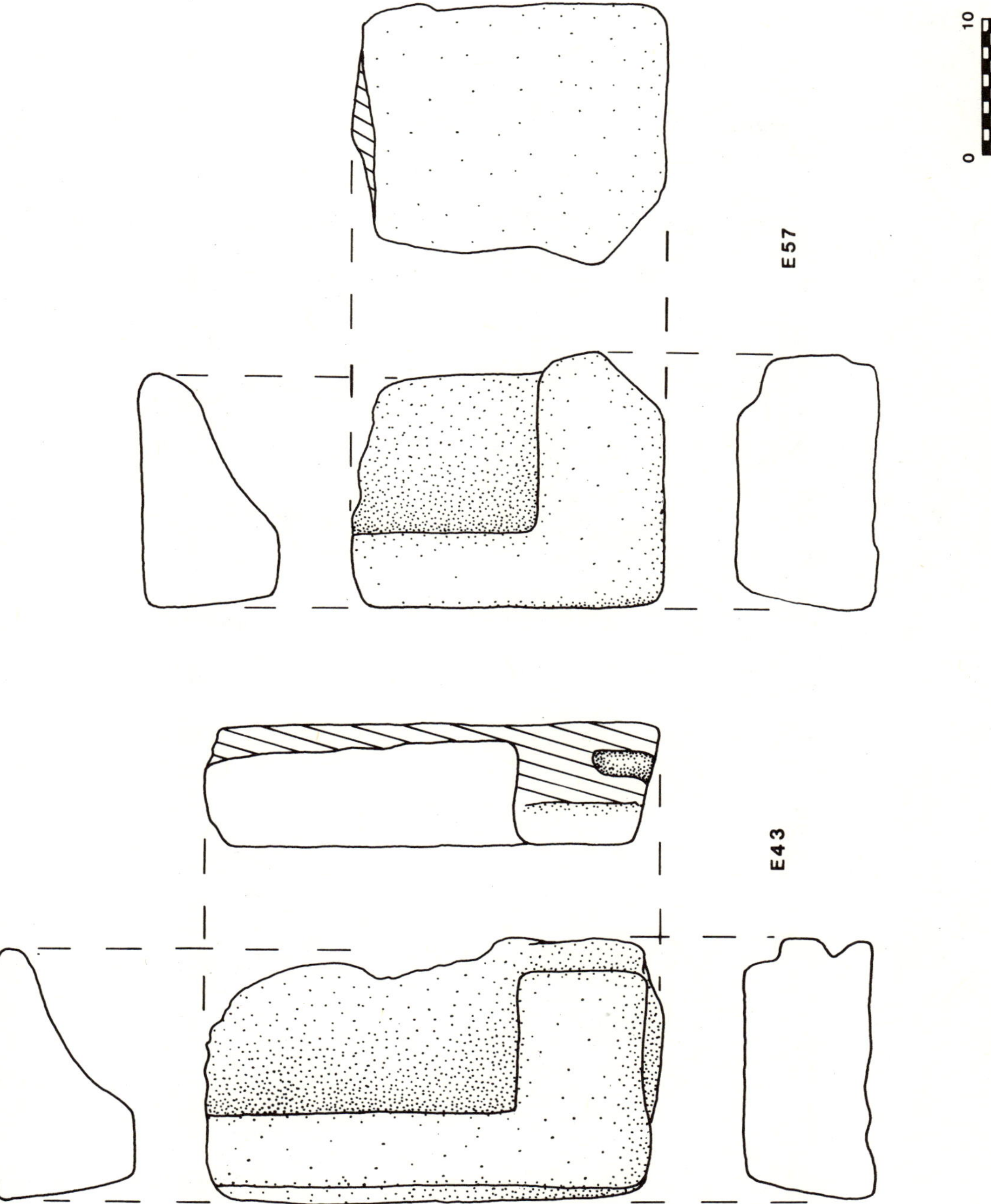

Fig. 108. Late Classical or later andesite hopper mills. One example (E43) preserves trace of a handle slot and a cutting let into the outer edge that was used to secure the handle to the table pivot. [Drawing from Runnels 1990.]

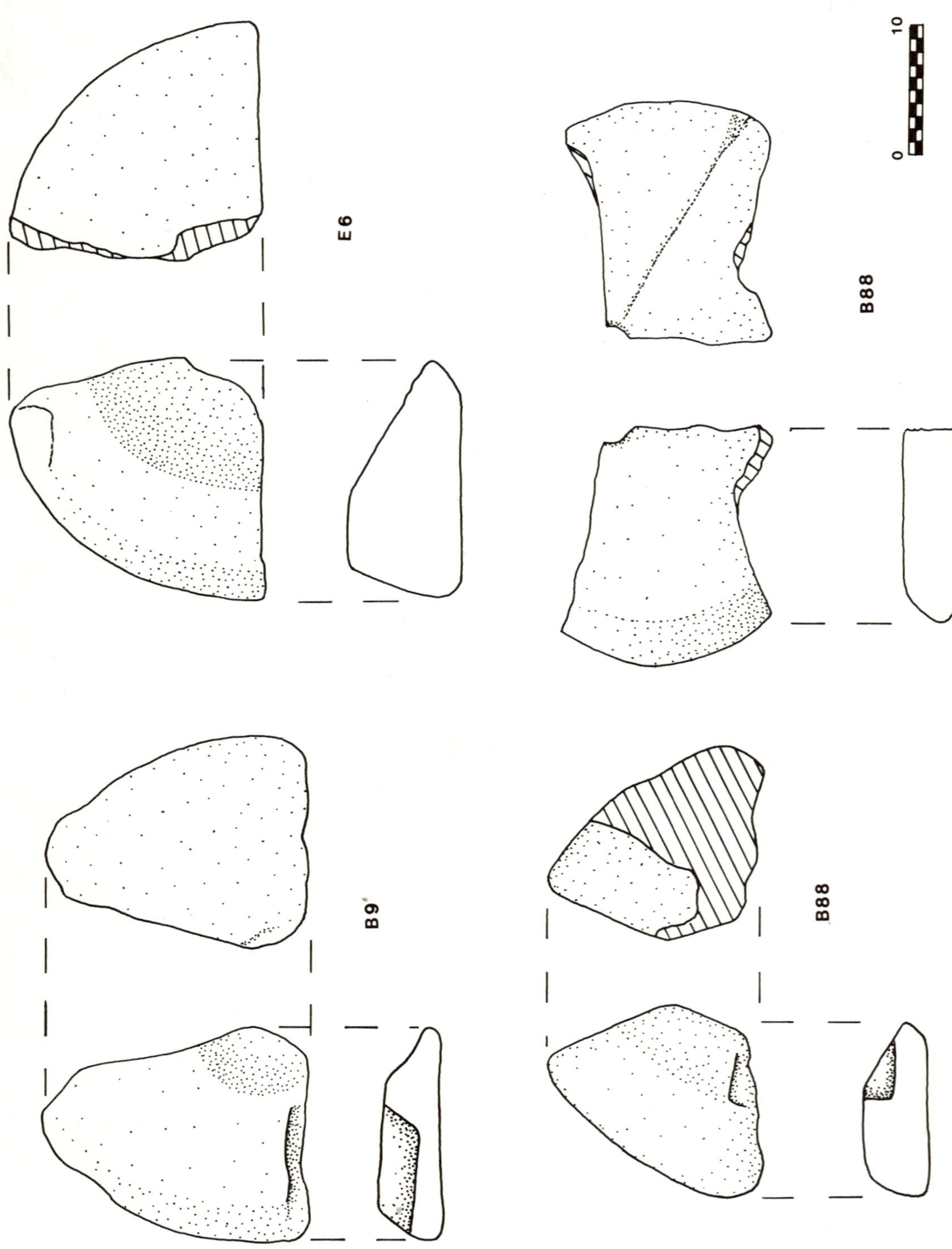

Fig. 109. E6, B88 (bottom, left): Roman rotary hopper querns, upper stones, andesite. B88 (bottom, right): Roman rotary flat quern, upper stone, andesite. B9: Medieval-Modern rotary flat quern, upper stone, andesite. Traces of handle slot cuttings are visible on B9, E6, and B88 (bottom, left). [Drawing from Runnels 1990.]

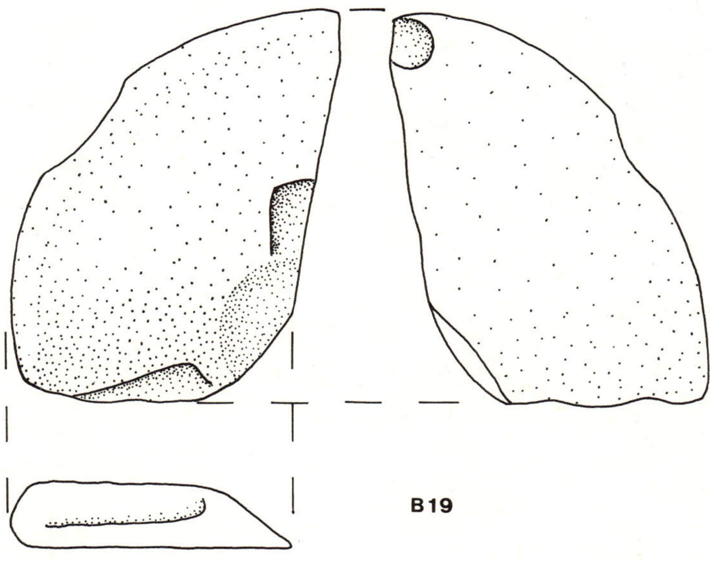

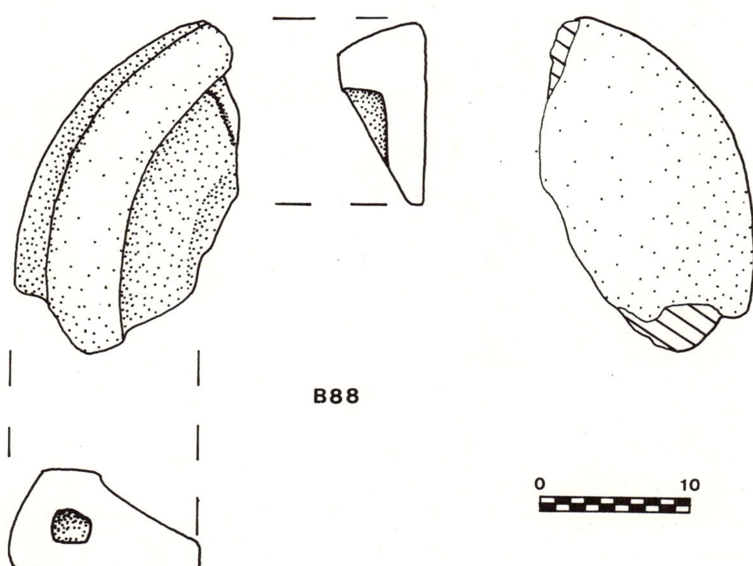

Fig. 110. B19, Late Roman rotary flat quern, upper stone, andesite, preserving traces of handle slot and rynd cuttings. B88, Late Roman rotary hopper quern, upper stone, andesite, preserving handle slot cutting on interior of hopper. [Drawing from Runnels 1990.]

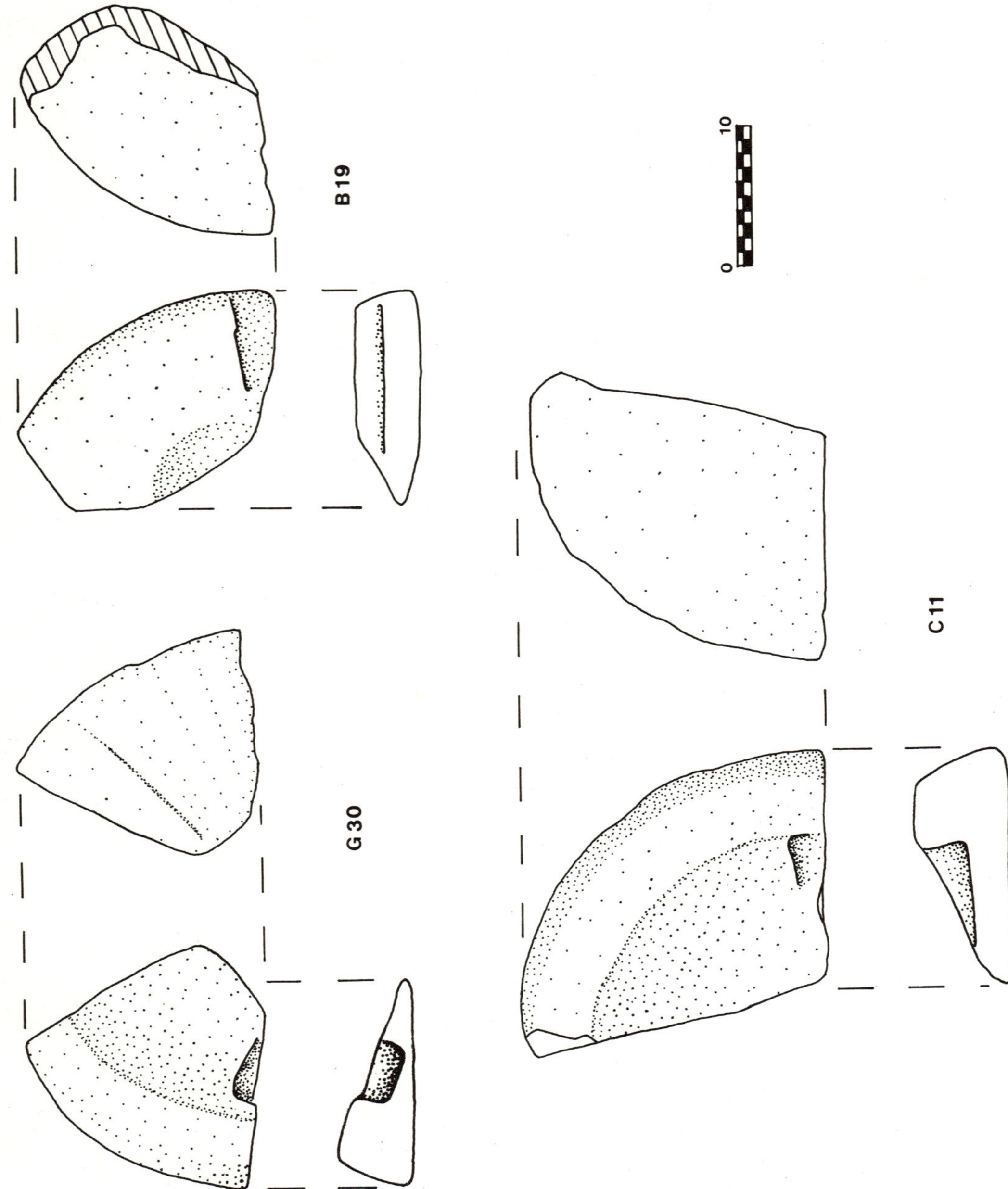

Fig. 111. G30, C11, Late Roman rotary hopper querns, upper stones, andesite, preserving traces of rynd cuttings, or handle slot cuttings; B19, Late Roman rotary flat quern, upper stone, andesite, preserving trace of handle slot cutting. [Drawing from Runnels 1990.]

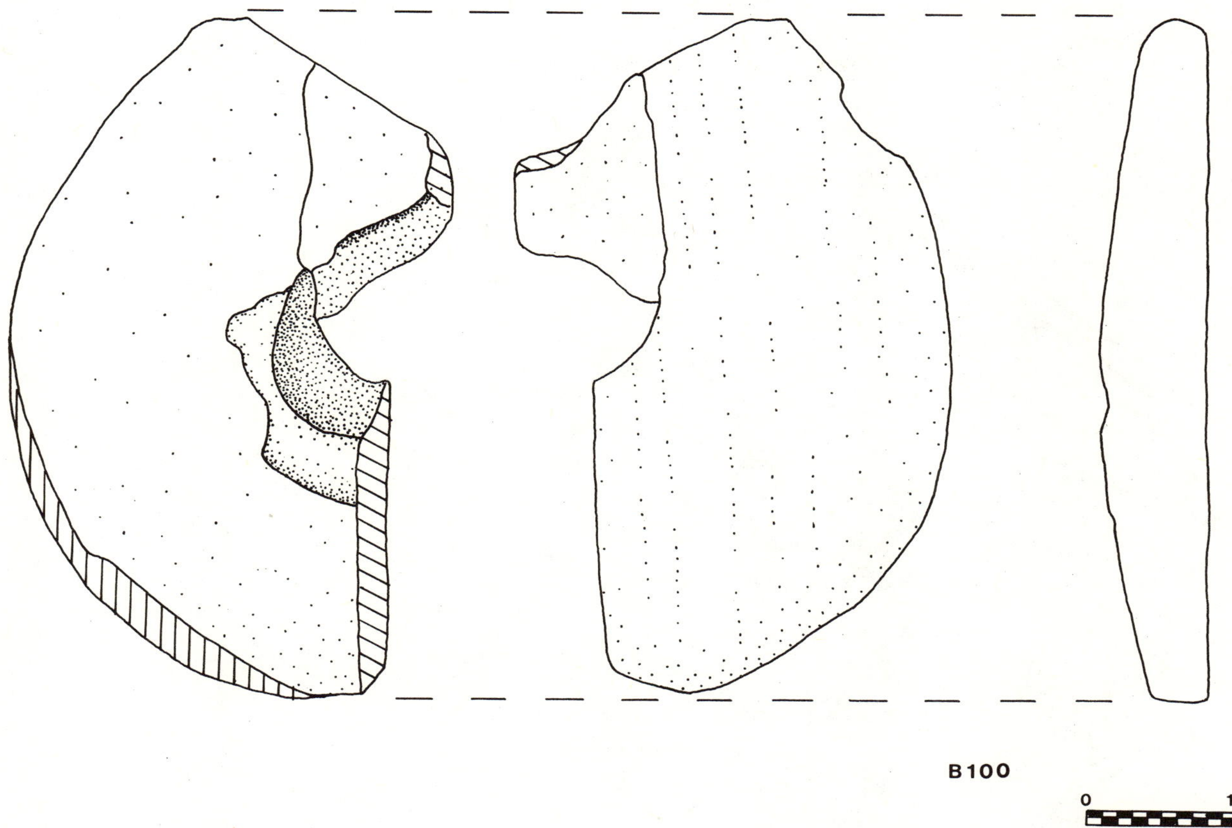

Fig. 112. Late Medieval rotary flat quern, upper stone, Rema stone, preserving traces of rynd cutting in the eye. [Drawing from Runnels 1990.]

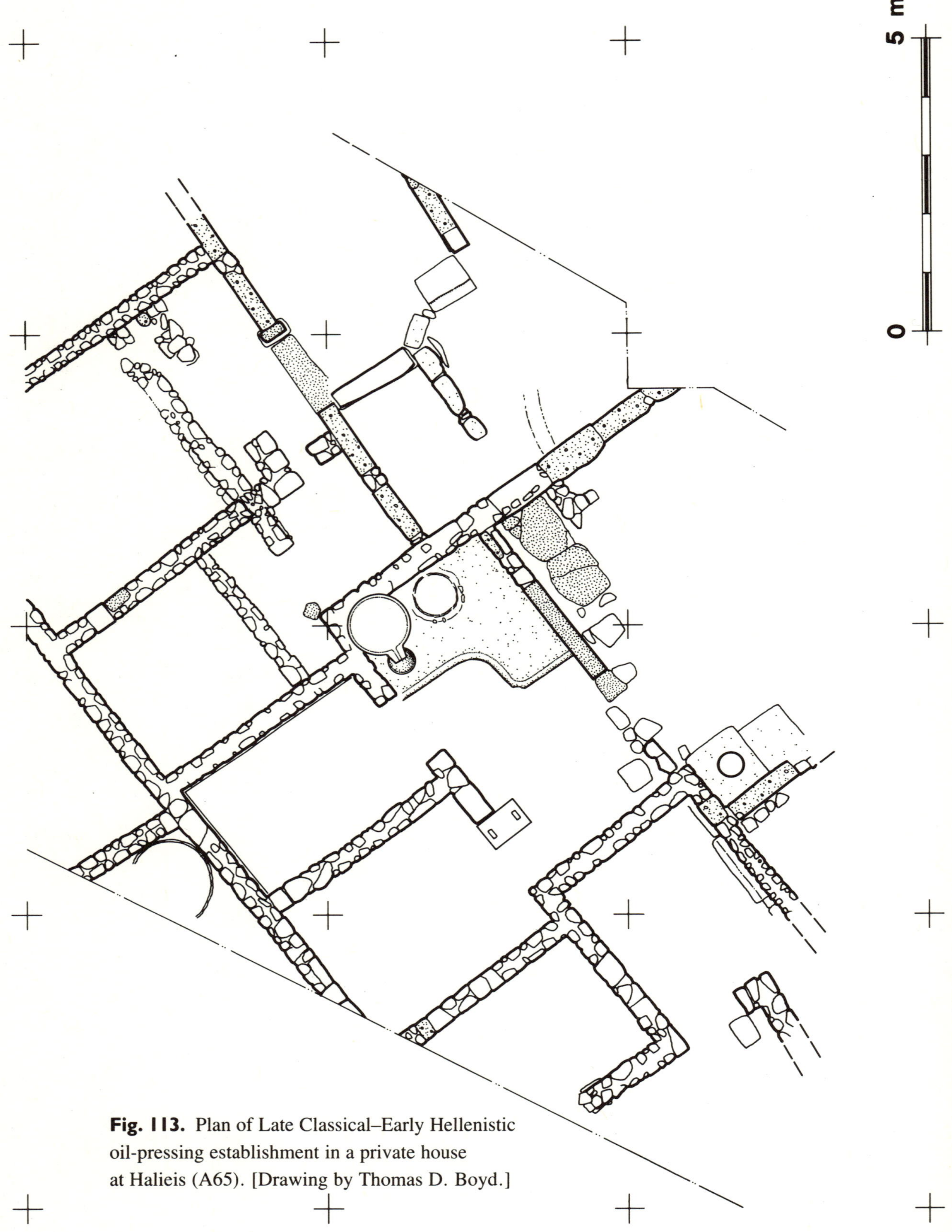

Fig. 113. Plan of Late Classical–Early Hellenistic
oil-pressing establishment in a private house
at Halieis (A65). [Drawing by Thomas D. Boyd.]

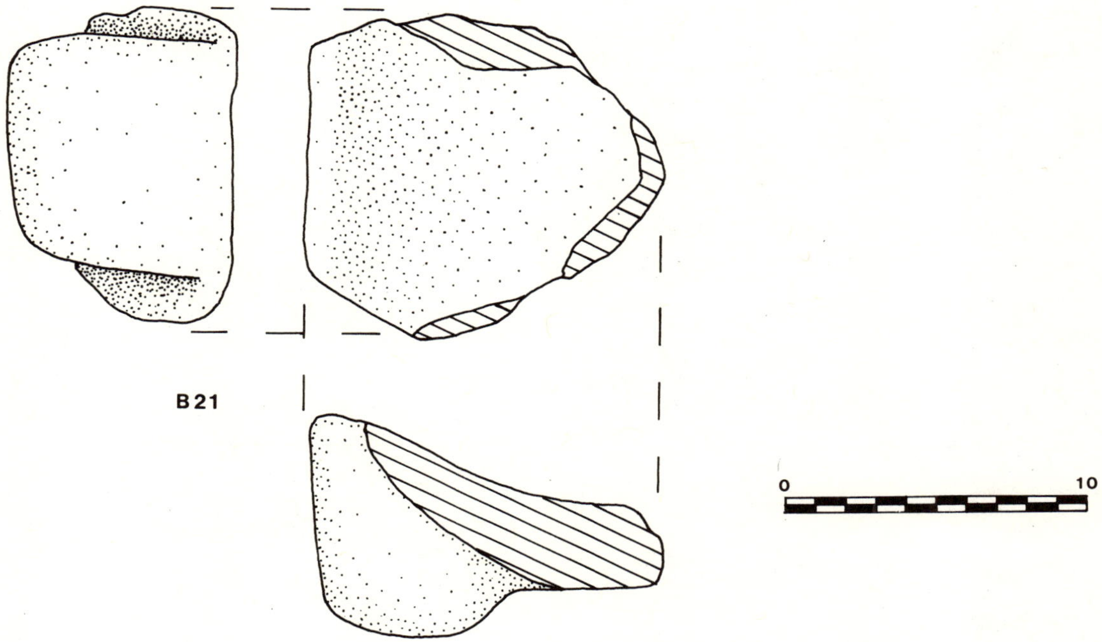

Fig. 114. Mycenaean tripod mortar, andesite, preserving one foot.

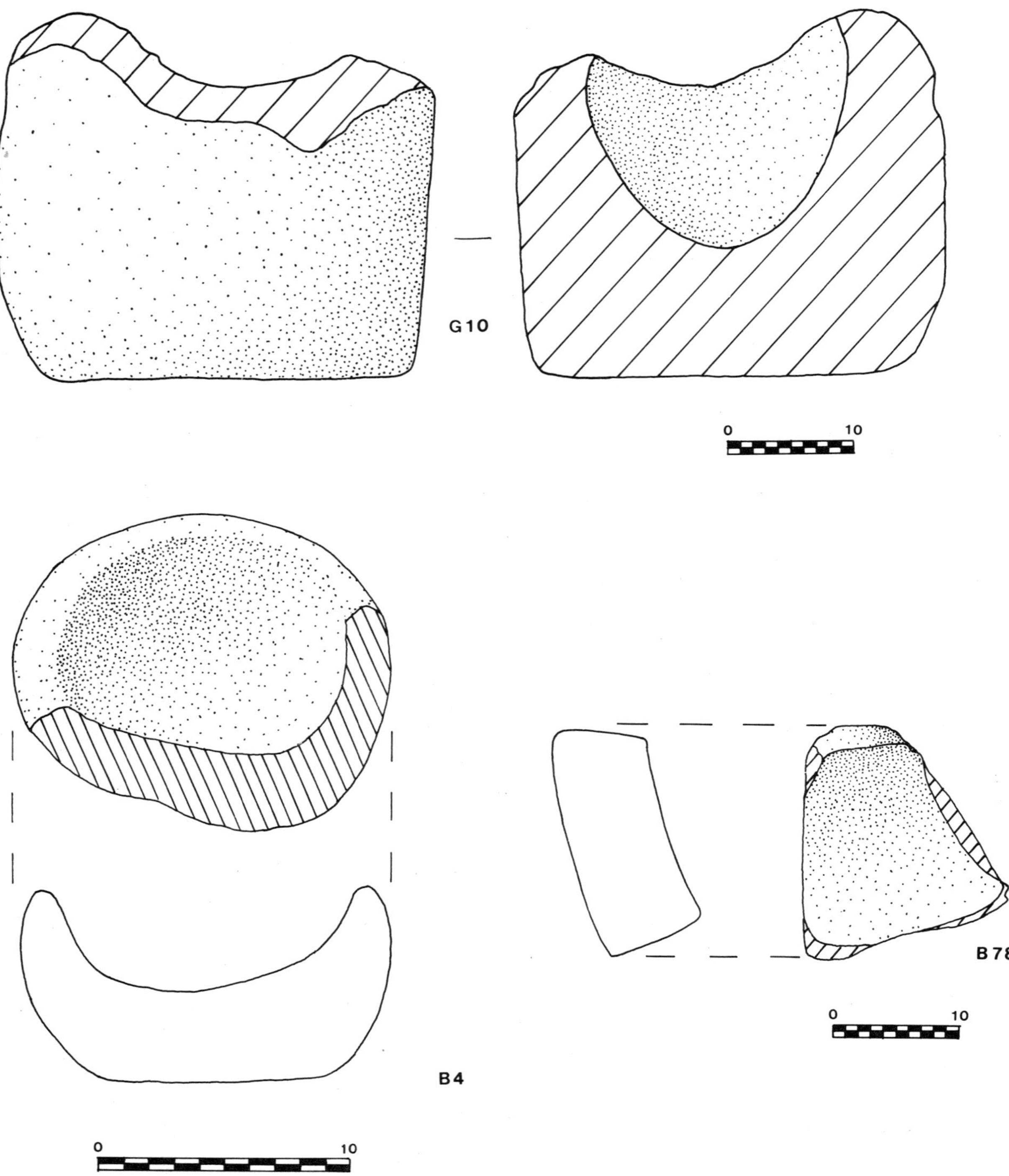

Fig. 115. G10, Classical mortar, andesite; B4, Late Roman mortar, andesite; B78, fragment of a mortarium from a trapetum (?), andesite.

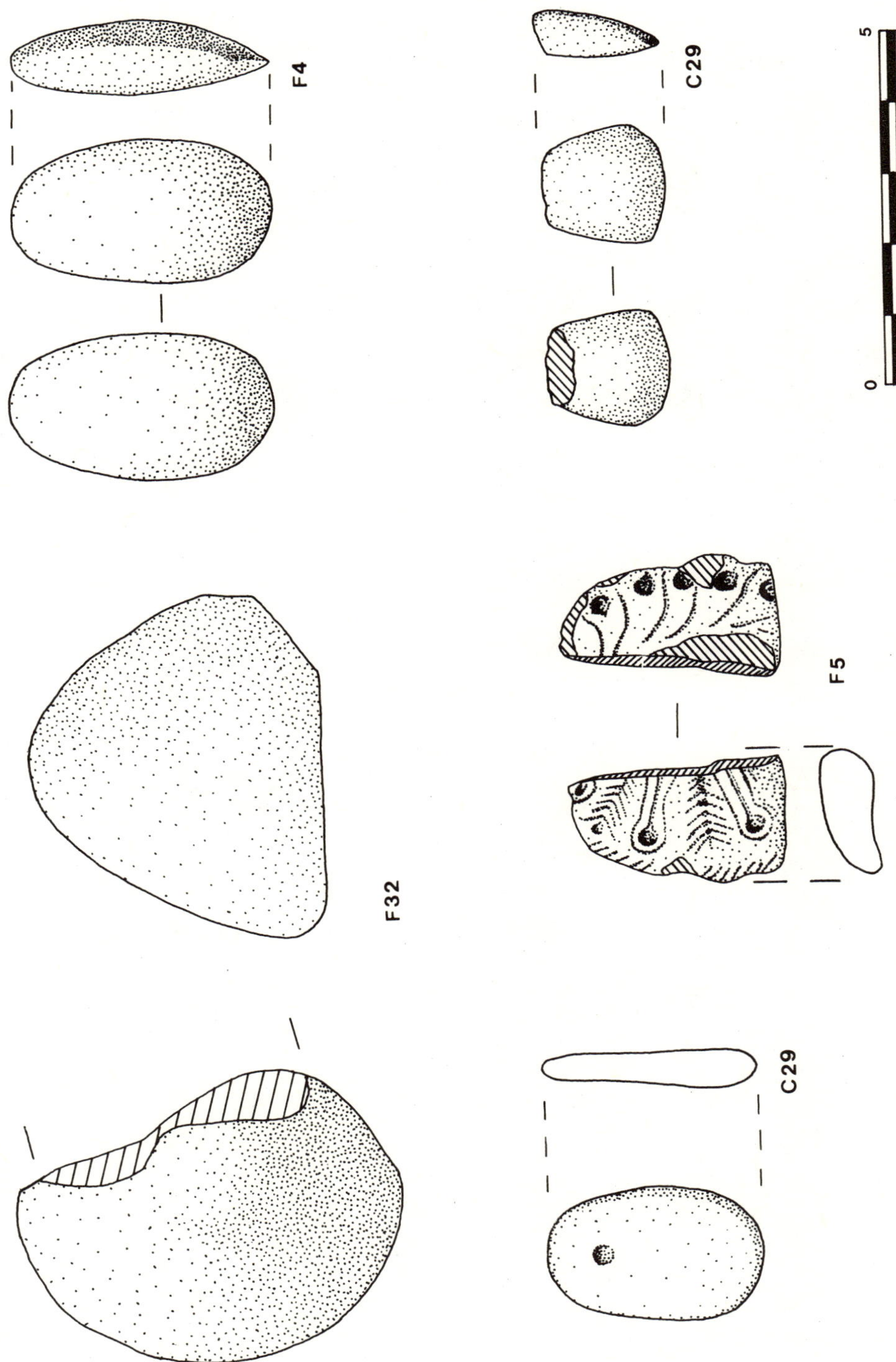

Fig. 116. F32, unidentified stone; F4 and C29, Late or Final Neolithic miniature celts, hard igneous greenstone; C29, Late or Final Neolithic unfinished perforated ornament, hard igneous greenstone; F5, fragment of Mycenaean relief vessel (?), talc.

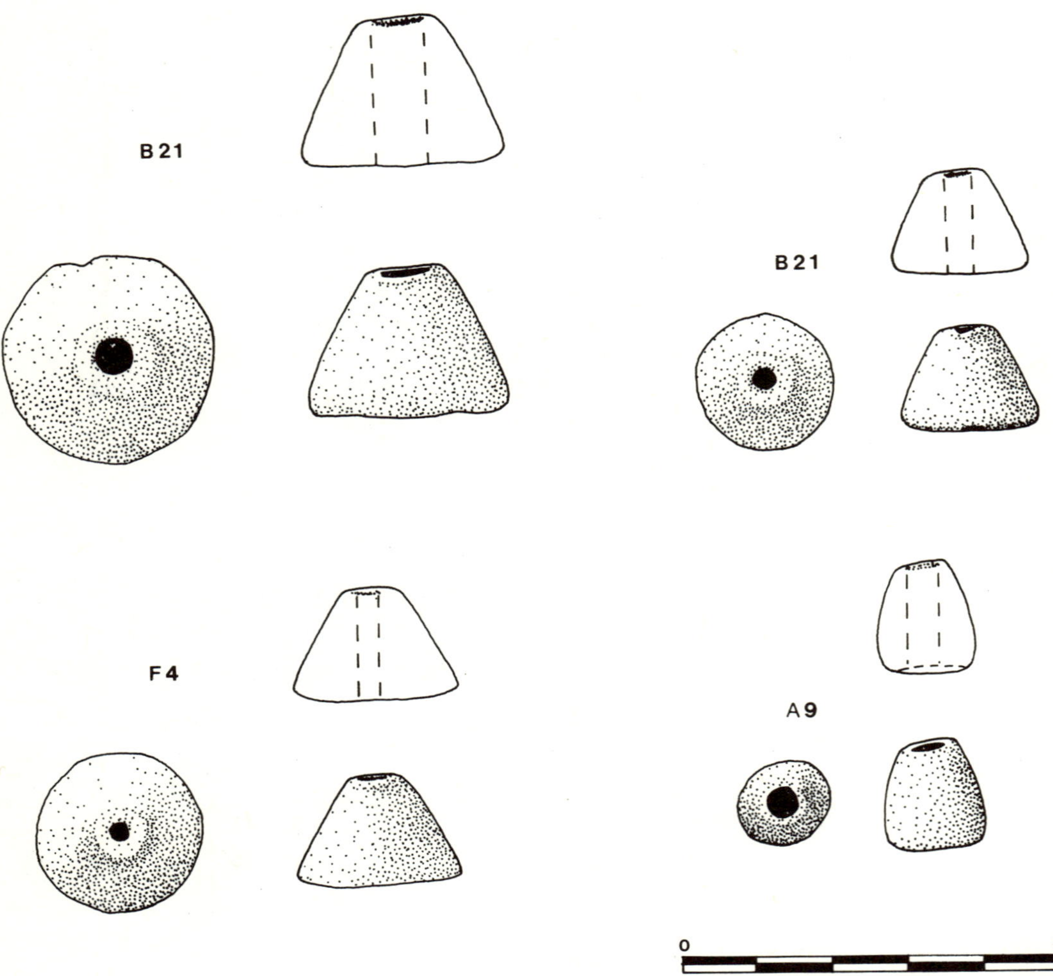

Fig. 117. B21, Mycenaean talc beads; F4, Mycenaean (?) talc bead; A9, Early Bronze Age (?) talc bead.

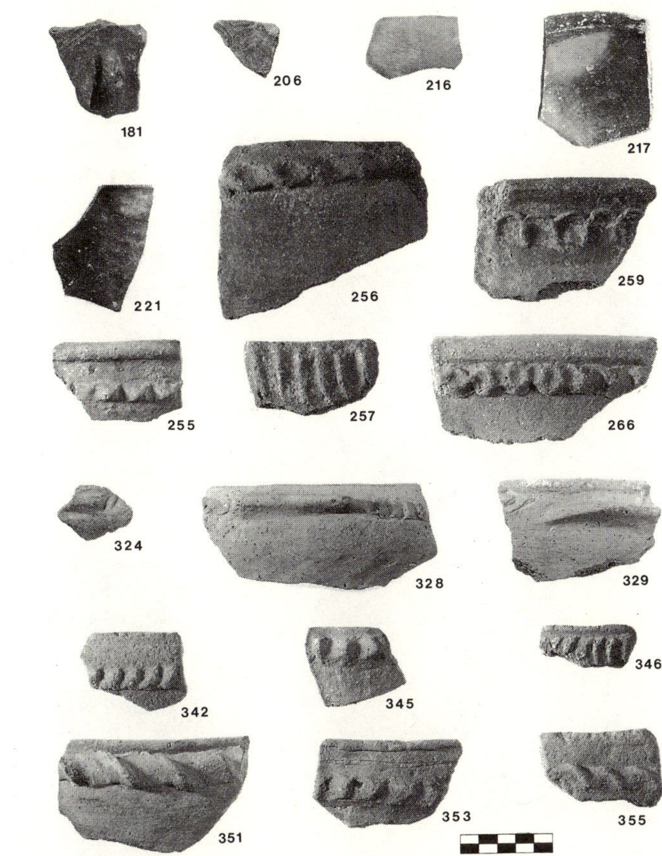

Fig. 118. Middle Neolithic vessel **3**; Late Neolithic vessels **8**, **10**, **14**, **16**, **17**; Final Neolithic vessels **29**, **30**, **57**, **60**, **64**, **66–68**; Early Helladic I vessels **111**, **114**, **117**, **118**, **161**, **163–165**.

Fig. 119. Early Helladic I vessels **181**, **206**; Early Helladic II vessels **216**, **217**, **221**, **255–257**, **259**, **266**, **324**, **328**, **329**, **342**, **345**, **346**, **351**, **353**, **355**.

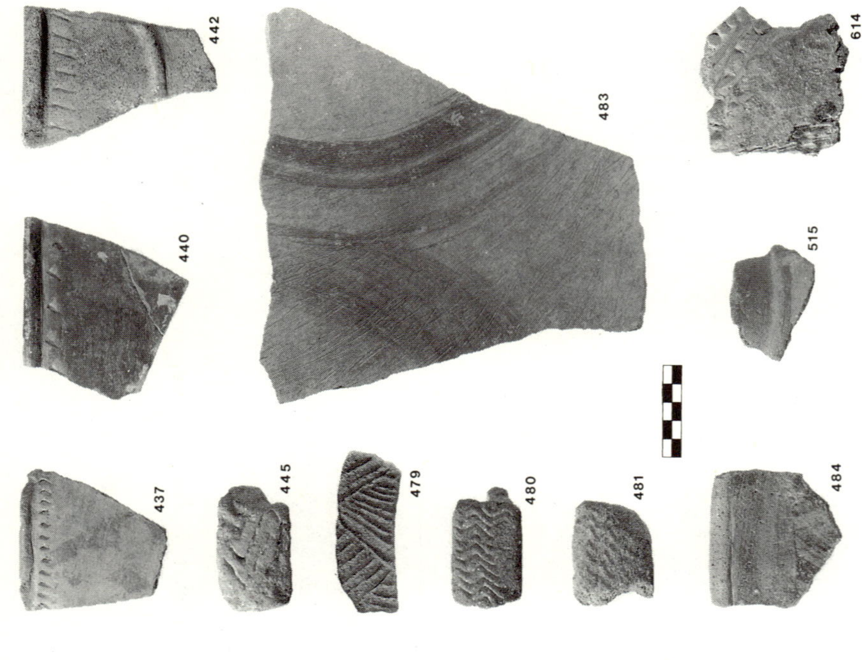

Fig. 121. Early Helladic II vessels **437, 440, 442, 445, 479–481, 483, 484, 515, 614.**

Fig. 120. Early Helladic II vessels **356, 357, 361, 365, 369, 372–375, 377, 379–381, 383, 388, 404, 418.**

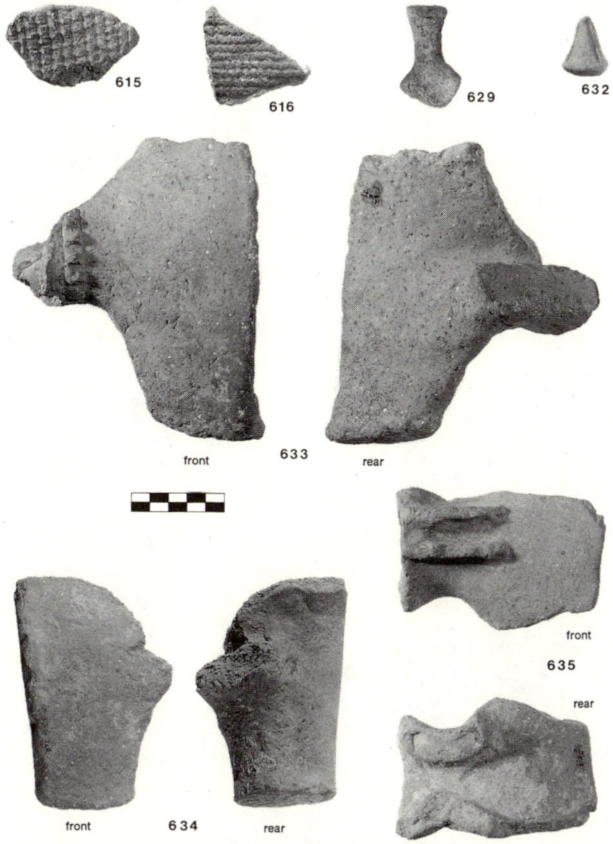

Fig. 123. Early Helladic II vessels **636, 637, 640, 645–647, 650, 651, 653, 655, 657, 659.**

Fig. 122. Early Helladic II vessels **615, 616, 629, 632–635.**

Fig. 125. Early Helladic III vessels **679, 681, 683, 697–703, 706, 707, 709, 711.**

Fig. 124. Early Helladic II vessels **662, 664, 666, A6-83-.**

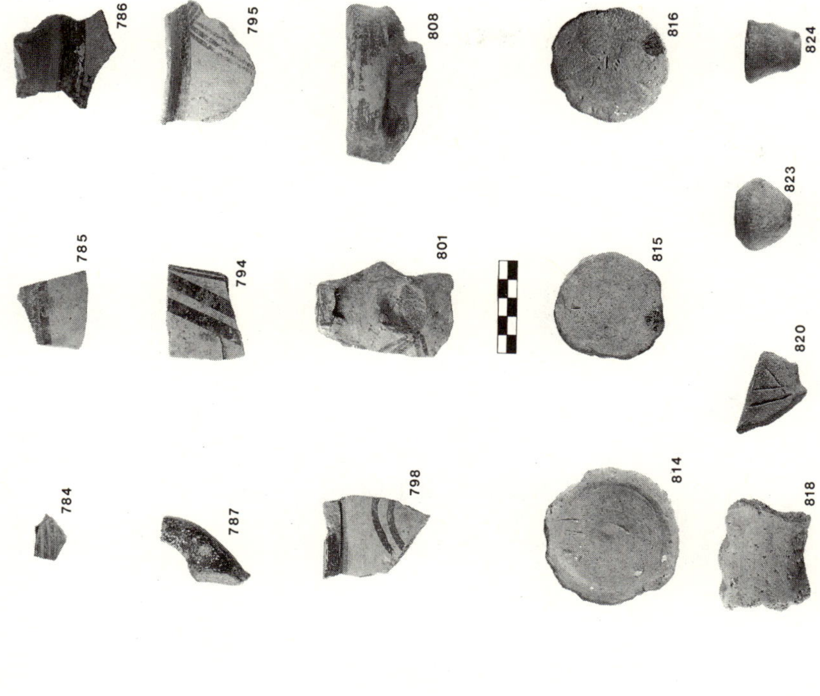

Fig. 127. Middle Helladic vessels **784–787, 794, 795, 798, 801, 808, 814–816, 818, 820, 823, 824.**

Fig. 126. Middle Helladic vessels **712, 715, 718, 723, 734, 745, 753, 755–757, 762, 767, 774, 776, 780, 781.**

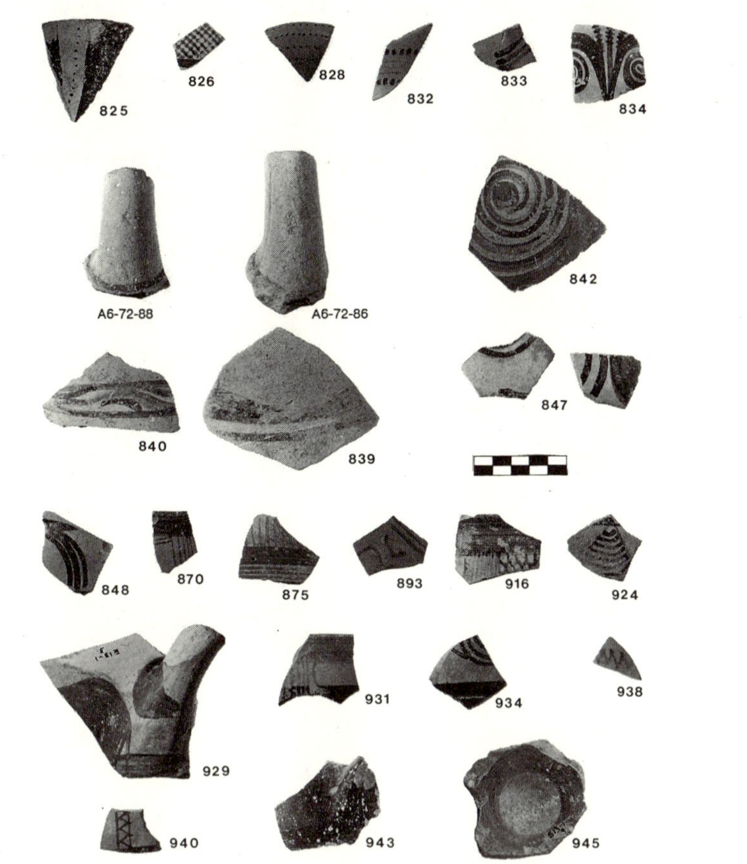

Fig. 128. Late Helladic IIA vessels **825, 826, 828**; Late
Helladic IIB vessels **832–834**; Late matt painted vessels
**A6-72–86, A6-72–88, 839, 840, 842, 847, 848, 870,
875**; Late Helladic IIIB vessels **893, 916**; Late Helladic
IIIC vessels **924, 929, 931, 934, 938, 940, 943, 945**.

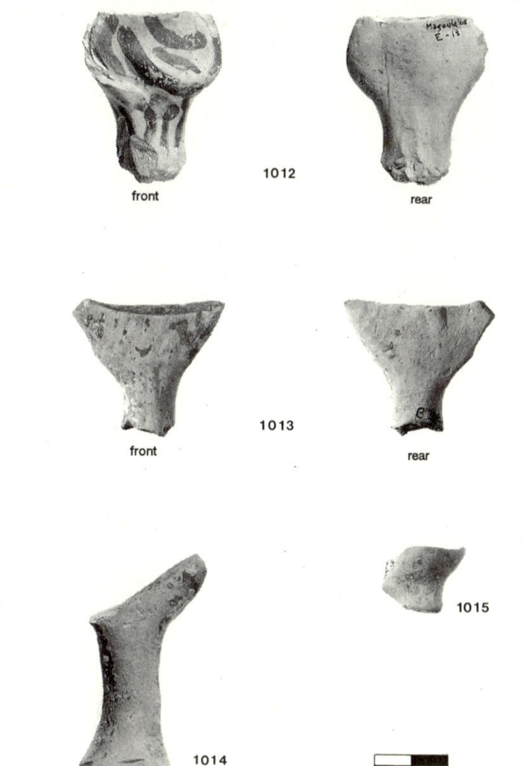

Fig. 129. Late Helladic terracotta figurines **1012–1015**.

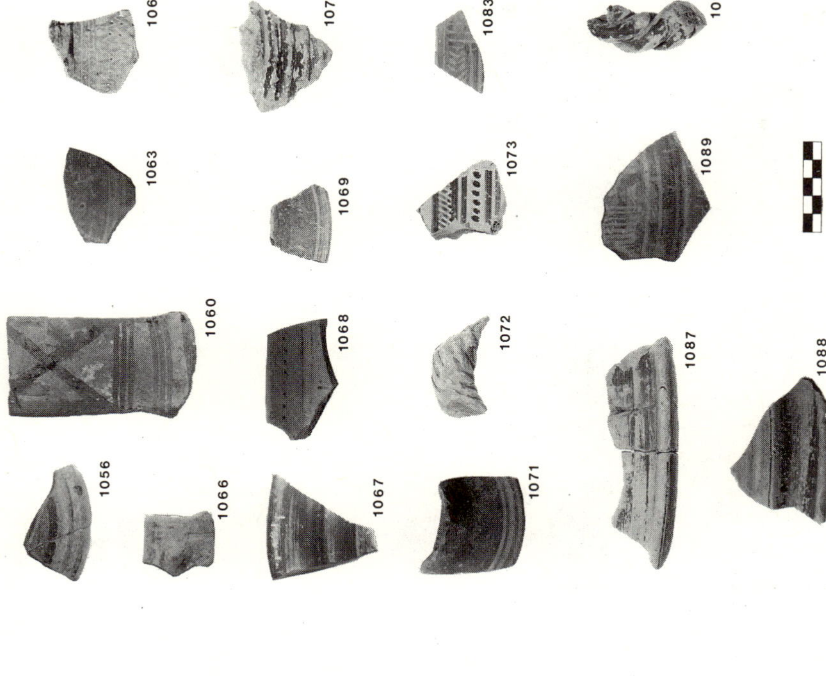

Fig. 131. Middle Geometric vessels **1056, 1060, 1063, 1065–1067**; Middle to Late Geometric vessels **1068–1073, 1083, 1087–1089, 1091.**

Fig. 130. Protogeometric vessels **1016, 1017, 1021, 1025, 1028–1031, 1033**; Early Geometric vessels **1036, 1037**; Middle Geometric vessels **1040–1042, 1044, 1047, 1049–1052.**

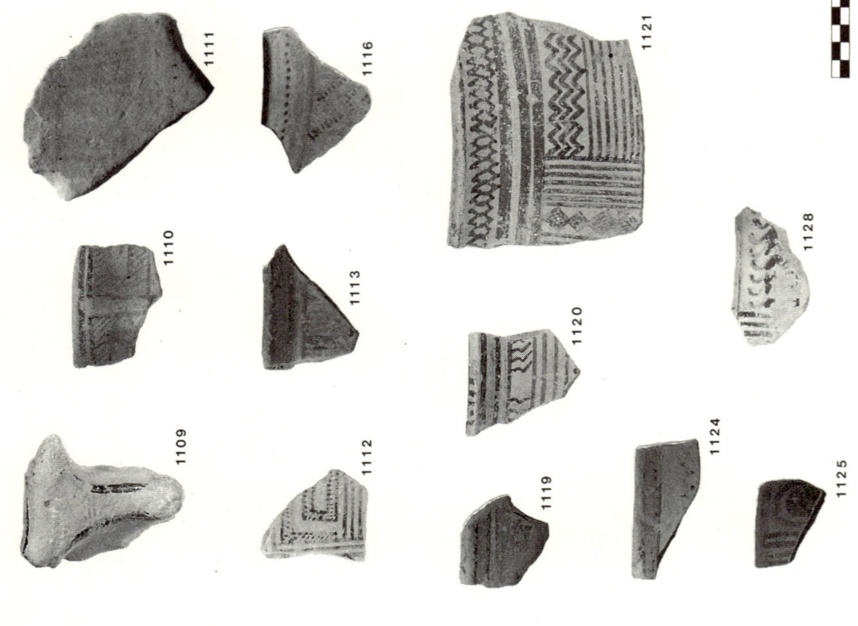

Fig. 133. Late Geometric I vessels **1109–1112**; Late Geometric II vessels **1113, 1116, 1119–1121, 1124, 1125, 1128.**

Fig. 132. Middle to Late Geometric vessels **1092, 1093, 1096, 1097**; Late Geometric I vessels **1098, 1103, 1104, 1108.**

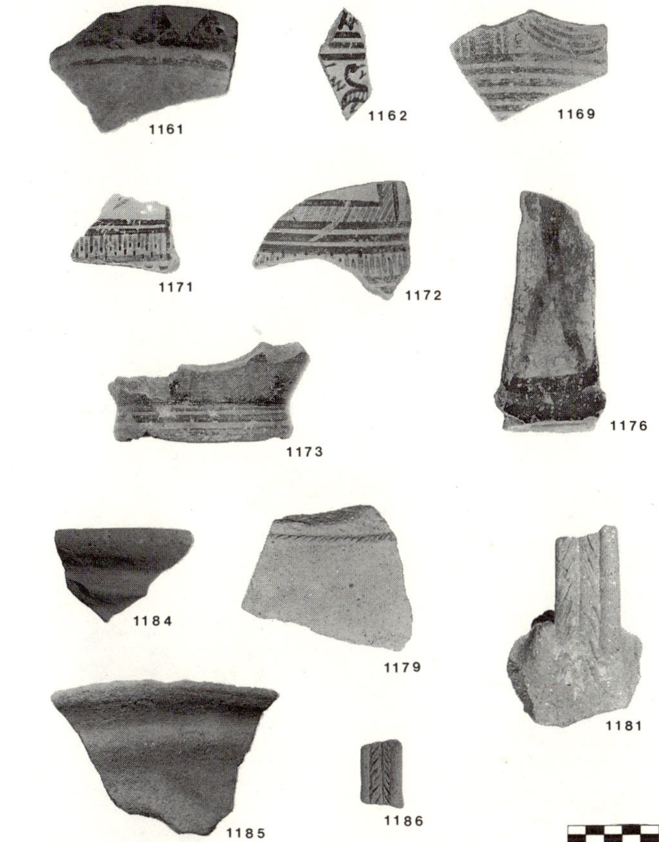

Fig. 134. Late Geometric II vessels **1129, 1132–1136, 1138, 1139, 1142, 1143, 1147, 1150, 1153, 1154, 1157–1160**.

Fig. 135. Late Geometric II vessels **1161, 1162, 1169, 1171–1173, 1176, 1179, 1181, 1184–1186**.

Fig. **136.** Late Geometric II to Subgeometric vessels **1189, 1191, 1197**; Subgeometric vessels **1198, 1200–1202, 1204, 1206, 1209–1212**, terracotta figurines **1213, 1214.**

References Cited and Index

References Cited

Full bibliographic references for all works cited in the text are given here.

Adams, W. Y. 1988. Archaeological Classification: Theory versus Practice. *Antiquity* 61: 40–56.

Aspinall, A., S. W. Feather, and C. Renfrew. 1972. Neutron Activation Analysis of Aegean Obsidian. *Nature* 237: 333–34.

Aupert, P. 1982. Argos aux VIIIe–VIIe siècles: bourgade ou métropole? *Annuario delle Scuola Archeologica di Atene e delle Missioni Italiane in Oriente* 60: 21–31.

Bailey, G. N., P. L. Carter, C. S. Gamble, H. P. Higgs, and C. Roubet. 1984. Palaeolithic Investigations in Epirus: The Results of the First Season's Excavations at Klithi, 1983. *Annual of the British School of Archaeology at Athens* 79: 7–22.

Banks, E. 1967. *The Early and Middle Helladic Small Objects from Lerna*. Ph.D. dissertation. University Microfilms. Ann Arbor, Mich.

Benaki Museum. 1978. *Exhibition of Ancient Greek Art from the N. P. Goulandris Collection*. Athens.

Bialor, P. A., and M. H. Jameson. 1962. Palaeolithic in the Argolid. *American Journal of Archaeology* 66: 181–82.

Biers, W. R. 1969. Excavations at Phlius, 1924: The Prehistoric Deposits. *Hesperia* 38: 443–58.

———. 1971. Excavations at Phlius, 1924. The Votive Deposit. *Hesperia* 40: 397–423.

Bikaki, A. H. 1984. *Keos IV: Ayia Irini, The Potters' Marks*. Philipp von Zabern. Mainz.

Binford, L. R. 1979. Organization and Formation Processes: Looking at Curated Technologies. *Journal of Anthropological Research* 35: 255–73.

———. 1980. Willow Smoke and Dogs' Tails: Hunter-Gatherer Settlement Systems and Archaeological Site Formation. *American Antiquity* 45: 4–20.

Blegen, C. W. 1921. *Korakou: A Prehistoric Settlement Near Corinth*. American School of Classical Studies at Athens. Boston and New York.

———. 1928. *Zygouries: A Prehistoric Settlement in the Valley of Cleonae*. Harvard University Press. Cambridge, Mass.

Blegen, C. W., H. Palmer, and R. S. Young. 1964. *Corinth XIII: The North Cemetery*. American School of Classical Studies at Athens. Princeton.

Bommelaer, J. F. 1972. Nouveaux documents de céramique protoargienne. *Bulletin de Correspondance Hellénique* 96: 229–51.

———. 1977. Review of *Les tombes géométriques d'Argos I*, by P. Courbin. *Revue Archéologique* 178: 330–32.

———. 1978. De la spécialisation artisanale en Argolide d'après l'étude de la céramique géométrique. *Ktèma* 3: 35–45.

———. 1980. Le premier motif figuré de la céramique argienne. In *Études argiennes. Bulletin de Correspondance Hellénique*, Supplement 6: 53–73.

———. 1985. L'apparition de la figure animée sur les vases grecs de style géométrique. *Ktèma* 10: 9–18.

Bordaz, J. 1969. Flint Flaking in Turkey. *Natural History* 78: 73–79.

———. 1970. *Tools of the Old and New Stone Age*. Natural History Press. Garden City, N.Y.

Bordes, F. 1961. *Typologie du Paléolithique Ancien et Moyen*. Publications de l'Institut de Préhistoire de l'Université de Bordeaux.

———. 1968. *The Old Stone Age*. Weidenfeld and Nicholson. London.

Bosanquet, R. C. 1904. The Obsidian Trade. In *Excavations at Phylakopi in Melos*. Journal of Hellenic Studies Supplementary Paper 4, 216–32. Macmillan. London.

Bossert, E.-M. 1960. Die gestempelten Verzierungen auf frühbronzezeitlichen Gefässen der Ägäis. *Jahrbuch des deutschen Archäologischen Instituts* 75: 1–16.

Boyd, T. D., and W. W. Rudolph. 1978. Excavations at Porto Cheli and Vicinity. Preliminary Report IV: The

Lower Town of Halieis, 1970–1977. *Hesperia* 47: 333–55.

Brann, E. 1960. Late Geometric Grave Groups from the Athenian Agora. *Hesperia* 29: 402–16.

———. 1961a. Late Geometric Well Groups from the Athenian Agora. *Hesperia* 30: 93–147.

———. 1961b. Protoattic Well Groups from the Athenian Agora. *Hesperia* 30: 305–79.

———. 1962. *The Athenian Agora VIII: Late Geometric and Protoattic Pottery*. American School of Classical Studies at Athens. Princeton.

Brézillon, M. 1971. *La dénomination des objets de pierre taillée*. Gallia Préhistoire Supplement 4. Paris.

Brouskari, M. 1980. A Dark Age Cemetery in Erechtheion Street. *Annual of the British School of Archaeology at Athens* 75: 13–31.

Bruneau, P. 1970. Tombes d'Argos. *Bulletin de Correspondance Hellénique* 94: 437–531.

Buck, R. J. 1964. Middle Helladic Mattpainted Pottery. *Hesperia* 33: 231–308.

Bulgarelli, A. 1977. The Lithic Industry of Tepe Hissar in the Light of Recent Excavations. *South Asian Archaeology* 1: 39–54.

Burr, D. 1933. A Geometric House and a Protoattic Votive Deposit. *Hesperia* 2: 542–640.

Cambitoglou, A. 1981. *Guide to the Finds from the Excavations of the Geometric Town at Zagora*. Archaeological Museum of Andros. Athens.

Cann, J., and C. Renfrew. 1964. The Characterization of Obsidian and Its Application to the Mediterranean Region. *Proceedings of the Prehistoric Society* 30: 111–33.

Caskey, J. L. 1960. The Early Helladic Period in the Argolid. *Hesperia* 29: 285–303.

———. 1971. Greece, Crete, and the Aegean Islands in the Early Bronze Age. In *The Cambridge Ancient History*, Third edition, Vol. 1, Part 2, ed. I. E. S. Edwards, C.J. Gadd, and N. G. L. Hammond, 771–807. Cambridge University Press. Cambridge.

Caskey, J. L., and E. G. Caskey. 1960. The Earliest Settlements at Eutresis: Supplementary Excavations, 1958. *Hesperia* 29:126–67.

Cherry, J. F. 1982. Register of Archaeological Sites on Melos. In *An Island Polity: The Archaeology of Exploitation in Melos*, ed. C. Renfrew and M. Wagstaff, 291–309. Cambridge University Press. New York.

Cherry, J. F., and R. Torrence. 1982. The Earliest Prehistory of Melos. In *An Island Polity: The Archaeology of Exploitation in Melos*, ed. C. Renfrew and M. Wagstaff, 24–34. Cambridge University Press. New York.

Cherry, J. F., J. L. Davis, A. Demitrack, E. Mantzourani, T. F. Strasser, and L. E. Talalay. 1988. Archaeological Survey in an Artifact-Rich Landscape: A Middle Neolithic Example from Nemea, Greece. *American Journal of Archaeology* 92: 159–76.

Childe, V. G. 1943. Rotary Querns on the Continent and in the Mediterranean Basin. *Antiquity* 17: 19–26.

Clark, J. E. 1982. Manufacture of Mesoamerican Prismatic Blades: An Alternative Technique. *American Antiquity* 47: 355–76.

———. 1986. From Mountains to Molehills: A Critical Review of Teotihuacan's Obsidian Industry. In *Economic Aspects of Prehispanic Highland Mexico*. Research in Economic Anthropology, Supplement 2, ed. B. L. Isaac, 23–74. JAI Press. Greenwich, Conn.

Coldstream, J. N. 1968. *Greek Geometric Pottery*. Methuen. London.

———. 1972. Knossos 1951–61: Protogeometric and Geometric Pottery from the Town. *Annual of the British School of Archaeology at Athens* 67: 63–98.

———. 1977. *Geometric Greece*. St. Martin's. New York.

———. 1978. Kythera and the Southern Peloponnese in the LMI Period. In *Thera and the Aegean World I*, ed. C. Doumas, 389–401. London.

Coleman, J. E. 1977. *Keos I: Kephala, a Late Neolithic Settlement and Cemetery*. American School of Classical Studies at Athens. Princeton.

———. 1985. "Frying Pans" of the Early Bronze Age Aegean. *American Journal of Archaeology* 89: 191–219.

Cook, J. M. 1953. Mycenae 1939–1952, Part III: The Agamemnoneion. *Annual of the British School of Archaeology at Athens* 48: 30–68.

Coulson, W. D. E. 1985. The Dark Age Pottery of Sparta. *Annual of the British School of Archaeology at Athens* 80: 28–84.

Courbin, P. 1953. Les origines du canthare Attique archaïque. *Bulletin de Correspondance Hellénique* 77: 322–45.

———. 1954. Argos. *Bulletin de Correspondance Hellénique* 78: 158–83.

———. 1955. Un fragment de cratère protoargien. *Bulletin de Correspondance Hellénique* 79: 1–49.

———. 1957. Une tombe géométrique d'Argos. *Bulletin de Correspondance Hellénique* 81: 322–86.

———. 1966. *La céramique géométrique de l'Argolide*. Bibliothèque des Écoles Françaises d'Athènes et de Rome. Paris.

———. 1974. *Tombes géométriques d'Argos, I: 1952–1958*. École Française d'Athènes. Paris.

———. 1977. Une pyxis géométrique argienne(?) au Liban. *Berytus* 25: 147–57.

Crabtree, D. 1968. Mesoamerican Polyhedral Cores and Prismatic Blades. *American Antiquity* 33: 446–78.

———. 1972. *An Introduction to Flintworking*. Occasional Papers of the Idaho State University Museum, 28. Pocatello.

———. 1975. Comments on Lithic Technology and Experimental Archaeology. In *Lithic Technology*, ed. E. Swanson, 105–14. Mouton. The Hague.

Cullen, T. 1985. *A Measure of Interaction Among Neolithic Communities: Design Elements of Greek Urfirnis Pottery*. Ph.D. dissertation. University Microfilms. Ann Arbor, Mich.

Cummer, W. W., and E. Schofield. 1984. *Keos III: Ayia Irini, House A*. Philipp von Zabern. Mainz.

Dakaris, S. I., E. S. Higgs, and R. W. Hey. 1964. The Climate, Environment, and Industries of Stone Age Greece, Part I. *Proceedings of the Prehistoric Society* 30: 199–244.

Davis, J. L. 1978. The Mainland Panelled Cup and Panelled Style. *American Journal of Archaeology* 82: 216–22.

———. 1979. Late Helladic I Pottery from Korakou. *Hesperia* 48: 234–63.

———. 1986. *Keos V: Ayia Irini, Period V*. Philipp von Zabern. Mainz.

Desborough, V. R. d'A. 1952. *Protogeometric Pottery*. Clarendon Press. Oxford.

———. 1954. Mycenae 1939–1953, Part IV: Four Tombs. *Annual of the British School of Archaeology at Athens* 49: 258–66.

———. 1955. Mycenae 1939–1954, Part VI: Three Geometric Tombs. *Annual of the British School of Archaeology at Athens* 50: 239–47.

———. 1972. *The Greek Dark Ages*. Ernest Benn. London.

Deshayes, J. 1966. *Argos: Les fouilles de la Deiras*. Études Péloponnésiennes 4. Paris.

DeVries, K. 1974. A Grave with a Figured Fibula at Lerna. *Hesperia* 43: 80–104.

Diamant, S. 1977. A Barbed and Tanged Obsidian Point from Marathon. *Journal of Field Archaeology* 4: 381–86.

Dickinson, O. T. P. K. 1974. The Definition of Late Helladic I. *Annual of the British School of Archaeology at Athens* 69: 109–20.

Dietz, S. 1982. *Asine II, 2: The Middle Helladic Cemetery, the Middle Helladic and Early Mycenaean Deposits*. Skrifter utgivna av Svenska Institutet i Athen 4, 24: 2, 75–83. Stockholm.

Dikaios, P., and J. du Plat Taylor. 1936. Acquisitions of the Cyprus Museum in 1936. *Report of the Department of Antiquities, Cyprus* 1936: 108–13.

Dousougli, A. 1987. Makrovouni - Kefalari Magoula - Talioti: Bermerkungen zu den Stufen FH I und II in der Argolis. *Praehistorische Zeitschrift* 62: 164–220.

Drennan, R. D. 1984. Long-Distance Movement of Goods in the Mesoamerican Formative and Classic. *American Antiquity* 49: 27–43.

Dugas, C., and C. Rhomaios. 1943. *Délos XV: Les vases préhelleniques et géométriques*. École Française d'Athènes. Paris.

Dunbabin, T. J., ed. 1962. *Perachora: The Sanctuaries of Hera Akraia and Limenia II*. Clarendon Press. Oxford.

Evans, J. D., and C. Renfrew. 1968. *Excavations at Saliagos near Antiparos*. Annual of the British School of Archaeology at Athens Supplement 5. Thames and Hudson. London.

Fahy, L. L. 1964. The Early Helladic Sauceboat. Unpublished M.A. thesis, University of Cincinnati. Cincinnati, Ohio.

Farnsworth, M., and I. Simmons. 1963. Coloring Agents for Greek Glazes. *American Journal of Archaeology* 67: 389–96.

Feder, K. L. 1980–81. Waste Not, Want Not: Differential Lithic Utilization and Efficiency of Use. *North American Archaeologist* 2: 193–205.

Foley, A. 1988. *The Argolid 800–600 B.C.* Studies in Mediterranean Archaeology 80. Paul Åström. Göteborg.

Foradas, J. G. 1989. Toward Intraformational Sourcing of Flint Using Normative Mineral Compositions: A Preliminary Study Using Flint Ridge Flint. Paper presented at the 54th Annual Meeting of the Society for American Archaeology, April 5–9, 1989. Atlanta.

Forbes, H., and L. Foxhall. 1978. The Queen of All Trees: Preliminary Notes on the Archaeology of the Olive. *Expedition* 21: 37–47.

Ford, S., R. Bradley, J. Hawkes, and P. Fisher. 1984. Flintworking in the Metal Age. *Oxford Journal of Archaeology* 3: 157–73.

Fossey, J. M. 1969. The Prehistoric Settlement by Lake Vouliagmeni, Perachora. *Annual of the British School of Archaeology at Athens* 64: 53–69.

French, D. 1972 [Notes on prehistoric pottery groups from Central Greece.] Privately circulated.

French, D., and E. French. 1971. Prehistoric Pottery from the Area of the Agricultural Prison at Tiryns. *Tiryns: Forschung und Bericht*. V. Philipp von Zabern. Mainz.

French, E. 1965. Late Helladic IIIA2 Pottery from Mycenae. *Annual of the British School of Archaeology at Athens* 60: 159–202.

———. 1969. The First Phase of LHIIIC. *Archäologischer Anzeiger* 1969: 133–36.

———. 1971. The Development of Mycenaean Terracotta Figurines. *Annual of the British School of Archaeology at Athens* 66: 101–87.

Frickenhaus, A., W. Müller, and F. Oelmann. 1912. *Tiryns I*. Deutsches Archäologisches Institut in Athen. Athens.

Friis Johansen, K. 1957. Exochi, ein frührhodisches Gräberfeld. *Acta Archaeologica* 28: 1–192.

Frizell, B. 1980. *An Early Mycenaean Settlement at Asine, the LHIIB-IIIA1 Pottery*. University of Göteborg.

Frödin, O., and A. Persson. 1938. *Asine: Results of the Swedish Excavations, 1922–1930*. Stockholm.

Fürtwangler, A. 1906. *Aegina, das Heiligtum der Aphaia*. Akademie der Wissenschaften. Münich.

Furumark, A. 1941a. *The Chronology of Mycenaean Pottery*. Skrifter utgivna av Svenska Institutet i Athen. Stockholm.

———. 1941b. *Mycenaean Pottery: Analysis and Classification*. Skrifter utgivna av Svenska Institutet i Athen. Stockholm.

Gabrici, E. 1913. Cuma. *Monumenti Antichi* 22: 1–448.

Gercke, P., and U. Naumann. 1974. Tiryns-Stadt 1971. *Archaiologika Analekta ex Athinon* 7: 15–24.

Goldman, H. 1931. *Excavations at Eutresis in Boeotia*. Harvard University Press. Cambridge, Mass.

Gorelick, L., and A. Gwinnett. 1981. The Origin and Development of the Ancient Near Eastern Cylinder Seal. *Expedition* 23: 17–30.

Hägg, R. 1962. Research at Dendra, 1961. *Opuscula Atheniensia* 4: 79–102.

———. 1965. Geometrische Gräber von Asine. *Opuscula Atheniensia* 6: 117–38.

———. 1971. Protogeometrische und geometrische Keramik in Nauplion. *Opuscula Atheniensia* 10: 41–52.

———. 1974. *Die Gräber der Argolis in submykenischer, protogeometrischer und geometrischer Zeit, I: Lage und Form der Gräber*. Boreas 7:1. Acta Universitatis Upsaliensis. Uppsala.

———. 1978. *Excavations in the Barbouna Area at Asine, II*. Boreas 4:2. Acta Universitatis Upsaliensis. Uppsala.

Hatzipouliou-Kalliri, E. 1983. An Early Helladic II Tomb by Lake Vouliagmeni, Perachora. *Annual of the British School of Archaeology at Athens* 78: 369–75.

Hay, C. A. 1977. Use-Scratch Morphology: A Functionally Significant Aspect of Edge Damage on Obsidian Tools. *Journal of Field Archaeology* 4: 491–94.

Hayden, B., ed. 1979. *Lithic Use-Wear Analysis*. Academic Press. New York.

Holmberg, E. J. 1944. *The Swedish Excavations at Asea in Arcadia*. C. W. K. Gleerup. Lund.

Holmes, W. H. 1919. *Handbook of Aboriginal American Antiquities, Part I. Introductory: The Lithic Industries*. Smithsonian Institution, Bureau of American Ethnology Bulletin 60. Government Printing Office. Washington, D.C.

Howell, R. J. 1968. The Pottery Phases 2–6. In *Excavations at Lefkandi, Euboea, 1964*, ed. M. R. Popham and L. H. Sackett. British School at Athens, London.

Iakovides, S. 1977. On the Use of Mycenaean "Buttons." *Annual of the British School of Archaeology at Athens* 72: 113–20.

Immerwahr, S. A. 1971. *The Athenian Agora XIII: The Neolithic and Bronze Ages*. American School of Classical Studies at Athens. Princeton.

Ives, D. J. 1984. Chert Sources and Identification in Archaeology: Can a Silk Purse Be Made from a Sow's Ear? In *Lithic Resource Procurement: Proceedings from the Second Conference on Prehistoric Chert Exploitation*, ed. S. C. Vehik, 211–24. Center for Archaeological Investigations, Occasional Paper No. 4. Southern Illinois University. Carbondale.

Jacobsen, T. W. 1969. Excavations at Porto Cheli and Vicinity, Preliminary Report II: The Franchthi Cave, 1967–1968. *Hesperia* 38: 343–81.

———. 1973a. Excavations in the Franchthi Cave, 1969–1971, Part I. *Hesperia* 42: 45–88.

———. 1973b. Excavations in the Franchthi Cave, 1969–1971, Part II. *Hesperia* 42: 253–83.

———. 1976. 17,000 Years of Greek Prehistory. *Scientific American* 234: 76–87.

———. 1984. Seasonal Pastoralism in Southern Greece: A Consideration of the Ecology of Neolithic Urfirnis Pottery. In *Pots and Potters: Current Approaches in Ceramic Archaeology*, ed. P. M. Rice, 27–43. Monographs in Archaeology 24. University of California at Los Angeles Institute of Archaeology.

Jacobsen, T. W., and D. M. Van Horn. 1974. The Franchthi Cave Flint Survey: Some Preliminary Results (1974). *Journal of Field Archaeology* 1: 305–8.

Jameson, M. H., C. N. Runnels, and Tj. H. van Andel. 1994. *A Greek Countryside: The Southern Argolid from Prehistory to the Present Day*. Stanford University Press. Stanford, Calif.

Jantzen, U., ed. 1975. *Tiryns: Forschungen und Berichte VIII*. Philipp von Zabern. Mainz.

Jones, R. E. 1986. *Greek and Cypriote Pottery: A Review of Scientific Studies*. Annual of the British School of Archaeology at Athens, Fitch Laboratory Occasional Paper 1. Athens.

Karageorghis, V., and J. des Gagniers. 1974. *La céramique chypriote de style figuré: âge du fer, 1050–500 av. J.-C.* Consiglio Nazionale delle Richerche. Rome.

Kardulias, N. P. 1992. The Ecology of Bronze Age Flaked Stone Tool Production in Southern Greece: Evidence from Agios Stephanos and the Southern Argolid. *American Journal of Archaeology* 96: 421–42.

Keeley, L. H. 1980. *Experimental Determination of Stone Tool Uses: A Microwear Analysis*. University of Chicago Press. Chicago.

Kelly, T. 1976. *A History of Argos to 500 B.C.* University of Minnesota Press. Minneapolis.

Kokkou-Viridi, K. 1977. Tessereis protogeometrikoi taphoi sto Argos. *Archaiologiki Ephemeris* 1977: 171–94.

Konsola, D. N. 1984. *I Proimi Astikopiisi stous Protoelladhikous Oikismous: Systimatiki Analisi ton Karaktiristikon Tis*. Athens.

Kourou, N. 1987. A propos de quelques ateliers de céramique fine, non tournée du type "Argien monochrome." *Bulletin de Correspondance Hellénique* 111:31–50.

Kraiker, W. 1951. *Aigina. Die Vasen des 10. bis 7. Jahrhunderts v. Chr.* Deutsches Archäologisches Instituts. Berlin.

Kraiker, W., and K. Kübler. 1939. *Kerameikos I: Die Nekropolen des 12. bis 10. Jahrhunderts*. Walter de Gruyter and Co. Berlin.

Krystalli-Votsi, K. 1980. Cratère géométrique d'Argos. *Études argiennes*. Bulletin de Correspondance Hellénique, Supplement 6: 85–92.

Kübler, K. 1954. *Kerameikos V. 1: Die Nekropole des 10. bis 8. Jahrhunderts*. Walter de Gruyter and Co. Berlin.

Langdon, S. 1989. The Return of the Horse-Leader. *American Journal of Archaeology* 93: 185–201.

Lavezzi, J. C. 1978. Prehistoric Investigations at Corinth. *Hesperia* 47: 402–51.

Luedtke, B. 1978. Chert Sources and Trace-Element Analysis. *American Antiquity* 43: 413–23.

———. 1979. Quarrying and Quantification: Estimates of Lithic Material Demand. *Midcontinental Journal of Archaeology* 4: 255–66.

Mackenzie, D. 1898. Excavations in Melos, 1898, the Successive Settlements. *Annual of the British School of Archaeology at Athens* 4: 11–36.

Mallouf, R. J. 1982. An Analysis of Plow-Damaged Chert Artifacts: The Brookee Creek Cache (41HI86), Hill Co., Texas. *Journal of Field Archaeology* 9: 79–98.

Maran, J. 1987. Anmerkungen zum Klassifikationssystem der mittelhelladischen Keramik aus Lerna. *Hydra: Working Papers in Middle Bronze Age Studies* 3: 26–28.

Marinatos, S. 1936. Le temple géométrique de Dréros II. *Bulletin de Correspondance Hellénique* 60: 257–85.

Marwitz, H. 1959. Kreis und Figur in der attisch-geometrischen Vasenmalerei. *Jahrbuch des Deutschen Archäologischen Instituts* 74: 52–113.

McDonald, W. A., W. D. E. Coulson, and J. Rosser, eds. 1983. *Excavations at Nichoria in Southwest Greece. 3: Dark Age and Byzantine Occupation*. University of Minnesota Press. Minneapolis.

Meeks, N. D., G. de Sieveking, M. S. Tite, and J. Cook. 1982. Gloss and Use-Wear Traces on Flint Sickles and Similar Phenomena. *Journal of Archaeological Science* 9: 317–40.

Miller, R. 1982. Pseudo-Tools Created by Livestock from Halawa, Syria. *Journal of Field Archaeology* 9: 281–83.

Millon, R. 1967. Teotihuacan. *Scientific American* 216: 38–48.

Mitten, D. G., and S. F. Doeringer. 1967. *Master Bronzes from the Classical World*. Von Zabern. Mainz.

Moritz, L. A. 1958. *Grain-Mills and Flour in Classical Antiquity*. Clarendon Press, Oxford.

Moss, E. H. 1983. Some Comments on Edge Damage as a Factor in Functional Analysis of Stone Artifacts. *Journal of Archaeological Science* 10: 231–42.

Mountjoy, P. A. 1976. LHIIIB1 Pottery Dating the Construction of the South House at Mycenae. *Annual of the British School of Archaeology at Athens* 71: 77–111.

———. 1981. *Four Early Mycenaean Wells from the South Slope of the Acropolis at Athens*. Miscellanea Graeca fascicle 4. Belgian Archaeological Mission in Greece. Ghent.

———. 1983. *Orchomenos V, Mycenaean Pottery from Orchomenos, Eutresis and other Boeotian Sites*. Bayerischen Akademie der Wissenschaften. Munich.

———. 1985. The Mycenaean Pottery. In *The Archaeology of Cult: The Sanctuary at Phylakopi*, ed. C. Renfrew. Annual of the British School of Archaeology at Athens Supplementary Volume 18: 151–208. London.

———. 1986. *Mycenaean Decorated Pottery: A Guide to Identification*. Studies in Mediterranean Archaeology 73. P. Åström. Göteborg.

Movius, H. L., N. David, H. Bricker, and R. B. Clay. 1968. *The Analysis of Certain Major Classes of Upper Palaeolithic Tools*. Peabody Museum, Bulletin 26. Cambridge, Mass.

Müller, K. 1938. *Tiryns IV: die Urfirniskeramik*. F. Bruckmann. Munich.

Murray, P., and C. Chang. 1981. An Ethnoarchaeological Study of a Contemporary Herder's Site. *Journal of Field Archaeology* 8: 372–81.

Mussche, H. F., et al. 1984. *Thorikos VIII, 1972–1976*. Comité des fouilles belges en Grèce. Ghent.

Mylonas, G. 1959. *Agios Kosmas, An Early Bronze Age Settlement and Cemetery in Attica*. Princeton University Press. Princeton.

———. 1965. *Mycenae and the Mycenaean Age*. Princeton University Press. Princeton.

———. 1972. *O taphikos kyklos B ton Mykenon*. Archaiologike Hetaireia. Athens.

———. 1975. *To dytikon nekrotapheion tis Elefsinos*. Archaiologike Hetaireia. Athens.

Nordquist, G. C. 1987. *A Middle Helladic Village: Asine in the Argolid*. Boreas 16. Acta Universitatis Upsaliensis. Uppsala.

Odell, G. H., and F. Cowan. 1986. Experiments with Spears and Arrows on Animal Targets. *Journal of Field Archaeology* 13: 195–212.

Odell, G. H., and F. Odell-Vereecken. 1980. Verifying the Reliability of Lithic Use-Wear Assessments by Blind Tests: The Low Power Approach. *Journal of Field Archaeology* 7: 87–120.

Paleologou, H. 1980. Vase géométrique figuratif d'Argos. *Études argiennes*. Bulletin de Correspondance Hellénique Supplement 6: 75–84.

Peacock, D. 1980. The Roman Millstone Trade: A Petrological Sketch. *World Archaeology* 12: 43–53.

———. 1986. The Production of Roman Millstones near Orvieto, Umbria, Italy. *The Antiquaries Journal* 66: 45–51.

Perlès, C. 1979. Des navigateurs méditerranéens il y a 10.000 ans. *La Recherche* 96: 82–83.

———. 1987a. *Les Industries lithiques taillées de Franchthi (Argolide, Grèce). Tome I: Présentation générale et industries Paléolithiques*. Excavations at Franchthi Cave, Greece, Fascicle 3, ed. T. W. Jacobsen. Indiana University Press. Bloomington.

———. 1987b. Les Industries du néolithique "précéramique" de Grèce: nouvelles études, nouvelles interprétations. In *Chipped Stone Industries of the Early Farming Cultures in Europe, Archaeologia Interregionalis*, 19–39. Warsaw University Press.

Pfaff, C. 1988. A Geometric Well at Corinth: Well 1981–6. *Hesperia* 57: 21–80.

Phelps, W. W. 1975. The Neolithic Sequence in Southern Greece. Ph.D. dissertation. University of London. London.

Podzuweit, C. 1979. Ausgrabungen in Tiryns 1977: Bericht

zur spätmykenischen Keramik. *Archäologischer Anzeiger* 412–40.

Pope, K. O., C. N. Runnels, and T.-L. Ku. 1984. Dating Middle Palaeolithic Red Beds in Southern Greece. *Nature* 312: 264–66.

Popham, M. R., and E. V. Milburn. 1971. The Late Helladic IIIC Pottery of Xeropolis (Lefkandi): A Summary. *Annual of the British School of Archaeology at Athens* 66: 333–52.

Popham, M. R., and L. H. Sackett, eds. 1979. *Lefkandi I. The Iron Age*. Thames and Hudson. London.

Protonotariou-Deilaki, E. 1971. Archaiotites kai Mnimeia Argolidokorinthias. *Archaiologikon Deltion* (Chronika) 26: 68–84.

Pullen, D. J. 1984. The Early Bronze Age in the Southern Argolid: Argo-Corinthian and Saronic Gulf Cultural Spheres (abstract). *American Journal of Archaeology* 88: 257.

———. 1987. The Earliest Phases of the Early Bronze Age at Tsoungiza Hill, Ancient Nemea. Paper delivered to 89th General Meeting of the Archaeological Institute of America, New York, December 1987.

Renfrew, C. 1972. *The Emergence of Civilization: The Cyclades and the Aegean in Third Millennium B.C.* Methuen. London.

———. 1982. Prehistoric Exchange. In *An Island Polity: The Archaeology of Exploitation in Melos*, ed. Colin Renfrew and Malcolm Wagstaff, 222–27. Cambridge University Press. New York.

Renfrew, C., and A. Aspinall. 1990. Aegean Obsidian and Franchthi Cave. In Catherine Perlès, *Les Industries lithiques taillées de Franchthi (Argolide, Grèce), Tome II: Mésolithique et Néolithique initial*. Excavations at Franchthi Cave, Greece, Fascicle 5, ed. T. W. Jacobsen, 257–70. Indiana University Press. Bloomington.

Renfrew, C., J. Dixon, and J. Cann. 1966. Obsidian and Early Cultural Contact in the Near East. *Proceedings of the Prehistoric Society* 32: 30–72.

Roes, A. 1953. Fragments de poterie géométrique trouvés sur les citadelles d'Argos. *Bulletin de Correspondance Hellénique* 77: 90–104.

Runnels, C. N. 1975. A Note on Glass Implements from Greece. *Newsletter of Lithic Technology* 4: 29–30.

———. 1976. More on Glass Implements from Greece. *Newsletter of Lithic Technology* 5: 27–31.

———. 1981. *A Diachronic Study and Economic Analysis of Millstones from the Argolid, Greece*. Ph.D. dissertation. University Microfilms. Ann Arbor, Mich.

———. 1982. Flaked-Stone Artifacts in Greece During the Historical Period. *Journal of Field Archaeology* 9: 363–73.

———. 1983a. The Stanford University Archaeological and Environmental Survey of the Southern Argolid, Greece. In *Archaeological Survey in the Mediterranean Region*, ed. D. Rupp and D. Keller, 291–94. B.A.R. International Series 155. Oxford.

———. 1983b. Trade and Communication in Prehistoric Greece. *Ekistics* 302: 417–20.

———. 1983c. Lithic Artifacts from Surface Sites in the Mediterranean Area. In *Archaeological Survey in the Mediterranean Region*, ed. D. Rupp and D. Keller, 143–48. B.A.R. International Series 155. Oxford.

———. 1985a. The Bronze-Age Flaked-Stone Industries from Lerna: A Preliminary Report. *Hesperia* 54: 357–91.

———. 1985b. Trade and Demand for Millstones in Southern Greece in the Neolithic and the Early Bronze Age. In *Production and Prehistoric Exchange: The Aegean and Eastern Mediterranean*, ed. B. Knapp and T. Stech, 30–43. Monographs in Archaeology 25. University of California at Los Angeles Institute of Archaeology.

———. 1988a. A Prehistoric Survey of Thessaly: New Light on the Greek Middle Paleolithic. *Journal of Field Archaeology* 15: 277–90.

———. 1988b. Early Bronze-Age Stone Mortars from the Southern Argolid. *Hesperia* 57: 257–72.

———. 1988c. The Rotary Querns. *Institute of Nautical Archaeology Newsletter* 15(3): 30–31.

———. 1990. Rotary Querns in Greece. *Journal of Roman Archaeology* 3: 147–54.

Runnels, C. N., and R. Cohen. 1981. The Source of the Kitsos Millstones. In *La Grotte Préhistorique de Kitsos (Attique)*, ed. N. Lambert, 233–39. École Française d'Athènes. Paris.

Runnels, C. N., and J. Hansen. 1986. The Olive in the Prehistoric Aegean: The Evidence for Domestication in the Early Bronze Age. *Oxford Journal of Archaeology* 5: 299–308.

Runnels, C. N., and P. Murray. 1983. Milling in Ancient Greece. *Archaeology* 36: 62–75.

Runnels, C. N., and Tj. H. van Andel. 1987. The Evolution of Settlement in the Southern Argolid, Greece: An Economic Explanation. *Hesperia* 56: 303–34.

Rupp, D., L. Sorensen, W. Fox, and R. King. 1984. The Palaipaphos Survey Project. *Journal of Field Archaeology* 11: 133–54.

Rutter, J. B. 1979. *Ceramic Change in the Aegean Early Bronze Age*. Occasional Paper 5. University of California at Los Angeles Institute of Archaeology.

———. 1982. A Group of Distinctive Pattern-Decorated Early Helladic III Pottery from Lerna and Its Implications. *Hesperia* 51: 459–88.

———. 1983. Fine Gray-Burnished Pottery of the Early Helladic III Period: The Ancestry of Gray Minyan. *Hesperia* 52: 327–55.

———. 1986. Some Comments on the Nature and Significance of the Ceramic Transition from Early Helladic III to Middle Helladic. *Hydra: Working Papers in Middle Bronze Age Studies* 2: 29–57.

Rutter, J. B., and S. H. Rutter. 1976. *Transition to Mycenaean: A Stratified Middle Helladic II to Late Helladic IIA Pottery Sequence from Ayios Stephanos in Lakonia.*

Monumenta Archaeologica 4. University of California at Los Angeles Institute of Archaeology.

Rutter, J. B., and C. W. Zerner. 1984. Early Hellado-Minoan Contacts. In *Minoan Thalassocracy: Myth and Reality. Proceedings of the Third International Symposium at the Swedish Institute in Athens, 31 May–5 June 1982*, ed. R. Hägg and N. Marinatos, 75–82. Svenska Institutet i Athen 4, 32. Stockholm.

Säflund, G. 1965. *Excavations at Berbati 1936–1937*. Stockholm Studies in Classical Archaeology. Stockholm.

Sahagun, Father Bernardino de. 1961. *Florentine Codex: General History of the Things of New Spain, Book 10—The People*, translated by C. E. Dibble and A. J. O. Anderson. Monographs of the School of American Research and the Museum of New Mexico 14, part 11. University of Utah Press. Salt Lake City.

Sarian, H. 1969. Terres cuites géométriques d'Argos. *Bulletin de Correspondance Hellénique* 93: 651–78.

Schiffer, M. 1979. Discussion: Experimental and Analytical Procedures. In *Lithic Use-Wear Analysis*, ed. B. Hayden, 365–73. Academic Press. New York.

Semenov, S. 1964. *Prehistoric Technology*, translated by M. W. Thompson. Cory, Adams, and Mackay. London.

Shafer, H. J., and T. R. Hester. 1983. Ancient Maya Chert Workshops in Northern Belize, Central America. *American Antiquity* 48: 519–43.

Smithson, E. L. 1961. The Protogeometric Cemetery at Nea Ionia, 1949. *Hesperia* 30: 147–78.

———. 1968. The Tomb of a Rich Athenian Lady, ca. 850 B.C. *Hesperia* 37: 77–116.

———. 1974. A Geometric Cemetery on the Areopagus: 1897, 1932, 1947. *Hesperia* 43: 325–90.

———. 1982. The Prehistoric Klepsydra. Some Notes. *Studies in Athenian Architecture, Sculpture, and Topography Presented to Homer A. Thompson*. Hesperia Supplement 20, 141–54. American School of Classical Studies at Athens. Princeton.

Snodgrass, A. M. 1971. *The Dark Age of Greece*. Edinburgh University Press, Edinburgh.

Sordinas, A. 1971. *Old Olive Oil Mills and Presses on the Island of Corfu, Greece*. Occasional Paper No. 5, Memphis State University. Anthropological Research Center.

Spence, M. W. 1981. Obsidian Production and the State in Teotihuacan. *American Antiquity* 46: 769–88.

Stillwell, A. N., and J. L. Benson. 1984. *Corinth XV (3): The Potters' Quarter*. American School of Classical Studies at Athens. Princeton.

Swanson, E., ed. 1975. *Lithic Technology-Making and Using Stone Tools*. Mouton. The Hague.

Theocharis, D. 1953–54. Asketario: Protoelladike Akropolis para ten Raphenan. *Archaiologike Ephemeris* 3: 59–76.

———. 1967. *I Avghi tis Thessalikis Proistorias*. Filarkhaiou Etaireias Volou. Volos.

———. 1973. *Neolithic Greece*. National Bank of Greece. Athens.

Tomlinson, R. A. 1972. *Argos and the Argolid from the End of the Bronze Age to the Roman Occupation*. Cornell University Press. Ithaca.

Torrence, R. 1979. A Technological Approach to Cycladic Blade Industries. In *Papers in Cycladic Prehistory*, ed. J. L. Davis and J. F. Cherry, 66–86. Monographs in Archaeology 14. University of California at Los Angeles Institute of Archaeology.

———. 1986. *Production and Exchange of Stone Tools*. Cambridge University Press. Cambridge.

Tringham, R., G. Cooper, G. Odell, B. Voytek, and A. Whitman. 1974. Experimentation in the Formation of Edge Damage: A New Approach to Lithic Analysis. *Journal of Field Archaeology* 1: 171–96.

Tylor, E. B. 1861. *Anahuac: Or Mexico and the Mexicans, Ancient and Modern*. Longman, Green, Longman, and Roberts. London.

Unger-Hamilton, R. 1985. Microscopic Striations on Flint Sickle-Blades as an Indication of Plant Cultivation: Preliminary Results. *World Archaeology* 17: 121–26.

van Andel, Tj. H., and C. N. Runnels. 1987. *Beyond the Acropolis: A Rural Greek Past*. Stanford University Press. Stanford, Calif.

———. 1988. An Essay on the "Emergence of Civilization" in the Aegean World. *Antiquity* 62: 234–47.

van Andel, Tj. H., and J. C. Shackleton. 1982. Late Paleolithic and Mesolithic Coastlines of Greece and the Aegean. *Journal of Field Archaeology* 9: 445–54.

van Andel, Tj. H., and C. J. Vitaliano. 1987. Water and Other Resources. In Tj. H. van Andel and S. B. Sutton, *Landscape and People of the Franchthi Region*, 17–20. Excavations at Franchthi Cave, Greece, Fascicle 2, ed. T. W. Jacobsen. Indiana University Press. Bloomington.

Van Effenterre, H., and M. Van Effenterre. 1969. L'Atelier des tailleurs d'obsidienne. In *Fouilles Exécutées à Mallia: Le Centre Politique, l'Agora (1960–1966)*, Études Crétoises 17, ed. H. Van Effenterre and M. Van Effenterre, 17–21. Geuthner. Paris.

Van Horn, D. M. 1976. *Bronze Age Chipped Stone Tools from the Argolid of Greece and Their Relation to Tools Manufactured from Other Materials*. Ph.D. dissertation. University Microfilms. Ann Arbor, Mich.

———. 1977. A New Greek Bronze Age Chipped Stone Tool Type: The Denticulated Tranchet. *Journal of Field Archaeology* 4: 386–93.

———. 1980. Observations Relating to Bronze Age Blade Core Production in the Argolid of Greece. *Journal of Field Archaeology* 7: 487–92.

Vaos, Z. A., and S. Nomikos. 1975. O Anemomylos ton Kykladhon. *Anthropos* 2: 91–114.

Verdelis, N. 1963. Neue geometrische Gräber in Tiryns. *Athenische Mitteilungen* 78: 1–62.

Vickery, K. D. 1983. The Flint Sources. In *Recent Exca-*

vations at the Edwin Harness Mound, Liberty Works, Ross County, Ohio*, ed. N. Greber, 73–85. MCJA Special Paper No. 5. Kent State University Press. Kent, Ohio.

Vitaliano, C. J. 1987. Map (plate 1): Geology of Ermioni Basin and Environs. In T. W. Jacobsen and W. R. Farrand, *Franchthi Cave and Paralia: Maps, Plans, and Sections*. Excavations at Franchthi Cave, Greece, Fascicle 1, ed. T. W. Jacobsen. Indiana University Press. Bloomington.

Vitelli, K. D. 1974. *The Greek Neolithic Patterned Urfirnis Ware from the Franchthi Cave and Lerna*. Ph.D. dissertation. University Microfilms. Ann Arbor, Mich.

Wace, A. J. B., and C. W. Blegen. 1916–18. The Pre-Mycenaean Pottery of the Mainland. *Annual of the British School of Archaeology at Athens* 22: 175–89.

Wagstaff, J. M. 1982. Post-Roman Melos. In *An Island Polity: The Archaeology of Exploitation in Melos* ed. C. Renfrew and M. Wagstaff, 58–71. Cambridge University Press. New York.

Waldstein, C. 1902. *The Argive Heraeum I*. Houghton Mifflin. Boston and New York.

———. 1905. *The Argive Heraeum II*. Houghton Mifflin. Boston and New York.

Walter, H., and F. Felten. 1981. *Alt-Ägina III, 1: die vorgeschichtliche Stadt: Befestigungen, Häuser, Funde*. Philipp von Zabern. Mainz.

Wardle, K. A. 1969. A Group of Late Helladic IIIB1 Pottery from Within the Citadel at Mycenae. *Annual of the British School of Archaeology at Athens* 64: 261–98.

———. 1973. A Group of Late Helladic IIIB2 Pottery from Within the Citadel at Mycenae: The Causeway Deposit. *Annual of the British School of Archaeology at Athens* 68: 297–348.

Warren, P. M. 1972. Knossos and the Greek Mainland in the Third Millennium B.C. *Archaiologika Analekta ex Athinon* 3: 392–98.

———. 1988. Knossos: Stratigraphical Museum Excavations, 1978–1982: Part IV. *Archaeological Reports* 34: 86–104.

Weinberg, S. S. 1937. Remains from Prehistoric Corinth. *Hesperia* 6: 487–524.

———. 1943. *The Geometric and Orientalizing Pottery, Corinth VII: Part I*. American School of Classical Studies at Athens. Cambridge, Mass.

Weisshaar, H.-J. 1981. Ausgrabungen in Tiryns, 1978, 1979: Bericht zur frühhelladischen Keramik. *Archäologischer Anzeiger* 1981: 220–56.

———. 1982. Ausgrabungen in Tiryns, 1980: Bericht zur frühhelladischen Keramik. *Archäologischer Anzeiger* 1982: 440–66.

———. 1983. Ausgrabungen in Tiryns, 1981: Bericht zur frühhelladischen Keramik. *Archäologischer Anzeiger* 1983: 329–58.

Wells, B. 1976. *Asine II: Results of the Excavations East of the Acropolis 1970–1974, 4: 1 and 2: The Protogeometric Period Parts 2 and 3*. Svenska Institutet i Athen. Stockholm.

Wells, B., C. Runnels, and E. Zangger. 1990. The Berbati-Limnes Archaeological Survey. The 1988 Season. *Opuscula Atheniensia* 18(15): 207–38.

Wide, S. 1896. Aphidna in Nord-Attika. *Athenische Mitteilungen* 21: 285–409.

Wide, S., and L. Kjellborg. 1895. Ausgrabungen auf Kalaureia. *Athenische Mitteilungen* 20: 296–326.

Wiencke, M. H. 1989. Change in Early Helladic II. *American Journal of Archaeology* 93: 495–509.

Williams-Thorpe, O. 1988. Provenancing and Archaeology of Roman Millstones from the Mediterranean Area. *Journal of Archaeological Science* 15: 253–305.

Wilson, D. E. 1986. Ayia Irini, Kea, in the Early Bronze Age: Helladic or Cycladic? (abstract). *American Journal of Archaeology* 90: 177–78.

Winters, H. D. 1969. *The Riverton Culture*. Reports of Investigation 13. Illinois State Museum. Springfield.

Wiseman, J. K. 1967. Excavations at Corinth, the Gymnasium Area, 1965. *Hesperia* 36: 13–41.

Yerkes, R. W. 1983. Microwear, Microdrills, and Mississippian Craft Specialization. *American Antiquity* 48: 499–518.

———. 1987. *Prehistoric Life on the Mississippi Floodplain*. University of Chicago Press. Chicago.

Young, R. S. 1938. Pottery from a Seventh Century Well. *Hesperia* 7: 412–28.

———. 1939. *Late Geometric Graves and a Seventh Century Well in the Agora*. Hesperia Supplement 2. American School of Classical Studies at Athens. Princeton.

———. 1949. An Early Geometric Grave near the Athenian Agora. *Hesperia* 18: 275–97.

Zeitlin, R. N. 1982. Toward a More Comprehensive Model of Interregional Commodity Distribution: Political Variables and Prehistoric Obsidian Procurement in Mesoamerica. *American Antiquity* 47: 260–75.

Zerner, C. W. 1978. *The Beginning of the Middle Helladic Period at Lerna*. Ph.D. dissertation. University Microfilms. Ann Arbor, Mich.

———. 1986. Middle Helladic and Late Helladic I Pottery from Lerna. *Hydra: Working Papers in Middle Bronze Age Studies* 2: 58–74.

———. 1987. "Middle Bronze Age and Late Bronze Age Pottery from Lerna in the Argolid." Middle Bronze Age Seminar, Argos Museum, August 5–6, 1987. (Privately circulated.)

———. n.d. Chart of Lerna V Minyan shapes. (Privately circulated.)

Zimmermann, J.-L. 1989. *Les chevaux de bronze dans l'art géométrique grec*. Philipp von Zabern. Mainz.

Index

In this index an "f" after a number indicates a separate reference on the next page, and an "ff" indicates separate references on the next two pages. A continuous discussion over two or more pages is indicated by a span of page numbers, e.g., "57–59." *Passim* is used for a cluster of references in close but not consecutive sequence.

Adze, 110, 133–34
AEP sites: A9 (Flamboura Magoula), 57, 61, 63, 71–72; B2 (Dhouroufi Ridge: Dhoukoulina), 57, 65, 72; B16 (Kastro), 57, 65, 72; B17 (Roadside), 57, 61; C12 (Vista), 57, 63, 65, 72; C13 (Franchthi Cave) 6f, 10, 40, 82, 86–93 *passim*, 103f, 112, 133, 136; C15 (Prehistoric site), 13; C17 (Mases), 57, 63, 65, 72; D3 (Dhidhima Cave), 6, 90; E5 (Kouverta), 7; E9 (Sambariza), 57–60 *passim*; E14 (Mouzaki Cave), 6; F32 (Fournoi Valley: Petres), 19, 30, 57, 65, 72, 106–8; G1 (Iliokastro), 57, 62, 65, 72; G9 (Kotena Cave), 7; importation of flint blades, 94; obsidian at, 77, 94, 104–6
AEP survey methods and procedures, 2–5, 42, 46, 52, 74ff, 81, 86, 107, 109
Agriculture, 39, 82, 89f, 94, 115
Aigina, 11, 44, 50, 69, 111–18 *passim*, 126. *See also* Andesite
Alabastron, 56
Alepotrypa, 10
Ammerman, A. J., 89

Amoriani, 67
Amphora, 54f, 60–64 *passim*, 68–71 *passim*
Amphoriskos, 67
Amyklai, 59
Andesite, 11, 111–16 *passim*, 121, 126, 133ff
Appliqué, *see* Plastic decoration
Argive Heraion, 69f, 72
Argive Minyan, 47
Argolid Exploration Project, *see* AEP sites; AEP survey methods and procedures
Argos, 59–73 *passim*, 143
Arrowheads, 91
Asine, 58ff, 64–68 *passim*, 72f, 143
Askos, 10, 36
Athens, 10, 53, 59–64 *passim*, 68ff. *See also* Attica
Attica, 42, 58ff, 68, 114–15. *See also* Athens
Axe, 110, 133–34
Ayia Irini, 21, 53
Ayios Iakovos (Cyprus), 71
Ayios Kosmas, 134
Ayios Stefanos, 93–97 *passim*

Backed blades, 83
Baking pan, 10, 36
Barbed and tanged point, 91
Barley, 39
Basalt, 111–12, 121
Base: button, 55–56; flat, 8, 19, 36, 56; hollow (raised), 8, 19, 35, 55f; ring, 22, 34–35, 55. *See also* Pedestal
Basin, 24, 47, 56. *See also* Bowl
Bead, stone, 135

Berbati, 61f
Bird, 64–70 *passim*
Black Minyan, 47
Blade, 77, 79, 83, 96f, 102, 106f. *See also* Lithics: production of
Blegen, C. W., 11
Boeotia, 42, 54
Boeotian stripe, 54
Bommelaer, J. F., 70
Bone implements, 94
Bowl, 8, 13, 24, 34, 44–51 *passim*, 70; broad-rim, 50f; deep, 15–16, 25, 54ff; hemispherical, 14; incurving, 14–15, 22–24, 25–30; inturned, 22–24; lipless conical, 56; outturned, 30–31; rolled rim (Kum Tepe Ib type), 10; saucer, 22; shallow, 13–14, 22–25; shallow angular, 56; small, 22–24; spouted, 30; spreading, 14, 24; spouted conical, 54f; stemmed, 53–56 *passim*; two-handled, 48, 50
Bridge-spouted jug, 53
Bronze, as medium of exchange, 93
Buck, R. J., 49
Burial, 61, 63
Button, stone, 135

Celt, 110, 133–34
Ceramic, *see* Fabric (ceramic); Non-vessel ceramics
Ceramic groups, regions, and imports: Anatolia, 10, 17; Argive Plain/Northern Argolid, 11ff, 19–22 *passim*, 28, 33–45 *passim*, 51, 57–73 *passim*, 141–42; Attica or Attic, 10, 20, 42, 53, 58–72 *pas-*

474   INDEX

sim, 141; Atticizing, 62, 64, 67; Boeotian, 23, 42, 54, 67; Corinthia or Corinthian, 7, 11–14 *passim*, 19–22 *passim*, 33, 37, 41, 59, 64, 68–73 *passim*, 141; Crete, 50, 71; Cycladic Islands, 11, 17, 21, 41f, 51, 53, 62, 67ff; Cypriot, 71; Early Helladic, 40–42, 141; Euboean, 67f; Laconian, 59, 72; Late Helladic, 55; Minoan, 50; Parian, 68; Peloponnese, 50; Protocorinthian, 68f, 71; Rhodian, 71; Saronic Gulf region, 11, 20, 41–44 *passim*, 50, 69, 141

Ceramic shapes, *see under individual shape names*

Cheese pot, 8, 10

Chert, *see* Flint

Childe, V. G., 140

Chisel, 82

Coarseware, 55–56

Coldstream, J. N., 62, 70

Complex societies, 93, 106

Concentric circles, 58–62 *passim*, 67

Conglomerate, 128, 133

Cooking pot, 55–56

Core, 77, 106

Corinth, 7, 37, 59, 64, 68–72 *passim*

Cortex, 79

Cortical flake, 79

Coulson, W. D. E., 59

Courbin, P., 58, 62, 66–70 *passim*

Craft specialization, 96–97

Crested blade (lame à crête), 77–78, 106

Crete, imported pottery from, 50

Crusted ware, 10

Cup, 44–49 *passim*, 53, 56, 60ff, 66

Cyclades, 41, 51

Cylinder seal impression, 38

Dating techniques, 85

Davis, J. L., 49

Debitage, 78–79

Delos, 68f

Delphi, 71

Dendra, 64, 68

Denticulated tranchet, 82

Desborough, V. R. d'A., 58f

Dhidhima Cave (AEP site D3), 3, 6, 90

Diamant, S., 83

Dipper, 37, 56

Double axe, 62f, 67

Dousougli, A., 13, 16–17, 28ff, 36

Dreros, 71

Dryopians, 68

Early Bronze Age, 93–97, 112. *See also* Early Helladic

Early Helladic, 4, 42, 134, 141–42; Early Helladic I, 4, 7, 10f, 15, 20, 41; Early Helladic II, 4, 15, 20, 41–42, 141–42; Early Helladic III, 4, 142

Early Iron Age, 4, 142–43

Egg cup, 49

EH, *see* Early Helladic

Ephyraean goblet, 53

Ermioni Magoula (AEP site E13), 113

Exochi, 71

F32 (AEP site), *see under* Fournoi Valley

Fabric (ceramic), 8–12 *passim*, 20–38 *passim*, 44–51 *passim*, 57–71 *passim*

Fahy, L. L., 21f

Figurine, 56, 71–72

Final Neolithic, 7–10 *passim*, 40–41, 133

Fine Burnished Non-Gray pottery, 45

Fine Gray Burnished pottery, 45

Fish, 67

Flake, 79

Flamboura Magoula (AEP site A9), 57, 61, 63, 71–72

Flint, 76f, 85ff, 100–108 *passim*, 121

FN, *see* Final Neolithic

Foley, A., 58, 63, 68, 70

Fournoi Valley, 42, 97, 106, 135, 143–44; Petres (AEP site F32), 19, 30, 106–8

Franchthi Cave (AEP site C13), 6f, 10, 40, 82, 86–93 *passim*, 103f, 112, 133, 136; importation of flint blades, 94; obsidian at, 77, 94, 104–6

Frankish presence in Cyclades, 127

Fruitstand, 13

Frying pan, 17, 19

FS 9 (krater), 54

FS 69 (amphora), 54

FS 105 (jug), 54

FS 128 (hydria), 54

FS 164 (stirrup jar), 54

FS 213 (cup), 53

FS 267 (carinated kylix), 56

FS 279 (ring-based krater), 53

FS 281 (krater), 54

FS 300 (spouted conical bowl), 55

FS 301 (spouted conical bowl), 55

Furumark, A., 52

Furumark shapes, *see individual FS numbers*

Fusco type krater, 70

Glass, 76f

Goblet, 53, 56

Gold mica, 44, 50

Grain impression, 39

Gray Minyan ware, 46–47

Greenstone, 121

Grinder, *see* Handstone

Grinding slab, 110, 112–18

Ground stone, 109–28 *passim*, 133–35

Gunflint, 83, 101

Halieis, 8, 57, 68f, 72, 116, 122, 129, 143

Handle, 7ff, 15, 18, 21, 27–28, 36, 47, 53

Handmill, 110, 124–28

Handstone, 110, 118, 121

Hansen, J. M., 39

Harvesting, 94

Hearth rim, 10, 38–39, 142

Hematite, 121

Hermion, 57, 72

Herringbone pattern, 32, 39

Honey flint, 104

Hopper mill, 121, 123

Hopper quern, 110

Horse, 67f, 70

Horseleader, 67

Hunting, 91

Hydria, 54f, 60, 63, 69

Iakovides, S., 135

Iliokastro (AEP site G1), 57, 62, 65, 72

Immerwahr, S. A., 10

Imported pottery, 44, 50f. *See also* Ceramic groups, regions, and imports

Impressed decoration, 26–36 *passim*

Incised decoration, 9, 13–18 *passim*, 26, 32–39 *passim*, 47f, 55

Incurving bowl, *see under* Bowl

Isthmia, 22

Ivory, 94

Jar, 8, 16–18, 33–34, 44–55 *passim*, 69

Jug, 34, 36, 49, 53f, 56, 60, 63, 69

Kalamaki, 22

Kalaureia, 71f

Kantharos, 44, 62, 66, 68f

Katafiki Gorge (AEP site E80), 88; (AEP site F25), 86; chert procurement, 103
Kea, 42. *See also* Ayia Irini; Kephala
Kephala, 97. *See also* Kea
Kephalari Magoula, 13
Keramidaki, *see* Corinth
Kerbschnitt, 31–32. *See also* Impressed decoration; Stamped decoration
Kitsos Cave, 112
Klithi Cave, 88
Koiladha Bay, 68–72
Kokkinopolis, 82
Kotena Cave (AEP site G9), 7
Kotyle, 62, 69
Koukou Cave (AEP site F35), 89
Krater, 30, 53f, 56, 68–72 *passim*
Kum Tepe, 10, 17
Kylix, 53–56 *passim*
Kyrenia shipwreck, 122

Ladle, 37
Lame à crête (crested blade), 77–78, 106
Late Helladic, 4, 47, 113, 134–35; Late Helladic I, 43–52 *passim*; Late Helladic II, 52–53; Late Helladic IIIA, 53–54, 56; Late Helladic IIIB, 54–55, 56; Late Helladic IIIC pottery, 54ff
Late Matt-painted pottery, 53
Late Neolithic, 91
Lavezzi, J. C., 7
Leaf, 64, 67f
Lefkandhi, 55, 59, 61
Lekythos, 60
Lerna, 12, 21, 39, 43, 51, 77, 93–96 *passim*, 107f
Levallois flake, 82, 87, 103
LH, *see* Late Helladic
Limestone, 128, 133
Lithics: dating of, 85; Early Helladic, 83; Final Neolithic, 83; historic periods, 74, 97–103, 143; production of, 76, 79, 83, 85, 90f, 96, 100–108 *passim*, 114, 141–42; typology, 76, 86; Upper Palaeolithic, 83; use, 74, 89, 101
Lug, *see* Plastic decoration

Makrovouni, 13, 28, 36
Mano, *see* Handstone
Mantinea, 70
Marble, 112
Mases (AEP site C17), 57, 63, 65, 72

Mastos, 62
Mat impression, 19, 36
Matt-painted pottery, 48, 50, 53
Meander, 64, 67f
Mechanical principles, 129
Meeks, N. D., 82
Melos, 76, 93, 101, 104–6, 111f, 124, 134
Mesolithic, 88–89, 136
Metallurgy, 93
Metal tools, 74, 100
Metate, 110, 112–18
Methana, 12, 41
MH, *see* Middle Helladic
Microwear studies, 81
Middle Helladic, 113, 135, 142; transition to Late Helladic, 43, 47, 51f
Middle Palaeolithic, 82–87 *passim*, 103
Migration, 41
Milling technology, 138
Mill, *see* Hopper quern; Rotary quern; Rotary olive mill; Saddle quern
Millstone, 110, 112–18
Minoan pottery, 50
Minyan, 46–48
Modern period lithics, 127
Mortar, 110, 134–35
Mortarium, 131
Motifs, painted, 33, 49–71 *passim*
Mousterian point, 82, 87, 103
Mouzaki Cave (AEP site E14), 6
Mug, 54
Muller, *see* Handstone
Mycenae, 59–69 *passim*, 142
Mycenaean pottery, *see* Late Helladic
Mycenaean stone relief vessel, 135
Mycenaean tripod mortar, 134–35

Nauplia, 63
Nea Ionia, 60
Nemea Valley, 12f, 41, 142
Neolithic, 4, 40–42, 89–91, 105, 112. *See also* Final Neolithic
Nichoria, 70
Nisyros, 111, 117, 121, 126
Nodule, 77
Non-vessel ceramics, 8, 19, 37–39, 51, 56, 69, 71

Oatmeal fabric, 48
Oats, 39
Obsidian, 76f, 79, 87–96 *passim*, 103–6 *passim*, 141–44 *passim*
Oinochoe, 59–62 *passim*

Olive oil, 131–33, 137–38
Olive press, 131
Olympia, 71
Olynthus mill, 110
Ornament, stone, 94, 115, 135

Painted decoration, *see* Motifs, painted
Pan, baking, 10, 36
Paneled cup, 49
Pastoralism, 94
Pattern burnishing, 9–10
Pausanias, 143
Pedestal, 19–20, 22, 35, 44, 61–66 *passim*
Pedogenic calcium carbonate assay, 85
Pendant, 136
Perachora, 13f, 17, 69
Perçoir, 81–82, 90–91, 94
Perrirhanterion, 135
Petrothalassa (AEP site B27), 87
Phelps, W. W., 7, 10
Pièce esquillée, 82
Pikrodhafni Valley (AEP site B102), 100
Pithos, 32f, 44, 55, 63, 69f
Plant impression, 39
Plaque, votive, 69
Plastic decoration, 9, 13–17 *passim*, 25ff, 32–35 *passim*, 44, 49. *See also* Taenia
Plate, 36, 68, 70
Platform, 83
Plow, 94
Population, 41, 142
Potter's mark, 51
Potter's wheel, *see* Pottery manufacturing techniques
Pottery decoration, *see* Impressed decoration; Incised decoration; Motifs, painted; Plastic decoration; Stamped decoration; Taenia
Pottery manufacturing techniques, 34–39 *passim*, 46–50 *passim*, 57–58. *See also* Fabric (ceramic)
Pottery shapes, *see under individual shape names*
Pottery surface treatments (non-decorative), 9, 13–35 *passim*, 44–51 *passim*. *See also* Fabric (ceramic)
Press bed, 110, 128–29, 131
Projectile point, 82–83, 91, 95, 102
Pyxis, 61–68 *passim*

Quarry, 100f, 105
Quern, 110, 115

Radiometric assay, 85, 87
Rema stone, 101, 112, 124, 127. *See also* Melos
Renfrew, C., 7, 104
Retouch, 79, 81, 84
Roller seal impression, 38
Rolley, C., 71
Rooftiles, 39, 142
Rotary mill, 143
Rotary olive mill, 110, 131–33, 143
Rotary quern, 110, 124–28
Rubber, *see* Handstone
Runnels, C. N., 82, 96
Rutter, J. B., 43
Rynd, 125

Saddle quern, 110, 112–18
Saliagos, 91
Sambariza (AEP site E9), 57–60 *passim*
Sandstone, 112, 121
Santorini, 111, 117, 134
Saronic Gulf, 41–42, 114, 121, 126, 135
Sauceboat, 19, 21f, 34
Saucer, *see under* Bowl
Scimatari, 54
Scoop, 37
Screw, principle of, 129
Seal, 37f
Semenov, S., 82
Serçe Limani shipwreck, 127
Serpent, 70–71
Serpentine, 111–12
Settlement pattern: Early Helladic, 41, 93, 142; Greco-Roman, 129–31; Middle Helladic, 142; Neolithic, 7
Shaft Grave period, 142
Shallow bowl, *see under* Bowl
Shallow cup, 56
Sickle blade, 82
Sickle element, 90, 102
Sidari, 88
Silica gloss, 94

Site, 140. *See also individual names of sites*
Skyphoid krater, 68
Skyphos, 59–69 *passim*
Small bowl, *see under* Bowl
SOS amphora, 68
Southern Argolid, as a region, 40, 57, 64–68 *passim*, 72–73. *See also* Ceramic groups, regions, and imports
Sparta, 59
Specialization, *see* Craft Specialization; Lithics: production of; Pottery manufacturing techniques
Spindle whorl, 19, 45, 51, 135
Spondylus, 115
Spoon, 37
Spout, 30
Stamnos or stamnoid krater, 70
Stamped decoration, 17, 30ff, 38–39
Stand, 19, 37–38, 62–63
Standardization, *see* Craft specialization; Lithics: production of; Pottery manufacturing techniques
Stemmed bowl, *see under* Bowl
Stirrup jar, 54
Stone tools, 76, 79, 81, 102
Stone vessel, 110, 135
Storage vessel, 61, 69f
Surface treatments, *see* Pottery surface treatments
Survey, surface, 1–2, 74f, 140
Synoikismos, 57

Table, 38
Taenia, 24–32 *passim*, 38. *See also* Plastic decoration
Talc, 135
Talioti, 13, 41
Tanged point, 82
Tankard, 44
Terracotta whorl, *see* Spindle whorl
Thebes, 23
Threshing sledge, 100
Tinderflint, 82, 101, 104

Tiryns, 23, 29ff, 38, 58–63 *passim*, 67ff
Torrence, R., 96, 105–6
Trade, 50, 74, 79, 94, 104–6, 111, 118, 122, 127, 142
Transhumance, 41
Trapetum, see Rotary olive mill
Tribula, 101
Tringham, R., 79
Tripod cooking pot, 55
Tripod mortar, 134–35
Trumpet lug, *see* Plastic decoration
Tsakmaki, 101
Tsoungiza, 12, 13. *See also* Nemea Valley

Upper Palaeolithic, 77, 83, 87–88
Uranium thorium series assay, 85
Urfirnis, 6, 20. *See also* Pottery surface treatments
Use-wear analysis, 81, 84, 118

Van Horn, D. M., 77, 82
Vapheio cup, 53
Vista (AEP site C12), 57, 63, 65, 72
Volcanic temper, 8, 11

Watermill, 138
Weight, stone, 135
Weight block, 110, 128–29, 131
Weisshaar, H.-J., 23–24, 29
Wells, B., 58f
Wheat, 39
Wheel, *see* Pottery manufacturing techniques
Whorl, *see* Spindle whorl
Windmill, 138

Yellow Minyan, 47–48
Yellow-blue slipped and burnished, 20–31 *passim*, 35, 37. *See also* Pottery surface treatments

Zerner, C. W., 46
Zygouries, 54

Library of Congress Cataloging-in-Publication Data

Artifact and assemblage : the finds from a regional survey of the
southern Argolid, Greece.
      v. ⟨1   ⟩   cm.
Vol. 1–   includes bibliographical references and index.
     Contents: v. 1. The prehistoric and early Iron age pottery and the
lithic artifacts / edited by Curtis Runnels, Daniel J. Pullen, and
Susan Langdon
     ISBN 0-8047-2065-7 (cloth)
     1. Argolis Peninsula (Greece)—Antiquities.   2. Iron age—Greece—
Argolis Peninsula.   3. Pottery, Prehistoric—Greece—Argolis
Peninsula.   4. Excavations (Archaeology)—Greece—Argolis Peninsula.
I. Runnels, Curtis Neil.   II. Pullen, Daniel J.
III. Langdon, Susan Helen.
DF221.A78A78   1995
938′.8—dc20
94-25691   CIP

⊗ This book is printed on acid-free paper.